DERIVATIVES HANDBOOK

WILEY SERIES IN FINANCIAL ENGINEERING

DERIVATIVES HANDBOOK

Risk Management and Control

Edited by

ROBERT J. SCHWARTZ

and

CLIFFORD W. SMITH, JR.

John Wiley & Sons, Inc.

New York • Chichester • Weinheim • Brisbane • Singapore • Toronto

Copyright © 1997 by Robert J. Schwartz and Clifford W. Smith.
Published by John Wiley & Sons, Inc.

Library of Congress Cataloging-in-Publication Data:

Schwartz, Robert J.
    Derivatives handbook : risk management and control / Robert J.
Schwartz and Clifford W. Smith.
      p.   cm. — (Wiley series in financial engineering)
    Includes index.
    ISBN 0-471-15765-1 (alk. paper)
    1. Derivative securities. 2. Risk management. I. Smith.
Clifford W. II. Title. III. Series.
HG6024.A3S39   1997
332.64'5—dc21   96-40295

Printed in the United States of America

10 9 8 7 6 5 4 3

To our families, especially our wives Gail and Bernie

Acknowledgments

We would like to extend special thanks to Republic National Bank of New York and the William E. Simon School of Business for the support and facilities provided during the conceptualization, organization, editing, and production of *Derivatives Handbook: Risk Management and Control.*

Cliff Smith acknowledges the financial support provided by Bradley Policy Research Center at the Simon School.

Bob Schwartz's colleagues Walter Weiner, Janet Norwood, Elias Saal, Dov Schlein, and Nathan Hasson were supportive throughout the effort. Bob acknowledges a particular debt to Jack Caoette, Marvin Moskowitz, and David Prichard who gave him the opportunity to enter the foreign exchange and interest rate risk management markets.

Michele Cox provided valuable assistance at various stages of the extensive correspondence with our contributors.

Jacque Urinyi worked tirelessly to bring this effort to fruition.

Finally, and most important, the contributors who made this book possible deserve the ultimate recognition, especially Tony Gooch and Linda Klein who acted as editors for the surveys of case law covering Canada, Australia, and the United Kingdom, as well as contributing their survey of case law in the United States. Thank you all.

The authors acknowledge the many ideas provided by Giovanna Righini, her role as a founding member of the derivatives market, and the loss to all of us with her passing in October 1996.

We also wish to recognize the visionary work of Peter Eccles who died in December 1996. Peter created what became the Citibank Swaps Group and started many market professionals on their careers.

Contributing Authors

Brandon Becker advises and represents clients on broker-dealer regulatory issues, related issues affecting financial market participants, and other matters involving capital markets such as derivative trading. He is the former director of the SEC's Division of Market Regulation and served as a staff member of the President's Working Group on Financial Markets as well as the CFTC's Financial Products Advisory Committee. Mr. Becker has taught courses on Corporations, Securities Regulation, Broker-Dealer Regulation, and Global Securities Markets at a variety of law schools.

Tanya Styblo Beder is a principal of Capital Market Risk Advisors, Inc., headquartered in New York. Prior to founding a consulting firm specializing in financial institutions, capital markets, and derivatives in 1987, she was a vice-president of The First Boston Corporation and was a consultant in the financial institutions practice at McKinsey & Company. She is currently a management fellow on the faculty of the Yale University School of Organization and Management and has been on the adjunct faculty at the Columbia University Graduate School of Business Administration. Her academic work focuses on global capital markets, off-balance sheet instruments, and the future of the financial system.

Harold Bierman, Jr., is the Nicholas H. Noyas professor of Business Administration at Cornell University. Professor Bierman formerly taught at Louisiana State University, the University of Michigan, and the University of Chicago. In 1987, he taught at INSEAD, and at KUL in Belgium in 1994. He has been a recipient of the annual Dow Jones Award from the American Assembly of Collegiate Schools of Business for outstanding contributions to collegiate business education. In 1985, he served as scholar-in-residence at the investment banking firm of Prudential Bache. In 1990, he served as a senior academic fellow at the Financial Accounting Standards Board. His industrial experience includes work with Corning Incorporated, Eastman Kodak, Emerson Electric Co., Anheuser-Busch, and Xerox Corp.

WENDY H. BREWER is the executive vice president and chief financial officer of Tokyo-Mitsubishi Derivatives Products (USA), Inc., and a senior vice president of the Capital Markets Group of the Bank of Tokyo-Mitsubishi. Prior to that she was an executive vice president and chief financial officer of Mitsubishi Capital Market Services, Inc., and senior vice president and chief financial officer for Mitsubishi Securities (USA), Inc. She joined Mitsubishi in 1989 to manage the back office and support functions for the start-up of the two subsidiaries. Before Mitsubishi, Ms. Brewer was the global head of Swaps Operations at the Chase Manhattan Bank, NA, which she joined in 1981.

MICHAEL S. CANTER is an analyst at Centre Financial Products, Limited, a risk management firm which specializes in securitizing and trading environmental, energy, and insurance risks. He has published scholarly articles on these subjects in the *Journal of Derivatives,* the *Journal of Futures Markets,* and the *Journal of Applied Corporate Finance.* He received a B.A. in economics and mathematics from Northwestern University and a Ph.D. in finance and economics from Columbia University Graduate School of Business.

ANDREW J. C. CLARK is a partner in the international law firm of Allen & Overy. He is based in Allen & Overy's London office and specializes in litigation and dispute resolution. He has extensive experience in international capital markets and banking litigation and has been involved in some of the most recent derivatives litigation cases to come before the English courts. He lectures widely on derivatives litigation and has written articles on the subject including in the *London Financial Times, International Financial Law Review,* and *Butterworth's Journal of International Bank Law.* Having spent some years of his career as resident partner of Allen & Overy's Middle East Regional Office in Dubai, United Arab Emirates, the author contributed to the United Arab Emirates section of Longman's encyclopaedia *Aircraft Finance, Registration, Security and Enforcement.* He holds an M.A. from Cambridge University and is a Fellow of the Chartered Institute of Arbitrators.

CHRISTOPHER L. CULP is the sole proprietor of Risk Management Consulting Services in Chicago, Illinois, and is senior fellow in Financial Regulation with the Competitive Enterprise Institute in Washington, DC. He was formerly senior examiner at the Federal Reserve Bank of Chicago and also has held positions with G.T. Management (Asia) Ltd. and TradeLink LLC. Culp has published over 50 articles on corporation finance, risk management, and regulation in academic journals, trade journals, law reviews, books, magazines, and newspapers, and is completing a Ph.D. in corporation finance at the Graduate School of Business, The University of Chicago.

DANIEL P. CUNNINGHAM is a partner of the law firm of Cravath, Swaine & Moore. He was the firm's resident London partner from 1986 to 1990 and was the firm's managing partner from 1990 through 1993. His corporate finance practice includes derivative instruments, mergers and acquisitions, and underwriting. Mr. Cunningham has participated since 1984 in the preparation by the ISDA Documentation Committee of standard master agreements for derivative transactions.

FRANKLIN R. EDWARDS is on the faculty of the Graduate School of Business at Columbia University and is a visiting scholar at the American Enterprise Institute. He also serves as director of the Center for the Study of Futures Markets at Columbia University. Professor Edwards has been a member of the Columbia Business School Faculty since 1966, and holds the Arthur F. Burns Chair in Free and Competitive Enterprise. His major areas of research and expertise are the regulation of financial markets and institutions and the economics of banking, securities, and derivatives markets.

GERALD D. GAY is chairman and professor of finance at Georgia State University in Atlanta. His research and professional interests center on the valuation and use of derivative instruments and the regulation of derivative markets. From 1990 to 1993, he served as the chief economist and the director of the Division of Economic Analysis for the U.S. Commodity Futures Trading Commission in Washington, DC. He received bachelors and masters degrees in industrial systems engineering from the University of South Florida and a Ph.D. in finance from the University of Florida.

ANTHONY C. GOOCH is a partner of Cleary, Gottlieb, Steen & Hamilton, based in the firm's New York office. He is the co-author of *Documentation for Derivatives* (Euromoney Publications, 1993) and its *Credit Support Supplement* (1995), as well as *Documentation for Loans, Assignments and Participations* (Euromoney Publications, 1996). His practice focuses in part on financial derivatives and in part on other international financial and investment transactions, including bank loans, debt and equity issues, and privatizations, with particular emphasis on Brazil and other Latin American countries. He holds J.D. and M.C.J. degrees from New York University and a diploma from the College of Europe, Bruges, Belgium.

WENDY LEE GRAMM serves on the boards of visitors of the Business School of University of Iowa and the Center for Study of Public Choice at George Mason University. She is on the International Capital Markets Advisory Committee to the New York Stock Exchange, the National Advisory Boards of the International Republican Institute, the Independent Women's Forum, and the Republican Women's Federal Forum. She serves as a director on the Boards of the Chicago Mercantile Exchange, Enron Corp., IBP, Inc., Kinetic Concepts, Inc., and State Farm Insurance Companies. She was named the 1995 Financial Executive of the Year by the Financial Management Association. Gramm served as chairman of the U.S. Commodity Futures Trading Commission from 1988–1993. She was administrator for information and regulatory affairs at the Office of Management and Budget from 1985–1988, the executive director of the Presidential Task Force on Regulatory Relief, and director of the Federal Trade Commission's Bureau of Economics.

ALAN GREENSPAN took office June 20, 1996 as chairman of the Board of Governors of the Federal Reserve System for a third four-year term ending June 20, 2000. Greenspan has also served as a member of President Reagan's Economic Advisory Board, a member of *Time* magazine's Board of Economists, a senior advisor to the Brookings Panel on Economic Activity, and a consultant to the Congressional Budget office. He received a B.S., an M.A., and a Ph.D. in economics, all from New York University.

MARGARET E. GROTTENTHALER is a partner of Stikeman, Elliott, based in the firm's Toronto office, where she is in charge of legal research and writing. She practices extensively in the area of financial derivatives and is currently co-authoring a text on the Canadian law of financial derivatives to be published by Carswells Legal Publishers in

1997. She is the editor and a contributing author to Matthew Bender's, "Doing Business in Canada." She holds an L.L.B. from the University of Western Ontario and a B.C.L. from Oxford University.

DOUGLAS E. HARRIS was senior deputy comptroller for Capital Markets at the Office of the Comptroller of the Currency (OCC) from May 1993 to June 1996. In his capacity at the OCC, Harris was charged with oversight of national banks in regard to issues such as risk management practices, derivative instruments, and new approaches to financial products.

LUDGER HENTSCHEL is an assistant professor of finance at the University of Rochester's William E. Simon Graduate School of Business Administration. He teaches courses in International Finance and Forecasting in the MBA program at the Simon School and the Simon School's Executive Development Programs. Prior to joining the Simon School faculty, Mr. Hentschel was an economist in the International Finance Division at the Board of Governors of the Federal Reserve System. He holds a B.S. in Mechanical Engineering from Yale University and M.A. and Ph.D. degrees in Economics from Princeton University.

JAMIE HUTCHINSON is with the Australian firm Mallesons Stephen Jaques. He has over ten years experience in banking and finance law and advises Australian and international market participants about derivatives documentation, regulation, and transactions. He is currently based in Sydney, but has also worked for Mallesons Stephen Jaques in London and for a German law firm in Stuttgart.

FRANK IACONO is an associate of Capital Market Risk Advisors, Inc. (CMRA), headquartered in New York. Mr. Iacono specializes in quantitative issues in derivatives and financial risk management including Value at Risk, stochastic processes, and contingent claim analysis. Prior to joining CMRA in August 1994, Mr. Iacono was with Wasserstein Perella & Co., Inc., a leading international investment banking firm.

JAMES V. JORDAN is professor of finance in the School of Business and Public Management at George Washington University. His research interests include fixed-income securities, derivatives, and financial risk management. He regularly consults in these areas. His publications include articles in the *Journal of Fixed Income, Journal of Futures Markets,* and *Journal of Finance.*

LINDA B. KLEIN is counsel in the New York office of Dewey Ballantine. She is the co-author of *Documentation for Derivatives* (Euromoney Publications, 1993) and its *Credit Support Supplement* (1995), as well as *Documentation for Loans, Assignments and Participations* (Euromoney Publications, 1996). In addition to financial derivatives, her practice includes a wide variety of international financial transactions, such as bank loans, loan participations and assignments, securitizations, issues of debt and equity securities, and public and private sector debt restructurings. Ms. Klein holds J.D. and Ph.D. degrees from Columbia University.

ANATOLI KUPRIANOV is an economist and research officer with the Federal Reserve Bank of Richmond. He has authored several articles on derivatives markets, including the chapters on interest rate derivatives included in *Instruments of the Money*

Market—a book on the U.S. money market published by the Federal Reserve Bank of Richmond. Before joining the Federal Reserve, Mr. Kuprianov taught economics at the Virginia Polytechnic Institute and State University and at the University of Virginia, and served as a consultant to the Rand Corporation in Santa Monica, California. He holds a Ph.D. in economics from the University of Rochester and a B.A. in economics and mathematics from Kent State University.

JAMES C. LAM has over twelve years of risk management and consulting experience in the financial services industry. His work has been focused on developing and implementing integrated approaches to managing all aspects of risk, including market, credit, and operational risks. Mr. Lam joined Fidelity in September 1995 as chief risk officer responsible for the Global Risk Management Department. His new function is responsible for ensuring that best practices are in place for measuring and managing all types of risk across Fidelity, including operational risk and control, credit risk management, and market risk management.

ROBERT J. MACKAY is professor of finance and director of the Center for Study of Futures & Options Markets in the Pamplin College of Business at Virginia Tech. He also has taught at the University of California-Berkeley, the University of Maryland, and Tulane University and was a visiting scholar at the Hoover Institution at Stanford University. He received his Ph.D. in economics from the University of North Carolina-Chapel Hill. Dr. Mackay has extensive experience in government, having served as chief of staff of the U.S. Commodity Futures Trading Commission following the stock market crash of 1987. During this time, he also served as a member of the senior staff of the President's Working Group on Financial Markets. After leaving the commission, he was appointed to the CFTC's Regulatory Coordination Advisory Committee and chaired its Working Group on International Competitiveness.

ROBERT M. MARK is an executive vice president at the Canadian Imperial Bank of Commerce (CIBC). His responsibilities at CIBC encompass corporate treasury and risk management functions. This is a CIBC-wide group that has global responsibility to cover all markets, trading related credit and operating risks for the wholesale and retail banks as well as for its subsidiaries. His corporate treasury responsibilities include actively managing the gap created by imbalances between interest rate repricings on assets and liabilities. His responsibilities also include managing the risk MIS, analytics, capital attribution, and risk advisory units. Dr. Mark works in partnership with CIBC managers and ensures that all risks are accurately measured, controlled, and managed. Prior to his current position at CIBC, he was the partner in charge of the Financial Risk Management Consulting practice at Coopers & Lybrand.

FRANCOIS-IHOR MAZUR is an associate at Sidley & Austin where he practices in the Corporate and Securities Group. "Oversight of Derivative Markets: Who's Responsible for What?" was prepared while Mr. Mazur served as an attorney in the division of market regulation at the Securities and Exchange Commission. Mr. Mazur attended the University of Pennsylvania where he received a B.A. in 1987 and a J.D. in 1991.

JOANNE T. MEDERO is managing director and chief counsel of Barclays Global Investors, N.A. Legal Group. Prior to joining BGI in January, 1996, she was a partner in the New York office of Orrick, Herrington & Sutcliffe, specializing in derivatives and market regulation issues. From 1989 to 1993 Ms. Medero served as general counsel of the Commodity Futures Trading Commission, the federal agency with oversight over the futures industry. Previously, she also served as associate director for legal and financial affairs, Office of Presidential Personnel, The White House (1986–1989). Her articles on regulation and derivatives have been published in books and professional magazines including *RISK, Institutional Investor,* and *Butterworth's Journal of International Banking Law.*

ANTONIO S. MELLO is currently assistant professor of finance at the University of Wisconsin-Madison. Prior to that he was in charge of research at the Central Bank of Portugal. He has also taught at MIT and INSEAD. Mr. Mello holds an M.A. and an M.B.A. from Columbia University and a Ph.D. from University of London.

MERTON H. MILLER is the Robert R. McCormick Distinguished Service Professor of Finance Emeritus at the Graduate School of Business, University of Chicago. Professor Miller was awarded the Nobel Prize in Economic Science in 1990 for his work in the area of corporate finance. A graduate school of business faculty member since 1961, Professor Miller has written extensively on a variety of topics in economics and finance. Along with Franco Modigliani of M.I.T., he developed the M&M Theorems on capital structure and dividend policy that are the foundations of the theory of corporate finance. Professor Miller is the author of numerous publications, including *Macroeconomics: A Neoclassical Introduction* (with C. Upton, 1974), *The Theory of Finance* (with E. F. Fama, 1972), and most recently, *Financial Innovations and Market Volatility.*

JOHN E. PARSONS is an expert in the field of corporate finance, securities, and financial markets. He has advised various U.S. and non-U.S. government entities on financial reform, privatization, and oversight of financial markets. Dr. Parsons has extensive experience in designing specialized securities and financial contracts, including derivative instruments and hedging programs. Much of his research in the field has involved applications to firms in the energy industry. Dr. Parsons is currently pursuing a study of the recently opened futures market in electricity.

ROBERT J. SCHWARTZ is an executive vice president of the Republic National Bank of New York. He is the Global Head of Derivatives and is a member of the Asset/Liability Management Committee. Prior to assuming those responsibilities, he managed and restructured the Emerging Markets Trading and Sales Desk. The International Swap and Derivatives Association elected Mr. Schwartz to its board of directors three times and he currently serves as co-chairman of the Market Survey Committee, and is a member of the Conference and Education Committees. He holds a B.S. (Mathematics) from Bucknell University, an M.Sc. (Information Science) from Lehigh University, and an M.B.A. (Finance) from the Harvard Business School.

JEFFREY L. SELTZER is a managing director of CIBC Wood Gundy Financial Products. He has global responsibility for the Advisory Group that provides product development and transaction structuring expertise with a special focus on the credit, legal, regulatory, tax, and accounting aspects of swaps, options, and structure across all markets. Mr. Seltzer is a member of the CIBC Wood Gundy New Initiatives and Finance Committee. Prior to joining CIBC Wood Gundy, he was a managing director of the Lehman Brothers Derivatives Department and a securities lawyer in private practice in New York City. Over the past 15 years, Mr. Seltzer has served as an advisor to the U.S. Department of Commerce, U.S. Trade Representative, U.S. Small Business Administration, Republican National Committee, and the National Policy Forum as well as numerous political campaigns. From 1991–1994, he served as chairman of the Securities Industry Association's Swap and OTC Derivative Products Committee and was instrumental in developing a proposal for a voluntary framework for supervision of the derivatives dealers.

CLIFFORD W. SMITH, JR. is the Clarey professor of finance at the William E. Simon Graduate School of Business of the University of Rochester. He has consulted with governments, leading financial institutions, and corporations around the globe. His research has resulted in numerous books and articles. He has a B.A. in economics from Emory University and a Ph.D. in economics from the University of North Carolina, Chapel Hill.

CHARLES W. SMITHSON is a managing director of CIBC Wood Gundy Financial Products where he is charged with developing the CIBC *Wood Gundy School of Financial Products.* Mr. Smithson's career has spanned the gamut, with positions in academe and in government, as well as in the private sector. Mr. Smithson taught for nine years at Texas A&M University, where his primary interests were in natural resource economics and regulation. In government, he served with both the Federal Trade Commission and the Consumer Products Safety Commission. In the private sector, he was the managing director for risk management research at Continental Bank (1988–1990). He served two stints with the Chase Manhattan Bank, as the developer of Chase's education program for derivatives (1985–1987) and as the managing director for risk management research and education (1990–1995). The author of scores of articles in professional and academic journals, Mr. Smithson is best known as the originator of the "building block approach" to financial products. He is the author of five books, including *The Handbook of Financial Engineering* and *Managing Financial Risk.*

THOMAS J. WERLEN is an associate at the law firm of Cravath, Swaine & Moore. His practice includes derivative instruments, corporate finance, and banking. He has extensive experience in derivatives documentation and netting issues, and provides counsel to a variety of derivatives dealers and end-users. He has been involved in a wide range of ISDA's documentation efforts. He has published several books and articles in the areas of derivatives and capital markets law in both Switzerland and the United States.

Contents

Introduction

ROBERT J. SCHWARTZ
CLIFFORD W. SMITH, JR.

Derivatives risk has been a billowing storm cloud, hanging over this market for much of the past decade. After the 1987 crash, equity derivatives were widely blamed for exacerbating the market decline. And in a speech in January 1992, then New York Federal Reserve Bank president Gerald Corrigan asked his audience—members of the New York Bankers Association—whether they knew the risks they were taking with derivatives and whether they knew how to control them. He suggested that they "take a very hard look" at these issues and added "I hope this sounds like a warning—because it is."

The financial press has echoed these concerns. The September 1992 *Institutional Investor* cover features a globe with a burning fuse protruding, overprinted with the words: "Derivatives: Just How Risky Are They?" Similarly, a March 1994 *Fortune* cover warns: "Financial derivatives are tightening their grip on the world economy. And nobody knows how to control them." This warning appears over a picture of a very large alligator—mouth agape. Yet as Don Chew, editor of the *Journal of Applied Corporate Finance* has noted about this cover, "Just what and how big this creature is cannot be made out from the photo because the perspective is so artfully distorted and the context altogether removed. And the same might be said about the cover story and its subject."

Articles that focus on derivatives risks regularly recount a series of derivatives debacles: Air Products, Barings, Codelco, Gibson Greetings, Glaxo, Kashima Oil, Metallgesellschaft, Orange County, Piper Jaffrey, Procter & Gamble, and Sumitomo. From these reports, several issues seem clear. First, these markets are large and growing; in part, this is a reflection of the risk-management benefits they offer the business community. Second, these instruments are effective risk management tools specifically because they are designed to isolate and be extremely sensitive to price changes in the underlying asset. Third, if ill-managed and poorly controlled, rather than reducing risks, derivatives can produce spectacular losses.

Appropriate derivatives policies for both dealers and their customers require a fundamental understanding of these products and their risks. Armed with this knowledge, managers can proceed to an understanding of how these risks can be measured, managed, and controlled. The collection of articles in this handbook—organized by topic—is designed to help managers achieve these goals. The articles reflect the thought of a broad collection of derivatives experts. Their areas of expertise cut across the business, legal, regulatory, and the academic communities.

In Part One, the articles focus on identification of risks in derivatives markets. In Chapter 1, Hentschel and Smith offer a systematic analysis of the risks in derivatives markets. Iacono examines the emerging market in credit derivatives. These instruments offer managers new tools to unbundle and better manage credit risk. Brewer focuses on operations risk. The process of recording, verifying, confirming, and settling derivatives transactions raises a number of challenges for an effective derivatives program. Brewer defines the role of operations in managing these risks, examines the tools available for controlling these risks, and suggests a basic strategy to limit these risks.

Part Two provides an overview of the current legal standing of derivatives. It begins with an overview of the case law affecting derivatives from important markets around the globe. Gooch and Klein focus on the United States, Grottenthaler on Canada, Hutchinson on Australia, and Clark on the United Kingdom. Cunningham and Werlen examine multibranch netting as a method of reducing exposures of a counterparty and thus the magnitude of default risks. National insolvency laws face major challenges in dealing with a multinational default such as that of the Bank of Credit and Commerce International (BCCI). Cunningham and Werlen examine the problems and suggest potential solutions. Gay and Medero examine provisions in the swap master agreement. They focus on how the structure of the contract reduces costs, mitigates credit risk, and ensures enforceability.

Part Three covers issues of risk measurement. Both Beder and Jordan and Mackay survey the current state of value at risk (VaR) methods. Beder notes that although VaR has been endorsed by regulators such as the BIS, the Federal Reserve, and the SEC, details of implementation are still being developed. Beder examines the challenges in structuring an effective VaR system. Jordan and Mackay focus on applying VaR to portfolios of equities and equity options.

Part Four focuses on risk oversight. Both Becker and Mazur and Smithson and Seltzer examine the role of the board of directors. Ultimately responsible for overseeing all corporate activities, the board plays a crucial oversight role with respect to derivatives. Smithson and Seltzer emphasize that effective board oversight does not require that board members be derivatives experts, but they do need to ask the right questions. They highlight critical board functions with respect to derivatives.

Mark, Lam, and Becker and Mazur discuss the role of senior management. They examine management's role in coordinating policies across the firm so that derivatives activities complement other aspects of the firm. Senior managers exercise important influence over derivatives activities within the firm through hiring, training, compensation, and retention.

Part Five examines regulatory issues associated with derivatives. Gramm and Gay focus on potential motives for effective regulation. They emphasize that for regulation to improve overall welfare, there must be some market failure; otherwise the participants have strong incentives to work out a private solution. They offer analysis of frequently offered rationales for derivatives regulations about the likelihood of changes in regulatory structure.

Both Miller and Culp examine financial regulation from the perspective originated by Stigler.[1] Stigler argues that regulation is designed and operated for the benefit of the regulated industry even though the regulation might originally been imposed over the industry's objection. Miller uses the Ministry of Finance in Japan as a specific example. These ideas are extended and focused more broadly on the derivatives markets by Culp.

Part Six focuses on the transparency of derivatives markets and disclosure issues. Federal Reserve Board Chairman Greenspan begins by examining the characteristics of OTC derivatives that determine their transparency and liquidity. He then identifies challenges that are created by using opaque and illiquid instruments. Finally, he offers suggestions on meeting these challenges.

Harris examines implications that the information technology has for understanding an institution's risk profile. He focuses on the information that specific participants require and on how timely such information needs to be. There are important tradeoffs between disclosing information that might be useful to investors versus protecting proprietary information. In structuring disclosure policies, these tradeoffs are critical.

Bierman provides a valuable survey of the accounting issues associated with hedging. When a financial instrument is used for hedging, special accounting rules are required to make the accounting consistent with underlying economic motives. There is a basic tension between marking derivatives positions to market to disclose gains and losses versus matching reported value changes on hedging instruments with value changes in the firm's underlying core business assets and liabilities. Marking to market only one leg of a hedge can increase the volatility of earnings even though the transaction hedges cash flows.

In Part Seven we offer a case study of one of the most spectacular examples of a derivatives program gone awry—Metallgesellschaft. In this set of articles, Miller and Culp, Edwards and Canter, Mellow and Parsons, and Kuprianov examine the company's use of derivatives in its U.S. oil subsidiary, MG Refining and Marketing (MGRM). These authors draw on the somewhat limited public information and analyze the derivatives strategy that was employed.

Miller and Culp suggest that MGRM used derivatives contracts as a low-cost method of what they call "synthetic storage." They argue that a reasonable strategy resulted in extraordinary losses because senior management ended the program because it failed to understand MGRM's combined marketing and hedging strategy. They liquidated the program in a way that created huge losses—losses that were largely avoidable. Both Edwards and Carter and Mellow and Parsons disagree (though to varying extents) with the Miller and Culp argument that the basic strategy was sound. They emphasize that the MGRM strategy faced a set of risks, especially the risk of rolling over a stack of short-dated derivatives to hedge a set of long-dated obligations. Miller and Culp then elaborate on and define their position. Finally, Kuprianov discusses both the Metallgesellschaft and Barings debacles. He analyzes these two cases offering implications for both senior managers and regulators.

A glossary of terms prepared by Beder, Schwartz, and Smith ends the book. As the market expands, jargon develops which makes discussions among professionals more streamlined and precise, yet at the same time renders aspects of those conversations virtually unintelligible to the uninitiated. We hope this glossary will help to demystify these discussions.

ENDNOTE

1. George Stigler (1971), "The Theory of Economic Regulation," *Bell Journal of Economics and Management Science, 2,* 2-19.

PART ONE

Derivatives: Risk and Control

Risk and Regulation in Derivatives Markets

LUDGER HENTSCHEL
CLIFFORD W. SMITH, JR.

The current public debate about derivatives has failed to provide either a systematic analysis of their risks or a convincing assessment of the likely effectiveness of regulation in limiting such risks. A major source of confusion in the popular debate is the proliferation of names to describe the various risks. Besides the "price risk" of losses on derivatives from changes in underlying asset values, there is "default risk" (sometimes referred as "counterparty risk"), "settlement risk" (or a variation thereof, "Herstatt risk,") "liquidity (or funding) risk," and "operations risk." Last, but certainly not least, is the specter of "systemic risk" that has captured so much congressional and regulatory attention.

In analyzing the risks associated with derivatives, we proceed in four stages. We begin with an analysis of price risk—that is, the potential for losses on derivatives from changes in the prices of underlying assets such as Treasury bonds, foreign currencies, and commodity prices. Second, we examine the risk of default by either party to a derivatives contract—a risk that has been largely misunderstood and hence overstated. (Although the reality of price risk has been demonstrated by a number of large, highly publicized losses, there are remarkably few examples of default in derivative markets—and we show why that trend can be expected to continue.) Third, we argue that systemic risk is simply the aggregation of the default risks faced by individual firms in using derivatives. Fourth and finally, we review various provisions of current regulatory proposals and assess their probable benefits and costs to the financial system.

We argue that the possibility of widespread default throughout the financial system stemming from the use of derivatives has been exaggerated, principally because of the failure to recognize the low-default risk associated with derivatives. For example, regulators as well as defenders of derivatives have observed that traditional measures of derivatives' exposure—notably, the notional principal of outstanding swaps—vastly overstate the amounts of capital at risk. These same observers argue that the actual "net" credit exposure on swaps amounts to no more than about 1% of notional principal. In this chapter, we argue that even this figure is misleading

Financial support from the John M. Olin Foundation and helpful conversations with S.P. Kothari and Charles Smithson are gratefully acknowledged. All errors are the authors' responsibility.

because it fails to acknowledge that the probability of default for most derivatives is significantly lower than the default probability associated with investment-grade corporate bonds.

Because of this overstatement of default risk, the many proposals for regulating derivatives now being contemplated in the United States and abroad should be viewed with some skepticism. There is another reason for urging caution. The authors of such proposals assure us that new regulations can be put in place with minimal costs. Yet, of all the risks described, the "regulatory risk" arising from the proposals themselves may represent the most serious threat to domestic and international capital markets.

PRICE RISK

The theory of option pricing, pioneered by Fischer Black, Myron Scholes, and Robert Merton, is one of the cornerstones of modern finance theory and practice. The central insight of the Black-Scholes option pricing model can be described as follows: The payoff from stock options (say, on 100 shares of IBM) can be replicated by the payoff on a portfolio consisting of the "underlying asset" (shares of IBM) and risk-free bonds (Treasury bills). The same Wall Street arbitrageurs who ensure that identical securities sell in different markets for the same prices also see to it that the prices of traded stock options respond rapidly, and in predictable fashion, to changes in underlying stock and T-bill prices.

The finance profession's current understanding of the value of broad classes of contingent claims—everything from LYONs and other convertible bonds to loan commitments and letters of credit—rests on this foundation of valuation by arbitrage. Moreover, this analysis has provided Wall Street with a set of practical tools that has resulted in more effective market-making in the options markets, as well as the creation of new instruments, markets, and strategies.

By building on and extending the theory of option pricing, such arbitrage-based derivatives pricing models have also had considerable success in valuing most other derivatives (including the large and growing variety of futures, swaps, caps, and collars). As with option pricing theory, derivatives pricing models are based on the ability of arbitrageurs to replicate the cash flows from the derivative contract with a portfolio of other securities that includes Treasuries in combination with the underlying asset (whether a given currency, bond, or commodity). For example, a forward contract to buy 1,000 barrels of light sweet crude can be replicated with a certain proportion of oil and Treasuries.

To be sure, the proportions of the assets in the replicating portfolios can vary considerably over time; and maintaining these replicating portfolios could involve extensive and costly trading. This means that derivatives, although "redundant" in the perfect markets of finance theory, usually cannot be replicated costlessly in real-world practice. (In fact, it is primarily the transactions-costs savings provided by most derivatives that justify their existence.)[1] But even if such trading costs introduce a degree of imprecision into the pricing process, virtually all derivatives can be valued with these arbitrage models.[2]

This ability to use arbitrage valuation methods in pricing derivatives has an important bearing on the current public debate on derivatives: *Because derivatives are equivalent to combinations of already trading securities, they cannot introduce any new, fundamentally different risks into the financial system.* What derivatives can and do accomplish, however, is to isolate and concentrate existing risks, thereby allowing for the more efficient transfer of such risks among market participants. Indeed, it is precisely this ability to isolate quite specific risks at low transactions costs that makes derivatives such useful risk-management tools.

Revisiting the S&L Problem

To see that derivatives can be effective tools in managing price risk, consider the predicament of Hometown Savings & Loan back in the early 1980s. Like most S&Ls, Hometown Savings was carrying 30-year mortgages with an average yield well under 10%, while funding itself with deposits whose costs had suddenly jumped well above 10%. Besides this mismatch between the maturities of its assets and liabilities, the fact that Hometown writes and refinances fewer mortgages in a high-interest-rate environment means that its fee income is also exposed to interest rates. In short, rising interest rates mean higher costs and lower revenues for this S&L and, hence, a reduction in its value.

Hometown's interest rate exposure—that is, the expected change in the S&L's market value for every 1% change in interest rates[3]—is illustrated by the downward-sloping line in Figure 1.1. When interest rates increase (that is, as you move right from the origin),[4] the value of the S&L's assets declines sharply, the value of its liabilities remains largely unchanged (because deposits are short-term and repriced frequently), and so the market value of Hometown falls.

FIGURE 1.1 Hometown's Exposures to Interest Rates

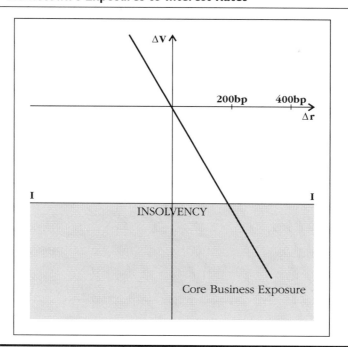

As Figure 1.1 also illustrates, if interest rates were to rise by as much as 200 basis points, net interest margins would shrink to the point where Hometown would likely become insolvent.[5] (In fact, it has been widely observed that if S&Ls in the early 1980s had been required to mark their assets to market, many of them would have reported negative net worths.)

Now, let's imagine the same S&L facing the interest rate environment of a year ago (fall of 1993). With 30-year mortgage rates as low as 7%, Hometown was flooded with applications for new mortgages and refinancings. But what if, soon after Hometown put all these new low-rate 30-year mortgages on its balance sheet, interest rates then increased by 200 basis points (as in fact they did the next year)? Would Hometown's current exposure still be large enough to make it insolvent?

As shown in Figure 1.2, Hometown has significantly reduced that exposure with an interest rate swap that pays fixed and receives floating (the exact reverse of the S&L's "natural" position of floating-rate liabilities and fixed-rate assets). The payoff to Hometown on the swap (as represented by the dashed, upward-sloping line in Figure 1.2) is designed to rise with increases in rates, thereby offsetting part of the decline in its market value.

The reduction in Hometown's exposure achieved by hedging with a swap is reflected in the less negative slope of the line in Figure 1.2. By reducing (though not eliminating) the S&L's exposure to rates, the use of derivatives has materially reduced the probability of insolvency.[6] As shown in Figure 1.2, interest rates would now have to rise by more than 400 basis points to push Hometown into insolvency.

But what about the risk of losses on the swap? After all, if interest rates fall sharply instead of rising, Hometown would be committed to making payments instead

FIGURE 1.2   Hometown's Exposure after Hedging

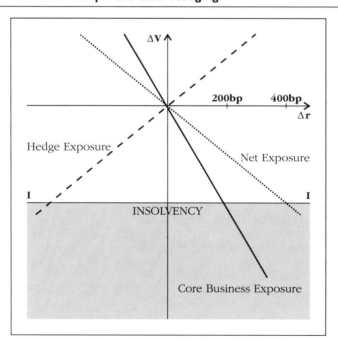

of receiving them. In these circumstances, it's important to recognize, Hometown's net interest margins would widen as the cost of its liabilities fell, and its origination and refinancing fees would increase. Thus, barring a wave of defaults by its borrowers caused by some factor other than interest rates, the S&L would be in a strong position to meet the payments required by the swap.

As this example illustrates, potential losses on derivatives are not a matter of concern *provided* companies are using derivatives to offset core business exposures and not to amplify them by taking "views" on interest rates. To the extent companies are using derivatives to hedge rather than to speculate, losses on derivatives will be more than offset by gains in operating values. (For this reason, complaining about losses on a swap used to hedge a firm's exposure is like objecting to the costs of a fire insurance policy if the building doesn't burn down.)

Whether companies are hedging or speculating becomes an even more important consideration in evaluating the default risk of derivatives—the subject to which we now turn.

DEFAULT RISK

As noted earlier, part of the confusion in the current debate about derivatives stems from the profusion of names associated with default risk. Terms such as credit risk and counterparty risk are synonyms for default risk. Settlement risk and Herstatt risk refer to defaults that occur only at a specific point in the life of the contract—the date of settlement.[7] These last two terms do not represent independent risks; they just describe a different occasion or cause of default.

As mentioned earlier, one of the greatest concerns voiced by regulators is systemic risk arising from derivatives. Although systemic risk is typically undefined and almost never assessed in quantitative terms, the systemic risk associated with derivatives is often envisioned as a domino effect in which default in one derivatives contract spreads to other contracts and markets, threatening the entire financial system.

For derivatives to cause widespread default in other markets, there first must be large defaults in derivatives markets. Because significant defaults on derivatives are a necessary (though by no means sufficient) condition for systemic problems, it is important to understand the probability of default on individual derivatives contracts before considering the possibility that such defaults could spread to other markets.

Default Risk on a Swap

To begin our analysis of default risk, let's return to the case of Hometown Savings and its use of an interest rate swap. Note what happens if interest rates do rise to the point where they endanger the S&L. A 400-basis-point (bp) increase, although much less probable than a 200-bp increase, is still possible. But if interest rates do rise by 400 bp and Hometown does becomes insolvent, the S&L will not default on its swap, even if the government forces it to close. Why? Because Hometown's swap will be "in the money"—that is, the S&L will then be *receiving* net payments from the swap.

There are *two* conditions that must hold simultaneously for Hometown to default on its derivative contract.[8] First, interest rates must fall so that Hometown owes money on the swap contract. (This occurs only to the left of the origin in Figure

1.2.) If rates rise, Hometown will instead receive payments. Second, the solvency (or at least liquidity) of Hometown must be sufficiently impaired that it is not able to make required payments on the contract. (This occurs only in the shaded region below the insolvency line "I" in Figure 1.2.) Hometown is expected to default on its swap only if both interest rates and its own net asset value fall at the same time—an unlikely combination of events.[9] (Therefore, the probability of default on the swap is represented by just the shaded area to the left of the origin in Figure 1.2.)

The small probability of default that remains can be attributed entirely to uncertainty about how Hometown's net asset value will actually change in response to interest rate declines. For if the negative correlation between Hometown's value and interest rates predicted in Figure 1.2 could be assumed to hold with complete confidence, the probability of its defaulting on the swap would be zero!

As this example is meant to suggest, then, *even if Hometown is the riskiest S&L in the industry, the default risk associated with its interest rate swap is likely to be negligible,* given the following: (1) the S&L's principal exposure has been correctly identified as interest rates (that is, there are no other major exposures—such as the risk of falling oil prices facing a Texas S&L—that would override the effect of interest rates on firm value); and (2) the swap position is being used to reduce, not to enlarge, the S&L's exposure to interest rates.

Counterparty Risk

What about Hometown's exposure to the party on the other side of the swap, the party that pays floating and receives fixed? Higher interest rates may make Hometown's counterparty unable to make good on the contract.

One potentially important consideration in evaluating counterparty risk is the credit rating of the counterparty. If the counterparty has a AA or AAA credit rating (as most swap dealers do), then any interest rate swap it enters into with Hometown will pose little counterparty risk for the S&L. The capital backing of AA-rated counterparties (and we will have more to say about swap dealers later) provides strong guarantees of performance.

But what if the counterparty is an industrial firm with a credit rating of Baa or lower? As we just saw in the case of Hometown, the most important consideration in evaluating counterparty risk in such cases (that is, holding credit rating constant) is likely to be the correlation between the replacement cost of the counterparty's swap position and the value of the counterparty's net assets. If there is a strong negative correlation—that is, if the counterparty (like Hometown) is also using its swap position to offset its own well-defined exposure—then, again, the default risk on the swap will be minimal.

To illustrate this point, let's begin with the (clearly unrealistic) assumption that Hometown does not use a swap dealer as its counterparty but instead enters into its swap with either one of two companies: (1) GoldCo, a commodity producer whose value rises with increases in interest rates; and (2) SpecCo, a trading firm whose value falls with increases in rates. Assume also that both GoldCo and SpecCo would have the same Baa credit rating *after* entering into this swap with Hometown. And let's begin with the case of GoldCo: Under what circumstances might it be expected to default?

Because the value of GoldCo is *positively* correlated with inflation and interest rates, its exposure to interest rates (as illustrated in Figure 1.3) is essentially the

FIGURE 1.3 Goldco's Exposures to Interest Rates

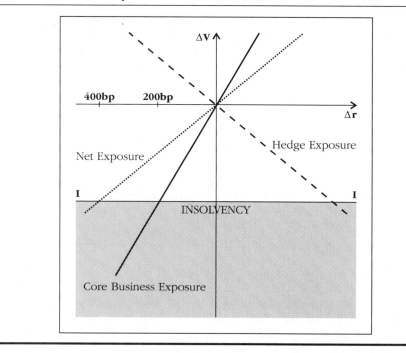

opposite of the S&Ls. By exchanging their opposite exposures through an interest rate swap, both GoldCo and Hometown reduce their net exposures to interest rates, thereby reducing the probability of insolvency and default on any outstanding liabilities.

Moreover, as we saw in the case of Hometown, GoldCo will default on the swap only if both of the following conditions hold: (1) interest rates must change in such a way (in this case, rise) that GoldCo owes a net payment on the swap; and (2) the decline in GoldCo's net asset value (when combined with the cashflows on the swap) is sufficient to make the firm insolvent.

As in the case of Hometown, the probability that both of these conditions will hold at the same time is low; if interest rates do rise, GoldCo's core business will most likely be prospering. Thus, the likelihood that GoldCo will default on the swap is also low. (In fact, as we demonstrate next, the probability that GoldCo will default on the swap is appreciably lower than the probability that it will default on its outstanding debt.)

But consider what happens if SpecCo instead of GoldCo is the counterparty to the swap with Hometown. In contrast to GoldCo (but like Hometown), SpecCo's value falls with increases in interest rates; that is, SpecCo's exposure is essentially the same as Hometown's as represented in Figure 1.1. By entering into this swap, SpecCo is effectively magnifying its own exposure to interest rates (it will be required to make net swap payments when interest rates rise—exactly when it can least afford it), thereby increasing the probability that it will default on its debt. Thus, Hometown's counterparty credit risk would be significantly higher in a swap with SpecCo than with GoldCo—again, *even if the two firms had the same credit rating* after entering into the swap.

It is in this sense of reducing or enlarging core business exposures that we speak of hedging and speculating with derivatives. Hometown and GoldCo may both retain some of their basic exposures to interest rates, but they reduce part of their exposure by means of the swap. SpecCo, by contrast, increases its exposure by entering into the swap.

Quantifying Default Risk

Default risk on a swap or other derivatives contract is the risk that losses will be incurred if a counterparty defaults. Default risk on swaps has two primary components: (1) the expected exposure (that is, the expected replacement cost of the swap at default less any expected recovery); and (2) the probability of default. Although these two components are generally not independent, we begin by discussing each separately and then consider their interaction.

The Expected Exposure

To estimate the default risk of swaps, then, one must begin by estimating how much capital is likely to be at risk when a firm defaults on a swap. As we noted in our introduction, the notional principal amounts used to estimate swap volumes grossly overstate the actual credit exposure. No principal is paid in an interest rate swap, and it is only price movements after the contract is initiated that cause one party to owe net payments to the other. In fact, as noted earlier, the U.S. General Accounting Office (GAO) estimates that the net credit exposure on swaps runs on the order of only 1% of notional principal.

As noted, however, the expected loss depends not only on the expected value of the swap at the time of default, but also on the amount of the expected recovery *after* the default. The GAO estimate effectively assumes the expected recovery is zero—an assumption that generally leads to a material overstatement of the expected loss. It's true that, in bankruptcy, most swaps are unsecured financial claims. But typical recoveries on even unsecured (senior) claims average about 50% of the claim. For those swaps that are collateralized (about 5% of the total, according to the GAO), average recoveries run on the order of 80%.[10]

Probability of Default

Perhaps the best way to quantify the probability of default associated with derivatives is to begin by looking at historical default rates on corporate bonds. Edward Altman's[11] 1989 study of corporate bond defaults reported that slightly under 1% (on a dollar-weighted basis) of all A-rated bonds issued between 1971 and 1987 defaulted during their first 10 years. Converted into an annual figure, Altman's estimate thus suggests an *annual* average default probability of roughly 0.1%.

How is the probability of default on a swap related to the probability of default on debt? As we have seen earlier, given the credit rating of the swap counterparty, the default probability of the swap relative to the same firm's debt depends principally on the use of the swap—that is, whether it is reducing or enlarging the firm's exposure. But, as we will now demonstrate, the probability of default on a swap depends not only on whether it is being used to hedge, but also on the size of the swap or, more precisely, on the *percentage of the firm's exposure* that is being hedged.

As a first step in this analysis, recall that the probability of default on a firm's swap can never be greater than the probability of default on its debt. Default on debt requires simply that the firm become insolvent. For a firm (rationally) to default on a swap, it must both be insolvent and owe payments under the swap.

Because both of these two conditions must hold simultaneously, the probability of default on the swap [Pr(D$_s$)] can be expressed as the product of two probabilities: (1) the probability of insolvency, Pr(I) (which is also the probability of default on the firm's debt); and (2) the probability of default on the swap *given that the firm is insolvent* [Pr(D$_s$|I)]. (The latter is referred to as a *conditional* probability.) In the form of an equation:

$$Pr(D_s) = Pr(I) \times Pr(D_s|I)$$

Thus, the probability of default on a swap rises with increases in both the probability of insolvency and the conditional probability of default on the swap. But the correlation between these two variables, as we now demonstrate, is far from a simple (or linear) one.

As illustrated in Figure 1.4, both the probability of insolvency [Pr(I)] and the conditional probability of default on the swap [Pr(D$_s$|I)] depend on the two factors cited above: (1) whether the firm is using the swap to hedge or to speculate; and (2) the percentage of the firm's exposure that is being hedged. With the aid of Figure 1.4, we now present a series of propositions about the relation between the default probabilities of debt and swaps.

FIGURE 1.4   Probability of Default on a Swap

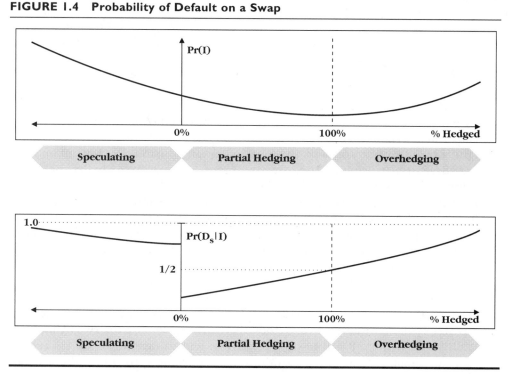

Panel A of Figure 1.4 shows how the probability of insolvency (and thus default on debt) varies with the use and size of the swap. Given that the firm is using the swap to hedge (that is, the percentage of the firm's exposure hedged in Figure 1.4 ranges between 0 and 100%), we can conclude the following: *The larger the percentage of its exposure a firm hedges, the lower is the volatility of the firm's value and hence the lower is the probability of insolvency.* Either decreases in the percentage hedged below 0% (which mean the firm is speculating) or increases above 100% (the firm is "overhedging") cause the probability of insolvency to increase.

Panel B of Figure 1.4 shows how the conditional probability of default on the swap varies with the use and size of the swap. As in the case of Panel A, if the firm is either speculating or overhedging with the swap (that is, as the percentage exposure hedged falls below 0% or rises above 100%), the conditional probability of default on the swap rises along with the probability of insolvency and approaches 1.0 (at which point the probability of default on the swap would equal the probability of default on the debt). By contrast—and this may seem surprising—given that the firm is using the swap to hedge, the smaller the percentage of its exposure a firm hedges, the *lower* is the probability of default on the swap if the firm becomes insolvent.

To see why this last proposition holds, consider a firm that hedges exactly 100% of its exposure to interest rates. In this case, the expected default probability of the swap will be *exactly one-half* the default probability of the firm's debt. This is true for the following two reasons: (1) Assuming that the firm is using an "at-market" swap and that future interest rates are equally likely to fall above or below the interest rate built into the swap, the firm is likely to owe payments on the swap in 50% of the cases where the firm might default. (2) The probability of insolvency (and thus default on the firm's debt) is not only reduced by the swap, but is now completely independent of rates—that is, rate changes have no effect on the probability of default, which is now equally likely across *all* interest rate outcomes.

Let's go back to the original case where Hometown (or GoldCo) was hedging *only part* of its interest rate exposure. Under these conditions (which, we will argue later, are more representative of actual corporate behavior), the default risk on Hometown's (or GoldCo's) swap is *less than half* the default risk on its debt. This is because in the interest rate environment in which the firm is most likely to be insolvent, the firm is receiving payments under the swap.

By putting together Panels A and B, we come up with the following propositions: Firms that hedge more than 100% (overhedge) or less than 0% (speculate) increase both the probability of insolvency and the conditional probability of default on their swap. And, as firms move further outside this range, the probability of default on the swap approaches the probability of default on the debt.

For firms hedging between 0% and 100% of their exposures, the two probabilities have offsetting effects. For example, in the case of an at-market swap, as the firm increases the percentage of its exposure hedged, the effect on the swap's default probability of the increase in $\Pr(D_s|I)$ dominates the effect of the decrease in $\Pr(I)$, and so the probability of default on the swap actually increases.

Summing Up

In the special case where a firm hedges 100% of its exposure, the credit risk on a swap is simply the product of two factors: the expected loss on the swap times the probability of default.[12] Based on this reasoning, and using Altman's 0.1% default estimate for single A firms cited earlier, a good working estimate of the average

annual default rate of an A-rated firm that completely hedges its interest rate exposure is 0.05%, or $\frac{1}{20}$ of 1%, of the expected exposure. And if we accept the GAO's estimate of that exposure as 1% of notional principal and assume that the expected
recovery is 50%, then credit risk is .00025% of notional principal.

To the extent that swaps and other derivatives are used to reduce exposures and
not to enlarge them, they have significantly lower default probabilities than the debt
issued by the same firm. And, if we assume that most companies are using derivatives as only partial hedges of their exposures, even this .00025% is too high.

At the same time, swaps and other derivatives that are used in attempts to convert the treasury into a profit center generally succeed only in adding financial risk
to business risk. Yet, even in the cases where companies double up their exposures
and increase the likelihood of insolvency, the probability of default on the swap cannot exceed the probability of default on its debt. And, given the default probability
on debt of .1% cited earlier, the credit risk on swaps in such cases is still likely to be
only on the order of .0005% of notional principal.[13]

Evidence on the Corporate Use of Derivatives

This brings us to the critical question: Are firms using derivatives to hedge rather
than to speculate? Although the evidence is admittedly preliminary at this point, the
answer appears to be, "Yes—for the most part."

The most comprehensive survey to date of the corporate use of derivatives was
conducted by Walter Dolde in 1993.[14] The overwhelming majority of the 244 Fortune 500 companies that responded to Dolde's questionnaire reported that their policy is to use derivatives primarily to hedge their exposures. Only about 20% of the
responding firms reported that they aim to hedge their exposures completely. Moreover, as theory would suggest, smaller firms—those likely to have lower credit ratings and hence greater default risk—reported hedging larger percentages of their
exposures than big companies.

About 90% of the firms in Dolde's survey also said they sometimes had a view on
the market direction of interest rates or exchange rates. And although roughly one in
six of even these companies hedged their exposures completely, the rest claimed to
modify the extent of their hedging to accommodate their view. For example, if they
expected rates to move in a way that would increase firm value, they might hedge
only 30% of their exposure. On the other hand, if they expected rates to move in a
way that would reduce value, they would hedge as much as 100% of the exposure.
Moreover, only 2 of the 244 firms responded that they choose hedge ratios outside
the 0% to 100% range. This means that less than 1% of the firms said they would use
derivatives to enlarge an existing exposure.

Some companies—particularly those in which the treasury operates as a profit
center—might be reluctant to respond to a survey admitting that they use derivatives
to increase an existing exposure. Moreover, some firms could be using derivatives in
a way that introduces new exposures; that is, a firm that has no interest rate exposure
may create one by, say, taking the floating side of an interest rate swap. But treasuries
that operate as profit centers are the exception rather than the rule (and, given the recent focus of the business press on derivatives losses by industrial firms, profit-center
treasuries are likely to become even more scarce).

In sum, the companies that use derivatives to hedge appear to outnumber significantly those that use them for speculative ends.[15]

SYSTEMIC RISK FROM DERIVATIVES

What Is Systemic Risk?

We define systemic risk as widespread default in any set of financial contracts that can be linked to default in derivatives. While this interpretation of systemic risk is *consistent* with most others, we believe that default is the most useful criterion because it has definite cash flow consequences and can be readily observed.[16]

System-wide derivative risk is simply the aggregation of the underlying risks faced by individual firms. But because the underlying risks are not independent, one cannot simply sum them to find the total. Indeed, in the case of derivatives, the underlying default risks are likely to be correlated through two channels.

First, default *within* derivative contracts is negatively correlated. That is, at any point in time, only the side of a derivative contract that is in the money can lose from default. Because the net supply of derivatives is zero, a simple summation of derivatives positions across the economy grossly overstates the total default risk.

The second channel is more complex. Some observers argue that widespread corporate risk management with derivatives increases the correlation of default *among* financial contracts. If risks are borne by more and different investors than before, more participants will be affected by the underlying shocks to the economy that occur from time to time. After all, even firms that use derivatives will be affected by such shocks.

What this argument fails to recognize, however, is that the adverse effects of such shocks on individual investors or firms should be smaller precisely because the risks are spread more widely. More important, to the extent firms are using derivatives to hedge their existing exposures, much of the impact of shocks is being transferred from corporations and investors less able to bear such shocks to counterparties better able to absorb them. For this reason, defaults in the economy as a whole, and hence systemic risk, are unambiguously reduced through the operation of the derivatives market.

As an illustration of a recent shock and how derivatives cope with it, consider the 200-bp increase in most interest rates that took place between October 1993 and October of 1994. Before the securitization of mortgages (which was made possible in part by interest-rate derivatives), S&Ls and other originators would have experienced large losses, and perhaps a wave of defaults. But this time there has been no rash of S&L or commercial bank failures, in large part because so many financial institutions have chosen to lay off part of their interest-rate risk to investors with opposite interest-rate exposures.

Perhaps the best evidence that such risks have been transferred are the handful of highly publicized instances in which mutual and pension funds have reported significant losses on hedge funds using mortgage-backed securities. Although the popular response is to deplore such losses, they can also be viewed as confirmation of a positive economic development: the shifting of interest rate risk from highly leveraged financial institutions like S&Ls to investors with longer term liability structures, such as pension funds and insurance companies. As long as 30-year, fixed-rate mortgages are available to the home-buying public, the risk of sharp increases in interest rates will be borne by some firms or investors (although there are ways for investors to hedge such risks using mortgage derivatives).[17] Institutional investors, such as pension funds, mutual funds, and insurance companies, are likely to prove

better able to bear these interest-rate risks once concentrated almost entirely on federally insured depositary institutions.

In sum, as a result of the expanded risk sharing that has been achieved with derivatives, a shock of a given size might affect more firms; but the average effect on
each firm will be significantly less. And because fewer firms default in response to
any given shock, systemic risk has been reduced.

How Bad Is It Likely to Be?

It is certainly conceivable that financial markets could be hit by a very large shock.
Take the stock market crash of 1987. If such a disturbance were to affect a large number of participants in the derivatives markets, it could expose them to systemic risk.
The effects of such a disturbance on derivatives markets and participants in these
markets will likely depend, however, on the duration of the shock.

Temporary Disturbances

If the shock were large but temporary—the liquidity effects of the stock market crash
of 1987 are a good example—many derivatives would be largely unaffected. Forwards, options, and swaps make relatively infrequent payments. Forwards and European options make payments only at maturity; and, although swaps make periodic
payments, standard swaps require payments only once every six months. A temporary disturbance would primarily affect only contracts with required settlements during this period. And, even if swap payments were literally impossible for some time,
a temporary reduction in liquidity would mean that only a small fraction of the total
payments would be missed.

This does not mean that temporary disturbances have no adverse consequences.
In response to the resulting uncertainty, market makers are likely to increase substantially the spreads they quote in order to receive sufficient compensation for the
risk they assume by carrying an inventory. Indeed, such behavior was evident during the 1992 upheaval in the European Monetary System, when many market makers
reportedly stopped quoting forward prices altogether for some European currencies
for several hours. Such an increase in trading costs makes the arbitrage between underlying instruments and derivatives more costly, which in turn is likely to slow the
origination of new derivatives contracts.

Longer Term Problems

If a shock persists for a long time, as did some of the valuation effects of the 1987
crash, it will affect derivatives in much the same manner that it affects other markets. If an underlying price falls substantially, positions that were effectively long in
the underlying security will lose; on the other hand, the corresponding short positions will gain. And, as noted above, since all derivatives contracts exist in zero net
supply, the gains will exactly equal the losses. As a group, therefore, participants in
the derivatives markets will be no worse off than they were before.

Nevertheless, for sufficiently large disturbances, there will—and probably
should—be defaults. Defaults followed by bankruptcies (and asset sales or, in some
cases, piecemeal liquidations) are an important means by which the economy
squeezes out excess capacity or eliminates otherwise inefficient operations. Moreover, the more costly it is (in terms of economic growth forgone through excessive
regulation) to reduce the probability of default, the larger is the optimal number of

defaults. As is true of all financial markets, regulators and other economic policymakers should aim to reduce the probability of default only if the benefits of fewer defaults exceed the costs of preventing them.

Independent and Correlated Disturbances

The critical question in evaluating systemic risk, however, concerns the extent to which defaults across derivatives markets, and financial markets in general, are likely to be correlated. In the analysis that follows, we begin by assuming that the derivatives defaults that could trigger systemic problems are largely independent across dealers, and then go on to explain the reasoning behind this assumption.

If we assume that defaults in derivatives markets are largely independent across market makers, then available data on corporate default rates can be used to provide a crude estimate of the likelihood of large-scale disturbances. Recall that, on that basis of Altman's estimate of the average annual default rate of A-rated corporate bonds, we earlier used 0.05%, or $\frac{1}{20}$ of 1%, as the expected annual default rate on swaps. (In using this number, keep in mind that Altman's default rates are for industrial firms; such rates are likely to be too high for the major financial firms that are active market makers in derivatives. In fact, they are likely to be much too high for the market makers in these instruments, because such firms typically have AA or AAA credit ratings.) We will now use this 0.1% estimate of annual corporate default probability on debt as a crude indicator of the probability that a large number of dealers default at the same time.

If default is independent across dealers and over time, then assessing the probability of defaults by dealers can be thought of as a coin tossing experiment—except that the coin is heavily loaded. Based on our estimate of the default probability, we will load the coin to come up "default" $\frac{1}{20}$ of 1% of the time—that is, only five times in 10,000 throws.[18] Probability theory can then be used to compute the probability that at least a certain number of firms default.

Just how quickly the numbers become incomprehensibly small can be illustrated with the following example: Consider the probability that several of the major dealers could default at the same time. If there are 50 major dealers, and we are worried about five or more defaulting during the same year (not the same quarter or month), the odds are one in 650 billion.

What grounds do we have for assuming that the risks are independent? First, we need to remember the private incentives that are at work in these markets. Market makers have strong incentives to do a thorough job of assessing the default risk of their swap partners. As suggested earlier, a very strong credit rating may be all the assurance a swap dealer needs to take the other side of a transaction. If the dealer receives a call from a AAA credit like DuPont expressing interest in a swap, the dealer is unlikely to care whether DuPont's treasury is hedging or taking a view; the company has such a strong balance sheet relative to the size of the transaction that default is extremely unlikely in either circumstance. But if, as we also saw earlier, a Baa-rated firm asks about the same kind of swap, the swap dealer is much more likely to investigate the firm's core business exposure to ensure that the swap is being used to offset, and not to enlarge, that exposure.

Second, as we have already noted, for firms using swaps to hedge their exposures, the interest-rate environment in which these firms are most likely to becomes insolvent is precisely the environment in which they will be receiving payments on their swaps or other derivatives. For these firms, defaults must be caused by shocks other than interest rate changes. (For example, the few defaults on swaps by S&Ls that have been reported to date occurred primarily among S&Ls in the oil patch. In such cases, the favorable impact of lower interest rates was overwhelmed by the negative effect of low oil prices on the creditworthiness of their loans.)

In this sense, defaults on swaps are significantly more "idiosyncratic"—that is, less predictably associated with systematic, economywide factors such as changes in interest rates—than are defaults on loans. For example, a large increase in interest rates is much more likely to lead to a rash of defaults on floating-rate bank loans than on interest rate swaps. And because the correlation among defaults on swaps is thus likely to be significantly lower than the correlation among defaults on loans, diversification is a more effective tool for managing the credit risk of swaps than loans. This is why swap dealers limit (and continuously monitor) their exposures to specific counterparties, industries, and geographical areas.

Finally, market makers with a carefully balanced book and substantial capital reserves can absorb defaults by their counterparties without defaulting on their other contracts. Swap dealers function somewhat like clearinghouses in futures markets. For a dealer to default, customer defaults would have to impair dealer capital. Moreover, a large number of financial institutions have set up well-capitalized, highly rated special purpose subs to conduct their derivatives businesses. Besides offering protection to the dealers' derivatives customers, such segregation of derivatives operations also reduces the risk that a wave of derivatives defaults could affect a bank's other operations.

Given all these risk-reducing arrangements along with the normal incentives for self-preservation in large, well-capitalized financial institutions, independent defaults are not as unlikely as a discussion of systemic risk might at first suggest. The default probabilities cited above are not intended as precise estimates; the fact that they are so small makes it unlikely that we could ever obtain very precise estimates of these phenomena—simply because we don't observe enough of them. And our assumption that expected defaults are independent across dealers is also clearly too strong. Nevertheless, given the capital that dealers devote to the support of their operations and the diversification of their derivatives portfolio, we believe that expected defaults among dealers are not far from being independent events. Even if we have understated the likelihood of systemic problems by a factor of a million, these default rates illustrate just how small these risks are likely to be.

REGULATION

Derivatives markets continue to attract a great deal of attention from regulatory bodies. In press accounts and in the popular debate, a few large losses have been cited as evidence that these markets are very risky. Proponents of greater regulation of derivatives then typically proceed to argue that regulations can reduce or eliminate these risks with minimal costs.

Establishing effective public policy, however, requires an accurate assessment of not only the risks associated with derivatives, but also of the benefits offered by the instruments and the potential costs of regulatory interference. We believe the benefits are substantial. As we have attempted to demonstrate, the derivatives markets have provided corporations with a powerful (and flexible) set of financial tools that can be used to manage their exposures to financial prices such as commodity prices, interest rates, and exchange rates.

Derivatives (like automobiles) can be used for destructive ends. Witness the recent run of stories in the popular financial press reporting speculative derivatives losses at industrial companies. Nevertheless, in contrast to most press accounts of derivatives, a growing body of academic evidence suggests that these tools are being used by firms primarily to reduce (not to enlarge) their exposures and to reduce funding costs, thereby increasing their competitiveness in global markets.

Largely for this reason, we believe the risks and hence potential costs of these markets have been materially overstated. To the extent that derivatives are being used primarily to hedge rather than to speculate, as we show in this paper, the default risk associated with derivatives has been significantly overstated. (For example, an interest-rate swap used by a B-rated firm to hedge its principal price exposure is likely to have significantly less default risk than even an AAA-rated corporate bond issue.) And, far from increasing systemic risk, we argue that derivatives markets act to reduce systemic risk by spreading the impact of economic shocks among a set of institutional investors and financial intermediaries in a better position (because most are well-capitalized and carefully diversified) to absorb them.

Such overstatement of default and systemic risk has led to regulatory proposals that would significantly raise the costs of—and thereby restrict access to—derivative instruments. By providing a clearer analysis of the risks and potential costs, we hope to encourage more productive regulatory initiatives—those designed to limit risks while preserving the efficiency of domestic and international capital markets.

Proposed Regulation of End Users

In the United States, the principal regulatory initiatives that would affect the users of derivatives involve new disclosure requirements. The proposals now on the table—particularly, those calling for periodic reporting of the market value of derivatives positions—have two obvious shortcomings:

1. They would necessarily be based upon GAAP accounting. Marking derivatives positions to market causes problems for corporations who are using them as economic or "macro" hedges of longer dated exposures. If the derivatives position used to hedge an exposure is required to be marked to market, but the underlying assets or liabilities being hedged must be carried at historical cost, then reported earnings will become more volatile—even when variability in the firm's value has been reduced through hedging. For this reason, the accounting system may have to be fixed to make the disclosures more useful to investors.
2. The second problem with disclosure requirements is that they effectively ignore the private incentives of companies to provide sufficient information to enable investors to value their shares accurately. Because investors discount shares for uncertainty, companies can be counted on (eventually, if not immediately) to provide additional information about their derivatives activities as long as the benefits of the new information outweigh the costs.

The good news about mandated disclosure, however, is that its capacity to impose additional costs is limited. Disclosure requirements are inefficient only to the extent they require companies to disclose more than investors are willing to "pay for" in the form of a higher stock price for reduced uncertainty. And, to the extent corporations are now providing less than the optimal amount of disclosure, disclosure requirements might even provide net benefits—at least insofar as they help initiate a beneficial process. The problem with this argument, however, is that disclosure requirements, even if modest at first, have a tendency to proliferate to the point where (like much SEC disclosure imposed on the largest U.S. corporations today) they end up imposing costs that exceed the benefits to investors.

Proposed Regulation of Dealers

Potentially more troubling than disclosure requirements, however, are the current risk-based capital requirements that affect derivatives dealing at banks and other regulated financial institutions, and the proposals to extend such requirements to unregulated market makers in derivatives. Without getting into the details of the calculations, the capital guidelines for banks apply a risk weighting to derivatives (as well as other on- and off-balance-sheet assets), and then compare the institutions' risk-adjusted assets to qualifying capital.

In our analysis, we argued that the credit risk of derivatives depends primarily on two factors: the credit standing of the counterparty and whether the derivative is being used to hedge or speculate. The capital guidelines, however, make no attempt to distinguish between a 10-year swap to a single-B credit that is using the swap to speculate on interest rates and a 3-year swap to a AAA credit that is hedging. In the first case, the guidelines might be too low; in the second, they are almost certainly too high.

Because these capital guidelines are such a blunt tool, their effectiveness in limiting the risk of a dealer default is questionable. Derivatives dealers have strong incentives to back their operations with appropriate levels of capital; in fact, a AA credit rating is almost a requirement to compete in the business. To the extent regulations specifying minimum capital requirements are set too high, they impose additional costs on dealers. The requirement for excess capital amounts to a tax; and, like all taxes, it raises costs and prices, thereby limiting access to the market.

In the process of raising costs, moreover, excessive capital requirements also have the potential to create precisely the opposite kind of incentives as those presumably intended by regulators. By burdening safer-than-average derivatives transactions with excessive capital charges, capital requirements that are too high encourage dealers to book riskier deals in order to justify the capital employed. To offer just one example, the current capital guidelines effectively create an incentive for banks and other dealers to structure the kind of leveraged derivatives that Bankers Trust sold Procter & Gamble (since the guidelines are keyed to notional principal, leveraged derivatives allow the dealer to support a larger effective exposure with the same amount of capital).

If you accept our basic contention—that the risks of derivatives have been exaggerated—then the regulatory history of derivatives can be explained simply as cautious responses by well-meaning regulators to rapidly growing markets in complex and unfamiliar products. But there may be a problem in effecting constructive policy changes. Just as derivatives dealers and users face important private incentives to manage risks in their operations, politicians have private incentives that influence legislative proposals to regulate this market. To the extent politicians are able to convince the public that the derivatives markets are fundamentally dangerous and that all that keeps the threat at bay is regulatory vigilance, they gain public and political support and so fortify their own positions.

This view of derivatives regulation reminds us of the story of a gentleman walking along a city street who would periodically stop and blow a whistle. When a policeman asked him why he did so, he replied, "It's a magic whistle; it keeps the tigers away." When the officer objected, "But there are no tigers around here," the fellow winked and said, "See, it works."

As long as this tiger whistle is relatively inexpensive, such political maneuvering will be fairly harmless. But if the regulation that results from the political process becomes too burdensome—which represents a very real risk to the derivatives markets—we will end up reducing the efficiency of the entire financial system.

ENDNOTES

1. Note that the trading required to replicate the payoffs depends critically on the other outstanding positions the firm is managing. Required trading costs for a market maker with an extensive derivatives book is generally dramatically less than the sum of the trades required to replicate the individual contracts.

2. In fact, to the extent transactions costs introduce a degree of imprecision into derivatives pricing models, the derivatives themselves are likely to provide more effective hedges than the "synthetic" derivatives sometimes used to hedge the same risks. A prime case was the performance of "synthetic puts" on the S&P 500 during the stock market crash of 1987. The puts were replicated by a dynamic futures trading strategy that was intended to provide "portfolio insurance" for stock market investors. Although actual put options would have protected investors, the replicating strategy generally employed at the time broke down when bid-ask spreads widened and trading became very costly or impossible.

3. This doesn't mean that the market value will necessarily change by that amount, only that a certain change in interest rates is expected to change its value by the amount. Factors other than interest rates also affect the S&L's value. For example, even in a very low interest rate environment, a Texas S&L could find an unusually high proportion of its loans going bad if oil prices go down. Thus, there is uncertainty, or a distribution of values, around this expected value.

4. More precisely, the figure shows the effect of unexpected changes in interest rates on firm value, since all expected changes should be incorporated into current prices.

5. As noted in footnote 4, unexpected positive or negative developments could delay or hasten insolvency.

6. There are other ways for S&Ls to hedge their interest rate risk. For example, they could sell many of the mortgages. But there are limits to the percentage of its mortgages that a mortgage originator can sell without recourse.

7. The term *Herstatt risk* derives from the name of a German bank that defaulted on contracts with foreign counterparties after receiving payments but before making them. The default exceeded the net payments due to different business hours.

8. The right to default can be viewed as a "compound option," one whose value depends on two uncertain outcomes—in this case, the change in firm value and the change in interest rates. For a more formal treatment of default risk as a compound option problem, *see* Herbert Johnson and René Stulz, "The Pricing of Options Under Default Risk," *Journal of Finance, 42* (1987), pp. 267–280.

9. In our discussion of default, we generally ignore technical default since it has no direct cash flow consequences. However, many derivative contracts have cross-default clauses which can place a party into technical default. Should the counterparty try to unwind the contract under the default terms but fail, then default occurs.

10. *See* Julian Franks and Walter Torous, "A Comparison of Financial Contracting in Distressed Exchanges and Chapter 11 Reorganizations," *Journal of Financial Economics, 35*(3) (June 1994), pp. 349–370.

11. Edward I. Altman, "Measuring Corporate Bond Mortality and Performance," *Journal of Finance, XLIV*(4) (September 1989), pp. 909–922.

12. In general, the relation is more complicated; but if a perfect hedge makes firm value independent of interest rates, this simple product is appropriate.

13. This assumes that the speculative use of derivatives is confined largely, if not exclusively, to firms with high credit ratings.

14. Walter Dolde, "The Trajectory of Corporate Risk Management," *Journal of Applied Corporate Finance* (Fall 1993), pp. 33–41.

15. Other preliminary academic evidence on hedging also bears out this corporate propensity to hedge rather than speculate. For example, a recent study by one of the present writers in collaboration with Charles Smithson and Deana Nance concludes that firms with tax or operating characteristics which theory suggests should make hedging more valuable in fact use more derivatives. If derivatives were used primarily to speculate, no such associations should be expected. *See* Deana Nance, Clifford Smith, and Charles Smithson, "On the Determinants of Corporate Hedging," *Journal of Finance* (1993), pp. 267–284.

16. The Bank for International Settlements (1992), for example, defines systemic risk to include "widespread difficulties." While this definition agrees with ours in spirit, it is not operational.

17. *See* Charles Stone and Anne Zissu, "The Risk of Mortgage Backed Securities and Their Derivatives," *Journal of Applied Corporate Finance* (Fall 1994), pp. 99–111.

18. That is to say, we assume that default has a binomial distribution with a default probability of 0.0005.

2

Credit Derivatives

FRANK IACONO

T his chapter provides a brief introduction to credit derivatives, discusses their
applications, and surveys issues surrounding their pricing and hedging. Following an introduction, credit derivatives are defined, and a general classification scheme for these products is provided. Using examples of products as much
as 100 years old, credit derivatives are shown to be a not new economic concept.
What is new is the emergence of a trading market for highly customized risks. We
then describe three types of credit derivative products and their applications. Next
we outline the challenges in pricing and hedging credit derivatives. Finally, we offer
a commentary regarding the potential future development of this market.

Credit risk is one of the oldest and best-understood risks in finance. Therefore, it
is surprising that credit risk derivatives were not publicly introduced until 1992 at
the ISDA annual meeting in Paris. Surprisingly, interest rate and foreign exchange
risk were little managed prior to the 1970s, yet by 1992 interest rate and FX derivatives were well-developed. Why did credit derivatives take so long to emerge? One
plausible explanation is that many credit-sensitive instruments are also interest rate-
sensitive, so the value of a credit derivative often requires more sophisticated
models than for pure interest rate or FX derivatives. An example is a spread-based
product, which derives its value from a risky bond (factor 1) and a comparable Treasury security (factor 2). The technology necessary to price and hedge two-factor
products is still under development, as evidenced by the continued use of single-
factor yield curve models and the practice of pricing convertible bond options as
simple equity options. Another explanation is that modeling credit risk depends on
discrete, not continuous events, so is more difficult to model than other capital market phenomena.[1] A possible historical explanation for credit derivatives' lag is that
through most of the 1980s, interest rate and FX risk were more on people's minds
than credit risk. Perhaps it took the LDC debt crisis, the collapse of real estate loans,
and the dislocation of junk bonds in 1989 to inspire the financial engineers to design
credit-risk management tools.

Despite credit derivatives' slow start, a critical mass of dealers has developed a
rich diversity of products. Bankers Trust was reportedly the first to make a market in
credit derivatives in 1992, and there are now several dealers who offer derivatives

---

The author wishes to thank Jams BeSaw, Sara Brumwell and Aliza Mezrich and for their excellent research assistance, and Tanya Styblo Beder for her valuable inputs regarding this chapter.

based on a broad set of credit-sensitive underlyings. Some common credit derivatives include:

- *Derivatives based on sovereign credits:* For Example, Brady Bond derivatives allow investors to take a view on the narrowing of Sovereign credit spreads or the differential between two measures of the same issuer's credit risk.
- *Derivatives based on corporate credits:* For example, derivatives based on a single company's credit are often used for liability management, to take customized views, or to effect "capital structure arbitrage."[2]
- *Derivatives based on bank loans:* For example, derivatives based on one or more loans are used by banks to diversify or neutralize concentrations of issuer-specific credit risk and offer investors favorable risk-return profiles.

Note that credit derivatives tend to be highly customized and the lack of fungibility of credits restricts transaction volume relative to other markets. As of 1995, market estimates were no higher than $10 billion in notional amount,[3] showing growth that had been far less spectacular than the early growth of the interest rate swaps market.[4] Recently, however, the market has taken off, and its size is now estimated to be "something north of $50 billion."[5] Moreover, the prospects for future growth are thought to be enormous as "[t]he potential uses are so widespread that some market participants argue that credit derivatives could eventually outstrip all other derivative products in size and importance."[6]

DEFINITION AND CLASSIFICATIONS

A credit derivative is based on the credit performance of some credit-sensitive asset or assets. Credit performance typically is measured by yield or price spreads relative to benchmarks, by credit ratings or by default status. A simple example is a credit spread swap under which one party makes payments based on the yield to maturity of a specific issuer's debt, and the other makes payments based on comparable Treasury yields. Given that changes in general interest rates impact the two yields similarly, the net payments under the swap will be driven by changes in the actual or perceived credit quality of the issuer (i.e., changes in the issuer's credit spread).

To illustrate, Figure 2.1a compares the yield to maturity of the 7.95% Kmart Bond maturing 2/1/23 and the 7.125% U.S. Treasury Bond maturing 2/15/23 for the period 2/93 to 6/96. Although Kmart's spread widened slightly between February 1993 and September 1995, the two yields largely moved together. They stopped moving together in October 1995 with the occurrence of some significant credit events. Figure 2.1b details this period. On October 2, 1995 Kmart was placed on credit watch. On October 20, Moody's downgraded $539 million of Kmart's long-term corporate debt from Baa1 to Baa2, and the spread began to widen. Note that this deterioration was exacerbated by the fact that $680 million of Kmart's debt contained a put provision that allowed the holders to force an early redemption if Kmart's debt were downgraded to below investment grade. On December 20, Kmart announced an agreement to eliminate this provision. The spread then tightened until January 12, 1996, when Standard and Poor's cut Kmart's senior debt from BBB to BB, triggering a widening spread. On February 2, Moody's downgraded Kmart's long-term debt to junk status, but included positive comments on Kmart's strengthening credit condition in its

FIGURE 2.1a   Yield to Maturity of Treasury Bond versus Kmart Bond

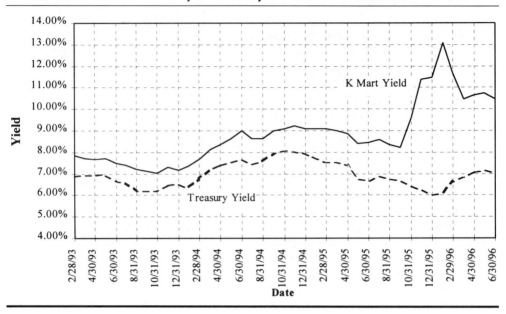

FIGURE 2.1b   Credit Spread of Kmart 2023 Bond

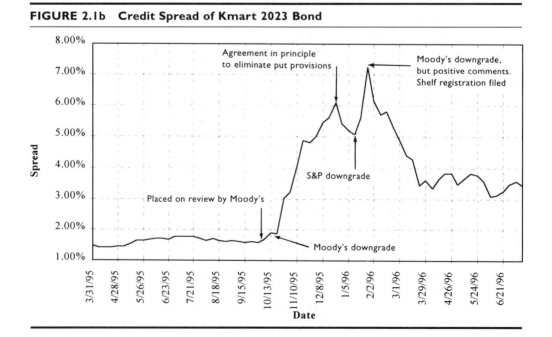

report. Also around this time, Kmart also filed a shelf registration in connection with a contemplated recapitalization plan.

There are many credit derivatives available to exploit such credit re-evaluations. Table 2.1 sets forth a two-dimensional classification scheme, with examples of each type. On the vertical dimension, credit derivatives are classified by the type of underlying credit. On the horizontal dimension, the credit derivatives are classified according to structure. To date, most credit derivatives have been based on Sovereigns, individual corporates and corporate baskets and indices. Brady Bond derivatives were popular prior to the devaluation of the Mexican Peso in December 1994 and provide an example of sovereign credit derivatives. An example of a corporate credit derivative is the yield swap described above which is based on a high-yield issuer such as Kmart. The payments on such a swap, which will be described in more detail below, are shown in Figure 2.2. Finally, examples of basket or index credit derivatives include an option on the BB/AAA spread, or a total return swap involving a portfolio of bank loans. In addition, credit derivative transactions have recently been executed on consumer debt, including pools of credit card receivables and home mortgage loans, and municipal credit underlyings.

For each type of underlying (municipals are rare), both option-based and forward-based (swap) products currently exist. Both basic types have been embedded

TABLE 2.1 Classifying Credit Derivatives by Underlying and Structure—Examples

	Trigger/Payout Variable		
	Price/Yield	*Credit Rating*	*Default Status*
Underlying			
Sovereign	Argentina Brady Bond—Bocon Pre2 contraction swap	Digital option which pays if Mexico is upgraded to investment grade status	Note which pays interest only if Russia does not default on its bonds
Individual Corporate	Corporate versus Treasury Bond relative performance option	Swap which becomes effective if Kmart is upgraded to investment grade status	Swap which pays an additional spread if Macy's debt defaults
Corporate Basket	BB index versus Treasury yield-linked note	Swap which identifies debt issues and provides for payments whenever one is downgraded	Note with a redemption equal to the % if issues in a bank loan portfolio which do not default
Municipal	Orange County vs. AAA Muni index total return swap	Swap which is canceled if the Triboro Bridge Authority is downgraded by Moody's or S&P	Note which pays no principal unless the City of Bridgeport defaults on its bonds

---

Figure 2.2   Payments under a Kmart Credit Spread Swap

YTM of Kmart Long Bond * $10 million

(YTM of Treasury Bond + 365 bp)*
$10 million

---

into structured notes. One structural dimension unique to credit derivatives is the trigger or payout variable, of which there are three types:

1. Changes in credit spreads or relative prices: An example of this type is a corporate credit spread swap in which payments are based on the yield of the issuer's debt relative to Treasury yields, regardless of credit rating or default status.
2. Rating upgrades and downgrades: An example of this type is a contract under which one party pays the other if the debt of a specific issuer (e.g., Kmart), is upgraded to investment grade status.
3. Default: An example of this type is a structured note under which the issuer's obligation to make interest payments is eliminated if and when a specified sovereign debt issue experiences an event of default.

Note that hybrids also exist, including contracts which provide for payments based on a credit spread in the event of a rating downgrade, and contracts under which one party receives the recovery value in the event of a default.

Consequences of this rich diversity of structures are the potential for arbitrage between credit-sensitive products, and the ability to implement custom-tailored views as never before. Just as interest-rate derivatives allow investors to bet against a perceived "yield curve bias,"[7] credit derivatives allow investors to exploit market mispricing of credit risk, discrepancies between different markets' pricing of the same risk (see Argentina contraction swap below), or simply different opinions or outlooks.

EARLIER FORMS OF CREDIT DERIVATIVES

Before modern credit derivatives, there were financial arrangements that were economically similar, if not identical. An example is the letter of credit (LC), a traditional commercial banking product known to exist at the turn of the century.[8] Under an LC, an issuer pays a bank an annual fee in exchange for the bank's promise to make debt payments on behalf of the issuer, should the issuer fail to do so. LCs are utilized to provide credit support for financial products which trade in markets which demand a high degree of credit quality, such as the commercial paper market. Similar to the LC is bond insurance, under which an issuer pays an insurer, such as FGIC, CAPMAC, or AMBAC, to guarantee performance on a bond. Bond insurance is used largely in the Municipal Bond market, where some 35% of the new issues in 1993 were insured.[9] Bond insurance dates back to 1971.[10]

Both LCs and bond insurance are similar to default swaps, as they provide for protection against nonpayment (Figure 2.3). There are, however, important differences, the most important being that LCs and bond insurance are contracts between the issuer and guarantor, so are not tradable separately from the underlying obligation.

Corporate issuers also embed credit derivatives in their debt securities. For example, callable and putable floating rate notes (FRNs), are one type which became popular in the 1980s.

Under a callable FRN, the issuer has the right to redeem the note prior to maturity at a prespecified price (e.g., par). Under a putable FRN, the investor has the right to force an early redemption. Since FRN coupons periodically reset to market interest rates, fluctuations in market value due to changes in interest rates are minimized. For this reason, the credit risk of the issuer will be the primary driver of an FRN's market value.[11] Thus, changes in credit quality determine whether option exercise is advantageous. In contrast to the FRN's option which is a pure credit derivative, the option in a callable bond is a partial credit derivative. A callable bond option has two underlyings—general interest rates and the credit quality of the issuer. For some issues, especially high-yield issues, the option value contributed by credit risk exceeds the contribution of general interest rates. While the credit derivatives embedded in corporate securities are not themselves tradable instruments, they may be stripped out via sophisticated financial engineering. In fact, a contribution of the current credit derivatives market is that for the first time such credit options can be separated, priced, and traded.

A third credit derivative predecessor is the *spreadlock*. Spreadlocks were developed in the late 1980s, and soon joined swaps, caps, floors, and swaptions as plain vanilla derivative structures. Simply put, a spreadlock is a contract which guarantees a market participant the ability to enter into an interest rate swap, at a predetermined spread over treasuries. Spreadlocks exist as option-based or forward-based

FIGURE 2.3   Credit Guarantees versus Default Swaps

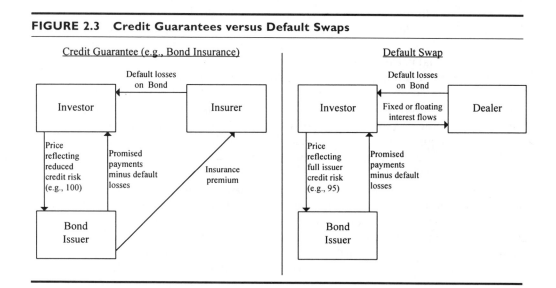

contracts. An example of a forward-based spreadlock is a two-way contract under which the parties agree that in one year's time, they will enter into a five-year swap under which one party pays LIBOR and the other pays the five-year Treasury yield as of the start date, plus 30 bp. Under an option-based spreadlock, one of the parties has the right to determine whether or not the swap becomes effective. Spreadlocks may be viewed as credit derivatives because one of the factors which drives the underlying swap spread is the general level of credit spreads.

EXAMPLES OF RECENT CREDIT DERIVATIVES

Brady Bond Derivatives

Pursuant to a plan sponsored by the Bush Administration, many less developed countries (LDCs) restructured their bank loans through the issuance of Brady Bonds.[12] Generally these bonds were denominated in the currencies of G7 countries (primarily U.S. dollars) and were traded in the global bond markets. Many of these issues also contained various forms of credit guarantees and protections. As early as the first quarter of 1993, dealers had created derivatives designed to isolate the credit performance of these securities. One such structure was the Argentina contraction swap.

The bellwether Brady Bond issued by the Republic of Argentina is the so-called Par Bond, issued in March 1993. The Par Bond is a U.S.-dollar security, paying a step-up coupon and maturing on March 31, 2023. In 1994, several dealers started to trade contraction swaps, which were transaction structures designed to exploit a perceived discrepancy between the credit risk premium embedded in the pricing of the Par Bond relative to the risk premium in the pricing of an Argentinean domestic issue known as the Bocon Pre2. The Bocon Pre2 is a dollar-denominated amortizing floating rate note issued by the Republic of Argentina, paying a coupon based on 1-month LIBOR, with a final maturity date of 4/1/02.

In the contraction swap, dealers employ financial engineering to isolate the credit spreads of the two securities. First, to capture the credit spread of the Par Bond, the principal payment at maturity (which is collateralized by U.S. Treasury strips) must be eliminated from the computation. To do so, the implied value of the Par Bond's coupon flows is computed as the difference between the Par Bond price less the value of the U.S. Treasury strip maturing closest to March 31, 2023. The resulting differential price is used to compute an internal rate of return for a synthetic investment in the coupon payments only. To neutralize general interest rate risk and isolate sovereign credit risk, this rate is compared to a U.S. Treasury yield. If the average life or duration of the resulting coupon flows is similar to that of a 10-year Treasury Note, the Argentine credit spread is computed as the difference between the IRR of the coupon flows and the yield to maturity of the 10-year Treasury Note.[13]

To capture the credit spread of the Bocon Pre2, it is necessary to convert the floating interest flows into fixed flows in order to compute a yield to maturity. An additional complexity comes from the fact that the Bocon Pre2 is not scheduled to pay any cash interest until 1997. One theoretical solution is to build a term structure of one-month LIBOR and to determine the cash flows of the Bocon Pre2 on the assumption that one-month LIBOR turns out as "predicted" by the forward curve. The resulting yield to maturity or IRR is then compared to a Treasury yield. If the average life or duration of the resulting cash flows is similar to that of five-year Treasury

Figure 2.4   Payments under an Argentina Par Bond/Bocon Pre2 Construction Swap

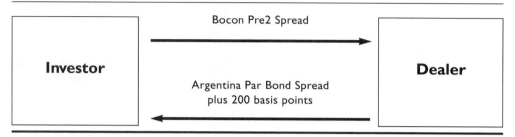

Note, the Argentine credit spread is computed as the difference between the IRR of the resulting flows and the yield to maturity of the five-year Treasury Note.[14]

In 1994, there was a large discrepancy between these two measures of the Argentine credit spread. At one point, the Bocon Pre2 spread was in the 900–1,000 bp range while the Par Bond spread was in the 600–700 bp range. It was believed that the higher spread on the Bocon Pre2 was caused by the lesser degree of liquidity in the local market, and by the fact that yield-hungry investors shunned the Bocon Pre2, which was not scheduled to pay a coupon until 1997. Over time, it was argued, the spreads would converge. In order to enable their customers to exploit this apparent arbitrage, several dealers began marketing "contraction" swaps, under which the customer pays the Bocon Pre2 spread and receives the Par Bond spread plus a fixed amount. If the two spreads come into line, the customer receives this fixed amount as profit on the trade. The payment flows of this swap are diagrammed in Figure 2.4. As the factors which drive the value of these transactions have been volatile, an investor's return in a contraction swap would have depended upon such details as the spread calculation, the trade date, the original maturity and, the unwind price, if any.

Bank Loan-Based Products[15]

Several factors are driving the development of this important credit derivative market, including:

- The size of the domestic Commercial and Industrial (C&I) loan market, including the leveraged loan sector: In 1995, the amount of leveraged syndicated loans was about $250 billion. In the first half of 1996, U.S. syndicated loan volume was almost $400 billion, of which more than $60 billion was leveraged.[16]
- The number and size of institutional investors who have been largely unable to participate in this market: For example, of the more than $250 billion in leveraged syndicated loans, institutional investors such as insurance companies and pension funds hold only $10 billion.
- Customer service versus risk diversification and regulatory capital considerations: The need for banks to diversify and/or hedge concentrations of credit risk while preserving banking relationships by keeping loans on their balance sheets.
- The risk-adjusted returns of bank loan portfolios: Many market participants cite bank loans' historically high risk-adjusted returns as a potential source of value to fuel growth in the credit derivatives market. It is argued that this

risk-return profile allows banks to compensate counterparties well for taking on credit risk. It should be noted, however, that since bank loans carry large administrative costs, as well as regulatory capital requirements, comparisons to other markets should be used with caution. The extent to which banks will be able to compensate their credit derivative counterparties will depend largely on whether regulatory capital requirements change to reduce the amount of capital that must be held against an asset which has been hedged through a credit derivative.

- The lower transactions costs and greater flexibility of credit derivatives relative to loan syndication: Credit derivatives allow banks to offload well-defined credit risks with simpler documentation, and less intensive marketing efforts.

In addition to actively trading credit swaps, some dealers offer credit-linked notes designed to exploit such opportunities. One example is the Bank Loan Asset-Backed Secured Trust Note, (BLAST Note). Under such a transaction, a Master Trust uses the note proceeds to purchase U.S. Treasury securities and simultaneously enters into a swap with the bank, under which the bank pays the coupon flows on a loan portfolio, plus or minus price changes and receives floating interest cash flows from the Trust. The investor receives the cash flows from the Treasury security plus or minus the Trust's net receipts under the swap with the bank. Advantages of this structure include:

- Investors, such as life insurers, who are required to use swaps for hedging purposes only, can gain the same economic result via the notes which are an allowable investment.
- The Treasury collateral earns the note an investment grade rating.
- The investor shares in the favorable banking spreads built into the pricing of the loan portfolio and gets a leveraged upside with downside protection.
- The leverage in the investment can be custom-tailored to meet the investor's risk appetite.
- The bank sells off a substantial portion of the credit risk in its loan portfolio.[17]

Figure 2.5 shows the payment flows under a sample BLAST Note[sm] transaction. In this transaction, the Note value is $10 million, while the underlying loans total $100 million, so the investor's upside is leveraged 10 times. Thus, if the value of the loans does not change, the investor earns a return of 18.5% (6% from the Treasury Note plus 10 times the 1.25% spread on the swap with the dealer). However, the BLAST Note[sm] is not without its risks. Due to the embedded leverage, a decline in the value of the loan portfolio by 1.85% (caused, for example, by a default) is enough to wipe out the investor's return for a year.

Corporate Credit Derivatives

Like bank-loan based products, credit derivatives based on individual corporate bonds have many forms. In sum, these products are used for corporate liability management, to take customized views with respect to credit risk, and to execute capital structure arbitrage by exploiting relative mispricing of different liabilities of the same or related issuers. We refer back to the Kmart Bond to illustrate. On 7/19/96, this bond was priced at 74.97, yielding 10.84%. The comparable Treasury Bond was priced at 100.44,

FIGURE 2.5   BLAST Note^{sm} Transaction

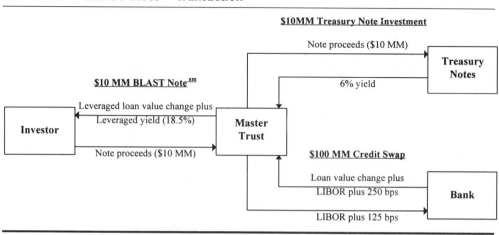

yielding 7.09%. Thus, the spread to Treasury was 3.75% or 375 bp. An investor enters into a swap under which a single payment is made on 7/19/97. On that date, the investor will pay the yield to maturity on the Kmart Bond and the dealer will pay the yield to maturity on the Treasury Bond plus 365 bp. Both payments are made on a notional amount of $10 million. Figure 2.2 shows the payments under the swap.

Through the swap, the investor takes the view that Kmart's actual or perceived credit quality will improve over the next year. To see why, assume that Kmart is upgraded to investment-grade status, so the value of the Kmart Bond increases substantially. Thus, the yield of the Bond declines, decreasing the investor's payment obligation under the swap. The investor could profit in a similar way from a direct investment in the Kmart Bond. A key advantage of the credit swap, however, is that the investor's exposure to changes in general interest rates is negligible compared to the interest rate risk inherent in a direct investment.

A second example is the use of a credit derivative as a corporate liability management tool. In the mid 1980s, ABC Corp issued a 30-year, fixed-rate bond. Two years after this issue, ABC was rumored to be a leveraged buyout target. The possibility that ABC's debt burden might increase dramatically caused the value of ABC's bond to fall substantially in the marketplace. The bond's spread to Treasuries quickly rose to 1.5 times its previous level. The corporate treasurer's office at ABC recognized this as an opportunity potentially worth millions of dollars. Management felt that there was little possibility the threatened hostile tender offer would materialize, was not interested in undergoing a leveraged recapitalization and forecast that the spread to Treasuries of the ABC bond would decline below even the prerumor levels within one year's time. The company did not wish to purchase the bonds directly, as a direct purchase by ABC would reduce the company's flexibility with respect to interest-rate risk management, would appear on the balance sheet (thus encouraging raiders), and might erode a substantial portion of the potential savings as the market reacted to news of the buyback. Ultimately, ABC entered into an OTC structure in which it purchased the 30-year bonds with a partner. An innovative provision in the Partnership Agreement specified that the change in the value of the bonds attributable to credit quality would be allocated to ABC. The partner was happy with this provision because it provided a substantial degree of credit risk protection. ABC liked the provision because it enabled ABC to take a large view on its own credit spread by investing only a fraction of underlying bonds' market value. As things turned out, ABC did not undergo a leveraged buyout or a recapitalization, and the credit spread of the bond narrowed substantially. The profit to the company as a result of this credit derivative transaction was in the millions of dollars.

These two examples involve directional bets on the credit quality of a corporate issuer. Another type of transaction, capital structure arbitrage, is designed to exploit differential pricing of the credit risk of an issuer or of related issuers. The idea and structure are similar to that of the Argentina contraction swap discussed above. In summary, through the credit derivative, the investor goes long the cheaper asset (the one with the higher credit spread) and short the more expensive asset on the expectation that the pricing of the two assets will come into line during the life of the trade.[18]

A SURVEY OF CURRENT MODELING TECHNIQUES

Pricing

The pricing of credit derivatives is a challenging problem with which practitioners and academics are grappling. To date, practitioners are adapting the modeling techniques used for other products, and applying them to credit derivatives. For example, pure forward-based products such as credit swaps are priced much like other swaps. The net present value of each leg is computed using the risk-neutral pricing assumption that the "expected" cash flow in each period equals the forward rate or price. To illustrate, the Kmart credit swap shown in Figure 2.2 is priced by computing the forward yields for both the Treasury Bond and the Kmart Bond. The present value of the Kmart leg is the product of the Kmart forward yield, the day count fraction (e.g., Act/365) and the one-year discount factor (most likely taken from the Eurodollar-swap yield curve). The present value of the Treasury leg is the product of the forward Treasury yield plus 365 bp, the day count fraction, and the same discount factor as used for the Kmart leg.

Options on price or yield differentials have been priced using the Margrabe model,[19] or some adaptation thereof. In essence, this model is a generalization of Black-Scholes,[20] used for options to exchange one stochastic asset for another or when the strike price of an option is equal to a stochastic capital market price or index. Although the Margrabe model works well for things like cross-currency options, and equity out-performance options, its use in this circumstance has its limitations. The most significant is that the model is based on a joint lognormal probability distribution in which any relationship between the Kmart yield and the Treasury yield is at least theoretically possible. Specifically, this model will assign a nonzero probability to the credit spread becoming negative. If the yield volatilities are high enough and their correlations low enough, this probability can be significant.[21]

One way to overcome this problem is to assume that the credit spread, rather than the yield of the credit sensitive asset, is lognormally distributed, and correlated with the comparable Treasury yield. This precludes the possibility of a negative credit spread. Although we have seen this approach applied in some risk management software for things like swap spreads, we have not seen it used in front-office credit derivative pricing by practitioners or in the academic literature. This seems surprising given that it is relatively simple, yet theoretically cleaner than applying the Margrabe model.[22]

Among academics, the pricing of credit derivatives, and credit-sensitive debt more generally, has been a topic of much research in the last several years. Generally, the academic models are more sophisticated than the models currently being used by practitioners. As noted by Das and Tufano,[23] this recent literature falls into two categories. The first category includes models which assume a stochastic process for the value of the issuer's assets, and treat risky debt as a contingent claim on those assets. This approach dates back to the early days of option pricing models.[24] One of the most significant advances in this recent literature is that the new models allow for a stochastic interest-rate process, which may be correlated with the stochastic process for firm value, as opposed to the static interest-rate assumptions of the old models.[25] The second category includes models which assume a stochastic process for the credit quality of each bond. An example of such an approach is Jarrow, Lando, and Turnbull,[26] which models the default process based on credit ratings. Specifically, the model assumes that the credit rating of a risky bond follows a Markov chain, and employs a matrix of probabilities for the transition between credit ratings (including default). Das and Tufano[27] build on this approach with a model which allows for a stochastic recovery rate in the event of default.

Each of the two approaches has its strengths and weaknesses. Approaches based on firm value are arguably theoretically cleaner, since they model default risk as a continuous economic process, avoiding the natural limitations of credit ratings as proxies for economic realities. On the other hand, since aggregate firm value is difficult or impossible to observe, parameter estimation is a challenge. Moreover, pricing one liability of the firm under this approach will in general require the valuation of other liabilities of the same firm. Models based on credit ratings are set up to make use of published credit-rating transition probabilities, thus mitigating the parameter estimation problem somewhat.[28] Moreover, for obvious reasons, these models are better suited to value derivatives based on credit ratings.

As noted above, market participants currently use much simpler models and approaches to price credit derivatives. Whether the marketplace will find that the benefits of the new models justify the additional programming, systems, training and data requirements remains to be seen.

Hedging

Although the pricing of credit derivatives presents complexities, it is unlikely that these will limit the development of the market. Hedging, however, is a different story. To date, the difficulty in hedging has limited the size and cost effectiveness of many types of products, and has made two-way market-making either impossible or impractical. To illustrate this point, the following discussion refers back to the Kmart credit spread swap discussed above, and shows the specific steps a dealer must take to hedge the transaction. As stated above, the Investor takes the view that Kmart's actual or perceived credit quality will improve over the next year. The Dealer, however, generally does not wish to take the market view opposite the Investor. Rather, as part of its general business practice the Dealer will enter into a series of transactions which hedge the market exposure created by the swap. The initial hedging transactions are diagrammed in Figure 2.6.

FIGURE 2.6   Initial Hedging the Kmart Credit Swap

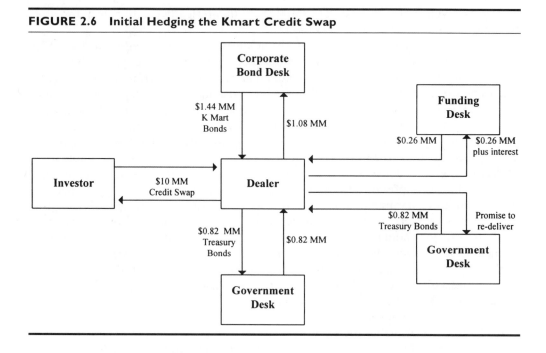

As can be seen from the diagram, the required hedging transactions are as follows:

1. Borrow the Treasury Bonds, in order to
2. Short-sell the Treasury Bonds,
3. Borrow additional funds, and
4. Use the proceeds to purchase the underlying Kmart Notes.

The amount of Kmart Bonds purchased and Treasury Bonds sold by the dealer depends upon how much the value of each changes with respect to changes in their respective yields to maturity (i.e., their durations). In this example, the face amount of Kmart Bonds purchased is approximately $1.44 million, while the face amount of Treasury Bonds shorted is approximately $0.82 million.[29] A few observations should be made here.

- The above shows the initial hedging transaction only. Since this swap is yield-based, the hedge must be dynamically managed. Due to convexity (i.e., the nonlinear relationship between prices and yields), the hedge is adjusted as the yields of the underlying instruments change.
- The above transactions do not leave the dealer perfectly hedged. In particular, during the time the dealer holds the Kmart Bonds, it receives the coupon payments therefrom (7.95% per annum). The dealer pays for this right in the pricing of the Kmart Bonds. However, if the Kmart Bonds default, the dealer loses these coupon flows. This exposure can only be hedged by shorting a near-term obligation of Kmart, or by entering into an offsetting credit derivative or insurance contract under which the dealer gets paid if the coupon is lost. These

hedges are generally not available. Absent a special provision in the swap confirm agreement (e.g., requiring the Investor to pay the coupon in the event of Kmart's default), the only way to address the problem is for the dealer to charge the investor a premium for the credit risk. Since most derivatives dealers generally prefer to hedge such risks, there is no reason to believe that the premium will be advantageous to the investor.

- The existence of the credit derivative does not change the fact that in order for the investor to take a view on Kmart's credit, the underlying Bonds must be purchased. The key difference is that the dealer, rather than the investor, does the actual purchase. Thus, absent alternative risk management techniques, the volume of corporate credit derivatives is limited by the size of the underlying market, and pricing and execution are subject to the same liquidity constraints. Potential ways to get around this limitation include diversification of underlyings by dealers, portfolio-level hedging with contracts based on broad baskets (e.g., single-B spread), or correlation hedging using the stocks of the underlying issuers. Whether the market will develop such alternative risk management techniques remains to be seen.

- The dealer is long convexity, since the convexity of the swap is negligible, the convexity of the long Kmart Bond position exceeds that of the short Treasury Bond position, and the Kmart Bond yield is almost certain to have a higher volatility than the Treasury yield.[30] On average, this is a benefit to the dealer which, under competitive market conditions, may be passed on to the investor in the form of more favorable pricing.[31] However, it should be noted that this convexity can conceivably work against the dealer if the Treasury yield makes a large move (in either direction) which is not accompanied by a comparably large move in the Kmart Bond yield. This can happen if, for example, there is a "short squeeze" in the Treasury Bond.

- In the swap, the investor takes the bullish view (i.e., that the credit spread will tighten). It would be much more expensive, if not impossible, for the investor to take the opposite view. This is due primarily to the cost and difficulty in shorting the Kmart Bonds, which the dealer would have to do as part of its hedge. To a lesser extent, the convexity also makes a bearish trade more difficult, since in the hedge, the dealer is net short convexity.[32] It is noteworthy that the majority of the corporate credit derivatives (and Brady Bond derivatives) in the market to date incorporate bullish views.[33]

CONCLUSION

Credit risk is one of the oldest and best understood risks in finance. Until recently, there were a limited number of tools available to manage it. One could diversify it, sell it or take it on through cash market transactions. Unfortunately, it was difficult to use combinations of these transactions to unbundle the risks which often accompany credit risk (typically interest rate and FX risk). Moreover, large cash commitments were required. The recent emergence of OTC credit derivatives promises to change that.

Although we share the view that credit derivatives could potentially become a large market, however, there are reasons to believe that this growth will be uneven. C&I loan-based products show great promise. Another area with comparable potential, not discussed in this chapter, are derivatives based on consumer credit. The sheer size of these markets, their comparatively generous pricing of credit risk, the existing concentration of the holdings of these assets, and the transactional efficiency of derivatives in general all point to tremendous growth potential. And much like the way that financial engineering in the MBS market contributed to more competitive pricing of home mortgages, credit derivatives may effect the same result in C&I loans and consumer credit. Another potential growth area for credit derivatives, albeit a more limited one, is Sovereign debt. The billions of dollars of Brady Bond derivatives done to date (primarily Latin America) could well be just the beginning as the debt for Eastern European and Far Eastern begins to trade on international markets. Given that Sovereign debt often contains varying degrees of FX and interest rate risk, as well as partial guarantees, credit derivatives could be instrumental in bringing about more transparent and efficient pricing of Sovereign credit risk. A final potential area for growth is the market for index credit derivatives (e.g., Treasury—BB spread), which we see as a potentially valuable investment and risk management tools for a broad range of institutions, and for corporate issuers.

In addition to these potential growth markets, we believe that there will continue to be a highly innovative market for customized, "one-off" products, such as the single-issuer corporate spread trade discussed above. Another area for additional development is Municipal credit derivatives. The desire to broaden participation in Muni credit risk beyond the market's natural clientele of high-bracket taxpayers and to develop new and more flexible forms of "bond insurance" could spur the development of specialty markets. Although such "one-off" products will continue to serve important investor needs, and to link disparate markets for credit risk, the hedging difficulties discussed above will likely limit the size of this segment of the market.

ENDNOTES

1. This is not to say that discontinuities are unique to credit events. Rather, the argument is that most changes in things like interest rates are small enough to be tolerably approximated with continuous-time math. For credit events such as downgrades and defaults, this is not so.

2. A capital structure arbitrage is a transaction designed to exploit a differential pricing of the credit risk of a single issuer or related issuers. For a simple illustration, assume XYZ Corp. has two 10% USD 10-year subordinated notes outstanding, and that both are well-traded issues. One trades in the U.S. domestic and is priced at par; the other trades in the Euromarket and is priced at 105. A capital structure arbitrage would involve purchasing the U.S. domestic note and shorting the Euro note.

3. "Credit derivatives: A new way to make some risky investments investable?" *Plan Sponsor,* May 1995, pp. 64–65. "Credit derivatives seen as next booming market," Reuters, December 2, 1994.

4. The first well-publicized interest rate swap transaction was actually a cross-currency swap executed in 1981 between the World Bank and IBM. Just two years later, the interest rate swap market was estimated to be $20 billion in notional. By 1984, the estimate had grown to $80 billion. Bank for International Settlements, *Recent Innovations in International Banking,* April 1986, pp. 39–43.

5. "Credit Derivatives Come Good," *Risk,* July 1996, pp. 22–26, quoting Blythe Masters of JP Morgan.

6. "Credit Derivatives Get Cracking," *Euromoney,* March 1996, pp. 28–34, byline written by Mark Parsley.

7. Many investors believe that the general upward slope of the yield curve creates biased forward rates that systematically "predict" that short-term rates will be higher than they usually turn out to be. Since arbitrage principles require that derivatives be priced off these forward rates, an investor can earn substantial profits from bull-market bets if short term rates decline, remain stable or even rise slightly. Many products developed in the early 1990s, such as inverse floaters and power swaps, were designed to exploit this view. Between 1991 and 1993, these products performed very well as

short-term rates were flat of declining for sustained periods of time. In 1994, however, many investors suffered substantial losses as short-term rates rose to levels higher than those "predicted" by the forward curve. Publicized examples of such losses include Orange County, Gibson Greetings, and Procter & Gamble.

8. Harold van B. Cleveland and Thomas F. Huertas, *Citibank 1812-1970,* 1985, p. 43.

9. Frank J. Fabozzi and T. Dessa Fabozzi (Ed.), *The Handbook of Fixed Income Securities,* 4th ed. (Chicago: Probus) p. 176.

10. Sanjiv R. Das, "Credit Risk Derivatives," *The Journal of Derivatives,* Spring 1993, pp. 7-23.

11. This assumes the FRN is a "straight floater," i.e., that coupon payments depend upon a single short-term index, multiplied by one, with no embedded caps or floors. If any of these conditions are not met, the FRN can exhibit a nontrivial degree of general interest rate risk.

12. This program was named for Treasury Secretary Nicholas Brady, who played a key role in its implementation.

13. Despite the degree of financial engineering involved in this computation, the resulting spread is still not a pure measure of Argentine credit risk, for at least two reasons. The first is that under the terms of the Par Bond, the two immediate coupon payments were collateralized by securities rated AA or better. Thus, the valuation of these two flows should also be independent of Argentine credit risk. The second reason is that since the coupon flows of the Par Bond go out until 2023, spreading their IRR to the 10-year Treasury yield leaves a slight Treasury yield curve play. To assess the potential impact of these factors, CMRA performed an analysis of a typical one-year trade based on this spread. Even if the true Argentinean credit spread had not changed between November 30, 1993, and December 1, 1994, we estimate that the spread as measured in the swap would have narrowed by approximately 32 basis points.

14. This methodology leaves the same type of yield curve play as for the Par Bond spread.

15. The following discussion of bank loan products is based largely on J. Gregg Whittaker and Sumita Kumar, "Credit Derivatives: A Primer," *The Handbook of Derivative Instruments, 2nd ed.,* 1996, Konishi and Dattatreya, eds., pp. 595-614; and J. Gregg Whittaker, "Credit Derivatives: New Structures and Applications," Talk given at the Chemical Securities Inc. Derivatives Summit '95.

16. Loan Pricing Corp. Gold Sheets.

17. In order to give the investor a leveraged upside combined with downside protection, the swap with the bank must be structured so that the bank absorbs some residual credit risk in the loan portfolio.

18. This type of trade is not really new. Going back at least as far as the 1980s, proprietary trading desks took such positions when, for example, the difference between the yield of an issuer's fixed-rate paper and the comparable swap rate exceeded the spread to LIBOR for the same issuer's FRNs. The contribution of the modern credit derivatives market is that now a broader range of market participants can participate in such arbitrages, in the form (e.g., note, swap, or option) which is best suited to individual needs and preferences.

19. W. Margrabe, "The Option to Exchange One Risky Asset for Another," *Journal of Finance,* March 1978, pp. 177-86.

20. Fischer Black and Myron S. Scholes, "The Pricing of Options and Corporate Liabilities," *Journal of Political Economy,* May-June 1973, pp. 637-59.

21. For example, on July 19, 1996, the spot spread of the Kmart Bond discussed above was 3.75%. Using forward yields, and the one-year historical volatilities and correlation, the joint lognormal distribution gives a 10% probability that the spread will be negative on July 19, 1997.

22. This is not to say that the suggested approach is perfect. For example, there may be difficulties with the lognormality assumption and parameter estimation. But these problems exist within the current approach as well.

23. Sanjiv Ranjan Das and Peter Tufano, "Pricing Credit—Sensitive Debt When Interest Rates, Credit Ratings and Credit Spreads Are Stochastic," *The Journal of Financial Engineering,* 5(2), pp. 161-198.

24. Fischer Black and Myron S. Scholes, "The Pricing of Options and Corporate Liabilities," *Journal of Political Economy,* May-June 1973, pp. 637-659. Robert C. Merton, "On the Pricing of Corporate Debt: The Risk Structure of Interest Rates," *Journal of Finance, 29,* 1974, pp. 449-470.

25. For examples using a Vasicek model, *see* Francis A. Longstaff and Eduardo S. Schwartz, "Valuing Risky Debt: A New Approach," UCLA Working Paper, 1993; and David C. Shimko, Naohiko Tejima, and Donald R. Van Deventer, "The Pricing of Risky Debt when Interest Rates are Stochastic," *The Journal*

of Fixed Income, September 1993, pp. 58–65. For an example using a Heath, Jarrow, Morton model, *see* Sanjiv R. Das, "Credit Risk Derivatives," *The Journal of Derivatives,* Spring 1993, pp. 7-23.

26. Jarrow, R., D. Lando, and S.M. Turnbull, "A Markov Model for the Term Structure of Credit Risk Spreads," 1994, Working Paper, Cornell University.

27. Sanjiv Ranjan Das and Peter Tufano, "Pricing Credit—Sensitive Debt When Interest Rates, Credit Ratings and Credit Spreads Are Stochastic," *The Journal of Financial Engineering, 5*(2) pp. 161-198.

28. However, to the extent that individual issues have transition probabilities which differ from the aggregate estimates, the need for issuer level parameter estimation resurfaces. Perhaps the approach can be enhanced by expanding the transition matrix to include, for example, an issue being placed on "credit watch."

29. The size of the hedges are determined by computing the relationship between changes in the value of the underlyings and changes in the present value of the swap payment flows for small changes in the respective yields.

30. Convexity is a measure of how quickly a bond's duration changes as its yield to maturity changes. Fixed-rate, noncallable securities have positive convexity, which means that as yields increase or decrease, the change in price is always more favorable than the first-order estimate based on duration. The value of convexity therefore depends upon the volatility of yields.

31. In addition, convexity might serve to offset coupon default losses if the default announcement causes a sudden and dramatic decline in the value of the corporate bonds. In this example, the convexity gain caused by a 20-point drop in the price of the Kmart Bond would be sufficient to cover the dealer's loss of coupon interest.

32. This latter problem can be addressed, however, by simply making the payout formula price-based.

33. An exception is the Argentinean spread swap discussed above, in which the investor effectively goes long the Bocon Pre2 but short the Brady Bond. This trade was made possible by the fact that the Brady Bond component serves as a natural hedge for the pure bullish trades sold by the dealer.

3

Minimizing Operations Risk

Wendy H. Brewer

With all the discussion of sophisticated models and methodologies for risk management, the capacity of any organization to effectively monitor risk can be distilled down to one basic concept: The information or database that is used as a building block must be correct. It is also helpful if the data is centralized, accessible, and complete.

This is why operations risk management is a critical part of the overall risk management profile of a company. Operations is responsible for verifying, confirming, and settling transactions, functions that determine the quality of the data and have a basis in external, observable reality. The examination of operations risk centers around the ability of a processing and control area to perform these duties correctly and efficiently and, just as importantly, to communicate the results to senior management.

The responsibility of operations in managing risk is complicated by the nature of derivatives products themselves. Unlike other traditional banking businesses, derivatives are tailored, flexible instruments that resist standardization and cohesive systems development. Multiple terms describe the transactions so deal capture becomes confusing and prone to error. Capital markets products are also long-term, with many events to monitor during the life of the deal, including amortizations, payments, resets, and the increasingly common option features. Derivatives can also cross product lines and thus require diverse knowledge as well as multiple systems, potentially resulting in an unclear picture of the transaction in its entirety. The average contract amount of derivatives has also increased to the point where $100 million to $500 million in notional principals are not uncommon and can be additionally leveraged. To compound this, a company's potential for earnings is predicated on the ability to deliver new products to customers or participate in short-term lucrative markets that force operations to react quickly and under significant pressure. These factors increase both the potential and impact of operations risks.

Although these are certainly challenges to the effective processing of derivatives, there is hope. It is possible to establish an effective operational risk management capability. Such efforts are occurring in most organizations and have been supported by the influx of recommendations and papers from the industry and regulators concerning best practices. There has also been an improvement in technology and in the caliber and recognition of derivatives operations specialists. However, as recent headlines concerning operational control failures indicate, there is still a lot of progress to be made.

In this chapter, an approach is presented to address operations risk in derivatives. The first step is to define the role of operations and the nature of the risks. Second, it is necessary to examine the common tools that are available to identify and control the risks. Finally, a basic strategy is suggested to limit the potential for operational failure and ensure the success of a comprehensive risk management policy in the future. Without effective operations, all other risk management efforts are meaningless.

ROLE OF OPERATIONS

There are generic operations responsibilities in any derivatives organization, even if the nomenclature or division of labor differs from company to company. Operations takes over after a transaction is entered into by the trading desk and provides a separation of function and independent control mechanism, as well as actual processing, confirming, and accounting for the trade. Operations also maintains and runs the processing systems and is responsible for the integrity of the data. Due to the highly publicized control failures of the 1990s, operations functions have expanded to include more verification and risk management duties that are usually performed by the "middle office." More traditional event processing and accounting functions are handled in the back office. The idea of the increasing functionality of operations is supported by an article in the *Wall Street Journal* in November 1995 that stated, "The responsibility of most banks' operations units include financial controls, risk management, clearing, and settlement." Now operations for derivatives commonly consists of a strong, highly automated processing area—the back office, combined with a specialized, more flexible middle office. Both these operations components have specific duties designed to provide a system of checks and balances to each other, and to the front office. Generic responsibilities of operations are designated in Table 3.1 with an example of a traditional breakdown of tasks.

The examination of the role and responsibilities of a derivatives operations department leads to an analysis of operational risk itself. The functions are relatively straight forward, yet can be prone to error based on the human element or the adequacy of the systems and controls.

DEFINITION AND IMPACT OF OPERATIONS RISK

The board of governors of the *Federal Reserve System Trading Activities Manual* identifies operational and systems risk as the "risk of human error or fraud, or that systems will fail to adequately record, monitor, and account for transactions or positions." It is further stated in the *Manual* that operational risk is "the risk that deficiencies in information systems or internal controls will result in unexpected losses." This is a rather nebulous description, but it brings to light the dichotomous nature of operational risk. On one hand, it is defined with a distinctly human element and, on the other, it is based on the adequacy of technology. This calls for a delicate balancing act between human resources and systems, each having significant risk potential.

TABLE 3.1   Generic Responsibilities of Operations: An Example

Function	Traditional Responsibility	
	Middle Office	Back Office
1. Data Capture		
Deal Ticket Review: Provide missing fields	Yes	No
Deal Entry: Input to process system	Yes	Sometimes
Market Data Input: Closing prices and volatility	Yes	No
External Verification: Comparison to observable source	Yes	No
Limit Monitoring: Trading, risk, and credit	Yes	No
Credit Exposure Calculation: Potential exposure by deal	Yes	No
Credit Limit Tracking: Available credit line	Yes	No
Static Data Maintenance: Payment instructions, contacts	Sometimes	Yes
2. Documentation		
Master Agreements: Preparation and negotiation	Sometimes	No
Confirmations: Outgoing and incoming	Yes	No
Documentation Tracking: Status of outstanding	Yes	Sometimes
3. Processing		
Daily Rate Reset Input: Floating rate, index	Sometimes	Yes
Payment/Reset Notifications: Advices to counterparties	Sometimes	Yes
Event Monitoring: Payments, fees, exercise dates	Yes	Yes
Settlement Instructions: Payment preparation/authorization	Sometimes	Yes
Audit Confirmations: Counterparty transaction verification	No	Yes
Hedge Processing: Futures, options, securities	No	Yes
Financing: Repurchase/reverse agreements, loans	No	Yes
Collateral Management: Monitor outstandings	No	Yes
4. Accounting		
Portfolio Valuation: Mark to market	Yes	Sometimes
Profit and Loss Preparation: Change in value	Yes	No
Profit and Loss Analysis: Actual versus estimate	Yes	No
Cash Management: Cash in/out reconciliation	No	Yes
General Ledger Entry: Financial accounting	No	Yes
Statement Reconciliation: Cash, positions	No	Yes

The specific responsibility breakdown between the Middle and Back Office can differ from organization to organization but the functions are the same. Some organizations now call everything except cleanup and cash disbursement "Middle Office." Various phases of the operational process as described above have specific risks that can be identified by function:

Middle Office
Incorrect Deal Entry: Incorrect/incomplete terms, missing deals
Unverified Market Inputs: Incorrect market assumptions, wrong prices
Careless Limit Monitoring: Unauthorized trading, positions
Late or Incorrect Confirmations: Unconfirmed or incorrect commitments

Back Office
Faulty Event Monitoring: Missed exercise/commitments
Incorrect Credit Monitoring: Incorrect exposure, collateral
Error in Payments: Fraudulent, missed, incorrect payments

Misstated Accounting: Incorrect financials, taxes, regulatory reports

Incorrect Master Agreements: Missed events, incorrect valuation methodology

Systems

Inadequate Testing: Incorrect payments, valuations, missed events

Lack of Functionality: Deals forced into system, manual calculations, inadequate information

Limited Integration: Multiple systems, incomplete views of transactions, inefficient processing

Inflexibility: Delay in delivering new products, lost competitive advantage, multiple systems

Weak Systems Security: Corrupted data, unauthorized access, no audit trail

Insufficient Back up: Processing delays, lack of timely information

These operational and systems risks also have an impact on other risks such as reputation and profitability. Errors in operations are highly visible. Incorrect payments can negatively impact the perception of the company in the marketplace resulting in a loss of business. In addition, the profitability of the institution is directly affected by missed option exercise dates or hedges based on incorrect deal terms. The relationship between operations risks and other risk types is further illustrated by reviewing the impact of processing failures on market and credit risk:

Operational Risk	Market Risk Impact	Credit Risk Impact
Incorrect data entry	Incorrect gaps, positions	Incorrect counterparty exposure
Unverified market data	Incorrect valuations, risks	Incorrect potential exposure, collateral
Careless limit monitoring	Limits exceeded, unauthorized trading	Limits exceeded, insufficient line
Incorrect confirmations	Inappropriate hedges	Incorrect counterparty exposure, netting
Faulty event monitoring	Missed exercise, increased risk exposures	Missed payments, increased exposure
Late reports	Trading blind	Unauthorized CPs

As well as a causal relationship, operations risk also has a compounding effect on market and credit risks. Incorrect valuations lead to exceeding limits and the potential for unauthorized trading or unknown risk positions and sensitivities. This can further result in an inability to react to changing market conditions. Difficulties in calculating potential exposure and credit line usage can result in undue concentration or a deficiency or excess of appropriate collateral. There have been many instances where incorrect or late information or merely human error have caused companies to double up on their risks instead of reducing them. A company's entire strategy in how to react to adverse market conditions relies heavily on the ability of its operations area to provide correct, timely information for stress testing, and portfolio analysis.

TOOLS TO DETECT AND DETER OPERATIONS RISK

The methods to control operations risk can be broken down into two categories for simplicity: internal controls and external verification.

Internal Controls

Internal controls are usually divided into primary and secondary controls. Primary controls prevent a mistake from occurring in the first place, and secondary controls act as a safety net by identifying results. Controls such as the separation of trading and operations responsibilities are provided by the structure of an organization it-self; others are contained in the operating procedures of the institution.

   1. *Separation of Function:* The delineation of responsibilities is designed to pro-vide an institutionalized primary control mechanism. Checks and balances are pro-vided by forced separation of function. The concept is clear: Those individuals responsible for committing an institution to a transaction should not also perform clearance or accounting functions. In September 1995, Daiwa Bank announced $1.1 billion in losses in the Treasury market over the past decade. These losses are a result of a blurring of the line between the front office and operations, as one individual was responsible for trading and processing securities transactions. He fraudulently covered unfavorable positions by forging customer statements over a significant pe-riod of time. This misconduct and the subsequent delay in disclosure has had impact on derivatives dealers in terms of increased scrutiny by regulators and the enforce-ment of strict separation of function standards. Within operations itself, payment au-thority should be separated from accounting and statement reconciliation. In addition, the front office should not perform the formal valuation of the portfolio or report the final profit and loss to management, especially if compensation is deter-mined by the result. The separation of function issue is addressed in depth by the Fed-eral Reserve Circular of December 1993, where it states that risk management and operations should not report to an individual involved in day-to-day trading. The best way to judge if functions should be separated is by analyzing whether fraud could be committed under the current structure and how long it would take to be discovered.
   As an addendum to the discussion of separation of function through appropriate reporting lines, there are unique characteristics in the way a derivative operations unit is structured that cause additional control difficulties. Derivative operations are diverse and constantly evolving and there is usually some level of manual interven-tion. The quality of the processing and the satisfaction of customers are the primary objectives. Therefore, especially for exotics, some derivative operations units are structured along product rather than functional lines. This allows for product and process flexibility but controls become complex and decentralized. A product-oriented structure makes it difficult to separate functions clearly. Therefore, the na-ture of derivatives themselves defines the processing structure which in turn forces a trade off between strong, institutionalized controls and customized processing. Derivatives business objectives are again at odds with traditional control techniques.
   2. *Dual Entry:* Another of the important primary operational controls is also the most basic. This is the simple double checking of work. Some organizations go so far as to have duplicate staff for each function, such as an input clerk and a verifier. Oth-ers use the hierarchy system of a supervisor who signs off on all parts of the process

performed by his or her staff. It is also common to have two-tier inputs to processing systems, where initial information is entered by the traders or the middle office and then checked and completed by the back office. Another approach is to have the system automatically match entries from two different sources which is extremely critical if more than one system is being used. Systems should also have the ability to flag data inconsistencies or a violation of limits. Whatever the methodology, some form of verification of the data entering into the systems is critical. As much as possible, controls should be front-loaded so that after all the terms of the transaction are in the system, manual intervention is limited. Again, derivatives have complex structures and multiple terms, so the difficulty of deal entry should not be underestimated. This is compounded by the inability of current systems to process all deal types easily. It is also why highly skilled staff members are necessary for data capture and are a good investment.

In the last quarter of 1994, Salomon Brothers learned the importance of correctly booking transactions the hard way. An article in the *New York Times* on February 28, 1995, titled, "Salomon Adds to Its Losses and Cites Bookkeeping Blunder," stated that Solomon revised its 1994 loss upward $35 million after taxes due to a previously undetected error in recording a 1988 transaction involving Japanese Yen. The restatement regarding this one deal would cover quite a few operations staff's salaries and functional redundancy.

3. *Reconciliations:* Comparing the output of various systems or reports is a strong secondary control. An example of a common comparison is of the traders' estimates or expected results to the profit and loss report prepared by middle office, a procedure that allows managers a modicum of comfort that the numbers are correct or at least equally incorrect. Reconciliations highlight potential failures in primary controls or systems. Although not the best solution, controls over output variances are a necessary evil in the current environment where institutions use multiple systems, and thus spend a great deal of time reconciling results. Other critical reconciliations are of cash movements, broker statements to positions and subsidiary to general ledgers.

The importance of these reconciliations is again illustrated by the case of Salomon Brothers. In addition to the loss for the incorrectly booked Yen deal, Salomon had already reported a loss of $126 million in the fourth quarter of 1994. A press release from Salomon Brothers dated February 2, 1995, explained that a detailed review of the company's general ledger accounts by Arthur Andersen, LLP to determine if proper support and reconciliations were in place resulted in a charge-off of $126 million after-tax to resolve unreconciled balances. It further cited that Salomon had been working for several years to develop a new global interest rate swap transaction processing system that required a reconciliation of the general ledgers of the company to the derivatives transaction database. Adjustments involved many different instruments, positions, and related currency effects dating back to the 1980s. Unpleasant surprises as a result of systems conversions or position comparisons are not uncommon and highlight the critical nature of timely reconcilements.

4. *Tickler Systems:* Most organizations use back-up procedures to ensure that critical events are not missed. The methods can consist of printing weekly or monthly settlements and exercise dates in advance, inputting them to a daily automated tickler file or, in less sophisticated areas, manually marking a calendar. In some companies, operations actually pulls the deal file for options prior to an exercise date and delivers it to the front office so that the actual cash settlement language on the confirmation can be reviewed. Most companies have had experience with missed exercise dates

that result in actual cash losses versus mere restatements of income. This is one of the more dramatic examples of operational failure and one of the most costly. Missed exercise dates occur often enough so that it is common for one counterparty to call another and remind them to exercise a beneficial position. This genteel practice should not be counted on as a primary control, however, and will probably not even be admitted to. The development of strong event-monitoring procedures is a wiser course.

5. *Amendments:* There should be very strict controls over the amendments of original deal tickets and systems data. The dual verification control outlined above is useless if changes and amendments circumvent the process. One common frustration of an operations function is that tickets are amended multiple times, especially when deals are with overseas locations or are for structured transactions. Amendments also originate from the confirmation process. If there are multiple systems used in processing the portfolio, these amendments can be very time-consuming to perform correctly. To avoid potential risk, all amendments should be treated with the formality of original deal tickets with a completed and authorized amendment form and adherence to normal workflows. The standardization of the process alerts management to a potential problem and ensures that all areas are aware of the changes.

External Verification

The second method of preventing operational failure is accomplished by external verification of the terms of the deal, market data, and the settlements. This is an extremely critical operations function as it is the true test of the integrity of the database and the accuracy of reports.

1. *Confirmations:* Confirmations are the single strongest external control mechanism for identifying and controlling risk because they represent what is agreed to by the counterparties. However, outstanding confirmations are the bane of the derivatives industry. The problem of outstanding confirmations has reached such proportions that the ISDA Operations Executive Committee considers the issue a top priority. The solutions that are being explored industrywide include deal slips for structured transactions, the automatic matching of confirmations via the SWIFT system, and even an actual face-to-face exchange of outstanding lists with peers. This last method has proved an embarrassing but effective way of resolving outstanding items among the larger dealers on the Committee. To address this problem in-house, general policies should be followed. Confirmations should be generated within 24 hours, ideally by the same database that produces the valuations and accounting reports. The status and aging of outstanding confirmations and other documentation should be tracked and pursued vigilantly. Deal tickets and internally generated confirmations and documentation received from the counterparty should be reconciled immediately and senior management should be formally apprised of any confirmation outstanding for more than five days. Confirmations are considered the medium for making a transaction legally binding as well as an affirmation of the database, so should be treated with significant attention.

2. *Verification of Prices and Volatilities:* One of the most controversial functions of operations is the external verification of closing prices and volatility assumptions used to create the yield curve. Many organizations have had to restate earnings based on incorrect or stale assumptions used to value the portfolio. A

famous example of the issue of unverified data reportedly concerns the Soros fund. According to legend, an outside consultant supposedly suggested that the assumptions used in the Soros valuation models did not reflect the market. The alleged response was, "The market is wrong." For institutions less willing to put their future on the line, an independent check of market inputs and the resulting prices against observable sources is recommended. This is easier now than it used to be since there are published levels for most indices and products. The current norm is for the middle office to check closing prices against screens, to poll brokers for spreads and volatilities, and generally "beat the bushes" for external sources that can verify internal assumptions for less liquid transactions. Some institutions use original methods such as measuring their assumptions against prices calculated for specific transactions in "Swaps Monitor," a biweekly derivatives newsletter. Regulatory bodies are increasingly recommending that volatilities be changed daily and the independent valuation of transactions be performed as part of a formal risk management audit. As an indication of the importance of this issue, some institutions have banded together to provide assistance to each other in verifying exotic transactions. In addition, valuation verification service bureaus have also been proposed and consulting firms are doing a booming business.

As a corollary to the external verification responsibility, each derivative practitioner should have the basic ability to value transactions in-house. Reliance on external sources for valuation proved unfortunate for Procter & Gamble, who announced losses of $157 million in April of 1994 through trading in highly leveraged interest rate swaps with Bankers Trust. The lack of ability of Procter & Gamble to value the transactions themselves and evaluate the risk, led to a highly publicized court case and opened up the issues of customer reliance and counterparty suitability. The German holding company Colonia also took a $76 million loss in mid-August 1994 when it was unable to value and monitor the exposure for eight exotic options in its equity and bond portfolio. These examples reinforce the importance of verification of valuations regardless whether the source is the trading desk or a counterparty.

3. *Authorizations:* The implementation and monitoring of authorizations and limits are the foundation of an effective internal control system. The Group of Thirty Recommendation number 17 reads, "Management of dealers and end-users should designate who is authorized to commit their institutions to derivative transactions." As the disinterested party, operations is responsible for not only monitoring the authorizations within their institution, but also those of counterparties. A signed confirmation is not an effective control if the signatory is not authorized. Authorization also includes a definition of what the individual is allowed to commit to. Limits should be established in writing for each trader, transaction, counterparty, product, risk factor, and profit and loss. It is the responsibility of operations to monitor these quantifiable factors and report exceptions to management. The minimum standard for trading and risk management limits appears in the *Federal Reserve Trading Activities Manual.*

4. *Settlements:* The payment process also provides a valuable external verification that the database is correct. Since payments are handled successfully by most processing systems, incorrect amounts or mismatches with counterparties on settlements often mean that there is a data discrepancy. Compensation claims by counterparties for missed payments or incorrect amounts and instructions can be an indication of potential operational problems. According to the Principles and Practices for Wholesale Financial Market Transactions, "A Participant should provide its

counterparty with standing payment and settlement instructions, and any modifications to those standing instructions should be communicated as quickly as possible to facilitate prompt settlement of transactions." This principle reduces settlement risk and should be followed religiously.

As another example of the control value of settlements, changes in the magnitude of settlements should alert management that something is amiss. Barings PLC reported a loss of $1.24 billion on February 28, 1995, from trades in the Nikkei Stock Average futures contract. A trader at Barings, Singapore bought stock index futures and also sold options on the Nikkei-225 index. Together, these transactions would result in huge losses if the market moved sharply in either direction. When the Japanese stock market fell 13% in the month after the Kobe earthquake on January 17, 1995, the trader doubled up on his positions instead of closing them out. By February 27, 1995, Barings had accumulated Nikkei-225 index positions that amounted to a $7 billion long bet on the Tokyo stock market. A *Wall Street Journal* article on March 2, 1995, titled, "Barings Was Warned Controls Were Lax But Didn't Make Reforms in Singapore," stated that the high volumes of settlements after the Kobe earthquake indicating massively increasing trading positions began to alarm some senior Barings executives. The unusually high volume of the trading operation was also noticed by outsiders, worried that the bank was taking unduly large risks. However, management did not react until it was too late. In hindsight, every 1% the Japanese stock market went down, Barings lost another $70 million due to its enormous position. Although there were other severe control problems at Barings, sudden large volumes and increased amounts of settlement activity can indicate potential risk. An operations area should bring to management's attention any unusual activity which is reflected in the settlement of transactions. Settlements, then, not only serve to verify that transaction data is correct but can also be used as a warning mechanism for market risk.

5. *Internal/External Audit Reports:* Examinations are an effective tool in identifying and reporting on potential weaknesses in operational controls. Although audits should not be the only method of determining the safety and soundness of operational environments, internal audits have warned of potential problems such as again in the case of Barings. In the summer of 1994, an audit team was dispatched to Singapore to review controls. The resulting examination identified the risks inherent in a situation where the trader responsible for amassing huge positions was also the head of operations as was the case at Barings, Singapore. The audit recommended that a separate control mechanism or a compliance officer should be established to monitor trading and settlement activities. The recommendations, scheduled for August 1st were not implemented by senior management, however. As a result of cases like Barings and other recent examples of fraud, examinations have become more rigorous with an emphasis on internal controls and risk management. In a press release on May 23, 1996, the board of governors of the Federal Reserve Bank announced that a formal rating of the risk profile of a bank "will be given significant weight in determining the overall effectiveness of management." Both external and internal auditors have built up staff to the point where the valuations of transactions and the risk management system of a company can be examined effectively. Deloitte & Touche, LLP has a special, structured finance division specifically charged with providing in-depth year end financial statement audits of derivative companies as well as consulting services by the same group of professionals. Although painful, unfavorable audits can warn management of risks especially in light of more advanced

audit personnel and diagnostic ability, but only if findings are acted on rapidly with special care to repeat items.

6. *Codes of Conduct:* Documented operating procedures are becoming more important in setting forth the standards of the company and providing a road map for processing. There has been an influx of best practice recommendations that can be used as a benchmark for evaluating an operation. At least yearly, procedures should be compared to the Group of Thirty Recommendations. According to the Principles and Practices of Wholesale Market Financial Market Transactions, "A Participant should maintain and enforce internal control and compliance procedures so designed that its transactions are conducted in accordance with applicable legal and regulatory requirements, internal policies and specific requirements contained in any agreements applicable to its transactions." Derivative practitioners have proved the ability to police themselves, as seen in the decrease of discussion concerning federal regulation, and there is a wealth of information on best practices now available for review. Using these guidelines or comparing them to internal policies is an effective reality check in managing risk.

It should be stressed that not all errors result in catastrophic disaster. To put these operational risk management tools in a more meaningful perspective, several case studies based on actual occurrences on a smaller scale are presented.

Example 1: Cash Settled Swaptions

Company A has a robust set of operational controls that include separate independent checking of confirmations against deal tickets, dual review of confirmations and multiple reconciliations between confirmations and systems. Errors in the database should be highly unlikely in this environment.

However, Company A's trading desk was informed by the back and middle offices of a swaption exercise date according to correct procedure. The front office calculated a cash settlement price and found it differed greatly from the counterparty's. In reviewing the documents, it appeared that the settlement methodology was different on the ticket and in the system from what was indicated on the counterparty's confirmation, yield to maturity versus zero coupon. Operations was immediately asked to explain how this could have occurred.

An analysis revealed that the documentation unit had iron-clad procedures for verification of confirmations that were generated in-house. However, within the fast-moving and complicated environment of derivatives, the documentation for swaption products is being developed by market participants and is always a little different, depending on the counterparty. Therefore, even though operations usually acted as the calculation agent and sent out its own confirmations, it sometimes found it more efficient to sign counterparty agreements for cash settled transactions.

The incoming counterparty agreements were compared with deal tickets, yet if there were differences, the trader was notified orally and if the confirmation was correct, a note was put on it and it was signed and sent back. The documentation unit assumed that the traders would process a deal amendment ticket and change their system but never followed up because no additional or amended confirmation was necessary. A comprehensive review showed at least 10 examples where the ticket did not match the confirmation. The system did not reflect the amendment in all cases.

Thus, existing control systems were no longer sufficient in a new environment. New controls were immediately developed concerning transactions where counterparties' confirmations were used. Also, procedures were implemented so that deal tickets always had to match confirmations before confirmations from counterparties were signed.

Lessons Learned

Confirmations are a critical control.

New developments require new controls.

Periodic review of unusual transactions from original documents is always valuable.

A separate database for confirmations and processing increases risk.

Example 2: Mutual Puts

Company A, again the one with the robust control system, has transactions with mutual puts. These transactions have an exercise date and a notification date. The notification date is quoted in relation to the exercise date (i.e., two New York or London business days prior). The problem with these transactions came to light as a by-product of the investigation into cash settled transactions, but highlights a different operational issue.

The back office was not tracking the notification dates on mutual puts as the system could not handle the additional field and the variable nature of its relationship to the exercise date. Although no financial impact was felt, a beneficial put opportunity could have been missed because notification dates of exercise were not captured in the system. Notification dates of exercise dates with separate holiday conventions for each, is another complication of cash settlement and is beyond the processing abilities of most systems.

Again, controls were developed and a manual tickler and hard copy reports were generated to track all deals with mutual puts since it was not done automatically by the system.

Lessons Learned

Systems capability will probably not stay abreast of market and product developments and should be reviewed for all elements of new transactions.

Details are important and correct data capture is essential.

Occasionally, manual controls are a necessary evil.

Operations risk management is a proactive activity.

OPERATIONS AND SYSTEMS STRATEGIES

Along with internal controls and external verifications, there are also longer term strategies that can be used in a more general manner to combat risk. The critical elements are senior management commitment, human resource management, and systems development.

Senior Management Commitment

For any successful operational risk management effort, the commitment of senior management is a necessity. In the last few years, the derivative's business has gone through a difficult period in terms of reputation and the reporting of large losses. As a result, the approach to the business has evolved. Specifically, two recent developments in the industry have helped focus senior management's attention on operational risk management.

First, senior management has changed. In general, senior management has become more aware of the importance of understanding the risk profile of its organization. According to the Group of Thirty Study, in 98% of the derivatives dealers surveyed, senior management set risk policy and reviewed procedures on a regular basis. The willingness and ability of senior management to emphasize and understand risk management issues are now common among most organizations.

Second, the role of derivatives operations areas has changed. As discussed earlier, operations now encompasses more functions including the middle office responsibilities, has a higher caliber of staff and a greater degree of accountability in managing risk. As the area responsible for the externally verified database, operations is the natural provider of information for supervisory reporting.

Thus, it appears that senior management wants to understand the risks it is exposed to, and that operations is growing in importance as a provider of critical information. It should be reasonable to assume that senior management would be fully committed to operational risk management efforts.

Unfortunately, this is not the case. For whatever reasons, whether there is some atavistic reluctance to take operational risks seriously, or that operations is not as interesting as other elements of the business, senior management still must be persuaded to support operational risk management objectives. An example of this is the previously mentioned Barings disaster, where senior management chose to ignore operational risks in favor of false profits. Therefore, ensuring senior management commitment to operational risk management is not simple. But, it can be made easier by following these basic principles:

1. *Information:* Ensure that the information being generated by the operations area is correct and meaningful in creating a picture of operational risk.
2. *Knowledge:* Train staff to be aware of what the issues are and what methods are used to control exposure both on the business side and in terms of operations.
3. *Communication:* Provide senior management with concise, clear reports on a regular basis and require acknowledgment.
4. *Participation:* Provide value-added support for the business side in new undertakings as well as acting as the control mechanism.
5. *Accountability:* Assume responsibility for mistakes and the well-being of the organization as a whole.

Although following these guidelines will not guarantee the commitment of senior management, these basic principles will improve the relationship and serve to assist in the development of a robust operational risk management environment.

Human Resources

Two years ago, Merrill Lynch and Chase Manhattan Bank finished first and second in the Euromoney Survey of Best Back Offices. When asked what the main contributor to their success was, both Operations Executives replied, "People." This response makes sense because processing failures are largely caused by human error. The human factor is therefore both the source and the solution for operations risk.

The caliber of operations staff has been steadily rising to keep pace with the demands of the derivatives industry. As deals and technology become more complex, high-level staff are required to understand and process the transactions correctly.

In addition, there is now an understanding that a different kind of talent is required for derivatives operations units than for other commercial bank processing functions. The traditional structure of a supervisor managing a large group of deal entry clerks is not applicable. The types of transactions, the product and process interrelationships, the large sums of money involved, and the amount of judgment required on the part of the operations professionals are substantial. This calls for a very high-level of operations/middle office staff. The Group of Thirty Recommendation number 16 reads, "Dealers and end-users must ensure that their derivatives activities are undertaken by professionals in sufficient number and with the appropriate experience, skill levels, and degrees of specialization. These professionals include specialists who transact and manage the risks involved, their supervisors, and those responsible for processing, reporting, controlling, and auditing the activities."

The actual implementation of the recommendation on professional expertise is somewhat more problematic, however. There is a natural reluctance to invest heavily in what is traditionally a burdensome cost center. Yet, with the very real possibility of operational disasters and the increasing role of operations as an active participant in rolling out new products, this is changing. In contrast to the 1994 Group of Thirty Study results where the upgrading of operations and systems staff was a concern to participants, the 1995 follow-up showed a decrease in concern. This can be attributed to the efforts to ensure quality resources that include the following steps:

1. *Hiring Practices:* Formalized hiring standards should be in place for operations staff and are in place as of 1995 in 70% of the dealers reviewed in the Group of Thirty follow-up study.

2. *Job Descriptions:* For staff that is already in place, specific job descriptions are necessary to ensure that responsibilities are clearly understood. Job descriptions have been implemented in 82% of the dealers polled in the Group of Thirty follow-up study.

3. *Training:* A specific training plan should be developed to add to the expertise of staff members and provide for cross training and exposure to larger issues. These programs could include seminars, continuing education, industry conferences, and job rotations. According to the Group of Thirty follow-up study, 73% of dealers provide training.

4. *Experience:* Formalized standards for experience requirements and special attributes such as PC or systems skills for operations staff should be on par with the levels required for front office functions. There are now derivatives operations specialists who are familiar with processing and reporting requirements. A "warm body" is not sufficient and adds to potential risk. As of 1995, 77% of dealers surveyed by the Group of Thirty had specific experience requirements for operations functions.

5. *Compensation:* The compensation levels and bonus amounts for derivatives operations staff should reflect the complexity of their function and will be higher than the salaries paid other operations personnel. A Towers Perrin study done in November of 1993 showed that a middle office position requiring two

to four years experience and strong PC and systems skills could expect a base salary of $50,000 to $70,000 with a $20,000 to $30,000 bonus. The relative magnitude of these numbers has not changed in the last few years and the demand for trained derivatives specialists is high.

6. *Career Planning:* Even though the processing of derivatives requires a high skill and experience level, not all the functions are especially challenging after a certain period of time. For example, even though deal terms can be extremely complex and many tasks need close attention to detail to perform reliably, the preparation of payment notifications or deal entry can become onerous. There has to be a potential for growth or advancement to keep staff fresh and morale high. Otherwise, functions are performed by rote and the potential for error is increased.

Executives of derivatives operations units have a difficult responsibility in managing these professionals. Turnover in sensitive positions can be devastating and the learning curve is steep. Operations' duties run the gamut from highly sophisticated profit-and-loss analysis to deal entry, sometimes contained within the same function and performed in some instances by a CPA or an MBA. Special skill is required to motivate and retain staff in this somewhat schizophrenic environment.

Systems Development

The availability of adequate technology to process derivatives is an on-going problem and the greatest challenge to operations managers. The difficulties are based on the nature of the business where models are developed by the front office to price new transactions while the back office is left behind. Transactions are also unbundled for booking purposes but must be reconstituted to confirm to the counterparties. It is nearly impossible to have one system that can satisfy both front office and operations requirements.

Even with these issues, the Group of Thirty recommends that, "Dealers and end-users must ensure that adequate systems for data capture, processing, settlement, and management reporting are in place so that derivatives transactions are conducted in an orderly and efficient manner in compliance with management policies." In the Group of Thirty follow-up survey, dealers were most concerned about strengthening the following elements of derivatives systems.

1. *Management Reporting Capabilities:* The ability to provide integrated information on credit risk and market risk, stress testing, and cash projections.
2. *Processing:* The systems' ability to perform all the processing functions from a common database throughout the operations workflow.
3. *Data Capture:* The ability to enter all of the transactions into the system without significant manual interventions or use of ancillary spreadsheets.
4. *Settlements:* The ability to calculate correct settlement amounts and provide a calendar for event monitoring such as notification dates.

The challenge is to address these concerns efficiently. The correct data and its completeness and accessibility are key to a derivatives risk management system. With this goal in mind, there are four areas concerning processing systems that should be analyzed: centralization, applications, integration, and security.

Most firms agree that the data for derivatives should be centralized in a common database on a global level. This allows for the monitoring of credit and risk exposure and the analysis of individual transactions and natural hedges. It also satisfies the Federal Reserve Bank criteria for consistent supervision and demonstrated adherence to stated risk postures. Reporting for regulatory and management purposes is also facilitated. The concept of a centralized database is also supported by the recent centralization of processing areas for cost efficiencies. The combined Chase and Chemical derivatives operation reportedly processes approximately 100,000 outstanding derivative transactions for multiple entities on a 24-hour basis from Brooklyn, New York. With quarterly resets, nearly 2,000 events a day would be processed and reported on around the globe. Clearly, the day of autonomous, stand-alone, regional systems has passed.

A centralized database, however, must have suitable applications for processing most deal types for the majority of operations functions. It is unrealistic to assume that 100% of all transactions will be captured, valued, reset, settled, and accounted for on the same system. Yet, to be effective, a core system should be able to process 80% to 90% of the transactions throughout the operational workflow. For plain vanilla deals, derivative operations can be more functionally organized and controlled. For the remainder of the transactions, the system should have the flexibility to accept uploads from other systems or downloads to a common platform where all transactions and associated fair values can be captured on a timely basis in order to produce necessary risk reports. It is not unreasonable to expect that current systems functionality will include most of the generic operations tasks. Since it will be continually externally verified, the core database should be used for as many purposes as possible including combined market and credit risk management reporting. Multiple systems generating different reports for confirmations, accounting and risk management increase the operations and systems risk potential and require extensive reconciliation. However, it is difficult to manage the trade off between consistency and security versus functionality and responsiveness. Solutions that are currently in use include various systems linked together via bridges and networks and flexible front end or middle office real time applications connected to a more robust transaction database and processing system.

This leads to the issue of integration. Since structured transactions include many different product types, a clear view of the whole is necessary for managing risk. A processing system that handles all associated products, hedges, financing, and derivatives is rare. Some derivative software vendors have attempted this using a modular approach, yet none seem to be completely successful. Some institutions have attempted to build this functionality in-house and are probably still trying. Although, many hard quants have been recruited from academia to the lucrative field of derivatives systems, their time is best spent developing new, proprietary pricing models. Therefore, a good axiom is to "buy the easy stuff and build the hard stuff." It is inefficient to program a futures or treasury processing system if a mature product with flexible functionality already exists. The result for derivatives processing will probably be a hybrid solution based on custom made, super-charged front-end systems attached to a core processing system and centralized data repository. This approach would allow multiproduct flexibility combined with stability and operational consistency. Traders would enter deals directly into systems with real time data feeds, since it is in their best interest to do so correctly and promptly, and middle office could complete and verify the data.

Operational consistency and the integrity of the database should be further enhanced by the systems security features which could be built into the core database. Once the data is verified and manual intervention is reduced as much as possible, strong systems administration procedures guarantee a secure environment. These include preventative and detective controls on unauthorized access, access hierarchies, systems and model change controls, contingency plans, and documentation.

Development efforts on the front end should remain more fluid via test environments to facilitate entry into new products. The production database, however, should be protected to allow for the accurate evaluation of risk exposures and the ability to add new products with confidence. As an interesting aside, three firms in London have recently been the victims of database corruption extortion which again demonstrates the importance of data and its security.

CONCLUSION

The examination of operations functions and the associated risks as well as the analyses of various approaches to counteract these problems can be somewhat daunting. The management of derivatives operations includes a sensitivity to the capricious human element, as well as an extremely technical analysis of the deal terms and systems applications. Strong operational staff and controls can also be a frightening concept, invoking images of a huge bureaucracy and rigid systems and procedures. The worst nightmare of some front offices is an operations person with a badge. To respond to the perception of the inmates running the asylum, a common goal throughout the organization should be stressed. The overall objective is an accurate, complete, and accessible transaction database that can be used as a platform for efficient processing and portfolio management. The old systems adage "garbage in, garbage out" is especially applicable in discussing operations risk, demonstrating the critical synergy between basic operational controls and sophisticated risk management techniques. It is this relationship that is the basis of an infrastructure for supporting an innovative and profitable derivatives business.

REFERENCES

Derivatives: Practices and Principles, Global Derivative Study Group, Group of Thirty, July 1993, Washington, DC, Recommendations.

Derivatives: Practices and Principles, Follow-Up Surveys of Industry Practice, International Swaps and Derivatives Association, Arthur Andersen & Co., Price Waterhouse, Group of Thirty, December 1994, Washington, DC.

The Principles and Practices for Wholesale Financial Market Transactions, Federal Reserve Bank of New York, August 17, 1995, New York, NY, Mechanics of Transactions.

SR-93-69 (FIS) Examining Risk Management and Internal Controls for Trading Activities of Banking Organizations, Board of Governors of the Federal Reserve System, Division of Banking and Supervision, December 20, 1993, Washington, DC.

Towers Perrin, Derivatives Position Evaluation (Proprietary). Based on Information submitted by 6 Institutions, November 3, 1993, Position 10: Trader Support.

Trading Activities Manual, Board of Governors of the Federal Reserve System, February 1994, Part I. Introduction and Back Office Operations.

PART TWO

Legal Risk

4

A Review of Case Law Affecting Swaps and Related Derivative Instruments

UNITED STATES CASE LAW
ANTHONY C. GOOCH AND LINDA KLEIN

We wrote the following in *A Review of International and U.S. Case Law Affecting Swaps and Related Derivative Products,* which dealt with lawsuits brought through August 1, 1992:

> *Only a few disputes involving swaps and related derivative products have come before the courts, and many of those suits have been settled out of court. In addition, the legislature changed the applicable law after the court's decision in some of the cases, so the issue examined in the case must now be analyzed under different rules. Market practitioners are actively lobbying for still further legislative changes to the law applied in some of the cases. Nevertheless, there are ample lessons to be learned from studying the sorts of disputes that have found their way before judges and juries, and the court decisions in some of the cases will be the applicable law for the future in the jurisdictions where they were decided.[1]*

The lawsuits described involved one or more of the following issues:

1. Whether enforceable contracts existed when the parties had exchanged correspondence about their trades and negotiated but not finalized formal agreements;[2]
2. Whether the confirmation of a trade was the final expression of the parties' agreement, thus precluding the introduction of extrinsic evidence to prove different terms;[3]
3. Whether transactions argued to be beyond the power to contract *(ultra vires)* of one of the parties were void;[4]

The authors and their law firms regularly represent a number of the entities involved in the proceedings described herein and, in some cases, have acted as counsel or filed *amicus curiae* briefs in connection with such proceedings. This material is current as of October 31, 1996.

4. Whether transactions violated public policy, as expressed in state anti-gaming and bucket-shop laws and the Commodity Exchange Act (the *CEA*), and, therefore, whether the defendant could avoid his obligations under the transactions;[5] and

5. Whether contractual provisions on early termination of transactions and on the calculation and payment of damages in connection with termination were enforceable in the event of a party's insolvency or inability to pay its debts as they fell due.[6]

As a general matter, those disputes served to remind participants in the OTC derivatives market of the need for due diligence in documenting their transactions, in verifying the power and authority of their counterparties to enter into transactions and in exploring the legal framework within which their agreements would be tested should a counterparty become insolvent or seek to avoid responsibility for a transaction that has become unfavorable to it.

This chapter discusses subsequent developments involving the U.S. cases described in the *1992 Review,* as well as more recent cases before the U.S. courts that have presented the same or similar issues and new issues. In the course of the discussion, we refer occasionally to legislative changes and initiatives of industry groups in the United States that are related to these issues, as well as administrative proceedings involving one or both of the parties to the lawsuits. The principal focus will, however, remain private civil actions brought or decided in the U.S. courts since August 1992. This review does not purport to be exhaustive.[7]

The first two sections of this chapter discuss disputes over the formation and existence of the contract and related legislative developments, involving, respectively, statutes of frauds and parol evidence rules. Section 3 covers cases relating to power and authority to enter into over-the-counter derivatives transactions,[8] and section 4 considers cases involving attacks on the legality of contracts based on commodities regulation and state gaming and bucket-shop laws. The fifth section discusses cases that presented issues involving choice of law and jurisdiction. In sections 6 through 9 we discuss cases that involve claims of breaches of duties alleged to have existed in connection with derivative transactions, common-law tort theories (fraud, negligence and the like) and alleged violations of anti-fraud and similar provisions of state and federal law, grouped in categories relating to the nature of the relationships, or alleged relationships, between the parties that served as the basis for the claims.

Section 6 covers cases brought by shareholders against company directors and management, seeking to hold them responsible for losses attributed to improper, speculative use of derivatives or to their failure to protect the company against risks through hedging. The seventh section discusses a case in which a principal sought to hold its broker liable for losses incurred in connection with derivatives transactions the broker had arranged, as well as cases in which the status of the defendant as a broker-dealer forms part of the underpinning for a claim of breach of duty. Section 8 covers cases in which it is alleged that one of the parties to OTC derivatives transactions acted as a fiduciary for the other party, even though no formal fiduciary relationship existed. The final section encompasses cases in which a purchaser of securities alleges that it was deceived in connection with the purchase because the issuer or an arranger or underwriter did not disclose to the purchaser that (1) the issuer of the securities had sustained significant losses on derivatives transactions or (2) the issuer of the securities had entered into a related derivatives transaction with an underwriter that had the effect of increasing the underwriter's compensation on the securities' sale.

There has been a tendency in recent years for plaintiffs, the press, concerned legislators and others to describe structured notes,[9] collateralized mortgage obligations (*CMOs*)[10] and other investment securities as "derivatives" or "derivative securities," or to liken them to OTC or exchange-traded derivatives because they involve some of the risk-shifting features of derivatives. Some of the disputes that we discuss form a small part of complex situations in which various parties are attempting to recover substantial losses incurred in connection with investments of those sorts. Our interest in those cases for purposes of this chapter is generally limited to their involvement with privately negotiated OTC financial derivatives, understood to include cash-settled forward transactions, swaps, options, caps, floors, collars, and similar transactions. We view the character of CMOs and structured notes as investment securities, their sale as such and the legal and regulatory framework applicable to them and to the relationship between the buyers and sellers of such securities as distinguishing them in important ways from the kinds of OTC derivatives involved in the lawsuits discussed in this chapter. We do not, therefore, deal here in detail with the many widely publicized cases involving these securities that have been brought against brokers, dealers, investment companies, and investment advisers or managers.[11]

1. Statutes of Frauds

As briefly described above, in *Homestead Savings v. Life Savings & Loan Ass'n,* the first of the cases described in the *1992 Review,*[12] the defendant relied on a statute of frauds as a defense to the plaintiff's suit for damages incurred as result of defendant's breach (repudiation) of contract relating to two interest rate swaps; the defendant took the position that a contract between the parties never existed because they had not executed full-blown agreements to cover the swaps, although lengthy negotiations on those agreements had taken place. The defense was rejected and a jury awarded damages to the plaintiff, apparently having found that the documents executed by the defendant, when viewed together with documents executed by the plaintiff and the circumstances of the case, were sufficient to indicate the existence of contracts.

Statutes of frauds are intended to protect against fraudulent claims based on alleged oral contracts supported by perjured testimony; they are not, however, "meant to be used as 'a means of evading just obligations' based on contracts 'fairly and admittedly made.'"[13] The jury's finding in *Homestead* indicated that a defense based on the statute of frauds was misplaced in that case.

Participants in the OTC derivatives market were aware before *Homestead* of a danger that a counterparty might raise a statute-of-frauds defense if market movements left it dissatisfied with the terms of a transaction agreed to orally, as most OTC derivative transactions are. *Homestead* showed that the danger was more than theoretical, and since that case market participants have naturally been concerned about a counterparty's failure of performance prior to its return of an executed confirmation, when an applicable statute of frauds requires such a signed, or subscribed, writing for the contract to be enforceable as such against the counterparty. At the time the *1992 Review* was published lobbying for a change in the applicable New York statutes of frauds was ongoing, in an effort to seek reasonable protection for parties to OTC derivatives against abuse of the statutes.

The changes sought became effective in September 1994, through amendments to various statutes of frauds in the Uniform Commercial Code as in effect in the State of New York and in New York's General Obligations Law. These amendments relate to "qualified financial contracts," a term defined to include a broad array of swaps, foreign exchange and other OTC derivatives in which neither of the parties is a natural person.[14]

One of the key features of the amended statutes is that qualified financial contracts will not be subject to otherwise applicable writing requirements contained in the statutes if the parties, by means of a prior or subsequent written contract, have agreed to be bound by the terms of the qualified financial contract from the time they reach agreement (by telephone, by exchange of electronic messages, or otherwise) on those terms. As a result, if a disputed oral contract is covered by a master agreement that includes such a provision, New York statutes-of-frauds defenses will no longer be available. An important consideration is the need to show a link between the oral agreement that is sought to be enforced and the agreement of the parties to be bound by oral agreements. The parties to master agreements governing their derivatives transactions may find it desirable to provide in their master agreements that all qualified financial contracts between the parties entered into after the date of the master agreement (as well as agreed previously existing transactions) will be subject to that agreement.

The second key feature of the amendments establishes new rules regarding the evidence that will be deemed to be sufficient to prove the existence of a qualified financial contract, even when there is no prior or subsequent written contract under which the parties have agreed to be bound by agreements not in writing. Under those rules, evidence adduced by a party to a qualified financial contract will be sufficient if (1) it consists of a confirmation that is sufficient against the sender, (2) the confirmation is received by the counterparty against whom enforcement of the contract is sought not later than the fifth business day after the contract is made (or such other period as the parties may agree to in writing), and (3) by the third business day (or such other period as is agreed) after receipt of the confirmation by the counterparty, the sender does not receive a written objection to a material term of the confirmation. For these purposes, the time of receipt of the confirmation or the objection is the earlier of actual receipt by an individual responsible for the transaction and constructive receipt, which occurs at the time when actual receipt would have occurred had the addressee organization exercised reasonable diligence.

Prior to the amendments a similar rule existed under a New York statute of frauds held applicable to certain foreign exchange transactions, as described in the *1992 Review* and *Documentation for Derivatives;* now the rule applies to all qualified financial contracts subject to those statutes of frauds provided a natural person is not a party. This change, therefore, affords substantial relief to the senders of confirmations. Market participants should carefully review the procedures they follow for reviewing and replying to confirmations they receive.[15]

Participants in the OTC derivatives market should not, of course, be lulled by these amendments into complacency about obtaining executed trade confirmations and complete agreements to cover their transactions. Even when the amended New York statutes of frauds are applicable to OTC derivatives, they impose, as described, certain requirements that must be satisfied. The amendments do not apply to OTC derivatives in which either of the parties is a natural person, and they may not be applied in actions brought outside New York against defendants who were acting from an office outside New York when they agreed to the transaction. Furthermore, special statutes of frauds may apply in some cases given the nature of the party against whom enforcement is sought[16] or given the nature of the obligations involved, as is illustrated by the next two cases.

Lehman Bros. Commercial Corp. v. Minmetals International Non-Ferrous Metals Trading Co.[17]

The *Minmetals* case is a reminder that special statutes of frauds may apply to the credit support provided for OTC derivative obligations. The case was brought by two companies in the Lehman Brothers group for breach of foreign currency option and forward contracts and a swap, after the transactions were terminated for failure by a Chinese company to post collateral as required. The plaintiffs also asserted claims against the defendant's parent company, based on an alleged guaranty of the defendant's obligations, which was stated to be governed by Delaware law. That claim was, however, dismissed on the basis of a statute-of-frauds defense because the court found that the plaintiffs had failed to plead facts sufficient to evidence satisfaction of a Delaware statute of frauds requiring obligations for the debt of another to be evidenced by a writing signed by the party to be bound, or some other person authorized in writing to bind that party.[18]

Daiwa America Corp. v. Rowayton Capital Management, Inc.[19]

A similar defense was raised in the *Rowayton* case, which involves a New York statute of frauds under which a "special promise to answer for the debt . . . of another person" is void unless "it or some note or memorandum thereof be in writing, and subscribed by the party to be charged therewith, or by his lawful agent. . . ."[20] The suit was brought alleging breach of contract by the named defendant (*RCM*) and RCM Global Long Term Capital Appreciation Fund Limited (*RCM Global* and, collectively with RCM, the *RCM Companies*), a fund described by the court as designed for highly speculative investments by non-U.S. residents in the off-shore foreign currency markets.[21] The plaintiff (*Daiwa*) sought both recovery of approximately $2 million in damages allegedly owed by the two defendants under FX transactions under identical Foreign Exchange Netting Agreements (the *Netting Agreements*) and a declaration that Daiwa had properly seized $33 million in assets from RCM Global to offset obligations owed by RCM under one of the Netting Agreements.

The Netting Agreements, like many agreements used to document spot and forward FX transactions, swaps and other derivatives, included a provision under which, in the event of a default by a party, the nondefaulting party would be entitled, first, to cancel or otherwise liquidate not only all transactions under the particular agreement with the defaulting party but also all other transactions between the nondefaulting party and the defaulting party or any of its affiliates and, second, to set off any obligation that it owed to the defaulting party or any of its affiliates against any obligations that the defaulting party or its affiliates owed to it or any of its affiliates. The Netting Agreements also included cross-collateralization language, in which each party granted, to secure any contractual obligation of that party to the other or to the affiliates of the other, a security interest in "all property heretofore held by or for" that party or its affiliates.

As described by the court, when Daiwa called for additional margin to cover a deficit in respect of the RCM Companies' accounts after giving effect to the netting contemplated in the agreements and requested an agreement confirming that each guaranteed the other and that any surplus in either of the accounts could be used to offset a deficit in the other, the request was refused. The RCM Companies' representative, who had executed the Netting Agreements and was alleged earlier to have indicated that the RCM Companies were virtually identical and that surpluses could be so used, purportedly for the first time claimed that RCM and RCM Global were not "affiliates." After notifying the RCM Companies that they were in default and that it planned to exercise its rights under the Netting Agreements, Daiwa liquidated the FX transactions in both accounts and applied the surplus in the RCM Global account to the RCM obligations, leaving an unpaid balance of the approximately $2 million in damages sought in the action.

Both defendants raised counterclaims seeking punitive damages: Among other things, RCM claimed that Daiwa had tortiously interfered with RCM's contractual relations with RCM Global,[22] and RCM Global claimed that Daiwa had tortiously converted the surplus in the RCM Global account and acted unlawfully in applying RCM Global's assets to RCM's obligations. In its April 1996 Order, the court dismissed that RCM counterclaim, dismissed both defendants' claims for punitive damages and denied defendants' motion for partial summary judgment, which was based, in part, on their statute-of-frauds defense.

The theory behind this defense was that the RCM Companies had refused to sign the requested confirmation of the RCM and RCM Global cross-guaranty, so Daiwa's claim against RCM Global for a debt of RCM was barred by the portion of the New York statute of frauds quoted above. The court rejected this theory, finding that the contractual netting provisions for setoff of obligations involving affiliates and the accompanying cross-collateralization language referred to above were sufficiently clear in constituting a guaranty to satisfy the requirements of that statute of frauds.

Under the RCM Companies' second theory, even if that language satisfied the statute of frauds, it applied only to "affiliates," and RCM Global should not be found to be an affiliate of RCM for that purpose because that term, which was not defined in the contract, should have the meaning given to the term in the standardized Master Agreement forms published by the International Swaps and Derivatives Association,[23] where its coverage depends on "control," defined solely by reference to ownership of a majority of the voting power of an entity or person. The court rejected that theory and, after reviewing New York authorities construing the meaning of the term "affiliate," found there was no basis to narrow the scope of the term from that which is commonly ascribed to it, which embraces entities under common management, control or ownership, with "control" intended to include the power to direct or cause the direction of the management and policies of another person. However, the court also found that the documents before it were inconclusive on the issue of control and affiliation and as to the authority of the person who signed the RCM Global agreement to bind RCM Global. The court, therefore, denied the RCM Companies' motion for summary judgment, without prejudice to renew it upon completion of discovery. The effort to recover the RCM Global funds seized by Daiwa has since shifted to voluntary bankruptcy proceedings in the Bankruptcy Court of the Southern District of New York.[24]

Although we have referred to these cases as new reminders of the need for attention to statutes of frauds and similar laws that may require executed agreements as a predicate to enforcement of contractual rights, they are also reminders that, in general, participants in the derivatives market should be paying closer attention to issues relating to contract formation that may arise in connection with guaranties and other types of credit support. For example, the representative of the alleged guarantor in the *Rowayton* case contended that he did not understand the implications of the cross-affiliate setoff and security provisions in the agreements he signed, and the guarantor entities in that case and in the *Minmetals* case both alleged that the persons who executed the alleged guaranties were not authorized to do so. These issues are especially likely to arise in connection with arrangements—like cross-affiliate close out and netting provisions—whose character as guaranties may not be a central focus of the parties' discussions, even though they may be a critical part of the credit protection sought by one of the parties. When the protection of a guaranty, whether styled as such or embodied in such a provision, is important, appropriate diligence should address compliance with any special statute of frauds applicable to guaranties, the power of the relevant party to provide a guaranty, the due authorization of the relevant agreement in the manner required for guaranties by that party, the authority of each relevant individual to execute a guaranty and the regulatory or fiduciary implications, if any, of such a guaranty.[25]

2. Parol Evidence Rules

Intershoe, Inc. v. Bankers Trust Co.[26]

As discussed in detail in the *1992 Review, Intershoe* was an action for damages involving a forward foreign exchange transaction in which Bankers Trust relied on a confirmation of the trade signed by Intershoe and Intershoe sought unsuccessfully to contradict the terms of the confirmation, arguing that it was not the final expression of the parties' agreement and, in fact, that the confirmation mistakenly reversed the parties' respective roles as the seller and buyer of the foreign currency involved (Italian lire). The court held that the parol evidence rule of Section 2-202 of the U.C.C. as adopted in New York precluded the plaintiff's reliance on extrinsic evidence to contradict the terms set out in the confirmation, finding that there was nothing about the confirmation or the parties' manner of dealing with each other to suggest that the confirmation was anything other than the final expression of the parties' agreement.

Intershoe stands for the proposition that, under the parol evidence rule in Section 2-202 of the New York U.C.C., the parties do not need to state in their trade confirmations that the confirmation is the complete and final expression of the financial terms of the relevant transaction. However, the *Intershoe* facts have since been distinguished in the following case involving FX transactions applying the same parol evidence rule, where the court found that there was reason to doubt whether trade confirmations constituted the final expression of the parties' agreement.

Compañía Sud-Americana de Vapores, S.A. v. IBJ Schroder Bank & Trust Co.[27]

Sud-Americana de Vapores was a breach of contract action in which the plaintiff alleged, among other things, that its agreement with IBJ Schroder relating to a course of FX trading included an oral promise, breached by the bank, to give the plaintiff preferred client status in setting the foreign exchange rates applicable to the transactions. In denying IBJ Schroder's motion for summary judgment based on the trade confirmations, which included no reference to agreed preferred rates, the court concluded that, because of the long history of the parties' foreign exchange dealings with each other, a jury could find that the confirmations were not the complete and final expression of the parties' agreement because there was an "overarching" prior oral agreement governing the totality of the parties' relationship.[28] This ruling raises some doubts about the comfort that the derivatives market took from the result in the *Intershoe* case, although it is very much based on the peculiar facts in the case.[29]

Participants in the OTC derivatives markets should also bear in mind that although the parol evidence rule applied in *Intershoe* and *Sud-Americana de Vapores* may be applicable in currency swaps and other foreign exchange transactions, if the same kind of dispute arose under New York law in connection with an OTC derivative of another kind, the source of the applicable parol evidence rule would be different, although the applicable principles generally appear to be the same. As stated by the courts in New York, the rule provides that, when the parties have reduced their agreement to writing, extrinsic evidence of prior or contemporaneous agreements may not be offered to contradict, vary or subtract from the terms of the writing, although, when the writing does not appear to express the entire agreement of the parties, evidence that the writing which purports to be a contract in fact is not a contract at all, or to explain any ambiguities or omissions in the writing, is admissible.[30]

In evaluating the lessons to be learned from these cases, market participants should weigh the desirability of brevity in confirmations against the possible benefits to be derived from additional language to the effect that the confirmation (together with the master agreement it supplements, where appropriate) is the complete and final expression of the parties' agreement on the terms of the transaction referred to in the confirmation. Inclusion of such a provision may be attractive to entities that believe they themselves will make few mistakes in the confirmations they send or sign and, in any event, would prefer to live with mistakes so as to avoid litigation, if necessary.

Another possibility, for institutions particularly concerned about the high cost of mistakes, is to consider a contractual provision that expressly permits the contradiction of a signed confirmation through at least certain kinds of contemporaneous extrinsic evidence. Section 8.3 of the International Foreign Exchange Master Agreement (*IFEMA*) includes such a provision for foreign exchange spot and forward transactions documented under those terms: "In the event of any dispute between the Parties as to the terms of an FX Transaction governed by these Terms . . . , the Parties may use electronic recordings as the preferred evidence of the terms of such FX Transaction, notwithstanding the existence of any writing to the contrary." Subject to appropriate safeguards relating to the legality and integrity of recordings, market participants that electronically record their OTC derivatives trades should consider whether this kind of provision is desirable.

In weighing the various considerations, professional market participants, in particular, should also consider the sorts of terms that sales personnel tend to discuss with clients in the process of shaping a transaction. In these discussions, sales personnel often touch on subjects, such as the firm's general willingness to unwind a transaction at the client's request, probably intending the discussion to be no more than an informal expression of the general way in which the firm seeks to accommodate client requests on terms to be negotiated at the time of the request. From the perspective of the professional participant in the market, a formal agreement on a price at which an unwind would be consummated would be tantamount to selling the counterparty an option to terminate the transaction, which would have to be hedged and would involve additional cost to the client. As two of the lawsuits discussed below indicate,[31] the client may mistakenly believe, or at least contend that it believed, that these discussions have become part of the parties' agreement on the terms of the transaction. The confirmation's statement that it (and the related master agreement, if there is one) represent the complete and final expression of the parties' agreement may be a desirable supplement to appropriate training of sales personnel about drawing clearer distinctions between general policies to be implemented pursuant to later negotiations, on the one hand, and the actual terms of the trade reflected in its pricing.[32]

3. Power and Authority to Enter into Derivatives Transactions

Standard practice in documenting swaps and related derivatives (sometimes relaxed for transactions between established dealers) requires that each party to an agreement deliver to the other evidence of the steps taken by the party to authorize its execution and delivery of the agreement and any confirmations thereunder, together with incumbency and specimen signature certificates for the persons signing the documentation on its behalf. In transactions with public-sector entities and other persons with limited powers, these documents are not, however, sufficient, if there is a risk that the transactions may be declared void if found to have been beyond the powers of the counterparty *(ultra vires)* or that the counterparty may avoid responsibility under the contract on the theory that its execution was not duly authorized. As we have written elsewhere, in these cases,

> *[l]egal opinions, though often dispensed with in transactions between dealers, should be required, and the substance of the opinions relating to the power of the entity to enter into the transactions and to the steps required for due authorization should be probed by counsel to ensure that the special concerns that arise in the area have been given informed attention. Indeed, a discussion of these concerns and of the contents of the legal opinion should be among the first things to happen when a public-sector entity considers engaging in derivative transactions, because it may not be prudent to enter into such transactions if counsel cannot furnish adequate assurance of the power and authority of the public-sector end-user to enter into transactions of the kind.*[33]

As described in the *1992 Review*, the importance of these considerations was impressed on the OTC derivatives market by the decision of the House of Lords in *Hazell v. Hammersmith & Fulham London Borough Council*,[34] where the many swaps and similar derivatives involved in the case were found to be *ultra vires* and, therefore, void. The decision of the House of Lords did not deal specifically with the financial consequences of unwinding the void derivatives transactions with the Borough of Hammersmith and Fulham and other English local authorities with similarly narrow powers. Therefore, as further noted in the *1992 Review*,[35] after the decision numerous proceedings were begun against British local authorities by their swap counterparties seeking repayment of amounts previously paid to the authorities, with interest, and press reports indicate that many such actions have been settled.[36] The status of those U.K. cases is described on pages 178–212.

Lawsuits brought in U.S. courts since the *Hammersmith & Fulham* decision should reinforce the lessons of that case and serve as fresh reminders that derivatives market participants with limited powers may seek to reverse their losses on transactions that have proved unfavorable by arguing that the transactions were beyond their powers or not duly authorized.

State of West Virginia v. Morgan Stanley & Co.[37]

The *West Virginia* case related, *inter alia,* to trading in when-issued Treasury securities and reverse repurchase agreements between West Virginia (the *State*) and Morgan Stanley and the sale by the State to Morgan Stanley of a put option on $200 million of seven-year Treasury notes.[38] In connection with these transactions, the State was investing approximately $2.5 billion of tax revenues, federal funds and various service fees, all collected and managed for the purpose of providing funding for State operations and capital improvement projects, as well as funds belonging to political subdivisions of the State. The transactions were part of a trading and investment program that the State's Investment Division pursued over several years, which led to losses in the hundreds of millions of dollars after earlier successes that were widely reported in the press.[39]

The State sought damages for its losses on various theories, two of which can be seen as ways of seeking to hold its counterparty responsible for the State's having entered into transactions beyond its powers. The first theory was that there had been a violation of a provision of state law (the *State investment policy*) requiring that any investment made by the State be made "with the exercise of that degree of judgment and care, under circumstances then prevailing, which men of experience, prudence, discretion and intelligence exercise in the management of their own affairs, not for speculation but for investment, considering the probable safety of their capital as well as the probable income to be derived."[40] The second was that there had been actual and constructive fraud and negligence and civil conspiracy by Morgan Stanley with staff of the plaintiff to commit unlawful acts by entering into the transactions in violation of the State investment policy. The other theories for recovery included alleged violations by Morgan Stanley of the anti-fraud provisions of the West Virginia securities laws and the federal Securities Act of 1933 (the *Securities Act*) and breach of an alleged fiduciary duty owed by Morgan Stanley, as a securities dealer, to the plaintiff.

The facts recited by the State in support of those causes of action may be summarized as follows:

> *(i) Morgan Stanley solicited the State to enter into the transactions and, therefore, under Securities and Exchange Commission (SEC), New York Stock Exchange (NYSE) and National Association of Securities Dealers (NASD) suitability rules, Morgan Stanley was required to use due diligence to learn the essential facts about the State as a customer, "including its liquidity needs, source of investment funds, investment objectives, investment policies, legal and other restraints to which the [State's] account was subject, etc., so as to have grounds for reasonable judgment with respect to the suitability of securities transactions recommended, encouraged or suggested" to the State.[41] In the case of the option sold by the State to Morgan Stanley, Morgan Stanley made no inquiry with respect to the knowledge of the State's investment staff about options or the appropriateness or permissibility of an option sale by the State, even though Morgan Stanley had never engaged in an option transaction with the State before.[42]*
>
> *(ii) The State investment policy and policy guidelines adopted by the State's Board of Investments (the Board) expressly prohibited State investments for speculation and required, inter alia, that any option positions taken on by the State be for the sole purpose of hedging. All persons that engaged in securities transactions with the State, including Morgan Stanley, had actual or constructive knowledge of these legislative and policy restrictions. Morgan Stanley's background was such that it had reason to know with certainty that transactions entered into by the State were required to be non-speculative, and Morgan Stanley therefore had a legal duty not to engage in speculative transactions with the State.[43]*
>
> *(iii) Morgan Stanley induced the State's investment staff to engage in speculative trading activity without adequately explaining to them either the risks*

involved in the trades or that the trades, being speculative in nature, violated the legal and policy restrictions on transactions permitted to the State; and Morgan Stanley knew the staff was not competent to evaluate those risks independently or to understand that the transactions were illegal. The staff's reliance on Morgan Stanley's much greater sophistication and expertise created a special trust relationship between Morgan Stanley and the State.[44]

(iv) Because the State's investment staff concealed the nature and results of its activities, the State did not contribute to its own losses from the illegal transactions because it could not have known, and did not know, of the wrongful transactions engaged in by the staff with Morgan Stanley, or the existence of the losses, until November 1988, when the State received the preliminary results of a special audit of the staff's investment activities.[45] *Morgan Stanley's trader knew of the concealment in respect of the State's loss position on the put option sold by the State but did not disclose the facts to the Board.*[46] *Morgan Stanley temporarily suspended its trading activity with the State in November 1986 because it had concluded that the heavy volume of trading was inappropriate and in violation of the applicable guidelines and, after being told by the staff (in a trip involving both business and legal personnel) that the prohibition in the guidelines against speculative activity could not be deleted from the guidelines, nonetheless resumed trading activities with the State, with the admonition that Morgan Stanley would continue to monitor the trading activity, but without seeking to discuss with any member of the Board the concerns that led Morgan Stanley to suspend the speculative trading. Thereafter, instead of monitoring that activity, Morgan Stanley greatly increased the activity, and it was not until mid-April of 1987 that Morgan Stanley ended the activity, when its attorney learned that it violated not only the previously known investment guidelines but also the statutory State investment policy.*[47]

(v) Morgan Stanley realized considerable and unwarranted profits and commissions from this wrongful conduct.[48]

The trial court awarded judgment to the State against Morgan Stanley for almost $57 million, approximately ninety percent of which resulted from a summary judgment ruling by the court to the effect that Morgan Stanley had knowingly aided and abetted the staff of the Board in violating their fiduciary duty by speculating in violation of the State investment policy.[49] The jury found for Morgan Stanley on the State's actual fraud claim but, in light of the court's jury charge on constructive fraud and the court's summary judgment ruling finding violation of the State investment policy, found for the State on the constructive fraud claim. That jury charge was, in part, as follows:

Constructive fraud is a breach of a legal or equitable duty, which, irrespective of any moral guilt on the part of the defendant, the law declares fraudulent because of its tendency to deceive others, or violate public or private confidence, or to injure public interests. Neither actual dishonesty of purpose nor intent to deceive is an essential element of constructive fraud. Constructive fraud includes violations of public policy or public rights or transactions affected by illegal conduct of any kind.[50]

On appeal, West Virginia's highest court reversed the summary judgment, ruling that the trial court should have submitted to the jury the matters it had decided as a matter of law, because the jury should have been permitted to determine as matters of fact both whether Morgan Stanley knowingly aided and abetted the Board's staff in violating the State investment policy and whether the transactions in question constituted speculation in violation of that policy. The court, recognizing that it was perhaps breaking new ground, also agreed with Morgan Stanley that, if the transactions were speculative and, therefore, in violation of the State investment policy, the trial court erred in failing to allow Morgan Stanley to reduce any amounts payable by it in respect of losses that the State suffered because of its aiding and abetting violations by the amount of profits that were made pursuing the same trading strategy, if the violation on Morgan Stanley's part was not intentional.[51] As indicated above, Morgan Stanley and the State subsequently settled the case.[52]

The lessons to be learned from *West Virginia* are the same as those offered earlier by the decision of the House of Lords in *Hammersmith & Fulham:* where a counterparty with limited power may seek the protection of the doctrine of *ultra vires* or of a statute like the one at issue in *West Virginia,* or may seek to avoid liability under a contract by arguing it was not duly authorized, the provider of a derivative transaction to such a counterparty can be at risk of losing the benefit it bargained for and, in effect, of being treated as the insurer of favorable results for the counterparty. It is, therefore, critical to identify such counterparties and to undertake appropriate legal diligence about their power and authority before entering into a transaction.

Market participants often take the view that these concerns may be disposed of through an opinion of counsel for the counterparty and the counterparty's own representations that it has the power to engage in a transaction and that it has taken all actions and obtained all approvals necessary to authorize the transaction. The value of such an opinion and of such representations will, however, vary from case to case and depend both on the factual circumstances and on the applicable law. In some situations, even if counsel for a counterparty has given a favorable legal opinion on the question of power and authority, and even if the counterparty itself has made representations of these kinds, in connection with a later challenge the opinion and representations may not preclude a decision that the transaction is void or that the counterparty may avoid its obligations thereunder, although the likelihood of a challenge undoubtedly is reduced when appropriate diligence is done and documented on these critical issues.

Lehman Bros. Commercial Corp. v. China International United Petroleum & Chemicals Co.[53] and Lehman Bros. Commercial Corp. v. Minmetals International Non-Ferrous Metals Trading Co.[54]

Other lawsuits brought in the U.S. courts since *Hammersmith & Fulham* illustrate that appropriate diligence can be critical with counterparties other than municipalities and sovereign states. Indeed, failure by a professional market participant to engage in such diligence may be cited in support of actions by counterparties to avoid contractual liability under various theories. For example, the failure to conduct due diligence may be alleged to support a theory that a market participant should have known that transactions were illegal for the other party or not properly authorized, because diligence would have disclosed it. Also, the counterparty may allege that a professional market participant breached a duty to the counterparty by failing to ensure that transactions between them were authorized, and that the market participant aided and abetted a breach of fiduciary duty owed to the counterparty by its own employee who participated in the transactions without authority (claims raised, as noted, in the *West Virginia* case). These concerns are illustrated by two cases that were brought before the U.S. District Court for the Southern District of New York.[55]

As described in Lehman's pleadings, the *Unipec* and *Minmetals* cases involved similar facts and substantial dealings in FX derivatives and swaps over prolonged periods. Unipec allegedly entered into more than 100 foreign currency transactions in 1993 and 1994, including FX forwards and options, with LBCC, pursuant to a Commodity Terms and Conditions Agreement and a Supplemental FX Facility Agreement,[56] and entered into eight swap transactions with LBSF pursuant to a Master Agreement prepared using an ISDA form. Unipec received approximately $6 million from Lehman in connection with the swap transactions over the course of a year. Minmetals allegedly entered into hundreds of foreign exchange transactions with LBCC from December 1992 through June 1994 and two swap transactions with LBSF, the first of which involved an up-front payment of $500,000 to Minmetals and the second of which was terminated by agreement of the parties.

Both Unipec and Minmetals agreed to post collateral from time to time in connection with their obligations under the FX transactions and, in the case of Unipec, under the swaps. Minmetals also agreed that LBSF had the right to terminate the swaps if the aggregate FX and swap exposure to Minmetals exceeded $5 million. An extended rise in U.S. interest rates and a fall in the value of the U.S. dollar beginning in early 1994 caused steadily increasing losses in the positions of both Unipec and Minmetals, and Lehman made a series of margin calls.

Some partial payments were made on the margin calls by Unipec, discussions about the unsatisfied calls on it were held with Unipec's president, and he acknowledged Unipec's responsibility to meet the calls and represented that they would be met with assets located outside China, because at the time it was impossible to use assets inside China for the purpose. Because Unipec failed to provide LBCC and LBSF with adequate assurance that the assets were actually owned by Unipec and these assets proved to be both difficult to value and illiquid, Lehman rejected Unipec's offer and Unipec was advised in July 1994 that stop-loss orders would have to be placed on its outstanding FX positions. Unipec's president agreed to the placement of several stop-loss orders and the market moved in Unipec's favor. LBCC and LBSF did not immediately liquidate Unipec's transactions, but Unipec's unrealized losses remained far in excess of the posted margin, so LBCC advised Unipec's president that stop-loss orders at revised prices should be placed. He refused and notified LBCC and LBSF that they would "bear the consequences" if stop-loss orders were placed and losses were incurred by Unipec as a result. LBCC placed a stop-loss order on the only remaining FX position and advised Unipec that the swaps would be liquidated if the related margin calls remained unsatisfied. The stop-loss level on the FX forward was reached and the transaction was liquidated, resulting in a Unipec obligation of over $22.8 million. The swaps were terminated, resulting in a Unipec obligation of over $29 million. In subsequent discussions, Unipec's president acknowledged the transactions and Unipec's obligations to post collateral but took the position that the liquidation of the FX forward and the termination of the swaps was unwarranted, that the transactions should be restored and that Unipec should be allowed to resume engaging in FX and swap transactions with Lehman, notwithstanding the unsatisfied margin calls. Lehman's combined claims for damages for breach of the FX and swap contracts, net of some amounts realized on a letter of credit that had been issued on Unipec's behalf, exceeded $43.8 million.

Similarly, Minmetals periodically posted collateral to keep Lehman's exposure below the agreed level for some time but later failed to make the necessary payments and, after having agreed to supply letters of credit to reduce the exposure, failed to produce them. Minmetals stated that certain of its delays were caused by a Chinese government freeze on payments to foreigners. After further calls for margin payments and other collateral were unavailing, Lehman liquidated the FX positions and terminated the remaining swap, leaving a Minmetals obligation of over $52 million.

Both Unipec and Minmetals raised the following, among other defenses: The individual who executed the alleged contracts was not authorized to do so; the transactions were illegal under Chinese law and were not authorized; the losses were caused by Lehman's own negligent, reckless or intentional acts or omissions; Lehman was estopped from seeking relief because of inequitable conduct and breaches of fiduciary duties owed by it to Unipec and Minmetals or because of fraud and misrepresentations or because the transactions violated the CEA; Lehman failed to take appropriate steps to mitigate damages; and Lehman failed to provide Unipec and Minmetals with information impliedly required by the contracts. Unipec also alleged that the contracts were void because Unipec's corporate seal was not affixed to them.

Unipec and Minmetals also asserted numerous counterclaims against the Lehman plaintiffs and, in the case of Unipec, against three other Lehman affiliates. Under these counterclaims, Unipec and Minmetals sought, among other relief, compensatory damages, and a minimum of $50 million in punitive damages, in the case of Unipec, and $100 million in punitive damages, in the case of Minmetals. Among other things, the counterclaims alleged the following in relation to the issues of power and authority: The plaintiffs owed Unipec and Minmetals, and breached, fiduciary duties, *inter alia,* by taking advantage of Unipec's and Minmetals' trust by recommending that they enter into transactions even though plaintiffs knew or should have known that the transactions were illegal under Chinese law and by failing to determine if the person trading in the name of Unipec or Minmetals had the authority to do so. Minmetals also alleged that Lehman induced the purported Minmetals representative to breach his own fiduciary obligations to the company by entering into the unauthorized transactions. The same conduct by the plaintiffs was argued by both Unipec and Minmetals to constitute negligence and fraudulent concealment, since the plaintiffs owed Unipec and Minmetals a duty to use reasonable care and competence to obtain authorization from Unipec and Minmetals for all transactions, as well as fiduciary duties.[57]

The alleged factual basis for the above-described defenses and counterclaims in *Unipec* relating to power and authority is as follows. Unipec is in the business of importing and exporting petroleum products and petrochemicals and related equipment and, under its business license, which was available for public inspection, Unipec was not authorized to engage in transactions of the types alleged by the plaintiffs, which, under Chinese law, could be engaged in only by companies with a governmental authorization that Unipec never received. The disclosure materials for a public offering that a Lehman affiliate had underwritten, as well as other evidence of Lehman business operations in and involving China, indicated that the plaintiffs were aware that this governmental authorization was required and that Unipec, without it, was prohibited from engaging in the transactions, and that it was illegal to trade foreign currencies with Unipec, or to solicit or induce Unipec or any of its employees to engage in such trading. The individual who executed the alleged contracts was not authorized to enter into them on behalf of Unipec and had resigned from his position with Unipec and moved from Beijing to Hong Kong, to work for a wholly unrelated company, by the time the plaintiffs entered into some of their alleged transactions with Unipec through him, and Lehman was aware of these facts when it engaged in transactions with him, dealing with him in Hong Kong.

Furthermore, according to Unipec, the documentation signed by Unipec's president purporting to authorize that person to enter into a swap referred to only one swap, did not mention FX transactions, did not expressly authorize the execution of any of the other contracts alleged by the plaintiffs, and was flawed because it did not have the corporate seal of Unipec. No board resolutions were issued granting that individual authority, and the plaintiffs failed to ascertain whether such approval had been obtained, did not require proof of the individual's authority, failed to take sufficient measures to assure that Unipec had legal capacity and authority to enter into swaps and, in connection with execution of the transactions, neither contacted anyone other than that individual at Unipec to verify his authority nor sought a legal opinion about these issues, although the Master Agreement apparently provided that an opinion would be required. Ultimately, when a legal opinion was obtained, it was not in the form required in the Master Agreement and, in addressing Unipec's power and authority, did not mention transactions in foreign exchange or swaps, but if the law firm that issued the opinion had been asked about those issues, it would have stated that such transactions were illegal for Unipec.

The alleged factual basis for the above-described defenses and counterclaims relating to power and authority in *Minmetals* is as follows. Minmetals and its parent are in the business of importing and exporting metals and mineral products. Under Minmetals' business license, which was available for public inspection, Minmetals was not authorized to engage in transactions of the types alleged by the plaintiffs, which, under Chinese law, could be engaged in only by companies with a governmental authorization that Minmetals never received. Moreover, only Minmetals' president and his delegees were authorized to act on the company's behalf. The prospectus for a public offering that a Lehman affiliate had underwritten showed that Lehman knew that Chinese companies are prohibited from engaging in transactions unless they receive special governmental approval to do so. A purported authorization by Minmetals' president for the Minmetals representative who signed the swap documentation was ineffective, since it was executed after the relevant transaction was entered into and since the president was misled as to the nature of the transaction.

In answer to the counterclaims, Lehman maintained in both cases, among other things, that: (1) the Chinese foreign exchange controls relied on by Unipec and Minmetals did not apply to transactions engaged in by Chinese companies outside China or financed by foreign exchange or other assets located outside China, and Unipec and Minmetals, and not any of the Lehman entities, bore responsibility for obtaining any permission from Chinese state agencies required for Unipec and Minmetals to engage in any of the relevant transactions and (2) Unipec and Minmetals had ratified, sanctioned and approved the actions of the individual alleged by them not to have had authority to enter into the transactions. In *Unipec,* Lehman also contended that the company's corporate seal was not required for any of the documents argued by Unipec to be without effect for lack of the seal, that the authorization of Unipec's president was relied upon by Lehman in forming a good faith view that Unipec was authorized to engage in the transactions (and Lehman did not need separately to ascertain whether board approval had been obtained), and that satisfaction of the Master Agreement's provision requiring a legal opinion was not a prerequisite to entering into a binding swap transaction. As affirmative defenses, Lehman argued, *inter alia*, in both cases that the counterclaims were barred by the doctrines of waiver and estoppel and because Unipec and Minmetals failed to take appropriate steps to mitigate damages, the transactions at issue were all ratified by Unipec and Minmetals; any losses incurred by Unipec and Minmetals in connection with the transactions were caused by their own negligent, reckless or intentional acts or omissions and, therefore, were not recoverable; and, to the extent the transactions required Chinese regulatory authorization, Unipec and Minmetals were responsible for obtaining it.

Section 1 of this chapter describes certain actions that were taken by the court in the *Minmetals* case in connection with the original complaint, where the Minmetals parent was named as a defendant on the basis of an alleged guaranty of Minmetals' obligations. As described above, when that action was dismissed with leave to amend,[58] the complaint was amended to allege that Minmetals was, in entering into the transactions at issue and throughout the contractual relationship, acting on behalf of and for the benefit of its parent, which dominated and controlled Minmetals in its transactions with the plaintiffs and, therefore, was responsible directly under those transactions as the alter ego of Minmetals. There is no indication in the record that further action has been taken by the court in the *Minmetals* case.

In *Unipec,* the court dismissed two of the Unipec counterclaims for failure to state a cause of action,[59] and the case has since reportedly been settled.[60]

Like the *West Virginia* case, the *Unipec* and *Minmetals* actions should impress upon professional participants in the OTC derivatives market that issues involving the power and authority of a counterparty to engage in a transaction may be used by the counterparty not only as a means of seeking to avoid its obligations, under the doctrine of *ultra vires,* expressed in one form or another, but also as a means of seeking to hold the provider of the transactions responsible for misconduct of an employee or representative of the counterparty in entering into allegedly unauthorized transactions. Whereas the traditional approach, under the *ultra vires* defense, involves a risk of loss of bargain for the professional market participant, the second approach, illustrated in the cases described above, also involves a risk of damage to the business reputation and franchise of the market participant. Therefore, as we have suggested elsewhere,

> If the power and authorization issues cannot be clearly disposed of in a favorable manner, the potential provider of a derivative transaction to such an end-user should explore what the consequences could be if the transaction proved to be ultra vires for the end-user or is not properly authorized. The following are some of the questions that should be considered. Would the law entitle the end-user to deny its liability with respect to the transaction at any time? If so, what relief, if any, might the counterparty obtain—only recovery of payments made by it? Not even that, with any certainty? Under the applicable law, could the end-user be estopped from denying its liability in respect of an ultra vires or improperly authorized transaction in some circumstances? If so, what are they, and do they exist in connection with the proposed transaction? In each of these areas, is there a difference between transactions that are ultra vires and those that suffer from some irregularity in the authorization process? If satisfactory answers to all these and related questions cannot be obtained, the end-user should be asked to seek a change in the law relating to its powers or to correct

any lapse in the authorization process before the transaction is consummated. If this is not possible, or if the end-user is unwilling to attempt it, then the market participant should carefully weigh the wisdom of entering into the transaction in light of the answers it has obtained about the consequences of entering into an ultra vires or improperly authorized transaction with that end-user.[61]

4. Commodities Regulation and State Gaming and Bucket-Shop Laws

The Appellate Decision in Salomon Forex, Inc. v. Tauber[62]

As noted above and described in detail in the *1992 Review,* the *Tauber* case involved a claim for damages for breach of FX forward and foreign currency option transactions in which Dr. Tauber argued that his obligations should be found unenforceable, *inter alia,* because they violated state gaming and bucket-shop laws and provisions of the CEA and regulations thereunder that, in the absence of an applicable exception, prohibit commodity futures contracts and commodity options unless they are conducted on or subject to the rules of a foreign board of trade, exchange or market or on or subject to the rules of a board of trade designated by the Commodity Futures Trading Commission (the *CFTC*) as a contract market for the relevant commodity.[63] In the trial court decision described in the *1992 Review,* the court held for the plaintiff, rejecting Dr. Tauber's state-law defenses and counterclaims as without merit and finding that the FX forwards and currency options in question were exempt from regulation under the CEA, under an amendment to the CEA sponsored by the U.S. Treasury Department (the *Treasury Amendment*) that modified Section 2 of the statute to provide, *inter alia,* that transactions in foreign currency are not governed by the statute unless such transactions involve the sale thereof for future delivery conducted on a board of trade.

The state-law defenses were disposed of on a motion for summary judgment, with virtually no discussion in the record of the court's rationale regarding the bucket-shop defense but with a clear indication on the gaming-law defense that the court was following New York precedent to the effect that the law was not intended to reach transactions entered into for a valid business purpose.[64] Since publication of the *1992 Review,* the *Tauber* decision has been affirmed by the United States Court of Appeals for the Fourth Circuit in an opinion that sheds light on the appellate court's approach to the bucket-shop law defense.

One feature of the dealings between Dr. Tauber and Salomon Forex was that, as a general matter, at the settlement date for an FX forward, the transaction would be settled through a new, offsetting contract, rather than through payment of the relevant currencies. This feature of the parties' dealings was pointed to by Dr. Tauber as an indication that the transactions were illegal, off-exchange futures contracts entered into in violation of Section 4(a) of the CEA. The decision of the Court of Appeals, however, focused on this aspect of the parties' dealings in concluding that a defense based on a violation of the New York bucket-shop law could not survive because one element of a violation of the statute[65] was absent: the requirement that an offending contract be made "without intending a bona fide purchase or sale" of the subject matter and with the intent to settle the account by reference to market quotations. The Court of Appeals noted as follows:

The agreements between Salomon Forex and Tauber were bona fide contracts, resulting in legal obligations to take delivery. They were not settled by reference to the dealings of others, but by further trading between the parties, who engaged in offsetting transactions. The New York statute does not ban legally enforceable trades settled by further transactions, but only sham transactions. As the Supreme Court noted more than eight decades ago in finding that offsetting transactions did not render futures sales violative of the Illinois bucket shop law:

> *It seems to us an extraordinary and unlikely proposition that the dealings which give its character to the great market for futures sales in this country are to be regarded as mere wagers or as pretended buying or selling . . . . A set-off is in legal effect a delivery.*[66]

The main part of Fourth Circuit opinion in *Tauber* deals with one of Dr. Tauber's rejected defenses based on the CEA. The trial court rejected his arguments that the FX forwards and currency options with Salomon Forex were illegal and therefore void or voidable off-exchange commodity futures and options by finding that the transactions were exempt from regulation under the Treasury Amendment to the CEA. As described in the *1992 Review*,[67] Dr. Tauber had argued at the trial level, among other things, that this exemptive provision is narrower than its words suggest[68] and applies only to transactions in foreign currency between financial institutions. At the appellate level Dr. Tauber also argued that the Treasury Amendment should be read to apply only to transactions "in" foreign currency, meaning those in which physical delivery of foreign currency is anticipated, and not to transactions more broadly involving foreign currency.

After considering the plain meaning of the CEA, its legislative history and the numerous *amicus curiae* briefs submitted in the case,[69] the Fourth Circuit rejected Dr. Tauber's arguments, concluding that "under the appropriate interpretation of the Treasury Amendment, all off-exchange transactions in foreign currency, including futures and options, are exempted from regulation by the CEA."[70] However, in the face of concerns expressed in some of these *amicus* briefs and Dr. Tauber's argument that affirmance of the trial court's decision would result in the use of the Fourth Circuit as a base for potentially abusive and unregulated sales of off-exchange currency futures and options to the general public, the court also stated its holding in *Tauber* narrowly, as follows: "We hold only that individually-negotiated foreign currency option and futures transactions between sophisticated, large-scale foreign currency traders falls within the Treasury Amendment's exclusion from CEA coverage."[71] The Fourth Circuit's opinion in the *Tauber* case will be its final disposition, since the Supreme Court has elected not to grant Dr. Tauber's request to be heard.[72]

CFTC v. Standard Forex, Inc.[73]

After the trial court decision in *Tauber* and before the ruling by the Fourth Circuit in that case, the U.S. District Court for the Eastern District of New York expressed its view on the scope of the Treasury Amendment in *Standard Forex,* an action charging that the company and its officers and employees violated the ban on off-exchange trading of commodity futures in the CEA by offering and selling foreign currency futures contracts to the public in markets not designated by the CFTC as contract markets, that they committed fraud in connection with such transactions and that certain of the defendants operated as unregistered futures commission merchants in violation of Section 4d of the CEA.[74] The preliminary relief sought and obtained by the CFTC in the case included a preliminary injunction barring all the defendants collectively and individually from engaging in further transactions in violation of the exchange-trading requirements of the CEA and barring Standard Forex and the account executive defendants from making fraudulent misrepresentations in violation of the CEA, as well as a protective order, pending disposition of the case, continuing a freeze of Standard Forex's assets. The defendants cross-moved for dismissal of the actions against them.

The *Standard Forex* discussion of the reach of the Treasury Amendment, in ruling on a motion to dismiss, reads the complaint liberally to determine whether it is sufficient to survive the motion. In this context, the court declined to dismiss the CFTC's action, noting that the language of the CEA is sufficiently ambiguous to permit a conclusion that the defendants' actions violated the CEA, as argued by the CFTC. The court suggested that it might reach this conclusion through various avenues. One possible conclusion is that the office in Queens from which the defendants marketed FX transactions to the public constituted a "board of trade" for purposes of the Treasury Amendment. If this were so, even though the relevant transactions were transactions in foreign currency, they would not be exempt from regulation pursuant to the Treasury Amendment, which does not exempt FX transactions involving "the sale thereof for future delivery on a board of trade."[75] On this theory, since the defendants' board of trade had not been approved as a contract market pursuant to the CEA, the CFTC could establish at trial that the defendants had engaged in transactions in violation of the exchange-trading requirements of the CEA.

The court also noted that it disagreed with the broad reading of the Treasury Amendment by the trial court in *Tauber* and was inclined to give deference to the CFTC's interpretation that "[a]ny marketing to the general public of futures transactions in foreign currencies conducted outside the facilities of a contract market is strictly outside the scope of the [Treasury] Amendment."[76]

CFTC v. Dunn[77] and CFTC v. Frankwell Bullion Ltd.[78]

The split in authority about the reach of the Treasury Amendment has also recently been compounded by two other decisions that have attracted some attention, both rendered in CFTC enforcement actions: *CFTC v. Dunn* and *CFTC v. Frankwell Bullion Ltd.,* decisions of the U.S. Courts of Appeals for the Second Circuit and the Ninth Circuit, respectively.

Dunn involved CFTC allegations of fraud by the defendants in soliciting funds from investors for trading in FX options and the CFTC's request that the trial court appoint a temporary receiver for the operations. The defendants challenged the court's subject-matter jurisdiction, arguing that the Treasury Amendment placed currency options beyond the reach of the CEA and the CFTC's regulatory authority. After the District Court ruled in favor of the CFTC, the Second Circuit affirmed, finding itself constrained to do so given an earlier decision by the Second Circuit.[79] The appellate court expressed some doubt about the correctness of the earlier decision, recognized that it is in conflict with *Tauber* and stated that it is up to the Supreme Court to resolve the conflict.

In *Frankwell Bullion,* the CFTC sought the appointment of a receiver for the defendants' operations, which were alleged to have involved solicitation of the general public for speculative precious metals and foreign currency contracts in violation of the CEA. The CFTC did not allege that the defendants had engaged in any fraudulent activity. A temporary receivership was established but later dissolved by the trial court, which also denied the CFTC's request for injunctive relief and granted summary judgment for the defendants.[80] The trial court's decision was based on the plain meaning of the Treasury Amendment and its rejection of the CFTC's interpretation under which the Treasury Amendment was intended by Congress to apply only to transactions in foreign currency between banks and other sophisticated parties.[81] The trial court also rejected the CFTC's argument that the term "board of trade" in the CEA is defined so broadly that any association selling foreign currency, including the defendants' businesses, should be found to constitute a board of trade subject to CFTC jurisdiction, except associations of banks and other sophisticated investors.[82] The trial court observed that this reading of the statute "would render the [Treasury] Amendment meaningless."[83] The Ninth Circuit affirmed the grant of summary judgment,[84] observing that (1) the Treasury Amendment applies to all transactions in foreign currency unless they involve futures conducted on a board of trade, and (2) in light of that sweeping exclusion from the CFTC's jurisdiction, the statute is rendered ambiguous by a literal application of the term "board of trade" as defined in the CEA. The court turned to the legislative history to resolve the ambiguity and found that Congress intended through the Treasury Amendment to exclude all transactions in foreign currency from the reach of the CEA and meant "board of trade," as used in the Treasury Amendment, to apply only to exchanges.[85]

The OTC derivatives market should soon see resolution to some of the uncertainty created by the disparate views on the reach of the Treasury Amendment expressed in the court decisions in the cases referred to above, since the Supreme Court has granted *certiorari* in the *Dunn* case, agreeing to hear the defendants' appeal on November 13, 1996. Since that case only involves application of the Treasury Amendment to currency options, however, in reaching its decision the Supreme Court will not be required to reach broader issues about the meaning of the term "board of trade" as used in the Treasury Amendment and, therefore, application of the Treasury Amendment to off-exchange currency futures or other OTC derivatives involving foreign currency that could be argued to fall within CFTC jurisdiction as futures or options. Resolution of those questions may have to await the Supreme Court's willingness to hear an appeal of the Circuit Court's decision in *Frankwell Bullion* or another case. In the meantime, the CFTC continues to pursue enforcement actions premised on its narrow view of the Treasury Amendment's reach but is also reported to be working with the Treasury Department to formulate a cooperative solution to CFTC jurisdiction in the off-exchange foreign currency markets[86] and an amendment to the CEA to deal with the subject of the CFTC's jurisdiction in the area may be expected.[87]

Title V of the Futures Trading Practices Act of 1992 and the CFTC's Exemptions for Swaps and Certain Contracts Involving Energy Products

At the time the *1992 Review* was being prepared, professional participants in the OTC derivatives market were lobbying for legislative change that would reduce the risk of cases like *Tauber* in which a party might seek to avoid its contractual obligations under derivatives by arguing that they violated state gaming and bucket-shop laws or the provisions of the CEA that, as indicated above, ban most off-exchange trading in commodity futures and options. Relief came in the form of Title V of the Futures Trading Practices Act of 1992 (*Title V*). This legislation amended the CEA to preempt state gaming and bucket-shop laws that might otherwise be argued to apply to OTC derivative transactions if the CFTC has exempted the transactions from the exchange-trading requirements of the CEA. Title V also authorized the CFTC to grant such an exemption to certain transactions between "appropriate persons," as defined in the statute.

Pursuant to that authority, the CFTC adopted an "Exemption for Certain Swap Agreements" (the *Swap Exemption*) from those requirements of the CEA, establishing an exemption when a "swap agreement is entered into solely between eligible swap participants at the time such persons enter into the swap agreement" provided that certain additional requirements are satisfied.[88] For these purposes, "swap agreement" is defined to include most OTC swaps and related derivatives, such as caps, floors and collars, as well as FX forwards and swaps and similar agreements, combinations of these transactions and any master agreement for any of the listed derivatives,[89] and "eligible swap participant" is defined to include banks, trust companies, savings associations, credit unions, insurance companies, investment companies subject to registration under the Investment Company Act of 1940, commodity pools, broker-dealers subject to regulation under the U.S. securities laws, regulated futures commission merchants, governmental entities and their political subdivisions, multinational and supranational entities and certain employee benefit plans subject to ERISA (the Employee Retirement Security Act of 1974), as well as most other companies and high net-worth individuals that participate in the OTC derivatives market today.[90] However, because not all OTC derivatives transactions are covered by the Swap Exemption, the *Tauber* case should continue to be a reminder to participants in the market of the kinds of challenges to the enforceability of their derivatives transactions that a non-performing counterparty may seek to raise.

Pursuant to Title V, the CFTC also adopted an "Exemption for Certain Contracts Involving Energy Products"[91] (the *Energy Contracts Exemption*) exempting certain bilateral, individually negotiated contracts for the future purchase and sale of crude oil, condensates, natural gas, natural gas liquids or their derivatives which are used primarily as an energy source from the CEA ban on off-exchange commodity futures, provided the transactions impose binding obligations on the parties to make or take delivery of the underlying commodity and are entered into by commercial participants, acting as principal, who, in connection with their business activities, incur risks, in addition to price risk, related to the underlying physical commodities, have the demonstrable capacity or ability—broadly defined[92]—to make or take delivery under the terms of the contracts, are legally permitted and otherwise authorized to engage in such transactions, are not formed solely for the specific purpose of constituting an eligible entity pursuant to the exemption and also fall within specific categories of "appropriate persons" contemplated in Title V: (1) banks or trust companies, (2) broker-dealers, (3) futures commissions merchants or (4) corporations, partnerships, proprietorships, organizations, trusts or other business entities with a net worth exceeding U.S.$1 million or total assets exceeding U.S.$5 million (or whose obligations under the contract are guaranteed or otherwise supported by specified eligible providers of support). The Energy Contracts Exemption also exempts the covered transactions if they are entered into by governmental entities or instrumentalities, agencies or departments of any of the foregoing, without any requirement that the governmental entity meet any of the other requirements applicable to those four categories of commercial participants.

The Forward Contract Exclusion

As noted, the Energy Contracts Exemption does not require the parties actually to settle their forward contracts through physical delivery; it permits settlement through individually negotiated "book-out" or offset or netting arrangements providing for a cash payment, so long as the parties are initially bound to make and take physical delivery of the relevant commodity and certain other requirements are met.[93] In this respect, for the specific energy products that it covers, the exemption formally expands on the so-called forward contract exclusion of the CEA[94] under which contracts for "future delivery" exclude "any sale of any cash commodity for deferred shipment or delivery," so those sales fall outside the CFTC's jurisdiction and the CEA's ban on off-exchange commodity futures.

As described in the *1992 Review*,[95] in *Tauber* the defendant argued that the forward contract exclusion did not save his forward FX contracts with Salomon Forex from the CEA's ban on off-exchange commodity futures, first, because the exclusion is applicable only to transactions in which future delivery is contracted for because immediate delivery is not commercially desirable,[96] whereas Dr. Tauber entered into his forward FX contracts with Salomon Forex for purely speculative purposes, as Salomon Forex knew, and second, because the exclusion is available only in cases where actual delivery of the relevant commodity occurs and is intended, whereas Dr. Tauber only actually took delivery of foreign currency under four of those contracts, settling the others through offsetting transactions pursuant to a general understanding with Salomon Forex that offset would be the normal procedure. Salomon Forex, for its part, pointed the court to evidence supporting the commercial motivation behind its transactions with Dr. Tauber (including Dr. Tauber's own admissions that his currency trading activities were not speculative) and to the modern and still evolving view that the forward contract exclusion does not require actual physical delivery of the relevant commodity in all cases, as well as case law supporting the view that offset constitutes delivery.

Among the sources cited in support of this view was the CFTC's pre-Title V Statutory Interpretation Concerning Forward Transactions,[97] which can be viewed as the precursor to the Energy Contracts Exemption. This Statutory Interpretation was adopted by the CFTC in response to market concern over a case in which certain Brent crude oil contracts, always thought of as within the forward contract exclusion, were treated by the court as illegal off-exchange futures contracts, because of the widespread practice of settling those contracts through "book-outs" with cash settlement payments, rather than actual physical delivery.[98] In the Forward Contract Statutory Interpretation the CFTC noted that Congress has not addressed the reach of the forward contract exclusion "in today's commercial environment," in which

> *transactions, which are entered into between commercial counterparties in normal commercial channels, serve the same commercial functions as did those forward contracts which originally were the subject of the . . . exclusion notwithstanding the fact that, in specific cases and as separately agreed to between the parties, the transactions may ultimately result in performance through the payment of cash as an alternative to actual physical transfer or delivery of the commodity.*[99]

The CFTC went on to state that the forward contract exclusion is applicable to private, individually negotiated commercial transactions conventionally used in the Brent crude oil market entered into by the parties in connection with their business, where the parties are capable of accepting delivery, even if they forgo delivery through individually negotiated book-outs with cash settlement payment, so long as such offset and cash settlement arrangements are not provided for in the contract and exchange-style offset is not possible.[100] The *Tauber* court reached its decision on the basis of the Treasury amendment and, so, did not make any determination about the applicability of the forward contract exclusion to the facts in that case, noting in the process that it could not do so in deciding a motion for summary judgment, because the determination would have required the resolution of disputed material issues of fact, and disposition on summary judgment is available only where material issues of fact are not in dispute.[101]

For OTC forward arrangements that fall outside the reach of the Swap Exemption and the Energy Contracts Exemption, unless another exemption or exclusion from the CEA's off-exchange ban on commodity futures (such as the Treasury amendment) is available, if the parties settle their transactions without physical delivery of the underlying commodity, there remains a risk that a nonperforming counterparty may seek to avoid contractual obligations by relying on that statutory prohibition, as did Dr. Tauber, because, as evidenced by the post-Title V enforcement proceedings described below, the reach of the forward contract exclusion continues to be a matter of some uncertainty.

In re MG Refining & Marketing, Inc.[102] and CFTC v. Noble Metals International, Inc.[103]

The *Dunn* and *Frankwell Bullion* enforcement cases discussed above were brought by the CFTC after passage of Title V and the CFTC's adoption of the Swap Exemption but in circumstances such that the defendants in those cases did not claim that the members of the public with whom they dealt were eligible swap participants for purposes of the Swap Exemption. Since adoption of the Swap Exemption and the Energy Contracts Exemption, the CFTC has also brought and settled enforcement proceedings against two U.S. affiliates of Metallgesellschaft AG, finding that one of them, MG Refining & Marketing, Inc.,[104] offered and sold illegal off-exchange energy product futures contracts to more than 100 independent gasoline stations and heating oil distributors in the United States as part of its overall energy contract business.[105] The facts in that case too were apparently such that neither the Swap Exemption nor the Energy Contracts Exemption applied, since MGR&M, which agreed in the settlement to tell its customers that the contracts were void, did not invoke either of the exemptions in its support. In submitting the Offer of Settlement accepted by the CFTC when it issued the order instituting and settling the proceedings, MGR&M did not admit or deny the findings, which are the market's guidance as to why the CFTC found certain contracts, referred to as Firm Fixed Price (45-Day) Agreements for the Sale of Petroleum Product (*45 Day Agreements*), to be illegal off-exchange commodity futures, rather than commodity forwards within the forward contract exclusion.

Both the commercial nature of the contracts and the question of delivery were at issue. Although the order describes the contracts as having been marketed, offered and sold "to commercial counterparties,"[106] it focuses on whether the contracts genuinely contemplated physical delivery of the underlying commodities or whether, instead, the contracts were entered into for speculative, rather than commercial, purposes. On this subject, the order's findings are as follows:

> The 45-Day Agreements purportedly provided for delivery of petroleum product to purchasers in the future at a price which was established by the parties at initiation. The purchasers could, if they desired, obtain delivery of product upon tendering 45 days advance notice to MGR&M. The 45 Day Agreements, however,

*did not require any ratable, monthly deliveries of petroleum product to customers.
In fact, delivery of any, or all, product pursuant to the 45 Day Agreements could
be deferred for a period of as long as five or ten years. The Agreements could also
be satisfied without any deliveries whatsoever pursuant to a so-called "blow-out"
provision in the contract. The "blow-out" provision enabled purchasers to terminate the contract and obtain a cash payment from MGR&M if the price of the underlying product (based upon price levels of energy futures contracts traded on
the NYMEX) reached a pre-established exit level.*

*Virtually all purchasers entered the 45 Day Agreements with the intent of in-
voking the "blow-out" provision for the purpose of speculating on the price of the
underlying product. This speculative intent was encouraged by MGR&M sales presentations which emphasized the likelihood that prices would reach the exit level
well before the expiration of the contract term and, if they did not, alternative
arrangements could be made to offset the contracts without delivery. Since 45
Day Agreements did not require ratable deliveries of product, and the delivery of
any product at all could be deferred for as long as five or ten years, the parties
reasonably expected that these contracts would never result in the actual payment for and delivery of petroleum product. In fact, no deliveries of product were
made pursuant to the 45 Day Agreements. These contracts, therefore, contain all
the essential elements of a futures contract: they call for the making or taking of
delivery of a commodity in the future at a price or pricing formula established at
initiation; they may be satisfied either by delivery of the commodity or by engaging in an offsetting transaction without delivery; the purpose of the transaction
is primarily to speculate or hedge the risk of price change in the commodity without actually acquiring the underlying commodity.*[107]

In the wake of the settlement order, concern has been expressed in the OTC derivatives market and by members of Congress that the CFTC might be narrowing its
view of the forward contract exclusion or seeking to expand its jurisdiction by including the recited, broad statement of the characteristics of a futures contract. In
response to a request that the CFTC clarify its intent, its chairperson responded as
follows:

> *The commission neither changed nor signaled a change in its view of what
> constitutes a futures contract or what constitutes a qualifying swap agreement
> under either its exemptive rule or the 1989 Swaps Policy Statement. . . .*[108] *The
> essence of the MG enforcement case was a response to a serious failure of MG's in-
> ternal controls. . . . The commission is very sensitive to questions of market and
> legal uncertainty in this regard.*[109]

That response has not, however, allayed market concerns about the weight that
will be placed on contract provisions for physical delivery and the parties' intent in
entering into forward contracts,[110] and those concerns have been heightened by the
court's decision in another enforcement proceeding, *CFTC v. Noble Metals International, Inc.*[111]

The *Noble* case was brought against Noble Metals International, Moorgate Ltd.,
a principal of Moorgate and a former sales manager of Moorgate for violation of the
CEA's ban on off-exchange futures contracts and alleged fraud in connection with
contracts for the purchase and sale of precious metals to members of the general

public under a program known as the "Forward Delivery Program." The trial court granted the CFTC's motion for summary judgment against all the defendants, and the appellate court generally affirmed that grant except for the fraud count against one of the individual defendants, which it remanded to the trial court. Under the program, customers paid a 15% administrative fee and agreed to make or take delivery of specified quantities of precious metals at an agreed price. The confirmation sent to customers provided that the administrative fee covered a two-year period commencing on the date an order was placed, and the customer, during that period, could elect to take or make delivery at any time during the period. If the customer did not do so, upon payment of additional administrative fees, the customer would be entitled to extend the obligation to make or take delivery for another three years, but the contract expressly stated in capital letters that all customers would be required to take or make delivery and further stated that delivery of transfer of title in return for payment were "of the essence" in the program and that no transaction could be liquidated through an offset.[112] Noble and Moorgate arranged for third parties to act as agents to receive and deliver metals on behalf of the customers, and customers taking delivery would receive legal title through an invoice delivered when the customer paid the full purchase price for the metals, but the third party, upon receipt, would sell the metal, so that, "[a]s a practical matter no actual metal would change hands; the third party would simply sell the metal back to Noble in a paper transaction. The third party would then receive a percentage fee, and the customer would receive the proceeds from the sale."[113]

In rejecting the defendants' argument that the program contracts were forward contracts within the forward contract exclusion, and not commodity futures, the Ninth Circuit cited its earlier decision in the *Co Petro* case to the effect that the exclusion is "unavailable to contracts of sale for commodities which are sold merely for speculative purposes and which are not predicated upon the expectation that delivery of the actual commodity by the seller to the original contracting buyer will occur in the future."[114] The Court then went on to state that it was undisputed that only a handful of the "vast number" of customers involved in the program contemplated actual delivery and rejected the defendants' argument that the delivery requirement was satisfied through delivery of title to the metals to the investor and delivery of the metals themselves to the third-party agents for sale: "To take advantage of the cash forward contract exclusion under the Act," the Court held, "the delivery requirement cannot be satisfied by the simple device of a transfer of title."[115]

The market has expressed considerable concern over this analysis and the adverse effect it can have on the cash forward market.[116] As one commentator has remarked about the *Noble* case and the CFTC's order settling with MGR&M:

> *Perhaps the most disturbing result of* Noble Metals *is the court's rejection of the argument that the delivery through a third-party depository constituted delivery for the purposes of the CEA. This holding suggests that any forward contract under which warehouse receipts or unallocated gold are delivered will be suspect as a futures contract because the contract does not involve delivery. . . .*
>
> *. . . [B]oth the MG Order and* Noble Metals *seem to represent either a reversion to the approach set forth in* Co Petro *(i.e., requiring delivery and related commercial purpose) or a failure on the part of the CFTC to make distinctions of the type necessary to assure the legitimate operation of the cash forward markets.*[117]

In fact, the court's conclusion regarding transfer of title is directly at odds with the CFTC's own statement in the Energy Contracts Exemption that "[c]ash market transactions in crude oil, petroleum products, natural gas and natural gas liquids, as well as other energy related commodities in which physical delivery is made, are effected through payment by the buyer and transfer of title by the seller to the buyer," and its related sanction of delivery through passage of title to a buyer that has itself, in another transaction, passed title to someone else.[118] CFTC action or legislation to amend the CEA to clarify the scope of the forward contract exclusion may ultimately be necessary to dispel the uncertainty and litigation risk perceived to exist as a result of these post-Title V cases.

5. Choice of Law and Forum Issues

When the parties to OTC derivatives execute agreements governing their transactions, they generally specify in the agreements that the law of a specified jurisdiction—often New York or England—will govern the contract and its construction. The parties do not, however, always appreciate that the law they have chosen contractually will not necessarily be applied to the resolution of all disputes between them relating to those transactions.

As suggested by the cases in section 3,[119] which involve power and authority to contract, those issues, and issues of governmental or similar approval, are generally governed, for each party, by the law of its home jurisdiction, and in cases involving a party acting from an office outside its home jurisdiction, some questions may be resolved through application of the law of the jurisdiction where the office is situated.[120] For that reason, as indicated earlier, it is often appropriate to obtain an opinion on these issues from local counsel in a party's jurisdiction of organization and, in some cases, a separate opinion from counsel in the jurisdiction from which the party is acting in connection with the derivatives transactions.

The cases covered in section 3 and in this section illustrate that, if a dispute arises, one of the parties may raise other issues under laws of jurisdictions other than the law chosen by the parties to govern the contract. This may be the law of the jurisdiction in which a party is organized or it may be the law of the forum in which a legal action is brought, particularly if the contract (say, a confirmation) does not specify a governing law or if a party perceives that the law of another jurisdiction may be more favorable and therefore brings an action there (i.e., if the party engages in forum shopping).[121]

This litigation risk may, to some extent, be managed through legal diligence, including an opinion of local counsel obtained before transactions are consummated between the parties. For example, an opinion of local counsel in the jurisdiction of a counterparty or provider of credit support may afford protection with regard to the enforceability of a contract where a statute of frauds concern exists, although, as described in section 1, in some circumstances special care should be taken to obtain the opinion through a process involving diligence about the ways in which the contractual provisions may be characterized (i.e., might a special statute of frauds apply if a provision is characterized as a guaranty), as well as diligence about any special rules that may apply if enforcement of the contract is sought against a receiver or similar official appointed for the counterparty in connection with its insolvency or financial distress.

Legal opinions of the kind generally obtained in connection with derivatives contracts go to the due authorization, execution and delivery, and enforceability, of documents. These opinions can also be helpful in identifying special public policy issues that may be raised by the parties' contract. They do not, however, and generally cannot, address the possibility that the particular factual circumstances surrounding the parties' dealings may give rise to claims under all parts of the law of a given jurisdiction, such as tort claims and claims based on the application of equitable principles or statutory expressions of public policy.

The legal opinion will, of course, relate to the laws of the jurisdiction of the lawyer rendering the opinion and thus will not necessarily cover the laws of all jurisdictions that may have an interest in the resolution of a dispute arising under the agreement. In particular, whether a court adjudicating a dispute will decide that the parties' contractual choice of law, either alone or together with a choice-of-forum clause, precludes claims brought under other laws, may depend on the forum in which the case is brought and, where laws expressing public policy are concerned, on the forum's perception of whether application of the law chosen by the parties, in the forum chosen by them, would be likely to operate to deny the claimant important remedies, thereby violating the public policy of the forum.

P.T. Adimitra Rayapratama v. Bankers Trust Co.[122]

This case illustrates how the issues were framed in an action involving what the court described as highly leveraged derivatives (a "Time Dependent Swap" and a "LIBOR Barrier Swap" that replaced the first transaction when it was canceled) between the plaintiff, an Indonesian company, and Bankers Trust International P.L.C., an English company. The swaps were documented under a Master Agreement, prepared using an ISDA form, that included a choice of English law to govern the contract and its construction and a nonexclusive submission to the English courts with respect to "any suit, action or proceedings relating to" the agreement, as well as waivers of any objection to the laying of venue in any such court and of any claim that any such suit, action or proceeding brought there had been brought in an inconvenient forum.

In this action, brought in a federal district court in New York, the plaintiff asserted fraud-based claims under the Racketeer Influenced and Corrupt Organizations Act (*RICO*) and the CEA,[123] as well as a number of other claims (for fraud, fraudulent concealment, breach of fiduciary duty, negligent misrepresentation, rescission, professional negligence and breach of warranty). The court's analysis began with an acknowledgment that the plaintiff's RICO and commodities law claims are not recognized under English law. The court concluded that English law does, however, provide "adequate remedies that would both vindicate the plaintiff[s]' substantive rights and protect the public policies established by" the relevant provisions of RICO and the anti-fraud provisions of the CEA, and ruled that the parties' contract "is the basic source of the claims" by the plaintiff and "there is no evidence suggesting that the choice of law clause was not intended to apply to all claims growing out of the contractual relationship."[124] The other claims were dismissed for lack of jurisdiction, since the court's jurisdiction over those claims was supplemental to its jurisdiction to hear the dismissed RICO and CEA claims under federal law. In reaching this conclusion and interpreting the effect of the choice-of-law clause, the court followed the reasoning and rulings in cases decided by the U.S. Court of Appeals for the Second Circuit.[125] The court also found that its rulings extended to defendant Bankers Trust, which was not a party to the agreement containing the choice-of-law clause, because the plaintiff had essentially conceded that Bankers Trust was an interested party in the swap transaction, and the facts thus supported the court's conclusion that Bankers Trust was an intended third-party beneficiary of the clause for purposes of the action.[126]

Procter & Gamble Co. v. Bankers Trust Co.[127]

The reasoning and conclusion of the *Adimitra Rayapratama* court were subsequently cited by a federal district court in Ohio in *Procter & Gamble Co. v. Bankers Trust Co.,* in connection with the court's dismissal of a claim under the Ohio Deceptive Trade Practices Act on the ground that the parties had made a contractual choice of New York law.[128] Moreover, in the same decision, in discussing several of the common-law tort claims presented by the plaintiff and its theory of breach of fiduciary duty, discussed below, the court applied and interpreted New York law.

It is not, however, necessarily true that every claim brought in a U.S. court in connection with an OTC derivative under a theory based on tort law, fiduciary principles or public policy will be found to be governed by the law chosen by the parties to govern their contract. Where statutes expressing public policy are concerned, market participants should be mindful that *Adimitra Rayapratama* was decided on the basis of a Second Circuit decision, but a trial court in the same circuit or in another circuit may reach a different result given the particular facts of a case brought before it. Indeed, after the Second Circuit decision followed in *Adimitra Rayapratama,* a federal district court in Texas, considering claims raised under a Texas statute and federal securities law, declined to enforce a contractual choice of an English forum and English law, in a decision that has been affirmed by the Fifth Circuit Court of Appeals.[129] The court reached its conclusion in the case after finding that the choice was induced by fraud and overreaching and that enforcing it would violate public policy as expressed in federal and Texas statutes. In the process, the court indicated its belief that the Second Circuit's decision in the *Adimitra Rayapratama* case was wrongly reasoned.

6. Duties of Care and Loyalty Owed by Directors to Shareholders

The corporation laws of the various American states and case law applicable to the relationship between a corporation and its directors and managers impose on these individuals a number of duties. These include the duty to manage the company's affairs in accordance with the applicable statutory standard and a duty of loyalty that prohibits placing the personal interests of the individuals above the interests of the company in the management of its business. The first case described below involves a claim for damages based on an alleged breach of the duty of care through failure to hedge. The second claim is based on alleged waste of corporate assets through use of OTC derivatives that had been described by management itself (in another context) as outside the scope of corporate policy.

Brane v. Roth[130]

This was a shareholder derivative action[131] against the directors of a rural grain elevator cooperative (the *Co-op*) for losses alleged to have been suffered in 1980 because of the directors' failure to protect the Co-op's position by hedging in the grain market. Damages plus interest were awarded, based on a finding that the directors breached their statutory duty of care to the Co-op under Indiana law. This duty required them to act in good faith, in the best interest of the corporation, and with such care as an ordinarily prudent person in a like position would use in similar circumstances.

The directors argued that they were entitled to rely on the manager of the Co-op, because the applicable statute allowed a director to rely on information, reports, and opinions of the corporation's officers and employees which the director reasonably believes to be reliable and competent, and on public accountants on matters which are reasonably believed to be within their professional competence. The facts indicated that the directors had authorized the Co-op's manager to hedge to protect the Co-op after three years of declining profits and a substantial loss in the prior year, followed by a recommendation from the Co-op's accountant that the Co-op hedge. However, only $20,050 in hedging contracts were entered into, although the Co-op had $7.3 million in grain sales. A second accounting firm later concluded that the primary cause of the Co-op's 1980 loss was the failure to hedge.[132]

The trial court found that the directors' conduct fell short of the statutory standard of care for various reasons: (1) the directors retained a manager inexperienced in hedging; (2) they failed to maintain reasonable supervision over the manager; and (3) they failed to attain knowledge of the basic fundamentals of hedging sufficient to enable them to direct the hedging activities of the Co-op and supervise the manager properly.[133] The court also found that the directors' gross inattention and failure to protect the grain profits caused the resultant loss for which damages against the directors were awarded. The appellate court affirmed, noting, in connection with the directors' reference to the statutory permission to rely on a manager, that the decision to rely must be an informed decision, citing a Delaware case to the effect that the business judgment rule does not protect directors who have abdicated their functions or, absent a conscious decision, failed to act; directors, wrote the court, have a duty to inform themselves of all material information readily available to make their decision.[134]

Brane v. Roth is sometimes casually referred to as a case illustrating that management can be held responsible for a company's losses attributable to insufficient hedging.[135] Its lesson, in fact, is broader. At the close of this section, we refer to some of the many guidelines that have been published in the last few years to assist management in defining its role in developing, applying, testing and reviewing risk management policies and procedures. *Brane v. Roth* is a reminder not only that management cannot abdicate this role but also that it may be held accountable if it fails to inform itself sufficiently about risk management tools, such as derivatives, to fulfill that role appropriately.[136]

Drage v. Procter & Gamble[137]

This shareholder derivative action was brought against P&G and certain of its directors and officers to recover damages sustained and to be sustained and other relief for corporate waste resulting from defendants' "allowing P&G to engage in concededly 'dangerous' derivative leveraged swaps,"[138] resulting in an after-tax charge of $102 million against the company's third quarter 1994 earnings. The plaintiff also sought an order that the Board of Directors and Audit Committee ensure that the company's investment policies be prudent and properly followed and an order that bonus compensation awarded or to be awarded for the 1992–93 or 1993–94 fiscal years to the individual defendants based on increased earnings due to the speculative practices complained of be returned or not awarded by P&G.[139]

The action was filed shortly after P&G issued a press release in which the company announced the after-tax charge "to close out two interest rate swap contracts . . . [that] were negatively affected by the recent dramatic increase in interest rates."[140] The complaint quotes a description of these swaps by one of the defendants in the press release as follows: "Unlike the other swaps the company has historically used, it turned out that the two leveraged swaps in question were based on highly complex formulas that multiplied the effect of interest rate increases. These types of transactions are inconsistent with the company's policy."[141]

The basic thrust of the complaint was as follows:

> *Investing in derivative leveraged swaps inherently involved a grossly unsafe and excessive level of risk, particularly for P&G in light of the Individual Defendants and management's utter and complete ignorance and inexperience in the field, their failure to keep informed, their failure to supervise, and was ultimately a waste of corporate assets. These reckless and completely imprudent actions constituted a breach of the defendants' duty of loyalty and due care for which P&G should be compensated.*[142]

The principal accusation underlying the claim of breach of duty of loyalty was that "[t]he Individual Defendants caused P&G to engage in the high risk derivative leveraged swaps described . . . to increase their bonus compensation . . . ."[143] The complaint also alleged that the defendants had a heightened fiduciary duty to ensure that P&G's investment policies and practices were prudent and that P&G was not engaging in "dangerous high risk investments such as derivative leveraged interest rate swaps"[144] because, in dealing with the company's use of swaps, its 10-K filing with the SEC for the fiscal year ended June 30, 1993 (which was signed by the individual defendants) described swaps as used to minimize exposure and to reduce risk. The case was dismissed on the ground that the plaintiff had failed to satisfy a procedural prerequisite to the filing of a complaint in a shareholder's derivative action, which is that the shareholder first demand that the corporation's directors bring the suit or that the shareholder plead with particularity why such a demand should be excused in the circumstances.[145]

Other Developments

Management's policies and practices regarding financial derivatives are subject to review not only through shareholder lawsuits of the kind described above but also through proceedings and investigations of kinds not within the scope of this chapter. Regulated entities (e.g., banks, broker-dealers and commodity trading advisors, and futures commission merchants) must be concerned about enforcement or other administrative proceedings against management, and the entity itself must establish policies and procedures that comply with any specific applicable regulations or more general mandates regarding safe and sound practices or duties to supervise. The derivatives activities of reporting companies and issuers of securities also require special attention when periodic reports and disclosure documents are prepared.

Among the most widely reported instances of such proceedings or investigations in the United States involving OTC derivatives have been those conducted by the Federal Reserve Bank of New York and the New York State Banking Department into the leveraged derivatives business of Bankers Trust in connection with losses incurred by Gibson Greetings, Inc.[146] and other clients and the related proceedings brought by the CFTC and the SEC against BT Securities, specifically involving only transactions with Gibson Greetings.[147]

The Federal Reserve inquiry culminated in a Written Agreement by and among various Bankers Trust entities and the Federal Reserve Bank of New York,[148] pursuant to which Bankers Trust agreed to introduce certain enhancements of the management and supervision of its leveraged derivatives business and to follow certain specific practices regarding information to be supplied to customers in connection with that business. The CFTC/SEC proceedings, which involved allegations of fraudulent conduct, were settled without admission or denial of guilt.[149] The SEC's theory for characterizing the relevant transactions as securities and, therefore, asserting jurisdiction, involved its conclusion that transactions with Gibson Greetings operated economically in the way options on securities do. The CFTC claimed that BT Securities was subject to its jurisdiction as a commodities trading advisor (or *CTA*) because Gibson Greetings had relied on its advice, but did not articulate a theory of how the relevant transactions might be said to have involved commodity futures or options as to which a CTA might be giving commodities advice. Neither regulatory position was adjudicated. The SEC's position, as argued in the private civil action brought by P&G against Bankers Trust and BT Securities discussed below, was rejected in the court's decision in that matter.[150]

Also of interest are the related proceedings brought against Gibson Greetings, its chief financial officer and its treasurer by the SEC.[151] These proceedings were settled without admission or denial of alleged violations of the Securities Exchange Act of 1934 (the *Exchange Act*), which included failure to include in reports filed with the SEC information about OTC derivatives entered into with Bankers Trust that were necessary to make the information filed by Gibson Greetings not misleading; failure to maintain books and records that accurately and fairly reflected in reasonable detail the company's transactions (*inter alia,* through failure to record the value of the relevant derivatives positions on a mark-to-market basis as required in light of the SEC's characterization of the positions as speculative); and failure to establish appropriate internal controls.

Market participants should also be aware, in this context, of the proceedings referred to above brought against two U.S. affiliates of Metallgesellschaft, AG, in connection with petroleum product contracts entered into with commercial customers and the related hedging of positions under those contracts with near-term futures contracts and OTC commodity-price swaps, a strategy that resulted in exhaustion of a credit line of approximately $900 million.[152] In each of these cases, the regulators involved seized upon the opportunity to require studies of, and improvements in, the internal risk management control and, where relevant, accounting and marketing procedures and policies of the respondents.

Also worthy of note is a report produced in July 1995 by the Legislative Audit Bureau of the State of Wisconsin on the practices of the State's Investment Board, which manages investments for the State's Retirement System and Investment Fund. The report was prompted by the Board's disclosure that it had incurred a $95 million loss from 12 derivative "investments," including leveraged OTC swaps,[153] and by the ensuing withdrawal by local governmental units of some $1.4 billion from the Fund's Local Government Investment Pool.[154] Recognizing the ultimate responsibility of senior management for oversight of the Investment Board's activities and policies, the Audit Bureau Report identified a lack of effective management oversight and called, among other things, for important organizational changes and improvements in reporting to management, as well as improvements in the information provided to the Board of Trustees of the Investment Board.

Groups of end-users and professional participants in the OTC derivatives markets, as well as others interested in the soundness of the marketplace, have produced significant documents embodying recommendations for the improvement of risk-management policies and techniques. The scope and purpose of these recommendations go well beyond the mere avoidance of shareholder lawsuits of the kinds described above and prevention of circumstances that might give rise to enforcement or other administrative proceedings, although mention of these studies is often accompanied by reference to these cases and proceedings, and to the disputes described herein.

As a general matter, these recommendations include a recognition of the need for senior management involvement in the following: (1) developing a formal risk management policy appropriate for the enterprise in light of the risks involved in its business or activities and addressing the parameters for the use of derivatives in the management of those risks; (2) developing and implementing procedures designed to ensure that the policy is being pursued; (3) monitoring compliance with the policy and procedures, through company personnel or external advisors with the necessary training and expertise, independent from those involved in the activities subject to the policy; (4) ensuring that the financial accounts and books and records of the enterprise are being maintained in a way that properly reflects the use of derivatives, as well as the other activities of the enterprise, in accordance with applicable accounting principles; (5) producing and reviewing periodic reports about the foregoing and, in light of the contents of the reports and changes in circumstances involving the enterprise and the environment in which it operates, reassessing and, where appropriate, modifying the policies and procedures already in place; and (6) senior management's informing itself sufficiently about derivatives to play an effective decision-making role and to choose competent advisors to assist it in doing so.

For example, in July 1993, the Global Derivatives Study Group of the Group of Thirty published a report entitled *Derivatives: Practices and Principles.*[155] The report consisted of a set of recommendations for dealers and end-users of derivatives and a set of recommendations for legislators, regulators, and supervisors; subsequent independent surveys of derivative dealers and end-users suggest that at least some of the recommendations are being widely followed by participants in the market.[156] The recommendations for dealers and end-users address five principal topics: Valuation and Market Risk Management; Credit Risk Measurement and Management; Enforceability; Systems, Operations, and Controls; and Accounting and Disclosure. The first Recommendation, on the role of senior management, is as follows:

> *Dealers and end-users should use derivatives in a manner consistent with the overall risk management and capital policies approved by their boards of directors. These policies should be reviewed as business and market circumstances change. Policies governing derivatives use should be clearly defined, including the purposes for which these transactions are to be undertaken. Senior management should approve procedures and controls to implement these policies, and management at all levels should enforce them.*

Since the publication of the Group of Thirty report, similar views have been expressed in two other widely-discussed documents produced by professional participants in the wholesale markets for financial instruments and derivatives.

The first of these is a report of the Derivatives Policy Group (*DPG*), a group of representatives of six of the largest nonbank OTC derivatives dealers[157] formed at the suggestion of the Chairman of the SEC to work with the CFTC and the SEC to design a voluntary oversight framework for the OTC derivatives activities of unregulated securities firm affiliates. The group's report, entitled "Framework for Voluntary Oversight,"[158] was published in 1995. The four main areas covered by this project were (i) the design and implementation of management controls for monitoring derivatives risks, (ii) enhanced voluntary reporting by the Report's participants to regulators about, *inter alia,* significant exposures to counterparties, (iii) the evaluation of capital and its sufficiency for the derivatives risks the participant firms are taking, and (iv) the development of statements to be given to counterparties about the nature of the relationship between the parties to a transaction, the risks involved in derivatives and standards to be followed in quoting prices. About the first of these topics, the DPG Report states:

> *This approach has two central themes that the DPG believes to be critical to effective management controls: (1) the integrity of the risk measurement, monitoring and management process, and (2) clarification of accountability, at the appropriate organizational level, for the definition of the permitted scope of activity and level of risk. The practices require that each firm's board or equivalent governing body should itself adopt, or authorize another body to adopt, written guidelines addressing:*
>
> - *the scope of permitted OTC derivatives activity,*
> - *guidelines for acceptable levels of credit and market risk, and*
> - *the structure and appropriate independence of the risk monitoring and risk management processes and related organizational checks and balances.*

The second of the recent industry initiatives mentioned above was published in August 1995 with the title "Principles and Practices for Wholesale Financial Market Transactions."[159] It was prepared by representatives of various associations of major participants in the OTC markets in the United States[160] in an effort to "articulate a set of best practices" that participants in the wholesale financial markets "should aspire to achieve" in connection with transactions in that market.[161] One of the main objectives of the report was to describe the basic assumptions that are made by professional market participants about the arm's-length nature of their relationship with other participants in those markets and thus to confront problems of the kinds that have led to the disputes described in sections 6 and 7 of this chapter.[162] However, the Principles and Practices recognize that those assumptions and the related recommendations about the handling of counterparty relationships can only function as part of coherent framework if each participant in the wholesale financial markets takes responsibility for the formulation and implementation of policies and procedures governing its own participation in the market. Therefore, like the Group of Thirty Report and the DPG Report, the Principles and Practices address the need for senior management of all market participants, at appropriate levels, to adopt policies relating, among other things, to the supervision and training of employees involved in transactions in the market, control and compliance procedures relating to such transactions and the risks they involve, the measurement of credit risk, the monitoring of the various risks involved in such transactions, the valuation of transactions internally or through the use of external valuations and, in the case of market professionals, the delivery of valuations to counterparties and reasonable measures to verify that a counterparty has the legal capacity and authority to enter into a transaction.[163]

Although each of these documents is worth close study, in a market that has recently seen the significant disputes described in this chapter between end-users and market professionals, perhaps more interesting as guidance for the nonprofessional side of the market are the October 1995 Voluntary Principles and Practices Guidelines for End-Users of Derivatives,[164] which were developed by the Government Relations Committee of the Treasury Management Association "to help treasury practitioners develop an appropriate framework of internal controls and disclosures specific to their organizations."[165] The following excerpts from that document place its guidance squarely within the topics at issue in the lawsuits reviewed above in this section: the duty owed by management to the stakeholders of a firm for determining when, and how much, to hedge, as expressed in formal policy, and management's responsibility to ensure compliance with that policy through appropriate procedures and controls:

> *Proper controls are necessary to ensure that derivatives are used appropriately to accomplish specific business objectives. They are also important for monitoring and measuring the risks to which a firm may be exposed as a result of dealing in derivatives products.*[166]
>
> *In accordance with the recommendations of the Group of Thirty study, end-users should use derivatives in a manner consistent with the overall risk management and capital policies approved by their boards of directors. Policies governing derivatives use should be clearly defined, including the purposes for which these transactions are undertaken. Senior management should approve procedures and controls to implement these policies, and management at all levels should enforce them.*[167]
>
> *While levels of responsibility will vary from company to company, treasury management and other financial management practitioners are likely to be directly responsible for applying policies and procedures to meet defined objectives for derivatives use. They will work closely with internal and/or external traders to ensure appropriate execution of transactions and management of information.*[168]
>
> *Usage [of external advisors] will vary greatly, depending on the nature of derivatives transacted, internal expertise, systems capabilities, etc. Independence of external advisors from counterparties is crucial.*[169]
>
> *A user of derivatives should maintain policies and procedures for the valuation of each derivative transaction at an interval appropriate for the type of transaction undertaken. . . .*
>
> *Before entering into a derivatives transaction, the user should ensure that he has the internal capability to value that transaction. If that capability does not exist, the user should obtain the necessary information from an independent outside party, clearly stating the desired characteristics. Users should not rely solely on valuations provided by the counterparty to the transaction. While such valuations may be useful, they should be validated by an independent source.*[170]
>
> *The expertise required to effectively manage derivatives programs and to achieve business objectives is extensive. . . . Before engaging in derivatives activities, the Board and senior management should ensure that the available resources and expertise are adequate and appropriate for the specific derivatives applications. Given the ever-changing environment, continuing staff development is essential. Derivatives users must stay current on regulatory change,*

technological change, and change in the financial services environment in which their counterparties operate.[171]

Without detailed internal expertise, it is both risky and imprudent to engage in derivative strategies. It is beyond the scope of this document to provide the specific knowledge required to be a competent financial risk manager, but many resources are available.[172]

If these and the other recommendations contained in the End-Users Practice Guidelines had been followed, and if its underlying principle of management responsibility had been acknowledged, many of the disputes described in the remainder of this chapter would never have arisen.

7. Duties of Advisers, Brokers, and Dealers

This section deals first with a case in which a formal fiduciary relationship existed between a swap broker and its principal, and the principal claimed that the broker should be held responsible for the losses on two swaps that it brokered. The remainder of the section deals with cases in which one of the parties to an OTC derivative transaction has claimed that the other party and one or more of its affiliates—registered securities broker-dealers—were acting as fiduciaries in connection with the negotiation and consummation of the transactions, although there was no formal agreement establishing the purported relationship. The discussion of those cases will focus on the underlying theories of breach of fiduciary duty as well as the other theories under which claims were asserted for fraud, misrepresentation and the like and, in some cases, for breach of implied contractual duties of disclosure based on the superior knowledge of the other party to the transactions.

Claims Involving Existence of a Formal Fiduciary Relationship

BankAtlantic v. Blythe Eastman Paine Webber Inc.[173] affirmed a decision in which the defendant and its law firm were sanctioned for violating a discovery order. In the underlying action that gave rise to the discovery order, the plaintiff sought damages for losses in excess of $30 million incurred in connection with two interest rate swaps brokered by the defendant.

The defendant had acted as a financial advisor to BankAtlantic (then known as Atlantic Federal Savings and Loan Association (*Atlantic*) in connection with matters other than rate risk management for a number of years, pursuant to a written engagement letter. According to the complaint, the defendant told Atlantic that the rate swap transactions were desirable because there was a mismatch between many of Atlantic's liabilities, which bore interest at variable rates, and its mortgage portfolio assets, which paid interest at fixed rates. The defendant warned that, if interest rates rose, Atlantic's cost of funds could become higher than the rate of return on its fixed rate mortgages. Atlantic entered into the swaps and subsequently suffered a loss, in part because interest rates fell during the period in question, and in part because Homestead Savings and Loan Association (*Homestead*), the swap counterparty, became insolvent.

Atlantic sought to recover its losses from the defendant on the grounds that the defendant failed to disclose to Atlantic a number of matters that it had a duty to disclose. This duty was said to have arisen because there was a fiduciary relationship between the parties, resulting from the engagement letter and the position of trust and confidence that the defendant had held as valued and trusted advisors of the plaintiff's management. Atlantic also argued that the broker's superior knowledge of the complexities of interest rate swaps and the related risks made the nondisclosure fraudulent, and that the nondisclosure constituted professional malpractice under a state investor protection act. There was also a claim of breach of contract (the engagement letter), which was abandoned at trial.[174]

Atlantic alleged that the broker should have disclosed that Homestead was not an appropriate counterparty for the transactions but failed to do so because there was a longstanding business relationship (involving mortgage loan servicing) between Paine Webber affiliates and Homestead. Atlantic further alleged that the broker knew, and should have disclosed, that, for a number of reasons, the swaps were inappropriate for Atlantic: "As marketed by . . . [the defendant], the interest rate swaps appeared to represent a solid and prudent vehicle to hedge against interest rate risk in the future," but "[i]n fact, [the defendant] . . . knew that these swaps . . . would provide no such protection for Atlantic Federal, but would in fact provide Atlantic Federal with only a lose/lose scenario."[175] More specifically, the complaint alleged that:

> *(i) Although the total principal amount of Atlantic Federal's deposits was nearly $1.5 billion, the notional amounts of the swaps were only $35 million and $50 million, so the total principal amount of swaps was not of adequate size to provide a meaningful hedge against another spike in interest rates.*
>
> *(ii) Even though one of the swaps, which provided for payments by Atlantic at a fixed rate of 12.45%, appeared to lock in a profit on $50 million of Atlantic's 13.50% mortgages, the benefit was illusory, since the average return on Atlantic Federal's mortgages was much lower than the fixed rate that Atlantic Federal would pay on the swap.*
>
> *(iii) If interest rates fell (as they did), customers would refinance their 13.50% mortgages, so the locked-in profit against the 12.45% cost of funds was doubly illusory.*
>
> *(iv) The results obtained through the swaps could have been achieved through less costly alternatives.*

The answer denied most of Atlantic's allegations, basically on the grounds that, at the time the defendant brokered the swaps, they appeared to represent a solid and prudent vehicle to hedge against future interest rate risk and Homestead appeared to be a suitable counterparty for the plaintiff. The broker also argued that Atlantic was in fact sophisticated with respect to interest rate risks and their management, had full knowledge of the terms of and risks inherent in the swaps, voluntarily assumed them and never complained about the swaps or sought to disaffirm them. In the defendant's view, the burden of considering alternatives to the swaps rested on Atlantic.

The jury found for the defendant, and the court refused to set aside the jury's decision, finding that there was substantial evidence to enable the jury to conclude, among other things, that Atlantic was aware of the risks associated with interest rate swaps, that Homestead was not an improper counterparty for the defendant to have recommended, and that the defendant's brokerage services were outside the scope of the advisory relationship between the parties under their engagement letter.[176] However, the appellate court upheld the sanctions ($350,078.80 plus BankAtlantic's costs in connection with the proceeding) imposed by the trial court on the defendant for violation of the discovery order through its failure to deliver documents relating to the relationship between the Paine Webber affiliates and Homestead.

The *BankAtlantic* decision recognizes that a party to derivatives transactions has independent duties of diligence and risk analysis that are not automatically shifted to a broker that is compensated for arranging transactions, and that the scope of a separate advisory relationship between the parties should not be extended to dealings outside the scope of the contractual relationship merely because the advisee has placed its trust and confidence in the advisor as the result of that relationship. The case further establishes that, even though a broker may have superior knowledge of the relevant risks, there is no heightened duty of disclosure where the customer is aware of the risks associated with the relevant transactions and there is only a brokerage, and not an advisory, relationship with respect to the transactions. It bears repeating that the *BankAtlantic* decision turned on its particular facts, so another case might well produce a different result, even under the same rules of law.

On the other hand, the *BankAtlantic* decision should also be viewed as a warning to professional participants in the OTC derivatives market that, given the multiple dealings that they and their affiliates may have with a single entity, procedures should be put in place to avoid even the semblance of undisclosed conflicts of interest in situations where the entity or one of its affiliates has a fiduciary relationship with a customer. The importance of this lesson was more recently driven home by the SEC's administrative proceedings against Lazard Freres & Co. LLC and Merrill Lynch, Pierce, Fenner & Smith Inc. in connection with contracts, negotiated by a former partner of Lazard Freres, pursuant to which the two entities would act together in originating, negotiating and arranging interest rate swaps to be entered into by Merrill Lynch affiliates and municipalities in the United States and would split the fees generated by successful marketing of the swaps. The proceedings were instituted and settled without the respondents' admitting or denying the SEC's findings, which included a determination that the contracts between the two entities created at least a potential conflict of interest for Lazard Freres that should have been disclosed when it was acting as financial advisor to municipal clients and a determination that Merrill Lynch, which had been told that the existence of the contracts had been fully disclosed to the municipal clients, failed to take adequate steps to ensure that the contracts and the facts and circumstances of transactions covered by them, including a fee-splitting payment to Lazard Freres, were in fact fully disclosed to the municipal parties in question—which the SEC concluded had not actually happened.[177]

Claims of Fiduciary Relationships by Association or Implication

Since *BankAtlantic* there have been other cases, some widely publicized, in which one of the parties to an OTC foreign exchange or derivatives transaction has claimed that the other and, in some cases, its affiliates, owed it, and breached, fiduciary duties of various sorts in connection with the transactions. Some of these lawsuits involved simple FX transactions; others involved complex transactions with a potential for greater rewards, reflecting the nature and magnitude (sometimes highly leveraged) of the risks that the transactions entailed.

These cases, like *BankAtlantic,* generally attribute to the defendants superior knowledge and expertise, allege that the plaintiff's lesser sophistication and its inability to gain access to certain information led it to misunderstand the risks involved in the transactions, and claim that this combination of circumstances gave rise to a higher of duty of disclosure on the part of the defendants. Some of the cases also present the theory that the dealer that provided the transaction (and, in some cases, purported to have tailored it to fit the customer's needs), knew or should have known that the transactions involved risks of kinds and magnitude unsuitable for the customer—that the customer's policy was to make only conservative investments and to engage in derivatives transactions only for hedging purposes, whereas the transactions in question were highly speculative and could not have functioned as hedges against any risks incurred in its business.

As suggested above, the theories of liability are in part based on failures to determine the suitability of a transaction for the customer, and on failures to disclose risks and profits and alleged breaches of a duty not to engage in churning, and involve attempts to extend to derivative providers rules applicable to securities broker-dealers and investment advisors with which they are affiliated, often accompanied by allegations that employees of those regulated affiliates played a role in arranging the transactions. The complaints name both the regulated and unregulated entities as defendants and then make claims against the defendants as a group based on rules and regulations of the SEC and the NASD, in the United States, and the Securities and Futures Authority, in the U.K., including rules that require securities professionals to use due diligence to know their customers so as to form a reasonable judgment with respect to the suitability for the customer of securities transactions recommended to the customer.

Unipec and Minmetals. Neither of the parties to the FX options and swaps involved in these cases, which are described at greater length above,[178] is a securities broker or dealer, but the counterclaims in both those cases were brought not only against the actual parties to the transactions but also against affiliates that are broker-dealers. The counterclaim defendants are consistently referred to, collectively, as "Lehman Brothers." There are frequent references to literature describing not only the derivatives expertise of the group but also Lehman Brothers' focus on advisory services to clients and a "commitment to clients [that] rose out of a culture that encourages cooperation and shared responsibility."[179]

The *Minmetals* counterclaims referred to a Japanese yen note purchase proposed by a Lehman entity, a securities broker-dealer, and point out that, at the request of a Minmetals representative, that entity had prepared a scenario analysis showing "the potential profit or loss [from the note] depending on different movements in the underlying interest rates."[180] Minmetals argued that, had the Lehman swap counterparty "fulfilled its fiduciary duty by disclosing such scenario analysis for his two swap transactions, [the Minmetals representative] would have understood how risky those transactions were, and would never have engaged in them."[181]

Finally, in the *Unipec* case and the *Minmetals* case, the counterclaims alleged, without recognizing any distinction between the various Lehman defendants, that, "[a]s brokers and investment advisors," the Lehman Brothers entities are subject, among other things, to suitability rules imposed by the SEC, the NYSE, NASDAQ, and other regulatory and self-regulatory organizations, and that the counterclaim defendants violated those rules by failing to determine whether the FX options and forwards and swaps at issue in the cases were suitable for Minmetals and Unipec when they recommended the transactions to those Chinese entities.[182] Again, based on the broker-dealer association, Unipec and Minmetals alleged that the Lehman entities owed those customers duties of full and fair disclosure of all material facts concerning the "investments" they recommended and of the risks and benefits of the proposed transactions and the profits the brokers or advisors were likely to make from the transactions,[183] as well as a duty not to generate excessive trading in customer accounts in order to increase their own income,[184] and a duty to effectively and diligently supervise and exercise control over their employees who dealt with and handled the Minmetals and Unipec accounts[185]—all duties allegedly breached.

Société Nationale d'Exploitation Industrielle des Tabacs et Allumettes v. Salomon Bros. International Ltd.[186] A similar approach is illustrated by the complaint recently filed in this case, an action involving interest rate swaps[187] purportedly entered into without due authorization by Seita, a French manufacturer and marketer of tobacco products that at the time was a state-owned company, and Salomon Brothers Holding Co., one of the defendants. Another defendant in the case is a U.K. securities broker-dealer in the Salomon Brothers group, one of whose officers is alleged to have been the primary contact in the relationship with Seita, and yet another is the principal U.S. broker-dealer in the Salomon Brothers group. Its role in the transactions appears to have been that of calculation agent for the swaps.

The complaint refers to the three affiliated defendants collectively as "Salomon" and refers to investment advisory relationships between Salomon and Seita outside the context of the swaps.[188] On the basis of that relationship and Salomon's 1993 Annual Report, in which it described itself as an international banking firm committed to recognition "by its customers and counterparties as reliable long-term partners who promise only what we can deliver and then deliver what we promise," the complaint alleges that Salomon held itself out as a fiduciary and that Seita relied on Salomon for advice, believing that Salomon was at all times acting on behalf of Seita's interests, as a broker and financial advisor.

According to the complaint,[189] Salomon violated its duty as fiduciary to Seita and failed to adhere to regulatory guidelines and internal controls by persuading Seita to enter into the swaps in question without disclosing, *inter alia,* the extent of the downside risks to Seita they involved and that Salomon was the true party in interest in the swaps, as opposed to a broker and advisor; that the transactions provided Salomon with the means of generating profits for itself at the expense of Seita, in structures that greatly favored Salomon's interests over Seita's, that the transactions were of a completely unregulated nature; and that Salomon had computer models and financial analyses that showed the true risks to Seita and benefits to Salomon of the swaps which Salomon would not make available to Seita.

The complaint also alleges that, even though Salomon knew Seita was a state-owned company that managed public funds and did not wish to and could not engage in risky or speculative transactions, it nonetheless induced Seita to enter into interest rate swaps that it knew served no hedging purpose for Seita by representing that the transactions had been structured to meet Seita's financial objectives, all in violation of suitability rules that Seita alleged are applicable to Salomon because some of the defendants grouped as Salomon are broker-dealers subject to such rules.

As an indication of the scope of the duties alleged by Seita to exist, the complaint refers to an annual report of Salomon, Inc. which stated that "[b]ecause derivatives often involve a high degree of leverage and are accounted for and settled differently than cash instruments, their use requires special management oversight"[190] and that oversight "should ensure that management understands the transactions to which they commit their firms and that the transactions are executed in accordance with sensible corporate risk policies and procedures."[191] According to the complaint, Salomon, therefore, had a duty to take steps to insure that the management of Seita understood the nature and risks of the swaps, and Salomon should not have induced Seita to enter into the transactions because it knew that they would not be in accordance with "sensible corporate risk policies and procedures" for Seita.

Salomon's conduct, according to Seita, violated Salomon's duties to "determine all the material facts with respect to the business, financial capacity, investment objectives and risk parameters of Seita, in order to determine if the Swap Transactions were suitable for Seita" and to determine if the person who purported to execute the transactions on behalf of Seita had authority to do so (which he allegedly did not),[192] as well as the duties of investment brokers and advisors like Salomon "to make full and fair disclosure of all material facts concerning the investments they recommend to their customers, including disclosure of the risks and benefits of the proposed transactions, of the profits the brokers or advisors are likely to make from the transactions, and of the suitability, or unsuitability of the investment for the customer."[193]

Finally, the complaint alleges that Salomon misrepresented Seita's position in the swaps at various times, represented that Salomon would "get Seita out of the Swaps when it appeared that Seita's principal was at risk,"[194] promised to immunize Seita on one of the swaps, failed to keep Seita fully informed of material developments in the transactions and misled Seita into believing that its "purported loss positions on the original swaps would be wiped out through offsetting paper payments by Salomon in exactly the same amount, reflected as up-front payments to Seita on the restructured Swap confirmations," when, in fact, the succession of restructurings engaged in by the parties "built the purported losses into the pricing and terms of the restructured swaps" on terms more onerous to Seita.[195]

Seita alleges that when it ultimately unwound the swaps, incurring losses in excess of U.S.$29.7 million, it did so to avoid the risk of further losses in light of its scheduled ensuing privatization and without waiving any of the objections to the swaps expressed in its complaint, seeking those losses as compensatory damages, as well as punitive and exemplary damages and certain other costs.

As we noted earlier in discussing the cases involving alleged undisclosed conflicts or potential conflicts of interest, it is common for professional participants in the OTC derivatives market to be engaged, or to have affiliates that are engaged, in other dealings with the same clients that involve advisory or other fiduciary relationships. As the *Seita, Unipec* and *Minmetals* cases further illustrate, this can occur because affiliated firms offer different services for regulatory reasons and because more than one firm in a group may be involved if one firm, located in the client's home jurisdiction, is involved in the development and maintenance of the relationship with the client but another firm in the group actually enters into or somehow lends assistance in connection with transactions with the client. These cases teach that, when this situation exists, professional participants in the markets should be far more scrupulous in defining the respective, limited roles, if any, played in specific transactions and businesses by the various affiliated companies that at the time have, or in the past have had, dealings with the same customer.

It may at first appear to be expedient to use a short form of a group name in a term sheet or other materials given to a client in marketing, or in face-to-face or telephonic dealings with a customer, but steps should be taken during the dealings, and over the course of an evolving relationship with a client, to ensure that it understands that the fiduciary roles played by one entity in the group, and the related duties imposed by that entity's regulators or self-regulatory organizations, where applicable, should not be confused with the nonfiduciary role played by its affiliates that enter into OTC derivatives as principals, to earn a profit—entities that may not be subject to the same sorts of regulatory or SRO duties and that in fact disavow any such duties in their principal-to-principal derivatives dealings.

8. Implied Duties of Principals to Derivatives Transactions

The cases discussed in this section focus directly on the relationship between the two parties to the OTC derivatives in question, without distracting arguments based on the affiliation of one of the parties with a broker or dealer, investment advisor or similar entity. In each of these cases one of the parties alleges that it relied on the other as a fiduciary, and that the other party, in violation of that trust, executed transactions that placed its own interests before those of the complaining party and failed to make material disclosures. The lawsuits also involve claims of fraud, negligent misrepresentation, negligence, economic duress and violations of the anti-fraud and similar provisions of federal and state laws.

Bank Brussels Lambert S.A. v. Intermetals Corp.[196]

This case involved FX dealings that the defendant (*Intermetals*) began with the plaintiff (*BBL*) for hedging purposes. Thereafter, Intermetals engaged BBL to enter into speculative FX transactions on Intermetals' behalf. BBL was given discretion in engaging in the transactions and extended credit to Intermetals in connection with them. After initial successes, the trading activities resulted in significant losses, and Intermetals sought to defend against BBL's claim for money owed it in connection with the losses by various allegations. Intermetals alleged that BBL had breached fiduciary duties owed to Intermetals and committed fraud by failing to disclose to Intermetals the risks of foreign exchange trading, by overstating the skill and expertise of its traders, by failing to disclose its fee and compensation structure (as in the later *Seita* complaint) and by failing to disclose that it was acting as a principal counterparty to Intermetals in many of the trades. Intermetals also claimed breach of contract, predicated on BBL's liquidation of positions at a time when Intermetals preferred that trading continue to seek to reduce its losses.[197] Intermetals (like *Seita*) further claimed that BBL had agreed to immunize Intermetals against losses above an agreed limit.[198] The court found for BBL and, in so doing, indicated, *inter alia*, the following:

> *(i) There was no evidence of a contractual understanding about a limit to Intermetals' liability, and Intermetals could not have thought that it was operating under a loss limit unless it believed that the bank was absorbing all the losses itself.[199]*
>
> *(ii) When Intermetals' speculative position had moved considerably against it, BBL may well have expressed "a present intention . . . [at a particular time] to stick with the position but it had no contractual obligation to adhere to that intention when the losses would soon have far exceeded any conceivable ability of . . . [Intermetals] to pay."[200]*
>
> *(iii) There was no showing that Intermetals ever asked BBL about fees and commissions or was ever given misleading information on that point, and it was not shown that BBL was under a duty to advise Intermetals of risks of foreign exchange trading. Intermetals' representative involved in the trading was*

an experienced businessman who may not have had any experience in such trad-
ing before it began with BBL but was aware of the risk of fluctuations in foreign
currency well before he began this speculative trading and indeed indicated that
knowledge by entering into the early hedging transactions.

With respect to BBL's statement of skill and expertise, the court found that Intermetals had shown nothing worse than permissible puffing. Regarding the claim that
BBL had failed to disclose its role as principal in many transactions, the court stated
that the practice, while "unhealthy" and "fraught with conflict of interest," is not
"inherently fraudulent," and stated that there was no showing of actual fraud in this
case.

Compañía Sud-Americana de Vapores, S.A. v. IBJ Schroder Bank & Trust Co.[201]

The *Sud-Americana de Vapores* case was a largely unsuccessful action for damages
alleging fraud, breach of fiduciary duty, breach of contract and violations of RICO in
connection with years of foreign currency transactions between the parties. These
transactions involved converting into U.S. dollars numerous foreign currency
amounts received by the plaintiff (*CSAV*) for its shipping services. After determining
the exchange rate to be used in a transaction, the defendant (*Schroder*) would telephone a designated person, usually the Chief Accountant in the Finance Department
of CSAV's wholly owned New York subsidiary, and that affiliate would then send the
information about the transaction to CSAV's head office in Chile by telex. Written
confirmations of the transactions, setting forth the amounts of foreign currency, exchange rate, U.S. dollar amount and value date for the transaction, were sent to CSAV
in Chile and its New York subsidiary.

CSAV alleged that, in over a thousand transactions over a period of approximately
six years, Schroder applied exchange rates that were unreasonably and grossly at variance from the prevailing market rates of exchange at the relevant times.[202] The variance allegedly increased over the years, averaging in Belgian franc transactions, for
example, 1.35% over the New York interbank rate in 1984 and 12.96% over that market
rate by 1990. CSAV alleged this conduct was fraudulent in light of:

> *(i) A promise from the bank that the plaintiff would be given favorable*
> *rates, was considered a "preferred client" within the bank and would be given*
> *"preferential treatment within the [foreign exchange] department," consisting of*
> *"rates at least as good as the best rates [Schroder] . . . gave its corporate customers*
> *and at or near the rates banks applied in transactions among themselves"; and*
> *(ii) Statements by bank personnel that the manner in which the bank con-*
> *verted foreign currencies for CSAV was "unique" and, "unlike a trading relation-*
> *ship, was actually a currency management service."[203]*

Against this background, CSAV argued that (1) Schroder knew that CSAV relied
on it to convert currencies at or near the interbank rate and not to treat CSAV as a
trading partner; and (2) Schroder's confirmations failed to reveal the prevailing market rates, the excess of its rates to CSAV over the market rate at which it actually
made the conversion (i.e., Schroder's margin or profit) and any administrative or
other expenses Schroder incurred on behalf of CSAV. Because of CSAV's reliance,
Schroder's disclosure in its confirmations of the rates provided to CSAV was not,
CSAV argued, sufficient to overcome CSAV's allegations of fraud.[204]

As described in section 2 of this chapter, the court denied Schroder's motion for summary judgment on the contract claim because the court concluded that the confirmations sent by Schroder to CSAV were not necessarily the final expression of the parties' complete agreement, since a jury could conclude that there was also an "overarching" prior oral agreement governing the totality of the parties' relationship involving hundreds of transactions over the years. Given that relationship, the court concluded that CSAV should be entitled to introduce extrinsic evidence regarding the parties' agreement about the exchange rates CSAV was entitled to receive.[205]

The court did, however, grant Schroder's motion for summary judgment on the claims based on breach of fiduciary duty and fraud. The court found, as a matter of law, that no fiduciary relationship existed between the parties,[206] describing CSAV's allegations as unjustified, conclusory statements about the existence of such a relationship and merely an effort to avoid the repercussions of its lack of diligence in monitoring the rates at which conversions were made for over six years.[207] The court stated that:

> New York law is quite clear . . . that "a conventional business relationship, without more, does not become a fiduciary relationship by mere allegation." . . .[208] Indeed, New York Courts have rejected the proposition that a fiduciary relationship can arise between parties to a business transaction[209] . . . and have concluded that "where parties deal at arms length in a commercial transaction, no relation of confidence or trust sufficient to find the existence of a fiduciary relationship will arise absent extraordinary circumstances."[210]

The court found that CSAV had failed to set forth evidence that the dealings between the parties were not arms' length or that there were extraordinary circumstances that would give rise to a fiduciary relationship. The court also pointed to evidence of CSAV's knowledge of the foreign currency market and noted that it had participated in complex foreign exchange swap operations, bought yen futures, engaged in dollar/yen forward swaps and reconversions, was absolutely familiar with the process of hedging foreign currency exposure and investigated sophisticated hedging devices. The court viewed the relationship between the parties as one designed to further the interests of both parties and suggested that CSAV's abrupt termination of its relationship with Schroder indicated that this was an arms' length relationship that would continue until CSAV found that it could get superior rates elsewhere.[211]

In granting Schroder summary judgment on the fraud-based claims, the court found that CSAV could not establish that its alleged reliance was justifiable—a fundamental requirement in a common-law action for fraud:

> [W]hen misrepresentations concern matters that are not peculiarly within [the maker's] . . . knowledge, as in this case, New York courts have rejected claims of justifiable reliance because:
>
> > [if plaintiff] has the means of knowing, by the exercise of ordinary intelligence, the truth, or the real quality of the subject of the representation, he must make use of those means, or he will not be heard to complain that he was induced to enter into the transaction by misrepresentations. . . .[212]

The court also cited cases indicating that, under New York law, where sophisticated businessmen engaged in major transactions enjoy access to critical information but fail to take advantage of that access, New York courts are particularly disinclined to entertain claims of justifiable reliance.[213] The court discussed CSAV's ability, and practice, of obtaining comparison quotations from other banks and indicated that officers of CSAV admitted that they were ultimately responsible for monitoring prices at which foreign exchange transactions with Schroder were undertaken.

With respect to CSAV's reliance on Schroder's failure to disclose market rates or its profit in its confirmations, the court noted that the Second Circuit Court of Appeals has rejected fraud claims based on the omission or nondisclosure of market rates, and that the remaining alleged omissions (i.e., about Schroder's profit) were irrelevant and immaterial because there was no evidence that Schroder had a duty to disclose such information.[214]

Procter & Gamble Co. v. Bankers Trust Co.[215]

Procter & Gamble involved a similar claim that a professional derivatives market participant, Bankers Trust, had fiduciary obligations to its customer, P&G, stemming from a relationship of trust and confidence between them and the superior knowledge of BT.

The parties entered into two highly leveraged swap transactions. Particularly in the case of the first swap, they engaged in lengthy negotiations to customize the terms of the transaction. In both cases, BT's payment obligations were to remain constant throughout the life of the transaction, but P&G's obligations might be reset in accordance with a formula to be applied at a later time to determine whether a spread should be added to the rate initially applicable for determining its obligations. The first swap, known as the *5s/30s Swap,* was structured so that P&G would receive a fixed rate and pay a rate substantially below the commercial paper rate, provided the ratio between the yield on 5-year Treasuries and the price of 30-year Treasuries was within certain limits on the reset date but, through application of the spread-setting formula, it could pay a sharply higher rate if that ratio fell outside the agreed limits.[216] The second swap (the *DEM Swap*) was somewhat similar, in that P&G was to receive a 1% stream of payments provided the reference Deutsche Mark swap rate stayed within an agreed band during a look-back period. However, the 1% payment would be eroded and P&G could take on significant net payment obligations, through application of the spread-setting formula, if the DEM swap rate moved outside the band. The relevant yields, prices and rates moved adversely to P&G, and the spread-setting features of both transactions were unwound. P&G subsequently commenced the lawsuit seeking rescission of the swaps, along with other relief, as described below, and BT counterclaimed for over $200 million in damages in respect of the two swaps.

With respect to the 5s/30s Swap, P&G argued that it had understood it would have the right at any time before the reset date to lock in its obligations at the highly favorable sub-commercial paper rate initially applicable and that it was unaware that its agreement with BT would not necessarily produce that result.[217] P&G alleged that BT was its fiduciary and stated that it had relied on BT to design a transaction that would produce the result that it expected.[218] P&G further alleged that it had been damaged because BT failed to keep it informed of its mounting losses on the swap (although there was no showing that P&G inquired about the swap's mark-to-market value). P&G's claims rested on a wide variety of legal theories, including fraud under federal and state securities law and federal commodity law, misrepresentation, negligence and violations of Ohio's Deceptive Trade Practices Act. P&G made similar claims with respect to the DEM Swap. On the basis of these theories, P&G sought rescission of the contracts, as noted, or reformation of their terms to reflect P&G's alleged view of what the contracts should have provided. In the alternative, P&G sought damages in the amount it would be required to pay BT under the transactions (or what it would have to pay in excess of the levels it alleged it was promised) plus punitive damages.

In the First Order, the court ruled that P&G was not entitled to the requested equitable relief with respect to the DEM Swap because, long before P&G raised its claims regarding that swap in an amended complaint, it had sufficient knowledge of BT's alleged fraud to have notified BT of its intent to seek rescission but did not do so. The court also found that P&G had earlier affirmed the DEM Swap by confirming its unwind to BT in connection with a stop-loss order it had negotiated as German swap rates were rising. The court observed that the right to disaffirm on grounds of fraud is lost by earlier affirmance, once a party is put on inquiry about the alleged fraud.[219] The court postponed its ruling on the rescission and reformation claims on the 5s/30s Swap until after the close of P&G's case at trial as to the matter of fraud. Settlement of the case precluded a ruling on that cause of action.

In the following discussion, we will take up the court's decision on each of P&G's main theories as follows:

- the alleged breach of a fiduciary relationship between the parties;
- the negligence claims;
- the fraud claims, and the court's related theory of an implied contractual duty of good faith and fair dealing;
- the securities law claims;
- the commodities law claim; and
- various other claims.

Fiduciary Relationship. In the Final Order, the court granted BT summary judgment on the claims that were premised on the existence of a fiduciary relationship between P&G and BT. The relationship, P&G argued, existed because of its disclosure of confidential corporate information to BT, BT's representation of itself as expert in derivatives, P&G's reliance on that expertise and BT's alleged statements that it would tailor the swaps to fit P&G's needs. Like the courts in *Intermetals* and *Sud-Americana de Vapores,* the *Procter & Gamble* court rejected the theory that these alleged facts gave rise to a fiduciary relationship, stating New York law on the matter as follows: "No fiduciary relationship exists . . . [where] the two parties were acting and contracting at arm's length. Moreover, courts have rejected the proposition that a fiduciary relationship can arise between parties to a business relationship."[220] The court further found, on the facts before it, that "P&G and BT were in a business relationship. They were counterparties. Even through . . . BT had superior knowledge in the swaps transactions, that does not convert their business relationship into one in which fiduciary duties are imposed."[221]

Negligent Misrepresentation and Negligence. The court also granted BT's motion for summary judgment on the claims of negligent misrepresentation, finding that, under New York law, that cause of action was not available to P&G because it depended on the existence of a "special relationship of trust and confidence between the parties"—a relationship that is not established by "an ordinary contractual relationship [or] a banking relationship, without more"[222] and that has been found not to exist between two "sophisticated financial institutions that came together solely to engage in an arm's length transaction."[223] The court found that no special relationship existed between BT and P&G, because they are sophisticated corporations whose dealings were on a business level.[224] Similarly, the court rejected P&G's theory that BT was negligent in failing to execute the swaps as P&G expected, ruling that "[w]here the parties' relationship is contractual, and the duty of good faith and fair dealing is implied in the contract, a negligence claim is redundant."[225] The court also granted BT's motion for summary judgment on the negligence claim that P&G had sought to establish on a malpractice theory.[226]

Implied Contractual Covenant of Good Faith and Fair Dealing. In its complaint and subsequent pleadings P&G never sought to base any of its claims on a breach by BT of the implied duty of good faith and fair dealing that New York law imposes on the parties to a contract. The P&G court, however, itself pointed to these implied duties to build a theory for the existence of a duty of disclosure on the part of BT that has attracted much attention in the derivatives market and that deserves close scrutiny in any attempt to assess the impact of *Procter & Gamble* on future cases.

The first aspect to note, in this regard, is the context in which the court offered its views. In presenting its analysis, the court stated it had to do so because P&G's claims based on fraud and misrepresentation required the court to determine what duties BT owed to P&G.[227] Therefore, although a motion to dismiss those claims was not before it, the court proceeded to state its view of the law that would frame the issues for the case.

In seeking the sources of the applicable rules, the court stated that it was required to look both at the parties' contract and at related principles of New York law. In looking at the parties' ISDA-based master agreement governing the two swaps, the court focused on the standard covenant of each party to supply the information specified in the agreement's Schedule or in a Confirmation and, in a very expansive reading of that provision, the court found that it gave rise to an obligation to furnish information relating to any documents specified in a Confirmation.[228] On the basis of that analysis, the court then found an implied duty of BT to supply documents that would have enabled P&G to make certain determinations about how its payment obligations would be set under the swaps—information regarding the correlation between the reference Treasury instrument yields and prices, sensitivity tables and spreadsheets regarding volatility, and documents relating to the yield curve.[229]

The court's analysis of the related principles of New York law involved two steps. First, the court noted that New York law imposes on each party to a contract a duty of good faith and fair dealing in its performance and enforcement.[230] The court then stated that "New York case law establishes an implied contractual duty to disclose in business negotiations . . . where (1) a party has superior knowledge of certain information; (2) that information is not readily available to the other party; and (3) the first party knows that the second party is acting on the basis of mistaken knowledge."[231] Applying those propositions to the case before it, the court concluded that BT had "a duty to disclose material information to plaintiff both before the parties entered into the swap transactions and in their performance, and also a duty to deal fairly and in good faith during the performance of the swap transactions."[232]

In assessing this aspect of the *Procter & Gamble* court's analysis, however, participants in the OTC derivatives market should consider several factors, in addition to the court's own statement of its limitation to the facts of the case.

First, there is a question whether the court's reading of the parties' contract was excessively broad. Under ISDA's form of master agreement, the parties agree to deliver the documents and other information listed in their original agreement and any further documents and information specified in the confirmations supplementing that agreement. The ISDA master also contains a provision (sometimes referred to as an "integration" or "merger" clause) to the effect that the parties' agreement, as supplemented by their confirmations, is their entire agreement and supersedes any oral agreements on the same subject. Accordingly, it would seem that there is no contractual duty to deliver information or documents that are not so specified, and the parties' express inclusion of a clause under which information could be required through confirmations, together with their decision not to call for any and the agreement's merger clause, all seem to support the conclusion that the court's interpretation of the P&G swap agreement with BT was wrong. Even in the context of a sale of securities by a securities professional, the seller is not required, in the absence of an express agreement on the subject, to supply the buyer with information, including the seller's view of the security's value, that will enable the buyer to determine from time to time whether it wishes to dispose of the security.

Second, the court's analysis of the duty of good faith and fair dealing did not take into account that the New York courts have limited this doctrine to a requirement of good faith and fair dealing in the performance of the parties' obligations as actually provided for in their contract, and have observed that the duty is not a license to the courts to modify the parties' bargain by imposing additional obligations or restricting the exercise of rights that are expressly provided for in the contract.[233] Indeed, one of the cases cited by the court states as follows:

> *The plaintiffs seek to invoke a covenant of good faith and fair dealing in the relationship. However, courts do not impose an obligation which would be inconsistent with other terms of the contractual relationship and for which the parties did not bargain.*
>
> > *[T]he implied covenant of good faith and fair dealing does not provide a court carte blanche to rewrite the parties' agreement. Thus, a court cannot imply a covenant inconsistent with the terms expressly set forth in the contract. . . . Nor can a court imply a covenant to supply additional terms for which the parties did not bargain.*[234]
>
> > *The implied covenant of good faith does not "operate to create new contractual rights."*[235]

Third, the *Procter & Gamble* court's statement about BT's initial and on-going duty of disclosure cannot correctly be taken as part of the holding of the case, because the court was not the trier of fact in the case but rather was merely analyzing the law that would be applied at trial. Therefore, the court did not consider whether the kinds of information it stated BT was obliged to deliver to P&G were readily available to P&G through independent sources or, for that matter, whether P&G should have asked BT for it. The case cited by the *Procter & Gamble* court in support of its statement of New York law, *Banque Arabe Internationale d'Investissement v. Maryland National Bank*,[236] was a tort action, not a decision involving contract law, and it involved superior information of the seller of a participation about delays in the granting of a governmental approval of a condominium conversion where there was discussion in the trial court's decision finding a duty of disclosure about whether the buyer could have discovered the information because it was the practice of the relevant governmental agency not to discuss the status of conversion plan approvals with outside parties. However, in the appellate court decision referred to by the *Procter & Gamble* court on the duty of disclosure where there is superior knowledge, the court in fact concluded that no duty of disclosure existed for reasons that have a bearing on the appropriate analysis in *Procter & Gamble*.

One reason was that there was no basis in the record for the *Banque Arabe* court to conclude that the seller knew the buyer was relying on it for the information in question or was acting on the basis of mistaken information. As the court there noted, "[s]uch knowledge is a prerequisite to a duty to disclose based upon superior knowledge."[237] The *Procter & Gamble* court did not, and at the stage of the proceedings involved at the time of the Final Order could not, find that P&G was relying on BT to disclose a material fact about which BT had superior knowledge or that P&G was acting on mistaken information about such a fact.

The *Banque Arabe* decision that no duty of disclosure existed in that case was also based in part on the court's conclusion that the particular information involved there was not "peculiarly within the knowledge" of the seller—another fundamental requirement and a prerequisite for finding that reliance is reasonable.[238] In reaching its conclusion, the court noted various trial court findings indicating that the relevant information was readily available to the participant or any interested party who cared to ask.[239] The *Procter & Gamble* court broadly concluded that BT "had a duty to disclose material information" to P&G "both before the parties entered into the swap transactions and in their performance" but it confined its conclusion "to the parameters outlined in this opinion" (the Final Order),[240] where the court had already stated that the documents required related to the correlation between the price and yields on the Treasury instruments involved in the 5s/30s Swap, sensitivity tables, spreadsheets regarding volatility and documents relating to the yield curve.[241] The court, in fact, never found—and it is doubtful it could have found— that this kind of information was not readily available to P&G. Indeed, much of it was given to P&G in connection with negotiation of the 5s/30s Swap and there was no indication that it would not have been given again had P&G "cared to ask," to use the *Banque Arabe* court's language.

In the absence of such findings of fact, the law applicable to the case about disclosure would be the rule of the *Banco Español* case, which is that in an "arms length transaction between sophisticated financial institutions, the law impose[s] no independent duty . . . to disclose information" that a party complaining of nondisclosure "could have discovered through their own efforts."[242] As indicated by the court in *Sud-Americana de Vapores*,[243] if access to critical information is available to a sophisticated party to a business transaction, under New York law, it cannot, by simply failing to take advantage of that access, shift the burden of supplying information to its contractual counterparty.[244]

Securities Laws. As a matter of first impression, in ruling on P&G's claims alleging violations of the anti-fraud provisions of state and federal securities laws, the *Procter*

& *Gamble* court ruled that the swaps in question were not securities and granted BT summary judgment on those claims. The court found that the swaps did not fall within any of the categories listed in the statutory definition of "security" that P&G relied upon: note or evidence or indebtedness, investment contract, options on securities or instruments commonly known as securities.[245]

Note or Evidence of Indebtedness. Regarding the theory that the swaps were notes, the court observed that one of the most basic features of a note—the payment or repayment of principal—was missing. Nonetheless, the court, seeking to follow the analysis prescribed by the Supreme Court in *Reves v. Ernst & Young,*[246] went on to inquire whether the swaps, if notes, would be any of the kinds of notes that should be treated as a security for purposes of the anti-fraud provisions of the Securities Act or the Exchange Act. This analysis required the court to consider four factors to determine whether the swaps bore a "family resemblance" to notes treated as securities.

The first factor was whether the motivations of the buyer and seller in entering into the transaction were commercial (which would not be indicative of a security) or to raise capital, in the case of the seller, and invest for profit, in the case of the buyer (which would be indicative of notes treated as securities). The court noted that there was no "neat and tidy" way to apply this prong of the test to the swaps in part because P&G and BT were counterparties, not the typical buyer and seller of an instrument. The court noted, however, that the parties' motivations were "tipped more toward a commercial than investment purpose" but that there was also "an element of speculation" driving P&G's willingness to enter into a transaction that was based on its expectations regarding the path that interest rates would take. In conclusion, the court found that this prong of the *Reves* analysis was not by itself a sufficient guide to make a determination on whether the swaps were notes that should be treated as securities.[247] It would seem that application of this analysis to the great majority of swaps engaged in today would probably lead to the same result, although a commercial purpose of the end-user would more clearly be present in the case of swaps entered into for hedging purposes.

The second factor considered by the *Procter & Gamble* court, applying *Reves,* was the "plan of distribution" of the instrument, to determine "whether it is an instrument in which there is 'common trading for speculation or investment.'"[248] Here the court noted that, while derivatives transactions are an important part of BT's business and "BT advertises its expertise in putting together a variety of derivatives packages," the test was whether the particular swaps in question were widely distributed. The court found that the swaps were analogous to notes found not to be securities on the basis that the plan of distribution was "a limited solicitation to sophisticated financial or commercial institutions and not the general public."[249] The court noted that the 5s/30s Swap and the DEM Swap were customized for P&G, that they could not be transferred by P&G without BT's agreement and that they were not part of a general offering. It, therefore, concluded that they did not meet the second prong of the *Reves* test for notes that would be treated as securities.[250]

The third factor considered by the court under *Reves* was the public's reasonable perceptions. The court found that this factor did not support treatment of the swaps as securities, noting that the swaps were not traded on a national exchange, "the paradigm of a security" in the public mind. It also recognized that some media refer to derivatives generally as securities and that some commentators assume that all derivatives are securities. It observed, however, that other commentators "understand that many swap transactions are customized, bilateral contracts not subject to regulation" and further stated that what is relevant "is the perception of those few who enter into swap agreements, not the public in general."[251] The court stated that "P&G knew full well that its over-the-counter swap agreements with BT were not registered with any regulatory agency. P&G's 'perception' that these swap agreements were securities did not surface until after it had filed its original Complaint in this case."[252]

The fourth *Reves* factor considered by the court was whether a regulatory scheme outside the securities laws would control and reduce the risk of the instrument, making application of the securities laws unnecessary. The court noted that various U.S. bank regulators had adopted guidelines relating to swaps around the time the swaps in question were entered into but also observed that those guidelines did not provide any direct protection to counterparties with whom banks enter into derivatives transactions. Nonetheless, the court found that this was not enough to bring the swap transactions within the statutory definition of a "note" for purposes of the securities laws.[253] In considering this aspect of the *Reves* test, market participants should also take into account, as did the *Procter & Gamble* court, that the Supreme Court has held that the U.S. congress did not "intend" the federal securities laws "to provide a broad federal remedy for all fraud,"[254] and it is not a foregone conclusion that financial or other transactions engaged in as unregulated businesses must be made to fit within an existing regulatory scheme. The factor was considered by the Supreme Court in *Reves* because it was faced with determining whether a note that fit squarely within the statutory definition of "security" should, nonetheless, not be treated as a security for purposes of the anti-fraud provisions.[255]

The court also concluded that the test of whether an instrument is a security as an "evidence of indebtedness" is essentially the same as the tests applied to analyze notes and, in large part because the swaps lacked terms for the payment or repayment of principal, declined to accept P&G's characterization of the swaps as evidences of indebtedness.[256]

Investment Contract. The swaps also were not securities as investment contracts, according to the court, among other things, because under the test prescribed by the Supreme Court, an investment contract must entail "an investment in a common venture premised on a reasonable expectation of profits to be derived from the entrepreneurial or managerial efforts of others,"[257] but no such common venture or enterprise existed in the swaps between BT and P&G:

> *P&G did not pool its money with that of any other company or person in a single business venture. How BT hedged its swaps is not what is at issue—the issue is whether a number of investors joined together in a common venture. Certainly, any counterparties with whom BT contracted cannot be lumped together as a "common enterprise." Furthermore, BT was not managing P&G's money; BT was a counterparty to the swaps, and the value of the swaps depended on market forces, not BT's entrepreneurial efforts.*[258]

Options on Securities. In rejecting the contention that the swaps were securities as options on securities, the court noted the parties' opposing analyses as follows. P&G described the 5s/30s Swap as "a single security which can be decomposed into a plain vanilla swap with an embedded put option" on the reference Treasury notes and bonds, where the option was "a put on the 30-year bond price with an uncertain strike price that depends on the level of the 5-year yield at the end of six months."[259] BT, on the other hand, argued that although both swaps contained terms that functioned as options, they were not options because they did not give either party the right to sell or buy anything and the only "option-like" feature was the spread calculation in each swap; any resemblance the spread calculations had to options on securities did not extend to the underlying swaps themselves, which had no option-like characteristics. The court agreed with BT, noting the lack of any right to take possession of any security and rejecting the theory that transactions with embedded option-like features should be treated as securities that Congress intended to regulate under the federal securities laws.[260] In so doing, the court expressly declined to follow the approach taken by the SEC, *inter alia,* in its settlement order referred to above in the enforcement proceedings brought by it against BT Securities. The findings in the orders in question, the court noted, by their own terms were solely for the purpose of the settlement, are not binding on any other person or in any other proceeding and were not binding on the *Procter & Gamble* court, in part because of the differences between the transactions involved. The court also observed, quoting the Supreme Court, that the "courts are the final authorities on the issues of statutory construction and are not obligated to stand aside and rubber-stamp their affirmance of administrative decisions that they deem inconsistent with a statutory mandate or that frustrate the congressional policy underlying a statute."[261]

Instrument Commonly Known as a "Security." The court's discussion in this part of the Final Order concluded with its analysis of whether either of the swaps in question could be found to be a security as an "instrument commonly known as a 'security.'" The *Procter & Gamble* court observed that, pursuant to the approach adopted by the Supreme Court in considering the same issue as applied to different kinds of instruments,

> *when a party seeks to fit financial instruments into the non-specific categories of securities, those instruments must nonetheless comport with the Howey test [the Supreme Court's statement of the attributes of an investment contract in SEC v. Howey], which "embodies the essential attributes that run through all of the Court's decisions defining a security. The touchstone is the presence of an investment in a common venture premised on a reasonable expectation of profits to be derived from the entrepreneurial or managerial efforts of others."*[262]

The court had previously found this test was not met by the 5s/30s Swap and DEM Swap and, therefore, rejected P&G's theory in this regard, noting too that, although P&G asserted that it knew of the fraud it alleged in mid-April 1994, it did not assert a claim for securities violations until after the SEC had issued its rulings in the *Gibson Greetings* matter. "If P&G itself had really thought it was dealing with securities," the court noted, "it is fair to assume that P&G would have included securities counts in its original complaint."[263]

The court's rejection of P&G's securities law claims under Ohio statutes was largely based on the same reasoning applied in its analysis of the federal securities law claims. To the extent that the Ohio claims were based on statutory language broader than that included in the 1934 Act, the court found the swaps in question fell outside the reach of the statutory provisions.[264]

Commodities Laws. The court's disposition of the claims brought under the anti-fraud provisions of the CEA and regulations thereunder was very complex. In summary, it can be said however, that the court concluded that no private right of action existed under the first of the provisions relied on by P&G,[265] because the court found such an implied right of action to exist only in connection with fraud engaged in by a person acting for or on behalf of another in connection with certain commodity futures;[266] BT was not acting for or on behalf of P&G in the swaps in question, but, rather, as a principal. The second CEA claim was rejected because the statutory provision in question applies by its terms only to fraudulent conduct by a commodity trading advisor,[267] and the court found that BT did not fall within the statutory definition of "commodity trading advisor."[268] The court recognized that representatives from BT Securities "had conversations with P&G regarding market conditions, past performance of Treasury notes and bonds, prognostications for the future, and the like," and gave P&G a sales pitch regarding the benefits of their product and involving P&G's view of interest rates, and the court stated that this activity "came close to giving advice," but that P&G's representatives "used their own independent knowledge of market conditions in forming their own expectation as to what the market would do in the 5s/30s and DM swaps. That expectation (central to the two swaps) was not based on commodity trading advice."[269] The court rejected the third basis for P&G's commodity-related claims[270] finding that it provides only for CFTC enforcement action, and not a private right of action.[271]

Other Claims. The court's disposition of P&G's claim under the Ohio Deceptive Trade Practices Act was, as described above,[272] dismissed based on the parties' contractual choice of New York law.

P&G's second amended complaint in the lawsuit had also introduced counts based on theories under RICO premised on a pattern of fraud involving P&G and others. These claims were not addressed in the First Order or the Final Order because the court had ruled that P&G first would have to prove to the jury that BT had engaged in fraud.

The various lawsuits described in this section illustrate that the parties to OTC derivatives should have a clear understanding at the outset about the nature of the relationship that exists between them, as should derivatives brokers with their principals. To avoid litigation, the parties should spell out in writing the extent to which each is entitled to rely on the other and clearly identify the information that is to be provided by each party from time to time. If it is not appropriate to do this in a master agreement that will cover future transactions whose nature cannot at the time be known, the parties' agreement on the subject can nonetheless set out their understanding about their relationship at the time the master agreement is executed and state that this description is subject, in relation to any transaction, to any contrary understanding expressed in writing in connection with that transaction. The agreement should make plain that it is intended to be the parties' entire agreement on the subject, subject to such subsequent written modification, so that obligations not bargained for are not implied. If, in fact, there is a subsequent change in the nature of the relationship, that should of course be documented at the time of the change.

In this context, it is worth considering that it may not be appropriate to treat the confirmation of a transaction as the vehicle for such subsequent agreements on the nature of the parties' relationship. This may be so for various reasons but one example should suffice. Although the parties to OTC derivatives sometimes prepare and review draft confirmations before they engage in transactions, this practice is the exception, not the norm. In the absence of an exchange of draft confirmations, the confirmation will generally be an unsuitable vehicle for the parties' agreement on a change in their relationship, because after the transaction has been executed at an agreed price (whether expressed as a premium or as one of the rates applied in the transaction), it would be untimely for one of the parties, in its reply to a confirmation of the agreed financial terms, only then to assert for the first time that it believes itself entitled to rely on its counterparty as an advisor in connection with the transaction.

The cases dealt with in this section also indicate that market professionals should, in order to reduce the risk of litigation, and as a matter of good business practice and client relations, carefully assess what kinds of information they will offer to supply to their counterparties, at the outset and on an ongoing basis, in light of the degree of complexity of the transactions being considered. End-users of derivatives, for their part, should also consider carefully exactly what kinds of information they want to receive from their counterparties before reaching decisions on whether to enter into a transaction. It is appropriate for the end-user to ask the professional market participant to warrant the accuracy of information that it creates and delivers. End-users should also consider what information they want their professional counterparties to agree to supply thereafter from time to time, particularly when the end-user's relationship with the dealer is conceived and documented as a principal-to-principal relationship. End-users should take particular care to understand the nature of valuation information they may receive from their counterparties. For example, an indicative quotation of the amount the counterparty would charge or pay to unwind a transaction might well be different from the counterparty's firm quotation. Moreover, even a firm quotation from a professional counterparty is subjective and is thus not necessarily a reliable indication of how others in the market would value the transaction. Unless the end-user has the in-house capacity to value the transaction, it would be well advised to obtain the necessary valuation information from one or more independent sources.

These steps can only help to establish good business relationships and to prevent good relationships from turning bad. They will not serve to prevent actual fraud or misrepresentation, but they will appropriately place on each party the burden of explaining to the other exactly what it expects from their dealings with each other, so that the other party can itself determine whether it wishes to participate in the relationship on those terms.

The same considerations are the underpinnings of the various sets of guidelines prepared by groups of end-users and professional participants described above in our discussion of the duties owed by the management of a company to its owners in connection with the entity's use of derivatives.[273] For example, a basic tenet of the Principles and Practices is that, unless informed by its counterparty that it views the parties' relationship differently, each participant in a transaction in the wholesale financial markets will assume that the parties are dealing with each other at arm's length, if both parties regularly engage in transactions in that market. Because the Principles and Practices are voluntary, a market participant may determine that it does not adhere to that fundamental principle, but if it would like to engage in a transaction other than on an arm's-length basis, and would like to rely on a counterparty's communications as recommendations or investment advice, it should, before entering into the transaction,

*(i) put its counterparty on notice in writing that it is relying on the counterparty,
(ii) obtain the counterparty's agreement in writing to do business on that basis,
and (iii) provide the counterparty with accurate information regarding its financial objectives and the size, nature and condition of its business sufficient to
provide such recommendations or investment advice.*[274]

The Principles and Practices acknowledge that "[c]ertain laws, rules or regulations
expressly provide that, in some situations, an oral agreement or the facts and circumstances of a relationship alone may give rise to an advisory or fiduciary relationship, in some cases even in the presence of a written agreement purporting to
negate such a relationship. Nonetheless, to avoid misunderstandings and disputes the
steps outlined above should be followed."[275]

Both the Principles and Practices, as an expression of industry assumptions, and
the End-Users Practice Guidelines, as an expression of the views of end-user treasury
practitioners, provide that a user of derivatives is itself obligated either to ensure
that it is capable, independently, of understanding and making independent decisions about the transactions it enters into or that it has such professional advice from
a third party as is necessary for it to be able to make its own decisions about its transactions. Both documents also recognize the need for participants in transactions to
be able to value their transactions either independently or on the basis of third party
valuations. The documents speak at length of the policies and procedures that
should be in place to ensure proper training and supervision of personnel to ensure
that these capabilities exist.

Nonetheless, in a section on Considerations Relating to Relationships between Participants, the Principles and Practices also suggest that professional market participants may want to maintain policies and procedures to deal with special cases in
which (e.g., a counterparty) does not have the capability to understand and make independent decisions regarding transactions; or a counterparty seems to have assumed
incorrectly that it may rely on the participant for recommendations or investment advice; or the amount of the risk to the counterparty involved in the transaction seems to
be "clearly disproportionate in relation to the size, nature and condition of the counterparty's business."[276] These procedures may involve, among other things, "(i) providing or obtaining additional information to or from the counterparty, (ii) involving
additional qualified personnel internally, (iii) involving additional qualified personnel
of the counterparty, (iv) entering into a written agreement specifying the nature of
the relationship or (v) not entering into the particular Transaction or type of Transaction with that counterparty."[277] In cases involving particularly complex or significantly leveraged transactions, the document also states that a participant may wish to
provide more information to a counterparty, such as loss scenarios.[278]

The participants in the DPG Report, for their part, have established certain
"guidelines [that] are designed to foster integrity and responsible conduct in the
market and are not intended to prescribe legal standards,[279] which state the principle that "OTC derivatives transactions are predominantly arm's length transactions"
but go on to provide:

*In cases where existing transaction documentation does not expressly address the
nature of the relationship between the professional intermediary and its nonprofessional counterparty and the professional intermediary becomes aware that the*

nonprofessional counterparty believes incorrectly that the professional intermediary has assumed advisory or similar responsibilities toward the nonprofessional counterparty with respect to a prospective OTC derivative transaction, the professional intermediary should take steps to clarify the nature of the relationship.

A professional intermediary should not make representations to a nonprofessional counterparty with a view to creating a misleading impression that the professional intermediary will assume advisory or similar responsibilities toward its counterparty in connection with an OTC derivative transaction.[280]

9. Duties of Disclosure in Sales of Securities

Many of the lawsuits discussed in earlier sections of this chapter relate to situations in which a litigant seeks to avoid responsibility for derivatives allegedly entered into by it in violation of applicable policy. In those cases—some relying on an *ultra vires* argument or on a purported lack of proper authorization, some on corporate waste and breach of management's duties, and some on an implied duty of the counterparty as fiduciary to have executed transactions only if they would have achieved the other party's permitted and claimed objectives—one of the parties is seeking to be restored to the position it would have been in had the transactions never been consummated. The relief sought (rescission or other equitable relief, on the one hand, or damages, on the other) is sought for one of the parties to the derivatives transaction itself. The lawsuits discussed in this final section are different, in that the plaintiffs were not parties to the relevant OTC derivatives transactions and are seeking to recover damages allegedly suffered as a result of faulty disclosure by the defendants in connection with the plaintiffs' purchases of securities.

The first of the cases arose out of the transactions between Gibson Greetings and Bankers Trust referred to above.[281] In a class action, the plaintiffs sought to hold Gibson's senior management responsible for the plaintiffs' damages from their purchases of Gibson shares at prices reflecting 1993 income as originally reported by the company, before disclosure to the public of significant losses that, in part, were attributable to those derivatives. The amount of recovery sought was the difference between the price at which the plaintiffs purchased the shares and the price at which they could have sold them after the company announced it would restate income to reflect the losses. The original reports of results for 1993, which were available to plaintiffs at the time they bought the shares, allegedly violated the anti-fraud provisions of the federal securities laws.[282]

The other two cases arose out of losses of approximately $46 million incurred by California's Orange County on purchases by it of structured notes and other securities issued by the Student Loan Marketing Association[283] and sold to Orange County by a member of the Merrill Lynch group, acting as an underwriter to sell the securities to the public. Orange County is seeking damages and other relief based on a variety of claims, including allegations of common law fraud and violation of the anti-fraud provisions of federal and state securities laws, through failure by Sallie Mae and Merrill Lynch to disclose, in connection with the sale of the securities, that Sallie Mae and another Merrill Lynch entity would be engaging in swaps in connection with the offering of the securities.

Gambal v. Gibson Greetings Inc.[284]

As noted, this action was brought on behalf of a class consisting of purchasers of stock of Gibson Greetings during the period from the day on which Gibson Greetings announced the results for its third quarter through the close of business on the day before it announced that it would be restating its 1993 net income to a figure it believed would be 20% lower than the figure previously reported. The restatement was necessary because of an overstatement of the inventory of its Cleo Division (which accounted for about 40% of its income), in what it believed to be a deliberate attempt by Cleo personnel to overstate income, and because of the accrual of unrealized market value loss on two derivatives transactions that did not qualify as hedges and the recognition of previously deferred gain from other derivative transactions, which also did not qualify as hedges. The company reported that the net effect of the derivatives adjustments, a loss of $1,118,000, was recognized in the 1993 consolidated financial statements because the adjustments became significant in light of the reduction in the company's overall net income resulting from the restatement of Cleo's inventory.

The complaint sought, *inter alia*, compensatory damages for the losses incurred by the plaintiffs as a result of their purchases of Gibson Greetings stock at prices inflated by the incorrect 1993 financial data. The incorrect reports were alleged to constitute violations of anti-fraud provisions in the U.S. securities laws and regulations thereunder[285] by various officers of Gibson Greetings and Cleo. Each of the defendants, the complaint alleged, knew or, but for gross negligence, should have known that the reports materially overstated Gibson Greetings' net income during the period when the plaintiffs purchased the company's stock. The complaint alleged that their motivation was a desire to enhance the value of their own Gibson Greetings securities and to protect and enhance their executive positions and maximize their compensation, including performance-based bonuses awarded to them on the basis of whether certain targeted income levels were achieved.

The Orange County Cases

There has been, and continues to be, a considerable amount of litigation surrounding losses of more than $1.8 billion by Orange County, California, in connection with an investment strategy pursued by a former county treasurer. As was the case with the aggressive investment strategy employed by West Virginia's Board of Investments,[286] the Orange County strategy produced very favorable results for some time. However, the continued success of the strategy required an environment of relatively stable or declining interest rates and, within that environment, relatively low short-term rates. This was so because the strategy involved, among other things, the leveraged purchase, through short-term funding, of structured notes and other securities designed to yield returns higher than those available on conventional fixed-income instruments so long as interest rates remained low, but that would yield returns lower than conventional fixed-income investments if rates rose. A chief source of the leverage was the repurchase agreement market, in which the provider of a so-called reverse repo effectively provides leverage on a short-term basis on the strength of the value of the underlying securities and, so, requires additional margin if their value declines.

The same unexpected turn in interest rates that led to the derivatives losses described above of Procter & Gamble, Gibson Greetings, Seita and others led to the decline in value of many of Orange County's investments and to calls for additional margin from its sources of funding. The ensuing liquidation of many of the investments when their market values had dropped led Orange County, in December 1994, to seek protection under the U.S. Bankruptcy Code in the largest municipal bankruptcy in U.S. history.

As described in the introduction to this chapter, we will not be discussing much of the related litigation, which involves the repurchase agreements and the structured notes and similar securities, because they are not OTC derivatives. The two cases described below, however, do deal with OTC swaps. They are actions that seek to recoup some of Orange County's losses by alleging that some of these securities were sold to it using disclosure documents that fraudulently failed to disclose that the issuer, Sallie Mae, was entering into swaps in connection with the issuance of the securities with an affiliate of the seller, in violation of federal and state laws and regulations. According to the complaints, the undisclosed swaps contained terms that materially affected the terms of the instruments sold to Orange County to the disadvantage of Orange County.

The complaint in one of the lawsuits, *County of Orange v. Student Loan Marketing Ass'n*,[287] was filed in June 1996. The second lawsuit, *County of Orange v. Merrill Lynch & Co.*,[288] was commenced in 1994, and a Second Amended Complaint including a counterclaim by Orange County based on nondisclosure of the swap was filed in October 1995. Both cases have been transferred from the Bankruptcy Court before which they were brought, whose jurisdiction had been questioned by the defendants, to the federal District Court for the Central District of California.[289]

As alleged by Orange County, the facts supporting its complaints are as follows:

1. The offering materials for the four issues in question appeared typical for Sallie Mae note offerings in that they disclosed "underwriting discounts" of 15 to 50 basis points for participating underwriters, consistent with Sallie Mae's practice of selling its securities through selling groups whose participating members would receive pre-set selling commissions of 10 to 50 basis points and agree to sell the securities at a single price.

2. In fact, however, the method used to sell an aggregate principal amount of $913 million of the notes to Orange County was completely different, in that, simultaneously with each sale "and as an integrated part of each underwriting," Sallie Mae and a Merrill Lynch affiliate entered into an undisclosed interest rate swap agreement under which the Merrill Lynch entity agreed to pay Sallie Mae the interest payments Sallie Mae was obligated to make under the notes and Sallie Mae, in turn, agreed to pay the Merrill Lynch entity an amount calculated on the note principal at a fixed or floating rate that was below "the lowest fixed or floating borrowing rate at which Sallie Mae could normally issue notes in the global capital market."

3. The combination of these agreements "effectively negated" Sallie Mae's obligation to pay interest under the notes, leaving Sallie Mae "with a net obligation to pay interest to Merrill Lynch or its affiliate at a fixed or floating rate that was below SALLIE MAE's borrowing cost."

4. Sallie Mae thereby "relinquished to Merrill Lynch the authority to determine the terms of the notes" and "had no financial interest in the terms of the notes," which were set by Merrill Lynch in a manner that was unfavorable to the purchasers of the notes, because its profit from the undisclosed swap depended on that.

5. The compensation to be received by Merrill Lynch for underwriting the notes was determined by Merrill Lynch and was "typically two to five times greater than the compensation that Merrill Lynch would receive from the sale of an equivalent amount of SALLIE MAE-issued notes where no swap was involved," since the true underwriting compensation was not the disclosed 15 to 50 basis points calculated on the note principal, which Merrill Lynch had in fact agreed to rebate, but, rather, profits to the Merrill Lynch affiliate from the undisclosed swap.

6. The opportunity to profit from this swap put Merrill Lynch in an undisclosed direct conflict of interest with its customers in recommending and selling the notes because Merrill Lynch or its affiliate "took market positions directly opposed to that taken by the County": "Merrill Lynch would simultaneously determine whether to (a) retain some or all of that market position, thereby continuing a market bet that was contrary to that of the County, or (b) lock-in enormous profit by hedging its positions in the futures market or in its swap book." In the latter case, this was a "virtually risk-free locked-in profit measured by the difference between (a) the fixed or floating interest rate that Merrill Lynch or its affiliate would be receiving from SALLIE MAE (on the first swap), and (b) the lower fixed or floating rate that Merrill Lynch or its affiliate would be paying to the counterparties (on the second swap)."

7. Merrill Lynch's profits "from hedging the opposite side of the County's position stemmed directly from the fact that Merrill Lynch put terms in the notes that resulted in the notes being overpriced by millions of dollars." These "embedded losses" were concealed from the County by "the absence of a competitive market for these exotic and illiquid instruments" and because Merrill Lynch and Sallie Mae "utilized false and misleading offering circulars to conceal the nature of their relationship."

8. The County believes that those "intimate relationships" between Merrill Lynch and Sallie Mae consisted of "a history of secretly extending favors to each other," and that those favors may have been the motivation for some of Merrill Lynch's purchase recommendations of Sallie Mae securities.

According to the complaint in the action against Sallie Mae, the latter's failure to disclose in the offering materials "Merrill Lynch's true underwriting compensation and pervasive conflicts of interest" constituted an omission of material facts necessary to make the disclosure of "underwriting discount" not misleading. As a result, Orange County contends that it would have been entitled to rescind its purchase of the notes if it still owned them but, since they had already been sold at the time the action was commenced, Orange County is entitled to rescissory damages of not less than $58.7 million, measured by the difference between (i) the price at which it bought the notes plus interest from the date of purchase and (ii) the value of the securities at the time they were disposed of by the County plus the amount of any income received on the securities by the County. The statutory bases cited for this claim of relief were various provisions of the California Corporations Code and the federal securities anti-fraud provisions in Section 10b of the Exchange Act and Rule 10b-5 thereunder. Orange County also seeks an injunction barring Sallie Mae from engaging in further violations of the same alleged kinds, an order requiring Sallie Mae to restore to the County the money received by Sallie Mae from the note issuances and punitive damages. Finally, Orange County also alleges that the same conduct on the part of Sallie Mae constituted aiding and abetting by Sallie Mae of Merrill Lynch's breaches of the fiduciary duties it owed to the County, *inter alia,* as broker-dealer and financial advisor to the County.[290]

In its Second Amended Complaint against Merrill Lynch & Co. and certain of its affiliates, Orange County predicated claims for damages substantially in excess of $2 billion on the same basic allegations of fact, as well as allegations to the effect that, in connection with the issuance of certain callable notes, the offering materials failed to disclose that the issuer would probably call the security if a related undisclosed swap between it and a Merrill Lynch entity were terminated.[291] The alleged misconduct was claimed to constitute fraud or deceit, or unfair or fraudulent business practices, in violation of the anti-fraud provisions of the federal securities laws and various provisions of California's Corporations Code, Civil Code and Business and Professions Code. On these grounds, Orange County also sought punitive damages, an order requiring Merrill Lynch to disgorge all moneys obtained through its allegedly wrongful acts and an injunction barring Merrill Lynch from engaging in further acts of the same kinds.[292]

Sallie Mae's answer to the Orange County complaint asserts, among other things, that the County's claims are barred by failure to join indispensable parties, failure to state a cause of action and, as to the alleged omissions or misstatements, that Sallie Mae had, after reasonable investigation, reasonable ground to believe, and did believe, that the statements made were true and correct and that there was no failure to state a material fact required to make the statements made not misleading. Sallie Mae denies that any material misstatements or omissions were made and, to the extent any were, alleges that the County's Treasurer knew or, in the exercise of reasonable care, should have known, of the alleged misstatements and/or omissions and that knowledge did not affect the decisions to invest in Sallie Mae securities, and the investments in fact were not made in reliance on the alleged misstatements or any facts allegedly made misleading through alleged omissions. In addition, Sallie Mae's answer generally avers that the County's losses were produced by the County's own actions.

Sallie Mae has also filed a motion to dismiss the County's state law claims brought under the anti-fraud provisions of California's securities laws (Corporations Code Sections 25401 and 25501) on the ground that these statutes require strict privity of contract between the plaintiff and the defendant in connection with a sale of a security, but no such privity existed between Sallie Mae and the County, since the latter purchased the Sallie Mae instruments from Merrill Lynch. The motion to dismiss also covers the County's claim of violation of California's Unfair Trade Practices Act (Business Professions Code Sections 17200 *et seq.*) because the courts have recently and repeatedly held that statute inapplicable to alleged securities law violations affecting interstate commerce.

In its reply to the Second Amended Complaint, Merrill Lynch too argues that the County's alleged damages were caused not by any actions of Merrill Lynch but, rather, by the negligent actions of the County and its advisors and denies the County's allegations supporting the counterclaims related to the swaps. Merrill Lynch's affirmative defenses apply generally to the County's many claims, and none of them refers specifically to the swaps.

The particular circumstances of the *Gibson Greetings* action described in this Section point to the need for management to be able, independently or with the assistance of a company's independent auditors, to determine the appropriate accounting treatment for its derivatives, to ensure that the derivatives in fact are accounted for in accordance with the applicable methodology and to determine how the company's derivatives activities, and its policies concerning the use of derivatives, should be reported to securities holders and others.

In many respects, a company's derivatives activities are little different from its investments in financial instruments or, with respect to disclosure, from other aspects of its business and activities that involve various kinds of risks. However, as participants in the market, regulators and the accounting profession itself have long lamented, the appropriate accounting treatment for derivatives is not always simple. Indeed, successive proposals by a task force appointed by the Financial Accounting Standards Board to consider the relevant issues, including the circumstances in which a derivative and a related investment or commitment, for example, should be accorded integrated, hedge accounting treatment, have yet to produce a result that users of derivatives will broadly endorse.[293] Similarly, insofar as disclosure is concerned, the need for improvement has been broadly recognized and called for over recent years, although the quality of the disclosure now being made in many quarters is considerably better than it was. In late 1995[294] the SEC issued its proposal on this subject; the complexities and practical impact of the proposal for many users of derivatives is still being studied.

The End-Users Practice Guidelines include the following, together with more specific and detailed recommendations, on these subjects:

> *A good understanding of accounting and tax rules relating to derivatives use and risk management strategies is essential, as well as changes being implemented or proposed. In addition to requirements by FASB, the SEC, the IRS, and others discussed elsewhere in this document, the derivatives user must understand any industry specific regulations and how a derivatives program must be tailored to comply.*
>
> *In the most basic terms, disclosure must address both internal and external audiences with explanations of what derivatives are being used, why derivatives are utilized, and how the usage of derivatives is controlled.*
>
> *A. Internal Disclosure*
>
> *Effective disclosure internally requires a structure of management controls . . . This structure can provide a reporting framework which ensures that senior management—including the Board—is aware of the potential impact of the use of derivatives on the organization. Reports need to provide understanding of the types of positions held, their purpose and the possible effects of market movements on the portfolio. Reports should provide a performance review of the program and an evaluation of its risks and benefits.*
>
> *B. External Disclosure*
>
> *Required external disclosures are intended to allow shareholders and others to understand—in relation to the organization's broad strategic goals:*
> * *Financial risks of the business.*
> * *Risks involved in the use of derivatives.*
> * *Purpose and size of the transactions.*
> * *Accounting for the transactions.*
> * *Fair value of derivatives instruments.*
> * *Amounts, nature, and terms.*
> * *Specific disclosures for hedges of anticipated transactions.*

- *Risk management policies and procedures.*
- *Nature and types of on- and off-balance sheet financial risks, including credit, market and liquidity.*
- *Any significant concentrations of credit risks, such as credit rating on investment grade of counterparties, regional or country risks, or currency risks.*

The two *Orange County* cases described in this section should be examined closely by participants in the derivatives market. Some of the arguments made by the County in framing its claims relating to the swaps are obviously unsound. For example, as a general matter a debt instrument and a swap used to manage obligations under the instrument are independent one from the other, and the issuer of the debt instrument generally remains liable to make payments under it whether or not the provider of the swap performs. Therefore, even if the full amount of each payment due under the debt instrument is matched by an offsetting receivable under the swap, the debt issuer must remain concerned about the reasonableness of the terms of its debt, and its ability to perform them. Unless the Sallie Mae structured notes purchased by Orange County and at issue in the cases were nonrecourse to Sallie Mae and payable only from the payments made to Sallie Mae under the related Merrill Lynch swaps—which does not seem to have been the case—the County's theories are flawed insofar as they depend on allegations that Sallie Mae's note obligations were "effectively negated" by the related swaps, that Sallie Mae, because of the swaps, had no "financial interest" in the terms of the notes and that, by entering into the swaps, Sallie Mae relinquished to Merrill Lynch the authority to determine the terms of the notes. Similarly, it is simplistic to conclude that the spread between the Merrill Lynch swap party's obligations to Sallie Mae under their swaps and the amounts payable to that Merrill Lynch party under offsettting, hedge transactions constitute hidden fees payable to a different Merrill Lynch entity in connection with its role in the sale of the notes to the County, because the risks under the sets of swaps offset each other. Financial intermediaries that engage in offsetting swap transactions receive such spreads as compensation for many reasons, only the most basic of which is the fact that the intermediary is required to perform under each swap it enters into regardless of whether it receives the performance owed to it under an offsetting, hedge transaction.

Nonetheless, the County's claims pose complex technical issues under the securities laws and regulations relating to duties of disclosure generally in connection with the issuance of securities and, in particular, in connection with potential conflicts of interest. Therefore, those who engage in derivatives in connection with the issuance of securities should be giving heightened attention to the allegations in the cases, regardless of how they are decided or whether they are settled. As is evident from this overview of many of the recent lawsuits involving OTC derivatives, whether or not new litigation theories succeed in the cases in which they are first presented, they often spawn copy cat suits in other jurisdictions. Therefore, when an issuer enters into OTC derivatives in connection with the issuance of securities, both the issuer and the underwriter and others involved in the distribution or placement of the securities should consider carefully whether the existence of the derivative should be disclosed, particularly when it is entered into by the issuer or one of its affiliates with the underwriter or placement agent or an affiliate of either of them.

Conclusion

We will not revisit here the various lessons we have drawn from the cases described in this chapter. We conclude with a few general observations.

The risk of litigation challenging the existence of contractual obligations under OTC derivatives continues to be very real. There have been positive developments in New York law, through amendments to various statutes of frauds, that in many cases will reduce the risk of a dispute over whether the parties to an OTC derivatives transaction are contractually bound. The amendments have no application to transactions in which either party is a natural person, however, and wealthy individuals are sometimes parties to such transactions. The amendments also do not apply to special statutes of frauds, such as those that may be applicable to guaranties of obligations under OTC derivatives. To benefit from at least some aspects of the amendments, participants in the derivatives market will need to ensure that they comply with the technical requirements of the statutes as amended. In addition, in some circumstances the parties' ongoing dealings with each other may be such that a court will permit one of the parties to introduce evidence other than the parties' confirmation to challenge whether the confirmation in fact fully sets forth the terms of the parties' agreement. Participants in the market should, therefore, be carefully examining whether their practices, including their practices in confirming transactions, should be altered to protect against this possibility or, conversely, to treat specified sources of evidence, such as the recording of a conversation in which a trade is concluded, as the best evidence of the complete and final terms of the parties' agreement, at least on the financial terms of their transactions.

The risk of challenges based on allegations that transactions are unauthorized continues to be serious, as does the risk that a counterparty will seek to hold a professional derivatives market participant responsible if its own employees and officers breach their duties to engage only in transactions that are within the counterparty's powers, properly authorized and consistent with its policies. This risk is present in dealing with the public sector and with private-sector counterparties with limited powers. In this area, professional market participants can seek to protect themselves through appropriate diligence.

Insofar as *ultra vires* doctrines and statutes with similar effect in the United States are concerned, only legislative change can bring the needed certainty to the market. If entities charged with a public trust are to be able to avail themselves of derivatives to manage their assets and liabilities, the rules on their power and authority to do so should be clear, so that their potential counterparties, acting as principals, and pricing transactions on the assumption that they are incurring only the risks that principals normally do, are not unexpectedly charged with the losses incurred by their public-sector counterparties as a result of the failed derivatives strategies pursued by them. It seems logical that the public sector should be held accountable for assessment and management of the risks that it undertakes, either through internal resources or through advisers paid to act as such. Financial markets do not operate efficiently when pricing does not accurately reflect risk.

The adoption of the CFTC's Swap Exemption and Energy Contracts Exemption has significantly reduced the risk of litigation over the legality and enforceability of many OTC derivatives on the theory that they violate state gaming or bucket-shop laws or the CEA's ban on off-exchange commodity futures and option transactions. However, even assuming that those exemptions are as broad as they reasonably should be for the specific classes of derivatives they cover, to reduce uncertainty in important sectors of the market, legislative change is still necessary to address the status of many OTC derivatives involving debt and equity securities and securities indices and the like, and to clarify the reach of the current exceptions from that CEA ban established pursuant to the Treasury Amendment and the forward contract exclusion. The expected Supreme Court decision in the *Dunn* case about the reach of the Treasury Amendment may bring some relief, but recent court decisions and CFTC statements relating to the forward contract exclusion and the features that characterize futures transactions remain troublesome in the meanwhile. In addition, the OTC derivatives market remains concerned that the CFTC has the power to modify its Swap Exemption and Energy Contracts Exemption; certainty in the marketplace would be better served through congressional action.

Several of the cases we have described illustrate how various tort theories and statutory anti-fraud provisions may be invoked to defend against suits for breach of contractual obligations or to seek to have contracts rescinded or reformed. We have also reviewed other contexts in which such theories and statutory provisions, as well as statutory and common-law rules relating to fiduciary duties, have been invoked in actions seeking to hold a company, its directors, and its officers accountable for losses allegedly incurred by a company's shareholders or purchasers of its debt securities. The circumstances that gave rise to much of this litigation would not have arisen if the parties involved had had better policies and procedures relating to the use of derivatives, in the case of the end-users, and relating to the marketing of derivatives, in the case of their professional counterparties. We have referred to the publication of various sets of guidelines about these subjects produced by both end-users and by professional participants in the market. Others have been provided by regulators for their constituencies. We are optimistic that the level of litigation of the kinds illustrated in sections 5 through 9 of this chapter will substantially abate with the heightened awareness that now exists among end-users and professionals alike of the need for improvement in the field of risk management.

As standards and practices in this field evolve, a guiding principle should be that parties contracting with each other must have a clear understanding about the nature of their obligations to each other, and this understanding is best stated in writing. For many years the derivatives market has operated on the assumption that derivatives documentation did not need to address this understanding because only sophisticated parties, acting in good faith, were participating in the market, and they would not seek to shift responsibility to their counterparties for their losses if the relevant rates or prices moved against them. These assumptions can no longer be accepted as correct. Just as participants in the loan participation market, to give just one example, have over the last two decades developed documentation that seeks clearly to allocate specific risks to the parties that negotiate the contract,[295] participants in the OTC derivatives market must address the need for contractual risk allocation that is more explicit. Valuable resources will be wasted if the parties leave to the courts the task of deciding what each of the parties expected, and is entitled to expect, from the other.

ENDNOTES

1. In ADVANCED STRATEGIES IN FINANCIAL RISK MANAGEMENT 387 (Robert J. Schwartz & Clifford W. Smith, Jr. (eds.), New York Institute of Finance 1993) (footnotes omitted) [hereinafter *1992 Review*].

2. *See* the discussion of Homestead Sav. v. Life Sav. & Loan Ass'n, which involved a defense based on a statute of frauds, in the *1992 Review* at 392–98 and the summary below of the case at p. 59 *infra.* The

case was commenced in the U.S. District Court for the Northern District of California, as Case No. C 85 1690 SAW, and was transferred to the District Court for the Northern District of Illinois, Western Division, where it was identified as Case No. 86 C 20268. The case is unreported.

3. *See* the discussion of Intershoe, Inc. v. Bankers Trust Co., 571 N.E.2d 641 (1991), which involved the application of a parol evidence rule to an FX forward transaction, in the *1992 Review* at 398–403, and the summary of that case at p. 63 *infra*.

4. *See* the discussion of Hazell v. Hammersmith & Fulham London Borough Council, [1990] 2 W.L.R. 17, [1992] Q.B. 697 (Div'l Ct. 1989), *aff'd in part and rev'd in part,* [1990] 2 W.L.R. 1039, [1992] Q.B. 697 (C.A. 1990), *reinstated,* 2 A.C. 1, [1991] All E.R. 545, [1991] 2 W.L.R. 372 (H.L. 1991), in the *1992 Review* at 403-12 and the summary of the case at p. 65 *infra.*

5. *See* the discussion of the lower court decision in Salomon Forex, Inc. v. Tauber, 795 F. Supp. 768 (E.D. Va. 1992), *aff'd,* 8 F.3d. 966 (4th Cir. 1993), *cert. denied,* 114 S. Ct. 1540 (1994), in the *1992 Review* at 412-22 and the description of subsequent developments in the case at p. 73 *infra.*

6. *See* the discussion of various cases in the *1992 Review* at 423-37.

7. Cases on settlement risk in OTC derivatives are not within the scope of this article. *See, e.g.,* Deutsche Bank v. Baring Bros. & Co., No. 104901/95 (N.Y. Sup. Ct. filed Feb. 28, 1995), and United States v. BCCI Holdings (Luxembourg), S.A., 833 F. Supp. 22 (D.D.C. 1993) (suits to recover monies paid under FX forwards to a party that failed to make its counterpayment). We also do not discuss disputes arising from the occurrence of events that were foreseeable but that the parties did not deal with in their agreement. *See, e.g.,* Caisse Nationale de Credit Agricole v. CBI Indus., Inc., 90 F.3d 1264 (7th Cir. 1996) (a dispute over the right to exercise a European-style swaption, where the expiration date was a Sunday, the following Monday was a holiday and the parties' contract was silent on whether the right to exercise would extend to the following Tuesday).

8. For a review of recent cases primarily involving exchange-traded commodity derivatives, *see* Kurt W. Hemr, *Commodity Litigation Update—1995,* Rev. Sec. & Comm. Reg., June 5, 1996, at 121.

9. "Structured notes are debt securities with derivative-like characteristics that are used by corporations and government-sponsored enterprises (GSEs), including the Federal National Mortgage Association, the Federal Home Loan Mortgage Corporation, and the Federal Home Loan Banks. Structured notes take various forms and often contain complex rate-adjustment formulas and embedded options (e.g., calls, caps, and collars)." Office of Thrift Supervision, *Structured Notes,* Thrift Bulletin 65, at 1 (Aug. 15, 1994). "There are [sic] a wide variety of structured notes, with names such as single- or multi-index floaters, inverse floaters, index-amortizing notes, step-up bonds, and range bonds. These simple, though sometimes cryptic, labels can belie the potential complexity of these notes and their possibly volatile and unpredictable cash flows, which can involve both principal and interest payments. Some notes employ 'trigger levels,' at which cash flows can change significantly, or caps or floors, which can also substantially affect their price behavior." Board of Governors of the Federal Reserve System, Division of Banking Supervision and Regulation, *Supervisory Policies Relating to Structured Notes,* Release SR 94-45 (FIS), at 2 (Aug. 5, 1994).

10. "CMO" is a generic term for securities backed directly or indirectly by real estate mortgages. *See* Gary L. Gastineau & Mark P. Kritzman, The Dictionary of Financial Risk Management 59 (1996). In a CMO structure, real estate mortgages or pass-through certificates representing mortgage obligations, such as the "Ginnie Maes" issued by the Government National Mortgage Association, are placed in a pool, and securities are issued, usually in tranches, representing the right to receive different portions of the mortgage payments that flow into the pool. For example, one tranche or group of tranches might be entitled to the interest payments received in the pool and another to the principal payments; each of those streams might in turn be further divided (for example, earlier payments might be separated from later payments) and allocated to different tranches.

11. For capsule descriptions of some of these cases, *see* Linda B. Klein, *An Overview of Recent Case Law Affecting Swaps and Other Derivatives, in* 2 Chicago-Kent College of Law, Seventeenth Annual Commodities Law Institute and Third Annual Financial Services Law Institute § 6 (Nov. 3-4, 1994); Lauren A. Teigland, *Derivative Disputes and Disappointments: The "SAD" Phenomenon of Derivatives Litigation,* 64 Banking Rep. (BNA) 703 (Apr. 3, 1995), and Lauren A. Teigland, *Derivative Disputes Revisited: How Litigants Have Fared in the Past Year,* 66 Banking Rep. (BNA) 891 (May 20, 1996).

12. At 392-98. *See also* Anthony C. Gooch & Linda B. Klein, Documentation for Derivatives 372–83 (Euromoney Publications 1993) [hereinafter Documentation for Derivatives], for further discussion of statutes of frauds generally.

13. Richard A. Givens, Practice Commentary on Section 5-701 of the New York General Obligations Law (McKinney 1989) at 279–81 (quoting from cases cited therein).

14. The amended statutes are Section 5-701 of the General Obligations Law and Sections 1-206 and 2-201 of New York's version of the Uniform Commercial Code [hereinafter U.C.C.].

15. *See* the discussion of the treatment of a confirmation as the final expression of the parties' agreement at p. 63 *infra*, in the *1992 Review* at 397–03 and in DOCUMENTATION FOR DERIVATIVES at 383–86.

16. *See* the discussion in DOCUMENTATION FOR DERIVATIVES at 379–83 of the special writing requirements that apply for contracts to be enforceable against the receiver or conservator for certain financial institutions in the U.S.

17. [1995–1996 Transfer Binder] FED. SEC. L. REP. (CCH) ¶ 99,001 (S.D.N.Y. 1995). Other aspects of this case are discussed at p. 68 *infra*.

18. *Id*. In dismissing the claims, the court granted the plaintiffs leave to amend the complaint. In June 1996, the plaintiffs filed an Amended Complaint in which they alleged that the parent was both directly responsible for the subsidiary's obligations, as an alter ego of the subsidiary, and liable on the guaranty.

19. No. 118148/95 (N.Y. Sup. Ct. filed July 24, 1995).

20. N.Y. GEN. OBLIG. LAW § 5-701(a)(2) (McKinney 1989).

21. The description of this case is based on the court's April 1, 1996 order granting the plaintiff's motion to dismiss some of the defendants' counterclaims and denying the defendants' motion for partial summary judgment.

22. This claim was premised, among other things, on allegations that Daiwa intentionally procured a breach of a Trading Advisory Agreement between RCM, as advisor, and RCM Global, its client, by improperly seizing RCM Global's funds to offset monies owed to Daiwa by RCM.

23. Hereinafter referred to as ISDA.

24. No. 9642635 (Bankr. S.D.N.Y. filed May 14, 1996).

25. For example, if a bank is asked to execute a guaranty or similar support, the parties should inquire into the bank's power to issues guaranties in the particular circumstances, and the bank itself should analyze whether the provision raises questions under regulations that may limit its ability to issue guaranties or that require the bank to receive security from an affiliate or other party whose obligations it guarantees. If the party asked to execute a provision that could operate as a guaranty is an investment company, limited partnership or other entity whose assets should, under fiduciary principles, be applied only for the benefit of its own equity investors or pursuant to obligations incurred for their benefit, both the entity agreeing to the provision and the counterparty seeking its protection should carefully examine the propriety of the provision.

26. 571 N.E.2d 641 (N.Y. 1991). Bankers Trust Company is referred to herein as *"Bankers Trust"* or *"BT,"* and its broker-dealer affiliate, BT Securities Corporation, is referred to herein as *"BT Securities."*

27. 785 F. Supp. 411 (S.D.N.Y. 1992).

28. *Id*. at 427–33. This case is discussed further in Section 8, p. 98 *infra*.

29. In another post-*Intershoe* case, the *Tauber* case described at p. 73 *infra*, the defendant—like the plaintiff in *Sud-Americana de Vapores*—contended that the plaintiff had breached an express representation of "best pricing" made by one of its sales persons by overcharging the defendant for the FX option and forward transactions involved in the case. Citing *Intershoe*, the trial court found that the N.Y. U.C.C. parol evidence rule barred the defendant from introducing extrinsic evidence to support this contention. Similar claims have been made in other cases discussed in Section 6, p. 84 *infra*.

30. *See* Aratari v. Chrysler Corp., 316 N.Y.S.2d 680 (App. Div. 1970).

31. *See* the discussions of the *Seita* case, p. 95 *infra*, and the *Procter & Gamble* case, p. 100 *infra*.

32. That is not to say that such additional language is necessary. Many of the standard agreements used in the OTC derivatives market include a general "merger" or "integration" clause to the effect that the master agreement, together with the confirmation of a transaction thereunder, form the entire agreement of the parties relating to the terms of the transaction covered by the confirmation. Arguably even if the parol evidence rule applicable in a particular case did not, without more, preclude the admission of extrinsic evidence on an alleged additional term absent from the confirmation, that sort of language in the master agreement would operate to preclude the evidence of the alleged additional term, and additional language in the confirmation would merely repeat the substance of the master agreement's integration clause.

33. Documentation for Derivatives 316.

34. [1990] 2 W.L.R. 17, [1992] Q.B. 697 (Div'l Ct. 1989), *aff'd in part and rev'd in part,* [1990] 2 W.L.R. 1039, [1992] Q.B. 697 (C.A. 1990), *reinstated,* 2 A.C. 1, [1991] All E.R. 545, [1991] 2 W.L.R. 372 (H.L. 1991).

35. At 411.

36. Unwinding a transaction by having the parties return the payments that have been made, with interest, may be contrasted with the standard market approach to compensation for early termination of a transaction, which calls for payment by the party for whom the transaction is out of the money of an amount calculated to approximate the cost to the other party of obtaining a replacement transaction. A transaction is "out of the money" to a party if the transaction represents a liability to that party, in the sense that the party would be charged by a third party contracting to take its place in a transaction with the same economic characteristics for the remaining term of the original transaction. The financial difference between the two approaches to unwinding a transaction can, of course, be very substantial.

37. State v. Morgan Stanley, 1995 W. Va. LEXIS 94, No. Civ. 89-C-3700 (June 5, 1995). The case has reportedly been settled. *See* Leslie Wayne, *Morgan Stanley Will Pay West Virginia $20 Million,* N.Y. Times, Aug. 15, 1996, at D2. Morgan Stanley & Co. Incorporated is referred to herein as *"Morgan Stanley."*

38. Other entities named as defendants in this case and other similar cases were Chase Securities, Inc., Citibank, N.A., County NatWest Government Securities, Inc., County NatWest, Inc., Goldman, Sachs & Co., Greenwich Capital Markets, Inc., Merrill Lynch & Co. and Salomon Brothers, Inc. *See* Wayne, *supra* note 37.

39. State v. Morgan Stanley & Co., 1995 W. Va. LEXIS, at *9–10.

40. *Id.* at *13 (quoting from W. Va. Code § 12-6-12 (1978)).

41. Complaint at 7, *West Virginia* (No. 89-C-3700).

42. *Id.* at 25.

43. *Id.* at 7–8.

44. *Id.* at 10–11.

45. *Id.* at 17.

46. *Id.* at 27.

47. *Id.* at 20–22.

48. *Id.* at 24.

49. State v. Morgan Stanley & Co., 1995 W. Va. LEXIS, at *12.

50. *Id.* at *18.

51. *Id.* at 36.

52. *See* Wayne, *supra* note 37, and *WV and Morgan Stanley Settle Suit over Fund's Losses in Derivatives,* [Aug. 26, 1996] Derivatives Litigation Rep. at 11.

53. [1995–1996 Transfer Binder] Fed. Sec. L. Rep. (CCH) ¶ 99,000 (S.D.N.Y. 1995). In the following discussion, Lehman Brothers Commercial Corporation is referred to as *"LBCC,"* Lehman Brothers Special Financing Inc. is referred to as *"LBSF,"* LBCC and LBSF are referred to collectively as *"Lehman,"* China International United Petroleum & Chem. Co. is referred to as *"Unipec,"* and the case is referred to as the *"Unipec case."*

54. [1995–1996 Transfer Binder] Fed. Sec. L. Rep. (CCH) ¶ 99,001 (S.D.N.Y. 1995). In the following discussion, Minmetals International Non-Ferrous Metals Trading Co. is referred to as *"Minmetals,"* its parent company, China National Metals and Minerals Import and Export Company, is referred to as the *"Minmetals parent,"* and the case is referred to as the *"Minmetals case."*

55. Other aspects of the *Minmetals* case are discussed at p. 61 *supra,* and other aspects of both cases are discussed at p. 94 *infra.* Similar claims were also raised in the *Seita* case discussed at p. 95 *infra.*

56. The Commodity Terms and Conditions Agreement and the Supplemental FX Facility Agreement are collectively referred to herein as the *"Commodity Agreement."*

57. Other counterclaims in the *Unipec* case are described at p. 94 *infra.*

58. See p. 61 *supra.*

59. *Unipec,* [1995–1996 Transfer Binder] Fed. Sec. L. Rep. (CCH) ¶ 99,000, at 93,881-82 (S.D.N.Y. 1995). The court dismissed a counterclaim in which Unipec alleged that Lehman representatives had engaged in business disparagement and a counterclaim in which it alleged that the Lehman entities

had interfered with prospective contractual relations of Unipec, *inter alia,* by issuing defamatory statements concerning Unipec.

60. *See* Sara Webb, *Lehman Settles Derivatives Feud with China Firm,* Asian Wall St. J., Sept. 10, 1996, at 1, *available in* 1996 WL-WSJA 10222455. A third action involving a Chinese counterparty and similar claims of lack of authorization was earlier settled. *See* Sinochem (USA) Inc. v. Lehman Bros., No. 96-CIV-0062 (S.D.N.Y. Jan. 4, 1996).

61. Documentation for Derivatives 316-17 (footnotes omitted). Other actions brought in the U.S. courts involving substantial losses from investments described as "derivative securities" have demonstrated the vitality of the *ultra vires* doctrine as a tool to seek recovery of losses by public bodies with limited powers. One such case is County Comm'rs v. Liberty Capital Markets, Civ. Act. No. DKC 95-2188, filed Sept. 2, 1994, D. Maryland. The complaint, as amended, sought damages, believed to be in excess of $7.5 million, on common-law and statutory theories of misrepresentation, breach of fiduciary duty and fraud, and in the alternative seeks rescission and repayment of the purchase price paid for securities then still held by Charles County, Maryland, together with all fees, commissions and interest, on *ultra vires* grounds. Another, more widely publicized *ultra vires* case involving "derivative securities" is County of Orange v. Merrill Lynch & Co., which is described in Section 9, p. 112 *infra,* in a different context.

62. 8 F.3d 966 (4th Cir. 1993), *cert. denied,* 114 S. Ct. 1540 (1994), *aff'g* 795 F. Supp. 768 (E.D. Va. 1992).

63. Section 4(a) of the CEA, 7 U.S.C.A. § 6(a) (Supp. 1996), is the relevant provision relating to futures contracts; Section 4c(b) of the CEA, 7 U.S.C.A. § 6c(b) (Supp. 1996), as implemented through regulations of the CFTC, has the same substantive effect as applied to "any transaction involving any commodity regulated under [the CEA] . . . which is of the character or, or is commonly known to the trade as, an option. . . ," subject to applicable exemptions. A summary of the relevant statutes appears in the description of *Tauber* in the *1992 Review* at 415-22, and further description of the case and of the relevant statutes is included in Documentation for Derivatives at 10-20.

64. *See* the discussion in the *1992 Review* at 419-22.

65. N.Y. Gen. Bus. L. § 351 (McKinney's 1988).

66. 8 F.3d at 978 (quoting from Board of Trade v. Christie Grain & Stock Co., 198 U.S. 236, 249-50 (1905) (deletion in original)).

67. At 415-19.

68. The relevant language is to the effect that "[n]othing in this chapter [the CEA] shall be deemed to govern or in any way be applicable to transactions in foreign currency . . . , unless such transactions involve the sale thereof for future delivery conducted on a board of trade." 7 U.S.C.A. § 2(ii) (Supp. 1996).

69. The Fourth Circuit's opinion in *Tauber,* 8 F.3d at 974, summarizes the various and to some extent opposing positions taken in these briefs by the CFTC, the Board of Trade of the City of Chicago, the Chicago Mercantile Exchange, the Idaho Department of Finance, the Securities Division of the Office of the Secretary of State of Nevada, the United States, the SEC, the Foreign Exchange Committee, and the Futures Industry Association.

70. *Id.* at 976.

71. *Id.* at 978.

72. Salomon Forex, Inc. v. Tauber, 114 S. Ct. 1540 (1994).

73. [1992-1994 Transfer Binder] Comm. Fut. L. Rep. (CCH) ¶ 26,063 (E.D.N.Y. Aug. 9, 1993). Standard Forex, Inc. is referred to herein as "Standard Forex."

74. 7 U.S.C.A. § 6d (Supp. 1996).

75. 7 U.S.C.A. § 2(i) (Supp. 1996).

76. *Standard Forex,* [1992-1994 Transfer Binder] Comm. Fut. L. Rep. (CCH) ¶ 26,063 at 41,455, 41,456 (quoting from the CFTC's Statutory Interpretation Regarding Trading in Foreign Currencies for Future Delivery, 50 Fed. Reg. 42,983 (Oct. 23, 1985) (footnotes omitted in the original)).

77. CFTC v. Dunn, 58 F.3d 50 (2d Cir. 1995). *See* Joanne T. Medero, *CFTC v. Dunn/Delta: Treasury Amendment Redux,* 14 Futures Int'l L. Letter 1 (1994), which describes the statutory background, the CFTC's position, the lower court decision in *Dunn* and various other cases that were pending at the time of the article.

78. 1996 U.S. App. LEXIS 27921 (4th Cir. Oct. 29, 1996), *aff'g* 904 F. Supp. 1072 (N.D. Cal. 1995).

79. 58 F.3d at 53, referring to the decision in CFTC v. American Bd. of Trade, Inc., 803 F.2d 1242 (2d Cir. 1986), where the court had found that the Treasury Amendment's reference to transactions "in" foreign currency did not include unexercised options, although the court indicated that the exercise of a foreign currency option would be a covered "transaction in foreign currency." *Id.* The *Tauber* decision had rejected this reasoning as involving a distinction without a difference. 8 F.3d at 976.

80. 904 F. Supp. 1072 (N.D. Cal. 1995). The State of California also sought relief in the action, relying on both the CEA and the state Commodity Law, Cal. Corp. Code Section 29500 *et seq.* The court dismissed the state law claims without prejudice, declining to retain jurisdiction over those claims after the federal claims had been dismissed. *Id.*

81. The court also granted the defendants' motion for summary judgment on the claims relating to trading precious metals, since the court found that there was insufficient evidence to support the claim. *Id.* at 1077-78.

82. *Id.* at 1075-76. The statute defines "board of trade" to mean "any exchange or association, whether incorporated or unincorporated, of persons who are engaged in the business of buying or selling any commodity or receiving the same on consignment." 7 U.S.C.A. § 1a(1) (Supp. 1996).

83. *Id.* at 1075.

84. 1996 U.S. App. LEXIS 27921.

85. *Id.* at *14-15. This analysis was based on the court's observation that: (1) in adopting the Treasury Amendment, Congress was responding to a letter sent in 1974 to the Senate Committee on Agriculture and Forestry by the Acting General Counsel of the Treasury Department, where he expressed concern that amendments to the CEA's definition of "commodity" then being considered were so expansive that the term would include foreign currency and that, therefore, the over-the-counter market in foreign currency futures would fall within CFTC jurisdiction and, thereby, be disrupted; (2) Treasury's amendment, proposed with that letter, was intended to make clear that the CEA's provisions "would not be applicable to futures trading in foreign currencies . . . other than on organized exchanges," and (3) Congress adopted Treasury's proposed amendment almost verbatim, indicating on more than one occasion that it too intended to be reserving CFTC jurisdiction over foreign currency futures only to transactions on organized exchanges. *Id.*

86. *See CFTC Working with Treasury on Forex Jurisdictional Issues, Tull Says,* 28 SEC. REG. & L. REP 419 (1996).

87. For example, a bill introduced on September 28, 1996 in the House of Representatives by Rep. Ewing, H. 4276, proposes, among other amendments to the CEA, a modification to the Treasury Amendment that would clearly establish CFTC jurisdiction over OTC currency options and futures (to the extent not otherwise excluded) if marketed to members of the general public but would exclude the same transactions from the CFTC's jurisdiction to the extent they were marketed to "appropriate persons," defined to include the same categories of persons treated as such in Title V of the Futures Trading Practices Act of 1992, which is described in the next paragraph. There is no expectation that this legislation will be adopted in the remainder of the Fall 1996 legislative session, but Representative Ewing has stated that he will reintroduce it early in the 1997 session.

88. 17 C.F.R. § 35.2 (1996), effective April 30, 1993.

89. 17 C.F.R. § 35.1(b)(1) (1996). The definition tracks the definition of the same term as it existed at the time in the U.S. Bankruptcy Code. The Bankruptcy Code definition has since been expanded to include spot FX transactions, 11 U.S.C.A. § 101(53B) (Supp. 1996), but that discrepancy is irrelevant to cases like those described in this section, since conventional spot FX transactions are not commodities futures or options of the kinds that could be argued to be void under the CEA's exchange-trading requirements if conducted over the counter.

90. A complete listing of these categories of eligible swap participants (including net worth and other tests) and of the additional requirements for exempted swap agreements is included in DOCUMENTATION FOR DERIVATIVES at 12-14.

91. 58 Fed. Reg. 21,286, 21,293 (1993).

92. These requirements focus on capacity to bear the economic risks of ownership of the relevant commodity and acknowledge that capacity to take or make delivery includes bona fide contractual arrangements for delivery with and through other persons and that "passage of title and acceptance of the commodity constitutes performance under a bona fide contract regardless of whether the buyer

lifts or otherwise takes delivery of the cargo or receives pipeline delivery, or as part of a subsequent separate contract, passes title to another intermediate purchaser in a 'chain,' 'string,' or 'circle' within a 'chain.'" *Id.*

93. *Id.* at 21,294; at 21,293 n.25 the CFTC, notes that "the terms 'book out' (crude oil) and 'book transfer' (other petroleum products) are cash market terms that generally refer to the cancellation or netting of physical delivery obligations between parties, the primary purpose of which is to prevent or minimize the uneconomic movement of the physical commodity." The CFTC also sanctions other sorts of subsequent contract arrangements providing for settlement other than by physical delivery so long as the second contract "is incidental to a pre-existing bona fide Energy Contract" and "one party cannot require the other to agree in advance to the establishment of the second contract as a condition of acceptance of the initial Energy Contract." *Id.* at 21,293.

94. Section 1a(11), 7 U.S.C.A. § 1a(11) (Supp. 1996).

95. At 416 n.108 & 418 n.117, respectively.

96. A source often cited for this description of the forward contract exclusion is CFTC v. Co Petro Mktg. Group, Inc., 680 F.2d 573, 577–78 (9th Cir. 1982), where the court noted that Congress created the forward contract exclusion for needs like those of farmers who wanted to sell part of the next season's harvest at a set price to a grain elevator or miller but needed to delay delivery until the miller or elevator had capacity to store or process the wheat.

97. 55 Fed. Reg. 39,188 (1990) [hereinafter *Forward Contract Statutory Interpretation*].

98. The case in question was Transnor (Bermuda) Ltd. v. BP North American Petroleum, 738 F. Supp. 1472 (S.D.N.Y. 1990).

99. *Forward Contract Statutory Interpretation,* 55 Fed. Reg. at 39,191.

100. *Id.* In so doing, the CFTC noted that the specific transactions in question create "substantial economic risk of a commercial nature to the parties required to make or take delivery thereunder" including "the risks of demurrage, damage, theft or deterioration of the commodity as well as other risks associated with owning the commodity delivered." *Id.* The CFTC also observed that by its interpretation of the CEA it was not addressing the applicability of the exclusion to transactions involving commodities that cannot be physically delivered. *Id.* n.15.

101. Salomon Forex Inc. v. Tauber, 795 F. Supp. 768, 771 n.8 (E.D. Va. 1992), *aff'd,* 8 F.3d. 966 (4th Cir. 1993), *cert. denied,* 114 S. Ct. 1540 (1994).

102. CFTC Docket No. 95-14 (July 27, 1995).

103. 67 F.3d 766 (9th Cir. 1995).

104. MG Refining & Marketing, Inc. is referred to herein as *"MGR&M."*

105. CFTC Docket No. 95-14 at 2. Note 152 *infra* and the accompanying text describe the thrust of the proceedings brought against the other entity, MG Futures, Inc., a futures commission merchant and commodity trading advisor registered with the CFTC, approximately 98% of whose business consisted, according to the CFTC in that order instituting and settling the proceedings, of clearing futures market transactions for affiliated entities such as MGR&M.

106. *Id.* at 3.

107. *Id.* at 3–4.

108. The reference is to the CFTC's Policy Statement Concerning Swap Transactions, 54 Fed. Reg. 30,694 (July 21, 1989), establishing a "safe harbor" for certain swap transactions that the agency would not seek to treat as illegal, off-exchange futures, which was adopted before Title V gave the CFTC the power to provide an exemption from the CEA's ban on off-exchange commodity futures. On this Policy Statement, *see* DOCUMENTATION FOR DERIVATIVES at 17 and the sources cited therein.

109. This response was addressed to the Chairmen of the House Agriculture and Commerce Committees, who are reported to have expressed concern about the possible collateral effects of the CFTC's statement of the features of a futures contract and to have asked whether the CFTC continued to be of the view that swap transactions covered by the Policy Statement referred to in the preceding note will not be subject to regulation under the CEA and that the Swap Exemption does not reflect any determination that the swap agreements covered by it are subject to the CEA, since the CFTC has not made and is not obliged to make any determination that they are subject to the CEA. The question posed and portions of Chairperson Schapiro's response quoted above are described in Sec. L. Daily (BNA Jan. 10, 1996) and Joanne Morrison, *CFTC Promises Not to Regulate Swaps Like Futures,* THE BOND BUYER, Jan. 23, 1996, at 6, and are excerpted in L. Clifford Craig et al., *Legal Theories in Lawsuits Against*

Derivatives Dealers in the Over-the-Counter Markets, 1 Derivatives 1996: Avoiding the Risk and Managing the Litigation 129, 159–60 (PLI Corp. L. & Practice Course Handbook Series No. 9-931, 1996). Further detail and additional quotations from the response appear in Joanne Morrison, *CFTC Action Threatens Swaps and Derivatives, Lawmakers Say,* The Bond Buyer, Dec. 22, 1995, at 6, and *Schapiro Reaffirms CFTC Position: Agency Will Not Regulate Certain Swaps,* Sec. Reg. & L. Rep., Apr. 28, 1995, at 656.

110. The CFTC's General Counsel has stated that the MGR&M order does not "create" uncertainty in this regard but does "illustrate" the difficulties in "drawing th[e] line" between commodity forwards and futures contracts. *Futures, Forwards Demarcation Needs Examining, CFTC Lawyer Says,* Sec. Reg. & L. Rep., Nov. 17, 1995, at 1819, 1820.

111. 67 F.3d 766 (9th Cir. 1995).

112. *Id.* at 769.

113. *Id.*

114. *Id.* at 772 (quoting *Co Petro,* 680 F.2d at 579).

115. *Id.* at 773.

116. *See, e.g., Court Ruling May Bring Forwards under CFTC,* Derivatives Week, Oct. 9, 1995, at 10 (citing an ex-CFTC attorney as saying that it is customary in the commodity markets to make delivery through the transfer of title, especially in the precious metals, oil and grain markets, and assuming that the commission "did not intend this result").

117. Frank C. Puleo, *CFTC Scope of Jurisdiction a Major Factor in the Location of Developing Derivative Markets,* Derivatives, Jan.–Feb. 1996 at 124, 125–26.

118. 58 Fed. Reg. 21,286, 21,293 n.24. The CFTC had earlier recognized passage of title as an acceptable form of delivery for purposes of the forward contract exclusion in the *Statutory Interpretation on Forward Contracts,* 55 Fed. Reg. at 39, 191–92.

119. *See* p. 17 *supra.*

120. This statement, of course, assumes a party that is a legal entity rather than a natural person. The issue of capacity to contract, for a natural person, is generally decided under the law of the jurisdiction where that person is domiciled.

121. Prevailing market practice is for the parties to agree to the nonexclusive jurisdiction of the courts in a specified jurisdiction; it is unusual for the parties to agree to exclusive jurisdiction clauses under which all disputes must be resolved in a contractually specified forum. As suggested below, even if the parties have agreed on the exclusive jurisdiction of a particular forum's courts, if one of the parties nonetheless brings suit in another forum, the courts of that forum may not necessarily enforce the parties' contractual choice if doing so would operate to violate an important public policy of the forum where suit was brought. In addition, as an offensive tactic, a party fearing that a suit may be brought against it in the chosen forum may bring suit in its own jurisdiction first and then seek to have the action brought against it dismissed or stayed pending resolution of the action it brought first in its own forum. *See* the discussion of the case involving Bankers Trust International PLC and PT Dharmala Sakti Sejahtera in the part of this volume dealing with lawsuits brought in England.

122. 2 Comm. Fut. L. Rep. (CCH) ¶ 26,508 (S.D.N.Y. Aug. 16, 1995). An appeal from the decision has reportedly been withdrawn as a result of a settlement.

123. Because the court granted the defendants' motion on the basis of the choice-of-law provision, it did not reach the defendants' other grounds for dismissal, which included lack of jurisdiction and failure to state a claim upon which relief might be granted.

124. 2 Comm. Fut. L. Rep. (CCH) ¶ 26,508 at 43,299.

125. In ruling on the effect of the choice-of-law clause, the court indicated it was following Turtur v. Rothschild Registry Int'l, Inc., 26 F.3d 304 (2d Cir. 1994), and in reaching its conclusion on the adequacy of the remedies available under English law, it indicated it was bound by Roby v. Corporation of Lloyd's, 996 F.2d 1353 (2d Cir.), *cert. denied,* 114 S. Ct. 385 (1993).

126. *Id.* at 43,299–300.

127. Procter & Gamble Co. v. Bankers Trust Co., 925 F. Supp. 1270, 1288–89 (S.D. Ohio 1996). The case is discussed in detail at p. 100 *infra.* Procter & Gamble is referred to herein as *"P&G."*

128. *Id.* at 1288–89. In support of its holding on this issue, the court also cited the *Turtur* case, *supra* note 125, and a decision by the U.S. Court of Appeals for the Sixth Circuit dismissing claims under

Alabama statutes where the contract was to be governed by Michigan law, Moses v. Business Card Express, Inc., 929 F.2d 1131 (6th Cir.), *cert. denied,* 502 U.S. 821 (1991).

129. *See* Leslie v. Lloyd's of London, 1995 WL 661090 (S.D. Tex. Aug. 20, 1995), *aff'd,* 85 F.3d 625 (5th Cir. 1996), one of many U.S. cases involving disputes between Lloyd's and U.S. "Names."

130. 590 N.E.2d 587 (Ind. Ct. App. 1992).

131. "Derivative," as used here, refers to the fact that the action was brought by a shareholder on behalf of the corporation.

132. *Id.* at 589-90.

133. *Id.* at 589.

134. *Id.* at 592 (citing Aronson v. Lewis, 473 A.2d 805, 812 (Del. 1984)).

135. In this context, it is worth noting that members of senior management of Compaq Computer Corporation were alleged in a class action brought by purchasers and sellers of options on the company's stock to have known (or recklessly disregarded) that the company had not hedged in such a way as to insulate its earnings from the adverse effects of the appreciation of the U.S. dollar against currencies of European jurisdictions where it operated. *See* Amended Consolidated Complaint at 39, Compaq Securities Litigation, No. H-91-9191 (S.D. Texas filed Sept. 6, 1991). The action did not, however, seek relief on that basis; the complaint was based on alleged violations of state and federal anti-fraud provisions through, *inter alia,* concealment of adverse material facts about the company's prospects, including the fact that the disclosed rate of growth of profits and revenues from the company's European operations was due, in large part, to favorable currency translations in an environment in which products were being sold there for local currencies that had appreciably strengthened against the U.S. dollar.

136. More recently, in a case involving securities referred to by some as "derivative securities," the trustees of a pension plan subject to the Employee Retirement Income Security Act (*ERISA*) have been charged with violation of their duties to the plan under the "prudent person" rule embodied in ERISA (Section 404(a)(1)(B), U.S.C.A. § 1104(a)(1)(B) (1985 & Supp. 1996)), which in many respects is the counterpart to the business judgment rules applicable under state corporation laws. The trustees were alleged in the complaint by the Secretary of the Department of Labor to have permitted an investment manager to invest substantial plan assets in mortgage backed securities, including inverse floaters, without an adequate understanding of the securities, to have inappropriately delegated to that person their investment discretion with respect to purchases and sales of the securities, which were alleged to be overly risky and inappropriate for the plan, and to have failed to establish guidelines to be followed by the investment manager and to have monitored him and the investments properly. *See* Complaint at 8-9, Reich v. Hassenmiller, No. 396CV01514 DJS (D. Ct. filed August 7, 1996).

137. The action (No. A9401998) was brought in April 1994 in the Court of Common Pleas, Hamilton County, Ohio.

138. Complaint at 1, Drage v. Procter & Gamble (No. A9401998).

139. *Id.* at 7.

140. *Id.* at 7-8.

141. *Id.* at 8.

142. *Id.* at 5-6.

143. *Id.* at 5.

144. *Id.* at 7.

145. The court's reasons for dismissing the action are stated in a Memorandum of Decision entered January 19, 1996, and judgment was entered dismissing the action on February 27, 1996.

146. Gibson Greetings, Inc. is hereinafter referred to as *"Gibson Greetings."* Various claims and legal theories raised in a related private action brought by Gibson Greetings are discussed in notes 215, 218, 219, 221 & 228 *infra.*

147. *See* In re BT Sec. Corp., CFTC, Rel. Nos. 33-7124, 34-35136, 3-8579 (Dec. 22, 1994), and In re BT Sec. Corp., SEC, Rel. Nos. 33-7124, 34-35136, 3-8579 (Dec. 22, 1994).

148. Docket Nos. 94-082-WA/RB-BC, 94-082 WA/RB-SM, 94-082-WA/RB-HCS (Dec. 4, 1994).

149. *See BT Sec. Corp.,* 1994 WL 711224 (CFTC Dec. 22, 1994), and *BT Sec. Corp.,* Securities Act Release No. 7,124, Exchange Act Release No. 35,136 (Dec. 22, 1994) [1994-1995 Transfer Binder] Fed. Sec. L. Rep. (CCH) ¶ 85,477, at 86,109.

150. *See* p. 100 *infra.* One of the results of these inquiries was that the Bankers Trust group was required to engage independent consultants to review and make recommendations concerning such matters as its compliance policies and procedures related to the marketing, offer, sale, purchase, amendment, termination or valuation of privately negotiated OTC derivative products. The publicly available product of that process is the Executive Summary and Recommendations of the Report on the OTC Derivatives Business of Bankers Trust During 1991-1994, dated June 30, 1996.

151. Gibson Greetings, Inc., Exchange Act Release No. 36357, 7 Fed. Sec. L. Rep. (CCH) ¶ 74,245, at 63,126 (Oct. 11, 1995), Accounting and Auditing Enforcement Release No. 730.

152. As described in note 105 *supra* and accompanying text, these proceedings were settled without the respondents' admitting or denying the CFTC's allegations. According to the CFTC, MG's strategy assumed that profits could be made continuously by rolling forward a barrel-for-barrel hedge in the futures market, in which the prices of near-term contracts were higher than those for deferred contracts. The strategy failed as near-term prices dropped below those for deferred contracts, resulting in a need to fund sizable margin calls at the same time losses were being incurred as the hedges were rolled forward and (in an effort to improve operating results for the year) the size of the customer book was being increased. According to the settlement order, reports submitted to the ultimate German parent did not adequately reflect the results of these operations. As described at p. 79 *supra,* the CFTC found in its Order that the contracts with the customers were void as illegal, off-exchange futures. However, CFTC officials have stated that the CFTC viewed that finding as secondary to its focus on compliance with reporting obligations owed to the CFTC by MG Futures, which had failed to file certified financial statements and to report to the CFTC the existence of material inadequacies in its accounting system, and internal controls and procedures. The Order spells out in detail some of the internal controls and risk management procedures that will be required in the future. *See* MG Refining & Marketing, Inc., CFTC Docket No. 95-14 (July 27, 1995).

153. The swaps involved leveraged exposure to movements in, *e.g.,* Italian lira and Spanish peseta interbank interest rates and the spread between the rates paid on certain Mexican government bonds and U.S. Treasury bonds. *See* State of Wisconsin, Legislative Audit Bureau, *An Evaluation of Investment Practices of the State of Wisconsin Investment Board,* Report 95-16, Appendix III (July 1995) [hereinafter *Audit Bureau Report*].

154. Audit Bureau, Audit Bureau Report 53.

155. The Group of Thirty consists of prominent individuals from the financial area, including commercial and investment bankers, regulators and academicians from many parts of the world.

156. For example, a survey conducted in 1994 by Arthur Andersen & Co. is reported to have shown that 93% of the dealers and 84% of the end-users surveyed had caused their boards of directors to review and approve their firm's risk management policies. *See* Paul M. Moore, *The Responsibilities of Directors of Corporate End-Users of Derivatives,* 1 Derivatives Use, Trading & Regulation 389, 393 (1995). According to the *Voluntary Principles and Practices Guidelines for End-Users of Derivatives, infra* note 165, at 1, the Treasury Management Association conducted a survey that indicated, as of early 1995, that 43% of corporate end-users of derivatives had written policy guidelines covering the use of derivatives.

157. The firms are identified as CS First Boston, Goldman Sachs, Morgan Stanley, Merrill Lynch, Salomon Brothers, and Lehman Brothers.

158. Hereinafter referred to as the *"DPG Report."*

159. Hereinafter referred to as the *"Principles and Practices."*

160. They were the Emerging Markets Traders Association, the Foreign Exchange Committee of the Federal Reserve Bank of New York, ISDA, the New York Clearing House Association, the Public Securities Association and the Securities Industries Association. The published version was released after a comment period of approximately six weeks during which the drafters invited comments on a first draft released March 20, 1995.

161. Principles and Practices § 1.2.

162. *See* pp. 84–91 *infra.*

163. Principles and Practices § 3.

164. Hereinafter referred to as the *End-Users Practice Guidelines.*

165. End-Users Practice Guidelines, at 1.

166. *Id.* at 3.

167. *Id.* at 4.

168. *Id.* at 6.

169. *Id.* at 7.

170. *Id.* at 9-10.

171. *Id.* at 10-11.

172. *Id.* at 13 (emphasis in the original).

173. 12 F.3d 1045 (11th Cir. 1994), *aff'g* 127 F.R.D. 224 (S.D. Fla. 1989).

174. BankAtlantic v. Blythe Eastman Paine Webber, Inc., 955 F.2d 1467, 1470 n.2 (11th Cir. 1992).

175. Complaint at 7, BankAtlantic v. Blythe Eastman Paine Webber, Inc.

176. *See* 955 F.2d at 1471, 1476.

177. The Order of October 26, 1995, instituting and settling the proceedings in the case, 1995 WL 630924 (S.E.C.), did not include any finding that any of the municipal parties involved (the Massachusetts Water Resources Authority, the District of Columbia and the Indian Trace Community Development District in Broward County, Florida) had incurred any damage but imposed significant civil penalties on both respondents and ordered them to make restitution of significant amounts paid by the first two municipal parties on the grounds that nondisclosure of the existence of the contracts between Lazard Freres and Merrill Lynch constituted violations of Rule G-17 of the Municipal Securities Rulemaking Board, which provides that, in the conduct of its municipal securities business, each broker, dealer and municipal securities dealer, shall deal fairly with all persons and shall not engage in any deceptive, dishonest, or unfair practice. *Id.* at *5-*6. The Order describes various steps that the respondents took prior to the date of the Order to revise their policies and procedures to avoid future violations of that Rule and requires both entities to comply with their undertakings to maintain those policies and procedures. *Id.* at *9.

178. *See* p. 68 *supra.*

179. Answer and Counterclaims at 21, *Minmetals,* [1995-1996 Transfer Binder] Fed. Sec. L. Rep. (CCH) ¶ 99,001 (S.D.N.Y. 1995).

180. *Id.* at 62.

181. *Id.*

182. Answer and Counterclaims at 39-41, *Unipec*, [1995-1996 Transfer Binder] Fed. Sec. L. Rep. (CCH) ¶ 99,000 (S.D.N.Y. 1995).

183. Answer and Counterclaims at 72, *Minmetals;* Answer and Counterclaim at 41, *Unipec.*

184. Answer and Counterclaim at 72, *Minmetals.*

185. *Id.* at 73.

186. No. 96-113154 (N.Y. Sup. Ct. July 23, 1996). The plaintiff is referred to herein as *"Seita."*

187. The first swap is described in the complaint as involving a single, final exchange obligation of each of the parties, with the Seita obligation fixed at U.S.$35 million and the Salomon obligation to be calculated at 121% on the same amount for the number of days, if any, during a 358-day period in which an agreed Deutsche Mark LIBO Rate was within an agreed band. The second transaction is described initially to have operated somewhat similarly, but with the Salomon obligation, if any, to depend on the number of days in the relevant period on which the U.S. dollar/Japanese yen spot exchange rate was inside a band, and to have been revised to behave more like the DEM transaction.

188. Salomon Brothers Inc., for example, is alleged to have acted as Seita's investment advisor from late 1990 through early 1995 in connection with a $10 million investment in the Salomon Brothers EMS Strategies Fund and to have advised Seita on a short-term investment of approximately 55 million French francs in mid 1990.

189. The following summary does not attempt to distinguish between the various theories under which Seita seeks relief, which are breach of fiduciary duty, fraud, reckless misrepresentation, negligent misrepresentation and negligence, all based on the same alleged acts and omissions, and breach of contract, based on an implied contractual duty to deal with Seita fairly and in good faith and an alleged contract to immunize Seita against losses on a swap.

190. Complaint at 12-13, *Seita* (No. 96-113154).

191. *Id.* at 13.

192. *Id.* at 31. The complaint also alleges that the swaps were unauthorized, that Salomon was aware of that fact and attempted to create the illusion of due authorization, *id.* at 23-25, and that the transactions were illegal under New York's bucket-shop law, *id.* at 32.

193. *Id.* at 32.

194. *Id.* at 18.

195. *Id.* at 39. As is discussed in section 2 of this chapter, if a trade confirmation or other document expresses the parties' final agreement on their contract, an applicable parol evidence rule may be found to preclude the introduction of extrinsic evidence offered to contradict, vary or subtract from the agreement so expressed. Allegations like Seita's about oral agreements at odds with the written contract are nonetheless not unusual and may be presented within the framework of a fraud claim so as to avoid the bar to extrinsic evidence on the nature of the parties' contract that would apply under parol evidence rules within the framework of a contract claim.

196. 779 F. Supp. 741 (S.D.N.Y. 1991).

197. *Id.* at 745.

198. *Id.*

199. *Id.*

200. *Id.*

201. 785 F. Supp. 411 (S.D.N.Y. 1992). References to language in the complaint are taken from the court's opinion.

202. *Id.* at 416-17.

203. *Id.* at 417, 418 (quoting from depositions).

204. *Id.* at 418.

205. *Id.* at 427-33.

206. *Id.* at 425.

207. *Id.* at 427.

208. *Id.* at 426 (quoting from Oursler v. Women's Interart Center, Inc., 566 N.Y.S.2d 295 (App. Div. 1991), and citing National Westminster Bank, U.S.A. v. Ross, 130 B.R. 656, 679 (Bankr. S.D.N.Y. 1991), which, in turn, cites Beneficial Comm. Corp. v. Murray Glick Datsun, 601 F. Supp. 770, 772 (S.D.N.Y. 1985)).

209. 785 F. Supp. at 426.

210. *Id.* at 426 (quoting from *National Westminster,* 130 B.R. at 679 (citations omitted in original)).

211. *Id.*

212. *Id.* at 419 (quoting from Mallis v. Bankers Trust Co., 615 F.2d 80-81, and citing Grumman Allied Indus., Inc. v. Rohr Indus., Inc., 748 F.2d 729, 737 n.13 (2d Cir. 1984)).

213. *Id.*

214. *Id.* at 422.

215. BT Securities, a registered broker-dealer affiliate of Bankers Trust, was also named as a defendant. The following summary refers to two decisions issued by the court before the case was settled: one dated April 11, 1996 (the *First Order*) and the other dated May 8, 1996, the day before the settlement was reached (the *Final Order*), which is reported at 925 F. Supp. 1270 (S.D. Ohio 1996). Many of the issues decided in *Procter & Gamble* were also raised in Gibson Greetings, Inc. v. Bankers Trust Co., No. C-1-94-620 (S.D. Ohio, filed Sept. 12, 1994). That suit was settled by the parties before the issuance of any decision by the court. We will, therefore, limit our discussion of *Gibson Greetings* to an occasional footnote observing where the claims and legal theories raised were the same or similar to claims in *Procter & Gamble. See* the references at p. 87 *supra* to related enforcement and administrative proceedings involving both Gibson Greetings and the two defendants in the case, Bankers Trust and BT Securities.

216. Initially the P&G obligations were to be determined at the commercial paper rate minus 75 basis points, which was modified to CP minus 88 basis points when the parties pushed back the date at which the additional spread, if any, would be determined in accordance with a formula set out at 925 F. Supp. 1270, 1276.

217. In this respect, P&G's claims were somewhat reminiscent of the theory rejected by the court in the *Intermetals* case, p. 97 *supra,* where the defendant alleged it was to be protected against losses from FX trades above a claimed level, although the trade confirmations had no term to that effect. *See also* the description of Seita's claim that it was to be protected in its swaps with Salomon, at p. 96 *supra.*

218. Similarly, Gibson Greetings alleged that it entered into the transactions at issue in reliance on the advice and representations of BT and valuation information that was in the control of BT and BT

Securities and could not be duplicated by Gibson Greetings. The focus of these claims was that BT did not share with Gibson Greetings the information it would have required to determine whether the valuations it relied on were accurate and, therefore, could not assess the risk that was involved in the transactions. Complaint at 7-8, *Gibson Greetings* (No. C-1-94-620).

219. As in *Procter & Gamble,* the losses at issue in *Gibson Greetings* came in the wake of rate rises that began in February 1994. It appears that the CFO, after consulting with the board, agreed to new transactions in March 1994 that were intended to reduce BT's increasing exposure resulting from the unrealized losses in Gibson Greetings' positions. According to Gibson Greetings, however, it was compelled to do so by unlawful economic duress, consisting of "threats to 'tear up' Gibson Greetings' outstanding positions and their demands of immediate payment." Plaintiff's Reply to Counterclaim at 7, *Gibson Greetings* (No. C-1-94-620). This theory, claims of fraud and misrepresentation and allegations of breach of fiduciary duty were the framework for Gibson Greetings' complaint. BT contended that (as with P&G), Gibson Greetings had never indicated that it disputed the validity of those transactions; rather, it intended to benefit from them as rates declined, leading BT to expend substantial effort and incur substantial cost in hedging its position in the transactions. As a result, according to BT's position in the case, Gibson Greetings had ratified the transactions and was estopped from complaining of their terms or seeking rescission.

220. *Procter & Gamble,* 925 F. Supp. at 1289 (quoting incorrectly from Beneficial Comm. Corp. v. Murray Glick Datsun, Inc., 601 F. Supp. 770, 772 (S.D.N.Y. 1985)). The *Beneficial Commercial* court actually used the expression "business transaction" and not "business relationship."

221. *Procter & Gamble,* 925 F. Supp. at 1289. In the *Gibson Greetings* case, in its reply to BT's counterclaim for breach of contract, Gibson Greetings argued: "Contrary to Bankers Trust's characterization of the relationship . . . as 'arms-length,' Bankers Trust specifically holds itself out as uniquely capable of managing the risks of its clients, publicly representing, for example: 'We will help you deal with the risk you can't. When Bankers Trust is beside you, risk is not to be feared' . . . Gibson further states that it was a long-term relationship of trust and confidence with Bankers Trust pursuant to which Bankers Trust and BT Securities had an advisory and fiduciary relationship to Gibson. . . ." Plaintiff's Reply to Counterclaim, at 3.

222. *Procter & Gamble,* 925 F. Supp. at 1291 (quoting from Banque Arabe et Internationale d'Investissement v. Maryland Nat'l Bank, 819 F. Supp. 1282, 1293 (S.D.N.Y. 1993), *aff'd,* 57 F.3d 146 (2d Cir. 1995)).

223. *Procter & Gamble,* 925 F. Supp. at 1291 (quoting from *Banque Arabe,* 819 F. Supp. at 1293, and citing Banco Español de Crédito v. Security Pac. Nat'l Bank, 763 F. Supp. 36, 45 (S.D.N.Y. 1991)).

224. *Procter & Gamble,* 925 F. Supp. at 1291.

225. *Id.* at 1292.

226. This theory was based on an effort to extend to BT the following principle stated in Section 299A of the Restatement (Second) of Torts:

> Unless he represents that he has greater or less skill or knowledge, one who undertakes to render services in the practice of a profession or trade is required to exercise the skill and knowledge normally possessed by members of that profession or trade in good standing in similar communities.

227. *Procter & Gamble,* 925 F. Supp. at 1289. Disposition of the claims of fraud and misrepresentation would have required findings of fact at a trial and, as the court noted, in the case of the fraud claims, would have required clear and convincing evidence by P&G, and not a mere preponderance of the evidence. *Id.* at 1291.

228. *Id.* at 1291. Gibson Greetings, similarly, argued, as an affirmative defense to BT's counterclaim for breach of contract, that the covenant gave rise to an obligation of BT to provide Gibson Greetings with information that was not materially incorrect or misleading and that BT's failure to do so constituted a breach of contract that should bar BT from seeking to recover based on the contract. Plaintiff's Reply to Counterclaim at 12, *Gibson Greetings.*

229. *Procter & Gamble,* 925 F. Supp. at 1290.

230. *Id.*

231. *Id.* (citing as authority Banque Arabe et Internationale d'Investissement v. Maryland Nat'l Bank, 57 F.3d 146 (2d Cir. 1995)).

232. *Procter & Gamble,* 925 F. Supp. at 1291.

233. *See, e.g.,* In re Bennett, 154 B.R. 126, 154 (Bankr. N.D.N.Y. 1992).

234. *Banco Español,* 763 F. Supp. at 44 (citing Hartford Fire Ins. Co. v. Federated Dept. Stores, Inc., 723 F.Supp. 976, 991 (S.D.N.Y. 1989)) (alteration and citations omitted in original).

235. *Banco Español,* 763 F.Supp. at 44 (quoting from Don King Productions, Inc. v. Douglas, 742 F.Supp. 741, 767 (S.D.N.Y. 1990)).

236. 819 F. Supp. 1281 (S.D.N.Y. 1993), *aff'd,* 57 F.3d 146 (2d Cir. 1995).

237. Banque Arabe et Internationale d'Investissement v. Maryland Nat'l Bank, 57 F.3d 146, 156 (2d Cir. 1995).

238. *Id.*

239. *Id.* at 157.

240. 925 F. Supp. at 1291.

241. *Id.* at 1290.

242. *Banco Español,* 973 F.2d at 56.

243. *See* text accompanying notes 201–213 *supra.*

244. A separate question is whether the information referred to by the *Procter & Gamble* court was truly relevant to P&G's theories. If P&G's theory was that it did not know, but BT did, that the 5s/30s and DEM Swap would operate differently from the way it believed they would, the relevant information on this question was all in the confirmations of the swaps, where their terms stated P&G's initial obligations and included the formulas to be used to calculate any spread that might later increase its obligations. If P&G's theory was that it did not know, but BT did, that if P&G sought to set the spread early, its obligations would be calculated in a way that would not necessarily secure for it the below-market rates it hoped to achieve, the information the court stated should be supplied would not have helped P&G. The confirmations did not include any term on how P&G's obligations would be set in any such circumstance because the parties did not bargain for such a term. In the absence of such an agreement, BT would price an early spread setting in light of circumstances at the relevant time and its valuation of its own position in the swaps. Indicative quotations of the price BT would quote would have given P&G information about this subject, but the court made no finding about whether such quotations should have been given or whether P&G in fact requested them.

245. *Procter & Gamble,* 925 F. Supp. at 1283. The court was analyzing the definition of "security" in the Securities Act, 15 U.S.C. Section 77b(1), which includes, unless the context otherwise requires, "any note, stock, treasury stock, bond, debenture, evidence of indebtedness, certificate of interest or participation in any profit-sharing agreement, collateral trust certificate, preorganization certificate or subscription, transferable share, investment contract, voting-trust certificate, certificate of deposit for a security, fractional undivided interest in oil, gas, or other mineral rights, any put, call, straddle, option, or privilege on any security, certificate of deposit, or group or index of securities (including any interest therein or based on the value thereof), or any put, call, straddle, option, or privilege entered into on a national securities exchange relating to foreign currency, or, in general, any interest or instrument commonly known as a 'security,' or a certificate of interest or participation in, temporary or interim certificate for, receipt for, guarantee of, or warrant or right to subscribe to or purchase, any of the foregoing." The court noted the Supreme Court's guidance to the effect that the definition of "security" in the Exchange Act (15 U.S.C. § 78c(a)(10)) is virtually identical and encompasses the same instruments. *Procter & Gamble,* 925 F. Supp. at 1277 (citing Reves v. Ernst & Young, 494 U.S. 56, 61 n.1 (1989)).

246. 494 U.S. 56 (1989).

247. *Procter & Gamble,* 925 F. Supp. at 1279.

248. *Id.* (citing the *Reves* court quoting from SEC v. C.M. Joiner Leasing Corp., 320 U.S. 344, 351 (1943)).

249. *Procter & Gamble,* 925 F. Supp. at 1279 (quoting from *Banco Español,* 763 F.Supp. at 43).

250. *Procter & Gamble,* 925 F. Supp. at 1279.

251. *Id.*

252. *Id.*

253. *Id.* at 1280.

254. *Id.* at 1277 (quoting from Marine Bank v. Weaver, 455 U.S. 551, 556 (1982)).

255. *Reves,* 494 U.S. at 67.

256. *Procter & Gamble*, 925 F. Supp. at 1280.

257. *Id.* at 1278 (quoting from United Hous. Found., Inc. v. Forman, 421 U.S. 837, 852 (1975)).

258. *Id.* at 1278.

259. *Id.* at 1281–82.

260. *Id.* at 1281.

261. *Id.* (quoting from SEC v. Sloan, 436 U.S. 103 (1978) (citations omitted in original)).

262. *Id.* at 1282 (quoting from *Forman,* 421 U.S. at 852).

263. *Id.* at 1283.

264. *Id.* at 1283–84. According to the court, if the statute's language covering "any instrument evidencing a promise or an agreement to pay money" were interpreted as broadly as P&G sought, every private agreement to pay money, including such things as credit card charge slips, would fall within Ohio's securities laws, and that was not the legislative intent. *Id.* at 1284. Regarding P&G's contention that the DEM Swap fell within the statutory language including most foreign currencies as securities, the court noted that P&G cited no authority for the proposition that the DEM swap, whose value was tied to a DEM swap rate, was the equivalent of German currency for this purpose. *Id.*

265. This was P&G's claim under Section 4b(a) of the CEA, 7 U.S.C.A. § 6b(a) (Supp. 1996), which makes it "unlawful . . . (2) for any person, in or in connection with any order to make, or the making of, any contract of sale of any commodity for future delivery, made, or to be made, for or on behalf of any other person . . ." to engage in certain fraudulent conduct. The discussion appears in *Procter & Gamble,* 925 F. Supp. at 1286.

266. *Id.*

267. The provision relied on was Section 4o of the CEA, 7 U.S.C.A. § 6o (Supp. 1996).

268. *Procter & Gamble,* 925 F. Supp. at 1287. The definition includes any person who, "for compensation or profit, engages in the business of advising others . . . as to the value of or the advisability of trading in" commodity futures traded on contract markets, or subject to the rules of contract markets, designated by the CFTC for the relevant commodity, commodity options authorized for trading by CFTC rules and certain CFTC-authorized leverage transactions, as well as any person who "for compensation or profit, and as part of a regular business, issues or promulgates analyses or reports concerning" any of those kinds of transactions. 7 U.S.C.A. § 1a(5)(A) (Supp. 1996).

269. *Procter & Gamble,* 925 F. Supp. at 1287.

270. This was Section 32.9 of the CFTC Rules, 17 C.F.R. § 32.9 (1996), which makes unlawful certain fraudulent conduct "in or in connection with an offer to enter into, the entry into, or the confirmation of the execution of, any commodity option transaction."

271. *Procter & Gamble,* 925 F. Supp. at 1288.

272. *See* p. 81 *supra.*

273. *See* pp. 87–89 *supra.*

274. Principles and Practices § 4.2.

275. *Id.*

276. Principles and Practices § 5.2.

277. *Id.*

278. "Where loss scenarios are part of the information voluntarily provided to a counterparty, or where loss scenarios are prepared at a counterparty's request and the counterparty does not stipulate some or all of the assumptions to be used in making the calculations, the Participant should attempt in good faith to use assumptions that provide information that is reasonable under the circumstances." Principles and Practices § 5.4.

279. DPG Report 37 ("Counterparty Relationships").

280. *Id.*

281. The enforcement and administrative proceedings involving Gibson Greetings and the two defendants in the case, Bankers Trust and BT Securities, are discussed at p. 87 *supra.* Various claims and legal theories raised by Gibson Greetings are discussed in notes 215, 218, 219, 221, & 228 *supra.*

282. The quality of the disclosure included in various periodic reports filed by Gibson Greetings with the SEC was also at issue in proceedings, described briefly at p. 87 *supra,* that the SEC brought against

senior Gibson Greetings management and that were settled without management's affirming or denying the SEC's findings that the disclosure was misleading.

283. Hereinafter referred to as *Sallie Mae.*

284. No. 94-CV-445 (S.D. Ohio filed July 1, 1994).

285. Section 10(b) of the Exchange Act and Rule 10b-5 thereunder, which prohibit the use of the means and instrumentalities of interstate commerce, among other things, to employ any device, scheme or artifice to defraud in connection with the sale of a security, including, under Rule 10b-5, the making of any untrue statement of a material fact and the omission of a material fact necessary in order to make the statements made, in light of the circumstances in which they were made, not misleading.

286. *See p. 87 supra.*

287. No. SA 94-22272 JR, Adv. No. SA 96 01625 JR, Bankr. C.D. Cal.

288. No. SA 94-22272 JR, Adv. No. SA 95 1045 JR, Bankr. C.D. Cal.

289. The *Merrill Lynch* case has been designated 96-CV-113; the *Sallie Mae* case, as 96-CV-766.

290. Alternative claims for relief are expressed in the complaint by Orange County as trustee for certain governmental entities and others whose funds were invested by Orange County pursuant to the investment strategy described above. Under the order approving the settlement of their claims against the County, certain of claims of those entities against third parties were assigned to Orange County.

291. There were also allegations related to "reverse to maturity" transactions involving some of the securities between Orange County, on the one hand, and Merrill Lynch or another counterparty, on the other, and the complaint does not specify what portion of the damages figure was allocable to those transactions and what portion to the claims related to the swaps.

292. As in the Sallie Mae complaint, there were also alternative claims for relief by Orange County as trustee. *See* note 290 *supra.*

293. The current FASB proposal, ACCOUNTING FOR DERIVATIVE AND SIMILAR FINANCIAL INSTRUMENTS AND FOR HEDGING ACTIVITIES, Proposed Statement of Financial Accounting Standards No. 162-B (Financial Accounting Standards Bd. 1996)(exposure draft), has met with significant disapproval. *See, e.g.,* Suzanne McGee, *Derivative Dealers Attack Proposals For Disclosure and Accounting Changes,* WALL ST. J., Sept. 25, 1996, at C16.

294. Proposed Amendments to Require Disclosure of Accounting Policies for Derivative Financial Instruments and Derivative Commodity Instruments and Disclosure of Qualitative and Quantitative Information About Market Risk Inherent in Derivative Financial Instruments, Other Financial Instruments and Derivative Commodity Instruments, [1995–1996 Transfer Binder] FED. SEC. L. REP. (CCH) ¶ 85,716 (proposed Dec. 28, 1995), *supplemented,* [1995–1996 Transfer Binder] FED. SEC. L. REP. (CCH) ¶ 85,750 (Apr. 9, 1996).

295. *See* ANTHONY C. GOOCH & LINDA B. KLEIN, DOCUMENTATION FOR LOANS, ASSIGNMENTS AND PARTICIPATIONS 247–61 & 264–96 (Euromoney Publications 1996).

DERIVATIVES LITIGATION IN CANADA
Margaret E. Grottenthaler

Fortunately for Canadian market participants, Canada is not a hotbed of derivatives litigation. No Canadian court has yet ruled on or considered any aspect of the enforceability of OTC derivative transactions. There have, however, been a few instances where derivative transactions have come into contact with the judicial process.

Of most immediate interest is a recent pending proceeding against financial advisor Nesbitt Burns by one of its clients seeking damages for losses incurred in options trading. So far only pleadings have been exchanged, but a review of the statements of claim and defense illustrates the type of claims that will typically be asserted under Canadian law.

The most prominent proceedings to date are the Ontario proceedings with respect to the insolvency of Confederation Life Insurance Company (CLIC) and its financing subsidiary, Confederation Treasury Services Limited (CTSL). The treatment of derivatives transactions in these proceedings received a great deal of attention at the time, but as will be discussed below, they are probably of little significance in Canada today given legislative reform. There is, however, one very recent decision arising out of the CLIC proceeding which should be of continuing interest.

Finally, there is an interesting case from the Manitoba courts dealing with the issue of the extent to which an insured must disclose to its insurer that it engages in derivatives trading.

Ukrainian (Fort William) Credit Union Limited, (In Liquidation) v. Nesbitt, Burns Limited, Zanewycz and Pilot, Proceedings Commenced November 8, 1995 in the Ontario Court (General Division)

The statements of claim and defense in the *Ukrainian (Fort William) Credit Union* case illustrate the various theories of liability that are most likely to be raised in Canadian litigation against a financial adviser for losses incurred in derivatives trading. The plaintiff in the case is a small financial cooperative that carried on business in a Northwestern Ontario city (the Credit Union). Its membership was largely made up of members of the Ukrainian community. The suit has been commenced by the liquidator of the Credit Union, namely the Deposit Insurance Corporation of Ontario (formerly the Ontario Savings and Deposit Insurance Corporation) (DICO). The defendants are the brokerage firm of Nesbitt, Burns Inc. (Nesbitt) and two of its employees, one a registered advisor (Zanewycz) and the other the manager of the local retail branch operation (Pilot). The Credit Union allegedly suffered significant losses primarily under option contracts, which eventually lead to the institution's financial collapse. The plaintiff has based its claim for damages of $8 million Cdn. on the defendants' breach of fiduciary duty, breach of contract, and negligence.

According to the claim, at the inception of their relationship, Nesbitt and the Credit Union engaged in a conservative investment program involving primarily investments in low-risk instruments, such as Canadian treasury bills. The Credit Union alleges that it was approached by Zanewycz, the defendant advisor, to develop a more profitable investment strategy which would deal with low-risk investments offering a stable rate of return. The proposed investment strategy primarily involved purchasing and selling put and call options on Government of Canada bonds that were listed on the Montreal Exchange.

As is to be expected with this type of litigation, the basic theory of the Credit Union's case is that it was an unsophisticated party that relied on the advice of Nesbitt and Zanewycz and that it did not understand the risk of loss that it faced with these types of "inappropriate" transactions. Lack of suitability of the transactions for a small community-based credit union is the primary ground upon which all three causes of action are based. Among the particular allegations supporting the claim that the plaintiff's trading account was mismanaged by the defendant in breach of the account agreement, in breach of fiduciary duty, and giving rise to a claim in negligence are that:

- The financial instruments purchased were of lower quality and higher risk than was prudent for a credit union subject to the investment restrictions of the *Credit Unions and Caisse Populaires Act.*
- There was inadequate disclosure to the Credit Union of the risks associated with the transactions and other facts material to the handling of the accounts.
- Nesbitt entered into an excessive number of transactions taking into account the nature of the business, the investment objectives, the statutory restrictions and the size of its accounts.
- Nesbitt knew or should have known that the Credit Union could not sustain the type of loss that was possible with the transactions that were entered into.
- Zanewycz misrepresented to the plaintiff that it was lawful for it to participate in option transactions. The illegality referred to appears to be a breach of the statutory requirement that credit unions not commit an aggregate amount exceeding 5% of its unimpaired capital, deposit and reserves in securities (including option contracts) and the statutory obligation to invest prudently.
- Nesbitt allowed the plaintiff to operate a margin agreement that it should have known conflicted with the terms of a General Security Agreement to which the credit union had entered into with the Province of Ontario.
- That Zanewycz's attempts to explain the transactions to the Credit Union's board of directors were incompetent and at the least should have made it clear that they were not understood by the board.
- Failure to specifically explain that a participant in options contracts should not purchase an option unless it is able to sustain a total loss of the premium and the commission charges for purchasing the option and should not write an option unless it is able to sustain substantial financial loss or unless, in the case of a call, it owns the underlying security.
- Failure to ensure that the Credit Union's personnel were properly authorized to transact business in the Credit Union's account and that Nesbitt should have reviewed the plaintiff's corporate charter or by-laws as required by the by-laws of the Montreal Exchange.

The Credit Union is expected to rely heavily on the "suitability" and "know your client" obligations imposed on registered investment dealers by Ontario securities laws, as well as comparable provisions in stock and futures exchange and the Investment Dealers Association's rules.

In its vigorous and extensive defense, Nesbitt paints quite a different picture. It alleges that the Credit Union's treasurer, Kozyra, was not only properly authorized by board resolution to engage in options trading, but was experienced and extremely knowledgeable regarding options trading. Some of the documentation and correspondence cited in the defense appears to support these statements. It also appears that the Credit Union executed the required account applications and agreements, most of which acknowledge its full capacity to engage in the trading, including margin trading, and its understanding of the risks of such trading, including trading in uncovered options. The defense further alleges that all trading was done only with the express instructions of the Credit Union. It also alleged that during a number of the years that it engaged in the options trading, the Credit Union achieved significant financial success which may have been due in part to its hedging strategy.

Nesbitt places the responsibility for ensuring the appropriateness and lawfulness of the trading on the credit union regulators. It alleges that each of the regulators was well aware of the trading and permitted it to continue for several years without any indication that they considered it inappropriate. In 1993 certain of the regulators asked to be informed of the policies and procedures which the Credit Union had in place and indicated some concern with "speculative" options trading, but took no action of any kind to stop it. In fact, the Credit Union appears to have responded to any regulatory inquiries with a vigorous defense of the prudency of its hedging strategy. Nesbitt relied on this implicit approval by the regulators of the Credit Union's activities. The Credit Union's statutorily mandated Supervisory Committee had reported to the Director of Credit Unions and to DICO that there were no deficiencies in the financial management of the Credit Union and the defendants allege that they relied on this report in dealing with the Credit Union. The defendants also claim that they relied on the fact that DICO was aware of the options trading and until several years had passed had not indicated in any way that it considered the trading inappropriate, unlawful or contrary to any agreements. As DICO is the liquidator of the Credit Union, it is now, according to the defendants, estopped from asserting that the trading was improper. Similar arguments are made with respect to the director of Credit Unions.

DICO apparently became more concerned about the short selling of bonds by credit unions generally in 1994 and threatened legal action unless the Credit Union stopped engaging in the practice. DICO later changed its position and said that the Credit Union could engage in issuing call or put options if it could clearly be shown to be hedging a current exposure. Nesbitt alleges that it is this intervention by DICO that caused the Credit Union's losses. After being unable to respond to a margin call in June 1994, DICO assumed management of the Credit Union and Nesbitt alleges that DICO's representatives caused the losses to occur by their own inadequate management of the account. Nesbitt has, in fact, asserted a third party claim against DICO claiming contribution and indemnity.

If this case proceeds to trial, the outcome will largely depend upon the facts. Although it is dangerous to make any predictions based only on a review of the pleadings, I venture to suggest that the plaintiff will have a great deal of difficulty in proving its case. In any event, in addition to some interesting factual issues, the judge in this case will have to deal with a few significant legal issues, including:

- The extent of a financial advisor's duty to its client to advise of the risks where the client is a regulated entity subject to statutory requirements of prudency.
- The extent to which a financial advisor can rely on contractual acknowledgments of risk and risk disclosure statements.
- The role and responsibility of financial institution regulators with respect to this type of trading.

The Confederation Life Insolvency, Ontario Proceedings Commenced August, 1994

The insolvency of the CLIC corporate group gave rise to two different but concurrent insolvency proceedings. Because of its status as a life insurance company, CLIC was subject to a liquidation proceeding under the *Winding-Up Act* (Canada). Its financing subsidiary, CTSL, was subject to a debtor in possession restructuring regime pursuant to the *Companies' Creditors Arrangement Act* (Canada) (CCAA). The court order in each proceeding included a stay on the termination of derivatives transactions, but each order was in quite different terms.

The CLIC Proceeding

The Winding-Up Order. The Superintendent of Financial Institutions had been monitoring matters at CLIC throughout 1994 and, in order to protect policyholders and other creditors, the Superintendent eventually took action. First, the federal Minister of Finance made an order under the *Insurance Companies Act* (Canada) permitting the Superintendent to take control of CLIC's assets. This appointment constituted a bankruptcy event of default under derivatives master agreements entered into by CLIC and as this order did not stay any contractual or other rights against CLIC, counterparties took the position that their agreements had terminated or could be terminated in accordance with their contractual rights. Very shortly after the order referred to was made, the Attorney-General of Canada brought an application to liquidate CLIC under the *Winding-Up Act.* The winding-up order restrained any parties to contracts with CLIC from exercising any right of termination, including rights arising under any "swap contract" or "derivatives transaction" triggered by the occurrence of any default or non-performance by CLIC or the filing of the winding-up proceedings or any allegation contained in the proceeding.

The Canadian Bankers Association Motion. Because counterparties had already terminated at the time the winding-up order was granted, it had no practical effect (subject to the Citibank proceeding discussed below). Nevertheless, members of the Canadian banking community were somewhat concerned by the unprecedented wording of the order. Until this time, insolvency advisors had generally been quite confident in advising that termination and netting rights were effective in a winding-up proceeding. The members of the Canadian Banker's Association were so concerned about the terms of the order that they brought a motion in the proceeding to set aside those parts of it relating to derivatives transactions. The judge that granted the order refused, however, to hear the motion on the basis that the Canadian Banker's Association lacked standing.

One can cite many reasons why the CLIC stay order was inappropriate and made without a legal basis. However, the point is now moot. In direct response to this unfortunate precedent, the federal government amended the *Winding-Up Act* [now the *Winding-Up and Restructuring Act*] to expressly provide that termination and netting rights under a very wide list of derivatives transactions, master agreements, and master master agreements are enforceable notwithstanding any order made under this Act.

The Citibank Application. Another application was brought by Citibank Canada (Citibank) seeking an order permitting it to set-off an amount held in a Citibank term deposit against obligations owed by CLIC to Citibank under, among other things, swap transactions and bond option agreements. The main issue on the application was whether Citibank was entitled to set-off against its obligation under a term deposit held by CLIC. Citibank relied on the statutory right of set-off under s.73 of the *Winding-Up Act* (now the *Winding-Up and Restructuring Act*). There was no general right of contractual set-off in either the deposit agreement, the bond option agreements or the swap agreements. Section 73 provides that the law of set-off applies in a winding-up proceeding. The reference to the law of set-off is generally understood to refer to legal set-off (i.e., the set-off of mutual liquidated claims) and equitable set-off (i.e., the set-off of fundamentally related claims whether or not they are mutual or liquidated), but arguably also refers to contractual rights of set-off. Among the issues argued were:

- Whether Citibank, as the nondefaulting party, was entitled to terminate the bond option agreements given that there was no master agreement (and, therefore, no express right of termination) by reason of CLIC's insolvency.
- If Citibank was entitled to terminate, whether it was entitled to use the ISDA method of calculating damages in the absence of a master agreement.
- Whether Citibank was entitled to set-off the net termination amounts calculated with respect to the bond option agreements and the swap agreements against the term deposit.

Among the requested relief was a declaration that an "Event of Default" pursuant to section 5(a) of the Interest Rate and Currency Exchange Agreements between CLIC and Citibank (an 1987 ISDA form of agreement) (the "CLIC Swap Agreement") and between CTSL and Citibank (the "CTSL Swap Agreement") had occurred on and was continuing on August 11, triggering an "Early Termination Date" immediately prior to the commencement of proceedings by CTSL pursuant to the CCAA. CLIC and Citibank had entered into four swap transactions. Citibank learned of the CTSL proceedings on August 12, took the position that the CLIC Swap Agreement had been terminated by reason of the admissions of insolvency in the CTSL materials and by reason of the anticipated appointment of the Superintendent to take control of CLIC and obtained the five required quotes from Reference Market Makers. The CLIC liquidator disputed that there had been an insolvency event of default; it argued that the materials filed in the CTSL CCAA proceeding did not admit the insolvency of CLIC and that the commencement of the CTSL CCAA proceedings was not, in and of itself, an Event of Default. The liquidator's alternative position was that if the CLIC Swap Agreement termination provisions were triggered, then they were contrary to public policy on the basis that they offended the principle of equitable and rateable distribution among creditors by granting a preference to Citibank as a creditor of CLIC. Further, it was argued that the damages calculation was not a liquidated amount as is required for a legal set-off as was indicated by the fact that the quotations received were widely divergent.

Although there was no master agreement with respect to the bond option agreements, Citibank treated the bond option agreements as having been terminated on August 11 by reason of the public declaration of insolvency implied by the Superintendent's statement of intention to take control of and potentially liquidate CLIC. Citibank took the position that when the winding-up order was made in respect of CLIC, its inability to honor its obligations both practically (due to its admission of insolvency on August 11) and legally (due to the winding-up order being made and the requirement of the Act that it cease carrying on business and liquidate its assets so as to meet claims of creditors) was made known and constituted a repudiation of the contracts. It went into the marketplace to seek quotations from five market dealers for replacement transactions and valued its damages based on those quotations. The parties had intended to enter into an ISDA form of agreement with respect to the bond option agreements, but had not done so at the time of the proceeding because of a few unresolved issues. The bond option agreements themselves called for an averaging of three quotes from three specified dealers upon expiry, but did not contain valuation mechanics that applied in a default situation.

The liquidator took the position that Citibank's right to payment under the bond option agreements was contingent and, therefore, could not be set-off. The obligation was said to be contingent because Citibank's right to payment was dependent, not merely on Citibank waiting until the Option Expiry Date, but also on the happening of an uncertain and contingent event, namely that the market price of the underlying security (a U.S. T-Bill) was less than the Strike Price on the Option Expiry Date. The liquidator further argued that it was not appropriate to imply a termination provision into the bond option agreements because there was insufficient evidence that such a term was consistent with custom and usage in this industry, the agreements themselves did not provide for termination and, at law, liquidation does not constitute grounds for termination. Finally, the liquidator argued that the claims were not liquidated (as required for a legal set-off) because they involved subjective calculations of damages. Relied on in support of this contention was the fact that the market quotes obtained by Citibank varied by as much as 33%.

CLIC had also guaranteed the liabilities of CTSL under a 1987 ISDA form of master agreement. Four transactions were outstanding at the time of the proceedings, two of which were in the money and two of which were out of the money. Citibank took the position that the CTSL transactions were automatically terminated by virtue of the CCAA proceedings (discussed below) and claimed to set-off the net amount against the obligations under the term deposit. The liquidator took the position that the CTSL swap obligations were contingent and not liquidated amounts at the date of the insolvency and that the guarantee obligation of CLIC was further contingent on notice of default being given at the date of the order. The winding-up order itself prohibited the giving of any such notice to CLIC. With respect to the notice issue, Citibank counterargued that this notice was for the purpose of allowing CLIC to cure a CTSL default and since CLIC was in liquidation there was no possibility that it could do so and, therefore, no requirement to give the notice. In any event, Citibank claimed to have provided notice on numerous occasions, including by means of copying the liquidator on the proof of claim filed in the CTSL proceedings.

Justice Blair denied Citibank's set-off claim. He treated the case as basically a set-off case. He began his analysis by stating that no question of contractual set-off existed. It is not clear whether the "law of set-off" referred to in s.73 of the *Winding-Up Act* includes only what are known as legal and equitable set-offs. By mentioning contractual set-off in the way that he did it is arguable that he impliedly recognized that contractual set-off is effective in a liquidation. However, this is probably reading too much into Justice Blair's statement.

The only serious basis for asserting set-off was legal set-off, namely the set-off off mutual liquidated debts. This set-off was denied on the basis that Citibank's claim was one sounding in damages; it was not a debt claim and it was not liquidated. In explaining that the claim was not a debt claim Justice Blair wrote:

> *Set-off does not exist for a claim that sounds in damages. Here, Confederation Life is being held to task—as a result of its insolvency and the winding-up Order—for not being in a position to honor its obligations under those agreements when they*

would later fall due. Because of this effective repudiation of future obligations, Citibank argues, the agreements have been terminated and it is entitled to go out into the market and replace the hedging instruments which have been lost as a result of the Confederation Life situation. These claims, in my opinion, sound in damages. The fact that the parties may have provided a formula in the contract for calculating the damages in such circumstances, or that an industry standard may generate a similar formula, does not alter the nature of the claim. Confederation Life's obligation under the Bond Option Agreements to pay the difference between the Strike Price and the T-Bill Price on the Option Expiry Date—if, indeed it turned out that such an obligation had been incurred—would be a debt; its obligation to reimburse Citibank for the cost of replacing the Bond Option Agreement as a hedging instrument as a result of its anticipatory breach of that agreement through insolvency and liquidation, gives rise to a claim for damages. As such the claim is not properly the subject of a set-off at law.

A similar analysis applies with respect to the Swap Agreements.

Later on he explained why the ISDA type formula did not give rise to a "liquidated" claim:

Calculation of the amount of a claim by means of a formula itself is not sufficient to constitute the claim a liquidated one—whether the formula emerges from a "termination methodology" which is standard in the industry, or from the contract in question between the parties, as it is said to do here. The technique used here was essentially the same with respect to both the bond option agreements and the swap agreements. However, the gathering of a number of quotations from specified or recognized experts and the averaging of those quotations according to some methodology for purposes of developing a sum payable depends upon the underlying opinion of the experts which is, in turn, based upon their assessment of any number of diverse factors at play in the bond option or swap agreement markets. It is not enough that at the end of the exercise a sum has been arrived at through the calculation. Where the ingredients of the formula depend upon the circumstances of the case and are fixed by opinion or assessment—as they are here—the characteristics of a liquidated amount are not present. Moreover, reasonableness is not a factor when determining whether a sum is liquidated or not.

Although the court denied Citibank's set-off claim, it did not take issue with the appropriateness of the ISDA method of assessing damages. Nor did it find that Citibank was not entitled to terminate by virtue of the commencement of the insolvency proceedings. However, having denied the set-off on the basis that the claims were not liquidated, the court did not have to directly address any of the other issues that were argued.

The CTSL Order

Of much more concern at the time was the order made by Justice Houlden in the CTSL proceeding. It dealt with derivatives contracts in a more detailed way; a reflection of the fact that they were a significant aspect of CTSL's business. The terms of the order dealing with derivatives were somewhat complicated and on their face it was difficult to determine exactly what CTSL's motivation was in framing the order as it did. In hindsight it appears that CTSL sought to achieve two purposes; one, to buy some time to review its derivatives contracts and effect an orderly termination and, two, to prevent parties from relying on limited two way payment (or walk away) clauses in those cases where the agreements contained such a term. CTSL would probably consider that it succeeded in its first purpose and that it partially succeeded in its second purpose. The terms of the order are of some interest.

General Restraint on Termination. The CTSL order restrained the right of any contracting party to assert or exercise any right of termination or other remedy available to it under what was defined as a Derivatives Contract. The term Derivatives Contract was inaccurately defined as a "swap contract, hedging contract, repurchase agreement, option contract relating to the price or value of a security, commodity, currency, interest or exchange rate, or on [*sic.*] index of any such securities, commodity currency, rate, or any other contract commonly referred to as a derivatives contract." Noteworthy is the fact that a master agreement relating to any such an agreement was not listed.

CTSL took the position that this stay prevented reliance by the counterparty on any automatic termination provision. However, arguably reliance on the automatic termination provision did not fit the wording of the order; it was not a "remedy" and did not constitute the assertion, enforcement or exercise of a "right" of termination. Termination required no positive act on the part of the counterparty; it was not a "right" vested in one party or the other. This ambiguity and the fact that there is an argument that the court lacked jurisdiction to grant such a stay order led counterparties to question whether the order operated to prevent automatic termination. There was also a question as to whether it could possibly have any effect on counterparties outside of the court's jurisdiction. Some counterparties took the position that automatic termination had occurred; others that it had been stayed. All, no doubt, were anxious in the initial period as to whether they had adopted the correct position. The timing issues that the uncertainty created are discussed next.

A 22(a) Notice. Notwithstanding the general restraint, the order permitted a party to terminate a Derivatives Contract with CTSL in certain circumstances. The first was a default by CTSL in making any regularly scheduled or periodic payment under "any of the Derivatives Contracts" between CTSL and the party. The second was if the counterparty received a notice from the Monitor within seven days of August 11, notifying it that CTSL would not honor its obligations pursuant to "one or more of the Derivatives Contracts" between CTSL and the counterparty. This was referred to as a 22(a) notice (since the permission to send such a notice was found in paragraph 22(a) of the CTSL Order). If the counterparty received such a notice, then it had to pay the settlement amount, if any, that would be payable under this contract as if CTSL was *not* considered to be a defaulting party under the contract.

A 22(b) Notice. A third circumstance in which a counterparty was entitled to terminate was set out in paragraph 22(b). In addition to the above grounds of termination, the order permitted CTSL to send a notice to the counterparty providing the counterparty with the "opportunity" to terminate "all of" the Derivatives Contracts between the counterparty and CTSL upon making payment of the "settlement amount" owing thereunder to CTSL. Unlike the case with paragraph 22(a), this paragraph did not expressly state that the settlement amount was to be calculated as if CTSL was not a defaulting party. If the counterparty did not take advantage of this opportunity to terminate within three days of such service, CTSL was permitted to assign its rights *and* its obligations under all of its Derivatives Contracts with the counterparty to any assignee with a credit rating of A or higher (an S&P rating or a rating of any other major rating agency). This assignment right applied notwithstanding any provision in the contract to the contrary. CTSL did send 22(b) notices to several counterparties, but did not purport to assign any Derivatives Contracts to any counterparties.

A 22(c) Notice. Finally, the order gave to CTSL the right to "enforce any of its [termination] rights under any Derivative Contract" and to become entitled to any payment "as a defaulting party." CTSL sent letters to various counterparties, referred to as 22(c) notices, purporting to exercise its termination rights.

Cherry Picking. A question that arose from the terms of the order was whether it permitted CTSL to cherry-pick transactions; bringing some to an end and keeping others in place. Because the definition of Derivatives Contract did not refer to a master agreement and because there were references to "any of" and "one or more of" the Derivatives Contracts in some places and references to "all of the" Derivatives Contracts in others, there was some fear that transactions could be dealt with individually. CTSL however, made no attempt to cherry pick and it did not appear that the terms of the order were drafted with the intention of permitting it to do so.

Limited Two-Way Payments. As stated above, a 22(a) notice allowed a counterparty to terminate and calculate the settlement amount so long as it treated CTSL as if it was not a defaulting party. Apparently this term was intended to prevent a counterparty from enforcing a so-called limited two-way payments or walk-away clause. CTSL was a party to a number of master agreements that had not altered the limited two-way payments provision. Although it is not clear, this provision of the order may also have been intended to allow CTSL to do its own calculations of the settlement amount even though it was the party in default; CTSL did obtain its own quotes in certain situations. It appears, however, that only a few counterparties received 22(a) notices.

Even though paragraph 22(b) of the Order did not specifically state that the calculation of the settlement amount was to be made on the basis that CTSL was not a defaulting party, in the 22(b) notices which it sent to various counterparties, CTSL took the position that this was how the calculation was to be made. In this way it also attempted to use 22(b) notices to avoid the limited two-way payments clause.

Another way in which CTSL attempted to avoid the limited two-way payments provision was simply to keep the agreements in effect. One counterparty, CCG Equipment Limited, which did not receive any notice permitting it to terminate and that had a limited two-way payments clause in it agreement brought a motion to challenge the proprietary of the Order and to permit it to terminate. Extensive affidavits sworn by U.S. derivatives experts were filed in support of each side's position and cross-examinations on the affidavits too place, but the motion was not brought to a hearing as the parties were able to settle the dispute. CCG was permitted to terminate and ended up paying an amount, but a significantly lesser amount than it would have owed in the absence of the limited two-way payments clause. Consequently, it remains the case in Canada that there is no judicial authority directly on the issue of the enforceability of limited two-way payments.

Timing and Valuation Issues. Many, if not most, counterparties received a 22(c) notice. This paragraph allowed CTSL to enforce any of its termination rights under any Derivative Contract. The obvious comment on this paragraph was that given that CTSL was the defaulting party, CTSL had no "right" to terminate. Nevertheless, CTSL it took the position, although not with all counterparties, that the order had given rise to automatic termination as of August 11 and that CTSL, therefore, had a right to treat the agreement as having terminated. Many counterparties received a notice from CTSL, ostensibly pursuant to this paragraph of the order, to the effect that it was terminating as of August 11. Unfortunately, these notices were received on August 15 or later at which time many had not treated the agreements as having terminated given the terms of the stay in the Order. Consequently, they had not removed or replaced hedges as of August 11. CTSL appeared insensitive to the significance of the timing issue and did not seem to see any inconsistency in taking the position with some parties that automatic termination had occurred while taking the opposite position with other counterparties. Those counterparties who received 22(c) notices and who had treated the order as not staying automatic termination turned out to have adopted the position most consistent with CTSL's. The 22(c) notices gave rise to several disputes between counterparties who had not terminated as of August 11 and CTSL as to the appropriate date of termination. Also, CTSL in many cases prepared its own quotes, which gave rise to disputes about valuation. It appears that most of these issues have been settled.

There is at the time of writing this chapter a Bill pending before Parliament that will amend the CCAA to expressly permit termination and close-out netting of derivatives transactions. Hopefully, by the time you are reading this, the legislation will be law.

Xcan Grain Ltd. v. Canadian Surety Company, [1995] 5 W.W.R. 730 (Man. Q.B.) Affirmed on Appeal, [1996] 1 W.W.R. 560 (Man. C.A.)

And now for something completely different—*Xcan Grain Ltd.* dealt with the issue of whether an insured makes a material nondisclosure where in applying for fidelity insurance coverage it does not disclose that it trades in derivatives.

An insurer that had insured Xcan Grain Ltd. with respect to its employees' dishonesty argued that the policy was void on the basis that Xcan did not disclose that it engaged in trading on commodities futures exchanges. Xcan was in the business of buying grain from pools and marketing the grain. To hedge against price risk, it traded extensively on commodities exchanges. In response to the question on the application for coverage with respect to the business of the insured, Xcan answered that it was a grain merchant, but did not mention its commodities trading activities. This was the first time that this insurer had provided fidelity insurance to a grain merchant and the insurer did not understand that grain merchants engaged in commodities trading. Had it known, then it would have declined to cover the risk; in other words, the activity was material to the risk. However, the court held that the disclosure obligation of an insured does not extend to facts which a reasonably competent underwriter is presumed to know and a reasonably competent underwriter of a grain merchant business would know that grain merchants universally engaged in such trading.

DERIVATIVES LITIGATION IN AUSTRALIA
JAMIE HUTCHINSON

Australia has seen a relatively small amount of litigation dealing specifically with derivatives. No doubt this will change in time. The cases form a fairly eclectic group and certainly do not cover all issues relevant to a person operating in the area. The law made in cases which have nothing to do with derivatives can be equally relevant to the area of derivatives and fill a gap where there has not yet been a case the facts of which relate to derivatives. This paper reviews some of the more significant derivatives litigation in Australia.

It is not just case-made law that is relevant for derivatives. The laws regulating derivatives are a mixture of legislation and case made law. Relevant legislation includes:

- Companies legislation which regulates various activities in connection with "futures contracts," "securities," and "prescribed interests."
- Legislation dealing with gaming and betting contracts and with insurance contracts.
- Legislation dealing with the powers of different types of entities to enter into contracts.
- Legislation dealing with misleading and deceptive conduct (e.g., the Commonwealth Trade Practices Act).
- Legislation dealing with insolvency.

This chapter refers briefly to some of the relevant legislation where it is necessary to give a framework to the cases discussed. However, the focus of the chapter is cases not legislation.

Generally Australian derivatives litigation has fallen into two categories:

- *Regulatory Litigation.* These are cases involving the regulation of derivatives by legislation. The main group of these cases has examined whether particular derivatives transactions are "futures contracts" for the purposes of the Corporations Law and the consequences of this. Later parts of this chapter review regulatory derivatives litigation.
- *The rest.* So far, there has only been a relatively small amount of litigation in Australia involving nonregulatory issues. No doubt more will come. Parts 2 and 3 look at some of the more interesting general derivatives litigation we have seen to date.

The Australian Legal System

Federal System

Australia has a federal legal system. The states and main territories are New South Wales, Victoria, Queensland, Western Australia, South Australia, Tasmania, the Australian Capital Territory, and the Northern Territory.

---

[1] This paper is designed to give an overview of some of the more significant derivative litigation we have seen in Australia to date. It reviews a selection of derivatives cases. It does not review every derivatives case we have seen in Australia. Nor does it review all laws (whether case law or legislation) that are relevant to derivatives. The outline of facts for cases are based on the case reports.

This paper is not intended to be an opinion which can be relied on in actual transactions or other real life situations. It is not a substitute for appropriate legal advice. The author accepts no liability for any losses suffered by any person arising from this paper or any errors or omissions in it.

Each of these states and territories has its own government, its own laws and its own court system. In addition, the Commonwealth (or federal) government makes laws that apply throughout Australia. There is also a federal system of courts.

Under the Australian constitution, the Commonwealth has a list of enumerated powers. For the Commonwealth to be able to make a law, the law must fit within one of the powers in this list. If it does not, the law is unconstitutional. On more than one occasion this has caused the Commonwealth government to be quite creative in searching for a head of power under the constitution to justify an action it has wanted to take. For example, some years ago the Commonwealth government wanted to prevent a hydro-electricity dam that would have devastated a wilderness area from being built in Tasmania. No power with respect to hydro-electricity was listed in the constitution. However, the Commonwealth does have the power to make laws relating to foreign affairs and had entered into an international treaty relating to the preservation of the environment. The Commonwealth was able to successfully rely on the foreign affairs head of power to justify it stopping the building of the dam.[1]

With a few exceptions, the states and territories on the other hand have the power to make laws on any issue they want, including issues on which the Commonwealth can also make laws. This can lead to a conflict between valid Commonwealth and valid state laws. The general position under the constitution is that if there is a true inconsistency between laws of a state or territory and laws of the Commonwealth, the laws of the Commonwealth prevail.

This means that in any given area (including derivatives) it is normally necessary to consider both Commonwealth and state laws. Sydney and Melbourne are the main financial centers in Australia, so that it is the state laws of New South Wales and Victoria, together with Commonwealth legislation, that have at least until now been most relevant for derivatives transactions. Laws of the other states and territories would of course be relevant if, for example, the derivatives transaction were entered in the state or territory or if a counterparty were established under the laws of the state or territory.

On occasions even where the Commonwealth does not have the power to make a law there has been sufficient justification and sufficient political will for the states and territories to enact uniform legislation. The Corporations Law (the main law governing corporate activity in Australia) is an example of such a scheme. The Corporations Law is state legislation that is effectively uniform throughout Australia. The way this has been achieved is by having legislation passed in one jurisdiction, in the case of the Corporations Law it was the Australian Capital Territory, and then for other states and territories to pass laws adopting that legislation.

Courts

Australia has a common law legal system, rather than a civil law system. Much of the law in Australia has been made by the courts rather than by a parliament. The courts also interpret legislation.

Each state and territory has its own court system, the highest court of which is the Supreme Court of the state or territory. Much of the Australian derivatives litigation to date has been before a single judge of a Supreme Court. It is possible to appeal a decision by a single judge of a Supreme Court to the Court of Appeal of the state or territory. The Court of Appeal involves three or more Supreme Court judges hearing the case. The Court of Appeal is the second last link in the chain. From there it is possible to appeal to the High Court. The High Court normally sits in Canberra and its members are appointed by the Commonwealth government.

FIGURE 4.1   Outline of Australian Court System. Each state or territory has its own court system. In addition, there is a federal court system which sits throughout Australia. In each case, ultimate appeal is to the High Court.

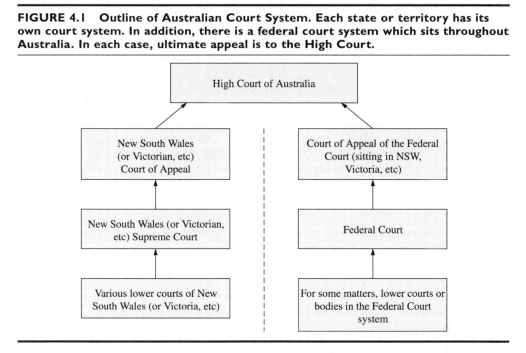

In addition to the state and territory courts, Australia also has a Commonwealth court system. These courts, called Federal Courts, sit in cities throughout Australia. Most cases are heard by a single judge, with it being possible to appeal to the Court of Appeal of the Federal Court (made up of three or more Federal Court judges) and ultimately to the High Court.

So far only a small number of derivatives cases have gone further up the chain than a single judge of a Supreme Court or a Federal Court.

General Derivatives Litigation

The AWA Litigation—Problems with Internal Controls

The AWA litigation is the most significant derivatives legislation in Australia to date. It has different lessons for different people. For auditors it is a case about what not to do. For directors and managers it is a case about directors' duties and the internal controls appropriate for a company's derivatives operations. For everyone it is about what can happen when your counterparty has a major problem.

AWA Limited is an Australian company involved in the manufacture, import and export of electronic and electrical goods. As AWA imported goods from overseas, it had a foreign currency exposure to hedge. The AWA litigation revolves around that hedging becoming speculation in 1986 and 1987.

The financial year of many Australian companies starts on 1 July. In the 1986/1987 financial year, the estimated costs of AWA's imports were $200 million. In contracts with the Department of Supply, one of AWA's main customers, the Department bore the risk of increases in the cost of goods imported from overseas as a result of exchange rate fluctuations. In the 1986/1987 financial year there was approximately $75 to $100 million worth of contracts for which the Department took the risk of foreign exchange fluctuations. After taking these contracts into account,

AWA's underlying exposure to foreign exchange movements was approximately $100 to $125 million.

Andrew Koval was originally hired by AWA as a trainee accountant. During 1984, he managed the short-term money market for AWA and in December 1985 was appointed as AWA's foreign exchange manager. The AWA case follows Koval's move from hedging to speculation and the extent to which AWA's management, directors and auditors should have known of those activities and been able to control them.

Unfortunately for AWA, Koval's speculation was not universally successful. Koval made losses on some of the contracts he entered for AWA, but was able to conceal the details of some of the contracts on which he made losses from AWA's management. According to the trial judge, contracts in loss were generally concealed by one of two means. First, Koval borrowed money on behalf of AWA from a large number of banks and used these borrowings to meet obligations under contracts on which AWA had made a loss. In some cases he borrowed from one bank to make a payment to another bank. Koval started borrowing small amounts in May 1986, but by November substantial loans were outstanding. Secondly, Koval concealed losses by rolling over contracts in a loss position at historical rates.

While AWA's derivatives activities might have started off as simple hedging, they quickly grew beyond that. In the 1986/1987 financial year, AWA's budget anticipated that 25% of its profit would come from hedging activities. Koval appeared to be "brilliantly successful." In February 1987 AWA's directors were told that AWA had realized profits of $26 million through foreign exchange transactions, of which $12 million had been realized in January 1987 alone. By February 1987, AWA's budgeted profits from its foreign exchange dealings had been exceeded by over 400% for the financial year.

By this time, AWA's activities had moved from hedging to major speculation. AWA made a loss of $3.8 million for March 1987. By the end of June 1987, it appears that AWA had open forward transactions in the order of US$800 million. This very significantly exceeded AWA's hedging requirements. By July 1987, Koval's activities had been discovered and in the litigation that followed AWA claimed that it had made losses of $49.8 million as a result.

The AWA litigation involved two quite separate proceedings. In the first proceedings[2] AWA claimed its auditors were negligent and the liability of the following people was examined:

- AWA's auditors, Deloitte Haskins & Sells. AWA claimed that the auditors had been negligent and so were liable to compensate AWA. The court agreed.
- The directors of AWA. The auditors claimed contributory negligence on the part of AWA. They said that the directors had been negligent. The case drew a distinction between Hooke, the chairman and chief executive officer, and AWA's nonexecutive directors. Hooke was held to have been negligent, but the nonexecutive directors were not.
- Senior management of AWA. The auditors also claimed that AWA's senior management had been negligent and that this negligence should be imputed to AWA for the purposes of determining contributory negligence. The court agreed.
- Two banks that provided foreign currency loans. The first claim against these banks was that by providing unauthorized foreign currency loans, the banks

had allowed Koval to conceal the losses he was making. The second claim against these banks was that they were negligent in not disclosing details about all their foreign currency loans and other transactions with AWA when asked for information by the auditors. The court rejected both of these claims against the banks.

These proceedings were first heard by a single judge of the New South Wales Supreme Court and then some issues went on appeal to the New South Wales Court of Appeal.

In separate proceedings,[3] claims were also made against:

- Koval himself.
- de Fries, a dealer at one of the banks with which Koval traded.
- The bank that employed de Fries.

This second case revolved around the quite different issues of the duties an employee owes his employer.

The Basic Problem

AWA's basic problem was that it allowed Koval to deal without adequate checks and controls on his activities. The deficiencies identified in the case are useful examples for anyone involved in setting up internal control systems. Some of the main deficiencies identified were as follows:

Inadequate Records

- Each time Koval entered a deal over the telephone he made a note of it on a pad in front of him. The pages of the pad were not numbered. From December 1985 to June 1986 details of transactions were written into a contract register known as the "green book." The green book did not form part of AWA's accounting system. Because of increased trading and the time it took to write up the green book, the green book was discontinued in June 1986. Apparently between June 1986 and the middle of August 1986 there were no systematic records of any type maintained for transactions entered by Koval.
- In the middle of August 1986, a computer-based spreadsheet system was introduced for recording transactions. The first spreadsheet system was later replaced by a second spreadsheet system, but it seems that neither of them worked accurately until July 1987.

  The spreadsheets were updated irregularly and the information put into them was provided by Koval. Unfortunately, it seems Koval failed to provide information about a large number of open contracts.

  The spreadsheet systems were not used to their best advantage and only gave details of realized profits and losses. Information for the spreadsheet system was obtained from bank statements (showing realized profits and losses). This information was not checked against contract notes or confirmations to ensure that it gave a complete picture of AWA's transactions. Furthermore, the systems did not show mark to market exposures for those transactions that did make it onto the system.

- Appropriate dealing slips for transactions were not written up or kept until July 1987.
- Koval was in charge of checking, signing and returning confirmations. Often he did not keep confirmations, and those he did keep were not filed in a systematic way.
- Senior management in AWA received reports based on the spreadsheets. However, there were no formal management meetings to discuss these reports. In any case, the information AWA's management received about open contracts was inadequate, as it was based on incomplete information being put in AWA's systems.

Inadequate Internal Controls

- Koval was involved in dealing, settling and maintaining accounting records for transactions. Front- and back-office functions were not adequately segregated. Nor does it seem that AWA had any official policy about the segregation of front and back office functions.
- Koval had access to accounting records and was able to authorize accounting journal entries.
- Koval was able to open his own mail.
- The other members of AWA's staff involved in foreign exchange had inadequate experience in the area.
- "Effective" dealing limits were not imposed on Koval. While Koval was informed about limits from April 1987, no steps were taken to inform dealers in other banks about AWA's limits.
- Realized profits or losses on contracts could be rolled at historical rates rather than receiving or paying cash. Koval was able to himself arrange foreign currency loans from various banks. Funds from at least some of these loans were used to cover losses.
- Koval himself set any stop-loss limits. Accordingly the stop-loss orders were not a sufficient internal control on Koval's activities.
- Koval's salary was linked to foreign exchange profits. This increased the temptation to overstate profits and understate losses.
- AWA's management did not exercise "effective" control over Koval. This in part appears to have been due to management's lack of experience in the foreign exchange area. However, another significant factor was that Koval appeared to be making big profits for AWA, so that management was keen to keep him happy.

These factors combined to allow Koval to engage in a pattern of trading that was well beyond that authorized by AWA's directors. When the losses that were suffered as a result became known, AWA claimed that its auditors had failed in their duties and so were liable to make good the loss.

The Case against the Auditors

Deloitte had been AWA's auditors for many years. Daniels was the partner in charge of AWA's audits. During the period on which the litigation focused, the auditors had conducted two audits for AWA. The first was an audit for the financial year ending 30 June 1986 which AWA was required to conduct under the Corporations Law. The second was an audit for the six months ending 31 December 1986 which was requested by the directors of AWA in anticipation of a possible takeover bid for AWA in 1987.

The First Audit

During the course of the first audit, the auditors became aware of various deficiencies in AWA's records, books and internal control systems. Daniels raised at least some of these deficiencies with AWA's senior management between June and July 1996. He did not raise them with AWA's directors at this stage. This is one of the main themes in the case. The court said it was one thing for the auditors to tell senior management about the deficiencies. However, as time passed without senior management having fixed the problems, the auditors should have gone straight to the directors.

In September 1986, Daniels attended a board meeting to discuss the foreign exchange figures in the draft accounts. By the time of the board meeting, senior management of AWA had known of the deficiencies in records, books, and internal controls for three to four months without having rectified the situation. Daniels did not tell the board about these deficiencies, as he wanted to make a more formal statement to senior management before going to the directors. The court held that Daniels should have informed the directors of the deficiencies in internal controls at this stage and was negligent in not doing so. At the board meeting, Daniels also referred to an article on hedging which said: "Forward cover remains a primary method of hedging foreign exchange exposure."[4] The trial judge said that Daniels was impliedly confirming to the directors that all forward transactions were hedges. Although there is contradictory evidence on the point, the trial judge also thought Daniels probably told the directors something to the effect that everything was in order.

An exit meeting was held for the first audit in October 1986. This meeting was attended by the auditors and by members of AWA's senior management. There were no directors present. Daniels again pointed to the inadequacies of AWA's records, books and internal controls and suggested that AWA prepare an appropriate accounting procedures manual. According to the trial judge, nothing Daniels said imported a sense of urgency. No manual was prepared and Daniels did not follow up the matter until March 1987.

In December 1986, Daniels sent a letter to AWA's directors suggesting a number of improvements to the internal audit department. The letter made no specific reference to the deficiencies in the internal controls of the foreign exchange department. By that time, these deficiencies had been known for six months, had been drawn to the attention of senior management and had still not been fixed. The letter came up for consideration in the December 1986 board meeting but because of other business was deferred until February 1987. Although not absolutely clear from the case report, it appears that at the board meeting in February 1987 it was decided to implement the letter's suggestions.

The Second Audit

By the time of the second audit for the six months up to 31 December 1986, the improvements suggested by the auditors at the first audit's exit meeting had still not been made. By this stage, the auditors had known of the deficiencies for over eight months.

A member of the audit team for the second audit identified deficiencies in the foreign exchange department which the trial judge summarized as follows:

(a) Koval was the only member of the department with FX operational experience.

(b) The dealing register was no longer being kept and telexes and some contract notes were being disposed of.

(c) The Macquarie software was not being used properly (it was only showing matured contracts) as data was only being entered from bank statements (showing realized profits and losses) rather than from contract notes and confirmations (originating documents).

(d) The staff had little technical experience in foreign exchange.

(e) Koval had influence over where funds went to or came from, i.e., he had some influence over the handling of assets.

(f) Mail was being delivered to Koval unopened.

(g) Stop-loss limits (with dealers) were being sent on Koval's own advice so they did not constitute an adequate internal control over his activity.

(h) Koval's salary was linked to foreign exchange profits (which increased the risk of overstatement of profit).

(i) There were weaknesses in the reporting system for divisional purchase requirements.

(j) The letters which, at the first step in the conduct of the audit, had been sent to foreign exchange dealers seeking confirmation of open contracts at 31 December 1986 had been addressed to the persons with whom Koval actually dealt rather than to the settlements department at each dealer.[5]

The trial judge thought that these deficiencies and the ways they could be remedied were quite obvious. The court of appeal agreed.

As part of the second audit process, various letters were sent to the banks AWA dealt with requesting information about AWA's dealings with the banks. The trial judge held that the first round of letters was inappropriate to obtain information from banks about foreign currency loans, foreign currency loan accounts or foreign currency settlement accounts. Two further rounds of letters seeking information were sent to some, but not all, banks. The first of these listed AWA's forward currency contracts and asked for confirmation about them for audit purposes and the second sought details of "outstanding foreign exchange contracts." In response to these letters, one bank wrote back indicating it had 12 transactions with AWA that did not appear on AWA's records. These 12 transactions involved unrealized losses of around $2.4 million. In the case Daniels gave evidence that he believed these transactions related to losses on speculation by Koval, but said he did not think it necessary to pursue them. Why he did not think it not necessary to pursue them is not clear from the case reports. Another bank wrote back indicating these were five discrepancies.

Despite all this, Daniels was prepared to sign a letter certifying AWA's financial position as at 31 December 1986 with an operating profit of around $16 million. According to the trial judge, the true result was a large loss.

The auditors met with AWA's management in March 1987 to discuss various deficiencies identified by the audit. Later that day a meeting was also held with AWA's chairman and chief executive officer, Hooke, to discuss the deficiencies.

Daniels attended a board meeting at the end of March 1987. The board was deeply concerned about the large profits apparently being made from AWA's "hedging" operations. Daniels confirmed that the reported profits had been realized. However, although the auditors were aware of them, Daniels did not mention the net unrealized losses that were not recorded in AWA's books which appeared from information provided by some banks in the course of the audit. Nor did he tell the board about the various concerns raised at his earlier meeting in March 1987 with Hooke. The trial judge said that he might well have assumed that Hooke had already told the board, but that Daniels should have told the board himself anyway.

The Auditors Were Negligent

In summary, both the trial judge and the court of appeal thought that the auditors had been negligent by not informing AWA's directors about the deficiencies in AWA's records, books and internal control systems at the board meeting in September 1986. True, the auditors had brought various problems to the attention of AWA's senior management, but that was not sufficient. Senior management had not fixed the problems and the auditors should have brought the matter to the attention of the directors themselves. This initial negligence was followed up by various other acts of negligence by the auditors, including signing off on the profit statements for the year ended 31 December 1986 and the information given to, and withheld from, the directors by the auditors at the meeting in March 1987.

The auditors argued that even if they had been negligent, their negligence did not result in AWA's loss so that they were not liable to pay AWA damages. The auditors submitted that their acts did not cause the loss on the following grounds:

- First, that even if they had told AWA's directors about the deficiencies, the directors would not have taken the steps necessary to avoid the losses made by AWA. After all, the auditors had given information about various deficiencies to AWA's senior managers and the problems had not been rectified. Why should the directors be any different? The directors said that had they known of the problems they would have sought expert advice, commenced an investigation of the position, dismissed Koval and ensured that proper internal controls were put in place. The court accepted that the directors would have done this, and so rejected the auditors' argument.
- Secondly, the auditors argued that losses would have occurred anyway even if Koval had traded within appropriate limits. The court rejected this, noting that if proper accounting records and internal controls had been put in place sufficiently early, Koval's losses would have come to light at a relatively early stage. The implication was that the directors would then have taken appropriate steps to remedy the position.
- The auditors also argued that Koval's conduct was not of a type that was very likely to occur, so that the damage was too remote. The court rejected this, saying that Koval's conduct was of a type that was quite likely to occur when an employee in Koval's position was almost completely unsupervised.

The auditors were held to have been negligent and this negligence was held to have been a sufficient cause of AWA's loss. But this was not the end of the matter, as the auditors claimed that they were not the only ones responsible. AWA, they claimed, was responsible too and so was liable in contributory negligence.

AWA's Contributory Negligence and the Case against the Directors

The court agreed that AWA had been negligent too. Balancing up the various factors involved, the court of appeal held that AWA was itself liable for 33⅓% of the loss, with the auditors being liable for the remaining 66⅔%.

In considering whether AWA had been negligent, the court examined separately the position of:

- AWA's senior management.
- Hooke, AWA's chief executive officer (i.e., the head of senior management) and chairman of the board of directors.
- AWA's nonexecutive directors.

Senior Management

The court held that senior management had been negligent in various ways, some of which were unknown to the auditors. This negligence included failing to adequately supervise Koval's activities, failing to report to the directors that there were inadequate internal controls and records and failing to react appropriately to information obtained from the auditors and various other sources. This negligence was imputed to AWA, so that the company itself was taken to have been negligent.

Hooke and the Nonexecutive Directors

From an Australian legal perspective, one of the most significant aspects of the case is the court's views on the liability of AWA's directors. Hooke, AWA's chief executive and chairman of the board, was held to have been negligent and this negligence was also imputed to AWA. The nonexecutive directors were held not to have been negligent. With one exception nonexecutive directors were entitled to rely on AWA's senior management. The exception was when the nonexecutive directors learnt of the large profits that were being made in early 1987, but the court held that the directors had not been negligent in their response to this.

In coming to these conclusions, the court traced through what Hooke and the nonexecutive directors respectively knew and should have done. What the court said has substantially changed the way many companies and their directors in Australia deal with derivatives.

AWA's foreign currency exposure was discussed at a board meeting in March 1986. Much evidence was given about precisely what was said and decided at that meeting, but in summary the trial judge held as follows:

> *(1) The board delegated to senior management the responsibility for conducting a foreign currency exposure protection exercise.*
> *(2) Subject to the requirements that:*
>   *(a) no substantial risk be taken;*
>   *(b) stop losses be in place;*
>   *(c) transactions be related to the company's [indulging] exposure it was for senior management to devise and implement managed trading in foreign currency contracts, including:*
>   *(i)   putting in place appropriate accounting and other record systems and internal controls;*
>   *(ii) hiring necessary staff;*
>   *(iii) ensuring compliance with conditions (a)-(c) above;*
>   *(iv) advising the auditors of the board's wishes and intentions.*[6]

The board had delegated to senior management the role of overseeing AWA's foreign exchange operations. They had delegated this subject to broad guidelines which, although not very detailed, were in a form that the court thought was sufficient. (That was in 1986. Today, courts might well expect directors to have a more sophisticated view of derivatives and to have more precisely developed derivatives policies and guidelines.)

At the board meeting in September 1986 after the first audit, Daniels, the auditor, did not tell the directors about the deficiencies as he wanted to give management formal notice first. He also said something to the effect that everything was in order and referred to an article which the trial judge said could have left the impression with the directors that all forward currency transactions were hedges. At least the nonexecutive directors were none the wiser about the deficiencies.

In November 1986, a letter was sent by one of AWA's counterparties to Hooke. The letter said that AWA had very large unrealized losses from rolling over contracts at historical rates. Hooke and two other senior managers of AWA had a meeting with the counterparty to discuss the matter. At the meeting someone from AWA said that it was AWA's policy to rollover contracts at historical rates to provide a "buffer" for adverse future foreign exchange movements. The trial judge noted that while this might have been appropriate for unrealized profits, it was hard to see how the policy applied to unrealized losses. Significantly, Hooke did not tell the other directors about the letter or the meeting.

In November 1986, Koval met the board. He discussed AWA's foreign currency contracts and the techniques he was using. The directors asked how it was possible for AWA to make such large profits from foreign exchange. Koval apparently responded that the profits were being made from hedge contracts and said that AWA was completely covered by stop loss orders. AWA's general manager was present at the meeting, but said nothing to contradict anything Koval had said.

At the February 1987 board meeting where the directors were told that AWA's foreign exchange operations had made a realized profit of $26 million for the financial year so far, the directors were greatly concerned about how such large profits that could be made from foreign exchange transactions that were supposed to be acting as hedges. The directors asked the auditors to confirm the profit figures. At the meeting, the directors also considered a letter from the auditors suggesting improvements to the internal audit department. The letter said nothing specifically about the deficiencies relating to AWA's foreign exchange operations, or that these deficiencies had been known by management for many months without being fixed.

Hooke and AWA management met with the auditors in March 1987. The auditors, Hooke and AWA management discussed various deficiencies in AWA's internal controls. Hooke seems not to have passed this information on to the other directors. In the same month, another of AWA's counterparties told Hooke that the profits being made by AWA were simply too large to be made from hedging activities. It seems that Hooke did not tell the other directors about this either.

In the March 1987 board meeting, the auditors confirmed that the reported profits which had so concerned the directors at the meeting in February had in fact been realized. This was true, in the sense that profits had been banked. However, the board was not told by the auditors about the unrealized losses that had been discovered in the course of the second audit, that the spreadsheet system was an incomplete record of transactions, or the other concerns the auditors had discussed with Hooke earlier in March.

AWA's directors had a further board meeting in May 1987. AWA made a loss of $3.8 million in March. A report from the general manager said this loss arose because AWA had decided to get rid of "doubtful" contracts. The general manager was not present at the meeting to discuss this report. The directors asked AWA's management to prepare a report on the nature and extent of foreign exchange dealings.

Largely based on what they knew at the relevant times, the court held that Hooke was negligent but that the nonexecutive directors were not. The nonexecutive directors delegated the role of overseeing AWA's foreign exchange operations to senior management. They were not told about the problems with the accounts, records, and internal controls in AWA's foreign exchange department and with one exception they were entitled to rely on AWA's senior management. That exception was when the nonexecutive directors learnt of the large profits made in early 1987, but the court held that the nonexecutive directors had not been negligent in their response to this. They had asked for confirmation from the auditors and this had been given. Hooke, on the other hand, had known much more. He had been given information by the auditors and by some of AWA's counterparties that the other directors did not have. Hooke was held to have been negligent.

The Case against the Banks

The auditors cross-claimed against two of AWA's banks claiming that they were also liable for contributory negligence. The court held that the banks were not.

Unauthorized Foreign Currency Loans

The auditors claimed that Koval did not have authority to borrow money on behalf of AWA, and that the banks should have known this. The auditors' argument continued that by lending money the banks enabled Koval to continue as he did, and that this was a reason for AWA suffering loss.

The trial judge rejected these claims, holding that Koval was in fact authorized to borrow money on behalf of AWA. The trial judge concluded that Koval had authority to do this for several reasons:

- It was true that the directors had not expressly authorized Koval to make foreign currency loans on behalf of AWA. However, the directors had, subject to some general guidelines, delegated the whole of AWA's foreign currency operations to senior management. Senior management had in turn delegated AWA's foreign currency operations to Koval. Tracing through this line of delegation, the trial judge held that Koval had actual authority to make the foreign currency loans.
- Koval had been held out to the banks as having responsibility for AWA's foreign exchange operations. One of AWA's senior managers had introduced Koval to people at one of the banks describing him as "Assistant finance manager and the person who looks after the foreign exchange and money market operations at AWA. If you want to talk about foreign exchange then Andrew is the person to talk to."[7] Later the same senior manager described Koval to a different person at that bank as AWA's "chief contact for money market and FX business."[8] When some time down the track one of the bank's employees tried to speak to AWA management about what they perceived as a move in AWA's foreign exchange transactions from being for hedging, she was told on various occasions to speak to Koval.

    On at least two occasions people from the second bank contacted senior management at AWA to check on the transactions Koval was doing, but on each case was told in effect that AWA was happy with what Koval was doing.

Furthermore, confirmations were not challenged by AWA and payments on the loans were actually made. Evidence was given that at the time the loans were made, neither Westpac nor Lloyds knew, nor had any reason to suspect, the deficiencies in AWA's internal controls. The trial judge thought that both banks were entitled to proceed on the basis that when AWA received written confirmations it would have realized that Koval had borrowed the money and, if appropriate, taken action to remedy the situation. This was the case even though it seems that at least one of the banks accepted the signature of the dealer on the confirmation.

- Even if Koval did not have actual authority, the trial judge held that the broad authority conferred by the directors on senior management, and by senior management on Koval, impliedly authorized him to do what was usual in the course of "a money market manager and FX dealer's business."[9] Detailed evidence was given about how the foreign exchange markets operated at the relevant time and largely based on this, the court held that this usual authority included the authority to borrow foreign currency.

The court held that the loans were authorized. Although it was not necessary for the decision, the trial judge indicated that even if the loans had been unauthorized, they might not have been a sufficient cause of the loss anyway. If Koval had not been able to borrow from these two banks, it seems he would have been able to borrow money from other banks. AWA's management had learned about loans made by some other banks but had not restricted Koval's activities as a result. The trial judge indicated that there was no reason to think AWA's management would have responded any differently if they had learned about the loans made by the two banks against which the auditors cross-claimed.

Negligent Response to Audit Request?

The auditors also claimed that the banks had been negligent in their responses to the information requested from them in the audit circulars. The court held that the banks had not been negligent in completing the audit forms. In the case of at least one of the banks, the letter requesting information had not been drafted in a way to obtain information about foreign currency loans. Furthermore, on the issue of causation the court noted that the auditors had received information about discrepancies from other banks, and thought that the auditors would not have acted in a different way even if they had received more information about the loans from the two banks in question.

The two banks were not liable.

The Proceedings against Koval

In the main AWA proceedings the auditors were held to be liable for 66⅔% of AWA's loss and AWA was held liable for 33⅓% of its loss as a result of contributory negligence.

In separate proceedings, AWA sued Koval himself. AWA claimed that Koval and Jonathan de Fries, a dealer at one of AWA's banks, obtained US$1,478,451 million from foreign exchange transactions entered into in the name of AWA. The bank at which de Fries worked was also sued, but settled the matter with AWA outside court. Koval filed a defense, but did not personally appear in the proceedings to give evidence. Accordingly, de Fries was the only defendant to appear and give evidence in court.

Both Koval and de Fries were on modest salaries in the region of $30,000 to $50,000 per year. Over a lunch towards the end of 1985, Koval told de Fries that AWA could not officially approve a wage increase sufficient to put Koval in line with other salaries in the foreign exchange market. However, he said that AWA's general manager had given Koval verbal authority to use a small portion of AWA's dealing limit with one institution to "split the profits of certain deals" that were "surplus" to AWA's trading requirements.[10] Koval said that the money that Koval and the dealer would make had to be after AWA had "made its money." He said the arrangement had to be oral because various people in AWA, including the board, had been starting to comment that AWA might be trading in foreign exchange too much. De Fries said he should tell his bank, but Koval said he could not. The reason Koval apparently gave for not telling the bank was that the bank was providing funding for some companies that were looking at taking over AWA and that he was concerned that relevant information (precisely what information is not clear) would be leaked. De Fries thought the matter over, and then decided to go along with the proposal. He said that one of the factors he took into account was that if he had not agreed to Koval's proposal, his bank would have lost AWA's business.

Koval and de Fries called the transactions on which they were to take the profits "RUDs." The name RUDs came from a U.S. Budgetary Act of which Senator Warren Rudman was a sponsor. De Fries told the court the transactions were designated as RUDs before they were entered, but the court held that Koval only decided whether or not a transaction would be a RUD after it was certain that the transaction would make a profit.

De Fries concealed what he was doing from his employer. A special U.S.-dollar bank account was opened and payments relating to RUDs paid into it. De Fries told his bank that the reason for this was that AWA was looking at acquiring a company in the US and did not want its name associated with the funds. This was not true. De Fries also breached his bank's internal rules prohibiting dealers from engaging in transactions on their own account. De Fries said he did not know about this prohibition, but the court did not believe him.

Koval and de Fries received money from 19 RUDs. De Fries decided to resign in October 1986 and in the last two month period Koval and de Fries made US$600,000 from RUDs.

AWA sued Koval and de Fries for breach of fiduciary duty. AWA claimed that Koval breached his fiduciary duties to his employer. The court agreed. The court held that using AWA's property (i.e., AWA's credit limits with Barclays) to make a profit for himself is a breach of duty. Even if Hooke or AWA's general manager had authorized Koval to do this, it was not within their power to authorize a breach of fiduciary duty. The directors had not been told what Koval was doing. De Fries claimed that he thought Koval did have authority to enter the RUD transactions and appropriate funds from them. He claimed he did not know that Koval was breaching his fiduciary duty. The court held that he did—and that this knowledge coupled with the assistance he gave Koval was sufficient to make de Fries himself liable for assisting a breach of fiduciary duty. The court held that Koval and de Fries had also been fraudulent.

The case report gives no hint about whether or not Koval and de Fries had sufficient funds to satisfy the judgment against them.

Some Other Cases

The AWA litigation is by far the most complex derivatives litigation we have seen in Australia to date. The following are examples of some of the more interesting other non-regulatory cases we have seen.

Another Auditors Case: Simonius Vischer v. Holt & Thompson[11]

The AWA litigation was not the first time in Australia that auditors had found themselves in difficulties because of derivatives. In *Simonius Vischer v. Holt & Thompson,* auditors were liable because of events that occurred in the 1960s.

Simonius Vischer was a wool buying firm based in Basel. It had several offices in Australia, including one in Sydney. Holt & Thompson were the company's auditors.

In Sydney, the company acted as a broker on the wool futures market. It also traded on its own account. Some of the trading on its own account was based on instructions from Basel to hedge exposure. In addition, the Sydney office had limited authority to trade on its own account for speculative purposes. From, at the least, the beginning of 1964, Sydney office only had authority from Basel to have 20 of these speculative contracts open at any one time. Furthermore, the speculative contracts were not supposed to be left open for longer than 14 days each. Unknown to Basel, Sydney office somewhat exceeded this limit. When a representative from Basel came to investigate the position in June 1965, he found that there were over 600 of these speculative contracts open. The contracts had been concealed from Basel by members of the Australian offices entering into the contracts in their own names or under false names.

In addition, Sydney office had been acting as a broker. However, it did not always obtain guarantees or margin calls from its clients and further losses resulted from this.

Holt & Thompson had prepared the accounts of the Australian offices. When they sent the accounts for the year ending 31 July 1964 to Basel, they confirmed that the books and records were kept "in a most competent and satisfactory manner." In fact the accounts gave a totally incorrect picture, and the profit that had been shown in the accounts was really a substantial loss.

When Basel sent a representative to Australia to examine the operation of the wool futures division, what had been happening quickly came to light. The company then closed out some of the speculative contracts, but forming the view that the market would probably fall decided to retain a portion of the speculative contracts. The market did not fall and the company made further losses from holding on to those contracts.

The company claimed that its auditors had been negligent. The court agreed. This negligence included:

- Failing to find out about the authority of the Australian offices to trade, to check on whether the Australian offices were acting within this authority and to report if they were not.
- Failing to determine and report the number of open contracts as at the balance date.
- Failing to make provision for these open positions.
- Failing to confirm and make provision for amounts owing on customer accounts (including doubtful debts on those accounts).

The trial judge held that Basel had not been aware of the extent Sydney office was exceeding its authority on speculative contracts to any material extent.

One of the defenses raised by the auditors was that on learning the true position the company should have closed out all the speculative contracts straight away. By not doing so, the auditors said that the company had failed to act reasonably to mitigate its loss. The court disagreed saying that in the circumstances the auditors had not proved that the company's conduct was unreasonable.

Who Is Your Counterparty? Qintex v. Schroders[12]

In Australia it is crucial that you identify the precise legal entity that is to be your counterparty. It is not enough to deal with a corporate group, without specifying which company in the group is your counterparty. The Qintex case illustrates the dangers of imprecision.

Schroders Australia Limited entered into various foreign currency transactions with the Qintex group. One of Schroders' dealers gave evidence that she dealt with particular people at Qintex and that it was not her practice to ask which of the Qintex companies was involved. Schroders only had one client coding for Qintex. Schroders' dealer indicated that she always assumed she was dealing with Qintex as a group, rather than with any of the companies in the group. Confirmations were addressed to "Qintex Group of Companies" and the counterparty was stated as being "Qintex." When Schroders was establishing credit limits, Qintex told Schroders to select whichever Qintex company Schroders felt most comfortable with, as it did not matter to Qintex. All this sets the scene.

In December 1989, Schroders closed out one of its foreign exchange contracts with Qintex, and as a result Qintex owed Schroders money. Schroders' appropriated funds from three accounts of Qintex Australia Finance Limited towards payment of the amount owed to it. In connection with a previous transaction, Schroders had paid a cheque (which had been expressed to be payable to Qintex Television Limited) into an account of Qintex Australia Finance Limited.

Qintex Australia Finance Limited argued that Schroders had no right to appropriate money from its accounts. The issue before the court was whether Qintex Australia Finance Limited was the counterparty, or in some way liable for the obligations of the Qintex counterparty. If it was not the counterparty, Schroders had no right to appropriate funds from its account.

The court was not sure which Qintex company was the counterparty, but on the facts before it did not think it was Qintex Australia Finance Limited. Had there been a confirmation issued in the name of Qintex Australia Finance Limited, the court noted that it would have been very difficult to argue that it was not the counterparty. However, there was no such confirmation.

Problems with Margin Calls—Rest-Ezi Furniture v. Ace Shohin (Australia)[13]

Rest-Ezi manufactured furniture. Michael Tobin, its managing director, had a degree in economics but little experience in commodities futures trading. A representative of Ace Shohin (Australia) contacted Tobin out of the blue and said that there was a bumper harvest of red beans in Japan which meant that Tobin could profit by investing in futures. Tobin was shown a document with various calculations, but nothing was said about margin calls. Tobin acknowledged that he had seen a reference to margins in the contract, but said that because of the jargon he did not realize what was involved. He asked Ace Shohin whether there were any costs and was told that the only costs were Ace Shohin's commission of $120 per contract. He was told that other costs referred to in the contract only applied if he wanted to take physical delivery of red beans.

Tobin invested $48,000 on behalf of Rest-Ezi through Ace Shohin in futures contracts. Unfortunately, the price of red bean contracts went down and Rest-Ezi was required to make various margin calls. In the end, the company lost just over $84,000—the original payment plus margin calls. This included $7,200 in commissions paid to Ace Shohin.

One of the most interesting features of this case is the example it gives of how easy it is for people to misunderstand the operation of derivatives markets. Tobin said that he thought the futures market was like the share market and that it was possible simply to hold onto contracts and decide when to sell them. He did not know that he might also be required to pay margin calls. If he had known, he said that he would have invested a smaller sum and retained some of his cash in reserve to make margin payments. The court believed him and held that Ace Shohin was liable to compensate Rest-Ezi.

According to the evidence, Ace Shohin had indicated that there were no costs other than the $120 commission it received per contract. In other words, Ace Shohin did more than simply being silent on the question of margin calls and how they worked. This particular company had other difficulties with margin calls and in another case was held liable for misrepresentation in connection with them.[14]

Option Investments (Australia) v. Martin[15]

Option Investments (Australia) had a totally different problem with its margin calls. Its client did not dispute that Option Investments had the right to make margin calls, but claimed that when margin payments were not made Option Investments should have promptly closed out in a way to avoid further loss for the client.

Option Investments bought cattle futures contracts on behalf of Martin. It was part of their arrangement that if the market moved, Martin might have to make margin payments. The market fell and Option Investments asked Martin to make a margin payment. He did not. The market continued to move and Option Investments asked Martin to make further margin payments. He did not pay any of them. Four months after the initial request was made for a margin payment, Option Investments closed out the contracts. Martin made a significant loss, and he claimed that Option Investments was liable to compensate him as his loss was caused by Option Investments not closing out quickly enough.

Martin based his case on two grounds. First, he said that in their initial discussions about the margin arrangements, Option Investments had told him that if a margin payment was not made straight away, Martin's position would be closed out. The court looked closely at the relevant conversations and held that they did not create a contractual obligation to close out straight away. Instead, in the context of the conversations the court thought that the statement by Option Investments that it would close out straight away was a warning.

That was not the end of the matter. Martin also claimed that Option Investments owed him a duty of care which it had breached by delaying the close out while the market fell. The court said that a broker who closes out is under a duty to act in good faith, but continued that generally this would be satisfied by a sale on an open exchange. However, the court thought that since the right to close out was for the protection of a broker's own interests, a broker is entitled to select the timing of the close out unless contractually bound to close out at a particular time. In this case, the court thought the broker was not contractually bound to close out at a particular time. While agreeing that in closing out a broker might owe a duty of care to its client, the court did not think Option Investments had breached its duty.

Significantly, the court thought Option Investments had not known what course Martin wanted to adopt. The court also thought that Martin knew this and was content to leave Option Investments in this state of uncertainty.

The end result was that Option Investments was not liable to Martin.

The Defense of Illegality—Ross McConnel, Kitchen & Co. v. Lorbergs[16]

Contracts entered for an illegal purpose can be unenforceable. This case is an example of this principle.

Lorbergs opened up two dealing accounts with his futures broker, one in his own name and one in the name of Gabriel Venus. While there is nothing in itself wrong with opening up dealing accounts in different names, the court held that Lorbergs' reason for opening up the two accounts was to avoid liability for income tax on profits that arose in connection with the Gabriel Venus account. The court noted that a contract which is not itself unlawful could be entered into for an unlawful purpose and that where this happens the person with the unlawful purpose cannot sue on the contract. The court held that both Lorbergs and the broker knew about the unlawful purpose, with the result that neither party could sue on the contracts between them.

An Exclusion Clause Works—Darlington Futures v. Delco Australia[17]

Darlington Futures was a broker in the commodities futures markets. Delco Australia was an engineering company. Delco entered into various futures contracts through Darlington. Darlington did not follow some of Delco's instructions about the timing of close out, with the result that Delco was in effect speculating on some of its contracts. Delco suffered a loss and it claimed against Darlington for that loss.

The court found that one of Darlington's employees had deliberately not followed instructions rather than having acted negligently. However, the contract between Darlington and Delco contained an exclusion clause limiting Darlington's liability to $100 for (among other things) "claims arising out of or in connection with the relationship established by the agreement." Having regard to the particular wording of the clause, the court held that an unauthorized transaction could have a connection with the broker-client relationship established by the agreement. The exclusion clause applied and Darlington's liability was limited to $100 per contract.

While not creating any particularly significant law in Australia, this case is useful as a reminder that exclusion clauses can in some cases work. Following this case, the business rules of the Sydney Futures Exchange were amended with a view to stopping members of the exchange relying on this type of clause. Furthermore, it is one of the rare examples of a derivatives case that has been considered by the High Court.[18]

Regulatory Litigation

The Corporations Law

The Corporations Law governs much corporate activity in Australia. It is the legislation under which most companies are incorporated and which regulates the nuts and bolts of their day-to-day operations.

As well as regulating the operations of companies, the Corporations Law also regulates activities relating to the following types of property or arrangements:

- *Futures Contracts:* Generally, these are a wide range of derivatives arrangements. Futures contracts are regulated by chapter 8 of the Corporations Law.
- *Securities:* These include certain debentures, stocks, bonds, shares and option contracts. They also include "prescribed interests." Securities are regulated by chapter 7 of the Corporations Law.
- *Prescribed Interests:* These can be of two types. The first is a right to participate in a time sharing scheme (e.g., a time share holiday house). The second is called a "participation interest," which is defined to cover a wide spectrum of profit-making schemes ranging, for example, from property unit trusts to interests in ostrich farms. Prescribed interests are a special type of "security." They are also regulated by chapter 7 of the Corporations Law.

Much of the derivatives litigation in Australia has focussed on whether a particular product is regulated as a futures contract, a security, a prescribed interest, or none of them. In the derivatives area, most of the cases have involved futures contracts with a smaller number involving securities and prescribed interests.

The Corporations Law is administered by the Australian Securities Commission. Before 1991 the Corporate Affairs Commission had this role. Many of the cases in this area involved the Corporate Affairs Commission trying to stop activity it thought breached the law.

The Regulation of Futures Contracts

The Corporations Law contains around 200 sections regulating futures contracts and activities relating to futures contracts.[19] A prime example that causes difficulties for many people operating in Australia is the general prohibition on conducting unauthorized futures markets. Section 1123 of the Corporations Law provides that:

A person must not establish or conduct, assist in establishing or conducting, or hold out that the person conducts, an unauthorized futures market.

Some Key Corporations Law Definitions Relevant to Derivatives	
Futures Contract:	Eligible commodity agreement.
	Adjustment agreement.
	Futures option.
	Eligible exchange traded option.
Security:	Debentures, stocks or bonds issued or proposed to be issued by a government.
	Shares in, or debentures of, a body.
	Units of such shares or of prescribed interests.
	An option contract within the meaning of Chapter 7.
	Prescribed interests (see below).
Prescribed Interest:	Right to participate in a time sharing scheme (e.g., a time share holiday house).
	Participation interest.

An unauthorized futures market is defined as a futures market that is not operating on an approved futures exchange and does not have an exemption. The exemption process is far from automatic. For section 1123 to apply there must be a futures contracts within the meaning of the Corporations Law.

The prohibition on unauthorized markets is just one example of how futures contracts are regulated by the Corporations Law. The sections of the Corporations Law dealing with futures contracts contain many other examples, including:

- Regulations about who may provide a clearing house facility (section 1128).
- Prohibitions on people dealing in futures contracts on behalf of other people without a license (section 1142).
- Prohibitions on people carrying on a futures advice business without a license (section 1143).

There are many more. Central to these provisions is the meaning of futures contract. Several Australian cases have considered precisely what it takes to make a contract a futures contract.

Corporations Law Definition of Futures Contract

The starting point is the definition of futures contract in the Corporations Law. The definition is unhappily complex, and to apply it involves reading definitions within definitions within definitions. The key definitions necessary to put the cases in context are as follows.

Section 72 of the Corporations Law defines a futures contract as:

(a) a Chapter 8 agreement that is, or has at any time been:
  - an eligible commodity agreement; or
  - an adjustment agreement; or
(b) a futures option; or
(c) an eligible exchange-traded option.

"Chapter 8 agreement" is Corporations Law-speak for a wide range of agreements, arrangements or understanding. It includes agreements, arrangements, or understandings:

- Whether formal or informal.
- Whether written or oral.
- Whether having legal or equitable force.

There are various exceptions to the definition of futures contract. For example, the definition excludes currency swaps, interest rate swaps, forward exchange rate contracts and forward interest rate contracts to which an Australian bank or a merchant bank, is a party (the definitions of Australian bank and merchant bank are quite restrictive).

Eligible Commodity Agreement

The key features of the definition of eligible commodity agreement are:

- The agreement must be a standardized agreement. A standardized agreement is a Chapter 8 agreement that is one of 2 or more Chapter 8 agreements each of which is a Chapter 8 agreement of the same kind as the other, or as each of the others, as the case may be. Agreements are of the same kind if, and only if, their provisions are the same, or not materially different, disregarding the fact that the parties or the amounts payable are different.[20] One of the big unanswered questions is how similar agreements really have to be for them to be standardized agreements; and

- The agreement must be a commodity agreement. A commodity agreement is a standardized agreement the effect of which is that a person is under a Chapter 8 obligation[21] to make or accept delivery:
  —At a particular future time.
  —Of a particular quantity of a particular commodity.
  —At a particular price or a price to be calculated in a particular manner.
- It appears likely that the obligation of the person to make or accept delivery will be discharged in either a way other than the person making or accepting delivery or by the person entering into an offsetting contract.

An example of an eligible commodity agreement would be a standardized agreement for the delivery of gold for an agreed price on an agreed future date, where it is likely that the contract will be cash settled rather than settled by physical delivery.

Adjustment Agreement

The key features of the definition of adjustment agreement are:

- The agreement must be a standardized agreement. Standardized agreement has the same meaning here as it does in the context of eligible commodity agreement.
- The effect of the agreement is that a particular person will be under a Chapter 8 obligation to pay, or will have a Chapter 8 right to receive, an amount of money.
- Whether the person will be under an obligation to pay, or will have a right to receive, the amount of money depends on a particular state of affairs existing at a particular future time (this includes a state of affairs relating to fluctuations in the value or price of a commodity or other property, or in an index or other factor).
- The amount of money will be calculated in a particular manner by reference to that state of affairs.

An example would be a standardized agreement under which the parties pay or receive money depending on the difference between a benchmark price for gold and the actual price of gold on a particular date.

Futures Options and Eligible Exchange-Traded Options

A futures option is in effect an option to enter into an eligible commodity agreement or an adjustment agreement. The precise definition of futures option in section 9 of the Corporations Law is as one would expect more complex than this.

An eligible exchange-traded option is in effect an option relating to a commodity or specified index entered into through an authorized futures exchange. The precise definition of eligible exchange-traded option in section 9 of the Corporations Law is also significantly more complex than this.

With this statutory background in mind, it is time to turn to the cases.

Cases Dealing with the Meaning of "Futures Contract"

As a preliminary point, to be regulated by Australian futures laws, the futures contract does not need to be an Australian futures contract. Contracts traded on the Chicago Board of Trade[22] and Japanese red bean, soya bean and silk cocoon futures[23] have been held to be futures contracts. In 1986 and 1987 there were a series of cases in which the meaning of futures contract was tested. While by no means revealing all the secrets of the definition, these cases have been helpful in clarifying some of the issues raised by it.

Shoreline Currencies Case[24]

Shoreline Currencies (Aust) entered into arrangements with its clients under which it was to purchase foreign currency on its clients' behalf. Under the contract used as an example in the case, Shoreline Currencies was to purchase Y7,488,021 for its client. The purchase price was US$46,888. This price was only payable if the client decided to take physical delivery of the yen. The client could at any time direct Shoreline Currencies to sell the yen, which would enable the client to take the benefit of any profit early. If, however, the value of the yen went down against the US dollar, the client would make a loss. The contract dealt with loss by saying that the client's loss was "insured" with a separate company called Inter-Exchange Insurance Limited and that, in effect, if the value of the yen went down against the US dollar, Shoreline Currencies would claim against this insurer rather than against the client. The client paid a fee of A$5,007 which was expressed to be a nonrefundable investment payment.

Shoreline Currencies advertised its product in the newspaper. In all, it seems that Shoreline Currencies entered into 218 contracts along those lines. 206 of them contained the same terms. The remaining 12 were on slightly different terms (e.g., they did not contain the "insurance" provision).

The Corporate Affairs Commission said that Shoreline Currencies' contracts were futures contracts and proposed to make an order prohibiting Shoreline Currencies publishing statements relating to them. Shoreline Currencies sought a court order that its contracts were not futures contracts, so that the Commission had no power to prohibit the publishing of statements relating to them.

The court held that the contracts were futures contracts as they came within the meaning of "eligible commodity agreements."[25] In coming to this conclusion the Court considered two aspects of the definition of futures contract:

- *What is a standardized agreement?* Shoreline Currencies argued that as the agreements were not on precisely the same terms they were not standardized agreements. Agreements must be standardized agreements to fall within the definition "eligible commodity agreement." The court rejected this argument. Since 206 of the contracts were on the same terms, with only a small group of 12 on different terms, and the contracts dealt with foreign currency purchases in the same way the court held that these contracts were sufficiently "of the same kind" to be "standardized" contracts.
- *Is foreign currency a commodity?* The court held that foreign currency could be a commodity for these purposes.

The Commission had also argued that the contracts were adjustment agreements. On this point the court made the following comments:

- *Is there an adjustment?* The court held that the agreement related to specific amounts of yen and US dollars and that these amounts did not fluctuate. Accordingly, under the terms of the contract itself, there was no person who had an obligation to pay, or a right to receive, money depending upon a particular state of affairs existing in a particular future time.
- *Looking through the written terms of the contract.* The Commission argued that even if the terms of the contract itself did not amount to an adjustment agreement, the way transactions were actually conducted between Shoreline Currencies and its clients did. While not conclusively deciding the point (given the conclusion on eligible commodity agreements it did not need to) the court indicated that this argument had merit. The implication is that people will not necessarily be able to hide behind the precise terms of their contracts if their real arrangements are different.

Since the contracts were futures contracts, the court held that the Commission was entitled to start the procedure necessary which would lead to it being able to prohibit Shoreline Currencies publishing statements about them.

Carragreen Currency Corporation Case[26]

Carragreen Currency Corporation entered into foreign currency options with its customers. The options could be exercised by the customer at any time up to 4.00 PM Sydney time on the expiry date. The contract provided that if the customer exercised the option, Carragreen Currency Corporation would "resell" the foreign currency and if the price it obtained was more than the price specified in the contract, Carragreen Currency Corporation would pay its customer the difference. The customer also had the right to require actual physical delivery of the foreign currency, although it seems no one actually ever required Carragreen Currency Corporation to do this. Carragreen Currency Corporation used the same form of contract for its transactions with all its customers.

Carragreen Currency Corporation hedged its exposure by itself entering into options to acquire foreign currency on the Chicago Futures Exchange. Occasionally, specific contracts with a customer were individually hedged, but normally Carragreen Currency Corporation hedged "in bulk" by entering into one hedging contract relating to its transactions with several customers.

Carragreen Currency Corporation attracted customers by advertising in various newspapers and by cold-calling over the telephone.

Carragreen Currency Corporation itself brought the case seeking a court declaration that its activities did not breach the prohibition on conducting unauthorized futures markets or dealing in futures contracts on behalf of other people. The main issue was whether or not the contracts were futures contracts.

Under the definition of commodity agreement, there must be an obligation to make or accept delivery at a particular time, and it was argued that as the customer had a discretion about when to exercise the option Carragreen Currency Corporation's contracts could not be commodity agreements. The court rejected this argument, indicating that the particular time may be specified by reference to an event—which could be the time of exercise of the option (which had to be sometime before 4:00 PM Sydney time on the expiry date).[27] Furthermore, the contracts were standardized agreements and foreign currency can be a commodity for these purposes. The court held that Carragreen Currency Corporation's contracts were eligible commodity agreements and therefore futures contracts.

The Commission also argued that the contracts were adjustment agreements. While agreeing that the contract in this case involved an adjustment, and so distinguishing the facts in this case from those in the Shoreline Currencies case, the court held that for there to be an adjustment agreement it was necessary for a person, depending upon the circumstances, either to be under an obligation to pay, or have a right to receive, an amount of money. It was not sufficient that a person might just have a right to receive money. In this case, on exercise of the option the customer would have a right to receive money. However, the arrangements did not contemplate that, depending on the future circumstances, the customer would have to pay money. In the court's view this meant that the contracts were not adjustment agreements. This was not significant for the final outcome of the case, since the court held the contracts were eligible commodity agreements.

That was not the end of the story. Carragreen Currency Corporation argued that even if its contracts were futures contracts it was not conducting in an unauthorized futures market. The court looked at Carragreen Currency Corporation's office, personnel, communications and general infrastructure, and held that they were a facility by means of which futures contracts were regularly made. This was sufficient for Carragreen Currency Corporation to be conducting a futures market. Carragreen Currency Corporation was breaching the then equivalent of section 1123 of the Corporations Law.

Although not much help for its long term business plans (given that the court said it was conducting an unauthorized futures market), Carragreen Currency Corporation won on the broking point. The court held that entering into back-to-back hedging contracts was not the same as dealing in futures contracts on another person's behalf, so that the company did not breach the legislative restriction doing this.

Lombard Nash International Case[28]

Lombard Nash attracted customers through newspaper advertisements and financial publications. The precise advertisements varied, but one was headed "You can make big profits fast." Potential customers were also contacted over the telephone.

The terms of the arrangements between Lombard Nash and its customers seemed to be rather vague, and there was no written agreement precisely setting them out. The materials sent to customers indicated that they would be leveraged and could, for example, control DM 125,000 by an investment of approximately $5,500. The materials indicated that if the foreign currency depreciated in value, the investors would receive any profit. However, in at least some cases the initial investment was not repaid. This meant that even although the value of the foreign currency increased, when taken together with the initial investment the customer could make an overall loss. Lombard Nash's literature did not indicate that the initial investment was non-refundable, and at least two customers gave evidence that they thought the purpose of the initial investment was just to cover decreases in the value of the foreign currency (i.e., to act as a margin) rather than to be a non-refundable payment. They said they were not informed that the amount of their initial investment could be lost even if the value of the foreign currency rose.

The Corporate Affairs Commission argued that Lombard Nash was conducting an unauthorized futures market. The Commission also sought an injunction to stop Lombard Nash inviting the public to invest in these contracts.[29]

On the facts, the court held that the arrangements offered by Lombard Nash were not futures contracts. The arrangements were not commodity agreements as there was no obligation to deliver a commodity. They were not adjustment agreements as it seemed that customers might have a right to receive money if the value of the foreign currency increased, but would not be under an obligation to pay money if the value of the foreign currency decreased.

As the contracts were not futures contracts, Lombard Nash was not conducting an unauthorized futures market. Lombard Nash won on this point, but was to lose on another issue.[30]

Romy & Brother Case[31]

Romy & Brother Pty. Limited advertised for clients in newspapers and by telephone cold-calling. It told its prospective customers that it traded in gold and currencies on behalf of its customers as agent. To trade it was necessary to open an account with Romy by depositing a minimum of $5,000. Trades were normally entered and closed out during the course of a single day, so that by the end of the day the customer would have made a profit or loss.

The court held that Romy's arrangements were "adjustment agreements" and so futures contracts. In coming to this conclusion the court made the following comments in the meaning of adjustment agreement:

- *Particular time.* For there to be an adjustment agreement, the obligation to pay or receive money must depend on a state of affairs at a particular future time. The court held that the time of closing out the trade could be a "particular future time" for these purposes.
- *Is there an adjustment?* Romy argued that there was no adjustment because the client paid a margin at the outset. At the time the adjustment was determined (the time of closeout) the customer would only receive money, and not have to pay money. The court rejected this argument, indicating that margin could be taken into account. (In the Lombard Nash International case, the upfront payment was non-refundable, rather than being margin, which explains why it was not taken into account in determining whether there was an adjustment.)

Since the contracts were futures contracts, the court held that Romy was both conducting an unauthorized futures market and breaching the prohibition on dealing in futures contracts on behalf of others.

The LEPO Case[32]

This case involved a clash between exchanges. Australian Stock Exchange Limited (commonly known as the ASX) is authorized to conduct markets in securities. Sydney Futures Exchange Limited (commonly known as the SFE) is authorized to conduct markets in futures contracts. The ASX proposed to start operating a market in LEPOs (low exercise price options). The SFE objected, claiming that LEPOs were futures contracts and that the ASX was not authorized to conduct a market in futures contracts. The SFE and the ASX went to court to resolve the matter.

LEPOs were to be written as options over parcels of 1,000 shares in an Australian listed company. The exercise price would generally be between 1 and 10 cents. Typically, they were to have a European expiry so that they could only be exercised on the last trading day of the LEPO (this point was significant for one of the judges). If the LEPO was exercised, the shares the subject of the LEPO were to be transferred using the FAST or CHESS systems. FAST and CHESS are electronic systems for recording the ownership of shares and for transferring shares. Shares under the FAST and CHESS systems do not have paper share certificates.

The court held that LEPOs were securities rather than futures contracts. Accordingly, it was appropriate for them to be traded on the ASX. In coming to this conclusion the court made the following comments about the definition of futures contract:

- *Is a share a commodity?* The SFE argued that LEPOs were a commodity agreement of a type that fell within the definition of futures contracts. For this argument to succeed, it was necessary to convince the court that a share is a commodity. The court was not convinced. To be a commodity for this purpose the property in question must be "capable of delivery pursuant to an agreement for its delivery" or "an instrument creating or evidencing a thing in action." The court held that a share was none of these things. Simple delivery of a share is not sufficient to transfer title. Furthermore, as the title to shares was recorded and transferred electronically through the FAST and CHESS systems, there wasn't any instrument creating or evidencing a thing in action.
- *Obligation to deliver?* For there to be an eligible commodity agreement a person must be under an obligation to make or accept delivery at a particular future time of a particular quantity of a particular commodity at a particular price. Two of the judges said that at the time the LEPO was entered there was no such obligation, as the obligation to make delivery would only arise after the exercise notice had been sent and the exercise price (albeit small) had been paid.[33] One judge went further, and said that even on exercise the LEPO does not become a commodity agreement. The reason he gave was that for an agreement to be a commodity agreement there has to be an obligation to make or accept delivery "at a particular future time." On exercise of the LEPO, there was an immediate obligation to transfer the shares—not a future obligation.[34]

The Regulation of Prescribed Interests

A prescribed interest is, in general terms, a right to a time sharing scheme or a right to participate in a profit-making scheme of a particular type. The definition covers a wide range of arrangements from property unit trusts to ostrich farm schemes. It can also cover some derivatives contracts.

The ways that the Corporations Law regulates prescribed interests include:

- Only public corporations may offer prescribed interests to others.
- A public corporation offering a prescribed interest to others must have a prospectus relating to the prescribed interest. The prospectus must comply with numerous detailed requirements.
- A public corporation wanting to offer a prescribed interest to others must structure the prescribed interest in a particular way. Normally a prescribed interest may only be issued under a trust deed which contains numerous provisions required by the Corporations Law and which has been approved by the Australian Securities Commission.[35]

As a result, a person who offers to enter into derivatives arrangements will normally want to make sure that the arrangement is not regulated as a prescribed interest.

The Corporations Law itself contains many exemptions. For example, the prescribed interest provisions will generally not apply to prescribed interests being offered to:

- A person who must invest a minimum amount of $500,000 (unfortunately, it is not always clear how the $500,000 test applies in the case of derivatives contracts).
- A person who controls not less than $10,000,000 for the purposes of investment in securities (this amount includes amounts held by associates and by trusts the person manages).
- A trustee of a superannuation fund that has net assets of not less than $10,000,000.
- A life insurance company that is registered under the Life Insurance Act 1945.[36]

These and many other exemptions mean that the activities of many participants in the derivatives markets will not be regulated as prescribed interests. However, if you have a product or are in any way dealing with an arrangement that falls within the definition of prescribed interest, it is important to check whether one of the relevant exemptions does in fact apply.

Corporations Law Definition of "Prescribed Interest"

Section 9 of the Corporations Law defines a prescribed interest as:

- (a) A "participation interest"; or
- (b) "A right, whether enforceable or not, whether actual, prospective or contingent and whether or not evidenced by a formal document, to participate in a time-sharing scheme." Time-sharing schemes are normally not relevant to people dealing with derivatives.[37]

Participation interest is defined to mean "any right to participate, or any interest:

- (a) In any profits, assets or realization of any financial or business undertaking or scheme whether in Australia or elsewhere;
- (b) In any common enterprise, whether in Australia or elsewhere, in relation to which the holder of the right or interest is led to expect profits, rent or interest from the efforts of the promoter of that enterprise or a third party; or
- (c) In any investment contract. . . . "Investment contract" is in turn defined to mean "any contract, scheme or arrangement that, in substance and irrespective of its form, involves the investment of money in or under such circumstances that the investor acquires or may acquire an interest in, or right in respect of, property, whether in this jurisdiction or elsewhere, that, under, or in accordance with, the terms of the investment will, or may at the option of the investor, be used or employed in common with any other interest in, or right in respect of, property, whether in this jurisdiction or elsewhere, acquired in or under like circumstances."[38]

The definitions of prescribed interests and participation interest contain some exceptions.

Some Cases

Derivatives contracts have been held to be "prescribed interests" in at least two Australian cases.

Carragreen Currency Corporation Case[39]

Carragreen Currency Corporation entered into foreign currency options with its customers. If the customer exercised the option, Carragreen Currency Corporation "resold" the foreign currency. The currency option arrangements were put to prospective customers as being designed to make profits from them. Carragreen Currency Corporation hedged its exposure. Carragreen Currency Corporation relied on the volume of trading to be able to hedge efficiently. The court thought that it was appropriate to treat the customer's profits as profits of the scheme and that Carragreen Currency Corporation was offering a right to participate, or an interest in, profits of a financial business undertaking or scheme. Accordingly, the arrangements fell within paragraph (a) of the definition of "participation interest" and so were prescribed interests.

The court also held that there was a common enterprise, so that the contract also fell within paragraph (b) of the definition of participation interest.

Lombard Nash International Case[40]

Lombard Nash was the company that advertised under the heading "You can make big profits fast." The court in this case thought it was rather unclear precisely what Lombard Nash was offering its customers, but thought that whatever it was offering was being sold on the basis that customers could participate in profits that resulted from Lombard Nash's bulk purchasing. The court held that this was sufficient to make the arrangement a participation interest and so a prescribed interest. Lombard Nash might have won on the futures contract point, but it breached the Corporations Law by not complying with the prescribed interest provisions.

The Regulation of Securities

The Corporations Law also contains a regime that regulates securities. Examples include:

- A person must not establish or conduct, assist in establishing or conducting, or hold out that the person conducts an unauthorized stock market (section 767).
- Prohibitions on people carrying on a business of dealing in securities without a license or exemption (sections 93 and 780).
- Prohibitions on people carrying on an investment advice business without a license or exemption (section 781).

As with futures contracts, there are many more provisions regulating securities.

Corporations Law Definition of Securities

As is also the case with the definition of futures contract, the definition of securities is complex and involves definitions within definitions. In general terms, the definition in section 92 encompasses:

- Debentures, stock, or bonds.
- Shares.
- Prescribed interests.
- Units in shares or prescribed interests.
- Option contracts within the meaning of Chapter 7.

Option contract is defined for the purposes of Chapter 7 to mean an option of a particular type relating to:

- Specified types of securities.
- Commodities, where the option contract is entered into on a stock market of one of a specified number of securities exchanges or an exempt stock market.
- The payment of an amount of money by reference to specified index (e.g., the Australian Stock Exchanges All Ordinaries Price Index) entered into on a stock market of a specified securities exchange or on an exempt stock market.

The precise definitions of securities, option contract, and the other terms referred to in those definitions are more complicated and there are also some exceptions. Notably, the definition of "securities" in section 92 states that it "does not include a futures contract."[41]

The point to note in the context of derivatives is that even if a derivatives contract does not fall within the definition of "futures contract" it is necessary to consider whether it is regulated as a security.

Gambling Laws

The Issue

Different state and territory legislation regulates gambling in Australia. Typically, as well as imposing penalties this legislation provides that gambling contracts are void. For example, the New South Wales Act provides as follows:

> *All contracts or agreements, whether by parole or in writing, by way of gaming or wagering shall be null and void, and no suit shall be brought or maintained in any court of law or equity for recovering any sum of money or valuable thing alleged to be won upon any wager or which has been deposited in the hands of any person to abide any event on which the wager has been made . . .[42]*

There is no general exemption for derivatives contracts. Accordingly, derivatives contracts in appropriate circumstances could be gaming or wagering contracts with the result that they could be void. This possibility was discussed in at least two cases.

Some Cases

Carragreen Currency Corporation Case[43]

In this case it was argued that the foreign currency options Carragreen Currency Corporation sold to its customers were gaming or wagering contracts. The court examined the meaning of gaming or wagering and referred to a passage in the English case of Thacker v. Hardy where Cotton L.J. said:

The essence of gaming or wagering is that one party is to win and the other to lose on a future event, which at the time of the contract is of an uncertain nature— that is to say, if the event turns out one way, A will lose, but if it turns out the other way he will win.[44]

The court referred to past cases establishing that for there to be a gaming or wagering contract it is not sufficient that there be speculation on only one side.[45] Carragreen Currency Corporation's position was fully hedged, and this was sufficient to mean that the contract was not a gaming or wagering contract. The fact that the customer could win or lose was not enough to make the contract a gaming or wagering contract. Accordingly, the contracts were not void as gaming or wagering contracts.

So, in this case the gambling laws did not cause a problem for the derivatives contract. However, the case is significant as it suggests that in appropriate cases derivatives contracts could be void as gaming or wagering contracts. If both Carragreen Currency Corporation and its customers had been speculating, it seems likely that the result would have been quite different. Also, the court thought it significant that Carragreen Currency Corporation hedged all its liabilities. If Carragreen Currency Corporation had only hedged some of its liabilities, the result for at least the unhedged contracts might also have been different.

Jackson v. Cheesman[46]

Around the same time a client was trying the gambling defense against his broker. In May 1985 Cheesman sold contracts for delivery of United States treasury bonds in June 1985. The markets moved against these contracts, and at the beginning of June 1985 Cheesman's broker closed them out. A large loss resulted.

The defendants argued that the contracts were gaming or wagering contracts with the result that they were unenforceable. The court reviewed various previous cases on gaming and wagering and confirmed the principle that it was necessary for both parties to be able to win or lose depending on movements in the market. The defendants on their side might well have been speculating, but their broker was not. Accordingly, the arrangements between the broker and its clients were not unenforceable on the basis of gambling and wagering.

In both of the Carragreen Currency Corporation case and Jackson v. Cheesman it was held that the contracts in question were not unenforceable as gaming or wagering contracts. Had the facts been different, they could have been unenforceable. Some derivatives contracts could be gaming or wagering contracts if both parties are speculating. This means that people dealing with derivatives in the Australian context should always consider whether or not their derivative arrangements could be gaming or wagering contracts.

A Limited Exception

Section 1141 of the Corporations Law provides a useful but limited exception to those gambling laws. It states:

Nothing in a law of this jurisdiction about gaming or wagering prevents the entering into of, or affects the validity or enforceability of, a future contract made:

(a) on a futures market of a futures exchange or of a recognized futures exchange; or

(b) on an exempt futures market; or

(c) as permitted by the business rules of a futures association, of a futures exchange or of a recognized futures exchange.[47]

Section 778 of the Corporations Law provides a corresponding exemption for option contracts entered into on a stock market of a securities exchange or an exempt stock market.[48]

Unfortunately, these exemptions are of very limited application. They will not help at all with most over the counter derivatives contracts.

Some Final Words

While no means forming a complete body of law, the derivatives litigation we have seen in Australia to date provides useful examples of some of the things that can go wrong. Many of these examples have an international appeal, as the issues could equally have arisen in many jurisdictions throughout the world. Others such as the Corporations Law regulatory cases are more Australian specific. There will be no doubt further examples of things that can go wrong over the coming years.

Legislation also changes and much thought is currently being given in Australia to restructuring the ways derivatives are regulated. At this stage changes are only at the discussion stage, but over the coming years it is likely that there will be amendments to the way the Corporations Law regulates derivatives.

From both a litigation and legislation perspective, we live in interesting times.

ENDNOTES

1. *See* Commonwealth of Australia v. Tasmania. The Tasmanian Dam Case (1983) 158 CLR 1 (High Court), where CLR stands for Commonwealth Law Reports.

2. These proceedings resulted in numerous judgments totalling several hundred pages in length including:

   • AWA Ltd v. Daniels trading as Deloitte Haskins & Sells & Others (1992) 7 ACSR 759 in which the trial judge, Rogers CJ in the NSW Supreme Court, examined the liability of the different people involved in the proceedings. ACSR are the Australian Corporations and Securities Reports.

   • AWA Ltd v. Daniels trading as Deloitte Haskins & Sells & Others (1992) 9 ACSR 383 in which Rogers CJ considered the issues of contributory negligence and apportioned the loss on a percentage basis between the people liable.

   • Daniels & Others (formerly practicing as Deloitte Haskins & Sells) v. Anderson & Others, Hooke v. Daniels & Others (formerly practicing as Deloitte Haskins & Sells), Daniels & Others (formerly practicing as Deloitte Haskins & Sells) v. AWA Ltd (1995) 16 ACSR 607 in which various matters decided by Rogers CJ were taken on appeal to the NSW Court of Appeal.

3. AWA Ltd v. Koval & Others, an unreported judgment of Rogers CJ in the NSW Supreme Court (no. 50018 of 1992; judgment date 24 February 1993).

4. 7 ACSR 759 at 814.

5. 6 ACSR 658 at 818–819.

6. 7 ACSR 759 at 789. "Indulging" should probably have been "hedging."

7. 7 ACSR 759 at 805.

8. 7 ACSR 759 at 805.

9. 7 ACSR 759 at 860.

10. AWA Ltd. v. Koval (unreported) at 5. See n.4 for the case reference.

11. Simonius Vischer & Co. v. Holt & Thompson [1979] 2 NSWLR 322 (NSW Court of Appeal). NSWLR stands for New South Wales Law Reports.

12. Qintex Australia Finance Ltd. v. Schroders Australia Ltd. (1990) 3 ACSR 267 (NSW Supreme Court).

13. Rest-Ezi Furniture Pty Ltd. v. Ace Shohin (Australia) Pty. Ltd., an unreported judgment of Yeldham J. in the NSW Supreme Court (no. 14267 of 1985; judgment date 25 September 1986).

14. Dennison v. Ace Shohin (Australia) Pty. Ltd., an unreported judgment of Lockhart J. in the Federal Court (no G179 of 1985; judgment date 17 July 1987). In this case the misrepresentations included that the margin call payments were not themselves at risk.

15. Option Investments (Australia) Pty. Ltd. v. Martin [1981] VR 138 (Victorian Supreme Court). VR stands for Victorian Reports. Martin appealed to the Victorian Court of Appeal claiming that the trial judge was wrong in his finding of fact. He was unsuccessful (Martin v. Option Investments (Australia) Pty. Ltd. (No.2) [1982] VR 464).

16. Ross McConnel Kitchen & Co. v. Lorbergs, an unreported judgment of Miles J. in the NSW Supreme Court (no. 13498 of 1980; judgment date 31 March 1983).

17. Darlington Futures Ltd. v. Delco Australia Pty. Ltd. (1986) 161 CLR 500 (High Court).

18. Daly v. Sydney Stock Exchange Ltd. (1986) 160 CLR 371 is another case that went to the High Court. That case was about whether a particular claim for inappropriate conduct by a broker could be made against a fidelity fund.

19. Most of the provisions in the Corporations Law regulating futures contracts are found in chapter 8 of the Corporations Law. The Corporations Law came into force at the beginning of 1991. Some of the cases referred to in this paper relate to legislation that preceded the Corporations Law. To avoid confusion, this chapter refers to the equivalent Corporations Law provision throughout.

20. The definition of "standardized agreement" is in section 9 of the Corporations Law. Section 54 of the Corporations Law sets out when Chapter 8 agreements are "of the same kind" as each other. However, even with these sections it is not certain how similar the agreements really need to be.

21. Under section 55 of the Corporations Law "Chapter 8 obligations," and "Chapter 8 rights," are obligations or rights whether or not enforceable at law or in equity.

22. Australian Securities Commission v. Dempster, an unreported judgment of French J. in the Federal Court (no. WAG3002/92, judgment date 24 February 1992). This case involved a farmer who had a long standing interest in charting wool and wheat prices. When his interest changed to a business, the Commission sought to prevent him carrying on a business as an unlicensed futures adviser.

23. Commissioner for Corporate Affairs v. Shintoh Shohin Pty. Ltd. & Another (1988) 6 ACLC 8 (Victorian Supreme Court). ACLC stands for Australian Company Law Cases.

24. Shoreline Currencies (Aust) Pty. Ltd. v. Corporate Affairs Commission (NSW) and Another (1986) 10 ACLR 847 (NSW Supreme Court). ACLR stands for Australian Company Law Reports.

25. The court only had to decide whether or not the contracts fell within the definition of "commodity agreement." The parties to the litigation had agreed that if they fell within the definition of "commodity agreement" they would also fall within the definition of "eligible commodity agreement" and so be "futures contracts" (page 852).

26. Carragreen Currency Corporation Pty. Ltd. v. Corporate Affairs Commission (NSW) (1986) 11 ACLR 298 (NSW Supreme Court).

27. Some of the views expressed in the LEPO case differ from the view expressed by the court in the Carragreen Currency Corporation case on this point.

28. Corporate Affairs Commission (NSW) v. Lombard Nash International Pty. Ltd. (No.2) (1987) 11 ACLR 866 (NSW Supreme Court).

29. This relates to the laws regulating prescribed interests rather than futures contracts. Prescribed interests are discussed later.

30. Lombard Nash lost on the prescribed interest point which is discussed later.

31. Corporate Affairs Commission (NSW) v. Romy & Brother Pty. Ltd. & Another (1987) 2 ACLR 289 (NSW Supreme Court).

32. Sydney Futures Exchange Ltd. v. Australian Stock Exchange Ltd. & Another (1995) 128 ALR 417 (Court of Appeal of the Federal Court). ALR stands for Australian Law Reports.

33. See Gummow J. at 451 and Lindgren J. at 477-478. Gummow J. is now a judge of the High Court. This differs from the Carragreen Currency Corporation case where the court—made up of a single judge—held that the currency options were eligible commodity agreements.

34. *See* Gummow J. at 452.

35. *See* Part 7.12 of the Corporations Law.

36. *See* section 66 of the Corporations Law and regulations 7.12.05 and 7.12.06 of the Corporations Regulations.

37. The section 9 definition of time sharing scheme requires the scheme to operate for at least 3 years to fall within the definition.

38. *See* section 9 of the Corporations Law.

39. *See* n.321 for the case reference.

40. *See* n.323 for the case reference.

41. Gummow J. in the LEPO case thought that these words did not necessarily mean that an arrangement that is a futures contract cannot be a security too (at page 447). Lindgren J. disagreed, saying that the words made futures contracts and securities mutually exclusive (at page 463). *See* n.327 for the case reference.

42. Section 16 of the Gaming and Betting Act 1912 (NSW). Section 16 has exemptions for contributing towards prizes and betting on a licensed racecourse with a bookmaker. Neither of these exemptions is aimed at derivatives contracts.

43. *See* n.321 for the case reference.

44. Thacker v. Hardy (1878) 4 QBD 685, 695 cited by Hodgson J. at 319.

45. Morely v. Richardson & Another (1942) 65 CLR 512 (High Court).

46. Jackson Securities Ltd. & Another v. Cheesman & Others (1986) 4 NSWLR 485 (NSW Supreme Court).

47. Section 1141(1). Section 1141(2) contains an exemption for certain arrangements prescribed under section 72A(1)(b).

48. Section 778(1). Section 778(2) contains a corresponding exemption for certain arrangements prescribed under section 92A(1)(b).

DERIVATIVES LITIGATION IN THE UNITED KINGDOM
ANDREW J. C. CLARK

Think of English swaps litigation and *Hazell v. Hammersmith & Fulham London Borough Council and others*[1] and the other local authority cases,[2] which gained such prominence in the early 1990s, immediately come to mind. These were the cases that confirmed that local authorities did not have the legal power to enter into interest rate swap transactions. But those cases also went on to clarify a number of other points of law of significance to swap transactions, including whether the parties to those void contracts were entitled to recover the payments made under the contracts. This chapter begins by summarizing two of the most prominent cases which followed *Hazell* and which endeavoured to resolve the uncertainties created by the local authority ultra vires decisions.

The local authority cases also highlighted for lawyers and practitioners the importance of credit risk management by ensuring the legal enforceability of derivative transactions through the old rubrics of due diligence and clear and careful documentation. More recently however the cerebral effort of derivatives lawyers and practitioners in England, like in the United States, has, in relation to over-the-counter derivatives transactions, focused less on the management of credit risk and more on an assessment of the litigation risks which may arise from the relationship between the parties to a trade. The focus has centered in particular on the extent to which banks and other financial institutions may owe duties to their counterparties which, in the event of any breach of those duties, may render the institutions liable for losses suffered by their counterparties. Whether a duty of care or a duty to advise may be owed to a counterparty under English law, and if so the extent of that duty, is briefly considered in this chapter by reference to some recent, and some not so recent, cases. In this regard the 1995 case of *Bankers Trust International Plc v. PT Dharmala Sakti Sejahtera*[3] is particularly significant. Finally, the Bank of England's London Code of Conduct is briefly considered in relation to derivatives transactions.

The Local Authority Cases and the Recovery of Money Paid under Void Swap Transactions

Turning first to the line of local authority cases, it should be appreciated that in the wake of the House of Lords' decision in *Hazell v. Hammersmith & Fulham*,[4] a large number of cases were brought to court by banks and local authorities who had entered into void swap transactions. Among the issues to be decided in those cases was the extent to which the parties could recover payments made under the swap contracts.

Westdeutsche Landesbank Girozentrale v. Islington LBC

The lead case on the issue of recovery of payments was *Westdeutsche Landesbank Girozentrale v. Islington London Borough Council*[5] which concerned a swap contract concluded on June 16, 1987. The terms of the contract were that during a 10-year period starting on June 18, 1987 the bank, as fixed rate payer, would pay interest to the local authority at the rate of 7.5% per annum on a notional principal sum of £25 million, and the local authority, as floating rate payer, would pay interest

The author wishes to thank Michael Hawthorne, an associate with Allen & Overy, for his valuable assistance with the production of this chapter. The material is current as of January 1, 1997.

on the same sum at the domestic sterling LIBOR rate. In addition, an upfront payment of £2.5 million was made by the bank to the local authority on June 18, 1987. The local authority paid the upfront payment into an account in which the authority kept other monies belonging to it, and used the funds in that account to meet the authority's general expenditure (it was accepted by the parties that as soon as the local authority paid the money into a mixed account it gained the legal title to the money). Half yearly payments were made during the period from June 18, 1987 to June 19, 1989, in which period the payments by the bank to the local authority exceeded those made by the local authority to the bank by £1,145,525.93.

The question of how those payments were to be returned was, superficially, a simple one. However, as Lord Goff commented in his judgement in the House of Lords:

> *This is a case concerned solely with money. All that has to be done is to order that each party should pay back the money it has receive or, more sensibly, to strike a balance and order that the party who has received most should repay the balance. It should be as simple as that. And yet we find ourselves faced with a mass of difficult problems, and struggling to reconcile a number of difficult cases.*[6]

The case, as it progressed from the Commercial Court through the Court of Appeal to the House of Lords, raised a number of very complex questions in relation to the English law of trusts and restitution, the details of which are beyond the scope of this chapter. In outline, however, the bank's primary argument was that, while it was accepted that the local authority had gained the legal title to the money the local authority had received, because the money was paid under a void contract, the equitable title to that money remained with the bank and the money was held by the local authority on a resulting trust for the bank.

The question of whether or not a resulting trust arose in respect of the upfront payment had a bearing on the award of interest which could be made. Under English law, there are only very few circumstances in which the courts may award compound interest. However, one of those circumstances is where a trustee mis-applies trust funds, and it is appropriate for an order for compound interest to be made against the trustee in order for it to account for the profits which the trustee has made from the trust funds.[7] The bank argued that the proper order for interest to be made against the local authority as a trustee was an order for compound interest.

In the Commercial Court, Mr Justice Hobhouse found that there had been no consideration for the upfront payment since the underlying agreement was ultra vires and void and the bank had not intended to make a gift of the money. Accordingly, he held that the bank could recover the balance of the upfront payment both at law by restitution, and also in equity. In the light of his finding that the local authority held the upfront payment as trustee for the bank, Mr Justice Hobhouse decided that it was within his discretion to award compound interest from the date on which the local authority stopped making payments, and made such an order.

In deciding what order for interest to make, Mr Justice Hobhouse took account of the fact that, but for the upfront payment, the local authority would have had to increase the level of its borrowing during the period of the swap in order to maintain its level of expenditure. He also took into account the fact that the bank had received an upfront fee of the same amount in a parallel swap transaction which it had entered into, and so held that the bank had not suffered any loss until the local authority stopped making payments. Both the local authority and the bank appealed to the Court of Appeal. The local authority appealed on the ground that the consideration for the payment of the upfront free had not wholly failed, by virtue of the fact that the local authority had made four payments under the void contract, and therefore restitution could not be ordered. The bank's appeal centred on its contention that interest should have been awarded from the date of the commencement of the contract, rather than from the date on which the local authority stopped making payments, on the ground that the local authority had had the use of the money for the whole of that period.

In the Court of Appeal it was held that, even though payments were made by the local authority before it realised that the swap was ultra vires, there had been no consideration for the upfront payment by the bank, and accordingly the remedy of restitution was available at law. However, since compound interest could only be awarded against the local authority if it held the money on trust for the bank, the Court of Appeal also had to consider whether, in the alternative, the local authority held the sums received under the void contract as trustee for the bank.

The Court of Appeal held that, since the local authority had received the upfront payment under a void contract, it had, from that date onwards, held it on a resulting trust for the bank, and so compound interest could be awarded. The Court of Appeal also held that the fact that the bank had received an equivalent amount in a parallel swap transaction was irrelevant to the local authority's obligation to pay interest on the upfront fee. The Court of Appeal was strongly influenced in deciding what order to make in respect of interest by the fact that the local authority would have had to borrow an equivalent sum had it not received the upfront payment. The Court reasoned that since that borrowing would have incurred compound interest, the local authority should be liable for compound interest for the entire period during which it had had the use of the balance of the upfront sum if it was not to benefit from its use of the trust monies. The local authority appealed the award of compound interest to the House of Lords.

The House of Lords overturned the award of compound interest, and instead made an award of simple interest from the date on which the bank's cause of action arose (namely the commencement of the void contract). In reaching this decision the House rejected the arguments in favour of the existence of a resulting trust which had prevailed in both courts below. The House found that it was not the intention of the parties that such a trust should arise, nor was the local authority's conscience affected in such a way as to justify the imposition of a trust.[8] Ordinarily, a resulting trust may arise where a payee receives money from a payer in circumstances where it knows that it is not entitled to keep it, but where the payee then, unconscionably, does keep the payment. That situation was contrasted to the position of the bank and the local authority, where both parties, at the time when the payments were made, believed the swap transaction to be valid. Whereas in the former situation the payee's conscience is affected by its retention of the sums paid over, the House of Lords considered that it could not be properly said that it was in any way unconscionable for the local authority to retain the upfront payment in the circumstances of this case.

It was accordingly held by the House of Lords that, where money is paid over under a contract which is subsequently found to be ultra vires and therefore void, and where, at the time the contract was made, neither the payer nor the payee could have known that the contract was void, the payee does not hold the money on a resulting trust for the payer, and the payer's only remedy is in restitution. The House of Lords was strongly influenced in reaching this conclusion by the practical consequences of imposing a trust, which could affect innocent third parties to whom the payee paid some or all of the money received from the payer. One such consequence would be that it would be possible for the payer to trace the funds into the hands of those to whom the payee paid those funds away. The House of Lords considered that this would unfairly favour the payer over those innocent third parties, and would run contrary to the desired policy of creating certainty in commercial relationships.

The Local Authority Cases and the Wagering Contracts Issue

One of the issues which arose from *Hazell* was whether, in some circumstances, a swap contract could be rendered unenforceable and void by the provisions of the Gaming Acts.[9]

As became apparent from the local authority swaps litigation, the number of swap transactions which local authorities had entered into prior to *Hazell* was considerable. When *Hazell* was decided in the House of Lords, the approximate statistics were that 77 local authorities, other than Hammersmith & Fulham, had entered into some 400 swap transactions. However, in addition to those local authorities, Hammersmith & Fulham had itself entered into 592 swap transactions, of which 297 were still outstanding by 31st March, 1989. While some of the local authority swap contracts were entered into to hedge against exposures under other swap contracts, it became clear that one purpose for which the local authorities had entered into such swap transactions was to increase their revenues by "speculating" on interest rate movements.

Morgan Grenfell & Co Limited v. Welwyn Hatfield DC

The question of whether the element of speculation rendered the swap contracts void under the Gaming Acts was considered by Mr Justice Hobhouse in *Morgan Grenfell & Co Limited v. Welwyn Hatfield District Council (Islington London Borough Council, Third Party).*[10] The facts of the case were that on June 22, 1987 Morgan Grenfell, as fixed rate interest payer, entered into a ten year swap contract with Welwyn Hatfield DC, as the floating rate payer. On June 23, 1987, as part of the same transaction, and through the same brokers, Welwyn Hatfield DC, as the fixed rate payer, entered into a ten year swap contract with the third party, Islington LBC, as the floating rate payer. The nominal principal in each contract was £25 million. So far as Welwyn Hatfield DC was concerned, the contracts were back-to-back. The payments of fixed and/or floating rate interest were identical in both contracts, but Welwyn Hatfield DC benefited to the extent of £210,00 by virtue of the difference in the upfront payment which it received from Morgan Grenfell and that which it was required to pay to Islington LBC. Welwyn Hatfield DC undertook no market risk, and did not believe that it was undertaking any legal or solvency risk.

Following the decision in *Westdeutsche* in the Commercial Court at first instance,[11] the state of the law was that the net payers under void contracts were entitled to recover from the payees the balance of the sums paid both at law and in equity. Morgan Grenfell and Welwyn Hatfield DC agreed to be bound by that decision, but Islington LBC raised a preliminary issue in the following terms:

> *Does the third party have a good defence to the Defendant's action for restitution on the grounds that (i) the interest swap transaction entered into by them on 23rd June, 1987 was within the ambit of section 18 of the Gaming Act 1845*

and/or Section 1 of the Gaming Act 1892; and (ii) the said interest rate swap transaction is not removed from the ambit of section 18 of the Gaming Act 1845 and section 1 of the Gaming Act 1892 by virtue of the provisions of section 63 and paragraph 12 of schedule 1 of the Financial Services Act 1986 on the grounds that it was not entered into by the Defendant and the Third Party by way of the business of either of them or each of them?

The net sum which was paid by Morgan Grenfell to Welwyn Hatfield DC was £1,918,458.90, and the net sum paid by Welwyn Hatfield DC to Islington LBC was £1,708,458.90. It was the latter sum which Welwyn Hatfield DC was trying to recover from Islington LBC in the Third Party proceedings. The questions to be decided was:

1. Apart from the Financial Services Act 1986, was the supposed contract a wagering contract?
2. If it was a wagering contract, was it entered into by either Welwyn Hatfield DC or Islington LBC by way of business within the meaning of section 63 of the Financial Services Act 1986?[12]
3. If the supposed contract was a wagering contract, and if it was not entered into by way of business, did that provide a defence to the claim for restitution?

In relation to the first question, Mr Justice Hobhouse held as follows:

The mere fact that there is a provision for the payment of differences does not mean that the contract must be a wagering contract. It merely raises that possibility or justifies an inference. If the other features of the relevant transaction show or confirm that it is a wagering contract, then it is unenforceable and void. If on the other hand the other features of the transaction do not confirm that its character was gaming or wagering, then the contract, notwithstanding that it provides payment of differences, is fully effective and enforceable.

. . . In the context of interest rate swap contracts entered into by parties or institutions involved in the capital markets and the making or receiving of loans, the normal inference will be that the contracts are not gaming or wagering but are commercial or financial transactions to which the law will, in the absence of some other consideration, give full recognition and effect.[13]

As to the second question of whether the contract was entered into by way of business within the meaning of section 63 of the Financial Services Act 1986, Mr Justice Hobhouse held that the local authority's purpose in entering into the contracts was to secure upfront payments in exchange for incurring a revenue liability to be spread over a period of 10 years. The local authority was motivated in its desire to enter into the transactions by its need to raise extra revenue. Mr Justice Hobhouse held that the speculative element of the transactions was secondary, and incidental to the contractual mechanism by which the local authority was trying to obtain, in its revenue account, loans from the later years to the first year. Mr Justice Hobhouse held as follows:

If there was an element of wagering in what Islington did, it was merely a subordinate element and was not the substance of the transaction and does not affect the validity and enforceability of the transaction.

As to the third question of whether, if not entered into by way of business, the contract was a wagering contract, Mr Justice Hobhouse held that the local authority was acting by way of business in entering into the transaction and therefore the issue did not arise. The argument that the local authority, when acting ultra vires, could not be acting by way of business was rejected.

Accordingly, it appears that in all but the most exceptional cases swap transactions will not be rendered void by the Gaming Acts. However, it still remains to be seen whether transactions of a highly speculative nature will be rendered void by the Gaming Acts and some commentators have suggested that they may be.[14]

Note that before a transaction can be rendered void by the Gaming Acts, the court has to find that both parties entered into the transaction for gaming or wagering purposes. Where one party is able to maintain that it entered into the transaction for a business purpose, the contract should be enforceable on the basis of section 63 of Financial Services Act 1986.[15] The limits to what the proper business purposes of a bank conducting derivatives transactions are for these purposes have yet to be fully tested, although the cases suggest that the English courts will be most unwilling to hold that the Gaming Acts render void derivatives contracts made between banks or other commercial institutions.

Duty of Care in OTC Derivatives

A duty of care under English law may arise by contract or under the law of tort (there is also a duty not to mis-state negligently material facts in relation to any proposed transaction and this is discussed below in relation to the law on misrepresentation). However, whatever the source of the duty of care, it is a general principle of English law that whenever a person assumes responsibility to perform professional or quasi-professional services for another and that other relies on the performance of those services, the relationship between the parties is itself sufficient to give rise to a duty on the part of the person providing the services, to exercise reasonable skill and care.[16] It should be noted that there are certain technical differences between a contractual claim and a claim based on the law of tort although these differences are beyond the scope of this chapter.[17] A party who has a claim in contract and in tort for breach of a duty of care can elect which claim to bring. As summarised by Lord Goff in a leading case:

> ... unless his contract precludes him from doing so, the plaintiff, who has available to him concurrent remedies in contract and tort, may choose that remedy which appears to him to be the most advantageous.[18]

Contractual Duty of Care

A contractual duty to advise with reasonable care and skill may arise by virtue of an express term of the contract, or by implication. In the case of a contract to give advice, a term is implied that the adviser will advise with reasonable care and skill.[19] This term implied by statute is similar in principle to the duty of care imposed by the courts in many of the cases referred to below.

The degree of care and skill required is that which is to be expected of a professional man of ordinary competence and experience.[20] The principle was summarised in a 1957 case as follows:

The test is the standard of the ordinary skilled man exercising and professing to have that special skill. A man need not possess the highest expert skill, it is well established law that it is sufficient if he exercises the ordinary skill of an ordinary competent man exercising that particular art.[21]

What is important is that the advice should be given carefully, and that it should be reasonable. The extent of the duty to advise does not depend on it being given by a member of a formal profession. Any banker or trader experienced in derivatives who advises on, for example, hedging risks, and who hold themselves out as competent to advise on such matters, will be required to obtain the statutory level of skill.

Duty of Care in Tort

A duty of case may arise between two parties, even where there is no contract between them, if the relationship between them is one in which one party undertakes to exercise its skills for the other party, and the other party relies on it to do so.

Hedley Byrne v. Heller

The leading case on the incidence of such a duty is *Hedley Byrne v. Heller.*[22] The facts in *Hedley Byrne* were that a bank made enquiries by telephone to a merchant bank concerning the financial position of one of its customers. The bank stated that it wanted to know this information in confidence, and without responsibility on the part of the merchant bank. The merchant bank replied that the customer in question was a good credit risk, and the information was duly passed on by the bank to one of its own customers who had sought the information. Relying on the information which it had received, the bank's customer entered into a transaction with the merchant bank's customer, which customer soon afterwards went into liquidation. The bank's customer claimed against the merchant bank that it had responded to the bank's enquiries negligently, and that consequently it had caused the loss suffered by the bank's customer as a result of the insolvency of the customer of the merchant bank.

At trial it was held that the merchant bank had been negligent in giving the credit reference, but that it was not under a duty of care to the bank. Accordingly, there were no grounds on which damages could be awarded. The Court of Appeal upheld the decision that there was no duty of care, and so did not go on to consider whether the earlier finding of negligence was correct. The decision that there was no duty of care was overturned by the House of Lords, although the House of Lords also held that the merchant bank was nevertheless not liable to the bank, since it had provided the information sought subject to an express disclaimer of liability. The circumstances in which the House of Lords held that a duty of care in tort arose appear in the following passage from *Hedley Byrne v. Heller:*

. . . if someone possessed of a special skill undertakes, quite irrespective of contract, to apply that skill for the assistance of another person who relies upon such skill, a duty of care will arise . . .

Furthermore, if in a sphere in which a person is so placed that others could reasonably rely upon his judgment or his skill or upon his ability to make careful inquiry, a person takes it upon himself to give information or advice to, or allows his information or advice to be passed on to, another person who, as he knows or should know, will place reliance upon it, then a duty of care will arise.[23]

It was held that the merchant bank owed the bank's customer a duty of care, notwithstanding the fact that there was no direct relationship between them. The reasoning applied by the House of Lords was that where a person gives advice in circumstances in which a reasonable man would know that trust was being placed in him, and that his skill and judgement was being relied on, if that person then goes on to give that advice without clearly disclaiming his responsibility for it, he accepts the duty to exercise due skill and care in giving that advice. If it is foreseeable that loss or damage will result from a breach of that duty of care, then the third party will have an action in negligence against the advisor.

The test of whether a party could reasonably rely upon the judgment and skill of the adviser is an objective test. If the adviser knew, or ought to have known, that the recipient of the advice was relying on the advice then there will be an assumption of responsibility.

When Will a Duty of Care Arise in a Derivatives Transaction?

There is little English case law on the circumstances in which a duty of care will arise specifically in a derivatives transaction. The best-known most recent case is *Bankers Trust International Plc v. PT Dharmala Sakti Sejahtera*[24] which is discussed in detail below. Apart from that case, it is necessary to look at the line of bank-customer cases for an understanding of when the English courts may impose a duty of care or a duty to advise. Some of the more important cases are set out below.

Woods v. Martins Bank Ltd

A case in which a bank was held to be under a duty of care to a customer was the 1959 case of *Woods v. Martins Bank Ltd.*[25] In that case, the defendant bank negligently advised the customer to invest in the shares of a company on the basis that the company was financially sound and that the investment was a wise one to make. In fact the company was in a poor financial condition, and had a considerable overdraft with the bank which, despite being continually pressed by the bank to repay, it did not repay during the time when the bank was advising the customer. The bank was held liable in damages for the negligent advice. In the course of giving judgment, Mr Justice Salmon said:

> *In my judgment, the limit of a banker's business cannot be laid down as a matter of law. The nature of such a business must in each case be a matter of fact and, accordingly, cannot be treated as if it were a matter of pure law . . .*

> *In considering what is and what is not within the scope of the defendant bank's business I cannot do better than look at their publications.*[26]

Mr Justice Salmon then went on to consider various booklets and advertisements published by the defendants in which there were various references to advice on financial matters being available to customers and concluded:

> *I find that it was and is within the scope of the defendant bank's business to advise on all financial matters and that, as they did advise [the plaintiff], they owed a duty to the plaintiff to advise him with reasonable care and skill in each of the transactions to which I have referred.*

The *Woods v. Martins Bank Ltd* case demonstrates what has subsequently become clearer in the more recent cases referred to below: that in assessing the existence and extent of any duty of care, an English court will look first at the facts in relation to each case to ascertain whether there was any express or implied assumption of responsibility by a bank or other financial institution to advise, and second at whether that advice was reasonably relied on by the plaintiff.

Box v. Midland Bank

The principles set out in *Wood v. Martins Bank Ltd* were followed in another case concerning the relationship between a bank and its customer, *Box v. Midland Bank Limited*.[27] In that case, the bank's customer was a businessman who required a substantial overdraft in order to perform what he hoped would be a lucrative contract. When the customer asked the bank manager if the overdraft would be granted, the bank manager told him that head office approval would be a "mere formality," and lead the customer to believe that he would almost certainly be granted the overdraft. The customer, in reliance on the representation made to him, proceeded to expend a large amount of money in anticipation of the overdraft being granted. The overdraft was not granted and the customer sued the bank for the losses which he claimed to have suffered as a result of the negligent advice of the bank manager that the overdraft would be granted.

The court held that the customer's affairs were, as the bank manager knew, in such a poor financial condition that there was never the slightest prospect of the overdraft being made available. It was also held that the bank manager was under no duty to advise the customer about the prospects of the overdraft being granted. However, once the manager undertook to give that advice, by proffering an opinion on the likelihood of the overdraft being granted, the manager was under a duty, which he had breached, to exercise reasonable skill and care. It was clear from the facts that the customer had relied on the advice which was proffered.

Royal Bank Trust Co. v. The Pampellonne

A case in which a duty of care was held not to arise in a financial contract was *Royal Bank Trust Co. v. The Pampellonne*.[28] In that case, the customer of a bank went to see his bank manager in relation to an investment which he proposed to make in a deposit taking company. The bank manager orally told the customer that he had in his possession a recent credit report on the company, and the bank manager explained to the customer the substance of the report. The bank manager then handed to the customer a brochure and application form for the deposit taking company, which the customer completed and in due course returned to the bank. The bank manger transferred a substantial amount of money from the customer's account to the deposit taking company. The deposit taking company subsequently went into liquidation and the customer lost the majority of his investment. The customer alleged that the bank manager had provided him with advice in relation to his investment, and that accordingly the bank manager was bound to do so with reasonable skill and care.

It was held by the court that the bank manager had only passed on to the customer the information about the deposit taking company which he had had in his possession, that he had not expressed any opinion as to the merits of the investment, and that he had left it to the customer to decide whether or not he considered the investment to be a good one. In the circumstances, it was held that the bank manager did not undertake to give the customer financial advice, and that the relationship between them was not one in which a duty to exercise due skill and care in giving financial advice arose. In reaching this conclusion, the court took into account the fact that there was no evidence that the customer had relied on any "advice" given to him by the bank manager. However, even if the customer had relied on the information given to him, it would probably have been held that the information he received did not amount to advice. The information which he was given enabled him to make his own decision. It is notable that although the customer was a personal customer he was not found by the court to be particularly financially naive. Where customers have shown a greater degree of financial naivety, the courts have been more willing to impose a duty of care on banks.

Verity and Spindler v. Lloyds Bank plc

A recent and well-publicised case where a duty of care was found to exist between a bank and its customer was *Verity and Spindler v. Lloyds Bank plc.*[29] Immediately after that case was decided there was a considerable amount of press comment which suggested that it represented an extension of the duty of care owed by a bank to its customer. In fact, the decision did not vary the duty of care owed by a bank to its customer. It is nonetheless illustrative of the type of relationship into which the courts appear to be willing to find a duty of care to advise and the kind of factors which the courts will take into account.

The bank's customers were a couple who maintained accounts with the bank in relation to their small business activities. They both owed money to the bank, and it was apparent that they were going to have to increase their income in order to discharge their borrowings. To do so, one of the customers wanted to buy a dilapidated property and renovate it for profit. The bank published a leaflet in which it offered to give business advice to customers starting small businesses and, accordingly, the couple went to see their bank manager to discuss the scheme and apply for a loan. The manager took an interest in their proposal and went to see the house in question. He also reviewed their projections for the expenses of the venture, although he later maintained that in doing so he was not giving business advice as offered in the leaflet because he did not see it as the type of business venture at which the leaflet offering advice was aimed.

Having seen their figures and the house in question, the bank manager approved the loan and the customers went ahead to buy and renovate the property. The renovations turned out to be much more expensive than that for which they had planned and, at the same time as the renovations were being carried out, the property market slumped to such an extent that when was the house was ultimately sold the customers were left with substantial debts to the bank. The customers alleged that their losses were caused by the negligent advice they had received from the bank manager, and, in particular, by his failing to warn them that the property would be more expensive to renovate than they had predicted, and that the value of the property would not necessarily increase as had been projected by the customers (the venture was premised on the assumption that the property would rise in value by 35% over the first year and 25% over the second year). It was accepted by the court that neither of the instances of "advice" referred to were matters which were within the exclusive, or normal, capacity of a bank to advise on. However, it was held that although a bank is not ordinarily under a duty to give financial advice to its customers, the manager had in this case undertaken to give such advice by visiting the property and reviewing the projected figures, and in the circumstances was under a duty to exercise reasonable skill and care in giving it. This was especially so in the light of the leaflet promoting the defendant bank's expertise in the start-up of small businesses and this leaflet was held by the court to apply to projects such as this.

The principal legal issues set out in the judgment were:

1. Whether the defendants owed a duty of care to advise as to the prudence of the transaction;
2. If so, whether they were in breach of that duty of care;
3. Whether the plaintiffs relied on the advice allegedly given by the defendants;
4. Whether the alleged reliance caused loss of a kind which was reasonably foreseeable and what loss had been suffered.

Duty of Care. On the question of whether the defendants owed a duty of care the judge considered several authorities in which a bank was not held to be under a duty of care. These were *Williams and Glynns Bank v. Barnes,*[30] *Goldsworthy v. Brickelle,*[31] and *Lloyds Bank Plc v. Cobb.*[32] In the *Williams & Glynns Bank* case, the decision was that the relationship of banker and customer did not impose a duty on the bank either to consider the prudence of lending from the customer's point of view, or to advise with reference to it. Such a duty could only arise: (i) as an express or implied term in a contract; (ii) upon the assumption of responsibility and reliance as stated in *Hedley Byrne v. Heller*[33]; (iii) in the case of a fiduciary duty; or (iv) as a result of an implied representation. In the *Goldsworthy* case, it was pointed out that because a banker has a pre-existing and conflicting interest in any loan transaction with a customer, he cannot be expected to have a duty of care to give disinterested advice. In the *Lloyds Bank* case, it was stated that if a bank examines the details of a project, this is merely for its own purposes as a lender and does not impose any duty to the customer.

However, the judge then went on to consider the 1959 case of *Woods v. Martins Bank Ltd* (see above), in which a bank was held to be under a duty of care to a customer. In that case, Mr Justice Salmon held that a bank owed a duty to its customer to advise him with reasonable care and skill in relation to the investment in question. In particular, if a bank offers to give and indeed advertises itself as able to give expert advice in all financial matters, then it is under a duty to use reasonable care and skill in giving such advice.

The plaintiffs therefore claimed that the bank manager had become their adviser in relation to the purchase of the property. The defendants threw doubt on the plaintiffs' recollection of events and also submitted that the plaintiffs had had their own views on the project and were not put off by the manager's reservations about the property market. The judge did not accept these contentions and found that the plaintiffs had specifically sought the advice of the manager on the prudence of this transaction and that the manager had encouraged them to proceed. The judge came to this conclusion for the following reasons:

1. Although the plaintiffs were well educated they were not knowledgeable about financial affairs.
2. The plaintiffs' project was plainly a business venture and the defendants had advertised that they gave free advice to customers on business matters.
3. The bank manager was in a good position to advise on the prudence of the transaction to the plaintiffs since he had access to information on the plaintiffs' financial position and had experience of the property market.

4. The bank manager's conduct and attitude were more consistent with the role of an adviser to the plaintiffs than with the role of their bank manager. In particular, the manager had thoroughly inspected both the properties which the plaintiffs were considering buying and indeed had advised against purchasing one of them.

Breach of Duty. The court heard expert evidence as to the standard of care required when giving financial advice. After hearing this evidence the judge concluded that the defendants had breached its duty of care in the following ways:

1. In giving financial advice the manager did not ascertain the objectives of the plaintiffs thoroughly and did not draw up a business plan to work out as accurately as possible the estimated profit or loss of the venture. Had he done so, he would have realised that the project was not viable.
2. The estimates which the plaintiffs relied on were based on their own guesswork and the manager failed to advise them to obtain true estimates.
3. A competent financial adviser would have warned the plaintiffs of the risks associated with the venture. These are listed in the judgment[34] and include, for example, the risks associated with the recent rises in interest rates, the risk of additional building costs, the risk of delay in selling the house, and the risk that the plaintiffs would lose their existing properties if the project failed.
4. The plaintiffs were not warned that their project depended entirely on property price inflation to achieve any profit and was therefore highly speculative. There was no margin of safety in the project and it required a high initial outlay for a modest return.
5. The manager was put on notice of the plaintiffs' circumstances but failed to advise them in the light of this. In particular he knew or ought to have known of the difficulties they were experiencing in meeting their financial obligations.
6. The manager failed to heed the plaintiffs' lack of experience in business matters.

For the defendants it was argued that this type of project was not a matter for a bank manager to advise upon. The manager had given the plaintiffs some warning about continuing property price inflation. Also, the defendants argued that, because this was not a business project, the defendants' offer of free legal advice did not extend to the venture. The court rejected these arguments and found that the manager had breached his duty of care by not advising the plaintiffs not to proceed with the project as it was clearly not viable.

Reliance on the Advice. The plaintiffs claimed that they had pursued the project because they had relied on the manager's encouraging advice. For the defendants it was argued, that, even had the manager given financial advice to the plaintiffs, they would have ignored it because they thought they knew better and because they were very enthusiastic about the project. However, the judge did not accept this argument and preferred the view that if proper advice had been given to the plaintiffs they would have abandoned the project for good.

Loss. The amount of damages which the plaintiffs could claim against the bank was calculated by comparing the plaintiffs' actual situation with the position in which

they would have been if they had never entered into the transaction at all.[35] A claim
for general loss of earnings on the grounds that the venture had had a damaging effect on the plaintiffs' respective careers was dismissed. However, it was held that
Mrs Verity (one of the plaintiffs) had a claim in principle for loss of earnings during
the period when she was working on the renovations to the house. The judge found
that if she had not been engaged on the project, she would have earned income from
elsewhere. As regards the claim for emotional distress, the judge noted that the law
was clear that such a claim could not be upheld if the object of the contract was
other than to provide peace of mind or freedom from distress.

The court therefore held that the bank manager had breached his duty of care by
failing to warn the customers of the probability that the proposed venture would not
be profitable, and in particular that the property market might not rise as predicted.
It was a feature of the case that the customers were held first to have been financially naive and inexperienced, and therefore likely to rely on the bank manager's advice, and second that they did so rely on the advice.

Fiduciary Duty and Undue Influence

As can be seen from the *Verity and Spindler* case, and more recently in the *Dharmala* case (see below) the question of reliance is of crucial importance in deciding
whether a duty of care exists. The greater the reliance placed by a counterparty on
advice given to the counterparty, the more likely it is that the adviser will assume a
duty of care to the counterparty to consider the counterparty's interests.

Lloyds Bank v. Bundy

The classic example of a case where a bank knew that a customer relied on it heavily
for investment advice is *Lloyds Bank Limited v. Bundy*.[36] Although an unusual case
on its facts, the principle of the case carries wider implications. The customer in that
case was a farmer who had a very limited understanding of financial affairs. The
farmer and his son banked with the same bank and the son had an overdraft facility
for his business which was guaranteed by a charge over the farmer's house. The son's
business fell into difficulties and the bank manager considered that he could only extend its overdraft if any additional borrowing was secured by a further charge over
the farmer's house. Accordingly, the son and the bank manager went to see the
farmer taking with them a charge form which was already completed and only required the farmer's signature. The son, in the bank manager's presence, explained to
his father that the son's difficulties had been caused by a number of bad debts. In
fact, the bank manager did not believe this to be the case, and considered that there
were more serious underlying problems with the son's business than the son disclosed. The bank manager did not, however, explain his reservations to the farmer,
even though he knew from past dealings that the farmer relied on him for financial
advice.

The son's business went from bad to worse, and in due course the charge over
the farmer's house was enforced. The court held that, in view of the customer's financial ignorance and his known reliance on the bank manager's advice, the bank
owed the customer so high a duty of care, that the charge was in fact procured by
undue influence exercised on the customer by the bank manager. The bank manager should have realised that, by virtue of his relationship with his customer, he

had a conflict of interest in advising his customer on extending the charge in favour of the son's business, and should therefore have advised him to take independent advice.

There are other cases which concern a bank's duty to advise a customer to take independent advice in analogous circumstances, typically where a wife charges her interest in a property for her husband's borrowings and later alleges that her consent was obtained by undue influence.[37] It is unlikely that a bank dealing in derivatives will have a relationship with many of its counterparties which is analogous to that in *Verity and Spindler* or *Lloyds Bank v Bundy;* the counterparties' greater financial sophistication would probably preclude it. It should be appreciated that almost all the English cases concern customers who are private individuals, usually claiming that they have been in some way unfairly persuaded or seduced into a financial commitment at a time when they did not appreciate the risks involved. If a corporate plaintiff were to claim in a derivatives transaction that a duty of care had arisen, in reliance on the bank-customer line of cases, the plaintiff would have to demonstrate that it is entitled to the same sort of protections under English law as have been given to unsophisticated individuals and that derivatives fall into the same category of transactions as the less complex types of transactions seen in the cases referred to above. At one end of the scale, it is obvious that as a matter of English law a bank or other financial institution is not under a duty of care to advise its counterparty of the wisdom of entering into a derivatives transaction where the counterparty is of very considerable, or even equivalent, financial sophistication and does not rely on the institution for financial advice. At the other end of the scale, it is conceivable that an institution might enter into a derivatives transaction with a financially unsophisticated counterparty which, by virtue for example of a course of dealing, has come to rely on the institution for financial advice. In such a circumstance the institution may well find itself under a duty to advise the counterparty as to the potential implications of the transaction, particularly where the counterparty is unsophisticated and the institution has aggressively marketed the transaction to the counterparty. In such a circumstance, the customer may also allege undue influence.

English law on undue influence is complex and not always clear. In general terms, if a counterparty is able to demonstrate that, in the particular circumstances of a case, a relationship did exist whereby a bank or other financial institution was able to influence the counterparty, then undue influence will be presumed if it can be shown that a transaction has taken place which was wrongful. Wrongful in this sense means that the institution has taken unfair advantage of the counterparty in a way that operates to the counterparty's manifest or obvious disadvantage.[38] The more detailed analysis of the law of undue influence is beyond the scope of this chapter but a failure to disclose the risk involved in a transaction has been held to operate as a type of undue influence.[39] It is not clear to what extent the law of undue influence has a role in the world of derivatives transactions but it is worth making the point that a counterparty is more likely under English law to be able to establish undue influence than to establish a fiduciary relationship between the parties. In an English context, it is therefore more useful to look at general duties of care and to acknowledge that, in appropriate circumstances, where a customer places reliance on a bank or other financial institution, a duty of care could arise. As discussed below in relation to the Bank of England's London Code of Conduct, best practice should ensure that a developing relationship with a customer in relation to potentially complex financial products is regularly appraised before it leads to unintended consequences.

Having said that, the general rule applied by the English courts and which the above cases (and the *Dharmala* case) illustrate, is that a bank or other financial institution does not owe a customer or counterparty a duty of care to advise the customer about the wisdom of any transaction, unless it agrees to proffer, or does proffer advice, which is relied on, and which the bank should have known was being relied on by the customer. Ultimately, whether a duty of care exists is a question to be decided by reference to the facts in each case. The relationship between the parties, the relative sophistication of the customer, the presence of reliance, and the assumption of responsibility by the relevant adviser, are all factors which can cause a duty of care to arise. Those factors are not exhaustive however, and in each case the court will look to the precise nature of the relationship to decide if a duty of care exists.

Breach of the Duty of Care

The existence of a duty of care is, of course, not in itself sufficient to give rise to liability. Only if the duty is breached and advice is not carefully (that is, negligently) given and the negligent advice causes loss to the counterparty,[40] will the bank or other financial institution advising be liable to the counterparty. This is because liability in negligence only arises when there is a failure to exercise the reasonable care of the competent or prudent banker.

However, exercising the reasonable care of the competent or prudent banker does not mean that the prudent banker always has to be right. An error of judgment on its own is not a breach of duty. In the words of an English High Court judge in a 1988 case:

> *The law does not require of a professional man that he is a paragon, combining the qualities of polymath and prophet.*[41]

The law does not say that the professional always has to be right, but he does have to be careful. Assessing whether there has been a breach of the obligation to exercise reasonable care and skill is often difficult. Conventionally, the test is by reference to the normal standards of performance which are considered acceptable in the relevant field. However, the standard of care required is not necessarily the standard that advisers with the relevant expertise do in fact achieve, but is the standard which ought to be achieved.[42] Thus, it is open to a court to hold that any particular conduct which may be normal in the market is nevertheless careless, and the fact that a bank or professional behaved competently by reference to the usual standard of practitioners in the field will not prevent such a finding.[43]

In analysing the standard of care of the prudent derivatives trader, then, as mentioned above, the starting point of English law is that generally there is no special duty on a bank or other financial institution to assume any obligation at all to a customer or counterparty in circumstances where the bank or other institution is itself a party to the transaction. There is no principle of law that banks must advise their customers about transactions they may be entering into. For example, in one case, the Court of Appeal stated:

> *. . . a banker, being a person having a pre-existing and conflicting interest in a loan transaction with a customer, cannot ordinarily be trusted and confided in*

so as to come under a duty to take care of the customer and give him disinterested advice.[44]

In another Court of Appeal case, Lord Justice Scott (as he then was) said:

> *. . . the ordinary relationship of customer and banker does not place on the bank any contractual or tortious duty to advise the customer on the wisdom of commercial projects for the purpose of which the bank is asked to lend money. If the bank is to be placed under such a duty, there must be a request from the customer, accepted by the bank, for some arrangement between the customer and the bank, under which the service is to be given.*

> *If a customer applies to the bank for a loan for the purposes of some commercial project, and the bank examines the details of the project for the purpose of deciding whether or not to make the loan, the bank does not thereby assume any duty to the customer. It conducts the examination of the project for its own prudent purposes as lender and not for the benefit of the proposed borrower. If the borrower chooses to draw comfort from the bank's agreement to make the loan, that is the borrower's affair. In order to place the bank under a duty of care to the borrower, the borrower must, in my opinion, make clear to the bank that its advice is being sought. The mere request for a loan, coupled with the supply to the bank of the details of the commercial project for whose purposes the loan is sought, does not suffice to make clear to the bank that its advice is being sought.*[45]

Although concerned with a bank loan, the principles set out by Lord Justice Scott in the above passage apply equally to the more sophisticated categories of banking relationships.

The Duty to Mitigate Loss

Where a counterparty suffers loss as a result of a breach of a contractual duty owed to it, including breach of a duty of care, the counterparty is obliged to take steps to mitigate its loss. It cannot sit back and allow its losses to accumulate unchecked, and if it does so some proportion of its losses may become unrecoverable.[46] The steps which a counterparty takes to mitigate its losses must, however, be reasonable, although that does not mean that the steps must be successful. Where a counterparty faces losses on a transaction, it may decide to mitigate its losses by closing out the transaction. Should the market subsequently move in such a way as to reduce the losses which would have been suffered had the position not been closed out, it may not be open to the defendant to argue that the counterparty should not, in hindsight, have taken the steps which it did.[47] This is especially the case if the counterparty takes the steps in mitigation after having taken advice.

The following passage in the House of Lords' judgment in the case of *Banco de Portugal v. Waterlow* is a concise summary of the law in this area:

> *Where the sufferer from a breach of contract finds himself in consequence of that breach placed in a position of embarrassment the measures which he may be driven to adopt in order to extricate himself ought not to be weighed in nice scales at*

the instance of the party whose breach has occasioned the difficulty. It is often easy after an emergency has passed to criticise the steps which have been taken to meet it, but such criticism does not come well from those who have themselves created the emergency. The law is satisfied if the party placed in a difficult situation by reason of the breach of a duty owed to him has acted reasonably in the adoption of remedial measures and he will not be held dissentitled to recover the costs of such measures merely because the party in breach can suggest other measures less burdensome for him that might have been taken.[48]

The overriding duty is to act reasonably in all the circumstances. It is no higher a duty than that.

Contributory Negligence

The Law Reform (Contributory Negligence) Act 1945 provides[49] that where a person suffers damage:

> *(a) as a result partly of his own fault and partly of the fault of another person . . . the damages recoverable in respect thereof shall be reduced to such extent as the court thinks just and equitable having regard to the claimant's share and the responsibility for the damage.*

It is clear that the contributory negligence of the plaintiff can under English law reduce the liability of the defendant for the breach of duty, including it would now seem breach of a duty to exercise care or skill expressly or impliedly imposed by contract.[50] There may be circumstances in which the losses which a party to a derivatives transaction incurs are partly caused by its own fault. For example, where a customer is financially sophisticated, but nevertheless establishes that the bank counterparty breached its duty of care to advise as to the consequences of a transaction, it may be possible for the bank to allege that the counterparty, by virtue of its own skill, should have appreciated the nature of risks inherent in the transaction, and should be responsible for some of the losses which it suffered. Alternatively, a counterparty may request a bank to enter into a derivatives transaction in order to hedge against a particular liability, and the counterparty may misapprehend the nature of the liability which it wishes to hedge itself against. In these circumstances, even if negligence can be established on the part of the bank, the counterparty may nevertheless have to bear some of its own losses by virtue of its failure to put the bank in a position where it could adequately advise the counterparty as to how the counterparty should hedge against the relevant risk.

Misrepresentation

In the absence of breach of a duty of care, the most likely claim that a counterparty to a derivatives transaction may make is that it was induced to enter into the transaction by a misrepresentation. The elements constituting a misrepresentation under English law are that a representation of past or present fact (as opposed to opinion or law) was made, that the representation was false, and that the false representation induced the representee to enter into the contract. False in this context means that the statement was substantially untrue, that the recipient of the statement gave the statement the meaning intended by its maker, and that the maker knew or ought to have known that the recipient would put this intended meaning on the statement. Liability for misrepresentation can arise whether or not an obligation to advise exists.

An actionable misrepresentation can be made fraudulently, negligently or innocently. A fraudulent misrepresentation is one in which either the representor knew the statement to be untrue, made the statement without believing it was true, or was reckless as to whether the statement was true or false. A negligent misrepresentation may give rise to liability under two heads, either in tort on the *Hedley Byrne v. Heller* principle (see above) or under the Misrepresentation Act 1967.[51] An innocent misrepresentation is where the representation was made neither dishonestly nor negligently.

Representations can be made orally or in writing, or may arise by implication from the words or conduct of the parties, but in whatever way a representation is made it must relate to a matter of present or past fact. Representations as to past performance of investments, or present rates of return, are easy to identify as being statements of past or present fact. Promises or forecasts as to future performance are not statements of past or present facts, and cannot therefore without more be representations. However, in relation to such matters as forecasts, it should be borne in mind that although forecasts properly made cannot of themselves be representations, as discussed above and as the *Dharmala* case confirmed, a bank or other financial institution does have a duty of care to its customer to provide such forecasts with reasonable skill and care.

As mentioned above, the misrepresentation must be one of fact, not law. But facts in this context can include statements of intention. If a derivatives trader tells a potential counterparty that the trader's institution tends to follow a particular policy in relation to its own risk management concerning a particular currency or interest rate exposure, and on the basis of that policy recommends a particular type of hedge to the counterparty, a misrepresentation will have been made if the institution does not in fact have such an intention.

The representation must be material for the customer to have relied on it. It should not merely be an obvious puff of the sort that may be common in advertising and promotional material, nor can a statement be a misrepresentation if it is too vague for the counterparty to have relied on it. Such statements are distinguishable from marketing material which actually holds out an institution as having particular expertise and which may impose on the institution in question an obligation to live up to the expectations represented. An old but illustrative example of the difference between puffing and misrepresenting particular facts is *Scott v. Hansen*[52] where a vendor described a parcel of fourteen acres of land which was for sale as "uncommonly rich water meadow land." Twelve of the acres were not "uncommonly rich," but as to those the court found that there was no misrepresentation. The other two acres were not water meadow land at all, and it was held that the vendor had misrepresented particular facts concerning the state of those two acres. An advertisement that promises good advice may well be construed as a representation that good advice will be given.[53]

Another limitation on liability for misrepresentation is where a complex series of representations is made; minor falsities will not render the general representation to be false if the overall effect of the representations is a faithful presentation of the facts. Again, the knowledge and experience of the representee is relevant to determining when a false representation is material, and when it is immaterial.

The relationship between the parties is also relevant in determining when a representation is a mis-representation. In order for a representation to be a misrepresentation, it must, at the time when it is acted on by the representee, be false. Whether or not a representation is false is determined by reference to whether a reasonable representee would have considered it false. The knowledge and experience of the representee is important in deciding whether he considered that a representation was false. This is especially so in relation to complex presentations, where some details may be incorrectly stated without the whole of the presentation being false. In the *Dharmala* case (discussed below), Mr Justice Mance described the importance of the knowledge and experience of the representee in the following passage:

> *The meaning and effect of words never falls to be viewed in a vacuum. It is shaped by the context of their communication, including the parties' respective positions, knowledge and experience. A description or commendation which may obviously be irrelevant or may even serve as a warning to one recipient, because of its generality, superficiality or laudatory nature, or because of the recipient's own knowledge and experience, may constitute a material representation if made to another less informed or sophisticated receiver. Even in the case of a written description, there may be cases where a proposal or presentation misrepresents the nature or working of the transaction to a particular reader, although another sophisticated, more analytical or legally qualified reader would have been expected to appreciate the real nature or working of the transaction. What is a fair and adequate presentation in one context between one set of negotiating parties may be unfair in another context. Whether there was any, and if so what, particular representation must thus depend upon an objective assessment of the likely effect of the proposal or presentation on the recipient. In making such an assessment, it is necessary to consider the recipient's characteristics and knowledge as they appeared, or ought to have appeared, to the maker of the proposal or presentation. A recipient holding himself out as able to understand and evaluate complicated proposals would be expected to be able to do so, whatever his actual abilities.*[54]

Liability for misrepresentation can arise from representations which are positively made, as well as from an omission to qualify a statement or a silence. Misrepresentation by silence only occurs when a representor is under a duty to disclose the existence of certain facts. If the representor fails to disclose those facts the representee may infer that those facts do not exist. The duty to state certain facts could, as discussed above, arise from the relationship between the parties. Alternatively, where a statement which is true when it was made subsequently becomes untrue, the representor is under a duty to correct it because a representation is treated, once made, as if it continues to be made at every moment until the contract is entered into by the representor and the representee. In some circumstances, a failure by a bank to discharge its duty to explain the nature of a transaction could also amount to a misrepresentation by silence. This is significant because misrepresentation gives rise to rescission of the contract in question (see below), whereas breach of duty gives rise only to a claim for damages.

Before a representor will be made liable for any of the remedies available for misrepresentation, the representee must show two further matters. First, the representee must establish that the representation was material, namely that it was a misrepresentation which would tend to affect the conduct of the representee. Second, the representee must establish that it did, in fact, induce the representee to enter into the contract. Materiality will be a question of fact for the customer to prove in each case. If the courts follow Mr Justice Mance's robust approach in *Dharmala,* materiality may prove to be a significant hurdle for some plaintiffs to overcome. However, it is not necessary for the misrepresentation to be the sole inducement which causes the representee to enter into the contract, but there must be some inducement.[55]

Remedies Available in Misrepresentation

The remedies available in misrepresentation depend upon the nature of the misrepresentation. Rescission of a contract is available as a remedy whether the misrepresentation is fraudulent, negligent or innocent. However, this remedy is not automatic and the party to whom rescission is available has the right either to elect to rescind the contract or to affirm it. The effect of rescission is that the contract is terminated and the parties are put back in the position in which they stood before the contract was entered into. Orders can be made to include the repayment of money paid under the contract, and payment of interest on that money.[56] Accordingly, in a swap contract for example, the parties will be able to recover payments made. Rescission is thus a very attractive remedy for a customer wishing to extract itself from an unprofitable transaction, and accordingly misrepresentation is often alleged by counterparties wishing to avoid their liability under transactions they have entered into.

Rescission is an equitable remedy and is therefore not available in all circumstances. Under the Misrepresentation Act 1967, the court has a discretion to award damages in lieu of rescission where there has been a non-fraudulent misrepresentation leading the parties to enter into a contract.[57] Also, if the contract has been affirmed or the party claiming rescission has delayed in seeking its remedy, then rescission may not be available.[58] However, damages in those circumstances are likely to be available.

Damages are available to a party who was induced to enter into a contract by a fraudulent misrepresentation for all consequential losses that it suffers. In other words, the misrepresentee can recover damages in respect of all losses resulting from the fraudulent misrepresentation. Damages are also available as a remedy for a negligent or innocent misrepresentation. There are complex rules regarding the calculation of damages for misrepresentation which are beyond the scope of this chapter.

The measure of damages for negligent misrepresentation is the same as for fraudulent misrepresentation, and is correspondingly wide. Recoverable losses include money paid to the representor under the contract, interest on that money, and other consequential losses which flow from entering into the contract.

Disclaimers and Exclusion Clauses

Section 3 of the Misrepresentation Act 1967 provides that contractual terms which purport to exclude or restrict any liability for misrepresentation, or the availability of any remedy for misrepresentation, are of no effect except in so far as they satisfy the requirement of reasonableness as set out in section 11(1) of the Unfair Contract Terms Act 1977.[59] That section, which also applies to terms which exclude liability for negligence, provides as follows:

In relation to a contract term the requirement of reasonableness is that the term shall have been a fair and reasonable one to be included having regard to the circumstances which were, or ought reasonably to have been, known to or in the contemplation of the parties when the contract was made.

The Unfair Contract Terms Act 1977 contains a number of guidelines for the application of the reasonableness test which include:

(a) *the strength of the bargaining positions of the parties relative to each other, taking into account (among other things) alternative means by which the customer's requirements could have been met;*

(b) *whether the customer received an inducement to agree to the term, or in accepting it had an opportunity of entering into a similar contract with other persons, but without having to accept a similar term;*

(c) *whether the customer knew or ought reasonably to have known of the existence and extent of the term (having regard, among other things, to any custom or trade and any previous course of dealing between the parties);*

(d) *where the term excludes or restricts any relevant liability if some condition is not complied with, whether it was reasonable at the time of the contract to expect that compliance with that condition would be practicable.*[60]

The requirement that a term excluding liability for misrepresentation should be fair and reasonable in the circumstances leaves open the question whether or not such an exclusion clause will be effective in any particular case. The relative knowledge and experience of the parties will again be important in deciding whether, in the circumstances of a particular transaction, it was fair and reasonable for liability for misrepresentation to be excluded.

St Marylebone Property Co. Limited v. Payne

There have been a number of cases, particularly in relation to property transactions, in which the question has been considered of whether terms excluding liability for misrepresentation are reasonable under section 11 of the Unfair Contract Terms Act 1977. One case where it was held that it was not reasonable to exclude liability for misrepresentation is *St Marylebone Property Co. Limited v. Payne.*[61] That case concerned the purchase of a property at auction by a builder (a buyer who could not be said to be naive or inexperienced). The property was described in a set of particulars which showed a picture of an attractive door which would have been a desirable feature of the property were if not for the fact that the door did not give access to the property. The builder inspected the property from the outside, but did not realise that the door in question did not give a right of access. The particulars contained exclusions of liability for misrepresentation which provided that the property was believed to be correctly described, but that no error should provide a ground for annulment or compensation, and that it was the purchaser's responsibility to satisfy himself as to the accuracy of the matters in the particulars. There was a further term in the contract that the purchaser was acting on his own judgement and was in no way influenced by any representation made by or on behalf of the vendor.

It was held by the court that, notwithstanding the conditions in the particulars, the picture constituted a representation. This was because the particulars purported to give both a verbal and a pictorial description, and in the circumstances the picture should be taken to be a clear representation as to the extent of the property to be sold. Because the sale was by auction, the buyer's opportunity to inspect the property was accordingly decreased, and it was held that it was unreasonable to attempt to exclude liability for the description in the picture, when it was clear that the buyer would rely on that description.

The circumstances which made it unreasonable to exclude liability for this representation were the difficulty which a potential buyer would have in verifying the facts represented, and the intended effect of the picture. The court considered the way in which the particulars would be read by a potential buyer and held that the exclusion clauses did not prevent the buyer from relying on the picture.

This case, dealing as it did with an auction sale, concerned a relationship between two parties where one was clearly in a better position to verify the facts than the other. As between a bank and a sophisticated counterparty, however, it is more likely that an exclusion clause would be held to be reasonable. The parties would have a more equal ability to verify the facts and to assess the risks in the proposed transaction. When dealing with a less financially sophisticated counterparty, however, there may well be a risk that any clauses inserted in the contract purporting to exclude liability for misrepresentation, will not be effective on the grounds that the clause is unreasonable.

A clause in a written contract between a bank and a counterparty which excludes liability for negligence will also be subject to similar considerations of reasonableness.[62] However, the Unfair Contract Terms Act 1977 provides that the Act does not apply to contracts of insurance, nor to:

> *any contract so far as it relates to the creation or transfer of securities or of any right or interest in securities.*[63]

It is arguable whether the effect of this provision is to include derivatives contracts amongst the contracts to which the Act does not apply. The matter has not been tested in the courts. However, assuming that the 1977 Act does not apply and that the issue of "reasonableness" is not therefore a factor, a well drafted clause should be successful in excluding liability for negligence as between two commercial parties dealing on a commercial basis.[64]

Some clauses excluding liability for negligence place a cap on the amount of damages which will be recoverable.[65] While such clauses are more likely to be effective than absolute exclusions, the question of whether the cap is reasonable will also depend on the circumstances of the parties. Accordingly, a capped liability may, if it places the liability at a level which seems too low in relation to the resources of the relevant party, be held to be unenforceable. The Unfair Contract Terms Act 1977 draws particular attention to the amount of money a party could have recourse to if found liable, and the extent to which it is possible for the party to take out insurance against the consequences of its liability for negligence.[66] Thus a clause limiting liability might be reasonable if imposed by a minor bank in a contract with a customer, but unreasonable if required by a major bank.

Duty of Care Between a Bank and a Counterparty

The issues of whether, and if so to what extent, a duty of care exists as between a bank and a counterparty in relation to a derivatives transaction, and of the extent to which a party may be liable in misrepresentation, were recently considered by the English Commercial Court in the so far unreported but nevertheless significant case of *Bankers Trust International plc v. PT Dharmala Sakti Sejahtera.*[67]

Bankers Trust International Plc v. PT Dharmala Sakti Sejahtera

The facts which gave rise to the dispute concerned a series of transactions which were entered into in the first half of 1994 between Bankers Trust and PT Dharmala Sakti Sejahtera, the holding company of the financial services division of an Indonesian group of companies which had subsidiaries in banking, finance, and capital markets.

The Swaps. The dispute arose from three transactions of increasing complexity: Swap 1, Swap 2, and an amended Swap 2. Swap 1 was for a notional principal amount of US$50 million. Its period was two years and interest payments were calculated by reference to LIBOR, defined as the LIBOR rate for six-month deposits in US dollars on Telerate as at 11AM London time on the relevant payment date. Swap 1 had two legs. Under the first leg, Dharmala was to pay interest at the six-month LIBOR rate, while Bankers Trust was to pay interest at that rate plus a margin of 1.25%. Under the second leg, Dharmala was to pay interest at 5% per annum, while Bankers Trust was to pay interest at 5% per annum multiplied by "N" over 183. "N" was defined as *the actual number of days in a six-month reference (or "look") period commencing August 15, 1994, during which the LIBOR rate was determined to be less than 4.125%, up to 183.*" Accordingly, if LIBOR exceeded 4.125% on every day during the reference period, Dharmala would receive no interest payment and would suffer a loss of 3|1\2|% per annum (the 5% per annum interest payment under the second leg less the 1.25% margin on the first leg). At the time of the swap, the six-month LIBOR rate stood at 3.625% per annum. An ISDA master agreement was signed by the parties in which they elected English law as the proper law of the agreement and submitted to the jurisdiction of the English courts.

Swap 1 was entered into on January 27, 1994. On February 4, 1994 the Federal Reserve Board raised its Federal Funds Rate by 25 basis points. This led to a corresponding rise in the projected rates for six-month LIBOR. In view of this rise in six-month LIBOR rates the parties agreed to cancel Swap 1 and replace it with Swap 2, a LIBOR barrier swap. The notional principal amount of Swap 2 was once again US$50 million and the life of the swap was again two years. It was agreed that under Swap 2, Dharmala would receive interest at the six-month LIBOR rate plus a margin of 1.25% per annum and would pay interest at the six-month LIBOR rate less 2.25% per annum but plus "Spread." It followed that, subject to the impact of the Spread, Dharmala would receive a subsidy of 3.5% per annum, instead of the maximum potential subsidy under Swap 1 of 1.25% per annum.

The Spread was calculated as follows: if the six-month LIBOR rate did not go above the barrier rate of 5.25% per annum at any time during the next year, the Spread was to be zero. However, if the rate did go above the barrier rate during the next year, the Spread for the two years of Swap 2 would be derived by dividing that six-month LIBOR rate by 4.5% and subtracting 1. The parties then agreed to further terms. They agreed that the principal amount notionally paid by Bankers Trust to Dharmala was in two tranches of US$25 million each and that in respect of one tranche, the barrier rate should be raised from 5.25% to 5.3125% per annum. It was also agreed that Dharmala would receive from Bankers Trust an upfront payment of

US$1.7 million. The bank treated this payment as an advance payment of the first year's subsidy (which was accordingly discounted from 3.5% to 3.36%).

Dollar interest rates continued to rise and within weeks the six-month LIBOR rate pierced the barrier. Approximately two months after entering into Swap 2 Bankers Trust wrote to Dharmala quantifying the Spread at around US$19 million for each of the two swap years. Shortly thereafter Dharmala orally agreed with Bankers Trust that it would forego the subsidy of 3.5% in the second year, in return for an increase in the respective barrier rates from 5.25% to 5.8125% per annum and from 5.3125% to 5.875% per annum. Within four days of the amendment, the negative value of this amended Swap 2 had risen from approximately US$34.5 million to approximately $45 million.

On May 13, 1994, Dharmala wrote to Bankers Trust stating that it did "not wish to proceed with the LIBOR barrier swap" and asserted that there had been:

> . . . gross misrepresentations on the point [sic] of Bankers Trust in highlighting the rewards but not the high risks associated with the LIBOR Barrier Swap plus wrongful advice on the economic outlook . . . .[68]

On August 8, 1994 Dharmala's Indonesian lawyers claimed misrepresentation against Bankers Trust and threatened a suit in damages. Six days later Bankers Trust issued proceedings in England for relief which included a declaration that Dharmala was not entitled to damages. Nine days later Dharmala began proceedings against Bankers Trust in Indonesia claiming that the spread had been mis-applied and alleging, inter alia, misrepresentation and lack of authority. During this time, U.S. interest rates were continuing to rise and in December 1994 Bankers Trust finally closed out on Swap 2 and served on Dharmala a Notice of Default under the terms of the ISDA Agreement. Bankers Trust then issued fresh proceedings in England against Dharmala in which they contended that the sum of US$64,702,981 was due to them from Dharmala.

The Defenses and Counterclaims of Dharmala. Amongst the defenses and counterclaims raised by Dharmala were allegations that Bankers Trust had misrepresented the terms and the risks involved in the transactions, and that Bankers Trust had breached the duty of care which it owed to Dharmala to:

> . . . explain fully and properly to [Dharmala] the operation, terms, meaning and effect of the proposed Swap 1, Swap 2 and amended Swap 2 and the risks and potential financial consequences to [Dharmala] of accepting them.[69]

Dharmala alleged that Bankers Trust owed it a very extensive duty of care, and that the duties owed by Bankers Trust had been significantly breached. The specific breaches of the duty of care alleged included:

1. Failing to establish what degree of skill and knowledge Dharmala possessed in such transactions;
2. Failing to give adequate warning to Dharmala as to the risks inherent in each transaction;

3. Failing to illustrate the financial consequences to Dharmala of each proposed transaction by reference to a range of possible circumstances;
4. Failing to advise Dharmala as to other possible means of limiting its exposure to movements in U.S. dollar interest rates; and
5. Failing to advise Dharmala to seek independent advice on each of the proposed transactions.

Misrepresentation Claim. Dharmala alleged that Bankers Trust had made various misrepresentations during the negotiations leading up to the transaction. The allegations of misrepresentation included allegations that Bankers Trust had misrepresented that:

1. Swap 1 was a suitable product for Dharmala;
2. Swap 1 and Swap 2 were safe products for Dharmala;
3. Only historical rates from January 1993 to January 1994 were given to Dharmala by Bankers Trust which showed the six-month U.S. dollar LIBOR rate as fluctuating between a high of 3.50 and a low of 3.19 during that period;
4. Swap 1 could be replaced at no cost to Dharmala if the barrier was reached;
5. Dharmala required a product with limited risk and downside but Bankers Trust had misrepresented that Swap 2 did not have substantial risk and downside.

Dharmala also claimed that the forecasts provided by Bankers Trust were incomplete, inaccurate and unreliable, that the representations made were deliberately or recklessly false and that worked examples of possible scenarios given by Bankers Trust to Dharmala were too limited.

Mr Justice Mance decided that the misrepresentations alleged by Dharmala in relation to Swap 1 had not been made and that Bankers Trust had explained the terms of the transactions adequately. The judge distinguished the enthusiasm of the relevant Bankers Trust officer who marketed the transaction to Dharmala from any impropriety. The judge stated:

> *He was no doubt an enthusiast, and capable of marketing the transactions which he helped to devise with considerable skill and persuasiveness. That does not mean he acted dishonestly or improperly or that he in any way misrepresented their effect.*[70]

Dharmala also contended that the expectation of substantial commission affected the judgment of the Bankers Trust officer. The judge commented:

> *I accept that the encouragement intended by bonus payments can work negatively in creating a temptation to misrepresent or exaggerate the advantages and to understate the risks of the derivative products being sold. It is not to be assumed without proof that this temptation has manifested itself in every or any particular case.*[71]

The judge distinguished between light-hearted puffing which may have been made by Bankers Trust and on which Dharmala placed no reliance and actual representations on which Dharmala would have relied. He found that the allegation by Dharmala that Bankers Trust had represented that the transactions were suitable was implausible and that the officers of Dharmala, who themselves had considerable financial experience, were well able to judge the suitability of the transactions and the significance of graphs regarding long-term interest rates. The judge also rejected the contentions made by Dharmala in respect of economic forecasts provided by Bankers Trust to Dharmala. He said that the views expressed by Bankers Trust were honestly and reasonably held and were properly researched and based on reasonable grounds. They did not purport to be a report on market views generally and therefore no liability could be imputed to Bankers Trust if their view differed from the majority of other leading US economic forecasts. Dharmala had its own internal information on interest rates and the likely direction of those rates.

However, Bankers Trust had also made representations (in correspondence and at a presentation) in relation to the nature of the risks involved in Swap 2 and the judge held that, having done so, Bankers Trust was obliged to ensure that the representations were accurate, to present the financial implications of the proposal by a properly constructed graph and letter and to present the downside and upside of the proposal in a balanced fashion. But on the basis that Dharmala and its two principal representatives in the negotiations were financially sophisticated and had significant previous experience of transactions of this nature, Mr Justice Mance found that Dharmala had failed to establish that any representation made by Bankers Trust made a difference to Dharmala's decision to enter into the transactions. He held that whilst not as expert or knowledgeable as Bankers Trust, Dharmala was in a position to work out and evaluate for itself the potential impact on the transactions of various possible market conditions. Further, Bankers Trust had made it clear to Dharmala that it expected Dharmala to satisfy itself about the risks associated with the transactions. In the event, Mr Justice Mance found that Dharmala did not rely upon any representation of Bankers Trust and that any representation made by Bankers Trust did not induce Dharmala to enter into the transactions.

Breach of the Duty of Care Claim. In considering the alleged duty of care contended for by Dharmala, Mr Justice Mance relied on previous case authorities regarding bank-customer relationships (see above). He decided that the appropriate test to be applied in determining whether Bankers Trust had assumed a duty of care was as follows:

> *A bank negotiating and contracting with another party owes in the first instance no duty to explain the nature or effect of the proposed arrangement to that other party. However, if the bank does give an explanation or tender advice, then it owes a duty to give that explanation or tender that advice fully, accurately and properly. How far that duty goes must once again depend on the precise nature of the circumstances and of the explanation or advice which is tendered.*[72]

Dharmala had argued that the wide ranging duty of care which it alleged arose from the fact that Bankers Trust had gone beyond stating the facts in relation to the transactions and that Bankers Trust had given advice to Dharmala. Dharmala relied on several cases (including *Box v. Midland Bank*[73]) in support of this proposition.

It was Dharmala's case that its officers who had dealt with Bankers Trust were not experienced in derivatives, and that their lack of experience and understanding was one factor in the relationship which gave rise to a duty of care. Dharmala also argued that Bankers Trust was under a duty to discover exactly how expert the Dharmala officers really were, and negligently failed to do so. In relation to this allegation, Mr Justice Mance rejected the onerous duty contended for. He held that

Bankers Trust was entitled to rely on the account of the officers' expertise which was given by the officers themselves, and was not obliged to check whether their experience was, in fact, as great as it appeared. This is in accordance with previous case law; a bank can take its customer to have the skill which the customer appears to have.

Mr Justice Mance found that both of Dharmala's officers had considerable commercial and financial expertise, and held themselves out as having that expertise. It emerged during the case that Dharmala had entered into several swap transactions previously, a fact to which the judge gave some weight. Mr Justice Mance held that once the officers had had the workings of the proposed transactions explained to them, they were sufficiently aware of the substance of the proposals, and had sufficient ability to form a view on the merits of the transactions. In reliance on these factors, the judge decided that the only duty owed by Bankers Trust to Dharmala was to represent fairly and accurately the facts and matters on which it made representations. There was no additional duty owed by Bankers Trust to Dharmala to explain fully and properly the operation, terms, meaning and effect of the transactions. The judge stated that the two representatives of Dharmala had deliberately interested themselves in transactions that they must have well understood to be speculative.

Notwithstanding the disparity in expertise between Dharmala and Bankers Trust, Mr Justice Mance did not hold that a general duty of care, in the terms alleged by Dharmala, arose. The judge found that Dharmala's representatives had sufficient understanding of the workings of the proposals to assess for themselves whether to take the risks inherent in the transactions. Mr Justice Mance further held that Dharmala did not ask Bankers Trust to act as its financial adviser generally, and in the absence of any representation by the bank that it was so acting, the relationship between Bankers Trust and Dharmala was not one which entitled Dharmala to assume that Bankers Trust would so act. It is notable, however, that the possibility that such a duty could be implied in different circumstances was left open.

In deciding the question of whether or not a duty of care was owed by Bankers Trust to Dharmala, Mr Justice Mance placed considerable weight on the relative expertise of the parties. However, he also pointed out that the relationship between the parties was, to both of their knowledge, a commercial one. It was not the conventional bank-customer relationship since Bankers Trust was marketing to existing or prospective purchasers derivative products of its own devising which were both novel and complex. The bank was soliciting the customer's business with a view to profit, and the customer equally sought to profit from the transactions. Mr Justice Mance emphasised that:

> . . . the courts should not be too ready to read duties of an advisory nature in to this type of relationship.[74]

Based on the same reasoning, Mr Justice Mance held that Bankers Trust was not under a duty to advise Dharmala of other possible transactions by which Dharmala could reduce its exposure to dollar interest rate movements. He stated that:

> . . . it would distort, rather than reflect the nature of this commercial relationship, in my judgement, to read into it duties on the part of [Bankers Trust] to consider or advise [Dharmala] about other possible transactions which might have

enabled [Dharmala] to extract itself from Swap 1, or might have offered the prospect of different profit on different terms.[75]

Had the relationship been one in which Bankers Trust had an advisory role, this position could well have been different.

It was argued for Dharmala that Bankers Trust's position on the transactions was one which it could sell for a substantial profit very soon after it had entered into both Swaps 1 and 2 and that this had a bearing on the duties which should be imputed to Bankers Trust. Whilst Mr Justice Mance referred to the early negative mark-to-market values of the transactions as "surprising features" he held that although this information would doubtless have caused Dharmala to think hard about the transactions had Dharmala been aware of it, it was not information which anyone at the time would have expected to be disclosed before the transactions took place. This was especially so in view of the fact that before entering into any of the transactions Dharmala did not seek any information or assurance from Bankers Trust as to the possible profit which Bankers Trust would make on the transactions.

Suitability. Mr Justice Mance decided that whether or not the transactions were "suitable" for Dharmala, in the sense of being appropriate or sensible for Dharmala, was a matter for Dharmala to judge for itself. He decided that Bankers Trust was justified in believing that it was dealing with people who would be able, and who could be expected, to undertake a close evaluation of the merits and risks of any proposal and to ask questions or seek further information if they did not understand any proposal or its implications.

Provision of Economic Forecasts. The *Dharmala* case also provides some guidance in relation to the provision of a bank's internal economic forecasts to a potential customer. Whereas Mr Justice Mance held that the customer did not rely on the alleged misrepresentations made by the bank in presenting proposals, he did hold that the customer was entitled to rely, and did rely, on the economic forecast which was produced by Bankers Trust's economists and that it was inherent in handing over any forecast that any representations made in the forecast were based on proper research and reasonable grounds. Although the Bankers Trust economic forecast may have proved to be wrong, the judge held that at the time when it was given, it was an honest and reasonable professional opinion concerning which the counterparty had no cause for complaint. The judge held that there was no obligation to provide an "average" market view.

Summary of Issues. Mr Justice Mance gave judgment in favour of Bankers Trust for £64,702,981 plus interest and costs and rejected Dharmala's counterclaims. Although, it is fair to say that *Bankers Trust v. Dharmala* turned substantially on its facts, it is apparent from Mr Justice Mance's judgement that he considered that the most important factors in determining whether a duty of care arises were: the nature of the commercial relationship; the knowledge of the customer (as held out by the customer); the presence of reliance; and the disparity in skills between the parties. In the absence of a duty to advise being assumed, the duty of a bank was not to mis-state material facts and to represent fairly and accurately the facts and matters on which it did make representations. The case is also an important decision of the English courts because it shows the courts' willingness to hold counterparties to their contracts and to enforce those contracts on their terms. The case concerned a relatively unsophisticated transaction and a counterparty who the judge found was well able to understand the transaction. In the circumstances, the judge was only prepared to allow a very limited duty of care owed by Bankers Trust to Dharmala and rejected the contention that the bank had assumed an advisory role.

It is always possible that a wider duty of care may be allowed by the English courts in, for example, a case involving a highly sophisticated transaction and a relatively unsophisticated counterparty. In those circumstances, the courts may be more likely to accept evidence that a bank had assumed a responsibility to advise the counterparty on issues such as risk and suitability. However, cogent and convincing evidence of the nature of the relationship and of the fact that the counterparty relied on a representation made or advice given, and that the representation or advice caused the loss, will be required. The *Bankers Trust v. Dharmala* case demonstrates how difficult a counterparty may find the production of that evidence. The mere fact that the bank is more sophisticated than the counterparty will not be sufficient.

The London Code of Conduct and the Market Best Practice

The London Code of Conduct is issued by the Bank of England and sets out the general standard and controls which should be adopted when transacting business in the relevant financial products, including OTC derivatives. The London Code of Conduct was referred to in the *Dharmala* case in relation to the existence of a duty of care between the bank and the customer. The confirmation sent by Bankers Trust in respect of Swaps 1 and 2 in *Dharmala* recorded that those transactions were subject to the London Code of Conduct. Mr Justice Mance relied on the passages of the Code in relation to "Know your customer" (in the then current edition of the Code) as demonstrating the market view that it is important for a bank to know its counterparty. He held that those requirements corresponded with his legal analysis: that in order to assess the existence and extent of its duty of care, a bank must first know how experienced is its counterparty.

The London Code of Conduct is a statement of the need and desirability of adopting high standards, rather than a statement of minimum standards and it is not a statement of the law. Accordingly, it is of more relevance as a guide on how a bank may prevent either a duty of care arising or a breach of any duty, than it is as a guide to the standard of conduct to be expected of a reasonably competent banker, particularly since being the Code of a regulator, it urges high, rather than merely competent, standards.

Nevertheless, the Code provides a valuable guide as to the standards of practice which a prudent bank should adopt. The following are amongst the more important provisions:

> 17 *When establishing a relationship with a new counterparty or client, firms must take steps to make them aware of the precise nature of firms' liability for business to be conducted, including any limitations on that liability and the capacity in which they act. In particular, broking firms should explain to a new client the limited role of brokers (see paragraphs 29 and 30 below).*[76]

> 21 *As a general rule core principals will assume that their counterparties have the capability to make independent decisions and to act accordingly; it is for*

each counterparty to decide if it needs to seek independent advice. If a non-core principal wishes to retain a core principal as its financial adviser it is strongly encouraged to do so in writing, setting forth the exact nature and extent of the reliance it will place upon the core principal. All principals should accept responsibility for entering into wholesale market transactions and any subsequent losses they might incur. They should assess for themselves the merits and risks of dealing in these markets. Non-core principals must recognise that it is possible for core principals to take proprietary positions which might be similar or opposite to their own.

It should be noted that although banks may assume that their counterparties have the capability to make independent decisions and therefore act accordingly, banks are nevertheless required under the Code to present the details of transactions to counterparties in a manner which is appropriate to the degree of financial sophistication possessed by each counterparty. In addition, the London Code of Conduct requires that the bank should do the following:

24 When entering into or arranging individual deals, dealers and brokers must ensure that at all times great care is taken not to misrepresent in any way the nature of any transaction. Dealers and brokers must ensure that:

The identity of the firm for which they are acting and its role is clear to their counterparties/clients to avoid any risk of confusion. This is particularly important, for instance, where an individual dealer acts for more than one company, or in more than one capacity. If so, he must make absolutely clear, at the outset of the deal, on behalf of which company or in which capacity he is acting.

It is clearly understood in which products they are proposing to deal.

Any claims or acknowledgements about, or relevant to, a particular transaction being considered should, as far as the individual broker or dealer is aware, be fair and not misleading.

Facts believed to be material to the completing of a specific transaction are disclosed before the deal is done, except where such disclosure would reveal confidential information about the activities of another firm. Unless specifically asked for more information, or clarification, a dealer at a core principal will assume his counterparty has all the necessary information for this decision making process when entering into a wholesale market transaction.

The third and fourth subparagraphs of paragraph 24 are particularly important provisions in attempting to minimise the possibility of future claims in misrepresentation. The Code requires that dealers and brokers must ensure that there is disclosure of the material facts relating to any deal, and that all claims and acknowledgments relevant to the deal should be fair and not misleading. These provisions are consistent with the duty not to misstate material facts which is discussed above. Aspects of the relationship between the bank and the customer which it is particularly important for banks to supervise closely are highlighted in the preamble to part III of the Code of Conduct, in the section headed "Know your counterparty":

> *Before agreeing to establish a dealing relationship in any of these wholesale market products, core principals should be mindful of any reputational risks which might arise as a result, and whether these risks might be greater when undertaking such transactions with noncore principals. In the absence of firm evidence to the contrary, noncore principals should be regarded as end-users (ie "customers") of the wholesale markets.*

The Code sets out, in paragraph 31, some of the criteria which should be considered when dealing for the first time with any counterparty in any wholesale market product. It is recommended that the approval process should apply both when granting an initial dealing line for a product and when that dealing line is subsequently changed or extended. The criteria set out in paragraph 31 include, in the case of all counterparties, whether the counterparty has the legal capacity to enter into the transaction. In the case of customers, the criteria include matters such as who initiated the relationship, whether there is a written agreement on which advice is given, what advice has been given, whether the respective responsibilities for losses of both parties are clear, and whether the core principal has any special legal responsibilities to the customer.[77] The provisions continue:

> *33 Once a customer dealing relationship has been established in one, or more, wholesale market product(s) it is strongly recommended that management at both parties periodically review it, against the above criteria.[78] It is also in their own interest for core principals to review periodically the totality of their business relationship with each customer against the same criteria.*

These rules of good practice are designed to ensure that a developing relationship of trust and confidence, or indeed reliance, is recognised by the bank so that is aware that it might, in some circumstances, incur a duty of care, or even a fiduciary duty, to its customer. The significance attached to the financial sophistication of the customer is shown by the following provision:

> *35 It is more likely, therefore, that small investors will ask for advice on the particular product being considered (for instance in terms of its risk profile, how this might differ from exchange traded instruments with which they may be more familiar, or how to value its worth over time, etc). It is the Bank's view (shared by the SIB) that where this is so they should not automatically be granted a new or extended dealing line for this product. If the product being considered is a derivative and/or leveraged, the Bank believes that it is in the interest of banks and other listed institutions to have in place a written agreement, which makes clear which products are concerned and the extent to which any reliance can be placed by the small investor on the advice given.*

This rule of good practice is clearly directed at the possibility that a duty of care may be more readily assumed in a relationship in which the bank's counterparty is particularly inexperienced. In addition to these general provisions, specific provisions in relation to undertaking derivatives transactions appear at paragraphs 70–72 as follows:

70 *When a core principal is dealing with any customer of the market in leveraged or derivative products it is good practice for its dealers to assist their opposite number by using clear concise terminology. It is however the responsibility of each party involved to seek clarification, before concluding a deal, on any points about which they are not clear. Each party should also consider whether it would be helpful for the core principal to send by electronic means (telex or fax) a pre-deal message setting out the terms upon which the deal will be priced and agreed by both parties. While this may not be judged appropriate for some customers (eg an experienced large corporate), it is likely to be helpful to send pre-deal messages to small investors (as defined earlier).[79] Such a message may also be particularly useful, for instance, where the product involved is relatively new to the customer, or where the individual dealer acting on behalf of the customer is not the regular contact point for undertaking such trades with that customer. The sending or receipt of such a message is not a substitute for the confirmation procedures described below.*

71 *The existence, or not, of such a message should not however be taken as undermining in any way the principle that each party must accept responsibility for entering into such trades and any losses that they might incur as a result of doing so. There are, of course, circumstances in which this principle might be brought into question; for instance if the dealer at the core principal had deliberately misled the customer by knowingly providing false and/or inaccurate information at the time the deal was being negotiated. It is therefore very important that great care is taken not to mislead or misinform.*

72 *To help minimise the scope for error and misunderstanding the Bank strongly recommends that management require their dealers to use standard pre-deal check lists of the key terms that they need to agree when entering into leveraged and/or derivative transactions.*

It is clear from the specific provisions that relate to derivatives transactions that the market view is that it is the responsibility of each party to a derivatives transaction to form a view as to the merits of entering into that transaction. However, particular emphasis is put on the need to take steps to ensure that counterparties are not misled or misinformed. Whilst the emphasis on taking steps to avoid misleading or misinforming counterparties is important, it is notable that the London Code of Conduct is not premised on the view that there is a duty of care on banks to advise their counterparties on the wisdom or otherwise of entering into particular derivatives transactions. In this regard, as Mr Justice Mance observed in *Bankers Trust v. Dharmala,* the Code of Conduct is consistent with the approach which has been taken by the English courts.

ENDNOTES

1. [1991] 1 All ER 545.
2. Inter alia, *Westdeutsche Landesbank Girozentrale v. Islington London Borough Council* [1996] 2 All ER 961.
3. The judgment of Mr Justice Mance was handed down on December 1, 1995.
4. [1991] 1 All ER 545.

5. [1994] 4 All ER 890 (Commercial Court and Court of Appeal), [1996] 2 All ER 961 (House of Lords).

6. [1996] 2 All ER 961 at 966.

7. *See Wallersteiner v. Moir* (No 2) [1975] 1 All ER 849.

8. [1996] 2 All ER 961 per Lord Browne Wilkinson at 990–992.

9. S18 of Gaming Act 1845 provides as follows:

> All contracts or agreements, whether by parole or in writing, by way of gaming or wagering, shall be null and void; and no suit shall be brought or maintained in any court of law and equity for recovering any sum of money or valuable thing alleged to be won upon any wager, or which shall have been deposited in the hands of any person to abide the event on which any wager shall have been made: Provided always, that this enactment shall not be deemed to apply to any subscription or contribution, or agreement to subscribe or contribute, for or towards any plate, prize, or sum of money to be awarded to the winner or winners of any lawful game, sport, pastime or exercise.

S1 Gaming Act 1892 provides as follows:

> Any promise, express or implied, to pay any person any sum of money paid by him under or in respect of any contract or agreement rendered null and void by the Gaming Act 1845 or to pay any sum of money by way of commission, fee, reward, or otherwise in respect of any such contract, or of any services in relation thereto or in connection therewith, shall be null and void, and no action shall be brought or maintained to recover any such sum of money.

10. [1995] 1 All ER 1.

11. [1994] 4 All ER 890

12. Section 63 provides as follows:

> (1) No contract to which this section applies shall be void or unenforceable by reason of—
>
>> (a) section 18 of the Gaming Act 1845, section 1 of the Gaming Act 1892 or any corresponding provisions in force in Northern Ireland; or
>>
>> (b) (applies to Scotland only).
>
> (2) This section applies to any contract entered into by either or each party by way of business and the making or performance of which by either party constitutes an activity which falls within paragraph 12 of Schedule 1 to this Act or would do so apart from Parts III and IV of that Schedule.

Paragraph 12 of Schedule 1 to the Financial Services Act 1986 provides as follows:

> 12. Buying, selling, subscribing for or underwriting investments or offering or agreeing to do so, either as principal or as an agent.

13. [1995] 1 All ER 1 at 5.

14. *See, for example,* Alistair Hudson in the *Law of Financial Derivatives,* Sweet & Maxwell 1996, at page 16 where the author states:

> The comfortable market consensus that there is no contract for differences problem with interest rates swaps, is, it is submitted, left in an equivocal position by Morgan Grenfell v. Welwyn Hatfield DC in some circumstances.
>
> On the facts in the decided cases, it has been held that the particular transactions were not entered into for speculative purposes. The position remains to be seen where the so-called "high octane" swaps transactions are considered. There are transactions where, rather than the return on a particular interest rate being paid to the counterparty involved, the counterparty pays or receives the return on a given rate squared. The return on such a transaction would be appear to be difficult to justify as a "quasi-insurance" measure.

15. *See* note 12.

16. *Henderson v. Merrett Syndicates Ltd* [1994] 3 All ER 506 (a case against underwriting agents in the Lloyds insurance market).

17. For example, there are differences in relation to the relevant period of limitation and the extent of damages recoverable.

18. *Henderson v. Merrett Syndicates Ltd* [1994] 3 All ER 506, per Lord Goff at 533.

19. Supply of Goods and Services Act 1982, section 13.

20. *Bolam v. Friern Hospital Management Committee* [1957] 1 WLR 582.

21. *Bolam v. Friern Hospital Management Committee* [1957] 1 WLR 582, per McNair J at 586.

22. [1964] AC 465. See also the decision of the House of Lords in *Spring v. Guardian Assurance* [1994] 3 All ER 129.

23. [1964] AC 465, per Lord Morris at 502–503.

24. The judgment of Mr Justice Mance was handed down on December 1, 1995.

25. [1959] 1 QB 55.

26. [1959] 1 QB 55 at 72–73.

27. [1979] 2 Lloyds Rep. 391.

28. [1987] 1 Lloyds Rep. 218.

29. [1995] NPC 148.

30. [1981] Com LR 207–208.

31. [1987] 1 Ch 378.

32. December 18, 1991, unreported.

33. [1964] AC 465 and *see above*.

34. [1995] NPC 148 and at page 33 of the judgment.

35. Note that exemplary or punitive damages are permitted under English law in very limited circumstances, none of which are likely to apply to derivatives transactions.

36. [1975] 3 All ER 757.

37. *See,* inter alia, *Barclays Bank plc v. O'Brien and another* [1993] 4 All ER 417.

38. *See Bank of Credit & Commercial International SA v. Aboody* [1989] 2 WLR 759.

39. *See Bank of Credit & Commercial International SA v. Aboody* [1989] 2 WLR 759.

40. Note that exemplary or punitive damages are permitted under English law in very limited circumstances, none of which are likely to apply to derivatives transactions.

41. Mr Justice Rose in *Eckersley and Others v. Binney and Others* 18 Con LR 1, February 18, 1988.

42. *See* for example *Sidaway v. Bethlem Royal Hospital* [1984] 1 All ER 1018 per Sir John Donaldson MR.

43. *See also Midland Bank Trust Co Ltd v. Hett, Stubbs & Kemp* [1978] 3 All ER 571.

44. Per Lord Justice Nourse in *Goldsworthy v. Brickell* [1987] 1 Ch 378 at 405.

45. *Lloyds Bank plc v. Cobb,* December 18, 1991, unreported.

46. *See,* inter alia, *British Westinghouse Electric Co. Ltd v. Underground Electric Railways* [1912] AC 673.

47. *See,* inter alia, *Lloyds and Scottish Finance Ltd v. Modern Cars and Caravans (Kingston) Ltd* [1964] 2 All ER 732.

48. [1932] AC 452, per Lord Macmillan at 506.

49. Section 1.

50. *See Vesta v. Butcher* [1989] AC 852; *Barclays Bank v. Fairclough Building Ltd* [1994] 3 WLR 1057.

51. Section 2(1).

52. (1829) 1 Russ & M 128.

53. *See also Verity and Spindler v. Lloyds Bank* [1995] NPC 148 referred to above.

54. Page 18 of the judgment of Mr Justice Mance handed down on December 1, 1995.

55. Reliance and inducement involve a similar analysis of the relationship between the parties, and, as with the arguments for the implication of a duty of care, the degree of "vulnerability" shown by the customer will have a significant bearing on its ability to show inducement.

56. *Westdeutsche Landesbank Girozentrale v. Islington London Borough Council,* [1996] 2 All ER 961, where it was held that interest, but not compound interest, could be awarded on the sums recovered (see above).

57. Misrepresentation Act 1967, section 2(2).

58. Rescission may also not be available in the event of acquiescence, affirmation, the obtaining by a third party of rights under the transaction or where various other technical defences apply.

59. Mention should also be made of the European Union Directive on Unfair Terms and Consumer Contracts (93/13/EEC) which imposes requirements of fairness in relation to contractual terms. The regulations by which the Directive was incorporated into English and Scottish law came into force on

1st July, 1995. Since the regulations only apply to individuals ("natural persons") under regulation 2(1), the Directive is unlikely to apply to derivative contracts.

60. Schedule 2 to the Unfair Contract Terms Act 1977.

61. [1994] E.G. 156.

62. Unfair Contract Terms Act 1977 section 2(c).

63. Unfair Contract Terms Act 1977 schedule 1 paragraph 1(e).

64. *See Tai Hing Cotton Mill Limited v. Liu Chong Hing Bank Limited* [1985] 2 All ER 947.

65. A cap on damages is within the statutory regime imposed by the Unfair Contract Terms Act 1977, *see* section 13(1)(b) of that Act.

66. Unfair Contract Terms Act 1977 section 11(4).

67. A judgment of 90 pages was handed down by Mr Justice Mance on December 1, 1995.

68. *See* page 3 of the judgment of Mr Justice Mance.

69. *See* page 13 of the judgment of Mr Justice Mance.

70. *See* pages 24 and 25 of the judgment of Mr Justice Mance.

71. *See* page 22 of the judgment of Mr Justice Mance.

72. *See* page 21 of the judgment of Mr Justice Mance.

73. [1979] 2 Lloyds Rep. 391 and *see* above.

74. *See* page 87 of the judgment of Mr Justice Mance.

75. *See* page 88 of the judgment of Mr Justice Mance.

76. Paragraphs 29 and 30 provide that a broker's role is (subject to certain exceptions) to act as an arranger of deals, but not as a principal. Brokers may pass on information which is in the public domain, but are not obliged to volunteer such information. Brokers must be particularly careful when called on to provide specific information which may involve their revealing confidential information or expressing an opinion on a matter, such as the creditworthiness of a counterparty, on which they do not have sufficient information to be qualified to advise.

77. The example given in the London Code of Conduct of a situation where a core principal may owe a particular legal duty to a customer which would require special consideration is where the core principal is asked to advise on the whole of, rather than part of, a customer's portfolio.

78. The criteria set out in paragraph 31 of the Code.

79. Individuals or small business investors as defined under the rules of the Securities and Futures Association.

5

Risk Reduction through Multibranch Netting

DANIEL P. CUNNINGHAM
THOMAS J. WERLEN

Although the globalization of finance is not necessarily a new phenomenon, recent years have seen a continued growth in cross-border finance activities. Not surprisingly, this continued growth corresponds with the trend toward the globalization of financial markets in general, as more institutions take advantage of the efficiencies and opportunities for profit available from cross-border operations. While from a business viewpoint, the significance of national boundaries has considerably decreased in the last decade, from a legal standpoint national boundaries and territorial sovereignty remain important.

Insolvency remains a major domain of territorial sovereignty. Although insolvency in its own right has become more important than ever in international commercial law, there is no multinational structure or multinational regime to deal with the failure of a multinational business. Indeed, there is a striking discrepancy between the internationalization of business and the lack of international approaches to deal with the insolvency of a global enterprise.

Recent international financial problems involving financial institutions, such as the Bank of Credit and Commerce International (BCCI) or Barings, have illustrated that the international insolvency system remains rudimentary. There is no formal structure that would provide for either an efficient reorganization of a multinational business in financial difficulty or an efficient distribution of its assets among its creditors in the event that a reorganization was not a viable prospect. The development of a framework that would provide organized solutions to multinational financial difficulties is lagging badly behind the possibility that those difficulties could develop into multinational financial disasters. There is very little in the way of international cooperation in place that would ensure that creditors in different jurisdictions would receive roughly equitable treatment and little prospect for that goal being achieved.

The applicability of national insolvency laws to multinational insolvencies and business transactions may in itself have impeded the even greater growth and development of international financial markets. For instance, in the case of a truly international business with assets and creditors located in a variety of jurisdictions it is currently impossible for any interested party to determine in advance in which jurisdiction or jurisdictions one or more liquidation proceedings would be commenced. Moreover, such elementary issues as the laws applicable to the determination of assets and claims and to the determination of the final payment for a given claim are not predictable.

This situation contrasts sharply with the efforts taken by the international legal community to ensure the enforceability of contractual rights before courts by way of choice of law clauses and choice of forum clauses. It is true that the contractual choice of law and/or forum may be challenged by one of the parties to the contract. Nevertheless, supported by a number of bilateral and multilateral treaties, choice of law clauses as well as choice of forum clauses have substantially increased the predictability of the outcome of international business litigation.

Interestingly enough the risks associated with an international insolvency of a globally operating financial institution have only recently come to the attention of both market participants and regulators. The difficulties created by the insolvency of international financial firms, such as BCCI and Barings, have alerted the international financial community. Against this background, senior management of global financial institutions has been made aware that the efforts taken in recent years to improve risk management will have to focus increasingly on reducing the legal uncertainties associated with an international insolvency.

In no area is the legal uncertainty caused by the discrepancy between globalization of business and local insolvency laws more apparent than in the activities in privately negotiated derivatives transactions, which are used by banks and other institutions to manage the risks associated with traditional financial activities. Privately negotiated derivatives transactions have brought increased scrutiny to the globalization of financial markets. Their use to manage risks throughout the world has drawn particular attention after the demise of Barings.

Increasingly, the view is taken by observers of the international financial markets that the legal uncertainty that arises from the inconsistencies between local insolvency laws and global financial activities may be also one potential source of systemic risk.[1]

This risk is particularly important where banks operate internationally through branches or agencies established in jurisdictions other than the jurisdiction where the bank itself is organized or incorporated. Unlike corporate subsidiaries that generally are independently incorporated and thus treated as legal entities separate from the parent corporation, branches of banks are not independently organized and are therefore deemed to be part of the parent bank itself for many purposes. For purposes of insolvency proceedings, however, some jurisdictions appear to treat branches of banks as separate entities thereby often trumping the expectations of the creditors of such bank and its branches. To prevent this result, in an insolvency of a major international bank, other financial institutions would probably immediately after the insolvency determine their credit exposures to the insolvent bank. For those financial institutions that had entered into transactions with various branches of the insolvent bank, the determination of the exposure would be likely to give rise to uncertainties, such as whether amounts due to one branch of the insolvent bank could be set off against amounts due from another branch of the insolvent bank.

For all these reasons, the quest for legal certainty in cross-border insolvencies should be of paramount importance to market participants, regulators, and legislators. Similar conclusions have been reached by other observers of the international financial markets. For example, a Discussion Draft on International Insolvencies in the Financial Sector prepared jointly by the Group of Thirty (a Washington DC—based think tank) and the International Association of Insolvency Practitioners

(INSOL International) and published in 1996 (the G-30/INSOL Discussion Draft), after examining the issues surrounding the Barings failure, has identified the systemic risks associated with the insolvencies of internationally active financial firms and made various recommendations to that end. Another survey conducted by the Global Derivatives Policy Group of the Group of Thirty recommended the removal of "any remaining legal and regulatory uncertainties" in several areas. One specific area of concern mentioned in that survey was the enforceability of multibranch netting arrangements in bankruptcy.[2]

This chapter first explores the deficiencies of the existing insolvency laws in dealing with the insolvency of a globally operating bank such as BCCI. Against this background, and with a view to other efforts taken by various institutions to come to grips with the problems related to an insolvency in the global village, we then present the efforts taken by ISDA to establish legal certainty through the use of multibranch netting provisions. Despite certain immanent limitations, multibranch netting is probably at this point the most efficient way to reduce the legal uncertainties for the creditors of an international bank. We present a Model Netting Act developed by ISDA that, if adopted, would ensure the enforceability of close-out and multibranch netting. The adoption of the Model Netting Act would eliminate remaining legal uncertainty of multibranch netting with respect to international insolvencies of banks active in privately negotiated derivatives transactions.

CROSS-BORDER INSOLVENCIES—PROBLEMS AND SOLUTIONS

The Problems

In any country, an insolvency involves a firm turning to a statutory procedure or to a law court for protection from its creditors. Alternatively, a firm is placed into a statutory or court-supervised procedure for the protection of its creditors and other private or public interests. In most countries, a fiduciary (or trustee or administrator) is appointed to manage the insolvency.[3] This fiduciary is endowed with three fundamental tasks: (1) locating, gaining control of and collecting the assets of the debtor; (2) compiling and sifting through creditor claims against the debtor, accepting valid claims and valuing and prioritizing them; and (3) distributing the assets of the debtor to satisfy the creditors' claims fairly.

A guiding principle for insolvency officials in facilitating the third task is the *pari passu* or "equal treatment" of creditors principle. This principle dictates that each creditor should receive, out of the debtor's limited pool of assets, the same priority. The "equal treatment" principle may be limited by priority rights granted to creditors holding security interests in the assets of the debtor. Also, certain claims of unsecured creditors (such as employees' claims and government claims) may be granted preferred treatment. Moreover, the principle of equal treatment of all creditors may be waived in favor of certain creditors that are at the same time debtors of the insolvent party by allowing them to set off their debt with their claims under certain circumstances.

These tasks can become exceedingly complex for cross-border insolvencies. In a cross-border insolvency a primary proceeding is started in the main place of business of the insolvent firm. Thereafter, secondary local proceedings concerning the same assets or debts may be started at the instigation of creditors or other involved local parties. Recent international insolvencies have shown that as the administration becomes localized in each of the jurisdictions in which the insolvent party formerly carried on business, different sets of creditors assert different rules, which almost always causes disappointment for certain creditors. In contrast to many other areas of law, there is no developed body of international insolvency law designed to address the issues that are likely to arise in a cross-border insolvency. There is a highly noticeable lack of attention among national governments toward implementing effective multinational or bilateral treaties in the insolvency area.

Not without justification, the status of international comity in the area of insolvency has been described as follows:

> *There are few areas of the law in which international comity has made as little progress as in bankruptcy. The call for an international bankruptcy system based upon notions of comity and equality of creditors was first voiced by 19th-century commentators . . . Subsequent efforts to achieve those ends have been notably unsuccessful . . . .*[4]

In theory, there are three major approaches to insolvency where assets and creditors are located in more than one country:[5]

1. The universalist approach whereby the courts of one country have exclusive jurisdiction over the insolvency of a particular debtor, and all the creditors have to bring their claims before that original bankruptcy court. Such a solution could only be achieved by means of a multinational treaty;
2. The strict territorial approach, whereby each country distributes the assets located within its jurisdiction according to its own law, and does not recognize the interests of foreign representatives of creditors and seek to cooperate with foreign courts;
3. A mixed or compromise approach, whereby the courts of each country exercise insolvency jurisdiction over the assets present in that country, but recognize the interests of foreign representatives of creditors and seek to cooperate with foreign courts. Such a solution can be achieved both by means of unilateral legislation of one country or by means of a multinational treaty.

In practice, in the absence of multinational treaties, many countries still operate with the territorial approach. As a limited exception to that rule, certain bankruptcy laws may provide for cooperation of insolvency officials of one country with those in other countries, in particular where a primary insolvency proceeding is existing or filed in the country where the main office of an insolvent party is located and the insolvent party has assets in that other country.[6]

Under the territorial approach, an insolvency official must attempt to apply local insolvency rules to address international issues even though such rules might not fit at all. For example, although some types of assets (e.g., real estate) are clearly located in a specific jurisdiction, other types of assets (e.g., accounts receivable and other contractual rights) might not be deemed to be located in a specific jurisdiction. In the absence of specific rules for determining the location of assets, the resolution of these issues is uncertain.

The second problem that arises in a cross-border insolvency is that more than one insolvency official may attempt to conduct this three-step process simultaneously. The marshalling of a limited pool of assets by more than one insolvency official inevitably leads to conflict. This conflict is exacerbated by the fact that each insolvency official may take a different view regarding where a particular asset or claim is "located," and, consequently, which insolvency official should have control of the disposition of the asset to satisfy local creditors.

Indeed, the main problem in an international bankruptcy where two or more insolvency fora are involved—and this situation would typically arise as soon as assets of an insolvent party are located in more than one jurisdiction—is that there are no established rules to predict how the insolvency officials in the jurisdictions concerned will cooperate with each other.

The problems associated with the insolvency of an international bank may be better explained in light of the BCCI experience.[7] The BCCI group, headed by Luxembourg-based BCCI Holding SA, and operating through two main banking subsidiaries, Luxembourg-based BCCI SA and Cayman Islands-based BCCI Overseas SA, was closed by the regulators in July 1991. The BCCI Group operated through branches or representative offices in 69 countries, each with its own legal system. The affairs of BCCI SA and BCCI Overseas SA were inextricably mingled. Worldwide cooperation was essential if the assets in the different jurisdictions were to be realized to the best advantage for the creditors. Therefore, in a pooling agreement meticulously worked out by liquidators in the main jurisdictions involved (i.e., Luxembourg, the Cayman Islands, and England), it was determined that the assets located in various jurisdictions would be transmitted to a central pool and that the creditors of both BCCI SA and BCCI Overseas SA would receive the same dividend from the pool in respect of allowed claims. This dividend was expected to be an initial 20 cents on the dollar. Also, it was agreed that the processing of creditors claims would be conducted, and distributions to creditors effected, by treating the liquidations of foreign branches of BCCI SA and BCCI Overseas SA as ancillary to the principal liquidations in Luxembourg and the Cayman Islands. The pooling agreement which was approved by the Luxembourg court on January 31, 1995, was intended to avoid the expense, difficulty and delay arising out of the multiplicity of local liquidations of the branches of BCCI SA and BCCI Overseas SA.

However, the same BCCI example shows that currently international cooperation is limited in its ability to overcome the lack of an international set of rules. Indeed, the very heart of the pooling agreement was upset by Vice-Chancellor Richard Scott in a ruling of the Chancery Division of the High Court of Justice dated August 6, 1996. The different insolvency rules in Luxembourg and in England, an ancillary forum only, have put the efficacy of the pooling agreement into doubt. The main problem is that under English insolvency set-off rules a particular creditor's debts and credits are automatically offset, which leaves only the net balance. Under Luxembourg law, however, a creditor must first pay his debts and only then is reimbursed for his claims on the same basis as everyone else. The English court decision stated that, for the purposes of the English ancillary liquidation, the English set-off rules would apply. It is reported that this would increase the English creditors' dividend to 40 cents on the dollar while the overall creditors dividend of 20 cents of the dollar seems now jeopardized.

At the same time, the U.S. assets of the BCCI Group were dealt with in a separate insolvency proceeding based on a strict territorial approach. BCCI SA had operated through uninsured state-licensed agencies in New York and Los Angeles. When BCCI SA failed, the U.S. assets were estimated at $550 million. Claims against the U.S. assets apparently were somewhat less than $20 million as well as a $200 million fine owed to the Fed. On October 15, 1991, 3 months after the failure, the Luxembourg liquidators agreed to a consent order in federal bankruptcy court that permitted the

California and New York State regulators to take control of the assets of the agencies pursuant to state liquidation rules. Pursuant to the rules applicable at that time to New York agencies of insolvent banks chartered outside the United States, a "territoriality" or "separate entity" approach was taken. Under that approach the assets of BCCI that were located in the United States were collected and applied to satisfy in the first instance creditors with claims against the local branch. Only the surplus, if any, was then distributed to creditors outside New York. New York has often been criticized because this approach is viewed as unfair towards the global creditors.[8] Indeed, ring-fencing may substantially limit the ability of a foreign receiver to reorganize a failed bank by taking away substantial assets. In addition, the failure to consolidate may also result in the inability of the other creditors to obtain the same pro rata share of all of the bank's assets that they would have obtained if the assets were consolidated. Apart from the difficulties of preferring some creditors of a bank at the expense of others, the assets of an agency or branch of a foreign bank may have little to do with their actual business activities. For instance, it was suspected that the BCCI banks shifted assets among branches to avoid detection of insolvency. The difficulty of sorting out assets between various offices of a bank illustrates the need for a consolidated bankruptcy proceeding.

However, as the BCCI experience shows, the liquidation of the New York agency was completed within a year after the insolvency and the creditors got 100 cents on the dollar, while at the same time the pooling agreement based on international cooperation has been upset, leaving many creditors with a result that is probably worse than if BCCI had been liquidated following a territoriality approach throughout the world.[9]

The Quest for Solutions

The legal uncertainties caused by the lack of multinational approaches to the insolvency of globally operating banks pose a considerable risk for market participants. Therefore, there is consensus among the financial community that the current uncertainties must be removed as soon as possible. There is also a belief that improvements for the international insolvency process may be pursued by both public and private initiative.[10]

Legislative Efforts

In recent years, many efforts have been made to address these issues, and various solutions have been developed. Current projects include the work of the International Bar Association (the IBA) on a Cross-Border Insolvency Concordat (the IBA Project),[11] the American Law Institute (ALI) Transnational Insolvency Project (the ALI Project) and the Joint Project of UNCITRAL and INSOL International on Cross-Border Insolvencies (the UNCITRAL Project).[12] In addition, the G-30/INSOL Discussion Draft provides valuable recommendations that, if adopted, would substantially reduce the legal uncertainties in global insolvencies.

The IBA Project provides a framework for harmonizing cross-border insolvency proceedings. The purpose of the IBA Project is to suggest generalized principles addressed to both legislators and insolvency practitioners to help render international insolvency proceedings reasonably predictable, fair, and convenient.

The ALI Project, the first multinational project of the ALI, has chosen the problems of cooperation in transnational insolvency cases within the NAFTA countries (Canada, Mexico, and the United States). The objective of the ALI Project is to establish cooperative procedures for use in business insolvency cases involving companies with assets and creditors in more than one of the three NAFTA countries.

The goal of the UNCITRAL Project is to develop rules of recognition and access for international insolvency proceedings that are predictable, quick and efficient. In order to be effective the model law would have to be implemented by national legislators. Even though the scope of the UNCITRAL Project is very limited its eventual adoption by many states would be a first step towards international cooperation in cross-border insolvencies.

Unfortunately, even if all these projects were realized today they would not eliminate all the uncertainties faced by the international financial markets in general and risk managers in particular. This is because they are limited either geographically, such as the ALI Project, or in scope, such as the UNCITRAL Project.

From a practical perspective, international harmonization of insolvency law is unlikely to happen in the near future. As the BCCI experience shows, the insolvency regimes in neighboring countries such as England and Luxembourg are fundamentally different in certain important respects. It is true that multinational insolvency treaties or conventions could, perhaps, ultimately be the highest form of international cooperation in the international insolvency field. However, a multinational project establishing a comprehensive scheme of substantive harmonization of international insolvencies will probably not be agreed upon anytime soon. Also, the time-frames involved in negotiating these kinds of arrangements are daunting to the point of despair. The deferral of territorial sovereignty to other countries or even supranational bodies has always been a sensitive issue and will continue to remain difficult to achieve, in particular on a more than regional level.

One effective initiative may be seen in the EU Convention on Insolvency Proceedings approved as of September 25, 1995, and signed by all the member states of the EU except the United Kingdom (the EU Convention), which focuses on procedural harmonization by establishing a system of insolvency conflict of laws rules within the EU. The EU Convention is a multinational undertaking that offers a comprehensive procedural harmonization of insolvency laws and might be best described as following the mixed approach. Indeed, rather than developing a common body of substantive insolvency law the project unifies the insolvency conflict of laws rules of the EU member countries thereby securing for each insolvency occurring in the EU a predictable jurisdiction. In order to protect local interests in one member state, the EU Convention furthermore permits local proceedings (governed by their own lex fori concursus) to exist parallel to the main universal proceeding and to cover the assets which are found in that specific member state. The EU Convention is, however, not applicable to insurance companies, banks, securities firms and mutual funds.[13]

Private Initiative Efforts—Multibranch Netting

Insolvency law is public law that is inherently difficult to change for the parties to a cross-border agreement. Therefore, it may be questioned whether the legal uncertainty associated with the insolvency of a globally operating market participant may be taken care of entirely by private initiative. This is because in the insolvency of a business entity a variety of private and public interests may be at stake the fair and equal representation of which is usually left in the discretion of public insolvency officials.

Nevertheless, there are opportunities for private parties to devise contractual solutions to cross-border insolvency concerns. The problem may be eliminated entirely by requiring a counterparty to book all of the transactions entered into through a single branch or even the home office. In addition, to minimize legal uncertainty in transactions with parties doing business in more than one jurisdiction, parties may enter into contractual agreements designed to clarify how their relationship will be dealt with following the insolvency of one of the parties. These contractual agreements can provide answers to two questions that would arise in a cross-border insolvency: (1) what is the proper measure of the value of the asset or liability represented by the contract; and (2) where is the asset or liability represented by the contract deemed to be located.

The most prominent example of the attempt to contractually preempt the problems of cross-border insolvencies is multibranch netting. By use of multibranch netting provisions in master agreements, parties define the nature and location of assets in cross-border insolvency proceedings. Their widespread use and the legal certainty as to their enforceability make them an important risk management tool for any market participant. This view is shared by many observers; for example, the G-30/INSOL Discussion Draft considers multibranch netting as a very important initiative to improve the international insolvency process.[14]

We will next describe how multibranch netting reduces the risks associated with international bank insolvencies.[15] Then we will explain the terms of a Model Netting Act that would further enhance the benefits of multibranch netting if adopted in key jurisdictions.

MULTIBRANCH NETTING AS A RISK REDUCTION TOOL

The Concept of Multibranch Netting

A brief summary of bilateral close-out netting will aid understanding the role that multibranch close-out netting provisions can play in a cross-border insolvency. Bilateral close-out netting provisions are contractual terms in a contract that call for the netting or set-off of amounts due to and from the two parties to the contract. Bilateral close-out netting provisions are often found in master agreements that document many privately negotiated derivatives transactions between the parties, such as the ISDA Master Agreements.

Under a master agreement, the parties will enter into multiple derivatives transactions, each calling for payments to or from one or both of the parties over time; each of these transactions is economically independent of the other, but all are subject to the master agreement that contains the bilateral close-out netting provisions. The master agreement generally calls for the close-out or termination of all transactions following certain events of default, including the insolvency of one of the parties. Following close-out or termination of each transaction, a close-out or termination amount is calculated for each transaction or group of transactions. These amounts represent the lost value to one of the parties for terminating the transactions prior to their intended maturity. The bilateral close-out netting provisions then call for the netting or set-off of all the close-out or termination amounts for all transactions. The bilateral close-out netting provisions thereby reduce all the close-out or termination amounts to a single net number due to or from one of the parties.

Multibranch close-out netting provisions operate in the same way as bilateral close-out netting provisions, except that they permit the netting or set-off of all close-out or termination amounts due to or from all the pre-designated branches of a multibranch party. Again, the intent of the multibranch close-out netting provisions is to reduce all the close-out or termination amounts for all transactions to a single net number due to or from one of the parties, regardless of the branch through which any or all the transactions are booked.

The Objectives of Multibranch Netting

Even though BCCI did not involve derivatives, the BCCI experience has shown that complex legal and practical problems can arise when there is an insolvency proceeding in the home country of the bank as well as separate proceedings for one or more branches in other countries. Multibranch netting is a contractual agreement that is intended to override the potential efforts by an insolvency official in one jurisdiction to apply the territoriality approach to ring-fence certain transactions booked under a master agreement through a local branch. Parties to a multibranch close-out netting agreement intend to treat all transactions and the master agreement as a single agreement, regardless of where the transactions are booked. This approach reduces the legal risks associated with having multiple agreements with different branches. It also reduces the potential credit risk that could arise if the nondefaulting party was owed a termination amount across all transactions, but was forced to pay a termination amount under only the transactions that were ring-fenced by an insolvency official in a branch jurisdiction.[16]

Enforceability of Multibranch Netting in Cross-Border Insolvencies

From an enforceability point of view,[17] netting agreements including multibranch close-out netting provisions pose three questions:

1. Are the multibranch close-out netting provisions enforceable according to the law of the jurisdiction where such party is incorporated or organized?
2. Are the multibranch close-out netting provisions enforceable according to the law of the jurisdiction in which the branch or the branches designated in the netting agreement are located?
3. Under the assumption that the multibranch close-out netting provisions would be enforceable in a certain jurisdiction both in a home country or a branch insolvency proceeding, would the fact that the parties booked transactions on a multibranch basis, including through one or more branches located in jurisdictions hostile to netting or where a satisfactory opinion cannot be obtained, jeopardize the enforceability of multibranch close-out netting in such jurisdiction? This is called the bad branch problem.

To provide its members with legal certainty as to the enforceability of the legal issues posed by multibranch netting, ISDA has asked local counsel to address the enforceability under the ISDA Master Agreements of multibranch close-out netting, both from the point of view of a bank chartered in the home jurisdiction, and from the point of view of a branch of a foreign bank located in the jurisdiction.[18] The multibranch netting provisions of the ISDA Master Agreements are similar to other multibranch netting provisions, such as those used in the International Foreign Exchange Master Agreement (IFEMA).

With respect to the first question, most jurisdictions would treat a bank and all its branches as a single entity. Therefore in an insolvency proceeding for a bank in its country of organization, the multibranch close-out netting provisions will be enforceable. The result, therefore, would be the same as if all transactions had been entered into through the home office.

With respect to the second question, most jurisdictions where multibranch netting is applicable will enforce multibranch close-out netting provisions in an insolvency of a branch located in such jurisdiction. However, some jurisdictions (notably Spain and Portugal) may not.

The third question is based on the concern that the presence of a "non-netting" branch under a multibranch master agreement could undermine the enforceability of the agreement as a whole and thereby "contaminate" such agreement. Unfortunately, such question is not a theoretical one given that certain jurisdictions such as Spain and Portugal may not recognize (multibranch) close-out netting. The refusal by an insolvency official in such a non-netting jurisdiction to honor the contract between the parties can reintroduce at least some of the legal uncertainty that the parties sought to avoid by entering into the multibranch netting agreement at the outset.[19]

In fact, many regulators share that concern. For instance, the Bank of England requires that transactions with a branch located in a non-netting jurisdiction may be included in master agreements for regulatory capital purposes only based on a legal opinion confirming that the netting agreement will not become void or voidable because the legal validity of netting is not recognized in relation to transactions connected with that branch.

Therefore, ISDA has thus far obtained supplemental non-netting jurisdiction opinions for six jurisdictions (England, France, Germany, Japan, Singapore and Switzerland) that confirm that the conclusions contained in the netting opinions for those jurisdictions would not change based on the actions of an insolvency official or court in a non-netting jurisdiction (such as Spain or Portugal). In particular, the supplemental opinions conclude that the presence of a "non-netting" branch would not undermine the enforceability of netting in the home country insolvency proceeding. This supports the theory that the entire agreement should be netted on a global, multibranch basis. During 1996, ISDA will expand the scope of these supplemental non-netting jurisdiction opinions to include other countries not yet covered.

Notwithstanding the conclusion that the presence of a non-netting branch should not affect the treatment of a multibranch master agreement in other jurisdictions, this situation does give rise to some legal uncertainty. Multibranch netting as a risk management tool is obviously most effective and valuable when close-out netting is enforceable in all jurisdictions involved. Therefore, there are strong arguments for working toward achieving legal certainty that multibranch close-out netting will be enforceable in insolvency in all relevant jurisdictions.

THE MULTIBRANCH PROVISIONS OF THE MODEL NETTING ACT

The Model Netting Act

Since 1989, laws expressly protecting the enforceability of netting for privately negotiated derivatives transactions in local insolvency proceedings have been enacted in many jurisdictions, including Belgium, Canada, the Cayman Islands, Denmark, Germany, France, Ireland, Luxembourg, South Africa, Sweden, Switzerland, and the

United States. In an ideal world for derivatives, lawmakers everywhere would adopt a uniform international bankruptcy statute recognizing close-out netting that would be broad enough to cover the unceasing innovations in derivative transactions.

ISDA has recently developed a Model Netting Act[20] that would ensure the enforceability of both bilateral and multibranch close-out netting if adopted in countries that do not yet have netting legislation. An additional goal of the Model Netting Act is to promote harmonization in netting regimes worldwide and to facilitate the proper and fair treatment of claims of creditors in multinational bank insolvencies, particularly if multibranch netting is involved.

The first part of the Model Netting Act presents the essential elements of a bilateral netting regime. Under the Model Netting Act, any agreement qualifying as netting agreement would be enforceable in an insolvency. For purposes of the Model Netting Act, netting agreement includes (1) any netting agreement in connection with one or more qualified financial contracts, (2) any master-master netting agreement and (3) any security agreement or arrangement or other credit enhancement thereto. To determine the transactions eligible for netting, the Model Netting Act utilizes both a list and a functional approach. Under that approach, any financial contract pursuant to which money payment or delivery obligations that have a market or an exchange price are due to be performed at a certain time or within a certain period of time would be treated as a qualified financial contract. This definition should include any and all transactions documented under ISDA Master Agreements because any derivatives transaction is time-sensitive.

In its second part, the Model Netting Act addresses specific issues arising under netting agreements that include multibranch provisions. The Model Netting Act provisions are based on the New York Banking Law provisions adopted after BCCI in 1993 that expressly enforce multibranch close-out netting for derivatives transactions in a constructive attempt to reconcile the ring fencing of New York branches and the interest in enforcing multibranch close-out netting.

The Multibranch Provisions of the Model Netting Act in Particular

Under the Model Netting Act, following the termination of a multibranch master agreement that is a "qualified financial contract," the single net termination amount shall be calculated on both a global and a local basis. The global net amount is the amount owed by or to the foreign party as a whole if *all* transactions across all branches subject to the multibranch netting agreement are considered (the Global Net Payment Obligation or Global Net Payment Entitlement). The local net amount is the amount owed by or to the foreign party after netting only the transactions entered into by the local branch or agency of the foreign party (the Branch/Agency Net Payment Obligation or Branch/Agency Net Payment Entitlement). The liquidator only shall be liable to pay to a non-defaulting counterparty the lesser of the Global Net Payment Obligation and the Branch/Agency Net Payment Obligation. Likewise, when a counterparty owes a net amount pursuant to a repudiated or terminated qualified financial contract, the liquidator may demand from the counterparty a payment of the lesser of the Global Net Payment Entitlement and the Branch/Agency Net Payment Entitlement. Any amounts to be collected or paid by the counterparty are reduced by amounts that have been collected or paid in other jurisdictions pursuant to the same qualified financial contract, thereby foreclosing the potential for double recovery or payment.

The operation of these provisions of the Model Netting Act can be illustrated through the use of a hypothetical multibranch master agreement between Party A and Party B, keeping in mind that the positive amounts represent amounts owed to Party A and the negative amounts represent amounts owed to Party B:[21]

Party A	Party B			
	London	New York	Tokyo	Madrid
New York		+$200 (T(2))		-$300 (T(1))
London	+$500 (T(3))			
Tokyo			-$100 (T(4))	

In an insolvency proceeding for the New York branch of Party B following Party B's insolvency, step one would be to calculate the Global Net Payment Obligation or Global Net Payment Entitlement. As shown above, the Global Net Payment Obligation of Party B under these four transactions is $300. The second step would be to calculate the Branch/Agency Net Payment Obligation or Branch/Agency Net Payment Entitlement. The Branch/Agency Net Payment Obligation of Party B's New York branch is $200 (under T(2)). Therefore Party A's claim against the New York liquidator will be limited to $200, which is the lesser of the Global Net Payment Obligation and the Branch/Agency Net Payment Obligation. To be made whole, if Party A collects the $200 in New York it will be required to file a claim for the additional $100 in the insolvency proceeding for the home office of Party B in England.

Two additional hypothetical examples provide further illustration of the operation of these provisions. The following matrix reflects different booking offices for Party B for T(2) and T(3):

Party A	Party B			
	London	New York	Tokyo	Madrid
New York		+$500 (T(3))		-$300 (T(1))
London	+$200 (T(2))			
Tokyo			-$100 (T(4))	

In this case, the Global Net Payment Obligation is still $300 (as expected, this amount will not change merely by changing the booking branches) but the Branch/Agency Net Payment Obligation is now $500. Party A therefore may file a claim for the full amount of its net multibranch claim ($300) in the insolvency proceeding for the New York branch, because the Global Net Payment Obligation is less than the Branch/Agency Net Payment Obligation.

Finally, consider the following matrix (modified from the original matrix) where Party B's booking offices for T(2) and T(1) are switched:

Party A	Party B			
	London	New York	Tokyo	Madrid
New York		-$300 (T(1))		+$200 (T(2))
London	+$500 (T(3))			
Tokyo			-$100 (T(4))	

Here the Global Net Payment Obligation is still $300 but the Branch/Agency Net Payment *Entitlement* is now −$300. Does Party A have to pay $300 to the New York liquidator? No, because the New York liquidator may only make a demand for the *lesser* of the Branch/Agency Net Payment Entitlement and the Global Net Payment Entitlement. Because there is, in fact, a Global Net Payment *Obligation,* the Global Net Payment *Entitlement* is deemed to be zero; because zero is less than $300, the New York liquidator may not make any demand on Party A for any amount, and Party A may not make any demand on the New York liquidator for any amount. Party A must make a claim in the insolvency proceeding for the home office of Party B for the full amount of its $300 claim against Party B.

The Merits of the Model Netting Act

Under the Model Netting Act the insolvency officials in each country would exercise insolvency jurisdiction over the assets present in that country, but would recognize at the same time the interests of foreign representatives of creditors. The Model Netting Act furthermore permits the branch proceeding to be governed by its own *lex fori concursus* and to cover the assets which are found in that specific jurisdiction. Therefore, the Model Netting Act is neither strictly territorial nor strictly universalist; rather, by combining global and local insolvency proceedings the Model Netting Act manages to achieve a balanced outcome that is much more likely to be recognized by insolvency officials in other jurisdictions. Therefore, the mixed approach employed by the Model Netting Act might be uniquely able to resolve the imminent clash between global or main and local or ancillary insolvency proceedings encountered for example in the BCCI insolvency.

Another particularity of the Model Netting Act is the fact that it contains substantive insolvency rules. These rules if applied equally by all jurisdictions involved in a given international insolvency would achieve a fair and reasonable distribution of the local assets subject to the multibranch netting agreement on a global basis to satisfy both local and global claims deriving from the termination of a qualifying multibranch netting agreement. The Model Netting Act thus offers a set of rules to address the main issues of substantive insolvency law, namely the determination of claims and assets and the distribution of the assets, if any, to the creditors.

The scheme of substantive insolvency rules contained in the Model Netting Act has a limited purpose; it deals exclusively with the treatment of the branch assets in an insolvency of a globally operating bank with respect to a limited number transactions entered into under a multibranch master agreement. Only claims deriving from qualified financial contracts documented in a multibranch netting agreement would benefit from special treatment. However, it may have been this limited scope that facilitated the enactment of similar rules in the New York Banking Law.[22] Indeed, it would probably have been too ambitious to propose internationally recognized substantive insolvency rules that would cover any and all transactions entered into by an insolvent party.

Moreover, international acceptance of the substantive insolvency rules contained in the Model Netting Act should be enhanced by the fact that those rules are not biased towards local creditors. In fact, the rules proposed by the Model Netting Act to determine to which creditors assets are to be distributed do not rely on whether their claims are local or global. This is a major difference from ring fencing. By using a distribution standard that is based on the balance of global and local obligations or entitlements, respectively, the Model Netting Act loses any touch of arbitrariness. Even if this standard is not the only possible, it is fair, clear, and predictable.

From the perspective of equal treatment of creditors, the Model Netting Act introduces—at least for the particular creditors to which it applies—a distribution principle that produces a predictable and clearly determinable result. Legal certainty in these situations is often preferable to elaborate attempts to provide equal treatment as the BCCI case proves.

The Model Netting Act can be adopted unilaterally by legislators in various jurisdictions, including those where there are questions concerning the enforceability of close-out netting under the currently applicable insolvency laws, such as Portugal and Spain. We hope that this facilitates its swift enactment.

CONCLUSION

The BCCI experience demonstrates that international cooperation of insolvency liquidators still needs to be substantially improved. For the time being, multibranch netting is probably the most efficient way to reduce the risks associated with the insolvency of international financial institutions. Reliance on comity and ancillary proceedings has proved to be very disappointing. Contractual remedies and netting laws will provide much better protection for creditors unless and until the bankruptcy laws of all the major countries are harmonized.

MODEL NETTING ACT

Part I: Netting

1. *Definitions*
    In this Act:
        "Bank" means the Central Bank of [   ];
        "insolvent party" is the party in relation to which an insolvency proceeding under the laws of [ ] has been instituted;
        "money" includes money in a currency other than the currency of [ ];
        "netting" means the termination, liquidation, acceleration, close-out, offset or netting of present or future money payment or delivery obligations or entitlements (including close-out values relating to such obligations or entitlements) arising under or in connection with one or more qualified financial contracts;
        "netting agreement" means (i) any agreement between two or more parties that provides for netting of present or future money payment or delivery obligations or entitlements arising under or in connection with one or more qualified financial contracts entered into thereunder by the parties to the agreement (a "master netting agreement"), (ii) any master agreement between two or more parties that provides for netting of the amounts due under two or more master netting agreements (a "master-master netting agreement") and (iii) any security agreement or arrangement or other credit enhancement related to one or more of the foregoing (a "security agreement");
        "non-insolvent party" is the party other than the insolvent party;
        "party" means a person constituting one of the parties to a netting agreement;

"person" includes [individuals], [partnerships], [corporations], [other regulated entities such as banks, insurance companies and broker-dealers], [governmental units];

"qualified financial contract" means any financial contract, including any terms and conditions incorporated by reference in any such financial contract, pursuant to which money payment or delivery obligations that have a market or an exchange price are due to be performed at a certain time or within a certain period of time. Qualified financial contracts include (without limitation):

(a) a currency, cross-currency or interest rate swap agreement;

(b) a basis swap agreement;

(c) a spot, future, forward or other foreign exchange agreement;

(d) a cap, collar or floor transaction;

(e) a commodity swap;

(f) a forward rate agreement;

(g) a currency or interest rate future;

(h) a currency or interest rate option;

(i) equity derivatives, such as equity or equity index swaps, equity options and equity index options;

(j) credit derivatives, such as credit default swaps, credit default basket swaps, total return swaps and credit default options;

(k) electricity derivatives;

(l) a repurchase or reverse repurchase agreement;

(m) a spot, future, forward or other commodity contract;

(n) an agreement to buy, sell, borrow or lend securities, to clear or settle securities transactions or to act as a depository for securities;

(o) any other agreement similar to any agreement or contract referred to in paragraph (a) to (n) with respect to reference items or indices relating to instruments such as (without limitation) interest rates, currencies, commodities, electricity, equities, bonds and other debt instruments and precious metals;

(p) any derivative, combination or option in respect of an agreement or contract referred to in paragraph (a) to (o); and

(q) any agreement designated as such by the Bank under this Act.

2. *Powers of the Bank.* The Bank may, by notice issued under this section, designate as "qualified financial contracts" contracts contained in Annex III of Council Directive No. 89/647/EEC of the European Communities of 18 December, 1989, as amended from time to time by any act of the European Union.

3. *Enforceability of a Qualified Financial Contract.* A qualified financial contract shall not be and shall be deemed never to have been void or unenforceable by reason of [the applicable law] relating to games and lotteries.

4. *Enforceability of a Netting Agreement.* (a) *General rule.* The provisions of a netting agreement will be enforceable in accordance with their terms against the insolvent party and, where applicable, against a guarantor or other person providing security for the insolvent party and will not be stayed, avoided, or otherwise limited by any other provision of law relating to bankruptcy, reorganization, composition with creditors, receivership, conservatorship or any other insolvency proceeding the insolvent party may be subject to, or by any other provision of law that may be applicable to the insolvent party, subject to the conditions contained in the applicable netting agreement.

(b) *Limitation on obligation to make payment or delivery.* The only obligation, if any, of a party to make payment or delivery under a netting agreement shall be equal to its net obligation to the other party as determined in accordance with the terms of the applicable netting agreement.

(c) *Limitation on right to receive payment or delivery.* The only right, if any, of a party to receive payment or delivery under a netting agreement shall be equal to its net entitlement with respect to the other party as determined in accordance with the terms of the applicable netting agreement.

(d) *Preferences and fraudulent transfers.* The liquidator of an insolvent party may not avoid

(i)   any transfer of cash, collateral or any other interests pursuant to a netting agreement from the insolvent party to the non-insolvent party; or

(ii)   any payment or delivery obligation incurred by the insolvent party and owing to the non-insolvent party pursuant to a netting agreement on the grounds of it constituting a [preference] [transfer during a suspect period] by the insolvent party to the non-insolvent party, unless there is clear and convincing evidence that the non-insolvent party (i) made such transfer or (ii) incurred such obligation with actual intent to hinder, delay, or defraud any entity to which the insolvent party was or became, on or after the date (i) such transfer was made or (ii) such obligation was incurred, indebted.

(e) *Preemption.* No stay, injunction, avoidance, moratorium, or similar proceeding or order, whether issued or granted by a court, administrative agency, or otherwise, shall limit or delay application of otherwise enforceable netting agreements in accordance with subsection (a), (b) and (c) of this section of the Act.

(f) *Scope of this provision.*

(i)   For the purposes of this section, a netting agreement shall be deemed to be a netting agreement notwithstanding the fact that such netting agreement may contain provisions relating to agreements or transactions that are not qualified financial contracts in terms of section 1 of this Act, *provided, however,* that, for the purposes of this section, such netting agreement shall be deemed to be a netting agreement only with respect to those contracts that fall within the definition of qualified financial contract in terms of Part I section 1 of this Act.

(ii)   For the purposes of this section, a netting agreement and all qualified financial contracts entered into thereunder shall constitute a single contract.

(iii) For the purposes of this section, the term netting agreement shall include the term multibranch netting agreement (as defined in Part II), *provided, however,* that in a separate insolvency of a branch or agency of a foreign party (as defined in Part II) in [ ] the enforceability of the provisions of the multibranch netting agreement shall be determined in accordance with Part II of this Act.

Part II: Multibranch Netting

1. *Additional Definitions*

"branch/agency net payment entitlement" means with respect to a multibranch netting agreement the amount, if any, that would have been owed by the non-insolvent party to the foreign party after netting only those qualified financial contracts entered into by the branch or agency and the non-insolvent party under such multibranch netting agreement.

"branch/agency net payment obligation" means with respect to a multibranch netting agreement the amount, if any, that would have been owed by the foreign party to the non-insolvent party after netting only those qualified financial contracts entered into by the branch or agency and the non-insolvent party under such multibranch netting agreement;

"foreign party" is a party whose home country is a country other than [ ];

"global net payment entitlement" means the amount, if any, owed by the non-insolvent party (or that would be owed if the relevant agreements provided for payments to either party, upon termination thereof under any and all circumstances) to the foreign party as a whole after giving effect to the netting provisions of a multibranch netting agreement with respect to all qualified financial contracts subject to netting under such multibranch netting agreement;

"global net payment obligation" means the amount, if any, owed by the foreign party as a whole to the non-insolvent party after giving effect to the netting provisions of a multibranch netting agreement with respect to all qualified financial contracts subject to netting under such multibranch netting agreement;

"home country" means the country where a party to a netting agreement is organized or incorporated;

"home office" means the home country office of a party to a netting agreement that is a bank;

"multibranch netting agreement" means a netting agreement between two or more parties under which at least one party enters into qualified financial contracts through—in addition to its home office—one or more of its branches or agencies located in countries other than its home country;

"party" means, for purposes of this Part II, a person constituting one of the parties to a multibranch netting agreement.

2. *Enforceability of a Multibranch Netting Agreement in an Insolvency of a Branch or Agency of a Foreign Party.*

   (a) *Limitation on the non-insolvent party's right to receive payment.*

   (i) The liability of an insolvent branch or agency of a foreign party or its liquidator under a multibranch netting agreement shall be calculated as of the date of the termination of such multibranch netting agreement in accordance with its terms and shall be limited to the lesser of (i) the global net payment obligation and (ii) the branch/agency net payment obligation. The liability of the insolvent branch or agency or the liquidator under this section shall be reduced by any amount otherwise paid to or received by the party in respect of the global net payment obligation pursuant to such multibranch netting agreement which if added to the liability of the liquidator under this section would exceed the global net payment obligation.

   (ii) The liability of the liquidator of an insolvent branch or agency of a foreign party under a multibranch netting agreement to any party thereunder shall be reduced by the fair market value or the amount of any proceeds of collateral that secures and has been applied to satisfy the obligations of the foreign party pursuant to the multibranch netting agreement.

   (b) *No limitation on the insolvent party's right to receive payment based on the terms of the multibranch netting agreement.* In the event that netting under the applicable multibranch netting agreement results in a branch/agency net payment entitlement, notwithstanding any provision in any such contract that purports to effect a forfeiture of such entitlement, the liquidator may make written demand upon the party to such contract for an amount not to exceed the lesser of (x) the global net payment entitlement and (y) the branch/agency net payment entitlement.

(c) *Limitation on the insolvent party's rights to receive payment based on payments made in accordance with insolvency proceedings relating to the foreign party in other jurisdictions.* The liability of the non-insolvent party under this section shall be reduced by any amount otherwise paid to or received by the liquidator or any other liquidator or receiver of the foreign party in respect of the global net payment entitlement pursuant to such multibranch netting agreement which if added to the liability of the non-insolvent party under this section would exceed the global net payment entitlement. The liability of the non-insolvent party under this section to the liquidator pursuant to such multibranch netting agreement also shall be reduced by the fair market value or the amount of any proceeds of collateral that secures and has been applied to satisfy the obligations of the non-insolvent party pursuant to such multibranch netting agreement to the foreign party.

(d) *Limitation on the terms of the multibranch netting agreement relating to a security agreement.* The non-insolvent party to a multibranch netting agreement which has a perfected security interest in collateral, or other valid lien or security interest in collateral enforceable against third parties pursuant to such multibranch netting agreement, may retain all such collateral and upon termination of such multibranch netting agreement in accordance with its terms apply such collateral in satisfaction of any claims secured by the collateral, provided that the total amount so applied to such claims shall in no event exceed the global net payment obligation, if any. Any excess collateral shall be returned to the insolvent party.

ENDNOTES

1. Legal uncertainty in such situations can increase the risk of systemic events in several ways. For example, parties may be unsure which local laws will determine the treatment of relationships with the local entity, whether contracts will be enforceable under applicable insolvency law, and how and where amounts due to and from the insolvent institutions will be valued and paid. Such uncertainty may lead institutions to withhold or refuse payments, which could lead in turn to reduced liquidity and a greater chance that the limited crisis will spread to other institutions or markets.

2. "Derivatives: Practices and Principles," Global Derivatives Policy Group of the Group of Thirty, p. 23 (July 1993).

3. The United States is a notable exception to that rule. Under "Chapter 11" of the Bankruptcy Code reorganization proceedings are usually undertaken by the shareholder-appointed management (subject to extensive court oversight) which remains in charge as "the debtor in possession." In a receivership or liquidation of a federally-insured bank, the Federal Deposit Insurance Corporation would be appointed as receiver or liquidator.

4. Warren and Westbrook, *The Law of Debtors and Creditors,* (1986) p. 721.

5. J.W. Woloniecki, "Cooperation Between National Courts in International Insolvencies: Recent United Kingdom Legislation" (1986), *International and Comparative Law Quarterly, 35,* p. 644.

6. For instance, *see* Sections 304 and 305 of the Bankruptcy Code that allows for an ancillary proceeding in the United States. An ancillary proceeding may ensure just, efficient and equitable treatment of all claims against the bankrupt entities, assure equitable distribution of the debtor's assets, and protect the U.S. assets of the debtor from any actions against them by U.S. creditors. Nevertheless, Sections 304 and 305 of the Bankruptcy Code are not detailed enough to eliminate any uncertainty that may arise for a creditor in determining its rights in that insolvency. In addition, it should be noted

that these provisions would not apply in an insolvency of a bank incorporated or organized in the United States or in any of the fifty States.

7. In that regard *see also* a Report by the Study Group on the BCCI Liquidation to the Basle Committee on Banking Supervision entitled "Case study of the insolvency liquidation of a multinational bank" published in 1992.

8. In the *Matter of the Liquidation of the New York Agency and other assets of BCCI SA* (587 N.Y.S.2d 524) Judge Baer of the Supreme Court of NY County ruled on August 3, 1992 that the liquidation procedures employed by the New York insolvency officials under the New York Banking Law do not violate the equal protection clause of the U.S. Constitution. The main argument was that they do not, directly or indirectly, give preference to New York creditors over those resident elsewhere but rather draw a distinction between creditors whose claims arise out of business done with BCCI SA's New York state agency and those claims arising out of dealings with the home office or other branches of BCCI SA.

9. There are further arguments for ring-fencing. One would be that the host country is at risk for the supervisory failures of the home country. This rationale is much stronger when the host country insures local depositors than when it merely seeks to protect their interests. In addition, ring-fencing might be necessary for a given country if its local financial system would be so vulnerable to a handful of foreign financial institutions that a local systemic collapse might result if one of them failed and the subsequent insolvency was managed globally. Finally, in the absence of established procedures of cooperation the uncertainties involved with respect to both timing issues and substantive issues might justify in a given instance to proceed unilaterally.

10. G-30/"INSOL Discussion Draft," p. 3/4.

11. The Cross-Border Insolvency Concordat is the product of the Committee J of the Section on Business Law of the IBA and was adopted by the Council of the Section on Business Law on September 17, 1995 in Paris.

12. *See* thereto the Expert Committee Report on Cross-Border Insolvency Access and Recognition (Draft 1, March 1995).

13. It should be noted, however, that the proposed EU Council Directive on the coordination of laws, regulations and administrative provisions relating to the reorganization and the winding-up of credit institutions (COM(85)788) would apply to any bank organized in a EU member state and to all its branches located in other EU member states. The proposal would deem each banking supervisor to have primary jurisdiction over banks organized in its jurisdiction; if a bank supervisor declared an insolvency of a bank under its supervision, that declaration would take effect in all EU member states where the bank had branches, regardless of local law in these EU member states.

14. G-30/INSOL Discussion Draft, p. 3.

15. In a recently published Discussion Paper, Daniel P. Cunningham and Craig T. Abruzzo have described in detail the potential of contractual multibranch netting provisions. *See* Cunningham/Abruzzo, "Multibranch Netting—A Solution to the Problems of Cross-Border Bank Insolvencies" published by the Capital Markets Forum of the Section on Business Law of the International Bar Association in 1995. Part III of this paper is based on the Discussion Paper.

16. An example printed in Cunningham/Abruzzo, op. cit., p. 15/16, helps to illustrate the intended operation of the multibranch netting provisions. Party A is a national bank chartered in the United States, with branches in England and Japan. Party B is an English bank with branches in the United States (a New York chartered branch), Japan and Spain. Party A and Party B agree to enter into a variety of privately negotiated derivatives transactions and enter into a master agreement to which all those derivatives transactions will be subject. That master agreement contains a multibranch close-out netting provisions that provides for the netting or set-off of the termination amounts for all transactions booked through any of the designated branches of either Party A or Party B. Party A plans to book transactions through all its branches, and therefore Party A lists its New York, London, and Tokyo branches as designated branches for close-out netting. Party B plans to book transactions through all its branches, and therefore Party B lists its London, New York, Tokyo, and Madrid branches as designated branches for close-out netting.

Subsequent to the execution of the master agreement, Party A and Party B enter into a variety of privately negotiated derivatives transactions, including interest rate swaps, commodity swaps, currency swaps, and equity swaps. Each of Party A and Party B books some of these transactions through its head office and some of these transactions through its branches in other jurisdictions. As long as both Party A and Party B are solvent and performing their obligations under the transactions, each of Party A and Party B can make and receive payments through its various branches. Upon an event of default (such as insolvency), however, the parties expect that a single net termination amount will be calculated for all transactions across all branches of both the parties. This expectation (expressed through the multibranch close-out netting provisions) holds for both parties, although neither party can anticipate if it will be the defaulting/insolvent party or the non-defaulting/solvent party. The agreement of the parties provides evidence that both parties believe that it is economically advantageous to effectuate multibranch netting following an insolvency, regardless of which party is insolvent.

17. At the same time keep in mind the quite similar capital adequacy requirements. For instance, the 1994 Amendment to the Basle Accord published by the Bank for International Settlements requires that if a counterparty is a multibranch party under a multibranch master agreement, then there must be a netting opinion for each jurisdiction where a branch is located through which transactions are booked. The requirements set forth in the BIS netting rules apply to any banking institution whose home country capital requirements are based on the amended Basle Capital Accord.

18. These opinions, updated as of January 1996, cover the enforceability of multibranch close-out netting in Australia, Belgium, Canada, the Cayman Islands, Denmark, England, France, Germany, Hong Kong, Indonesia, Italy, Japan, Luxembourg, Malaysia, The Netherlands, New Zealand, Portugal, Singapore, South Africa, Spain, Sweden, Switzerland, Thailand, and the United States. With the exception of Italy, Portugal, and Spain, these opinions conclude that multibranch close-out netting is enforceable under local insolvency law.

19. To illustrate the problem we refer again to an example used in Cunningham/Abruzzo, op. cit., p. 30. We assume that in the example discussed in FN 16, Party B has become insolvent, and is subject to insolvency proceedings in England, New York, Japan, and Spain. The Spanish insolvency official, however, may not recognize close-out netting and therefore may seek to ring-fence the transaction booked through the Madrid branch; that official therefore views the Madrid branch as having a, say $300 claim against Party A. The Spanish insolvency official would make this claim despite the fact that *on a net basis* across all four transactions, Party A is owed $300 from Party B.

   Although Party A might refuse to pay the $300 claim to the Spanish insolvency official, the Spanish insolvency official may have the option to either (1) attach Party A's assets located in Spain or (2) obtain a default judgment and attempt to enforce the judgment against Party A in another jurisdiction outside of Spain. In the first situation, Party A must assess whether it will be able to amend its claim in another jurisdiction to include the $300 collected by the Spanish branch in violation of the terms of the master agreement. Party A could attempt to make a claim for $600 (representing its $300 net claim plus a claim to recover the $300 wrongfully collected by the Spanish insolvency official), but it is unlikely that Party A could be given any assurances that such a claim would be honored. In the second situation (where the Spanish insolvency official attempts to enforce a default judgment), Party A must determine if a court in another jurisdiction will honor the judgment against Party A obtained in Spain, or if a court will consider the multibranch close-out netting provisions to provide a valid defense to the judgment. Again, the outcome is uncertain at best. To a large degree, therefore, the presence of a non-netting branch can undermine a portion of the legal certainty provided by a multibranch master agreement.

20. The Model Netting Act is attached in Annex I.

21. This example as well as the other two examples are used in Cunningham/Abruzzo, op. cit., pp. 26–28.

22. Section 618-a(2)(c)–(e) of the New York Banking Law.

6

The Economics of Derivatives Documentation: Private Contracting as a Substitute for Government Regulation

Gerald D. Gay
Joanne T. Medero

T he rapid growth and complexity of the over-the-counter (OTC) derivatives market, particularly swaps, and the perceived risks to the financial system, continue to stimulate debate on regulatory controls. Too often minimized in these debates are the industry's own efforts and incentives to produce superior mechanisms for controlling risks—in terms of both effectiveness and efficiency— than those imposed through regulation. While product innovation is certainly a hallmark of the derivatives industry, so too has been its ability to develop market-based solutions for addressing risk.

This article examines one such successful solution—the swap master agreement—that has seen significant innovations as the swaps market has grown and matured. The use and design of master agreements has evolved in response to demands for better documentation that reduces negotiating costs, addresses counterparty credit risk, and helps ensure contract enforceability. Indeed, the importance of sound documentation for reducing derivatives losses is emphasized in the 1993 report prepared by the Group of Thirty Global Derivatives Study Group and forms the basis of major recommendations.[1]

We begin by providing a brief review of the general risks that master agreements are intended to address, primarily credit and legal risk. We then discuss how the major components, including the basic agreement, schedules, and confirmations, are negotiated and fit together. We take as an example the International Swaps and Derivatives Association (ISDA) Multicurrency Cross-Border master agreement, focusing on the provisions that have the greatest importance for reducing transaction costs and for controlling credit and legal risks.

This copyrighted material is reprinted with permission from *The Journal of Derivatives*, a publication of Institutional Investor, Inc., 488 Madison Avenue, New York, NY 10022. The authors thank Peter Dadalt, Jouahn Nam, Thomas Noe, Michael Rebello, and Marian Turac for helpful comments.

We examine how these provisions address these risks by allowing for both up-front and ongoing risk assessment, which facilitates monitoring and helps alleviate contracting problems associated with potential information asymmetries between counterparties.[2] Among these provisions are various ex post risk control mechanisms that help deter moral hazard and provide event risk protection.

Throughout our analysis, we point out how many innovations in these provisions have occurred in response to accepted industry practice and market growth as well as to specific market events. The conclusion provides additional illustrations of the way the derivatives industry has responded to recent potential credit-threatening situations through contractual solutions.

CREDIT AND LEGAL RISKS IN SWAPS

Although they are not unique to OTC derivatives, several risks require attention in a well-functioning risk management operation. Among them are market and liquidity risk, operational risk, credit (or performance) risk, and legal risk. The master agreement is specially suited to help address the latter two.[3]

Credit risk refers to the risk of loss arising from counterparty default. Generally speaking, the analysis of credit risk in swaps is similar to that for more traditional lending arrangements such as debt or commercial loans. An interesting feature of swaps as a credit vehicle is the aspect of two-way credit; each counterparty has a potential exposure to the other. In addition, both the direction and magnitude of the exposure may vary through time. While significant advances have been made in quantifying the credit risk of a swap in terms of both current and potential replacement costs, the focus here is on how documentation is and can be used to address credit risk.

Legal risk refers to the risk of loss resulting from an unenforceable swap contract. Factors potentially contributing to legal risk include inadequate documentation, lack of authority for a counterparty to enter the contract, uncertain payment procedures associated with the bankruptcy process, and the threat that a contract may be deemed illegal by a decision of a court or legislative or regulatory body and thus void or voidable.

Economic researchers have largely overlooked the role and importance of legal risk in financial markets.[4] But, as stated in the Group of Thirty Global Derivatives Study Group report, "Enforceability presents the greatest risk participants face in derivatives transactions" (Appendix 1, p. 43).

Inadequate documentation may be a simple failure to document in writing an important term negotiated orally. There could be a long delay between an oral agreement and the signed writing of the agreement. During a delay, a counterparty could attempt to avoid a loss by disaffirming the oral agreements.[5]

Documentation is also important if a counterparty may attempt to avoid a loss through a determination that transactions are beyond their legal capacity to enter into (*ultra vires*). The most well-known instance involves the case of *Hazell v. The Council of the London Borough of Hammersmith and Fulham and Others.*

In this case, the Borough of Hammersmith and Fulham had entered approximately 600 swap and other derivatives transactions during the 1980s. Following an adverse move in interest rates that produced significant losses, a district auditor sought a declaration that the swap transactions entered into by the local municipalities were beyond their authority and were thus unlawful. This argument was predicated on the grounds that Parliament had not formally authorized local authorities to enter swap transactions.

The case was first heard in May 1989 by the Divisional Court, which eventually ruled that the Transactions were invalid, a decision subsequently overturned by the Court of Appeals. In January 1991, however, the House of Lords overturned the Court of Appeals decision, ruling that local authorities had no power to enter into swap contracts.

According to a 1992 ISDA survey, counterparty losses due to default resulting from this single episode were approximately $178 million. This represented about one-half of total swap losses due to default reported to that date. A more recent attempt to use this "defense" has arisen in the Orange County investment pool—Merrill Lynch case.

Legal uncertainty can also arise upon the insolvency of a counterparty, especially regarding the status of close-out netting agreements provided for in contracts such as swaps. Another source of legal uncertainty is the risk that swaps may be deemed illegal off-exchange futures contracts, although this source of risk was mitigated substantially by the Futures Trading Practices Act of 1992 amendments to the Commodity Exchange Act (CEA). These changes give the CFTC authority to define conditions under which swaps are exempt from provisions of the CEA, including the exchange trading requirement, and thus not illegal, even if found to be a futures contract. Finally, some derivatives transactions have been subject to the risk that they may be deemed gambling contracts under state laws.

Many of the provisions of the master agreement are aimed specifically at mitigating credit and legal risk. Broadly speaking, master agreements address these risks by allowing for (1) upfront risk assessment such as the provision of documents concerning credit risk as well as representations concerning enforceability; and (2) ongoing risk assessment, including the periodic provision of documents, maintenance of covenants, use of collateral, and mark-to-market margining. Provisions of these two types help alleviate potential information asymmetries between counterparties and facilitate monitoring.

A master agreement also includes (3) ex post risk control mechanisms such as provisions for terminating the agreement early to limit exposure brought about by the occurrence or discovery of specific events. Early termination serves to protect parties from the risk of significant credit and legal developments arising from factors that may or may not be the fault of or under the control of the counterparty (event risk protection), or that may result from ex post opportunism by counterparties (moral hazard). In addition, it may serve as an additional mechanism to help address problems with information asymmetries, for example, to deter parties for making false or misleading representations.

THE ARCHITECTURE OF A MASTER AGREEMENT

In the early days of the swaps market, active participants often developed their own in-house forms, with each differing from company to company. Lack of uniformity in definitions and basic terminology made negotiations difficult and time-consuming, particularly for counterparties with little capital markets experience. Each transaction was often separately documented even between the same counterparties.

As a result, documentation for even simple transactions was excessive, and there were often significant delays in completing the documentation for transactions that had already taken place. Obviously, delays in completing the documentation increased legal and credit risk. In addition, lack of uniformity sometimes occurred in agreements between the same counterparties, hampering netting and making inefficient use of credit lines.

The movement to develop standardized documents for general industry use received a major boost from the efforts of a small group of industry representatives who subsequently in 1985 organized themselves as ISDA (then known as the International Swap Dealer Association). Over time this group has produced several documents recommended for general industry use.[6]

Today, in a typical derivatives transaction between a dealer and end-user, the dealer will provide its preferred form of master agreement (usually an ISDA agreement) to the counterparty soon after discussions have begun about a possible trade. The ISDA master agreement involves a preprinted master agreement (either local jurisdiction-single currency or multicurrency-cross-border), a schedule, and a form of confirmation.

Generically, these three documents are often referred to together as an *ISDA Master*. The schedule is used to make certain elections and any modifications (additions and deletions) to the standard terms in the preprinted form. Confirmations provide the specifics of each trade between the two parties. Together with various definitional booklets (incorporated by reference), these documents form a single agreement between the parties. If appropriate, credit support documents (guarantees and pledge agreements) are also annexed to the master agreement.

Once negotiated between the parties and executed, the master agreement and schedule form the basis for all subsequent derivatives transactions and need not be renegotiated, absent unforeseen changes in circumstances. If deal-specific modifications need to be made, changes made in the confirmation override the schedule modifications and the master agreement standard terms.

Standardization of format permits dealers to reduce their transaction costs, and end-users who may have relationships with more than one dealer can quickly develop expertise using the ISDA or similar formats and thus reduce their costs as well. Besides lowering the cost of transacting in OTC derivatives, the increased use of standardized masters has contributed to an increase in the general level of market transparency, facilitated assignability, increased liquidity, and, for dealer banks, permitted the more efficient use of capital and credit lines resulting from netting.[7]

THE ISDA MULTICURRENCY-CROSS-BORDER MASTER AGREEMENT

Several standardized master agreements are currently available; they differ mainly in the underlying product to be transacted. There are standardized masters for foreign currency, energy products, and single and multicurrency swaps. Our discussion focuses on the current most widely used master, the 1992 ISDA Multicurrency-Cross-Border agreement.[8] While this agreement includes much boilerplate language, it retains broad flexibility, by permitting parties to make certain elections as provided for in the accompanying schedule and to amend the basic agreement through the schedule and addenda.

We focus mainly on the master's provisions that have the greatest importance for reducing transaction costs and for mitigating credit and legal risk.

Interpretation

Section 1(c) (Single Agreement) specifies that the master and all transactions under it form a single agreement. The ability to bind all transactions under a single master document is economically advantageous to the counterparties as it significantly reduces both the time and the costs of bargaining. The many terms and conditions of a contract that two counterparties would agree are fairly routine and repetitive can typically be negotiated once, and then specified in the master agreement. This leaves only the terms unique to each subsequently executed transaction (rates, notional amount, payment dates) to be negotiated, and these are documented in separate confirmations.

Besides reducing transaction costs, the recognition that all transactions form a single agreement is important for mitigating credit risk, especially as it relates to the legality of close out netting in the event of early termination.

Obligations

Section 2(c) entitled "Netting" is perhaps the most significant part of this section as it addresses *payment* netting (not to be confused with *closeout* netting, which we discuss later). The agreement states that there will be automatic netting of payments in the same transaction due on the same day and in the same currency. For example, in a simple fixed-for-floating interest rate swap, the two payments are netted into a single, smaller cash flow to be made by the counter-party with the larger liability. Similarly, payment netting may be applied to cash flows resulting from multiple transactions where payments again occur on the same date and in the same currency, if parties so elect in the schedule or in the confirmation.

Payment netting is a significant transaction cost-reducing feature that eliminates the need for the individual collection and processing of offsetting payments. It is also an extremely important practice for addressing credit risk, particularly as it significantly reduces the probability of not receiving payment due to settlement risk. Settlement risk arises out of the nonsynchronous timing of payments or deliveries by counterparties to each other. When only a single cash flow, typically a fraction of the original two payments, occurs, settlement risk and thereby credit risk is reduced, as the number of potential default events over the life of the swap is reduced.

Payment netting, however, does not reduce settlement risk when counterparty payments are denominated in different currencies or occur in different time zones—often referred to as Herstatt risk (following the 1974 failure of the *Bankhaus Herstatt* because of settlement losses in foreign exchange trading). A popular industry practice when a significant time zone differential occurs is to incorporate escrow provisions into the agreement, specifying that payments are not to be released until both parties have made payments.

Section 2(d), "Deduction or Withholding of Tax," is also a measure to help control credit risk. This provision stipulates that payments are not to be affected by tax deductions or withholdings unless required by law. If the tax is an "indemnifiable tax," the party required to deduct or withhold will pay an additional amount (gross-up) that will ensure that the net amount aid to the counterparty is the same had no withholding occurred. The payer does not have to gross-up if the receiving party failed to disclose its true tax obligations.

This provision may be viewed as a feature to control an asymmetric information aspect of the bargaining agreement. Neither party is required to determine the tax effects of the transaction on the other—any tax liabilities are the responsibility of the party liable for them.

Representations

Several upfront risk assessment measures for mitigating credit and legal risk are addressed in this section. First, each party attests to its legal authority to enter into the agreement through basic representations regarding, for example, its organizational status, its power to execute the agreement, and that such execution does not violate or conflict with any law. Each party also indicates that it is not in default, that there is no litigation that is likely to affect performance or the legality of the contract, and that other specified information furnished is accurate.

Each of these various representations acts as a "bonding" mechanism. Clearly, there are up-front costs to making such representations. While paper costs are likely to be negligible, there may be non-trivial amounts involved such as fees to attorneys, auditors, or other third parties to certify that the representations are true. Other costs incurred could include record-keeping to protect against the possibility of legal action if a counterparty subsequently doubts a party's truthfulness (the counterparty might be on the losing end of a transaction), thus requiring the party to be able to verify the accuracy of its representations.

Still, the cause of efficiency is promoted, as it is likely to be more economical for a party to stipulate certain facts than to have the counterparty incur the cost of an investigation to discover the same information for itself. Furthermore, the bonding is a credible mechanism, as there are costs incurred if a party is found to have made an inaccurate representation (whether the cost of a legal action for false stipulation, the loss of market reputation, or the cost of having to terminate the position early).

Agreements

The agreements section provides measures for conducting ongoing risk assessment, especially as it relates to credit risk. Often the schedules and confirmations will stipulate that a particular party is to furnish specified information to the other party or to a government or taxing authority. Again, this can be viewed as a mechanism for helping address asymmetric information concerns.

For example, to monitor certain covenants one party may require the periodic provision of financial statements or other reports. The information in these reports may be useful in helping the party anticipate any upcoming defaults (and therefore possibly renegotiate). Another important aspect of this section is that parties agree to make all reasonable efforts to maintain their legal authorizations.

On occasion, swaps participants will use financial covenants, perhaps specified in the schedule as additional agreements. The use of financial covenants as a means for controlling credit risk in swaps is not widespread at this time, which is surprising, especially in light of their frequent use in other arm's-length transactions such as private placements.[9]

Possible reasons for not incorporating financial covenants with any regularity include (1) the relatively high creditworthiness of most swap participants (the vast majority are investment-grade); (2) the shorter average maturity or tenor of swaps than of private placements; (3) the lower initial and potential credit exposure of swaps than traditional creditor arrangements; the initial exposure is typically zero, and the potential exposure is a relatively low percentage of notional amounts; and (4) the ability of parties to free-ride on the monitoring of other creditors or on covenants in other lending arrangements.[10]

Because financial covenants involve costs, including increased monitoring, the particular benefit from their inclusion is likely not as high as other credit enhancement arrangements such as the use of collateral. Infrequent just a few years ago, the use of collateral by market participants is growing significantly as a credit enhancement mechanism.

According to a 1994 year-end global survey of derivatives dealers conducted by Arthur Andersen on behalf of ISDA, the amount of counterparty collateral pledged was found to be approximately 8.9% of the net replacement value of outstanding swaps and related derivatives transactions. More recently, according to *Swaps Monitor* (April 8, 1996), six large derivatives dealers electing to disclose collateral information for fiscal year-end 1995 positions reported holding collateral covering between 7% and 43% of their net replacement value, with the average equaling 16%.

The growing use of collateral may be attributed to market growth and hence increasing potential exposures, increasingly longer maturity structures, low monitoring costs, and perhaps the entry of less credit-worthy counterparties. An additional factor may be the 1990 amendments to the U.S. Bankruptcy Code, which among other things, permit a counterparty to a bankrupt entity to seize and sell any posted collateral in a swap agreement to satisfy a claim.

Typically, the election to use collateral is made in the schedule of the agreement, with terms specified in a separate annexure. In response to the increasing popularity of collateral arrangements, ISDA has developed a standardized collateral document that can be included as an addendum to the master agreement.

Participants have found collateral arrangements quite flexible for handling a variety of credit issues. They may be either unilateral or bilateral with respect to whether one party or both parties are required to post collateral. Collateral may also take a variety of forms, including cash, government or marketable securities, or letters of credit. Under some arrangements, fixed mark-to-market dates are established for collateral postings to be made to cover a calculated exposure or replacement amount. Alternatively, threshold exposure amounts are established that trigger collateral movements when the exposure levels are reached.

In bilateral arrangements, it is common for parties to establish differing threshold levels; the more highly rated counterparty is assigned a higher level. Besides threshold levels, triggering events for the posting of collateral may be keyed to credit downgrades, falling capital ratios or, for collective investment fund counterparties, substantial decreases in net assets.

Events of Default and Termination Events

In addition to the upfront and ongoing risk assessment provisions described above, the agreement also provides for ex post risk control mechanisms. It specifies a list of events whose occurrence or discovery could trigger the early termination of some or all transactions under an agreement. The listed events fall into two groups: those that would categorize a counterparty as being in default with respect to the *entire* agreement (events of default), and those that could lead to the termination of a *particular* transaction or *set* of transactions conducted under the agreement (termination events).

Generally speaking, events of default are those that are within the control of, or are the fault of, a particular party, while termination events are viewed as the fault of neither party.[11] The rights of the parties under either event are described in the agreement's early termination section.

Events of Default

Eight events of default are specified in the agreement, and the parties have the option to list additional ones. It is noteworthy that the events apply not only to the contracting party, but also, if applicable, to any specified entity or credit support provider (CSP), such as those providing letters of credit or third-party guarantees. This is important, as that party's credit standing may be the one used in pricing the potential credit risk of the swap.

The events of default include:

1. Failure by a party to make a payment or delivery.
2. Failure by a party to perform other obligations (breach of agreement) such as a violation of a covenant.[12]
3. "Credit support default," which would include the termination of a CSP or its failure to comply or perform.
4. Misrepresentation.
5. "Default under specified transaction:" which refers to default in another swap or transaction between the parties so specified in the schedule.
6. "Cross default" if so specified in the schedule and in excess of a threshold dollar amount for the specified form of indebtedness.
7. Bankruptcy.
8. "Merger without assumption," in which the resulting entity or the CSP fails to assume the original obligations under which the agreement was negotiated.
9. Any others that the parties agree to include, the most common being a material adverse change in the financial condition of a party.

As the occurrence of any of these events can lead to early termination of the agreement, thus limiting a party subsequent exposure, these provisions are effective in mitigating problems owing to asymmetric information and ex post opportunism (moral hazard) as well as providing event risk protection. Information asymmetries, for example, are addressed when the parties make various representations regarding their credit and legal standings. Inclusion of a "misrepresentation" clause discourages parties from providing false or misleading information, as discovery of such could lead to termination of the agreement.

The "merger without assumption" clause clearly provides event risk protection, and may also help address information asymmetries. A party knows more about the possibility that it may be acquired than its counterparty. Absence of this provision could allow a party to enter into a swap without divulging knowledge of a potential merger event that might give it a negotiating advantage.

The *cross-default* provision assumes that a default on one obligation may be followed by a default on others. Hence, this provision promotes early detection and better monitoring of a firm potentially going into financial distress or becoming of lesser credit quality. Inclusion of a *material adverse change* clause could be useful in deterring counterparties from engaging in ex post opportunism, materially altering the risk profile of the firm subsequent to the transaction through asset substitution or because of a significant change in business strategy.

Termination Events

Several termination events are specified including:

1. An *illegality,* in which a party is unable to perform based on changes in law or regulation.[13]
2. A *tax event* that causes a party to make an additional payment (gross-up) or to have an amount withheld from a payment as a result of a change in the tax law.
3. A *tax event upon merger,* that, similar to the above, arises as the result of a merger.
4. A *credit event upon merger* in which the creditworthiness of the merged entity becomes *materially weaker* than that of the original entity (again this helps protect a party from an unanticipated decrease in the credit quality of the counterparty).

Each of these four events can be viewed as providing event risk protection. Also listed is:

5. Any additional termination event that is so specified in the schedule or a confirmation.

One additional termination event that is increasingly specified in the schedule as a credit enhancement mechanism is credit downgrade provisions. These are often designed so that the right to terminate is triggered if a counterparty's credit rating is downgraded below a certain level, (e.g., below investment-grade or Moody's Baa3). Credit downgrade provisions are a useful bonding mechanism as they are inexpensive to monitor and can also serve to reduce moral hazard by, for example, reducing incentives to engage in asset substitution.

Iben and Brotherton-Ratcliffe [1994] and Lucas [1995] provide interesting analyses of the efficacy of downgrade provisions in reducing credit risk. Both studies demonstrate that such provisions provide significant reductions in credit risk. Lucas analyzes placement of the downgrade provision relative to the initial credit rating. The placement of a downgrade trigger is important, as the counterparty must still be able to make the full termination payment, which may be a problem if it is experiencing significant difficulties as a result of financial distress.

Iben and Brotherton-Ratcliffe analyze the marginal benefit of downgrade provisions beyond that provided by closeout netting. While the additional impact of the downgrade protection is found to be substantially smaller than that of netting, expected losses from default are still reduced significantly. Furthermore, the authors report that the impact of downgrade provisions would be much greater in jurisdictions where the enforcement of netting provisions is not certain in the event of bankruptcy. The downgrade provision may act as "synthetic netting," because in many cases it is reasonable to expect that it will be possible to unwind transactions following a downgrade but before default actually occurs.

Early Termination

Upon the occurrence and continuation of an "event of default," the nondefaulting party may, with up to 20 days' notice, designate an early termination date for all outstanding transactions. The right to set this date appears to give the nondefaulting party some bargaining power over the defaulting party. Furthermore, the time frame gives the nondefaulting party an opportunity to possibly rehedge its market exposure.

In the 1987 version of the master, this option did not apply in the case of one particular event of default, bankruptcy. Instead, bankruptcy immediately triggered an automatic early termination. In the 1992 version, bankruptcy is incorporated into the schedule as an option.[14] This change thus allows nondefaulting parties greater certainty about their ability to reestablish a hedge prior to terminating the agreement, and allows them to continue the transaction when there is adequate security.

In the case of a "termination event," the affected party must give prompt notice upon becoming aware of the event and share information about the event with the other party. In addition, before designating an early termination event, an affected party must make reasonable efforts to transfer its rights and obligations to an affiliate to avoid the termination event.

Transfers are subject to and conditional upon the approval of the counterparty, thus protecting it against an unexpected increase in credit risk. The counterparty cannot deny consent, if, given the terms proposed, its normal policies would permit it to enter into the transaction with the transferee.

If both parties are affected by a termination event, both parties are to make reasonable efforts to avoid the event. If the parties are not able to avoid the event or to complete a transfer of the affected transactions, the entitled party may designate a termination date following which applicable payments are calculated.

To determine the appropriate compensation following the designation of a termination date, the agreement provides for parties to elect in the schedule both a choice of a payment measure ("market quotation" or "loss") and a payment method ("first method" or "second method"). Market quotation calls for determining the replacement cost according to available quotations. Loss is used for computing damages for products not typically quoted or for highly customized swaps for which quotes are not readily available.

The payment method option is applicable only to events of default, as termination events are always settled by the second method. This is because the first method is essentially "limited two-way payment," where possibly only the defaulting party is subject to having to make a payment, thus permitting the nondefaulting party to enjoy a possible windfall payment.

Under the second method, often referred to as "full two-way payment," either party may be liable for making a payment depending on the net value of the relevant transactions. Since parties affected by a termination event are typically viewed as not at fault, the second method applies.

It might be argued that limited two-way payment is an additional tool for exerting pressure on management to avoid default. In fact, selection of this option is increasingly falling out of favor. Potential reasons include the existence of more efficient contracting means to control the actions of counterparties, the increased bargaining power of lower-rated counterparties, changes in methodologies for computing bank capital requirements, and uncertainty surrounding the willingness of courts to uphold limited two-way payment agreements.[15] Many also believe that full two-way payment provisions serve to reduce credit risk as well as system risk by facilitating the unwinding or transfer of the swap portfolios of failed entities.

The practice of netting the value of the transactions (i.e., full two-way payments) between two counterparties in the event of early termination due to insolvency or bankruptcy is recognized as an important tool for managing credit exposure. Several studies and commentators have noted the risk reduction that netting affords.

For example, Alan Greenspan has written that the Federal Reserve System estimates that netting of interest rate and currency contracts reduces credit exposure by approximately 40% to 60% relative to gross replacement costs. The Government Accounting Office (GAO) reports in its survey of major OTC derivative dealers that approximately 75% of OTC derivatives contracts (in terms of notional dollar amounts as of December 1992) were subject to enforceable netting agreements. In addition, the GAO survey finds that netting agreements reduced the dealers' combined gross credit exposure by 36%.

More recently, results of a global survey of swaps dealers released by ISDA in July 1995 for year-end 1994 outstanding positions indicate that gross replacement costs of $172.6 billion were reduced to $77.9 billion after netting, a 59% reduction that is attributable to the regulatory recognition and legal enforceability of netting.

The ability to achieve these significant levels of risk reduction available through netting provisions depends critically upon the legal certainty of enforceability. Under the insolvency laws in the United States, corporations and financial institutions are provided a high degree of legal certainty. For corporations, under 1990 amendments to the U.S. Bankruptcy Code, an important step is recognition of the enforceability of closeout netting provisions. This provision has the added benefit of effectively preventing counterparties from "cherry picking," or demanding payment on winning trades and renouncing losing trades.

For financial institutions in receivership or conservatorship, similar treatment is provided to the netting of swaps (or qualified financial contracts) under the Financial Institutions Reform, Recovery, and Enforcement Act of 1989 (FIRREA) and the FDIC Improvement Act of 1991 (FDICIA). Laws in other G-10 countries where there may be counterparties to U.S. firms are also increasingly recognizing the enforceability of netting.[16]

The 1990 amendments to the U.S. Bankruptcy Code produced several other major advantages for reducing counterparty credit risk in swaps and related derivatives contracts, advantages not enjoyed by most other claimants against a bankrupt entity. Included are provisions explicitly permitting the nonbankrupt party to use the filing of a bankruptcy petition as a basis for the termination of the agreement. In addition, despite the automatic stay provision of the Code, a counterparty to a bankrupt entity may seize and sell any posted collateral to satisfy a claim.[17] Further, a trustee is substantially limited in its ability to use its powers to avoid transfers under a derivatives claim (e.g., payments made under the terms of a swap contract or adjustments to collateral).

Transfer

The transfer section includes language that restricts transfer of the agreement by either party without prior written consent of the counterparty. This provision serves to protect parties against a potentially credit risk-increasing transfer that is not considered in the original negotiations. Exceptions include transfers to an entity resulting from a merger or consolidation (assuming no material change in credit quality) and transfers by the nondefaulting party of amounts owed it by a defaulting party.

Contractual Currency

Payments on a swap are to be made in the contracted currency, which is usually specified in the confirmation. If a party receives payment in a noncontracted currency, the party is entitled to appropriate compensation, after conversion of the funds, for any shortfall in the full amount due. Any excess must be refunded promptly.

Miscellaneous

A miscellaneous section includes a series of boilerplate provisions that signify the arm's length nature of the negotiation between the two principal negotiating parties. For example, Section 9(a), "Entire Agreement:" states that the agreement constitutes the entire agreement and understanding of both parties and supersedes all oral and other prior written communications between the two parties. While the agreement does not void certain common law protections and statutes covering fraud, fiduciary responsibilities, and duties regarding principal-to-principal transactions, it otherwise serves as the explicit vehicle for contracting any understandings between the two parties.

Recently, however, in light of several highly reported instances of firm losses involving derivatives, several commentators and government agencies have questioned the conditions under which swaps and other over-the-counter transactions may indeed be viewed as arm's length.[18] For example, in the case of Gibson Greetings, the CFTC brought an enforcement action against Bankers Trust alleging that BT had an advisory relationship with Gibson. Following this action by the CFTC (and other reports around this time of several end-users' larger derivatives losses), many dealers began amending the schedule to include explicit language that the firms have not entered into an advisory capacity.

In this regard, on March 6, 1996, ISDA released standardized wording to be included in the master agreement for counterparties to document their understanding of the nature of their relationship. Included is language pertaining to (1) nonreliance (e.g., each party is acting for its own account, has made its own independent decision as to the merits of the transaction, and is not relying on the other party for investment advice); (2) assessment and understanding (e.g., each party is capable of assessing the merits of and understanding the risks of the transaction); and (3) status of parties (one party is not acting as a fiduciary for or an advisor to the other with respect to the transaction). ISDA suggests that such language be included in the schedule or as a new section.

CONCLUDING REMARKS

A well-functioning risk management operation should consider all facets of risk emanating from derivatives usage. While models and computer analytics have been developed for pricing, measuring, and managing market risk, the industry has also made substantial progress in formulating contractual solutions to address credit and legal risk. Development of the swap master agreement is a good example.

The swap master agreement, while standardized in many ways, can accommodate the unique characteristics and contractual needs of counterparties. This is in sharp contrast with many regulatory approaches, whose "one size fits all" approach may be a counterproductive obstacle to innovative practices. The master agreement has evolved in response to both market growth and broad industry acceptance of particular practices. Specific market events will continue to affect its development.

Consider recent developments pertaining to the Japanese interest rate environment during the Fall of 1995. At the time, there was a substantial volume of outstanding yen interest rate swaps having floating legs with payment terms based on a spread under yen-LIBOR. As yen interest rates plummeted, swap payments on the floating leg increasingly became negative.

Several market participants contended that counterparties normally expecting to receive a floating payment are obligated to make a payment for the negative amount (in addition to their fixed payment), while others argued that there is an implicit floor struck at zero, thus preventing a negative payment from occurring. This issue was not one contemplated by drafters of the standard swap agreement or by actual counterparties, and an adverse legal interpretation could precipitate a large number of defaults.

In response, on November 15, 1995, ISDA issued a memorandum suggesting language for inclusion in either the schedule to the master agreement or in a confirmation. Alternative language was provided for either interpretation of the treatment of negative interest rates.

A second recent development with a disruptive potential for derivatives markets pertains to the creation of the European Monetary Union. Plans are for member countries of the monetary union to convert to a proposed single currency, the Euro, and a single interest rate governed by the new European central bank. This conversion of the several national currencies, scheduled for January 1, 1999, raises significant concerns regarding the treatment of affected interest rate and currency derivatives currently scheduled to mature after that date.

One concern is that counterparties could declare that contracts were "frustrated," and walk away from trades on the theory that the contracts were invalid because the original terms no longer applied. A second concern is that counterparties may bring claims against dealers for failing to warn them of the potential impact of the conversion on their trades. Although the potential events remain a few years off and could be delayed even further, earlier this year ISDA set up four working groups to examine the various issues raised and perhaps recommend amendments to current documentation.

REFERENCES

Das, Satyajit. *Swap & Derivative Financing.* Chicago: Probus, 1994.

"Derivatives: Practices and Principles." The Group of Thirty, Washington, DC, July 1993.

"Financial Derivatives: Actions Needed to Protect the Financial System." U.S. General Accounting Office, Washington, DC, May 1994.

Iben, Ben, and Rupert Brotherton-Ratcliffe. "Credit Loss Distributions and Required Capital for Derivative Portfolios." *Journal of Fixed Income,* Vol. 4, No. 1 (1994), pp. 6–14.

Kahan, Marcel, and Bruce Tuckman. "Private v. Public Lending: Evidence from Covenants." Working paper, New York University, June 1994.

Kwan, Simon H., and Willard T. Carleton. "The Structure and Pricing of Private Placement Corporate Loans." Working paper, University of Arizona, July 1993.

Lucas, Douglas. "The Effectiveness of Downgrade Provisions in Reducing Counterparty Credit Risk." *Journal of Fixed Income,* Vol. 5 (1995), pp. 32–41.

Marshall, John F., and Kenneth R. Kapner. *The Swaps Market,* 2nd ed. Miami: Kolb, 1993.

"OTC Derivative Markets and their Regulation." Commodity Futures Trading Commission, Washington, DC, 1993.

Overdahl, James, and Barry Schachter. "Derivatives Regulation and Financial Management: Lessons from Gibson Greetings." *Financial Management,* Vol. 24 (1995), pp. 68–78.

Smith, Clifford W., and Jerold B. Warner. "On Financial Contracting: An Analysis of Bond Covenants," *Journal of Financial Economics,* Vol. 7 (1979), pp. 117–161.

Winton, Andrew. "Costly State Verification and Multiple Investors: The Role of Seniority." *Review of Financial Studies,* Vol. 8 (1995), pp. 91–123.

Zinbarg, Edward. "The Private Placement Loan Agreement." *Financial Analysts Journal,* Vol. 31 (1975), pp. 33–35, 52.

ENDNOTES

1. Recommendation 13 states

   Dealers and end-users are encouraged to use one master agreement as widely as possible with each counterparty to document existing and future derivatives transactions, including foreign exchange forwards and options. Master agreements should provide for payments netting and close-out netting, using a full two-way payments approach.

2. The economic design and role of financial contracts has received popular attention in academic circles. Smith and Warner (1979) analyze the corporate bond indenture as a vehicle for mitigating shareholder-bondholder conflict, while Zinbarg (1975), Kwan and Carleton (1993), and Kahan and Tuckman (1994) analyze the structure of private placement loan agreements compared to public debt issues.

3. We contend that documentation has played and continues to play an important part in mitigating derivatives losses. Reports on the low incidence of derivatives losses to date include a 1992 survey, commissioned by ISDA, of derivatives dealers. Over a ten-year period ending in 1991, respondents reported total losses amounting to only $358 million.

   In its May 1994 study, the General Accounting Office (GAO) reported that, according to data provided by a survey of fourteen major U.S. derivatives dealers, 1992 losses as a result of counterparty default amounted to $250 million, or only 0.2% of the combined gross credit exposure. For the three year period 1990-1992, losses were reported to total $400 million.

   More recently, *Swaps Monitor* (March 25, 1996) reports that the level of derivatives losses continues to be very low as disclosed in the annual reports of major U.S. dealers. The publication notes that Citicorp reported gross credit losses from derivatives of $6 million in 1995 and that BankAmerica reported losses of only $3 million. The reports of other dealers note mainly that losses were minor.

4. Overdahl and Schachter (1995) are an exception. They examine the unintended consequences of regulatory actions on contracting costs and market innovation.

5. Most jurisdictions have a statute of frauds generally requiring the execution of a written contract when performance does not occur within one year.

6. Das (1994) and Marshall and Kapner (1993) provide chronologies of the development of these various documents.

7. A discussion of the importance of documentation appears in "OTC Derivative Markets and their Regulation" (1993). Particularly interesting is the discussion regarding Olympia and York Development, a large Canadian real estate developer. Because it was perceived as creditworthy at the time it

entered several swap contracts, the firm was able to dictate many of the terms, including the use of its own document. When the firm began experiencing financial difficulties, swap dealers had little interest in acquiring the contracts because of their unique terms relative to industry practice.

8. Before revision in 1992, this master was referred to as the 1987 Interest Rate and Currency Exchange Agreement.

9. Kahan and Tuckman (1974) document the more frequent occurrence of covenants, especially financial covenants, in private debt offerings than in public offerings. They attribute these differences to lower renegotiation costs and better monitoring abilities of lenders in private offerings.

10. Some agreements may incorporate by reference covenants appearing in other debt contracts of a party. Also, the cross-default provision as a specified "event of default" in effect captures violations of covenants in the counterparty's other lending arrangements that lead to default. Winton (1995) discusses the advantage of lenders who are marginal (hold lower-priority claims) bearing most of the costs of monitoring.

11. The distinction between an event of default and a termination event is becoming less significant as market practice overwhelmingly adopts "full two-way payments" as compensation for early termination.

12. Unless otherwise provided, each party has a three-business day cure period to remedy a failure to pay or deliver, and thirty days to remedy a breach of agreement.

13. If an event could be treatable as both an illegality (a termination event) and as an event of default, it shall be treated as an illegality.

14. This change may have been prompted by the 1990 amendments to the U.S. Bankruptcy Code that made the "automatic stay provisions" inapplicable to swaps, thus reducing the need for automatic early termination upon bankruptcy.

15. For banks, swap positions written under a single master agreement can be netted prior to the calculation of capital requirements if the second method (full two-way payment) has been elected, and legal opinions have been received that support the enforceability of closeout netting in bankruptcy or insolvency.

16. For a survey of issues regarding legal enforceability in other jurisdictions, see Appendix II of "Derivatives: Practices and Principle" (1993).

17. In the absence of a collateral agreement, the nondefaulting counterparty should find itself in a position no worse than that of a senior unsecured claimant.

18. For discussion of the potential economic implications of these actions for the market for swaps, see Overdahl and Schachter (1995).

PART THREE

Risk Measurement

7

Report Card on VaR: High Potential but Slow Starter

TANYA STYBLO BEDER

For all its cachet, value at risk is no cookie-cutter risk management solution. Implementation has been hampered by the need to make simplifying assumptions. Differences in VaR methodology and the many modeling assumptions required mean that risk managers should have a clear understanding of the components of their VaR measures and must combine it with other risk tools.

While Value at Risk (VaR) shows increasing promise as a risk measurement tool, there are more questions than answers after three years of use. Despite this, the concept is widely endorsed by regulators such as the Bank for International Settlements, the Federal Reserve, the Office of the Comptroller of the Currency and the Securities and Exchange Commission. It is mandated for many under Generally Accepted Accounting Principles, is part of the rating process by agencies, and is encouraged by key industry groups such as the Group of Thirty, the Derivatives Policy Group, and the International Swaps and Derivatives Association. But implementation of VaR is harder than grasping the simplicity of its concept. First, not all VaRs are equal. Second, vast quantities of data and significant modeling or systems efforts may be required. Third, firms must design and implement risk management add-ons to address VaR's limitations and weaknesses. While dealers typically are further along with VaR implementation than end-users, few if any are finished with the process. This article surveys the current realities of VaR and what we have learned to date.

TYPES OF VaR

VaR is the great equalizer. It translates the risk of *any* financial instrument into its potential loss under specific assumptions.[1] There are three main types of VaR:

This copyrighted material is reprinted with permission from *Bank Accounting & Finance,* a publication of Institutional Investor, Inc., 400 Madison Avenue, New York, NY 10022. The author wishes to thank Frank Iacono for his valuable input regarding this chapter.

- *Variance/Covariance[2] VaR:*   Under this methodology, financial instruments are decomposed (or mapped) into delta equivalents[3] consisting of basic financial building blocks or market factors. Once historical or other distributions for these market factors are specified, VaR and other measures are computed using standard statistical techniques. In most cases, historical data are used to build the variance/covariance matrix for the market factors, making this aspect of the calculation dependent upon the time period selected. Over the past two years, data sets have become available which provide distributions for many common market factors (for example RiskMetrics[4]), as have commercial software packages which perform VaR computations.

- *Historical VaR:*   Under this methodology, financial instruments are analyzed over the number of days in the historical observation period (e.g., 100 days) and the *actual* change that was experienced in the value of each financial instrument is calculated using the desired time horizon (e.g., overnight). Note that while most users analyze financial instruments specifically, some translate their financial instruments into "equivalent" building blocks or market factors, and calculate the changes on these. Once the changes in value are calculated, each change is added to today's value for the financial instrument or its "equivalent" to produce an array of observations. As this replicates historical behavior, the risk view depends upon the time period selected. To complete the calculation, the array is analyzed statistically. For example, if there are 100 observations, the 5th lowest observation value would be the one-day 95% confidence interval VaR.

- *Simulation VaR:*   Under this methodology, the theoretical probability distribution of changes in value for each financial instrument or its "equivalent" is calculated for the desired time horizon (e.g., over two weeks) as per the distribution parameters specified in the simulation. Typically, correlations and lognormal or other distributions are incorporated. The theoretical changes in values are then added to today's value for the financial instrument or its "equivalent" and arrayed as in the case of historical VaR to produce the desired confidence interval VaR. The process is often completed under varying sets of parameters.

Each type of VaR has its strengths and weaknesses. Variance/covariance VaR is the least computationally intensive and free data are available. However, it is based on normal or lognormal distributions so misses fat-tailed behavior[5] and does not properly incorporate options or other nonlinear instruments. Historical VaR is the easiest to implement from a systems perspective and may be the easiest to explain to the nonmathematically inclined. However, its output depends heavily on the time period selected (simply stated, history must repeat itself). Simulation VaR can incorporate any joint distribution for the market factors so offers the greatest flexibility for sensitivity analyses regarding market plus model issues, and fully captures nonlinear instruments. However, it has the greatest systems, programming and data needs.

SEVEN LESSONS ABOUT VaR

Beginning in 1994, dealers focused on implementing at least *some* VaR measure and devoted their resources to data, systems and programming challenges. Risk management software vendors took a similar approach, focusing primarily on the need to expand their systems to include at least *one* VaR alternative. At first, most implemented variance/covariance or historical VaR calculations. Larger corporations implemented VaR as well, with the goal of comparing the Treasury area's performance versus an established internal benchmark. Some institutional investors and investment managers (particularly insurance companies, mutual funds and "manager of managers") began to implement VaR over the past six to twelve months, with the goal of calculating risk adjusted portfolio performance. Many smaller corporations as well as pension funds, public funds, foundations and endowments have started to address VaR more recently.

To date and in general, the theoretical discussions of VaR far exceeded firms' actual practices.[6] This is due to the many practical issues which complicate and surround its implementation. However, valuable lessons have been learned, and these are being addressed as VaR approaches its third year of use in the risk management arena. Seven lessons follow:

Lesson One: For Instruments with Nonlinear Price Function, Variance/Covariance VaR Understates Risk

The variance/covariance approach significantly understates risk for portfolios with options or financial instruments with nonlinear price functions,[7] particularly during periods of large volatility or with large changes in the price of the underlying. Most dealers with significant nonlinear exposures have implemented or are switching over to simulation-based VaR calculations for at least the nonlinear books within their businesses. This presents aggregation issues regarding VaRs calculated with different methodologies over different time horizons. Research is underway regarding risk management add-ons to a variance/covariance approach that better reflect nonlinear risks.

Lesson Two: Historical VaR and Simulation VaR Can Differ Drastically

The historical VaR and simulation VaR approach may produce vastly different results, especially when the historical period comprises a heavily trending market. This is due to the fact that the key variables in simulation VaR are computed according to the user's expectations or may be computed randomly and often differ substantially from those for the recent historical period. There are many types of simulation, each determined by the user's preferences and parameters. Monte Carlo simulations are the most common type of random simulations. Note that to the degree random or user-specified expectations vary from trending market expectations, differences will be magnified between the two approaches. Note that the choice of simulation parameters is itself an important determinate of the VaR result so some dealers and end-users are beginning to stress test the sensitivity of the VaR result to alternate sets of parameters. Note that appropriate stress tests vary and depend upon factors such as portfolio composition, holding period, risk appetite, systems capabilities, and so on.

Lesson Three: Mapping Can Impair VaR Calculations

For large dealers and end-users, the historical VaR and simulation VaR[8] require vast quantities of data plus numerous pricing models. To enable calculation of VaR as models and data bases are built or to reduce the total amount required, most VaR users have resorted to some degree of mapping financial instruments into equivalents and/or matrix pricing. This often results in significant differences between the risk/reward profile of the actual financial instrument and its mapped equivalent. Research is underway regarding the degree to which this impacts the VaR result, particularly in the case of nondiversified portfolios, heavily engineered instruments, exotic instruments, and so on. We reviewed several cases in which the VaR calculation was performed correctly but the accuracy lost through mapping or matrix pricing produced misleading results for the actual portfolio.

Lesson Four: Poor Assumptions about Diversification Can Lead to Flawed Results

The variance/covariance approach requires mapping financial instruments into market factors which are contained in the matrix. To facilitate this process, entire instrument classes are often mapped into market indices. For example, all domestic stocks may be mapped into the S&P 500 or all corporate bonds into a swap index. For several portfolios we have reviewed, mapping an undiversified portfolio into an assumed diversified portfolio produced misleading results. Research is underway to analyze the relationship between the quality of the VaR result after such mapping and varying degrees of diversification.

Lesson Five: Combining Adjusted VaRs from Different Time Periods Can Be Misleading

Many VaR users employ different time horizons for different trading areas or asset classes. For example, an overnight horizon is used for the forward foreign exchange positions while a longer time horizon is used for real estate or illiquid/exotic financial instruments. To obtain a firmwide VaR statistic for a comparable time period, adjustments are made using statistical approximations such as the square root of time. To the degree that markets do not follow linear price behavior and normal distributions (most markets do not), and to the degree that drift should be considered, misleading results will be produced by such approximations.

Lesson Six: VaRs May Be Less Comparable Than They Appear

Performance measurement and capital allocation are common goals of VaR users. The desire is to allocate capital to those areas which have the greatest performance with the least amount of risk. However, many financial instruments and markets are inefficient and have risk profiles that change over time. Thus the VaR for highly liquid, diversified portfolios may be compared to the VaR for highly illiquid, nondiversified portfolios, and results are often noncomparable. Furthermore, two portfolios or business areas with equivalent VaR and return may have different risk tails, thus producing different expectations of loss outside of the confidence bands. Research is underway regarding what can be learned from analyzing the changes in VaR over time (i.e., the first derivative with respect to time). Other research is studying the relationship between downside risk and the degree of diversification to determine how these risk dimensions should be incorporated into performance measurement and the capital allocation decision.

Lesson Seven: Accounting and Economic Measures
May Not Mix

Many corporations use VaR in conjunction with a benchmark in the Treasury area. For many, the goal is to manage the volatility of earnings. Two common problems arise with this approach. First, accounting realities may differ significantly from economic realities. To the degree that the benchmark is accounting-based and the VaR calculation is economic-based, this problem will be exacerbated. Second, earnings occur continuously and involve all business activities of the company while VaR typically is based on a snapshot of selected activities of the corporation. Both require adjustments in how VaR is employed.

WHICH VaR SHOULD YOU USE?

VaR research to date primarily has involved portfolios of simple, highly liquid financial instruments such as Treasury strips, equity index options, and forward foreign exchange contracts. Our review of dozens of dealers' and end-users' risk management techniques revealed vast differences not only in the type of VaR calculation, but also in the VaR statistics produced. Variances in the VaR statistic ranged by as much as 14 times for the same portfolio, depending on the type of VaR calculation and the time horizon.[9] Large variances in VaR have been corroborated by others' research, particularly for portfolios which contain options.[10] Yet other research suggests that variances in VaR may be less significant for portfolios which do not contain options or other instruments with nonlinear price behavior, especially over one-day holding periods,[11] and that the length of sampling periods plays an important role.[12]

Which VaR methodology to select depends on several factors. Typically, dealers and end-users with complex portfolios set a goal of implementing a consistent, firmwide VaR which reflects their outlook preferences and the complexity of the portfolio. For portfolios with options or significant nonlinear price behavior, the historical VaR and simulation VaR produce superior results to the variance/covariance VaR. However, the systems, model, data, personnel, educational and time requirements of the historical and simulation VaRs often result in the use of variance/covariance VaRs or multiple VaR methodologies on an interim basis. The choice between historical and simulation VaR resides largely with the user's outlook preferences and the desire to perform sensitivity analyses. Historical VaR is based on actual, past market experience whereas simulation VaR is based on the user's outlook and expectations. Full sensitivity analyses only can be performed on the latter.

Once the outlook preferences and the complexity of the portfolio are analyzed, and one or more VaRs are selected, users must make decisions regarding several important dimensions of the calculation:

1. *The length of the VaR horizon (overnight, 2 weeks, longer, etc.).* VaR requires the firm to select a time horizon for analyzing risk in the context of expected losses. For example, dealers often select overnight time horizons while pension funds and corporations often select longer horizons.

One challenge in selection of the time horizon is that while a model may produce adequate views of capital at risk on an overnight or weekly basis, it may produce inadequate risk views over time horizons of several months, a year, or longer. For example, the calculation of one-day or overnight VaR may be misleading for customized or exotic products that cannot be analyzed, action decided upon and liquidated in such a time frame. The 1995 Basle Amendment suggests that firms employ a single time horizon of two-weeks (10 business days) for VaR calculations. Note that this may be short relative to the life of many asset classes and other exposures, and potentially too long versus highly liquid instruments.

A second challenge is that while longer time horizons may be preferred for instruments such as illiquid, path-dependent options, some mathematical functions are inaccurate beyond small market moves. For example, many mathematical models are incapable of handling discontinuities such as market gapping, or require linearity to produce accurate information, yet these are used in pricing models which are part of the VaR calculation. Over the past two years, dozens of dealers and end-users announced losses due to differences between estimated short-term profits and actual experience over longer time horizons. This suggests that firms should test the sensitivity of the VaR calculation to alternate assumptions regarding pricing models (see 4 below) and time horizon.

For some firms, a third challenge is to compare and combine VaRs calculated over alternate time frames and under different methodologies. As discussed above, the translation of long-horizon VaRs into short-horizon VaRs (and vice versa) typically assumes linearity, joint normal relationships (i.e., that the square root of time is sufficient) or static relationships (i.e., no drift) which may produce misleading results.

2. *Database.* VaR requires data covering all relevant market factors and variables on which to perform the calculations. Vastly different risk views may be produced by alternate data sets. For example, during a recent 24-hour-period the 10-year U.S. Treasury traded at as high a price as 103 for three hours, but only at par for one hour. Thus, time of day (or intraday data versus end-of-day data), can produce contrary risk views via VaR. Different risk views can also be created by the use of historical versus market-implied data. Note that historical end-of-day data are most often employed to calculate VaR, but the historical period selected varies significantly from firm to firm. Some firms employ the most recent 90-day time horizon while others use the past year at a minimum. Other firms expand the time horizon to capture periods of stressful market moves such as market crashes or dislocations. The proposed Basle Amendment suggests that firms employ a 1-year minimum data set for VaR calculations.

Length of time is not the sole criterion to establish and test regarding the data set. As discussed, mapping procedures are a critical part of most VaR processes. Furthermore, sampling frequency and independence of data also can impact VaR significantly. For example, a one-year data base comprised of twelve, end-of-month data points may be no more relevant than a data set of twelve points selected through random chance. Alternately, theoretical mark-to-model prices for customized or illiquid instruments may be far from market prices at the time of transactions. Such data issues can cause unpleasant surprises as experienced in 1994 by many mutual funds, pension funds, and municipalities who monitored engineered mortgage securities and/or inverse floaters at month-end based on theoretical values.[13]

Another decision regarding the data is whether to exclude certain data points. For example, should the data set include "outlier" events caused by one-time events, market gapping or other dislocations? Such occurrences are often characterized as extreme but low-probability events. Recent examples are the devaluation of the Mexican peso, the 1987 stock market crashes, and commodity volatility during the Gulf War. Note that two databases, distinguished by inclusion of outlier events, are likely to produce different VaR calculations.

Yet another challenge is to determine whether an outlier event is an indication of structural change in the market. For example, fundamental change in the prepayment patterns for mortgage-based securities in the United States occurred over the past few years, driven by mortgage broker activity and education of the homeowner. Prior to the change, conventional wisdom dictated that a drop in interest rates had to prevail for two to three months before refinancing occurred. Subsequently, this refinancing lag shortened from months to weeks and the mortgage market demonstrated new prepayment patterns during the rally that ended with the Federal Reserve's interest rate hike in February of 1994. Thus, use of historical prepayment data was misleading in predicting the expected life (and therefore return) of many mortgage securities.

Some firms employ data sets based on implied market information to reduce dependence on historical data. Whatever the data set, firms should stress test the sensitivity of the VaR calculation not only to exclusion of any data points but also for sampling error and the use of specific historical periods and/or mark-to-model dependence. The goal is to determine whether alternate data sets drive large differences in the value of VaR for the same portfolio or exposures.

3. *Correlation assumptions.* VaR requires that the user decide which exposures are allowed to offset each other and by how much. For example, is the Japanese yen correlated to movements in the Italian lira or the Mexican peso? Is the price of Saudi Light correlated to movements in the price of natural gas? If so, by how much? VaR requires that the user determine correlations not only *within* markets (for example, USD currency underlyings vs. USD commodity underlyings) but also *across* markets (for example, how do changes in the bond market in the United States relate to changes in the equity market in Australia?). Note that mapping procedures have additional embedded correlation assumptions. For example, mapping individual stocks into the S&P 500 or fixed income securities into the swap curve translate into the assumption that individual financial instruments move as the market overall. While this may be a reasonable assumption for well diversified portfolios, it may not be reasonable for nondiversified or illiquid portfolios.

Dealers, end-users, regulators, and financial theorists espouse wildly different views on the topic of correlation relationships both within and across markets. For instance, pension funds have tackled correlation issues for decades in analyzing strategic versus tactical allocation of assets. Pension funds with a *lack* of diversification across asset classes (e.g., stocks versus bonds) or capital markets (e.g., domestic versus foreign) may well be considered to be in violation of the "prudent man" standard of ERISA. Financial theory[14] demonstrated the value of diversification, both within and across markets, decades ago. While cross-border *legal* and netting risks may exist, these risks typically are managed and reserves are taken separately from *market* risks. Despite the use of separate reserves and risk calculations, The 1995 Basle Amendment allows only the extreme position of correlation *within* asset classes. For purposes of calculating VaR, the Amendment assumes a correlation of 1 between long positions, and a correlation of −1 between long and short positions. While this may be of little consequence for some relationships (for example, the correlation between strong currencies and interest rates in EC countries), it is of huge consequence for others (for example, the correlation between the price of a restaurant stock in Sri Lanka and a Yankee bond issued by the Canadian telephone company). Not surprisingly, the rigid correlation methodology in the 1995 Basle Amendment raises VaR significantly relative to more common correlation assumptions.[15]

Additional challenges exist. What happens if a market breaks through its historical or implied trading pattern and violates the correlation assumption in place? A recent example is provided by the many currencies that previously displayed little or no historical correlation to the Mexican peso, but made sympathy moves during the peso's devaluation. What happens if some temporary phenomenon alters correlations significantly? For example, barrier options on spreads (also known as knock-out or knock-in options) has been blamed for unexpected, high correlations during periods that market levels approach strike levels, with both the writers and the buyers of the barriers suspected of large trading volume to influence the outcome in their favor.

In CMRA's review of different approaches to VaR, some firms assumed that all cash flows were correlated across all markets, while others assumed a lower degree of correlation. Sophisticated mean-variance models, for example the one used to compute the RiskMetrics data set, allow correlation for all instruments across all markets that are covered. At the other extreme are models such as The 1995 Basle Amendment which require correlation of 1 or −1, depending on what is least favorable to the VaR calculation.

4. *Mathematical engine and quantitative approach.* All VaR calculations require the use of mathematical models to value individual instruments (or their components or assumed equivalents) as well as to value the aggregate portfolio. Valuation variances produced by widely accepted models (termed mark-to-model risk) are well-documented and the subject of numerous research articles.[16] For example, the Black-Scholes versus Hull and White options models can produce differences of 5% or more in pricing, even when all input data and curve construction (i.e., cross-over from futures to cash, interpolation, extrapolation) are identical. In addition, the selection of probability distribution(s)[17] in one model versus another varies from firm to firm, and is a topic of great debate among theoreticians and practitioners alike.

While many dealers and end-users are well-versed in testing the behavior of an individual position or portfolio, given market moves (for example, what happens if interest rates rise or fall by 1 basis point or by 200 basis points?), they have only recently commenced testing the behavior of individual positions or portfolios for changes in *model* assumptions. Given the increased pace of losses due to model risk (the risk that the market price will be different than that calculated theoretically by a model), firms should test the sensitivity of the VaR calculation to alternate mapping and model assumptions. The goal is to determine how much the risk picture changes if one changes either the underlying mathematical model or one or more assumptions regarding the data source, time of collection, curve creation, probability distribution, mathematical process or other factors to reflect the VaR approaches described in The 1995 Basle Amendment, the RiskMetrics Technical Document or other common VaR models. To the degree that other commonly used models indicate an aggressive stance by the firm, an adjustment to the VaR calculation may be appropriate, or a higher VaR factor may be appropriate to protect the firm's capital from a market risk perspective. Such model risk adjustments should be taken in addition to those for credit risk, market risk, liquidity risk, operations risk, or other standard risk reserves.

5. *Percentage of outcomes to be considered.* The VaR methodology requires the firm to select the percentage of outcomes which will be used to determine the expectation of loss. For example, some firms calculate VaR under the requirement that

the outcome or a worse outcome is expected approximately 1% of the time (often called a 99% confidence interval). Others pose a lower requirement of expecting the outcome approximately 10% or 5% of the time. Perhaps due to the confidence interval terminology, some firms make the mistake of equating their VaR expectation to a *certainty* that the firm will not lose more than the stated amount. This is incorrect.

An important challenge in selecting the percentage of outcomes is to address the firm's need for an absolute loss limit. For example, a 95% confidence interval dictates that losses *are expected* to exceed the VaR limit at least once every 3 weeks. Users should address how large these losses may become through stress testing and establish limits accordingly. Furthermore, users may wish to address the potential for cumulative losses, none of which exceed the VaR limit individually, to be greater than the risk appetite of the firm. What if the amount of the VaR limit is lost continuously over contiguous time horizons (e.g., daily for an entire month?).

6. *Other risk management and risk measurement tools combined with VaR.* Most users combine VaR with stress testing to address questions such as "How much do I expect to lose the other 1% of the time?" As with VaR, the quality of the answer depends on the inputs, including the financial engineer's ability to select appropriate scenarios. Both the European Currency Crisis and the Gulf War demonstrated that predicting factors such as "maximum" volatility is difficult, and that correlation relationships can change substantially during extreme market moves. The increasing complexity and optionality of many derivatives and engineered securities makes relevant scenario selection even harder. Given such challenges, firms often resort to designing stress tests which analyze large historical market moves.

In CMRA's experience, portfolios do not necessarily produce their greatest losses during extreme market moves. Whether asset-based or asset plus liability based, portfolios often possess Achilles' heels that require only small moves or changes between instruments or markets to produce significant losses. Stress testing extreme market moves does little to reveal the greatest risk of loss for such portfolios. Furthermore, a review of a portfolio's expected behavior over time may reveal that the same stress test that indicates a *small* impact today indicates embedded land mines with a *large* impact during future periods. This is particularly true of options-based portfolios that change characteristics due to time, rather than due to changes in the components of the portfolio. For this reason, it is paramount to employ stress testing to reveal:

- For those market variables or model assumptions that have a high likelihood of change, what is the impact of small and large changes on VaR?
- For those variables or exposures considered to offset each other, how do alternate correlation assumptions impact VaR?
- How wide is the variance of results produced by other commonly used VaR approaches versus yours?

The Mexican peso devaluation in December of 1994 illustrates the difficulty in using stress testing to analyze crises. The devaluation and subsequent market dislocation caused a 30% drop in the value of holdings in 5 days, with average losses ranging between 15% and 50%. Over 400 funds and most emerging market derivatives portfolios held TELMEX stock, so experienced significant, unexpected losses. How should such dramatic market moves be captured by the VaR calculation or other tests? In virtually all cases, the VaR calculation considered the likelihood of

occurrence minuscule (far less than a 1% expectation) when analyzing either historical or expected movements of the peso. In virtually all cases, firms' stress tests considered far less dramatic market moves. Today, firms remain divided regarding
inclusion of such a low-probability event in future calculations. Firms are divided as
well on the inclusion of the December 1994 peso move in historical data sets. In
other words, the peso move is considered to be an "outlier," so some firms remove it
from their historical data sets when calculating VaR. Regardless of whether such
moves are included, a valuable post mortem is to *assume* such an event occurred
and to determine whether losses expected under VaR equal those incurred. Back-
testing a firm's qualitative and quantitative risk management approach for actual, extreme events (whether market dislocations or the actions of a rogue trader) often
reveals the need to adjust reserves, increase the VaR factor, adopt additional poli-
cies/limits/controls/procedures or to expand risk calculations plus reporting.

The Mexican peso crisis was not a standalone event in terms of magnitude, suggesting the importance of such back-testing. *At least one* major market (*not* an
emerging market) makes a ten or more standard deviation move every year. For example, there have been 9 Hong Kong market declines greater than 20% and 2 more
than 50% over the past 15 years. The devaluation of the Italian lira, the stock market
crashes of 1987, and the oil shocks in the 1970s are further examples of market
moves far beyond the two to three standard deviation assumption used in most VaR
calculations. In the case of the 1982–87 U.S. bull market followed by stock market
crash (508 point plunge on October 19, 1987), within 6 months, the markets stabi-
lized and in less than 2 years the markets returned to pre-crash levels.

Many risk variables such as political risk, personnel risk, regulatory risk, phan-
tom liquidity risk, and others are difficult or impossible to capture through quantitative techniques. Yet as demonstrated by recent, well-publicized losses, such
variables can cause significant risk. For this reason, VaR must be supplemented not
only with stress testing, but also with prudent checks and balances, procedures,
policies, controls, limits, random audits, appropriate reserves and other risk measures. These are summarized in Figure 7.1.

FIGURE 7.1   Risk Management Framework

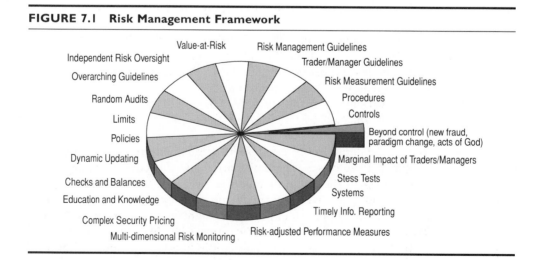

VaR IN PRACTICE

In this section, five different variance/covariance, historical and simulation VaRs are calculated and compared for a hypothetical portfolio consisting of Treasury strips plus S&P 500 equity index contracts and options. Table 7.1 sets forth the portfolio as of May 25, 1995, comprised of long positions in 2-year and 30-year U.S. Treasury strips,[18] and a long position in the S&P 500 equity index contract plus long and short options on the same index. The net investment in the portfolio is $2 million.

Variance/covariance VaR is calculated once, using the JP Morgan RiskMetrics data set. Historical VaR is calculated twice, using 250-day and a 100-day prior historical periods. Simulation VaR is calculated twice, using correlations and volatilities from the RiskMetrics data set (Simulation A) and from the 10 years prior (Simulation B). The results of the calculations appear in Table 7.2 and Figures 7.2 and 7.3.

The actual VaR statistics are set forth in Table 7.2 and may be interpreted as follows: under the *assumptions specific to the particular VaR calculation,* there is a 1% (or 5%) expectation that the portfolio will suffer a loss greater than or equal to the statistic shown. Thus *under the assumptions made* to perform historical VaR over a 250-day period, and assuming a two-week holding period, there is a 1% expectation of loss equal to or exceeding 1.08% of the $2,000,000 investment in the portfolio (i.e., a loss greater than or equal to $21,600).

The distributions for the VaR calculations are set forth in Figures 7.2 and 7.3. For both the 1% and 5% expectation of loss results, the alternate methods produce quite different results. Several observations may be made:

- In all cases, Simulation B produces much higher expected loss levels. This is due to the fact that all four other VaR calculations depend significantly upon a more recent historical period, whereas Simulation B is based upon correlations and volatilities drawn from a 10-year prior period.
- The 100-day and 250-day historical VaR calculations produce quite different downside and upside risk expectations. For example, the 1% expectation of

Table 7.1   The Strip and Equity Index Portfolio

Portfolio Composition Instrument	2-Year Strip			30-Year Strip		Total Portfolio
Yield	5.91%			6.85%		
Price	89.12			14.94		
Face Amount	$779,778			$2,041,424		
Purchase Amount	$694,964			$305,036		$1,000,000

Instrument	Jun 520	Jun 545	Sep 530	Dec 540	S&P 500	
Type	Put	Call	Call	Put	Long	
Strike vs. market	+20	+45	+30	+40	0	
Price	1.95	0.60	14.90	18.45	528.59	
Number	4,157.4	−28,723.8	19,784.8	11,617.0	945.9	
Purchase Amount	$ 8,107	($17,234)	$294,793	$214,335	$499,999	$1,000,000
Total Portfolio						$2,000,000

Table 7.2   VaR Results

1 Day VaR for the Portfolio

	1%	5%
Variance/Covariance	0.80%	0.57%
Simulation A	0.77%	0.57%
Simulation B	1.14%	0.89%
Historical—250 Days	1.08%	0.74%
Historical—100 Days	0.73%	0.48%

10 Day VaR for the Combined Portfolio

	1%	5%
Variance/Covariance	2.54%	1.80%
Simulation A	3.00%	2.51%
Simulation B	8.91%	3.21%
Historical—250 Days	2.89%	2.56%
Historical—100 Days	1.71%	1.24%

loss for VaR in the case of the 100-day historical simulations is a *single* data point, consisting of the largest loss over a *single* overnight, and over a *single* 10-day trading period. Furthermore, there is high autocorrelation in the data set. In other words, not only does a 1% probability consists of only 1 of the 100 observations, but there are only 10 distinct 10-day periods. During the 100-day and 250-day periods included in the historical VaR calculations, the value of Treasury strips largely appreciated. Had a period of rising interest rates been selected, the opposite result would have been produced. The danger in basing

FIGURE 7.2   Distribution of One-Day Returns

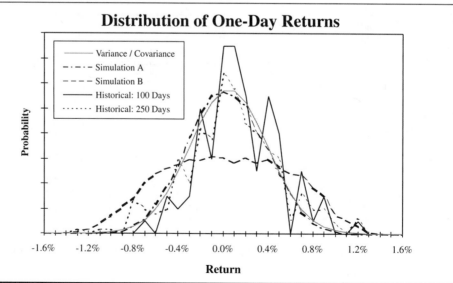

FIGURE 7.3   Distribution of Two-Week Returns

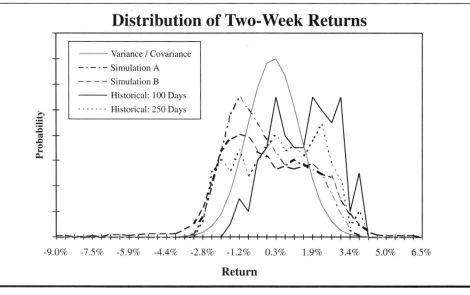

Distribution of Two-Week Returns

VaR estimates on direct historical observations, and over short data periods, is apparent—history must repeat itself for this method to provide an accurate expectation of future loss.

- The loss of the fat tails due to the nonlinearity of both the options and the Treasury positions is clear when the variance/covariance VaR distribution is compared to all other results.

VaR: ONLY ONE ASPECT OF RISK MANAGEMENT

A final observation is that while firms typically select a single VaR measure, it is important to determine the degree to which the answer changes under different methodologies. Furthermore, several important dimensions of VaR are under research which may provide insights into adjustments which may be practicable across different methodologies:

1. The impact of time horizon.
2. The impact of nonlinearity.
3. The degree of price opacity (reverse engineering complexity, illiquid underlyings, illiquid instruments, lack of historical data, etc.).
4. The degree of residual error (differences between the actual and the mapped portfolio, equivalents, etc.).
5. The impact of diversification (whether it magnifies, dampens, or does not impact differences across VaR calculations).
6. The impact of sampling issues (sufficiency of sample period, size, and breadth).

VaR, while an important advance in market risk measurement, is *only* one aspect of an overall risk management program. Different VaR methodologies and selection of the key decision factors for VaR are appropriate for different firms, and depend upon many factors. These include the types of exposures, other qualitative and quantitative risk management techniques employed, and the firm's risk appetite relative to its capital base. However combined with the appropriate additional risk management and risk measurement tools, VaR gets high marks.

ENDNOTES

1. Mathematically, VaR quantifies the amount of expected loss based on the probability of certain market events occurring during a stated time period.

2. Sometimes also referred to as analytic VaR.

3. A delta equivalent is a linear estimate of a security's value based on its first derivative with respect to a specific factor or factors.

4. RiskMetrics is perhaps the most widely-used of available data, and assumes normal distributions.

5. Fat-tailed behavior, also known as leptocurtosis, refers to distributions in which there is a broad range of values at the tails (e.g., 1% of the time).

6. To quote Charles Smithson of CIBC Wood Gundy who summed it up very well in a recent discussion regarding VaR, "The talk to action ratio is very high."

7. Nonlinear price functions exist not only for options, derivatives with exponential functions and leveraged instruments but also in the case that yields are mapped into prices (e.g., basic bonds). For an example of how these impact VaR, *see* for example Tanya Styblo Beder, "VAR: Seductive but Dangerous," *Financial Analysts Journal,* September–October, 1995.

8. It is possible to run a simulation VaR which uses variance/covariance data such as RiskMetrics. This technique is illustrated in the section, "VaR in Practice."

9. *See* Tanya Styblo Beder, "VaR: Seductive but Dangerous," *Financial Analysts Journal,* September–October, 1995.

10. *See* for example, J.V. Jordan and R.J. Mackay, *Assessing Value at Risk for Equity Portfolios: Implementing Alternative Techniques,* Handbook of Firmwide Risk Management, Beckstrom, Campbell and Fabozzi, (Eds.), forthcoming 1996, as reported in *Risk* magazine, January 1996. Differences of over 10 times are set forth in this data.

11. *See* for example, Darryll Hendricks, "Evaluation of Value-at-Risk Models Using Historical Data," *FRBNY Economic Policy Review,* April 1996.

12. *See* for example, Philippe Jorion, "Risk^2: Measuring the Risk in Value at Risk," *Financial Analysts Journal,* forthcoming.

13. Learning from these mistakes, firms often limit the portion of their portfolio or overall exposure that is based on theoretical mark-to-model values or erratic/infrequent data points. In addition, firms often impose the requirement that risk management, audit, IRO, or custodian obtain outside pricing from a different dealer than the dealer from whom the customized or illiquid securities were purchased.

14. The seminal work by Markowitz.

15. *See* Tanya Styblo Beder, "VaR: Seductive but Dangerous"

16. *See* for example, "The Realities of Marking to Model," by Tanya Styblo Beder, *Journal of Bank Accounting and Finance,* Institutional Investor, Summer 1994.

17. An assumption of anticipated or experienced market behavior.

18. The market yield for each strip as of May 25, 1995, is stated on an Actual/365 basis with semi-annual compounding. The price of each strip is stated as a percentage of face amount.

Assessing Value at Risk for Equity Portfolios: Implementing Alternative Techniques

JAMES V. JORDAN
ROBERT J. MACKAY

Defining and measuring market risk is not a simple task. First, a useful measure of market risk must be applicable not only to a single financial instrument (e.g., a share of stock, a treasury note, or an interest rate swap) but also to portfolios of those same instruments (e.g., stock, bond, or interest rate swap portfolios) and directly related instruments (e.g., stock, bond, or interest rate option portfolios) as well as to overall portfolios combining these different types of instruments and underlying risks. Second, a useful measure of market risk must be capable of accounting for all the various risk factors—absolute price change, convexity, volatility, correlation, time decay, and discount rate. Third, a useful measure must account for these different market risk factors in a consistent and coherent fashion. These risk factors must be reduced to a single common denominator that measures both the market risk of individual instruments and can also be aggregated to measure the risk of subportfolios and, ultimately, the overall market risk of an entire institution or portfolio. Finally, a useful measure of market risk must be capable of being communicated in a form that is readily understandable and helpful in controlling market risk.[1]

Value at Risk (VaR) is one measure of market risk that satisfies these criteria. While most applications of Value at Risk techniques to date have dealt with the market risk of the derivatives portfolios of dealers and end-users, the theoretical concepts and empirical techniques underlying the Value at Risk concept are quite general. They can be applied, for example, on a firmwide basis to both financial and nonfinancial firms to assist in the management of overall market risk. They can also be applied on a portfoliowide basis to the management of market risk for institutional investors, such as pension funds and mutual funds.

The authors are grateful to Mark Brickell, Ted Barnhill, Christopher Culp, Spiros Martzoukos, Lyle Minton, and Charles Smithson for many valuable conversations on this subject. We would especially like to thank Shuchi Satwah for her excellent research assistance on the empirical portions of this chapter.

The application of these Value at Risk techniques to equity portfolios, both stock-only and stock-plus-option portfolios, is the focus of this chapter. The next section defines Value at Risk, describes the three general approaches to estimating Value at Risk and discusses how Value at Risk can be used in managing market risk. With this as background, the next section explains and illustrates (using real data for a portfolio of sample stocks) how the various approaches to measuring Value at Risk can be implemented. The results of each approach are compared and contrasted with the other approaches. The next section extends the analysis to the more technically complex situation in which an equity portfolio contains both stocks and options.[2] Again, the alternate approaches to implementing Value at Risk are illustrated and compared. The final section offers some concluding thoughts on the application of Value at Risk to equity portfolios and the need for supplementing this analysis with stress testing of the portfolio.

DEFINING, MEASURING, AND USING VALUE AT RISK

Defining Value at Risk

We start with a precise (but hopefully intuitive) definition of Value at Risk.

> *Definition: Value at Risk (VaR) is that dollar amount such that the likelihood of experiencing a loss in the market value of a financial instrument or a portfolio of instruments in excess of that amount, due to an "adverse change" in market risk factors over a specified "risk horizon," is less than a specified "tolerance level."*

For example, if the chosen risk horizon is one day and the tolerance level is 2.5%, then a VaR of $1 million for a particular portfolio means that the likelihood of that portfolio experiencing a one-day loss in excess of $1 million is less than 2.5%. Alternatively put, the expectation is that the actual daily loss will exceed $1 million only one day out of 40. The flip side of the 2.5% tolerance level, of course, is a "confidence level" of 97.5% implying that the likelihood of experiencing a one-day loss of *less than* $1 million is 97.5%.

A "Worst Case" Scenario

The choice of the risk horizon and tolerance level determines the size of the adverse change in market risk factors—that is, the severity of the "worst case" scenario chosen for quantifying market risk. The Value at Risk approach to measuring market risk involves developing a statistically and economically plausible worst case scenario for quantifying both the magnitude and likelihood of the losses that would result from this adverse change in market risk factors. The focus of the analysis, however, is on those worst case scenarios that could occur under "normal" market conditions—that is, when normal market responses and relationships hold.[3] In particular, VaR accounts for the normal patterns of volatilities in and correlations across market risk factors. These patterns, in fact, are central to the VaR approach and distinguish it from certain other approaches to measuring market risk.[4] Alternative methods of implementing VaR account for these patterns either directly as inputs in the calculation of VaR or indirectly as they are imbedded in simulated distributions of prices. These methods also assume normal sensitivities of market values to changes in these risk factors.

Risk Horizons and Tolerance Levels

Depending upon the particular market risk management problem at hand, VaR can be calculated for alternative risk horizons (e.g., a day, a week, a month, or a quarter) and tolerance levels (e.g., 2.5%, 5%, 10%, or 15%). The choice of risk horizons should correspond to key decision-making or performance-evaluation intervals. The choice of tolerance level should depend upon several factors including: the tolerance of an institution's board and senior management for lower-probability, extreme losses versus higher-probability, modest losses; the capital base of the institution; the level of experience and sophistication of management and staff; and the institution's business or investment strategy.

Calculating Value at Risk

For a given risk horizon and tolerance level, the calculation of VaR is quite straightforward if one knows the "true" distribution of future value change or rate of return for the instrument or portfolio of interest. Figure 8.1 shows the "true" frequency distribution, $f(r|b)$, or a portfolio's future rate of return at a specified risk horizon of "b" periods.

If the chosen tolerance level is $x\%$, then this defines a *critical* rate of return such that the area under the lower tail of the frequency distribution equals $x\%$. This critical rate of return, denoted $r(x\%,b)$, is the adverse market move or worst case scenario implied by the chosen risk horizon and tolerance level. The VaR corresponding to this risk horizon and tolerance level, denoted $VaR(x\%,b)$, is given by

$$VaR(x\%, b) = -r(x\%, b)V_o \tag{1}$$

FIGURE 8.1 Frequency Distribution of a Portfolio's "True" Rate of Return for a Risk Horizon of "h" Periods and the "Worst Case" Return and VaR at a Tolerance Level of x%

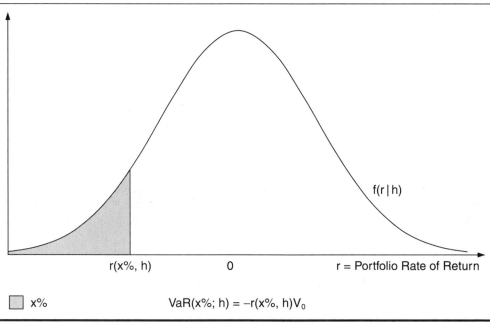

$$VaR(x\%; h) = -r(x\%, h)V_0$$

where V_o is the initial value of the portfolio. If the true frequency distribution is stable over time, then we would expect on average that $x\%$ of the losses experienced over risk horizons of b periods would equal or exceed the calculated VaR.

Measuring Value at Risk

Unfortunately, the true distribution of future value change or rate of return is seldom, if ever, known. As a result, the measurement of VaR must instead rely upon estimates of this frequency distribution. There are three general approaches to estimating the frequency distribution of future value change or rate of return. These approaches include:

- Historical simulation;
- Estimation of portfolio mean and variance; and,
- Monte Carlo simulation.

Each of these approaches is summarized below and detailed examples of how to implement each of these approaches (using real data for a sample of stocks and options) are presented in the next two sections for stock-only portfolios and portfolios with both stocks and options. Variations on each approach are also discussed.

Historical Simulation

A large sample of prices for the individual financial instruments comprising the portfolio can be constructed from an observed time series of actual prices over, say, the last 200 or more trading days. This historical sample of prices can be transformed into observed percentage price changes or rates of return for alternative risk horizons. Given a distribution of historical returns for a desired risk horizon, the "true" distribution of future returns can be simulated or estimated by assuming that "the future will look like the past"—that is, that the trends and pattern of volatilities and correlations among returns embedded in the historical sample will be repeated in the future. The historical sample distribution, in other words, is simply taken as an estimate of the true frequency distribution of future returns.[5]

Figure 8.2 shows a discrete distribution of historically simulated returns for a particular portfolio over a selected risk horizon of b periods. The portfolio's VaR, implied by this particular distribution of rate of return, can be found by determining that critical rate of return such that $x\%$ of the sample returns is less than the critical return. In Figure 8.2, the heavily shaded bars represent $x\%$ of the cumulative frequency. The estimated VaR is then found by multiplying the negative of this critical rate of return by the initial value of the portfolio.

A historical time series on stock prices can be used to calculate *non-overlapping* samples of daily, weekly, monthly, or quarterly rates of return for the individual stocks and for a portfolio of these stocks, given portfolio weights for each of the stocks. The longer the risk horizon chosen, however, the smaller the number of observations in non-overlapping samples. This problem of small sample size can be addressed, however, through a sampling technique known as "bootstrapping." A large sample of actual daily rates of return, for example, can be randomly sampled (with replacement) to generate a time series of random daily returns that can then be strung together to create bootstrapped samples of weekly, monthly, or quarterly

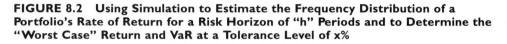

FIGURE 8.2   Using Simulation to Estimate the Frequency Distribution of a Portfolio's Rate of Return for a Risk Horizon of "h" Periods and to Determine the "Worst Case" Return and VaR at a Tolerance Level of x%

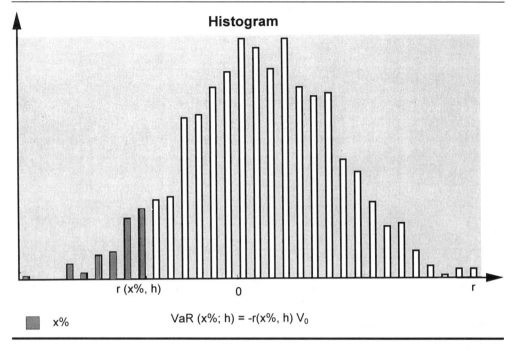

returns.[6] These samples, in turn, can be used to estimate VaR for weekly, monthly, or quarterly risk horizons.

Estimation of Portfolio Mean and Variance

If rates of return for the individual securities or financial instruments comprising the portfolio are all normally distributed, then the rate of return on the portfolio will also be normally distributed. If the portfolio return is normally distributed, then the mean and variance of portfolio returns completely describe the distribution of returns. In this case, estimates of these two parameters are all that is necessary to calculate VaR. The mean and variance of the portfolio's future return distribution, moreover, can be estimated directly from historical estimates of the means, variances, and covariances of the individual instruments using standard statistical formulas. With the portfolio's rate of return normally distributed, the critical rate of return for a desired risk horizon and tolerance level is then given by

$$VaR(x\% \ or \ k, h) = -(\hat{\mu} - k\hat{\sigma})V_o \tag{2}$$

where $\hat{\mu}$ and $\hat{\sigma}$ are estimates of the portfolio's mean and standard deviation and k is the number of standard deviations corresponding to a tolerance level of $x\%$. (See Figure 8.3.)

As pointed out above, the portfolio's mean and variance can be estimated directly from the means, variances, and covariances of the underlying securities. Alternatively,

FIGURE 8.3   Using Estimates of the Mean and Variance of the Frequency Distribution of a Portfolio's Rate of Return for a Risk Horizon of "h" Periods to Determine the "Worst Case" Return and VaR at a Tolerance Level of x%

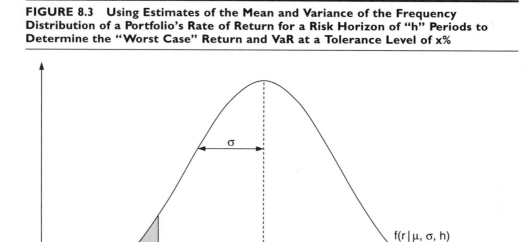

they can be estimated from the individual factor sensitivities implied by a multi- or single-factor model of stock returns combined with estimates of the means and variances of the factor or factors. Both of these methods for estimating VaR are illustrated and compared in the next section.

Monte Carlo Simulation

For a given stochastic model describing the evolution of the price or rate of return on individual financial instruments, the distribution of future returns on a portfolio of these instruments can be estimated through Monte Carlo simulation techniques. Depending upon the specific application (e.g., an equity or fixed income portfolio), a particular stochastic model may be most appropriate. In the case of individual stocks, for example, stock prices are frequently modeled as if they followed *geometric Brownian motion*. Given a set of estimates of the drifts, volatilities, and correlations for a sample of stocks, the distribution of value change or rate of return for a portfolio composed of these stocks can be estimated through Monte Carlo simulation techniques. Changes in initial stock prices over a chosen time interval or risk horizon can be randomly generated by simulating geometric Brownian motion for each of the stocks, incorporating both estimated volatilities *and* correlations. Summing the resulting value changes for each stock, allowing for the appropriate portfolio weights, gives the change in portfolio value for this simulation run. The process can be repeated a large number of times, generating a sample distribution of value change or rate of return as an estimate of the future distribution of value change or rate of return. The end result of the simulation is a sample frequency distribution such as that shown in Figure 8.2. Given this distribution, calculation of the estimated VaR proceeds in the same manner as described above for historical simulation.

Using Value at Risk

Value at Risk provides a relatively comprehensive and consistent approach to market risk management based on a common conceptual framework for identifying, measuring, monitoring, limiting, reporting, and hedging market risk. The use of VaR for identifying and measuring market risk was discussed above. These other uses are discussed below.

Monitoring and Limiting Market Risk

Dealers in financial instruments and institutional investors alike should establish market risk limits that are consistent with their measures of market risk taken on in various dealing books or portfolios. These limits should be in line, both individually and in the aggregate, with the maximum exposures authorized by their boards and senior management. As a result, risk limits should be comparable across instruments, across trading books and nontrading activities, across individually managed portfolios, and should be capable of being integrated and aggregated on a portfolio- and institutionwide basis.

While limits can be set and frequently are set on other bases (e.g., limits on net or gross positions, on risk equivalent position in a baseline instrument, or on allowable losses), VaR provides a particularly attractive and coherent framework for setting limits. This is the case because risk limits based on VaR can be:

- Directly compared across distinct instruments, subportfolios or books, and overall balance sheets or portfolios;
- Aggregated across instruments, books, portfolios, branches, and profit centers to determine an institution's or portfolio's aggregate risk limits; and
- Easily monitored and compared with actual risk taking (also measured on a VaR basis) facilitating effective management oversight and prompt corrective action.[7]

Reporting to Management

Technical and quantitative information generated by the front-office as part of investment or trading activities and by the back office as part of risk measurement and monitoring activities must be translated into a language and format that is easily understood by senior managers and directors if it is to be used effectively in controlling market risk. Value at Risk provides a readily understandable measure of market risk that can be easily communicated and yet provides a coherent and relatively comprehensive measure of market risk for any position or set of positions. Well-designed VaR reports allow senior management and boards to check that risk limits and exposures are consistent with authorizations and in line with the board's expressed risk tolerances.[8]

Hedging Market Risk

Value at Risk can be used not only to measure, monitor, and limit market risk but also to determine the best hedge of market risk. Using relative VaR to determine hedge ratios is superior to certain, more traditional, hedging techniques that ignore the actual volatilities and correlation of prices and yields, assuming instead that prices and yields shift in some arbitrary fashion. Value at Risk provides a straightforward and coherent approach to hedging since the net exposure of even a complex book or portfolio of instruments can be measured by its overall VaR and this exposure, in turn, can be matched or offset, at least in part, by adjusting the VaR of the hedging instrument and, hence, the VaR of the combined position (i.e., the hedged position and the hedge item) through the setting of the hedge ratio.[9]

IMPLEMENTING VALUE AT RISK TECHNIQUES FOR PORTFOLIOS OF STOCKS

Defining Portfolio Return

Consider a portfolio composed of m stocks. The rate of return on the ith stock, denoted r_i, is defined as

$$r_i = \frac{D_i + \Delta S_i}{S_i} \tag{3}$$

where S_i is the stock price at the beginning of the period, D_i is the dividend payment, and ΔS_i is the change in the stock price over the period. Figure 8.4 shows the daily stock prices and rates of return (calculated using equation (3)) for Ford Motor Company for a two-year period from January 1992 through December 1993.

The change in value of a portfolio of these m stocks, denoted ΔV, can be written as

$$\Delta V = \sum_{i=1}^{m} x_i (D_i + \Delta S_i) \tag{4}$$

where x_i is the number of shares of the ith stock held in the portfolio. Using equation (3), the rate of return on the portfolio, denoted $\Delta V/V$, can be written as

$$\frac{\Delta V}{V} = \frac{1}{V} \sum_{i=1}^{m} x_i S_i r_i \tag{5}$$

For further compactness of notation, we define the proportion of portfolio value invested in the ith stock (i.e., $x_i S_i / V$) as y_i. Then,[10]

$$\frac{\Delta V}{V} = \sum_{i=1}^{m} y_i r_i \tag{6}$$

This analytical framework is quite general, accommodating long positions, short positions, and leverage or borrowing. Consider, for example, a portfolio consisting of a long position in 100 shares of stock 1 at a current price of $50 per share, which have been purchased on 50% margin; a short position in 200 shares of stock 2 at a current price of $25; and $5000 in cash or money market instruments.

FIGURE 8.4   Daily Stock Prices and Rates of Return for Ford Motor Company from January 1992 through December 1993

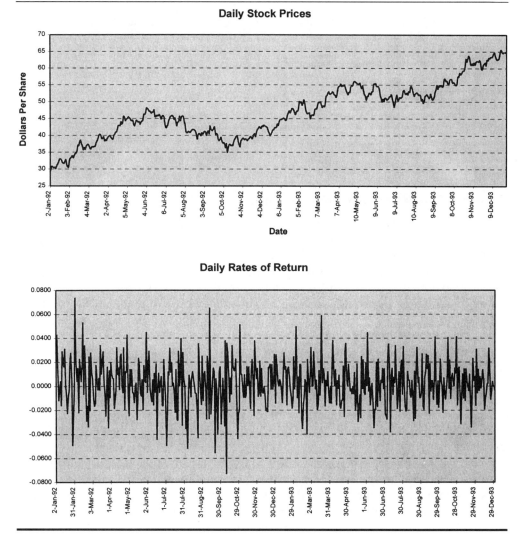

The total portfolio value is $2500 as shown in Table 8.1. The portfolio weights are also calculated and sum, as expected, to 1.

If we knew the true joint distribution for the changes in share prices (i.e., the ΔS_i's) or the rates of return (i.e., the r_i's), then we could determine the true distribution of value change or rate of return for the portfolio using equations (4) or (6) respectively. This true distribution could then be used to calculate VaR for a given risk horizon and tolerance level. In practice, however, the true distribution is seldom, if ever, known and must instead be estimated. Three methods of estimating the true distribution of the change in portfolio value and, hence, estimating VaR are examined in this section for a stock-only portfolio.

TABLE 8.1

		Portfolio Value		Portfolio Weights	
	$5,000	Long stock position.	y (long stock)	= $5,000/$2,500 =	2
+	5,000	Money market position.	y (money market) =	5,000/2,500 =	2
−	2,500	Margin loan.	y (margin loan)	= −2,500/2,500 =	−1
−	5,000	Short stock position.	y (short stock)	= −5,000/2,500 =	−2
	$2,500	Total Value			

$$\sum_{i=1}^{m} y_i = 1$$

Historical Simulation of Portfolio Returns

The distribution of future portfolio returns can be estimated using historical simulation based on the actual return distributions observed over various risk horizons. In this method, historical data on stock returns is collected and is used to calculate corresponding returns on the portfolio of interest. The sample of observed portfolio returns is assumed to be drawn from a stable population distribution—a distribution of portfolio returns that is not changing over time. The historical distribution is assumed to be the best estimate of the future returns that might be drawn from the population, and VaR is based on the histogram of the distribution.

Non-Overlapping Samples of Returns

We illustrate historical portfolio calculations (and other calculations) in the rest of this chapter, using a sample of two years of daily data on five stocks. The sample stocks are American Airlines (AMR), Ford Motor Company (Ford), International Business Machines (IBM), Time-Warner, and Seagrams. Daily prices and returns were taken from the Center for Research in Security Prices (CRSP) tape for the period January 2, 1992 to December 31, 1993. Table 8.2 shows the means, variances, and standard deviations of daily, weekly, and monthly rates of return for all five sample stocks.[11] The weekly return was defined as the return over a seven-day calender period. Since our data started on a Thursday, the weekly return is for the Thursday through Wednesday period each week. Typically, then, there are five daily returns (i.e., trading day returns) in a calendar week, with one of the daily returns extending over the weekend from Friday through Monday. The monthly return was defined in a similar manner. The daily, weekly, and monthly samples have 507, 104, and 24 observations, respectively.

Figure 8.5 shows the histograms for the daily and non-overlapping samples of weekly and monthly returns on an equally weighted portfolio of the sample stocks. These distributions can be used to estimate this portfolio's VaR. The smaller sample size for the weekly returns and especially the monthly returns, however, reduces our confidence in estimates of VaR based on these distributions.[12] One alternative would be to obtain a longer time series of returns. There is, however, a trade-off between sample relevance and sample size. In this context, the larger sample size results from a longer time series making it more likely that the population distribution is changing over the sample period. If this is the case, then the returns from farther back in

TABLE 8.2   Means, Variances, and Standard Deviations of Daily, Weekly, and Monthly Rates of Return a Sample of Stocks

	American	Ford	IBM	Time Warner	Seagram's
		Daily Returns			
Mean	0.000062	0.001961	−0.000554	0.001580	−0.000032
Variance	0.000325	0.000367	0.000327	0.000310	0.000125
Standard Deviation	0.018040	0.019170	0.018090	0.017598	0.011166
		Weekly Returns			
Mean	0.000155	0.009440	−0.002409	0.007489	0.000154
Variance	0.001226	0.001426	0.001601	0.001114	0.000779
Standard Deviation	0.035012	0.037763	0.040013	0.033370	0.027906
		Monthly Returns			
Mean	0.000100	0.041253	−0.010440	0.032973	−0.000497
Variance	0.004485	0.006618	0.009087	0.005318	0.003191
Standard Deviation	0.066971	0.081349	0.095325	0.072926	0.056491

time are drawn from a different (and possibly less relevant) population distribution than are more current returns.[13]

Bootstrapped Samples of Returns

An alternative to increasing the length of the sample period is to simulate a larger sample size for the weekly and monthly returns. This can be done using the actual sample of daily returns and a simulation technique called *bootstrapping*. To bootstrap a sample of, say, weekly return observations from a sample of actual daily returns, we would:

- Draw five daily returns at random from the historical sample of actual daily returns;[14]
- Calculate one weekly return from the random sample of five daily returns;[15] and,
- Repeat the process as many times as desired to obtain a sufficiently large sample of weekly returns.

Using this technique the sample size of the weekly and monthly return distributions can be made comparable to the size of the daily return distribution. The histograms of weekly and monthly returns for bootstrapped samples containing 500 observations each are shown in Figure 8.6.

VaR for Alternative Risk Horizons and Tolerance Levels

Using historical simulation, the probability of the future portfolio return being *equal to or less than* any particular level of return can be estimated directly from the histogram of returns calculated over a holding period equal to the risk horizon. To calculate daily VaR at a 2.5% tolerance level, for example, we need to identify the critical return, $r(2.5\%, 1\ \text{day})$, in the histogram of daily returns at which 2.5% of the observations are at or below that return or 97.5% of the observations are at or above that return. For the 507 observations of daily portfolio returns, the critical return

FIGURE 8.5   Histograms of the Daily, Weekly, and Monthly Rate of Return on a Portfolio of Sample Stocks for Non-Overlapping Samples of Returns

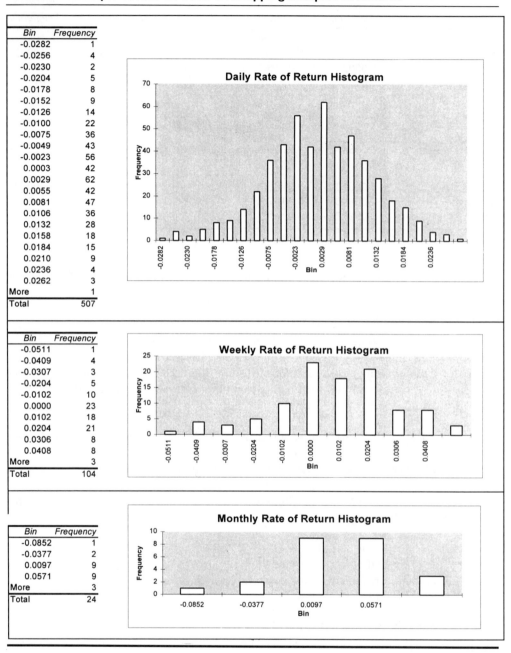

Bin	Frequency
-0.0282	1
-0.0256	4
-0.0230	2
-0.0204	5
-0.0178	8
-0.0152	9
-0.0126	14
-0.0100	22
-0.0075	36
-0.0049	43
-0.0023	56
0.0003	42
0.0029	62
0.0055	42
0.0081	47
0.0106	36
0.0132	28
0.0158	18
0.0184	15
0.0210	9
0.0236	4
0.0262	3
More	1
Total	507

Bin	Frequency
-0.0511	1
-0.0409	4
-0.0307	3
-0.0204	5
-0.0102	10
0.0000	23
0.0102	18
0.0204	21
0.0306	8
0.0408	8
More	3
Total	104

Bin	Frequency
-0.0852	1
-0.0377	2
0.0097	9
0.0571	9
More	3
Total	24

FIGURE 8.6 Histograms of the Weekly and Monthly Rate of Return on a Portfolio of Sample Stocks for Bootstrapped Samples of Returns

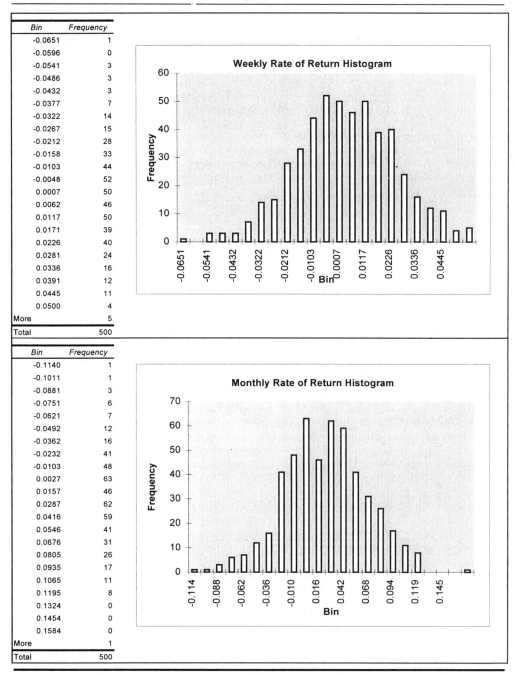

Bin	Frequency
-0.0651	1
-0.0596	0
-0.0541	3
-0.0486	3
-0.0432	3
-0.0377	7
-0.0322	14
-0.0267	15
-0.0212	28
-0.0158	33
-0.0103	44
-0.0048	52
0.0007	50
0.0062	46
0.0117	50
0.0171	39
0.0226	40
0.0281	24
0.0336	16
0.0391	12
0.0445	11
0.0500	4
More	5
Total	500

Bin	Frequency
-0.1140	1
-0.1011	1
-0.0881	3
-0.0751	6
-0.0621	7
-0.0492	12
-0.0362	16
-0.0232	41
-0.0103	48
0.0027	63
0.0157	46
0.0287	62
0.0416	59
0.0546	41
0.0676	31
0.0805	26
0.0935	17
0.1065	11
0.1195	8
0.1324	0
0.1454	0
0.1584	0
More	1
Total	500

lies between the 12th and 13th observation measuring from the bottom of the histogram (i.e., .025 (507) = 12.675). Visually, in Figure 8.6, we see that $r(2.5\%, 1\ \text{day})$ is approximately -0.0204, or -2.04%. BESTFIT[16] software identifies the critical return as $-.020207$ or -2.0207%. For a $1 million position in the equally-weighted portfolio of the sample stocks, there is a 2.5% probability of a *loss* greater than or equal to:

$$\text{VaR}\ (2.5\%,\ 1\ \text{day}) = -r\,(2.5\%,\ 1\ \text{day})V_o$$

$$= -(-.020207)\,(\$1\ \text{million})$$

$$= \$20{,}207$$

Thus, the daily VaR at 2.5% is $20,207. This estimate can be described in several ways. "On only 1 day out of 40 should we expect to lose more than $20,207." Or, "We can be 97.5% confident that our loss over the next day will be less than $20,207."

For comparison purposes, we calculated the critical return and the VaR for a $1 million portfolio for alternative tolerance levels (i.e., 2.5%, 5.0%, and 10.0%) and for various risk horizons, (i.e., daily, weekly, and monthly) using both non-overlapping and bootstrapped samples of returns. These results are shown in Table 8.3. At the 2.5% tolerance level, the portfolio's VaR ranges from $20,207 for daily VaR, to $40,800 for weekly VaR, and to $69,750 for monthly VaR using the bootstrapped samples of returns. Note that use of the non-overlapping samples results in a substantial increase in the estimate of the portfolio's VaR for all tolerance levels and risk horizons. The largest percentage increase (i.e., 41%) is for a 5% tolerance level and a monthly risk horizon; whereas, the smallest percentage increase (i.e., 4.3%) is for a 10% tolerance level and a weekly risk horizon. Estimates of VaR are quite sensitive to the choice of sampling method (i.e., non-overlapping versus bootstrapping) in historical simulations. Given the relatively small sample sizes resulting from the use of non-overlapping samples, however, we would place more confidence in the estimates of VaR based on bootstrapped samples, especially for longer risk horizons such as a month or more.

TABLE 8.3 VaR for Alternative Risk Horizons and Tolerance Levels Based on Historical Simulations of the Portfolio's Rate of Return

	At x% = 2.5%		At x% = 5.0%		At x% = 10.0%	
	r(x%)	VaR*	r(x%)	VaR*	r(x%)	VaR*
Daily	−0.020207	$20,207	−0.016142	$16,142	−0.011956	$11,956
Weekly						
(Non-overlapping)	−0.046207	46,207	−0.042902	42,902	−0.026272	26,272
(Bootstrapped)	−0.040800	40,800	−0.033600	33,600	−0.025200	25,200
Monthly						
(Non-overlapping)	−0.085160	85,160	−0.076684	76,684	−0.040880	40,880
(Bootstrapped)	−0.069750	69,750	−0.054400	54,400	−0.035200	35,200

* For $1 million portfolio.

Estimation of Portfolio Means and Variances

Normally Distributed Stock Returns

As we discussed in the previous section, if the individual stock returns are normally distributed with expected value μ_i and standard deviation σ_i (i.e., $r_i \sim N(\mu_i, \sigma_i)$), then the portfolio return is also normally distributed with expected value, μ_p, and standard deviation, σ_p, (i.e., $\Delta V/V \sim N(\mu_p, \sigma_p)$). The sum of normally distributed random variables is also normally distributed. As a result, the first two moments of the portfolio's return distribution, μ_p and σ_p, completely describe the distribution of returns. Estimates of these parameters are all that is necessary to calculate VaR. The derivation and estimation of μ_p and σ_p are described next.

Defining Means, Variances, and Covariances

Based on equation (3), the expected rate of return on the ith stock, denoted μ_i, is defined as

$$\mu_i = \frac{E(D_i + \Delta S_i)}{S_i} \tag{7}$$

The variance of the rate of return, denoted σ_i^2, is defined as[17]

$$\sigma_i^2 = E[r_i - \mu_i]^2 \tag{8}$$

The standard deviation of the rate of return, denoted σ_i, is defined as the square root of the variance. That is,

$$\sigma_i = \sqrt{\sigma_i^2}.$$

The covariance between the rate of return of the ith stock and the jth stock, denoted σ_{ij}, is defined as[18]

$$\sigma_{ij} = E(r_i - \mu_i)(r_j - \mu_j) \tag{9}$$

Calculating Portfolio Mean and Variance

It was shown above in equation (6) that the rate of return on a portfolio could be expressed as

$$\frac{\Delta V}{V} = \sum_{i=1}^{m} y_i r_i \tag{10}$$

where y_i is the proportion of portfolio value invested in the ith stock. In his pioneering work on portfolio theory, Markowitz showed that the portfolio's expected rate of return, denoted μ_p, and variance of return, denoted σ_p^2, are given by[19]

$$\mu_p = \sum_{i=1}^{m} y_i \mu_i \tag{11}$$

and

$$\sigma_p^2 = \sum_{i=1}^{m} \sum_{j=1}^{m} y_i y_j \sigma_{ij} \tag{12}$$

Note that each individual stock position contributes its own variance of return, σ_i^2 or σ_{ii}, and its covariances, σ_{ij}, with every other stock return. As more stocks are added to the portfolio, its own variance effect becomes less and less important. In a 50-stock portfolio, for example, each stock contributes 1 variance and 49 covariances. Even though a stock's variance tends to be larger than its covariance with any other stock, the sum of the covariances ultimately swamps the variance in terms of the stock's contribution to portfolio variance.

The set of return variances and covariances for the individual stocks can be written in a more compact way using the variance-covariance matrix, Σ. The matrix for m stocks is

$$\Sigma = \begin{bmatrix} \sigma_{11} & \sigma_{12} & \cdots & \sigma_{1m} \\ \sigma_{21} & \sigma_{22} & \cdots & \sigma_{2m} \\ \vdots & \vdots & \ddots & \vdots \\ \sigma_{m1} & \sigma_{m2} & \cdots & \sigma_{mn} \end{bmatrix} \tag{13}$$

This matrix is a standard form for presenting variance-covariance information. The use of matrix notation allows portfolio mathematics to be written in a more condensed form. Let the expected returns and portfolio weights be written as vectors, μ and y, where $\mu' = (\mu_1, \mu_2, \ldots, \mu_m)$ and $y' = (y_1, y_2, \ldots, y_m)$. The "prime" indicates the transpose of a vector; the untransposed vectors are column vectors. Then,

$$\mu_p = y'\mu \tag{14}$$

and

$$\sigma_p^2 = y'\Sigma y \tag{15}$$

These matrix expressions, equations (14) and (15), have the same meaning as equations (11) and (12).[20]

An equivalent version of equation (12) uses the correlation between the returns on the ith and j^{th} stocks, denoted ρ_{ij}, in lieu of the covariance. The relationship between correlation and covariance is given by

$$\sigma_{ij} = \rho_{ij}\sigma_i\sigma_j \tag{16}$$

This expression can be substituted into equation (12) so that the variance of portfolio return is written as

$$\sigma_p^2 = \sum_{i=1}^{m} \sum_{j=1}^{m} y_i y_j \rho_{ij}\sigma_i\sigma_j \tag{17}$$

The correlation matrix, denoted P, is used in some applications instead of the variance-covariance matrix. For the m-stock portfolio, the correlation matrix is

$$\Sigma = \begin{bmatrix} \rho_{11} & \rho_{12} & \cdots & \rho_{1m} \\ \rho_{21} & \rho_{22} & \cdots & \rho_{2m} \\ \vdots & \vdots & \ddots & \vdots \\ \rho_{m1} & \rho_{m2} & \cdots & \rho_{mn} \end{bmatrix} \qquad (18)$$

The portfolio variance can then be written,[21]

$$\sigma_\rho^2 = y' \sigma \, P \sigma y \qquad (19)$$

where

$$\Sigma = \begin{bmatrix} \sigma_{11} & 0 & \cdots & 0 \\ 0 & \sigma_{22} & \cdots & 0 \\ \vdots & \vdots & \ddots & \vdots \\ 0 & 0 & \cdots & \sigma_{mm} \end{bmatrix} \qquad (20)$$

Estimating Portfolio Mean and Variance

Table 8.4 shows alternative estimates of the variances and covariances of daily, weekly, and monthly returns for the sample stocks. Estimates for the weekly and monthly returns are shown for both non-overlapping and bootstrapped samples. These estimates for the variances and covariances of individual stock returns, along with the estimates of mean returns shown in Table 8.2, are used to calculate estimates (based on equations (11) and (12)) of the mean and variance of daily, weekly, and monthly rates of return for an equally weighted portfolio of the sample stocks. These estimates of the mean and variance of portfolio returns are shown in Table 8.5.

Value at Risk for Alternative Risk Horizons and Tolerance Levels

Using these estimates of the portfolio's mean and variance, probability statements about the return on the portfolio can be made based on the standardized normal distribution. The standardized normal distribution is the distribution of the variable z, defined by

$$z = \frac{r - \mu}{\sigma} \qquad (21)$$

If $r \sim N(\mu, \sigma)$, then $z \sim N(0,1)$. The cumulative frequency associated with a particular value of z is the probability of drawing z or less. For example, $Pr\ (z < = -1.96)$ is 2.5%, which we can indicate by $z(2.5\%) = 1.96$. Substituting this value of z into equation (21) and using the portfolio mean and standard deviation for a holding period or risk horizon of, say, one day, we can define the critical rate of return, $r(2.5\%, 1\ day)$, as

$$\frac{r(2.5\%, 1\ day) - \mu_\rho}{\sigma_\rho} = -1.96$$

or

$$r(2.5\%, 1\ day) = \mu_\rho - 1.96\sigma_\rho \tag{22}$$

Substituting the daily estimates of μ_ρ and σ_ρ reported in Table 8.5 into the above expression, we see that the implied estimate of the critical rate of return is approximately −0.0188 (i.e., 0.0006 − 1.96 (0.0099)) or −1.88%. For a $1 million position in

TABLE 8.4 Variances and Covariances of Daily, Weekly, and Monthly Rate of Return for the Sample Stocks

	American	Ford	IBM	Time Warner	Seagram's
		Daily Returns			
American	0.000325	0.000087	0.000053	0.000058	0.000034
Ford	0.000087	0.000367	0.000050	0.000087	0.000042
IBM	0.000053	0.000050	0.000327	0.000016	0.000033
Time Warner	0.000058	0.000087	0.000016	0.000310	0.000033
Seagram's	0.000034	0.000042	0.000033	0.000033	0.000125
		Weekly Returns (Non-Overlapping)			
American	0.001226	0.000538	0.000086	0.000244	0.000251
Ford	0.000538	0.001426	0.000366	0.000289	0.000406
IBM	0.000086	0.000366	0.001601	0.000215	0.000184
Time Warner	0.000244	0.000289	0.000215	0.001114	0.000218
Seagram's	0.000251	0.000406	0.000184	0.000218	0.000779
		Weekly Returns (Bootstrapped)			
American	0.001383	0.000411	0.000347	0.000100	0.000206
Ford	0.000411	0.001598	0.000338	0.000280	0.000177
IBM	0.000347	0.000338	0.001716	0.000065	0.000130
Time Warner	0.000100	0.000280	0.000065	0.001481	0.000171
Seagram's	0.000206	0.000177	0.000130	0.000171	0.000603
		Monthly Returns (Non-Overlapping)			
American	0.004485	0.001208−	0.001314	0.000414	0.001432
Ford	0.001208	0.006618	0.001459	0.002576	0.001602
IBM	−0.001314	0.001459	0.009087	0.002345	0.000917
Time Warner	0.000414	0.002576	0.002345	0.005318	−0.000249
Seagram's	0.001432	0.001602	0.000917	−0.000249	0.003191
		Monthly Returns (Bootstrapped)			
American	0.006336	0.001072	0.001128	0.000943	0.000725
Ford	0.001072	0.007992	0.000699	0.001442	0.000817
IBM	0.001128	0.000699	0.006023	0.000346	0.000896
Time Warner	0.000943	0.001442	0.000346	0.006550	0.000566
Seagram's	0.000725	0.000817	0.000896	0.000566	0.002632

TABLE 8.5 Estimates of the Means and Variances of Daily, Weekly, and Monthly Rates of Return for a Portfolio Based on the Means, Variances, and Covariances of the Sample Stocks

	Mean (m_p)	Variance (s_p)	Standard Deviation (s_p)
Daily	0.000603	0.000098	0.009876
Weekly			
(Non-overlapping)	0.002966	0.000470	0.021668
(Bootstrapped)	0.000627	0.000449	0.021195
Monthly			
(Non-overlapping)	0.012678	0.001979	0.044488
(Bootstrapped)	0.016240	0.001872	0.043267

the equally weighted portfolio, this estimate implies that there is a 2.5% probability of a daily *loss* greater than or equal to $18,754. That is,

$$VaR\ (2.5\%,\ 1\ \text{day}) = -(\mu_p - 1.96\sigma_p)V_o$$

$$= -(-0.018754)\ (\$1\ \text{million})$$

$$= \$18,754$$

For comparison purposes, we again calculated the critical return and the VaR for our $1 million equally weighted portfolio at alternative risk horizons and tolerance levels. These estimates are shown in Table 8.6. At the 2.5% tolerance levels the portfolio's estimated VaR ranges from $18,754 for Daily VaR, to $40,914 for Weekly VaR, and to $68,563 for Monthly VaR using the bootstrapped samples of returns. In other words, the estimate of VaR increases by 2.2 times when the risk horizon goes from one day to one week and by 3.7 times when the risk horizon goes from one day to one month.[22] Looking across tolerance levels, the Monthly VaR estimates range from

TABLE 8.6 VaR for Alternative Risk Horizons and Tolerance Levels Based on Estimates of the Mean and Variance of the Portfolio's Rate of Return

	Mean (m_p)	Standard Deviation (s_p)	At x% = 2.5%		At x% = 5.0%		At x% = 10.0%	
			r(x%)	VaR*	r(x%)	VaR*	r(x%)	VaR*
Daily	0.000603	0.009876	−0.018754	$18,754	−0.015642	$15,642	−0.012054	$12,054
Weekly								
(Non-overlapping)	0.002966	0.021668	−0.039503	39,503	−0.032676	32,676	−0.024804	24,804
(Bootstrapped)	0.000627	0.021195	−0.040914	40,914	−0.034236	34,236	−0.026536	26,536
Monthly								
(Non-overlapping)	0.012678	0.044488	−0.074518	74,518	−0.060500	60,500	−0.044337	44,337
(Bootstrapped)	0.016240	0.043267	−0.068563	68,563	−0.054930	54,930	−0.039211	39,211

* For $1 million portfolio.

** $r(x\%) = \mu p - k\sigma p$ where k = 1.96, 1.6449, and 1.2816, for 2.5%, 5%, and 10%, respectively.

a high of $68,563 at a 2.5% level, to $54,930 at a 5% level, and to $39,211 at a 10% level. Unlike with the historical simulations of VaR, the estimates based on the non-overlapping samples are not always greater than the bootstrapped estimates. They are somewhat larger for the monthly risk horizon but smaller for the weekly horizon.

These estimates of VaR can also be compared with the estimates based on historical simulation (Table 8.3). These two methods of estimating Value at Risk lead, in this case, to roughly similar results for the bootstrapped samples. At some risk horizons and tolerance levels, one method produces larger estimates than the other, but there is no clear pattern in which one method consistently produces larger estimates than the other. The differences are more pronounced for the non-overlapping samples with the historical simulation method tending to produce substantially larger estimates. For a one day risk horizon, for example, the VaR based on historical simulation using bootstrapped samples exceeds the mean-variance estimate by 8%, 3%, and −1% at the 2.5%, 5%, and 10% tolerance levels, respectively. That is an average difference of 3%. For a one week risk horizon, the average difference is −2.4% for the bootstrapped samples and +18% for the non-overlapping samples.

The assumption of normality is an assumption of convenience, based on the roughly symmetrical character of stock return distributions. We can test the validity of the assumption by testing the stock return distributions for normality. Figure 8.7 provides a visual comparison between the actual daily returns and a normal distribution with the same mean and standard deviation. Table 8.7 shows the results of two tests for normality, the Anderson-Darling test and the Kolmogorov-Smirnov test.[23] The results of the two tests agree in most cases. The general impression from Table 8.7 is that the assumption of normality has strong empirical support. The assumption is rejected most often for daily individual stock returns (i.e., three of the five stocks for both tests). Yet for the daily portfolio return normality is not rejected. This suggests that the assumption of normality for stock portfolio returns may be acceptable even if some of the individual stock returns are not normally distributed. It is also interesting (and somewhat surprising) that as the risk horizon is lengthened, the assumption of normality appears to become more acceptable for individual stock returns.

It is worth emphasizing that these results are merely illustrative and by no means a thorough empirical study of the issue. In a recent study, Richardson and Smith cite a number of earlier studies and comment that the general conclusion of these studies is that stock returns are not normally distributed.[24] They then conduct their own study using monthly returns on the 30 Dow Jones industrial stocks and reject the normality hypothesis for 12 of them. They also reject the hypothesis that the returns are drawn from a multivariate normal distribution. Before abandoning techniques based on the normality assumption, however, it is useful to note that there are a number of different tests, and that the reliability of the different tests depends on the types of departures from normality that may be present in the data.[25] It is probably safe to say that the last word on this issue has not been written.

Factor Models of Portfolio Returns

A factor model of stock returns with k factors is written[26]

$$r_i = a_i + b_{i1}F_1 + b_{i2}F_2 + \ldots + b_{ik}F_k + e_i \tag{23}$$

This model assumes that the return on any stock can be decomposed into a component of returns explained by the k factors (i.e., $b_{i1}F_1 + b_{i2}F_2 + \ldots + b_{ik}F_k$) plus a

FIGURE 8.7 Comparison of Actual Frequency Distribution and Normal Distribution for Daily Rate of Return and Bootstrapped Monthly Rate of Return for Ford Motor Company Stock

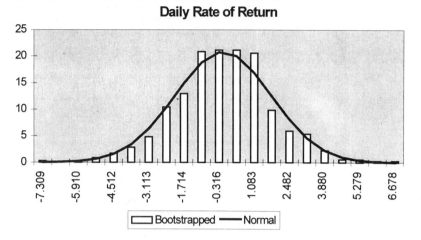

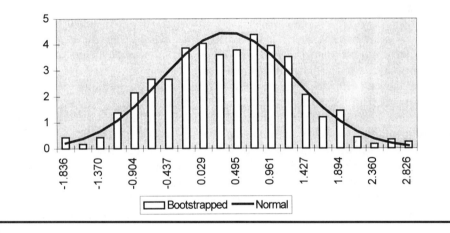

component of return that remains unexplained (i.e., $a_i + e_i$). The factors should be "systematic" in the sense that they influence returns on all stocks. Examples of factors that have been widely used in empirical research include changes in real economic growth, changes in the slope of the term structure of interest rates, and unexpected inflation.[27] The unexplained component of stock returns is made up of the expected unexplained return, a_i, and the random unexplained return, e_i.

The principal value of a factor model for risk management purposes is that portfolio risk (variance of return) is decomposed into a systematic component and an unsystematic component. In many circumstances, systematic risk will be of primary concern to the risk manager, since a "worst case" move in the systematic factors will affect all positions in the portfolio, in contrast to the unsystematic moves in each stock which tend to be uncorrelated and not the major influence on portfolio value.

TABLE 8.7 Tests for Normality of Daily, Weekly, and Monthly Rates of Return for the Sample Stocks and a Portfolio Composed of Those Stocks*

	American	Ford	IBM	Time Warner	Seagram's	Portfolio
			Anderson-Darling Test			
Daily	N	N	R	R	R	N
Weekly						
(Non-overlapping)	N	N	N	N	N	N
(Bootstrapped)	N	N	N	R	N	N
Monthly						
(Non-overlapping)	N	N	N	N	R	N
(Bootstrapped)	R	N	N	R	N	N
			Kolmogorov-Smirnov Test			
Daily	R	N	R	R	R	N
Weekly						
(Non-overlapping)	N	N	N	N	N	N
(Bootstrapped)	N	N	N	N	N	N
Monthly						
(Non-overlapping)	R	N	N	N	R	N
(Bootstrapped)	N	N	N	N	N	N

* Table shows rejection (R) or nonrejection (N) of the null hypothesis of normality at the 5% significance level.

For a factor model to correctly divide the variance of return into systematic risk and unsystematic risk, four conditions must hold: (1) the expected value of the error term for each stock must be zero; (2) the correlation between the error term and the factors must be zero; (3) the correlation between the factors must be zero; and (4) the correlation of the error term for each stock with every other stock must be zero. When a factor model is estimated by regression, the first two conditions are satisfied because of the mathematics of the regression technique. The third condition can generally be satisfied by the way the factors are defined and estimated. There is, however, no way of assuring that the fourth condition is satisfied.[28] With these assumptions, the only linkage *between* stock returns is through the systematic factors. The expected return, variance, and covariance for the ith stock are given by

$$\mu_i = a_i + b_{i1}\mu_{F_1} + b_{i2}\mu_{F_2} + \ldots + b_{ik}\mu_{F_k}, \tag{24}$$

$$\sigma_i^2 = b_{i1}^2\sigma_{F_1}^2 + b_{i2}^2\sigma_{F_2}^2 + \ldots + b_{ik}^2\sigma_{F_k}^2 + \sigma_{e_i}^2, \text{ and} \tag{25}$$

$$\sigma_{ij} = b_{i1}b_{j1}\sigma_{F_1}^2 + b_{i2}b_{j2}\sigma_{F_2}^2 + \ldots + b_{ik}b_{jk}\sigma_{F_k}^2. \tag{26}$$

Equation (25) for variance shows that the total risk has been divided into systematic risk (i.e., $b_{i1}^2\sigma_{Fi}^2 + b_{i2}^2\sigma_{F2}^2 + \ldots + b_{ik}^2\sigma_{Fk}^2$) and unsystematic risk (i.e., σ_{ei}^2). Equation (26) for covariance shows that all covariance comes from the relationship of the ith and j^{th} stocks with the factors (the "factor betas") and the variances of the factors, and none from the error terms.

The equations for the individual stock returns allow portfolio return to be expressed directly as a function of the factors. That is,

$$r_p = a_p + b_{p1}F_1 + \ldots + b_{pk}F_k + e_p \tag{27}$$

where[29]

$$a_p = \sum_{i=1}^{m} y_i a_i \tag{28}$$

$$b_{p1} = \sum_{i=1}^{m} y_i b_{i1}, \ldots, b_{pk} = \sum_{i=1}^{m} y_i b_{ik}, \text{ and} \tag{29}$$

$$e_p = \sum_{i=1}^{m} y_i e_i. \tag{30}$$

In diversified portfolios, e_p should be small and perhaps negligible due to the averaging-out of the ups and downs of each company's fortune unrelated to the systematic factors. Even in portfolios for which this is not true, the primary focus of risk management may be systematic risk.

Estimating a Single-Factor Model

To illustrate the use of factor models in VaR analysis, we estimated a one-factor model for the sample stocks using non-overlapping weekly returns.[30] The chosen factor is the return on the S&P 500 index. Data for this factor is taken from the CRSP tape for the same period described above. The one factor model to be estimated is

$$r_i = a_i + b_{i1}F_1 + e_i \text{ for } i = 1, \ldots, 5 \tag{31}$$

where the means, variances, and covariances of the individual stock returns are given by

$$\mu_i = a_i + b_{i1}\mu_{F_1}, \tag{32}$$

$$\sigma_{i1} = b_{i1}^2 \sigma_{F_1}^2 + \sigma_{ei}^2, \text{ and} \tag{33}$$

$$\sigma_{ij} = b_{i1}b_{j1}\sigma_{F_1}^2. \tag{34}$$

In this single-factor model, portfolio return is given by

$$r_p = a_p + b_{p1}F_1 + e_p \tag{35}$$

where a_p, b_{p1}, and e_p are defined as in equations (28)–(30). Table 8.8 shows the regression results for the single-factor model applied to the sample stocks using the

TABLE 8.8   Means, Variances, Covariances, and Betas of the Actual Weekly Rate of Return for the Sample Stocks Based on Regression Results for a Single-Factor Model Using the S&P 500 Index

		American	Ford	IBM	Time Warner	Seagram's
Index	S&P 500					
Mean	0.001256					
Standard Deviation	0.013820					
Factor Model Results						
Regression R-Square		0.148217	0.100582	0.036633	0.210937	0.242519
a		−0.001070	0.008351	−0.003106	0.006096	−0.001095
b		0.975366	0.866617	0.554166	1.108994	0.994439
Var(e)		0.001044	0.001283	0.001542	0.000879	0.000590
Mean		0.000155	0.009440	−0.002409	0.007489	0.000154
Standard Deviation		0.035012	0.037763	0.040013	0.033370	0.027906
Variance-Covariance Matrix						
American		0.001226	0.000161	0.000103	0.000207	0.000185
Ford		0.000161	0.001426	0.000092	0.000184	0.000165
IBM		0.000103	0.000092	0.001601	0.000117	0.000105
Time Warner		0.000207	0.000184	0.000117	0.001114	0.000211
Seagram's		0.000185	0.000165	0.000105	0.000211	0.000779
Portfolio Results						
Portfolio Mean		0.002966				
Portfolio Variance		0.000368				
Portfolio Standard Deviation		0.019188				
Portfolio Beta		0.899917				

S&P 500 index as the factor. The estimated regression parameters are shown in the rows labeled "a" and "b." The variance-covariance matrix based on the "b's" and the factor variance are also shown. Note that the means, variances, and standard deviations are the same as shown in Tables 8.2 and 8.4. The estimated covariances, however, differ from those shown in Table 8.4 and this results in different portfolio variance and standard deviation than in Table 8.5.[31]

In the single-factor model, portfolio exposure to systematic risk is given by the portfolio's "beta," denoted b_{p1}, which is defined as

$$b_{p1} = \sum_{i=1}^{m} y_i b_{i1}$$

From Table 8.8, we can calculate the beta of an equally weighted portfolio of the sample stocks. In this case, b_{p1} equals .8999 (i.e., (⅕) Σ (.9754 + .8666 + .5542 + 1.1090 + .9944)). In this case, Time-Warner with its beta of 1.1090 makes the largest contribution to the portfolio's exposure to systematic risk. With unequal weights, of course, the contribution of a stock to portfolio risk is a function of both its beta and its weight.[32]

Estimating Factor Returns

If the risk manager is only interested in *systematic* risk, the estimates from the factor model can be combined with an estimate of the future distribution of factor returns

FIGURE 8.8   Histogram of the Actual Daily Rate of Return on the S&P 500 Index

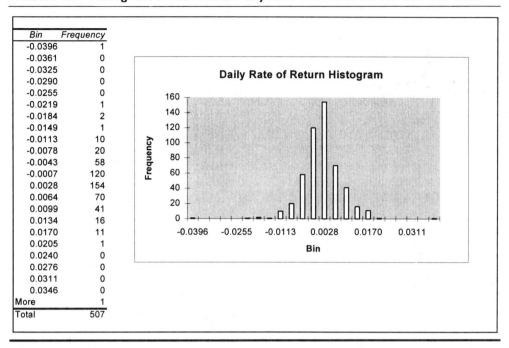

Bin	Frequency
-0.0396	1
-0.0361	0
-0.0325	0
-0.0290	0
-0.0255	0
-0.0219	1
-0.0184	2
-0.0149	1
-0.0113	10
-0.0078	20
-0.0043	58
-0.0007	120
0.0028	154
0.0064	70
0.0099	41
0.0134	16
0.0170	11
0.0205	1
0.0240	0
0.0276	0
0.0311	0
0.0346	0
More	1
Total	507

to make probability statements and calculate Value at Risk. Figure 8.8 shows a histogram of the actual daily rate of return on the S&P 500 index. Similar distributions can be calculated for weekly and monthly rate of returns on the S&P 500 index using both non-overlapping and bootstrapped samples.

If these distributions are normal they can be characterized by their mean and standard deviation. Table 8.9 shows the estimated mean, variance, and standard deviation the rate of return on the S&P 500 index measured for various risk horizons. These estimates can be combined with the portfolio's estimated beta to calculate estimates of VaR.[33]

TABLE 8.9   Estimates of the Mean, Variance, and Standard Deviation of the Daily, Weekly, and Monthly Rate of Return for the S&P 500 Index

	Mean $(\mu_{s\&p})$	Variance $(\sigma_{s\&p}^2)$	Standard Deviation $(\sigma_{s\&p})$
Daily	0.000240	0.000039	0.006276
Weekly			
(Non-overlapping)	0.001256	0.000191	0.013820
(Bootstrapped)	0.001042	0.000186	0.013634
Monthly			
(Non-overlapping)	0.004848	0.000363	0.019044
(Bootstrapped)	0.008616	0.000851	0.029166

VaR for Alternative Risk Horizons and Tolerance Levels

The VaR for a one-day horizon at a 2.5% confidence level can be calculated as follows. The critical rate of return on the S&P 500 index, denoted r_{s+p} (2.5%, 1 day), equals -0.0121 (i.e., $0.00024 - 1.96 (0.00628)$) or -1.21%. The VaR due to this change in S&P 500 index can be estimated as follows:[34]

$$VaR(2.5\%, 1 \text{ day}) = -b_{p1}r_{s\&p}(2.5\%, 1 \text{ day})V_o$$
$$= -(-.8999)(0.012061)(\$1 \text{ million})$$
$$= \$10,854$$

Thus the daily "systematic" VaR at 2.5% is $10,854. This estimate can be restated as "We can be 97.5% confident that our loss over the next day *due to movements in the S&P 500 index* will be less than $1."

For comparison purposes, we again calculated the critical return on the S&P 500 and the VaR for a $1 million portfolio for alternative risk horizons and confidence levels. These results are shown in Table 8.10. At the 2.5% tolerance level, the portfolio's systematic VaR ranges from $10,854 for daily VaR, to $23,110 for weekly VaR, and to $43,692 for monthly VaR for the bootstrapped samples. These estimates are roughly consistent with the "square root of time" rule for both weekly and monthly returns relative to daily returns. The estimates of weekly VaR are roughly the same whether non-overlapping or bootstrapped samples of S&P 500 index returns are used. For monthly VaR, however, the bootstrapped estimates are much larger (i.e., 48% on average across tolerance levels) than the non-overlapping estimates.

The results of this technique for estimating VaR can be compared to the results of the historical simulations method reported in Table 8.3 and the results of basing the estimates on portfolio mean and variance estimated directly from the means, variances, and covariances of the underlying stocks reported in Table 8.6. The estimates of systematic daily VaR average 44% less than the estimates of VaR based on historical simulation. Similar results hold for the other method also. These differences, of

TABLE 8.10 VaR for Alternative Risk Horizons and Tolerance Levels Based on Estimates of the Portfolio's Beta and the Mean and Variance of the Daily, Weekly, and Monthly Rate of Return for the S&P 500 Index

Portfolio Beta   0.8999

	Mean $(\mu_{s\&p})$	Standard Deviation $(\sigma_{s\&p})$	At x% = 2.5% r(x%)**	VaR*	At x% = 5.0% r(x%)**	VaR*	At x% = 10.0% r(x%)**	VaR*
Daily	0.000240	0.006276	−0.012061	$10,854	−0.010084	$ 9,074	−0.007803	$ 7,022
Weekly								
(Non-overlapping)	0.001256	0.013820	−0.025830	23,245	−0.02147	19,327	−0.016455	14,808
(Bootstrapping)	0.001042	0.013634	−0.025681	23,110	−0.021385	19,244	−0.016431	14,787
Monthly								
(Non-overlapping)	0.004848	0.019044	−0.032478	29,228	−0.026477	23,827	−0.019559	17,601
(Bootstrapping)	0.008616	0.029166	−0.048551	43,692	−0.039360	35,421	−0.028764	25,885

* For $1 million portfolio.
** r(x%) = $\mu - k\sigma$, where k = 1.96, 1.6449, and 1.2816 for x% = 2.5%, 5%, and 10%.

course, are due to the factor model's focus on systematic risk rather than total risk in this small portfolio of five stocks.

Monte Carlo Simulation of Stock Returns

The previous section assumed that the rates of return on individual stocks and the S&P 500 index were normally distributed. With normally distributed stock returns portfolio returns are also normally distributed. Moreover, normally distributed stock and portfolio returns imply that stock prices and portfolio values are also normally distributed.[35] While the assumption of normally distributed stock returns greatly simplifies portfolio analysis, in general, and Value at Risk estimation, in particular, we know that stock returns cannot really be normally distributed. A normal distribution for rates of return and, hence, stock prices, would imply that stock prices could be negative. The minimum stock price, however, is clearly zero. A distributional assumption about stock returns and prices that does not permit negative prices would be preferable.

Choosing a Stochastic Process for Stock Returns

An assumption that retains much of the tractability of the normal distribution and yet is consistent with a range of stock prices defined only over 0 to $+\infty$ is that the *continuously-compounded* stock return is normally distributed. The continuously compounded rate of return, r_c, is defined by

$$S_{\Delta t} = Se^{r_c \Delta t} \tag{36}$$

where $r_c \Delta t$ is the continuously compounded return over the interval Δt, S is the initial stock price, and $S_{\Delta t}$ is the stock price after an interval of time Δt. This equation can also be written

$$r_c = \frac{1}{\Delta t} \ln\left(\frac{S_{\Delta t}}{S}\right) \tag{37}$$

Because of the properties of the logarithmic function, as $S_{\Delta t} \to 0$, $r_c \to -\infty$, and as $S_{\Delta t} \to +\infty$, $r_c \to +\infty$. Thus, the reasonable range for stock prices of zero to $+\infty$ produces the range of the normal distribution, $-\infty$ to $+\infty$, for the continuously compounded return. Assuming r_c is normally distributed means that $\ln(S_{\Delta t})$ is normally distributed. When the logarithm of a variable is normally distributed, that variable is said to be lognormally distributed. Thus, a normal distribution for the continuously compounded rate of return implies a lognormal distribution for stock prices.

Stock Prices and Geometric Brownian Motion

Assuming that the continuously compounded rate of return is normally distributed is equivalent to assuming that the movement of stock prices through time can be described by a stochastic process known as geometric Brownian motion.[36] The equation for geometric Brownian motion for stock prices is

$$\frac{dS}{S} = \mu dt + \sigma\varepsilon\sqrt{dt} \tag{38}$$

where dS is an infinitesimal change in the stock price, dS/S is the instantaneous return on the stock, dt is an infinitesimally small period of time, μ is the instantaneous expected return on the stock, σ is the standard deviation of the instantaneous return, and ε is a standardized normal variable, $\varepsilon \sim N(0,1)$. Because ε is normally distributed, dS/S is normally distributed. This model says that after each instant of time, dt, the (instantaneous) return on the stock, dS/S, is drawn from a normal distribution with mean μdt and standard deviation $\sigma\sqrt{dt}$.[37]

Given the assumption of geometric Brownian motion, it can be shown that the continuously compounded rate of return over a finite period of time, $r_c \Delta t$, is normally distributed.[38] That is,

$$r_c \Delta t = \ln\left(\frac{S_{\Delta t}}{S}\right) \sim N\left[\left(\mu - \frac{\sigma^2}{2}\right)\Delta t, \sigma\sqrt{\Delta t}\right] \tag{39}$$

Given values of μ and σ, probability statements can be made about the continuously compounded stock return and, hence, the stock price after any horizon Δt. Since $r_c \Delta t$ is normally distributed, this implies that ε defined as

$$\varepsilon = \frac{\ln\left(\frac{S_{\Delta t}}{S}\right) - \left(\mu - \frac{\sigma^2}{2}\right)\Delta t}{\sigma\sqrt{\Delta t}} \tag{40}$$

is a standardized normal variable. That is, $\varepsilon \sim N(0,1)$. Rewriting equation (40) gives us an explicit solution for the continuously compounded rate of return. That is,

$$r_c \Delta t = \ln\left(\frac{S_{\Delta t}}{S}\right) = \left(\mu - \frac{\sigma^2}{2}\right)\Delta t + \varepsilon\sigma\sqrt{\Delta t} \tag{41}$$

This equation can be solved, in turn, for $S_{\Delta t}$ and $\Delta S = S - S_{\Delta t}$. That is,

$$S_{\Delta t} = Se^{(\mu - \frac{\sigma^2}{2})\Delta t + \varepsilon\sigma\sqrt{\Delta t}} \tag{42}$$

and

$$\Delta S = S_{\Delta t} - S = \left[e^{(\mu - \frac{\sigma^2}{2})\Delta t + \varepsilon\sigma\sqrt{\Delta t}} - 1\right]S \tag{43}$$

The geometric Brownian motion assumption has two advantages: (1) it produces a lognormal distribution of stock prices, which means no negative prices; and (2) it is consistent with the assumptions made in most stock option pricing models. A disadvantage of the assumption, however, is that we cannot write down a simple analytic expression for the distribution of portfolio returns. In other words, the return on a portfolio composed of stocks with multivariate lognormally distributed returns is not lognormally distributed. Neither is it normally distributed. Thus, although we can compute portfolio mean return and variance of return as in the standard portfolio theory, we cannot make precise probability statements based on these two parameters alone as we can with the normal distribution. We can, however, use the geometric Brownian motion assumption to stochastically simulate the continuously compounded rate of return and the price of each stock. These results can then be aggregated, given portfolio weights, to determine the new portfolio value and the change in its value.

Suppose we wish to model all stocks in the portfolio by geometric Browning motion. Then the measurement of each stock price is described by the following system of simultaneous, stochastic differential equations.

$$\frac{dS_1}{S_1} = \mu_1 dt + \sigma_1 \varepsilon_1 \sqrt{dt}$$

$$\frac{dS_2}{S_2} = \mu_2 dt + \sigma_2 \varepsilon_2 \sqrt{dt} \qquad (44)$$

$$\vdots$$

$$\frac{dS_m}{S_m} = \mu_m dt + \sigma_m \varepsilon_m \sqrt{dt}$$

Each stochastic *term,* ε_i is distributed $N(0,1)$. Because stock returns tend to be correlated, however, we do not want to assume that the ε's are independent of one another. We assume, instead, that $\varepsilon_1, \varepsilon_2, \ldots, \varepsilon_m$ are distributed as multivariate standardized normal variables.

In actual simulations, the above equations would be expressed in discrete form and then transformed into equations, such as equation (42) or (43), for $S_{\Delta t}$ or ΔS for each stock. The procedure for simulation of the individual stock prices is as follows:

- Draw a uniformly distributed random variable (e.g., RAND ( ) in Excel). Transform the uniformly distributed random variable into a value of the standardized normal variable, z.[39] Do this for each of the m stocks, thus producing m values of z in each iteration of the simulation.
- Use the m values of z to determine $\varepsilon_1, \varepsilon_2, \ldots, \varepsilon_m$ from a multivariate normal distribution, taking account of all the estimated correlations.[40]
- Given each stock's ε, μ, σ and the chosen risk horizon, $\Delta t,$ calculate $S_{\Delta t}$ from (42) and, given the initial value of $S,$ calculate ΔS from (43).
- Sum the ΔS's, appropriately weighted, to get the change in portfolio value.
- Repeat the prior steps as many times as desired.
- Tabulate the histogram of portfolio value change and compute the portfolio's VaR at the chosen tolerance level.

Estimating Means, Variances, and Covariances

Table 8.11 presents estimates of the annualized means, variances, covariances, and correlations of the continuously compounded returns for the sample stocks back on actual weekly returns (i.e., $ln\ (S_{\Delta t}/S) = ln\ (1 + r)$) calculated from the non-overlapping sample of weekly returns. The estimated variance-covariance matrix and the correlation matrix are also presented. These estimates provide the parameters for the Monte Carlo simulation described above.

TABLE 8.11   Estimates of the Annualized Means, Variances, and Covariances of the Continuously Compounded Rates of Return for the Sample Stocks Based on Actual Weekly Returns

	American	Ford	IBM	Time Warner	Seagram's
Mean	−0.022665	0.434902	−0.161422	0.346006	−0.011615
Standard Deviation	0.248005	0.265910	0.288949	0.233514	0.197768
Variance-Covariance Matrix					
American	0.061506	0.026511	0.004500	0.012011	0.012532
Ford	0.026511	0.070708	0.018872	0.014607	0.020206
IBM	0.004500	0.018872	0.083492	0.010637	0.009100
Time Warner	0.012011	0.014607	0.010637	0.054529	0.010873
Seagram's	0.012532	0.020206	0.009100	0.010873	0.039112
Correlation Matrix					
American	1.000000	0.402010	0.062802	0.207403	0.255518
Ford	0.402010	1.000000	0.245620	0.235246	0.384222
IBM	0.062802	0.245620	1.000000	0.157650	0.159241
Time Warner	0.207403	0.235246	0.157650	1.000000	0.235440
Seagram's	0.255518	0.384222	0.159241	0.235440	1.000000

Individual stock returns and changes in portfolio value for an equally-weighted portfolio were simulated for 500 iterations over risk horizons of one day, one week, and one month. Histograms of these 500 observations on changes in portfolio values were plotted at each risk horizon and BESTFIT was used to estimate the critical portfolio return and VaR at tolerance levels of 2.5%, 5%, and 10%. The results of these calculations are shown in Table 8.12.

First, it is useful to note that under the assumption of geometric Brownian motion, there is usually no need for bootstrapping into various return measurement intervals. Once μ, σ, and ρ are estimated from a particular sample of historical data (e.g., weekly), the distribution of stock returns and price changes for any finite time interval, Δt, are given by equations (41) and (43). The Monte Carlo simulation VaRs in Table 8.12 can be compared to those in Table 8.3 (Historical Simulation), and Table 8.6 (Portfolio Mean/Variance) to see the sensitivity of estimates of VaR to the alternative methods or techniques of estimation. For example, at a tolerance level of 5% and a one day risk horizon, although Monte Carlo simulation gives the largest

TABLE 8.12   VaR for Alternative Risk Horizons and Tolerance Levels Based on Monte Carlo Simulation of Geometric Brownian Motion Using Estimates of the Annualized Means, Variances, and Covariances of the Continuously Compounded Rates of Return for the Sample Stocks

	At x% = 2.5%		At x% = 5.0%		At x% = 10.0%	
	r(x%)	VaR*	r(x%)	VaR*	r(x%)	VaR*
Daily	−0.020074	$20,074	−0.016268	$16,268	−0.012276	$12,276
Weekly	−0.037164	37,164	−0.030272	30,272	−0.025615	25,615
Monthly	−0.072518	72,518	−0.062427	62,427	−0.047954	47,954

* For $1 million portfolio.

estimate of VaR, the differences are relatively small (less then $1,000 of the assumed $1 million portfolio value, or 0.1%). For tolerance level of 5% and a 1 month risk horizon (and ignoring the non-overlapping samples), the differences are approximately $2,000, (0.2%).

IMPLEMENTING VALUE AT RISK TECHNIQUES FOR PORTFOLIOS OF STOCKS AND OPTIONS

The change in value of a portfolio of m stocks and n options is given by

$$\Delta V = \sum_{i=1}^{m} \left[\sum_{j=1}^{n} w_{ij} \Delta C_{ij} + x_i \Delta S_i \right] \tag{45}$$

where C_{ij} is the price of the jth option on the ith stock and w_{ij} is the number of shares of the ith stock subject to the jth option. Determining VaR for this portfolio is, for the most part, a straightforward extension of the methods used for stock-only portfolios. Because ΔC is a function of ΔS, the values of ΔS used in the historical simulation and Monte Carlo simulation methods create corresponding values of ΔC, allowing a distribution of values of ΔV to be calculated. The exception is the portfolio mean-variance method. Because option prices are non-linear functions of stock prices, stock-and-option portfolio price changes (and returns) will not be normally distributed.[41] Consequently, mean and variance are inadequate descriptors of the value change and return distributions.

An additional characteristic of options, which creates a problem for VaR analysis by any method, is that an option price is affected by more variables than just the stock price. Standard option pricing models, for example, show an option price to be a function of six variables:

$$C_{ij} = C_{ij}(S_i, E_{ij}, d_i, \sigma_i, r_{ij}, T_{ij}) \tag{46}$$

where E_{ij} is the option exercise price, σ_i is the stock "volatility," r_{ij} is the risk-free rate, d_i is the dividend yield on stock, and T_{ij} is the time to expiration of the option.[42] Value at Risk analysis based only on ΔS will not tell the risk manager how portfolio value is affected by changes in these other variables.

Both the nonlinearity problem and the multiple-sources-of-risk problem can be addressed through an extremely useful approximation—that is, a Taylor series expansion for the change in option price. This mathematical technique allows ΔC to be decomposed into additive terms each of which captures the dependence of ΔC on one of the underlying variables. In turn, this allows VaR analysis to be focused on a single term or several terms, depending on the degree of approximation that can be tolerated.

The Taylor series approximation for the change in the option price is[43]

$$\Delta C_{ij} = \frac{\partial C_{ij}}{\partial S_i} \Delta S_i + \frac{1}{2} \frac{\partial C_{ij}^2}{\partial S_i^2} (\Delta S_i)^2 + \frac{\partial C_{ij}}{\partial \sigma_i} \Delta \sigma_1 + \frac{\partial C_{ij}}{\partial r_{ij}} \Delta r_{ij} + \frac{\partial C_{ij}}{\partial d_1} \Delta d_i + \frac{\partial C_{ij}}{\partial T_{ij}} \Delta \partial t \tag{47}$$

Each partial derivative has acquired a name from the Greek alphabet: respectively, delta (Δ), gamma (Γ), lambda (Λ) (or vega, or kappa), rho (Pr) of the interest rate, rho (Pd) of the dividend yield and theta (Θ).

$$\frac{\partial C_{ij}}{\partial S_i} = \Delta_{ij}; \frac{\partial^2}{\partial S_i^2} = \Gamma_{ij}; \frac{\partial C_{ij}}{\partial \sigma_i} = \Lambda_{ij};$$

$$\frac{\partial C_{ij}}{\partial r_{ij}} = \text{Pr}_{ij}; \frac{\partial C_{ij}}{\partial_i} = Pd_i; \frac{\partial C_{ij}}{\partial T_{ij}} = \Theta_{ij}.$$

(48)

The option's "delta," Δ_{ij}, is the linear approximation to the change in the option price for a change in the underlying stock price. For an infinitesimal change in price and no changes in the other variables, the option's delta gives the exact option price change. The option's delta can also be considered the share equivalent of that option for small stock price changes. For example, if Δ_{ij} equals .5, then an option on one stock is equivalent to a position in one half of a share, in terms of the effect on portfolio value for a small stock price change. An option on w_{ij} shares is the share equivalent of $w_{ij}\Delta_i$ shares. Note that a stock position of x_i shares has a delta of x_i, since the delta of a single share of stock is +1. Thus an option of w_{ij} shares and a stock position of x_i shares has a share equivalent of $w_{ij}\Delta_{ij} + x_i$.

Because the option price is a non-linear function of the stock price, for any finite change in the stock price the option's delta is only an approximation. The approximation, moreover, gets worse as the absolute size of the stock price change increases. The option's "gamma," Γ_{ij}, improves the approximation by accounting for some of the non-linearity or convexity in the option's price. The other factors—lambda, rho, and theta—give the linear approximations of the change in the option's price for finite changes in the volatility (σ) of the underlying stock, the spot interest rate appropriate to the time to expiration of the option, the dividend, and the passage of time, respectively. Note that stock positions have no gamma, lambda, and rho exposures, although under the assumption of geometric Brownian motion, they do have theta exposures.[44]

Defining and Measuring Market Risk for Portfolios with Stocks and Options

Position Exposures and Full Valuation

In the Taylor series approximation, the exposures of all the positions related to one underlying stock can be summed to produce the *position exposure* for that stock. Substitution of equations (47) and (48) into equation (45) gives

$$V = \sum_{i=1}^{m} \left[\sum_{j=1}^{n} w_{ij} \left[\Delta_{ij}\Delta S_i + \frac{1}{2}\Gamma_{ij}(\Delta S_i)^2 + \Lambda_{ij}\Delta\sigma_i + P_{ij}\Delta r_{ij} + \Theta_{ij}\Delta t \right] + Pd_i\Delta d_i + x_i\Delta S_i \right] \quad (49)$$

As shown in equation (49), for each underlying stock, both the option positions and the stock position are affected by ΔS_i. The total (linear) response to ΔS_i is the position delta, denoted Δ_i, given by

$$\Delta_i = \sum_{j=1}^{n} w_{ij} \Delta_{ij} + x_i \tag{50}$$

Similarly, for each underlying stock, the position gamma, denoted Γ_i, is given by

$$\Gamma_i = \sum_{j=1}^{n} w_{ij} \Gamma_{ij} \tag{51}$$

and the position lambda, denoted Λ_i, is given by

$$\Lambda_i = \sum_{j=1}^{n} w_{ij} \Lambda_{ij} \tag{52}$$

We do not define a position interest-rate rho, because some of the options on a stock may have different times to expiration. In this case, unless the term structure of spot interest rates undergoes a parallel shift, different interest rate changes will be involved.

The option theta terms are unique in that they involve exposure to the passage of time, Δt, which is common to all positions. Thus, they can be added over all positions to define the *portfolio exposure*. The portfolio theta, denoted Θ_p, is given by

$$\Theta_p = \sum_{i=1}^{m} \sum_{j=1}^{n} w_{ij} \Theta_{ij} \tag{53}$$

With these substitutions, the change in portfolio value becomes

$$\Delta V = \sum_{i=1}^{m} \left[\Delta_i \Delta S_i + \frac{1}{2} \Gamma_i (\Delta S_i)^2 + \Lambda_i \Delta \sigma_i + \sum_{j=1}^{n} w_{ij} \, \mathrm{Pr}_{ij} \, \Delta r_{ij} + P d_i \Delta d_i \right] + \Theta_p \Delta t \tag{54}$$

To illustrate the calculation of stock-and-option position exposures and the implementation of alternative VaR techniques, we created a portfolio of option and stock positions based on the same five stocks used in the stock-only illustrations. Table 8.13 shows the individual positions. AMR remains a stock-only position of 100,000 shares (long). Ford becomes a conventional put-protected position, long 100,000 shares in the stock and the put. IBM is an option-only position, a put money spread, long the 80-exercise-price option and short the 85 option. The Time-Warner position is a call calendar spread, long the July expiration and short the October expiration. Finally, Seagram is an outright long call on 20,000 shares.[45, 46]

Table 8.14 shows the exposures of the positions to the various risk factors—the "Greeks." A display such as this allows a risk manager to see which positions are creating the greatest exposures to the various sources of risk. The largest position delta, for example, is the stock-only AMR position. This stock only position, moreover, has no gamma, vega, theta, or rho exposure. The effect of put "insurance" can be seen in the Ford position, with a net position delta reduced from $100,000 to $39,475 by adding the put. The Ford position also has the largest gamma and vega exposure.

TABLE 8.13   Description of Sample Portfolio with Stocks and Options

	Stock Data			Option Data						Portfolio Data		
	Stock Name	Market Price	Dividend Yield	Option Type	Option Price	Exercise Price	Expiry Date	Settlement Date	Risk-Free Rate	Units of Shares	Position	Portfolio Value
Company 1	American Air	$67.250	0							100,000	Long	$ 6,725,000
Option 1				None								
Option 2				None								
Company 2	Ford	28.375	0.046							100,000	Long	2,837,500
Option 1				Put	$2.50	$30.00	9/15/95	5/19/95	0.0585	100,000	Long	250,000
Option 2				None								
Company 3	IBM	93.250	0.011							0		—
Option 1				Put	0.0625	80	7/14/95	5/19/95	0.0561	100,000	Long	6,250
Option 2				Put	0.25	85	7/14/95	5/19/95	0.0561	100,000	Short	(25,000)
Company 4	Time Warner	39.250	0.009							0		—
Option 1				Call	1.8125	40	10/15/95	5/19/95	0.0585	10,000	Short	(18,125)
Option 2				Call	1	40	7/14/95	5/19/95	0.0561	10000	Long	10,000
Company 5	Seagram	28.500	0.021							0		—
Option 1				Call	4.5	25	11/17/95	5/19/95	0.059	20,000	Long	90,000
Option 2				None								
												$9,875,625

While the position exposures are of great interest, the risk manager would also like to determine the entire portfolio exposure. It is tempting to sum down each exposure column to determine total portfolio exposure to each risk factor. For theta, this is no problem, since one value for Δt applies to every position. Based on the theta portfolio exposure shown in Table 8.14, the value of this portfolio will decline by approximately $118 (i.e., −$556 + 474 −26 −110) in one day or approximately −$590 in 5 days due simply to the passage of time, given no change in the other risk factors. This calculation of portfolio theta nets out the erosion of time value across all option positions.

TABLE 8.14   Estimates of Market Risk Exposures on a Position Basis for the Portfolio of Sample Stocks and Options

Company	Type	No. of Units	Position	Market Price	Market Value	Delta	Gamma	Theta	Vega	Rho of Rate	Rho of Dividend Yield
American Air		100,000	Long	$67.25	$6,725,000	$100,000	$ 0.00	$ 0.00	$ 0.00	$ 0.00	$ 0.00
Option 1		0		0	0.00	0.00	0.00	0.00	0.00	0.00	0.00
Option 2		0		0	0.00	0.00	0.00	0.00	0.00	0.00	0.00
Position 1				6,725,000	100,000	0.00	0.00	0.00	0.00	0.00	
Ford		100,000	Long	28.375	2,837,500	100,000	0.00	0.00	0.00	0.00	0.00
Option 1	Put	100,000	Long	2.5	250,000	(60,525)	9,234	(556)	610,376	(678,948)	619,851
Option 2		0		0	0.00	0.00	0.00	0.00	0.00	0.00	0.00
Position 2				3,087,500	39,475	9,234	(556)	610,376	(678,948)	619,851	
IBM		0		93.25	0.00	0.00	0.00	0.00	0.00	0.00	0.00
Option 1	Put	100,000	Long	0.0625	6,250	(2,173)	689	(324)	189,650	(33,842)	26,963
Option 2	Put	100,000	Short	0.25	(25,000)	7,942	(2,189)	799	(539,821)	124,054	(104,721)
Position 3				(18,750)	5,769	(1,501)	474	(350,172)	90,212	(77,758)	
Time Warner		0		39.25	0.00	0.00	0.00	0.00	0.00	0.00	0.00
Option 1	Call	10,000	Short	1.8125	(18,125)	(5,114)	(843)	102	(89,099)	(63,015)	67,295
Option 2	Call	10,000	Long	1	10,000	4,536	1,299	(128)	60,846	27,229	(28,091)
Position 4				(8,125)	(578)	455	(26)	(28,254)	(35,786)	39,204	
Seagram		0		28.5	0.00	0.00	0.00	0.00	0.00	0.00	0.00
Option 1	Call	20,000	Long	4.5	90,000	16,093	995	(110)	106,980	194,672	(204,875)
Option 2		0		0	0.00	0.00	0.00	0.00	0.00	0.00	0.00
Position 5				90,000	16,093	995	(110)	106,980	194,672	(204,875)	

Theta exposure, however, is the only exposure that can be summed for the whole portfolio in this manner without making more restrictive assumptions. For example, the total portfolio delta of $160,759 could be multiplied by an assumed change in all stock prices, $\Delta S_i = \Delta S$ for all i, to get an estimated change in value of the portfolio. If all stock prices, for example, change by $1 in this sample portfolio, the portfolio value will change by approximately $160,579 considering only the portfolio delta (and by $160,579 + 9,183 = 169,942$ considering portfolio delta and gamma). This "all changes equal" assumption is analogous to the assumption of a parallel shift in the yield curve that is not uncommon in the risk analysis of portfolios of interest-rate derivatives.[47] In both cases, this assumption ignores the different volatilities in and correlations across prices (or rates) and, for this reason, is not appropriate for estimating VaR. Moreover, if the risk manager is willing to assume particular changes in stock prices, volatilities, and interest rates, then the "full valuation" of the option positions at each new set of variable values makes more sense than the "position exposure" approach.

A simplified approach to estimating VaR that does allow for use of volatilities and correlations is the "delta-only" approximation.

Delta-Only Approximation of Portfolio Exposure

The delta-only approximation drops all the Taylor-series terms except the ΔS term and in some cases the Δt term. Thus, this approach is based on the assumption of small changes in ΔS, so that the non-linear or convexity effect is negligible, and that changes in volatility, interest rates, and dividends are negligible. Equation (54) becomes [48]

$$\Delta V = \sum_{i=1}^{m} (\Delta_i) \Delta S_i + \Theta p \Delta t \tag{55}$$

Each position in the portfolio is now simply a share equivalent position, with Δ_i shares instead of x_i.[49] In return form, the equation is

$$\frac{\Delta V}{V} = \sum_{i=1}^{m} \delta_i r_i + \Theta_v \Delta t \tag{56}$$

Where δ_i equals $(\Delta_i) S_i / V$ and Θ_v equals Θ_p / V.

Estimating VaR Based on Historical Simulation of Portfolio Returns

VaR and Delta-Only Approximation

The historical distribution of stock returns can be used with the delta-only share equivalents just as it is used in stock-only portfolios. The results are shown in Table 8.15.

VaR and Delta Plus Gamma Approximation

Table 8.15 also shows the results of estimating VaR allowing for delta and gamma exposure in valuing option positions. (These estimates also account for theta.) Finally, Table 8.15 shows the results of full option valuation at the new stock prices implied by each historical return. This more accurate method of option valuation

TABLE 8.15   VaR for Alternative Risk Horizons and Tolerance Levels Based on Historical Simulation of Stock Returns with Delta-Only, Delta Plus Gamma, and Full Valuation of Option Positions

	At x = 2.5%	At x = 5.0%	At x = 10.0%
Daily			
Delta-Only Valuation	$ 257,356	$ 208,629	$156,199
Delta and Gamma Valuation	256,225	210,397	158,473
Full Valuation	256,201	210,765	158,576
Weekly			
(Non-overlapping)			
Delta-Only Valuation	465,325	434,293	381,945
Delta and Gamma Valuation	487,834	428,188	383,227
Full Valuation	497,549	431,524	384,139
(Bootstrapped)			
Delta-Only Valuation	591,680	506,099	393,515
Delta and Gamma Valuation	607,856	504,508	397,471
Full Valuation	609,702	508,830	404,632
Monthly			
(Non-overlapping)			
Delta-Only Valuation	1,276,646	1,179,623	635,332
Delta and Gamma Valuation	1,265,527	1,175,090	711,765
Full Valuation	1,261,727	1,171,588	664,824
(Bootstrapped)			
Delta-Only Valuation	959,943	832,126	699,169
Delta and Gamma Valuation	1,038,865	875,136	706,497
Full Valuation	1,077,823	886,771	723,865

provides the best indication of the usefulness of the other two approximations. For daily returns, even the delta-only approximation is quite good, differing from full valuation by only at most 1.4% (for a tolerance level of 10.0%). The delta-gamma approximation for daily returns is virtually exact. For short risk horizons, such as one day, the delta-only approximation to VaR gives good results that are slightly improved by more refined techniques capturing the options' convexity.

The two approximations also perform fairly well for weekly returns. The delta-only estimate is about 3% less than the full valuation at tolerance levels of 2.5% and 10%; delta-gamma estimates never differ from the full valuations by more than 2%. For monthly returns, however, the delta-only error reaches a maximum of nearly 11% for a 2.5% tolerance level, 6% error at the 5% level, and 3.4% error at the 10.0% level. The delta-gamma error is 3.6%, 6.2%, and 2.4% at 2.5%, 5%, and 10.0% tolerance levels respectively. Note that although in percentage terms these errors might seem acceptable, the dollar VaR error is increasing with the horizon due to the expected growth in portfolio value and standard deviation of value. For example, the monthly error at a tolerance level of 2.5%, although only 3.6%, is almost $50,000.

Given that full valuation is unlikely to be substantially more time consuming than the two approximations, these results suggest the use of full valuation with historical simulation with longer risk horizons such as a month.

Estimating VaR Based on the Mean and Variance of Portfolio Returns

As noted above, the non-normality of stock-and-option portfolio price changes and returns prevents the full use of the portfolio mean-variance method that can be easily applied to stock-only portfolios. Since the non-normality is a result of the nonlinear relationship between option and stock prices, however, the delta-only approach (which ignores the nonlinearity) can be used with the mean-variance analysis. Alternatively, the mean-variance analysis is also useable with a single-factor model, as will be illustrated.

VaR with Delta-Only Approximation

Since the delta-only approximation creates share equivalent positions, the equations for portfolio mean and variance apply with δ_i instead of γ_i weights. Portfolio mean return is given by

$$\mu_p = \sum_{i=1}^{m} \delta_i \mu_i \tag{57}$$

and variance of return by

$$\sigma_p = \sum_{i=1}^{m} \sum_{j=1}^{m} \delta_i \delta_j \sigma_{ij} \tag{58}$$

Table 8.16 shows VaR estimates based on the normal distribution assumption for the sample stock-and-option portfolio.

The VaR estimates in Table 8.16 can be compared to those in Table 8.15 to see the effect of the different assumptions. Comparing "delta-only" estimates in the two tables, we see large differences for weekly and monthly time intervals (e.g., $506,099 for weekly historical simulation at a 5.0% tolerance level and $477,538 for weekly mean-variance (bootstrapped)). Also, the weekly and monthly estimates of VaR based on the portfolio mean-variance method are, for the most part, further away from the full valuation result attained using historical simulation. For the daily interval, the

---

TABLE 8.16 VaR for Alternative Risk Horizons and Tolerance Levels Based on Estimates of the Means, Variances, and Covariances with Delta-Adjusted Option Positions

	Mean (μ_p)	Standard Deviation (σ_p)	At x% = 2.5%		At x% = 5.0%		At x% = 10.0%	
			r(x%)	VaR*	r(x%)	VaR*	r(x%)	VaR*
Daily	0.000229	0.013317	−0.025871	$ 255,712	−0.021675	$214,274	−0.016837	$166,496
Weekly								
(Non-overlapping)	0.001035	0.026595	−0.051092	506,081	−0.042711	423,322	−0.033049	327,904
(Bootstrapped)	−0.002366	0.027865	−0.056982	564,250	−0.048201	477,538	−0.038078	377,563
Monthly								
(Non-overlapping)	0.004080	0.049142	−0.092238	917,423	−0.076753	764,504	−0.058900	588,193
(Bootstrapped)	0.008612	0.058118	−0.105299	1,046,408	−0.086986	865,557	−0.065872	657,041

* For a $9,875,625 portfolio when the portfolio weights are based on the value of the delta-adjusted position in each stock relative to the overall portfolio value.
** r(x%) = μp − kσp where k = 1.96, 1.6449, and 1.2816, for 2.5%, 5%, and 10%, respectively.

mean-variance and historical delta-only VaR estimates are similar (although, approximately $10,000 different, or over 6% different, at a tolerance level of 10.0%).

These results suggest that the portfolio mean-variance approach applied to delta-adjusted option positions should only be used for daily risk horizons.

VaR with Beta-Adjusted Delta-and-Gamma Exposure to a Single Factor

For portfolios large enough that unsystematic risk is negligible, and in any case when systematic risk is considered the major risk to be analyzed, factor models can be used with the Taylor series approximations to obtain factor exposures. In a k-factor model, the stock price is a function of the k factors,

$$S_i = S_i\left(F_1, F_2, \ldots, F_k\right) \tag{59}$$

and ΔS_i is given by

$$\Delta S_i = \frac{\partial S_i}{\partial F_1} \Delta F_1 + \frac{\partial S_i}{\partial F_2} + \Delta F_2 + \ldots + \frac{\partial S_i}{\partial F_k} \Delta F_k \tag{60}$$

It can be shown, based on the factor model, that each partial derivative is given by

$$\frac{\partial S_i}{\partial F_j} = b_{ij} \frac{S_i}{F_j}$$

Thus,

$$\Delta S_i = b_{i1} \frac{S_i}{F_1} \Delta F_1 + b_{i2} \frac{S_i}{F_2} \Delta F_2 + \ldots + b_{ik} \frac{S_i}{F_k} \Delta F_k \tag{61}$$

Anywhere ΔS_i appears in the risk analysis, its factor equivalent, (i.e., equation (61)), can instead be used. The factor model, therefore, reduces the number of ΔS risk factors from m (i.e., one for each stock) to k (i.e., one for each factor).

With the single factor model, this simplification is significant. With a single factor model, the Taylor series expansion for portfolio value change due only to ΔS_i and $(\Delta S_i)^2$ becomes

$$\Delta V = \sum_{i-1}^{m} \left[\Delta_i b_{i1} \frac{S_i}{F_1}\left(\Delta F_1\right) + \frac{1}{2}\Gamma_i\left(b_{i1} \frac{S_i}{F_i} \Delta F_1\right)^2 \right] \tag{62}$$

The term $\Delta_i b_{i1} (S_i/F_i)$ in the first term of equation (63) is the *systematic* delta for the ith stock—that is, the change in its value for a unit change in the value of the factor. Summed over all stocks, this quantity is the portfolio's systematic delta with respect to the single factor, denoted $\Delta_{p\iota}$. Similarly, each stock's *systematic* gamma with respect to the single factor can be defined in the second term as $\Gamma_i (b_{i1} (S_i/F_i))^2$ and summed over all stocks to compute portfolio systematic gamma, denoted $\Gamma_{p\iota}$. The equation for the estimated change in portfolio value becomes

$$\Delta V = \Delta_p\left(\Delta F_1\right) + \frac{1}{2}\Gamma_p\left(\Delta F_1\right)^2 \tag{63}$$

The critical rate of return for the S&P 500 at a specific risk horizon and tolerance level gives the critical value of ΔF_p, which then can be substituted into equation (64) for estimating VaR. Table 8.17 shows these results. These estimates of *systematic* VaR, of course, are much smaller than the estimates of VaR based on total risk presented in the previous tables.

Estimating VaR Based on Monte Carlo Simulation of Stock Returns

For stock-and-option portfolios, the Monte Carlo simulation method works in a similar manner to the way it works for stock-only portfolios. Each stock price drawn in the simulation is used to calculate an option price (under full valuation) or to approximate an option price change (under delta-only and delta-plus-gamma approximations). Table 8.18 shows the results of the Monte Carlo simulation based on estimates of VaR for the sample stock-and-option portfolio. We see once again that for daily and weekly risk horizons, the delta-only method provides a good approximation of VaR, relative to the other two methods. See also Table 8.15 for comparison. For the monthly risk horizon, however, full valuation appears to provide a sufficiently different and hopefully more reliable estimate so as to be worth the additional trouble.

TABLE 8.17   VaR for Alternative Risk Horizons and Tolerance Levels Based on Estimates of the Portfolio's Beta and the Mean and Variance of Return for the S&P 500 Index with Delta-Only and Delta Plus Gamma Valuation of Option Positions

Portfolio Beta-Adjusted Delta	0.8363								
Portfolio Beta-Adjusted Gamma	0.1639								

	Mean $(\mu_{S\&P})$	Standard Deviation $(\sigma_{S\&P})$	At x% = 2.5%		At x% = 5.0%		At x% = 10.0%	
			r(x%)**	VaR*	r(x%)**	VaR*	r(x%)**	VaR*
Daily	0.000240	0.006276	−0.01206	−0.01008	−0.00780			
Delta-Only Valuation				$ 99,834		$ 83,500		$ 64,667
Delta Plus Gamma Valuation				119,353		99,818		77,295
Weekly								
(Non-overlapping)	0.001256	0.013820	−0.02583		−0.02148		−0.01646	
Delta-Only Valuation				214,857		178,892		137,426
Delta Plus Gamma Valuation				256,659		213,647		164,056 <
(Bootstrapped)								
0.001042	0.013634	−0.02568		−0.02138		−0.01643		
Delta-Only Valuation				213,619		178,138		137,228
Delta Plus Gamma Valuation				255,179		212,745		163,819
Monthly								
(Non-overlapping)	0.004848	0.019044	−0.03248		−0.02648		−0.01956	
Delta-Only Valuation				274,756		225,196		168,054
Delta Plus Gamma Valuation				327,316		268,045		199,706
(Bootstrapped)	0.008616	0.029166	−0.04855		−0.03936		−0.02876	
Delta-Only Valuation				407,503		331,599		244,084
Delta Plus Gamma Valuation				486,074		395,297		290,634

* For $9,875,625 portfolio.

** r(x%) = $\mu - k\sigma$ where k = 1.96, 1.6449, and 1.2816 for x% = 2.5%, 5%, and 10%.

**TABLE 8.18   VaR for Alternative Risk Horizons and Tolerance Levels
Based on Monte Carlo Simulation of Stock Returns with Delta-Only,
Delta Plus Gamma, and Full Valuation of Option Positions**

	At x = 2.5%	At x = 5.0%	At x = 10.0%
Daily			
Delta-Only Valuation	$ 214,136	$181,989	$147,010
Delta and Gamma Valuation	215,274	186,544	149,736
Full Valuation	214,603	187,605	149,759
Weekly			
Delta-Only Valuation	504,421	431,155	334,780
Delta and Gamma Valuation	506,323	431,014	333,351
Full Valuation	507,585	433,536	335,427
Monthly			
Delta-Only Valuation	942,505	805,242	599,065
Delta and Gamma Valuation	982,735	830,306	645,627
Full Valuation	1,002,379	865,146	678,393

CONCLUDING REMARKS

The VaR approach to measuring market risk relies on estimates of the volatility in and correlations of the relevant market risk factors. The approach also relies on estimates of the responsiveness of market value to changes in these risk factors. Using the first set of estimates a "worst case" (or almost "worst case") scenario is developed based on an "adverse" movement in the market risk factors. Although the calculation of VaR may rely upon an unusual market move (e.g., a 2 or 3 standard deviation drop in the S&P 500), the factors underlying the determination of the size of the adverse move—volatilities and correlations—and the responsiveness of market values to these changes are assumed to remain constant. Looked at another way, the more or less "normal" market conditions under which these volatilities, correlations, and price sensitivities were estimated are assumed to remain unchanged. This assumption allows us to make more or less precise probability statements about the likelihood of certain losses due to market risk.

It is precisely this assumption, however, about unchanging or stable market conditions—predictable volatilities and correlations and predictable price sensitivities due to adequate market liquidity and easy access to markets—that is likely to be violated in more extreme, abnormal market conditions. As a result, VaR measures of market risk must be supplemented by *stress testing* for a truly comprehensive approach to market risk management. From this perspective, the purpose of stress testing is to examine and, if possible, quantify how sensitive the market value of an institution's portfolio is to those parameters and factors taken as given in the estimation of VaR. In other words, the goal is to stress the portfolio looking for the weak points, if any, that are particularly vulnerable to breakdowns in the normal market relationships taken for granted in VaR analysis.

The analysis of VaR for equity portfolios presented in the previous sections provides a useful framework for identifying those parameters and factors that should be the focus of stress testing. These parameters include:

- Estimates of the volatilities of stock prices;
- Estimates of correlations between stock prices;
- Estimates of the sensitivity of stock prices to various factor indices (i.e., individual stock "betas" and the portfolio "betas");
- Estimates of the sensitivities of option prices to underlying risk factors (i.e., the Greeks).[50]

The following types of questions need to be addressed in designing stress tests. What would happen to the value of the portfolio, if the previously predictable volatilities jumped, either on their own or in tandem with the adverse move in market prices? Or, if the previously predictable lack of substantial correlation between various stock prices (e.g., U.S. equities versus foreign equities) reversed itself in a worldwide decline of stock prices? Or if the responsiveness of a highly concentrated equity position to an overall market factor should suddenly change? Or, if a major market move in a single stock or sector of the market or the overall market disrupts normal pricing relationships due to a drying up of liquidity? Evaluation of such abnormal market scenarios is critical to good risk management.[51]

ENDNOTES

1. In addition, it would be desirable if the measure of market risk could be combined with consistent measures of other risks, such as credit risk, to provide an aggregate risk measure that could be used, along with other inputs, to measure risk-adjusted performance for capital allocation and incentive compensation purposes.

2. This section is particularly relevant to the management of market risk for those firms making markets in equities and equity options.

3. Stress testing, by contrast, focuses on the quantification of losses for various worst case scenarios under "abnormal" market conditions—that is, when normal market responses and relationships break down. Attention to both is necessary for a comprehensive and sound system of market risk management.

4. For fixed-income portfolios, for example, market risk is often measured by the portfolio's net DVO1 (i.e., dollar value of one basis point), assuming all yields shift in a parallel fashion. This approach fails to account for the different volatilities and correlations of yields along the term structure.

5. Our version of the historical simulation approach differs from some other accounts in that normality of the true distribution is not assumed. In lieu of any formal distributional assumptions, we simply use the histogram for calculating probabilities.

6. The problem of small sample size with non-overlapping samples could also be addressed by using overlapping or rolling samples to calculate, say, monthly or quarterly returns. Using overlapping samples to increase the number of observations will, however, induce artificial correlation in the sample series. By drawing the daily returns at random with replacement, bootstrapping avoids this problem.

7. Within any limit system, account managers and traders may at times exceed their risk limits. The seriousness of a particular limit exception or even a sequence of such exceptions depends upon management's approach to setting limits and the size of limits involved relative to the institution's capital. Limit exceptions should nevertheless receive prompt management attention and repeated exceptions should lead to careful review of both positions *and* the assumptions underlying the calculation of VaR.

8. A major (but often overlooked) advantage of a VaR approach to identifying, measuring, monitoring, reporting, and controlling market risk is that it fosters and facilitates discussions at each link in the chain of risk management. A common language is imposed on all the conversations and focuses the discussion on the right issues. Account managers and traders constrained by risk limits can question and test the assumptions underlying the VaR calculation. Risk managers can challenge account managers and traders with repeated limit exceptions, while reviewing their own assessments of the VaR calculations. Senior management and the board can promptly question the managers of particular books or

portfolios when limits are violated and question risk managers when estimated market exposures are inconsistent with actual loss experiences.

9. *See* H. Green and R. Marks, "Managing a Portfolio of Positions," in *The Handbook of Interest Rate Risk Management,* (Homewood, IL: Irwin Professional Publishing, 1993) for an excellent introduction to the use of Value at Risk in hedging a portfolio's exposure.

10. Portfolio theory has developed in terms of stock returns and many of the available databases (e.g., the CRSP data files) contain return data. In this chapter, we work primarily with returns; but, as equations (3) through (6) show, any statement about returns can be algebraically transformed into a statement about price or value changes.

11. During this period, the mean daily, weekly, and monthly returns of IBM were negative, as were the mean daily and monthly returns for Seagrams. Thus, a pure historical simulation approach would impose the assumption that the future probability distributions of returns on these stocks have negative means. Is a negative expected return a reasonable forecast? Perhaps, if the analyst has information about the stock that suggests the stock price will fall. But in the absence of a strong view about the prospects for a stock, we would expect the return on a stock to be positive. Because stocks are risky investments, we would not expect investors to buy them unless there is sufficient positive expected return to compensate for the risk. If enough investors begin to expect a negative return, the stock price should quickly fall to a level at which the expected return is positive. This problem could possibly be explained by "sampling error." While the population distribution for the return on IBM may have a positive mean, it is possible, of course, for a particular sample to have a negative mean.

12. It would be possible to measure more than 104 weekly returns by using overlapping observations. For example, the first weekly return would be calculated from daily returns 1 through 5, the second weekly return from returns 2 through 6, etc. The resulting series of weekly returns, however, would be artificially correlated and consequently could not be treated as a sample of independent observations from the population. Although there are statistical corrections for this problem, it is better to use nonoverlapping samples and rely on bootstrapping techniques to generate larger sample sizes.

13. The RiskMetrics™ approach to volatility estimation does not assume that the return distribution is stable. They instead estimate future volatility by an exponentially-weighted moving average of past volatilities, so that recent volatilities are given more weight than past ones. *See* "Introduction to RiskMetrics™," Morgan Guaranty Trust Company, Market Risk Research, New York, October 25, 1994, pp. 53–66. There are many variations. In univariate time series models, the return is a function of its past values, and may have trend, seasonal and irregular components. The expected return will then also depend on past return. The variance in such models may be constant (homoskedastic) or nonconstant (heteroskedastic). In recent years heteroskedastic variance models, known as generalized autoregressive conditional heteroskedastic (GARCH) models, have been extensively used in financial modeling. There are models in which the expected return depends on the past variance (ARCH-M), and there are multivariate time series models. Recent reference works for these models include Walter Enders, *Applied Econometric Time Series,* (New York: John Wiley, 1995) and James D. Hamilton, *Time Series Analysis,* (Princeton: Princeton University Press, 1994). A complete examination of these models in the context of risk management and Value at Risk estimation is an important topic for future research.

14. The random drawing can be accomplished as follows:

- Number the actual daily returns as $1/N, 2/N, \ldots,$ and $N/N,$ where N is the total number of daily returns. In our example, $N = 507,$ so the returns are numbered .00197, .00394, . . . , and 1.
- Draw a random number from a uniform probability distribution defined over 0 to 1. Most spreadsheet and statistical software have such a random number function. In Excel, for example, the function is RAND( ).
- If RAND( ) lies in the first interval, 0 – .00197, then choose the first daily return as the first observation. If, instead, RAND( ) lies in the second interval, choose the second daily return as the first observation. And so on.
- Continue this process until you have drawn a random sample of five daily returns.

15. The weekly return can be calculated using the following equation:

$$r_{\text{weekly}} = (1 + r_{\text{day1}})(1 + r_{\text{day2}}) \ldots (1 + r_{\text{day5}}) - 1.$$

16. *See BESTFIT,* (Newfield, NJ: Palisade Corporation, March 1995).

17. The symbol for variance can also be written as $\sigma_{ii}.$ In this chapter, we use both notations as is convenient.

18. If variances and covariances in terms of stock price changes are needed, these can be obtained from the following formulas:

$$\sigma_i^2 = \frac{\text{variance } (\Delta S_i)}{S_i^2}$$

$$\sigma_{ij} = \frac{\text{covariance } (\Delta S_i, \Delta S_j)}{S_i S_j}$$

These formulas are based on the assumption that dividend uncertainty is negligible.

19. *See* Harry Markowitz, *Portfolio Selection: Efficient Diversification of Investments,* (New York: John Wiley and Sons, 1959).

20. Many computer software programs (e.g., Lotus and Excel) have matrix manipulation capability, making matrix equations particularly easy to use in portfolio analysis.

21. *RiskMetrics*™ presents forecasts of volatilities and correlations in a matrix format.

22. If daily returns are uncorrelated, then the standard deviation of a sequence of n daily returns equals the daily standard deviation times $\sqrt{n}$. This is the "square root of time" rule. Then VaR for one week would be approximately $\sqrt{5} * (VaR)$, for 1 day. The increase in VaR as the risk horizon goes from one day to one week is roughly in line with the "square root of time" rule while the one week to one month increase is substantially less than predicted by the rule, based on using 21 as the number of trading days in a month.

23. Both tests are based on dividing the data into intervals and computing the difference between the actual and theoretical number of observations in these intervals. The Anderson-Darling test is more sensitive to discrepancies in the tail of the distribution and, thus, may be more appropriate for Value at Risk applications. *See BESTFIT,* (Newfield, NJ: Palisade Corporation, March 1995), pp. 2-17, 2-18.

24. Matthew Richardson and Tom Smith, "A Test for Mulivariate Normality of Stock Returns," *Journal of Business,* 1993, vol. 66, no. 2, 295-321.

25. For a review of a number of tests (although not Anderson-Darling), *see* Albert Madansky, *Prescriptions for Working Statisticians,* (New York: Springer-Verlag, 1988), Chapter 1.

26. Factor models are also called *index* models. The name *index* suggests the factors are returns on indices of types of securities, such as a stock market index, an industry index, a bond index, etc. The name *factor* suggests a more general concept that can refer to such variables as real economic growth and inflation as well as security indices. The names can be used interchangeably.

27. These factors were included in the model proposed by Nai-fu Chen, Richard Roll, and Stephen Ross, "Economic forces in the Stock Market," *Journal of Business,* 59 (July 1986), pp. 386-403. Some versions of factor models use market and industry indices, and others define purely statistical factors based on the variance-covariance matrix of a sample of stock returns. *See* Edwin J. Elton and Martin J. Gruber, *Modern Portfolio Theory and Investment Analysis,* 5th edition, (New York: John Wiley & Sons, 1995), Chapters 7, 8, and 16, for a review of the literature and a detailed explanation of factor models.

28. One criterion for judging factor models, then, is the extent to which residuals from the estimated models are uncorrelated across stocks.

29. The y_i's are defined as before—as the proportion of the portfolio value invested in each stock.

30. Just as in estimating return distributions, estimating beta requires choices about sample size, return measurement interval, and overlapping vs. non-overlapping observations. We have chosen not to explore these issues further in the context of beta estimation.

31. Which way is best for estimating covariances? This question has been addressed in several empirical studies. There are really two issues. How well does the factor model represent the past, and how good are the results for forecasting future portfolio variances. Clearly, this factor model does not represent the actual past covariance. No factor model will do this perfectly, because of the assumption of no correlation between the error terms. The purpose, however, is to estimate what may happen in the future. Elton and Gruber have found that the covariances produced by factor models provide better estimates of future portfolio variances than the directly-estimated historical covariances. Apparently, the historical covariances contain "noise" which the factor models screen out. They also find that a single-factor model outperformed multi-factor models, at least the ones they

tested. However, the best predictor of future covariances was the "overall mean" model, in which every covariance is assumed to be equal to the average covariance of all stocks. Similar results have been found by others, although there is also some contrary evidence, and only some multi-factor models have been tested. *See* Elton and Gruber, *ibid.,* Chapter 8 for a review of these studies. An excellent reference for the more general topic of estimation risk is Gordon J. Alexander and Jack Clark Francis, *Portfolio Analysis,* 3rd Edition, (Englewood Cliffs: Prentice-Hall, 1986), Chapter VI.

32. There are estimation issues for factor model coefficients with which we do not deal. For example, single-factor model betas appear to "mean revert" over time. Corrections for such time series properties have been developed. *See* Elton and Gruber, Chapter 7, for further discussion and references.

33. Value at Risk estimates for a factor model could also be based on historical or Monte Carlo simulation of the factor returns.

34. This estimate of VaR could be modified to include the "expected" component of unsystematic risk (i.e., a_p).

35. Over a time period of length Δt, the return on a stock (ignoring dividends) is $r\Delta t = (S_{\Delta t} - S)/S$ or, rearranging, $S_{\Delta t} = (1 + r\Delta t)S$, where $S_{\Delta t}$ is the end-of-period stock price and S is the beginning-of-period stock price. Since $r\Delta t$ is assumed to be normally distributed and S is constant, $S_{\Delta t}$ is a linear function of a normally distributed random variable and, hence, must be normally distributed itself.

36. This is the same assumption about stock prices which Black and Scholes used to derive their famous option-pricing model, and it is the basis for many other option pricing models.

37. That is, $E\,(ds/S) = \mu dt.$ var $(dS/S) =$ var $[\sigma\varepsilon\sqrt{dt}\,] = \sigma^2 dt$ [var (ε)], and var $(\varepsilon) = 1$.

38. *See* John Hull, *Options, Futures, and Other Derivative Securities,* (Englewood Cliffs, NJ: Prentice-Hall, 1993), Chapters 9 and 10. Hull uses stochastic calculus to prove that r_c is normally distributed, applying Ito's Lemma to ln $(S_{\Delta t}/S)$. For an alternative derivation not using stochastic calculus, see Robert A. Jarrow and Andrew Rudd, *Option Pricing,* Section 7-5.

39. There are various transformations. After some experimentation, we used the simple method given by Hull, p. 332. For further discussion of methods, *see* Averill M. Law and W. David Kelton, *Simulation Modeling and Analysis,* 2nd ed., (New York: McGraw-Hill, 1991), Chapter 8.

40. Hull, pp. 332–333, sketches this methodology. A more complete treatment is in R.Y. Rubenstein, *Simulation and the Monte Carlo Method,* (New York: John Wiley, 1981), Chapter 3. A very detailed description is in *OPAL,* the World Bank, Washington, DC, 1991.

41. For example, consider a "put-protected" stock-and-option portfolio consisting of a long stock position "protected" by a long put position whose time to expiration equals the risk horizon. The minimum value of this portfolio occurs at the option exercise price. Thus, the portfolio ΔV (and $\Delta V/V$) distribution is truncated for stock prices less than the exercise price.

42. The stock volatility, σ_i, is the standard deviation of the continuously compounded rate of return of the stock, the same σ that appears in equation (38). The risk-free rate is subscripted "ij" to make clear that, except in the unusual case of a flat term structure of interest rates, a particular default-free interest rate applies to each option maturity. For simplicity, we are assuming an option pricing model based on dividend yield.

43. A Taylor series contains an infinite number of terms. The approximation shown here is the standard one used in measuring option exposure. It neglects many (an infinite number of) exposures, such as exposures to $(\Delta S)^3$, $(\Delta\sigma)^2$, and interaction terms such as $(\Delta S\Delta\sigma)$. The particular approximation chosen is a judgment made by the analyst based on the extent to which the neglected exposures are believed to be negligibly small.

44. Stocks, in fact, do have rho exposures. The basis of stock valuation is discounted cash flow. As interest rates and dividends change, stock values change. This dependence is suppressed in standard portfolio theory, because the sources of stock returns are not addressed. Some factor models (e.g., Chen, Roll, and Ross) have factors based on interest rates.

45. This type of portfolio might resemble that of a small market maker, in which several traders take positions based on views of price movements or quasi-arbitrage opportunities.

46. To simplify the valuation task for these illustrations, we use dividend yield in the option valuation formula. For individual stocks, the explicit dividend approach might be more accurate, but the difference does not affect this discussion.

47. For example, *see* Chapter 18 in Charles W. Smithson, Clifford W. Smith, Jr., and D. Sykes Wilford, *Managing Financial Risk,* (New York: Irwin, 1995).

48. We choose to keep the theta term in our "delta-only" analysis. The theta term causes no complications and improves accuracy somewhat, particularly for longer time intervals.

49. Table 8.14 shows that the delta-only share equivalents of the portfolio are 100,000 shares of AMR; 39,475 of Ford; 5,769 of IBM; short 578 of Time-Warner and 16,093 of Seagram.

50. To some extent these factors can be accounted for and incorporated into the VaR analysis by treating these factors not as parameters but as random variables that can be modeled.

51. Simulations can be used to develop contingency plans for such events. A special focus should be placed on examining the firm's ability to adjust hedges and liquidate positions. The inability to hedge or liquidate positions in a particularly volatile situation may lead to an unexpected lengthening of the at risk period causing the risk exposure to greatly increase relative to normal VaR measures.

PART FOUR

Risk Oversight

9

Oversight of Derivative Markets: Who's Responsible for What?

Brandon Becker
Francois-Ihor Mazur

F inancial losses attributed to derivatives[1] continue to highlight the mercurial nature of these instruments and the need to manage their risks carefully.[2] Despite these losses, derivatives undeniably are valuable as tools for financial risk management. They allow users to manage risk by hedging against fluctuations in interest rates, currency values, and other forms of price risks. When used properly, various derivative strategies can serve to lower funding costs, make asset management more efficient, improve hedging abilities, provide a more liquid means of attaining a desired exposure, and take position or directional risk (i.e., speculate).[3] At the same time, the complexity and leverage of derivatives can pose substantial risks if the products are used improperly.

Derivatives have become an indispensable component of global financial markets, yet their ever increasing complexity, combined with the tremendous upsurge in the volume of derivatives transactions, make it essential that the risks associated with them are identified, managed, and monitored. To a great extent, self-preservation and the fear of loss of reputation motivate dealers and end-users to manage derivatives risk. Moreover, dealers and end-users are in a position to appreciate the risks specific to their derivatives activities.[4] Hence, the dealers and end-users who actually use derivatives are also best able to establish and implement a comprehensive framework of derivatives risk management and controls that are tailored to their situation. The hope is that these entities live up to that ideal, but reality often falls short of this goal. Hence the regulators' concern.

We wish to thank Howard Kramer, senior associate director, and Caite McGuire, chief counsel, Division of Market Regulation, SEC; David M. Levine, special assistant to the general counsel, and Christopher P. Gilkerson, attorney, Office of the General Counsel, SEC; Wayne M. Carlin, assistant regional director, SEC Northeast Regional Office; and Jennifer Yoon, National Economic Research Associates, formerly accountant/economist, Division of Market Regulation, SEC, for the helpful comments and suggestions they made in the course of the preparation of this chapter. Any mistakes remain ours.

This chapter is adapted from a longer piece that appeared in 21 J. Corp. L. 177 (1995).

As a matter of policy, the SEC disclaims responsibility for any private publication or statement by any of its employees. The views expressed herein do not necessarily represent the views of the SEC or its staff.

For a dealer or end-user, the obvious goal of any derivatives risk management structure is to reduce firm-specific risk. For regulators, this structure has the less obvious but important goal of reducing systemic risk by making derivatives risk management ubiquitous. Systemic risk is the risk that a disruption at a firm, in a market segment, or to a settlement system could cascade to other firms or other market segments, thereby affecting the financial system as a whole.[5] Such concerns include the possibility that market liquidity could deteriorate if many market participants were to attempt to liquidate their positions at the same time, or that attempts to hedge derivatives exposure through trading in the cash market could lead to further disruption.[6] A single firm employing a flawed trading strategy can have tragic consequences for that one firm. Many firms employing such a strategy can have broader repercussions.[7] Thus, from a regulatory perspective, it is the potential systemic risk posed by market activity in derivatives[8] that makes sound risk management practices imperative. Ultimately, dealers, end-users, and the investing public in general benefit from a well-managed financial marketplace.

The guidance provided by the financial industry and its regulators regarding derivatives risk management demonstrates a belief that entities bear a responsibility to manage the risks posed by derivatives. Regulators and regulatory groups including the SEC;[9] the Commodity Futures Trading Commission (CFTC),[10] the United Kingdom Securities and Investments Board (SIB),[11] the Office of the Comptroller of the Currency (OCC),[12] the General Accounting Office (GAO),[13] the International Organization of Securities Commissions (IOSCO),[14] and the Basle Committee on Banking Supervision (Basle Committee)[15] have issued reports and papers on this subject. At a meeting in Windsor, England hosted by the SIB and the CFTC, financial futures regulatory authorities from 16 countries[16] issued the Windsor Declaration outlining measures to strengthen regulatory cooperation regarding the international futures markets.[17] More recently, the Basle Committee and IOSCO issued a joint statement announcing their common goal of "improving the quality of supervision worldwide and responding to financial market developments in a timely, effective and efficient manner."[18] Industry groups such as the G-30[19] and the Derivatives Policy Group (DPG)[20] also have considered the issue of derivatives risk management.[21] For these recommendations to be of any use, however, they must be implemented by those who actually engage in derivatives transactions.[22]

This chapter provides an overview of derivatives risk management practices, including guidance regarding the role of dealer and end-user directors and senior management in the oversight of risk management, and the means by which specific kinds of risk posed by derivatives can be addressed.[23] These risks include market, credit, liquidity, operational, legal, and systemic risk. Although these risks are not unique to derivatives, the need to understand and manage them is magnified by the complexity and potential leverage of derivatives products.

RISK MANAGEMENT OVERSIGHT

The oversight of an entity's overall risk management framework begins with its board of directors (or comparable body).[24] The board of directors should understand and approve all significant policies relating to a company's risk management, including the risk management of derivatives activities. The board is responsible for establishing the nature of the entity's derivatives activities and the appropriate guidelines governing those activities. The board of directors should define the company's fundamental risk management policies and ensure that these policies are consistent with the company's broader business strategies, management expertise, capital strength, and overall appetite for risk. Because board of directors' responsibilities are continuous, a board regularly should evaluate derivatives risk management policies and procedures, with a special emphasis placed on defining its risk tolerance for these activities.[25] Communication between the board of directors and management responsible for operating the risk management process should be maintained.

The role of senior management, in general, is to ensure that effective derivatives risk management policies and procedures are implemented and maintained. Senior management should address matters such as managerial oversight and responsibilities, the scope of derivatives activities, risk tolerance, the means by which risk is to be measured and reported, and the operational controls that will be in place.[26] In addition, senior management should keep itself regularly informed of the company's risk exposure, and any material deviations from policy should be reported to the board.[27] Senior management must ensure that all approvals are obtained and that appropriate risk management procedures and systems are in place prior to entering into derivatives transactions.[28] Before engaging in derivatives transactions management should provide the following information to the board of directors, as applicable: an explanation of the financial products, markets, and business strategies; the resources required to establish risk management systems and to hire individuals with the necessary professional expertise in derivatives; whether the derivatives activities are appropriate given the firm's financial condition and capital levels; the risks associated with derivatives transactions, and the procedures that will be used to measure, monitor, and control those risks; relevant accounting guidelines; and relevant tax treatment. Finally, a determination should be made whether the entity legally is permitted to enter into derivatives activities, and whether there are any legal restrictions on those activities.[29] In keeping with the foregoing, senior management should evaluate the entity's risk management procedures regularly. Finally, it should be recognized that, especially for highly leveraged derivative transactions, compensation structures should seek to reinforce prudent risk taking by the firm and discourage traders from thinking they receive all the short-term profits while the firm retains all the long-term risk.[30]

Policies and procedures should be implemented prior to entering into derivatives transactions. An entity's policies and procedures should address such issues as measuring market and credit risk; criteria for appropriate counterparties, strategies, and products; risk monitoring procedures; hiring personnel with derivatives expertise; separating trading from risk management; and management controls over accounts, traders, operational staff, and systems.[31] The board of directors and senior management should ensure that they understand the risk management and reporting procedures and find that they are appropriate.[32] In addition, effective procedures are essential to ensure that derivatives activities are carried out in accordance with authorized policies and are subject to appropriate operational controls.[33] Any significant change in derivatives activity should be approved by the board of directors or designated senior management.[34]

Large derivatives-related losses do not occur in a vacuum. An environment of lax management controls provides the opportunity for an individual to embark on a disastrous derivatives strategy. Moreover, these examples demonstrate the rapidity with which such events arise and unfold.[35] The lesson to be learned from these massive losses is the need by both broker-dealers and end-users to have effective risk management procedures and controls.

MANAGING SPECIFIC RISKS

Derivatives can represent various kinds of risk, including market risk, credit risk, liquidity risk, legal risk, and operational risk. Because any one of these risks can pose danger for an entity, it is important that an entity understand and address each of these risks.

Market Risk Management

As with other financial instruments, the market risk of a derivative product is the risk of adverse price, interest rate, index level, volatility, and other fluctuations, typically in the underlying instrument.[36] Losses by corporate and governmental entities suggest that directors and senior management sometimes may not fully appreciate the market risk, amplified by leverage,[37] to which they are exposed in connection with their derivatives activities.[38]

There is much that dealers and end-users can do to manage the market risk that may arise from their derivatives transactions. Available methods include marking to market,[39] using a portfolio approach to managing market risk, hedging, and understanding the risks associated with different categories of derivatives. These methods are applicable to end-users as well, although the degree to which end-users should adopt them will depend on the nature and scope of their derivatives activities.

Market participants should mark their derivatives positions to market at least once a day. This allows dealers and end-users to measure the current value of derivatives cash flows and provides information about market risk and how to hedge that risk. A company then can implement appropriate hedging responses.[40] Marking to market currently is a widespread practice among dealers.[41] Intraday or real time mark to market valuations provide further benefits.

Effectively marking to market naturally requires appropriate market valuation methodologies. One approach is to employ bid/offer quotes to determine the market value of an entity's derivatives portfolio. End-users either may mark at the bid-longs (the price at which they can sell to dealers), or mark at ask-short (the price at which they may buy from a dealer). Dealers may use inside-bid or inside-ask prices (the prices dealers quote to each other when trading for their own inventories) to mark to market. In the absence of actual dealer quotes, an entity may use a mark to model approach by relying on pricing and risk measurement models. In relying on such models, however, an entity should evaluate carefully their accuracy.[42]

An alternative approach is to base valuation on midmarket levels, less specific adjustments (the adjustments made to midmarket levels are assumed implicitly in the bid or offer method). Such adjustments include taking into account the degree of credit risk reflected in a portfolio and the costs of administering a portfolio. For portfolios that are not perfectly matched, two additional adjustments are necessary: "close-out costs adjustment" (cost of buying or selling hedge instruments to eliminate market risk from the unhedged portion of the portfolio); and "investing and funding costs adjustment" (cost of funding and investing cash flow mismatches).[43]

It is essential for an entity to calculate the market risk of the positioning of its derivatives. To do so, an entity should select a consistent measure that will allow it to evaluate the degree of market risk it is undertaking in comparison to the limits of its market risk. One measure of market risk is "value at risk."[44] The value at risk approach seeks to predict the amount of money that a portfolio could lose from an adverse market movement with a specified probability over a particular period of time (e.g., two or three standard deviations and two week exposure). The market conditions are based on assumptions regarding implied or historical volatility and the degree of probability, also called the confidence interval, that the assumed level of volatility will not be reached.[45] In measuring the effectiveness of value at risk in market risk management, estimated market risk exposure should be compared to the actual behavior of an entity's positions.[46] Deviations between actual and expected behavior would warrant adjustments in the assumptions underlying a firm's value at risk analysis.[47] Value at risk measurements can provide a firm with invaluable information for establishing position limits for traders, but they do not represent the liquidation value of a given portfolio. Instead, value at risk can be seen as measuring the degree of risk that a firm must hedge over a given time period and, thus, the amount of risk to be controlled.[48]

In conjunction with a value at risk analysis, dealers should identify revenue sources, the amount of revenue those sources generate, and the degree of risk they pose. This process permits a better understanding of the risks and rewards that flow from various derivatives strategies. Revenue sources include origination revenue, credit spread revenue, and returns of derivatives activity.[49] Entities periodically should evaluate expected cash investing and funding requirements associated with their derivatives activities.[50] As part of developing risk management systems, models, and procedures, derivatives users should ask the question whether the results are consistent with those one would expect from the value being put at risk.[51]

Value at risk is useful for examining a firm's day-to-day market risk exposure, but it may not accurately reflect the effects of a once-a-year event.[52] Moreover, value at risk relies on the assumption that historical data necessarily will serve as a predictor of the future.[53] Because this is not necessarily the case, an entity should perform stress tests to determine how its portfolio would perform under conditions of extreme market volatility. Employing a broad range of stress scenarios that reflect both past and potential future events provides the most useful information regarding the effect of severe market shocks on a given portfolio of securities.[54] Such stress scenarios should evaluate the effects market shocks would have on an entity's capital and its earnings.[55]

Financial entities should ensure that the market risk monitoring function is clearly independent of the trading and sales function, and that the individuals charged with managing market risk have the authority to develop and implement market risk policies and procedures. Appropriate policies and procedures relating to market risk include: establishing risk limits and ensuring that such limits are adhered to by monitoring transactions and positions, developing stress tests, generating revenue reports that compare the revenue generated by each risk component to the amount of risk reflected by such components, ensuring that portfolio volatility corresponds to expectations, and reviewing and approving pricing models and valuation systems. Market risk management should be administered by someone at board or near board level.[56]

End-users, when determining the valuation and market risk management practices to implement, should take into account the scope and complexity of their derivatives program.[57] Relevant practices include marking to market, forecasting cash investing and funding requirements, and establishing an independent and authoritative risk management structure. According to the G-30, end-users enter into derivatives transactions that are designed to address the specific market risks of their business activities.[58] Thus, an entity with derivatives activities that are limited to its business position and are of relatively low volume may require a less complex risk measurement system than would a derivatives dealer.[59]

Credit Risk Management

Credit risk is the risk that a derivatives contract counterparty could default.[60] The amount of credit risk a particular contract represents can be expressed as the positive value, if any, the contract has to the non-defaulting party when neither party has defaulted, less any amount that the non-defaulting party has been able to collect from the defaulting party. Thus, it is the replacement cost or market value of the contract.[61] A related credit risk is settlement risk, the risk that funds or instruments will not be delivered to a firm when expected.[62] In the context of OTC derivatives, an entity is exposed to the credit risk posed by its counterparty. Thus, each counterparty depends on the other's continued financial well-being for payment on its contract. In contrast, standardized exchange-traded derivatives rely on a clearing agency, such as the Options Clearing Corporation, to stand between each buyer and seller, guaranteeing the performance of each contract. Counterparty credit risk thereby is reduced because the clearing agency collects margin from each member to guarantee all participant transactions. In effect, the risk of each individual transaction is mutualized across all clearing agency participants.[63] With respect to OTC derivatives, credit risk can be reduced and controlled by establishing procedures to measure and monitor credit risk exposure, master agreements for netting purposes, counterparty selection criteria, and collateral.[64]

Dealers and end-users should measure credit risk exposure in terms of current exposure and potential exposure. Current exposure represents credit risk at a given moment and can be expressed as the aggregate value of an entity's outstanding contracts, taking into account legally enforceable netting, if applicable.[65] Dealers should measure their current exposure daily, while the frequency with which end-users should undertake such monitoring depends on the extent of their derivatives activities.[66] Potential exposure is an estimate of the degree to which the current exposure of a portfolio could increase over a selected time period.[67] Thus, potential exposure represents the future replacement costs of derivatives transactions. Assessing potential exposure is more difficult and requires reliance on simulation analysis and options valuation models. This process includes evaluating the effects of movements in the prices of underlying variables. Once potential exposure has been evaluated, it should be reflected as an "add-on" to current exposure when evaluating the total credit risk that an entity's portfolio represents.[68]

Dealers and end-users should aggregate their derivative and other credit exposures with respect to each of their counterparties. Aggregated credit exposures should take into consideration enforceable netting arrangements. Another good practice is to avoid concentrating transactions with a single counterparty. Dealers and end-users should calculate exposures regularly and compare them to the counterparty credit limits. A separate credit limit should be established for each counterparty prior to entering into a derivatives transaction with such a counterparty, and the credit limit should be considered together with that counterparty's other credit obligations to the entity.[69] Current exposure involves summing the positive and negative exposures represented by transactions in a portfolio. Potential exposure requires modeling the effects of various changes in prices and volatilities on the entire portfolio.[70]

As part of managing credit risk, dealers and end-users should seek, when possible, to enter into master agreements with each of their counterparties to document existing and future transactions.[71] Under a bilateral closeout netting agreement, upon a party's default, obligations from the derivatives transactions covered by the netting agreement are based on the net value of those transactions. Thus, a single net closeout amount for similar contracts with the same counterparties is paid following the default of one of the counterparties.[72] In its proposal to recognize the validity of bilateral netting agreements for determining credit exposures, the Basle Committee on Banking Supervision stated that netting agreements would be recognized if legally enforceable in all applicable jurisdictions, but netting agreements with walk-away clauses (allowing a nondefaulting counterparty to avoid paying its obligations to the defaulting party) would not be recognized.[73] As new products are developed, dealers and end-users should address the legal enforceability of such products.[74] Guarantees for credit enhancement purposes can be provided by banks, insurance companies, and parent companies for their subsidiaries.[75]

Dealers and end-users should consider using credit enhancements and related arrangements such as collateral, letters of credit, guarantees, and special purpose vehicles.[76] In addition, an entity should consider limiting the extent to which its assets are encumbered because they are being used as collateral.[77] Collateral as a credit enhancement between financial counterparties often occurs on a bilateral basis. Thus, neither party will post collateral at the initiation of a contract, but if the obligation of one counterparty to the other reaches a prescribed level, an obligation on the part of that counterparty to post collateral is triggered. In situations where one of the counterparties is a weaker credit, the stronger credit might impose a one-way collateral agreement. The weaker credit would then have to post collateral at the agreement's inception.

Independent credit risk management is critical both for dealers and end-users. The credit risk management function is responsible for: (1) approving credit exposure measurement standards, (2) setting credit limits and monitoring adherence to such limits, (3) reviewing counterparty creditworthiness and concentration of credit risk, and (4) reviewing and monitoring risk-reduction arrangements. Dealers should have their credit exposure monitored by an independent credit risk management group. For end-users, this function need not necessarily be performed by a separate group, although this task still should be performed by someone independent from dealing personnel. Independence is essential to prevent conflicts of interests and to ensure objective credit exposure assessment.[78]

Liquidity Risk Management

Liquidity risk comes in two forms. Market liquidity risk is the risk that an entity may be unable to unwind or offset a derivatives transaction in a timely manner,[79] or at or near the previous market price.[80] Market liquidity risk can arise because the size of a particular transaction could affect the market for a specific instrument, or from sudden or unexpected shifts in prices or volatility.[81] Funding liquidity risk[82] is the risk that an entity cannot meet its payment obligations on settlement date, or meet margin calls due to mismatches of inflows and outflows of funds.[83]

As part of managing market liquidity risk, an entity must first understand the characteristics of a particular market, including its size, depth, and liquidity. A loss of liquidity can arise when an entity's or its counterparty's creditworthiness declines, or during periods of overall market stress. Under such conditions, an entity may find it more difficult and costly to hedge its exposures, as its ability to obtain access to particular financial markets may be curtailed.[84] Even the deepest markets can suffer a loss of liquidity under conditions of severe financial turmoil. This was underscored by the October 1987 market crash,[85] when flawed assumptions regarding market liquidity were revealed. Portfolio insurance, which was prevalent prior to the 1987 crash, depended on infinite liquidity, and institutions relied on such insurance to protect themselves in a declining market. Institutions would sell futures as the index underlying such futures would lose value. Later, the futures would be repurchased at a lower price, generating a profit that would offset the losses on the underlying equity portfolio that the institution held. An institution could benefit further if the value of the market later rose. To be successful, portfolio insurance required an endless supply of market liquidity to perpetuate the strategy. The preconception of infinite liquidity turned out to be "an illusion of liquidity."[86] As the 1987 crash unfolded, the inability of the futures and equity markets to absorb the selling pressures was magnified by sell orders spilling over from one market to the other.[87]

Another example of market liquidity risk arose when interest rates rose sharply in early 1994, and the liquidity of the CMO market vanished (reflected by bid/ask spreads increasing to 10%).[88] Reports in the press have suggested that this loss of liquidity resulted from the hesitancy of the original dealers who had sold CMOs to make markets for their customers.[89]

Market liquidity risk concerns should be addressed in an entity's guidelines, which should consider the availability of alternative markets or require that enough collateral be set aside to cover certain circumstances.[90] Extreme transaction concentration in a single market, particularly one where liquidity cannot be assured absolutely, is to be avoided. In addition, an entity can diversify the types of derivatives transactions in which it engages and implement exposure limits for individual types of products. Finally, requiring traders to warn risk managers of indications of market illiquidity is advisable.[91]

Funding liquidity risk can arise in connection with the management of an entity's derivatives portfolio. An entity should have procedures in place that address the funding requirements caused by market changes and their effect on cash flows, collateral, and margin requirements. Specifically, procedures should be in place to identify and address timing mismatches in offsetting payment and delivery obligations. Such mismatches can be caused by contractual terms such as early termination provisions.[92] The possible need to rebalance portfolios, provide extra collateral, and manage potential defaults also should be considered.[93]

A firm should assess realistically its assumptions concerning the interrelation of different markets and the funding liquidity risk implications they present. MG demonstrates the need to assess market liquidity risk, and the possibility that even the most seemingly liquid markets are not always so.

Legal Risk Management

Legal risk arises from the possibility that an entity may not be able to collect on a winning position, or enforce a hedge, because a contract may not be enforceable.[94]

Legal risk can arise from inadequate documentation; actions of a counterparty without authority or subject to certain legal restrictions; the uncertain legality of the contract itself, including contractual provisions requiring collateral;[95] and the effect that the bankruptcy or insolvency of a counterparty can have on contractual remedies, such as netting provisions.[96] The issue of legal risk is particularly vexing regarding derivatives because many existing laws were written before the types of transactions to which they might apply were even imagined.[97] Often, the form rather than the substance of a particular derivatives transaction can determine the applicable legal framework.

Inadequate documentation of OTC derivatives transactions can raise issues regarding legal risk, although such concerns have been alleviated in recent years. Standard industry forms, such as the International Swaps and Derivatives Association's (ISDA) Master Agreement,[98] now exist and are flexible enough to reflect the many varied terms of OTC transactions. Of course, the very flexibility of such forms requires that the parties to an OTC transaction ensure that the form chosen is appropriate and that the effects of the particular provisions selected are well understood.[99]

State law statute of frauds requirements applicable to a given OTC derivatives transaction can pose another form of documentation risk.[100] OTC derivatives transactions are often entered into by telephone, to be followed later by a writing setting forth the terms of the agreement.[101] A large market movement against one of the parties prior to a written confirmation of the terms of an oral agreement could cause that party to attempt to repudiate the contract.[102] In New York, recent amendments to the New York Commercial Code have eased concerns about such oral agreements by creating an exception for "qualified financial contracts."[103] An agreement that constitutes a qualified financial contract is not void for lack of a writing if there is either sufficient evidence that a contract has been made,[104] or the parties agree by prior or subsequent written agreement to be bound by such a contract from the time they reach agreement (by telephone, e-mail, or otherwise).[105] It has been noted that New York's statute of frauds exemption does not include all financial contracts. Oral contracts with a natural person as a counterparty are not covered, and master agreements must be checked to ensure they apply to oral contracts.[106]

The enforceability of netting agreements in bankruptcy also poses questions of legal risk. Therefore, it is especially important that such agreements be evaluated carefully to ensure that they are legally enforceable in all applicable jurisdictions before they are relied upon.[107] Concerns have been expressed regarding the viability of netting agreements in certain jurisdictions should a counterparty became bankrupt or insolvent. Specifically, there is concern that a bankruptcy court could "cherry-pick" those transactions beneficial to the bankruptcy estate, and that termination procedures pursuant to an agreement could be affected by bankruptcy automatic stay provisions that exist in certain jurisdictions.[108] The enforceability of close-out netting agreements in the United States is for the most part assured.[109] Less certain is the enforceability of such agreements vis-a-vis entities organized outside the United States.[110] An entity also should ensure that it can exercise its rights regarding any collateral or margin that it receives from a counterparty.[111]

Effective legal risk management occurs before an entity enters into a transaction and essentially requires that the proper homework has been done. An entity's legal counsel, in consultation with its risk management personnel, should develop the policies and procedures relating to legal risk to address issues such as the authority of the individual representing the counterparty to enter into a transaction and the legal and regulatory authority of the entity itself to enter into a particular transaction. Agreements that govern derivatives transactions should be evaluated to determine the sufficiency and legality of their contents.

Operational Risk Management

Operational risk is the risk of loss arising from human error, management failure, and fraud, or from shortcomings in systems or controls.[112] The inherent complexity of derivatives only heightens such risks.[113] Operational risk management sometimes is seen as a discrete aspect of overall risk management. For purposes of this chapter, however, a broader view of operational risk is taken. Thus, if all other risks have been considered and addressed properly, there remains the risk that the unknown and unexpected may arise. The goal of managing operational risk, then, is to recognize that certain events, such as fraud, the departure of key personnel, and computer errors, will occur. A firm should be prepared to address such events when manifested in a manner that minimizes their harmful effects.

To manage the operational risks of derivatives transactions, a firm should put in place an effective framework of systems, operations, and controls. Specifically, three elements must be considered: the people involved in derivatives transactions, the framework within which the activities are undertaken, and the systems that are used.[114]

Senior management should devote sufficient resources to employ individuals with the requisite skills and experience to transact in, and manage the risks of, derivatives, as well as to process, report, control, and audit the derivatives activities of the company.[115] Similarly, those who supervise such persons should be familiar with these matters.[116] An entity's management should designate those individuals who are authorized to enter into derivatives transactions, clearly delineate the lines of responsibility for managing the risks of derivatives activities, and communicate this information to potential counterparties. The last point is important because an entity may be liable for a transaction undertaken by an employee lacking the authority to enter into that transaction, but who appears to have that authority. The competency of those chosen to undertake derivatives and related risk management activities should be reassessed periodically.[117]

As part of an entity's control framework, its board of directors (or comparable body) should ensure that the market and credit risk management controls are independent of its trading operations.[118] Independence should be both managerial and financial. Thus, the salaries and bonuses of those involved with the risk management function should not depend on the profits derived from trading activities or selling efforts, nor should such persons answer to anyone whose compensation is related to such profits.[119] Similarly, an entity should ensure that the legal and accounting consequences of its derivatives activities, including how such activities will be booked, are considered by persons independent of the trading function.[120]

A firm's control framework should include a compensation plan that reflects the risk-taking associated with derivatives activities, as well as their profitability. Otherwise, a company may find itself creating a moral hazard where employees may be tempted to engage in excessive risk-taking to maximize their pay. This is especially so because profits tend to be booked immediately, whereas their related risks only may manifest themselves much later when the responsible employee already has pocketed his bonus and may be long gone. Of course, it is easier said than done to temper profit making by factoring in adherence to prudent risk management. Policies that can reign in excessive risk taking are generally those that tie an employee's compensation to a firm's long-term well-being. For example, a salary plus bonus system may be preferable to a purely commission-based system. Similarly, offering compensation in terms of an equity interest in the firm and rewarding employees for exercising sound risk management judgment should be considered.[121]

An effective control framework should ensure, as a matter of routine, that cash flows are being tracked. This permits a firm to verify that the trades a trader is reporting correspond to those being recorded by the back office. Keeping track of cash flows also allows risk managers to compare trading activities with trading limits.[122] As commentators have noted, firms should be just as concerned with unexpected profits as unexpected losses.[123] By tracking and understanding the sources of its revenue, a firm is in a better position to assess the potential risk of loss that a given technique presents.[124]

A board should ensure that an internal audit system exists that is undertaken by competent professionals who are knowledgeable about derivatives. The purpose of such an audit is to review risk operations to ensure that an entity's risk management policies and procedures are adhered to, including compliance with limits on derivatives activities.[125] The audit system should evaluate the existence of potential weaknesses in an entity's internal controls.[126] An external audit provides added protection that internal controls are not being overridden.[127]

Sufficient resources must be allocated so that appropriate data processing facilities are available to ensure adequate accounting, risk management, and information systems for data capture, processing, settlement, and management reporting. This involves the establishment of appropriate systems and their maintenance. Planning the appropriate allotment of resources should be undertaken as part of an entity's program to implement the use of derivatives.[128] The sophistication and extent of risk management systems should be commensurate with an entity's expected level of derivatives activities. At a minimum, such systems should have the capability to monitor an entity's exposure arising from its derivatives activities, including the degree of market and credit risk,[129] and the ability to communicate that information to management.[130]

An entity's front and back office systems for derivatives should be integrated with a firm's other management information systems to enhance efficiency and reliability.[131] More generally, the greater the degree of integration among an entity's trading and back office systems, the greater that firm's ability to measure the amount of risk its activities present. There are several obstacles that may prevent this goal from being realized. First, financial activities often are fragmented among several segments of a firm, each with its own expectations regarding its activities, and communication among segments often can be piecemeal. Second, each segment may have its own, sometimes incompatible systems. Such systems often are established at different times to fulfill different needs. Third, until recently, off-the-shelf systems products have tended to be designed for a specific kind of product or risk, requiring that any fully integrated system be developed in-house.[132] The third obstacle now may be less problematic than it once was. Despite past limitations of commercially available risk management products, apparently some progress has been made in creating product specific systems that can be integrated with other systems.[133] Firms will have to determine whether such systems are appropriate for them. In the absence of integrated systems, not surprisingly, a firm may find it difficult to aggregate in a meaningful way data relating to its financial activities. The presence of integrated systems allows the firm to manipulate data firm-wide according to specific parameters such as product type and customer identity. A firm also will find it easier to realize a goal of real-time risk measurement.[134]

CONCLUSION

Properly used, derivative products provide a valuable contribution to the nation's capital markets. Although the development of such products will continue to raise issues regarding how those products should be integrated within the existing oversight structure (e.g., capital standards,[135] accounting rules,[136] disclosure requirements, and sales practices[137]), the one area where there is a well developed consensus is the need for sophisticated risk management strategies. In this regard, derivatives are not unique in raising concerns regarding the management of highly leveraged, complex products,[138] but they do highlight the need for managers and regulators to evaluate such products carefully to ensure that their benefits are not overwhelmed by their risks.

ENDNOTES

1. For the purposes of this chapter, the term derivative will be used broadly to include financial instruments that derive their value from the performance of underlying securities, currencies, commodities, interest rates, or indices; or that form a constituent part of and derive their value from underlying whole securities. Such instruments often are characterized as being leveraged and having a limited life. Derivative instruments include standardized exchange-traded options and futures; individually negotiated over-the-counter (OTC) options, swaps, and forwards; structured notes with embedded options; and a wide variety of debt instruments, such as collateralized mortgage obligations (CMOs), that have payoff characteristics reflecting embedded derivatives, or have option characteristics, or are created by "stripping" particular components of other instruments such as principal or interest payments.

A broad range of financial instruments have been described as falling within the ambit of the term "derivative." So many instruments have been characterized as derivatives that there is currently a debate over what instruments properly are called derivatives and whether the term has been bled of meaning. *See, e.g.*, Henry T.C. Hu, *Hedging Expectations: "Derivative Reality" and the Law and Finance of the Corporate Objective*, 73 TEX. L. REV. 985, 996–1000 (1995), *reprinted in* 21 J. CORP. L. 1 (1995) (providing an overview of the way the term "derivative" has been defined and used by various commentators and market participants); Saul S. Cohen, *The Challenge of Derivatives*, 63 FORDHAM L. REV. 1993, 1994 (1995) (arguing that the term "derivatives" "operates without definitional borders").

The Group of Thirty's (G-30) Derivatives Study Group defines an OTC "derivatives transaction" as:

> a bilateral contract or payments exchange agreement whose value derives . . . from the value of an underlying asset or underlying reference rate or index. [D]erivatives transactions cover a broad range of "underlyings"—interest rates, exchange rates, commodities, equities, and other indexes.

GLOBAL DERIVATIVES STUDY GROUP, G-30, DERIVATIVES: PRACTICES AND PRINCIPLES 28 (1993) [hereinafter G-30 REPORT].

The SEC has proposed amendments to Regulation S-X, Regulation S-K, and various forms, including Form 20-F, relating to requirements for financial statement footnote disclosures of registrants' accounting policies for derivative financial instruments, as well as to the disclosure of outside financial statements of qualitative and quantitative information about market risk inherent in derivative financial instruments, other financial instruments, and derivative commodity instruments. Proposed Amendments to Require Disclosure of Accounting Policies for Derivative Financial Instruments and Derivative Commodity Instruments and Disclosure of Qualitative and Quantitative Information About

Market Risk Inherent in Derivative Financial Instruments, Other Financial Instruments, and Derivative Commodity Instruments, Release Nos. 33-7250, 34-36643, IC-21625, 61 Fed. Reg. 578 (1996) [hereinafter Accounting Release]. In defining "derivative financial instrument," the SEC relies on DISCLOSURES ABOUT DERIVATIVE FINANCIAL INSTRUMENTS AND FAIR VALUE OF FINANCIAL INSTRUMENTS, Statement of Financial Accounting Standards No. 119, ¶¶ 5-7 (Fin. Accounting Standards Bd. 1994) [hereinafter FAS 119]. FAS 119 defines a "derivative financial instrument" to be a futures, forward, swap, or option contract, or other financial instrument with similar characteristics. FAS 119, ¶¶ 5-7. The Accounting Release defines "other financial instruments" to include trade account receivables and payables, mortgage-backed securities, interest-only and principal-only obligations, indexed debt instruments, deposits, and other debt obligations. Accounting Release. Finally, the Accounting Release defines "derivative commodity instrument," to the extent such instruments are not derivative financial instruments, to include commodity futures, commodity forwards, commodity swaps, commodity options, and other commodity instruments with similar characteristics. Id.

The question whether a given type of derivative financial instrument is a security under the federal securities laws does not have a ready answer. Compare In re Gary S. Missner, Release No. 34-7304 (June 11, 1996) and In re BT Securities Corp., Release No. 34-7124 (December 22, 1994)(finding certain types of derivative financial instruments to be securities) with Proctor & Gamble Co. v. Bankers Trust Co. and BT Securities Corp., 925 F.Supp. 1270 (S.D. Ohio 1996)(finding instruments not to be securities for federal securities law purposes). See also Brandon Becker & Joshua Fisher, OTC Derivatives and the Federal Securities Laws after Procter & Gamble v. Bankers Trust, in Swaps and Other Derivatives in 1996 (PLI Corp. Law & Practice Course Handbook)(forthcoming Oct. 1996)(attempting to reconcile the P&G v. BT opinion with the SEC's views on whether a swap can be a security).

2. In recent years there have been many articles discussing the potential and actual risks posed by derivatives. See, e.g., Carol J. Loomis, Untangling the Derivatives Mess, FORTUNE, Mar. 20, 1995, at 50 (describing several losses suffered by companies in 1994 and early 1995 attributable to derivatives activities); Suzanne McGee, Commodities: 'Plain Vanilla' Derivatives Can Also Be Poison, WALL ST. J., Mar. 20, 1995, at C1 (stressing that exchange-traded derivatives are no less risky than OTC derivatives); Terence P. Pare & Tricia Welsh, Learning to Live with Derivatives, FORTUNE, July 25, 1994, at 106, 107 (stating that "[o]ver the past 12 months, virtually every kind of institution that handles other people's money has taken a hit from derivatives"); Carol J. Loomis, The Risk that Won't Go Away, FORTUNE, Mar. 7, 1994, at 40 (describing the types of risks presented by derivatives); The Regulators Balk, ECONOMIST, Apr. 10, 1993, at 30 (stating that derivatives do not present too much risk so long as they are managed properly); Saul Hansell & Kevin Muehring, Why Derivatives Rattle the Regulators, INSTITUTIONAL INVESTOR, Sept. 1992, at 49 (describing the growth of derivatives, the types of risk they pose, and the need to address those risks); Steven Lipin & William Power, "Derivatives" Draw Warnings from Regulators, WALL ST. J., Mar. 25, 1992, at C1 (describing regulators' concerns regarding derivatives).

For a compendium listing more than 100 examples of financial losses attributed to derivatives, see Brandon Becker & Jennifer Yoon, Derivative Financial Losses, 21 J. CORP. L. 215 (1995).

3. Balvinder S. Sangha, Financial Derivatives: Applications and Policy Issues, BUS. ECON., Jan. 1995, at 46; see also Roger D. Blanc, Policy Issues Presented by Derivatives Trading, INSIGHTS, June 1994, at 10; James H. McCord & Allan C. Martin, Derivatives—Power Tools for Pension Funds, FIN. EXECUTIVE, Nov. 1993, at 19; OFFICE OF THE COMPTROLLER OF THE CURRENCY BANKING CIRCULAR 277, RISK MANAGEMENT OF FINANCIAL DERIVATIVES 3 (1993) [hereinafter OCC BC-277] (replacing OCC BANKING CIRCULAR 79, NATIONAL BANK PARTICIPATION IN THE FINANCIAL FUTURES AND FORWARD PLACEMENT MARKETS (1983)); Equity-Index-Linked Swaps, Go Global, Stay at Home, EUROMONEY, Aug. 1992, at 36.

Derivatives can be viewed as a market stabilization device, acting as private insurance replacing government action. The end of Bretton Woods and the fixed exchange rate system in the early 1970s, together with the deregulation of bank activities, has created a need for those exposed to financial price fluctuations to manage those risks. See John Plender, Through a Market Darkly: Is the Fear that Derivatives are a Multi-Billion Accident Waiting to Happen Justified?, FIN. TIMES, May 27, 1994, at 17; cf., Timothy A. Canova, The Transformation of U.S. Banking and Finance: From Regulated Competition to Free-Market Receivership, 60 BROOK. L. REV. 1295 (1995). Canova argues that bank deregulation led banks to offer higher rates to depositors and concomitantly caused them to take on greater risks to pay those rates. Id. at 1327-28. Such risk taking, Canova argues, eventually led to the savings and loan crisis. Id. at 1333.

4. Henry T.C. Hu, Misunderstood Derivatives: The Causes of Informational Failure and the Promise of Regulatory Incrementalism, 102 YALE L.J. 1457, 1503 (1993). Hu states:

The comparative, if not absolute, advantage of private entities lies in the production of bank-specific risk information, while regulators have a comparative advantage in the production of systemic risk information. Comparative advantage dictates that the private sector produce bank-specific risk information and the public sector produce systemic risk information.

Id.

5. G-30 Report, *supra* note 1, at 61 (citing Bank for International Settlements, Recent Developments in International Interbank Relations 61 (1992) [hereinafter Promisel Report]).

6. Derivative Markets: Hearings Before the Subcomm. on Agriculture/Environment, Credit and Rural Development of the House Comm. on Agriculture, 103d Cong., 2d Sess. 40 (1994) (testimony of Brandon Becker, Director, Division of Market Regulation, SEC) [hereinafter Becker Testimony].

SEC Chairman, Arthur Levitt, stated in testimony:

[E]ven though [derivatives] may serve to reduce risk in many situations, in an aberrant, stressful market the leverage, complexity, liquidity risk, and global nature of OTC derivatives may make dealing with exigent circumstances more difficult. This is because derivatives, both listed and OTC, tend to link different market segments. Thus, a failure in one part of the system, such as the insolvency of a major intermediary or a sharp fall in a specific market, potentially could reverberate throughout the financial markets. Although these concerns may not be unique to derivatives, this is an area where we are concerned that a difference in degree becomes a difference in kind.

Derivative Financial Markets: Hearings Before the Subcomm. on Telecommunications and Finance of the House Comm. on Energy and Commerce, 103d Cong., 2d Sess. 192 (1994) [hereinafter Levitt Testimony].

The Presidential Task Force on Market Mechanisms, established following the 1987 market crash to determine its causes, noted that stocks, stock index futures, and stock options have become closely related and effectively constitute one market. Report of the Presidential Task Force on Market Mechanisms vi (1988) [hereinafter Brady Report]. Similarly, the Promisel Report noted that one effect of the presence of derivatives has been the strengthening of interrelatedness among markets. Promisel Report, *supra* note 5, at 19. Nevertheless, the Promisel Report noted that financial entities view their exposure to risk in isolation from the potential systemic risk that could exacerbate other types of risk at the individual firm level. *Id.*

There is debate among economists and financial analysts regarding the effects of derivatives activities on volatility in the equities markets. *See, e.g.,* Laura E. Kodres, *Existence and Impact of Destabilizing Positive Feedback Traders: Evidence from the S&P 500 Index Futures Market,* Finance and Economics Discussion Series, Div. of Research and Statistics, Div. of Monetary Affairs, Federal Reserve Board 94-9 (1994) (finding some positive feedback); Ali F. Darrat & Shafiqur Rahman, *Has Futures Trading Activity Caused Stock Price Volatility?,* 15 J. Futures Markets 537, 553 (1995) (arguing that futures activity does not cause jumps in volatility of equity markets).

7. One example cited in the Brady Report is the role played by portfolio insurance during the 1987 market crash. Brady Report, *supra* note 6, at ch. 6. For a more complete discussion regarding the 1987 market crash, see *infra* notes 85–87 and accompanying text.

8. *See, e.g.,* G-30 Report, *supra* note 1, at 61 (noting that ordinary market activities can pose systemic risk).

9. *Municipal Securities Market: Hearings Before the Subcomm. on Telecommunications and Finance of the Comm. on Energy and Commerce,* 103 Cong., 1st Sess. 4 (1993) (testimony of Arthur Levitt, Chairman, SEC); Levitt Testimony, *supra* note 6, at 31.

10. Report of the Commodity Futures Trading Commission, OTC Derivative Markets and Their Regulation (1993) [hereinafter CFTC Study]. The Conference Report to accompany P.L. 102-546, the Futures Trading Practices Act of 1992, directed the CFTC to examine whether the OTC derivatives markets required additional regulation, analyze the public policy implications of two court decisions, and consider the need for a single financial markets regulator. The CFTC Study concluded that although the current regulatory framework is sound, greater cooperation and the establishment of an interagency council to address issues regarding OTC derivatives is desirable. *Id.*

11. OTC Derivatives Oversight, Statement of the SEC, CFTC, and SIB (Mar. 14, 1994) (joint statement regarding OTC derivatives oversight setting forth ways to cooperate in regulating OTC derivatives).

12. OCC BC-277, *supra* note 3. OCC BC-277 includes recommendations regarding risk management practices for national banks, and federal branches and agencies that act as sellers and end-users of

derivative products. In defining its scope, OCC BC-277 states that although financial derivatives represent only a portion of the total risk to which banks currently are exposed, the complexity of derivatives transactions has caused banks involved in such transactions to develop sophisticated approaches in managing risk. Nevertheless, the applicability of these approaches is not limited to derivatives. *Id.; see also* OFFICE OF THE COMPTROLLER OF THE CURRENCY, RISK MANAGEMENT OF FINANCIAL DERIVATIVES, COMPTROLLER'S HANDBOOK (1994). The Comptroller's Handbook provides guidance and procedures for bank examiners to use in evaluating the risk management of derivatives by national banks and nationally chartered federal agencies and branches. *Id.* at 1.

13. GENERAL ACCOUNTING OFFICE, FINANCIAL DERIVATIVES: ACTIONS NEEDED TO PROTECT THE FINANCIAL SYSTEM (GAO/GGD-94-133) (1994) [hereinafter GAO REPORT]. The GAO Report discusses derivatives risk, risk control, and whether additional regulation is necessary. *See also* Letter from Arthur Levitt, Chairman, SEC, to The Honorable John D. Dingell, Chairman, Committee on Energy and Commerce, United States House of Representatives (July 18, 1994) (on file with the authors). Chairman Levitt's letter describes SEC efforts to implement the GAO's recommendations, including efforts to improve the collection of information regarding derivatives activities, and reviewing the capital requirements applicable to registered broker-dealers. *Id.* at 2.

14. OPERATIONAL AND FINANCIAL RISK MANAGEMENT CONTROL MECHANISMS FOR OVER-THE-COUNTER DERIVATIVES ACTIVITIES OF REGULATED SECURITIES FIRMS (Technical Committee of the International Organization of Securities Commissions Working Party No. 3, 1994) [hereinafter IOSCO PAPER]. The IOSCO Paper describes its purpose as to provide guidance to securities regulators regarding the types of risk management control mechanisms they might seek to encourage in their respective jurisdictions for entities engaged in OTC derivative transactions. *Id.* at 2.

15. BASLE COMMITTEE ON BANKING SUPERVISION, RISK MANAGEMENT GUIDELINES FOR DERIVATIVES (1994) [hereinafter BIS PAPER]. The BIS Paper seeks to provide guidance for supervisory authorities and banking organizations regarding the risk management of derivatives activities. *Id.* at 1.

A survey of derivatives market activity undertaken by the Bank for International Settlements (BIS) placed the total notional amount of OTC contracts outstanding at 40.7 trillion dollars. BANK FOR INTERNATIONAL SETTLEMENTS, CENTRAL BANK SURVEY OF DERIVATIVES MARKET ACTIVITY (1995); *see* Nicholas Bray, *Survey Offers Detailed Look at Derivatives,* WALL ST. J., Dec. 19, 1995.

16. Representatives of the regulatory authorities from the following countries participated: Australia, Brazil, Canada, France, Germany, Hong Kong, Italy, Japan, The Netherlands, Singapore, South Africa, Spain, Sweden, Switzerland, the United States, and the United Kingdom. WINDSOR DECLARATION, May 17, 1995. [hereinafter WINDSOR DECLARATION].

17. The Windsor Declaration sets forth four points of consensus among the 16 regulatory authorities. WINDSOR DECLARATION, *supra* note 16. First, they agreed that cooperation among the authorities improves the prompt communication of relevant information regarding material exposure and other matters of regulatory concern. *Id.* Second, to protect customer positions, funds, and accounts, the adequacy of existing arrangements relating to the risk of loss posed by insolvency and misappropriation should be reviewed. *Id.* Third, the regulatory authorities should promote mechanisms that facilitate the prompt liquidation or transfer of positions, funds, and assets from insolvent futures exchange members. *Id.* Fourth, the regulatory authorities agreed they should improve mechanisms relating to international cooperation among market authorities and regulators, and support measures that enhance emergency procedures for financial intermediaries, market participants, and markets. *Id.*

18. BASLE/IOSCO JOINT STATEMENT (April 1996) (on file with the authors), at 1.

19. G-30 REPORT, *supra* note 1. Published in July 1993, the G-30 Report was the first among several broad initiatives that sought to provide an overview of sound risk management practices in the face of increased financial derivatives activity. Specifically, the G-30 Report focuses on OTC derivatives transactions between dealers and end-users.

The G-30 Report has been described as an attempt to add a degree of self-regulation to the OTC derivatives market in response to increasing attention from regulators. *Roundup,* WALL ST. J., Aug. 21, 1992, at B7. By way of comparison, the SEC's regulatory approach regarding securities, including standardized derivative securities, can be described as one based on a tripartite system of broker-dealer oversight. This tripartite system relies first on broker-dealer internal controls; second, on the oversight of self-regulatory organizations; and finally, on periodic inspections and enforcement actions by the SEC itself. Brandon Becker, *A Regulatory Perspective on the Global Securities Market,* 1987 COLUM. BUS. L. REV. 309, 309-10 (1987); *see also* Jerry W. Markham, *"Confederate Bonds," "General Custer," and the Regulation of Derivative Financial Instruments,* 25 SETON HALL L. REV. 1, 2

(1994). Markham suggests an approach to OTC derivatives regulation based on the example of regulating the government securities market. *Id.* at 72–73.

20. DERIVATIVES POLICY GROUP, A FRAMEWORK FOR VOLUNTARY OVERSIGHT OF THE OTC DERIVATIVES ACTIVITIES OF SECURITIES FIRM AFFILIATES TO PROMOTE CONFIDENCE AND STABILITY IN FINANCIAL MARKETS (1995) [hereinafter DPG REPORT]. The DPG Report sets forth a framework for the voluntary oversight of the OTC derivatives activities of the unregulated affiliates of six of the largest U.S. investment banks. *Id.* at 1–2. Among the issues identified by the DPG Report are the desirability of increased information regarding the risk exposure of professional intermediaries, the means by which such exposure is controlled, and the responsibilities of professional intermediaries to, and their relationship with, nonprofessional counterparties. *Id.* at 1, 9. The DPG Report also addresses the types of internal controls firms should implement to monitor and measure the risks of OTC derivatives, and provides for the DPG participants to submit periodic quantitative reports regarding credit risk exposure and other information relating to OTC derivatives. *Id.* at 2–3.

21. Under the coordination of the Federal Reserve Bank of New York, a set of principles and practices was issued that seeks to provide guidance for dealing in OTC financial transactions. This effort was the result of a joint undertaking by representatives of the Emerging Markets Traders Association, the Foreign Exchange Committee of the Federal Reserve Bank of New York, the International Swaps and Derivatives Association, the New York Clearinghouse Associations, the Public Securities Association, and the Securities Industry Association. EMERGING MARKETS TRADERS ASS'N ET AL., THE PRINCIPLES AND PRACTICES FOR WHOLESALE FINANCIAL MARKET TRANSACTIONS (1995).

Some end-users have expressed less than whole-hearted support for these guidelines. Among their concerns are that the drafting committee did not include end-user representatives, and that the proposed guidance seems to represent an attempt by dealers to avoid legal liability for their actions by placing the onus for understanding and appreciating the risks of a prospective transaction on the end-user. *See* Joanne Morrison, *Dealers Guidelines Draw Fire from Derivatives Users,* BOND BUYER, Aug. 22, 1995, at 1; *see also End-User Group Faults Swaps Guidelines,* INS. ACCT., June 12, 1995, at 1 (commenting on the Mar. 20, 1995 draft guidelines); *Pension Group Slams Fed-Sponsored Wholesale Project,* DERIVATIVES WK., Aug. 14, 1995, at 4; Joanne Morrison, *End-Users Group Calls its Input Essential to Guidelines,* BOND BUYER, May 30, 1995, at 27; *End Users Demand Big Changes in Wholesale Code,* DERIVATIVES WK., May 29, 1995, at 1, 11.

22. "The best defense any system of investment can have against major loss is an effective risk management system and stringent internal control mechanisms." Arthur Levitt, Shareholder Interests as the Director's Touchstone, Remarks Presented at Directors' College, Stanford, California (Mar. 23, 1995) (on file with the authors) [hereinafter Levitt Stanford Speech].

23. Although the focus of this Article is on the actions that dealers and end-users can take to manage the risks, including the systemic risk, that financial derivative products can present, there exist many regulatory approaches designed to reduce systemic risk. These include revised capital and accounting rules for derivatives, *see* Accounting Release, *supra* note 1, enhanced sales practices requirements, improved disclosure standards for public companies that engage in derivatives activities, and improved disclosure and controls for mutual funds. *See* Becker Testimony, *supra* note 6. The regulation of financial activities by governmental entities plays a crucial role in the management of systemic risk. But effective regulation requires thoughtful action. One argument urges that incremental regulation is the preferred approach for contending with the challenges of financial innovation. *See* Hu, *supra* note 4, at 1496. Just as the first rule of medicine is "do no harm," so too must regulators tread carefully when evaluating a new course of regulation. An incrementalist approach reduces the potentially deleterious collateral effects of regulation and generally makes the reversal of new regulation easier if it proves undesirable. *Id.* This type of regulatory approach also underscores the importance of effective risk management and internal controls because they represent the first line of defense that derivatives dealers, end-users, and the financial system have against major losses. *See* Levitt Stanford Speech, *supra* note 22.

24. G-30 REPORT, *supra* note 1, at 9; OCC BC-277, *supra* note 3, at 4–5, 8 (noting derivatives activities should be consistent with the board of directors' overall risk management philosophy); *see also* Levitt Stanford Speech, *supra* note 22, at 7. It is to be hoped that the regulatory scrutiny that has been visited upon derivatives has helped focus the attention of dealers and end-user board of directors on derivatives and the development of new risk management techniques. *See* Tracy Corrigan, *Survey of Derivatives,* FIN. TIMES, Oct. 20, 1993, at 1 (discussing the effect of regulatory scrutiny vis-a-vis risk management).

25. BIS Paper, *supra* note 15, at 5; *cf.* OCC BC-277, *supra* note 3, at 7–8. Senior management should evaluate risk management policies and procedures at least annually; the board of directors periodically should approve significant policies. *Id.*

26. OCC BC-277, *supra* note 3, at 8.

27. BIS Paper, *supra* note 15, at 5; G-30 Report, *supra* note 1, at 9; *see also* IOSCO Paper, *supra* note 14, at 9.

28. *Cf.* Matt Murray & Paulette Thomas, *Management: After the Fall: Fingers Point and Heads Roll,* Wall St. J., Dec. 23, 1994, at B1 (describing how several companies that suffered large losses on derivatives investments later fired or demoted those who made the investment decisions). Obviously, disciplining individuals after a large loss begs the question of how those employees were able to expose their companies to potential large losses in the first place.

29. BIS Paper, *supra* note 15, at 5–6; *cf.* OCC BC-277, *supra* note 3, at 5 (concerning proposals to undertake derivatives activities).

30. *See* Eugene A. Ludwig, Comptroller of the Currency, Remarks at the European Institute's International Roundtable Seminar (Apr. 28, 1995) (on file with the authors) [hereinafter Ludwig Speech] (discussing the role of bank regulation); *see also* Marcus W. Brauchli et al., *Broken Bank-Barings PLC Official May Have Been Aware of Trader's Position,* Wall St. J., Mar. 6, 1995, at A1; David Nusbaum, *Are Your Internal Controls a Match for Operations Risk?,* Futures, June 1995, at 62, 63; *infra* note 121 and accompanying text (discussing the issue of compensation).

31. BIS Paper, *supra* note 15, at 5; G-30 Report, *supra* note 1, at 9; *see also* IOSCO Paper, *supra* note 14, at 9.

32. OCC BC-277, *supra* note 3, at 6–7. BIS Paper, *supra* note 15, at 5 (stating that the board of directors should approve all significant risk management policies, including those relating to derivatives activities); *see also* G-30 Report, *supra* note 1, at 9 (noting that the board of directors should articulate the purposes for undertaking derivatives transactions); OCC BC-277, *supra* note 3, at 5, 7 (stating that the board of directors, one of its committees, or designated senior management should approve any derivatives activities, and describing recommended contents of proposals to undertake such activities).

33. BIS Paper, *supra* note 15, at 5; G-30 Report, *supra* note 1, at 9; IOSCO Paper, *supra* note 14, at 9 (asserting that risk management policies and procedures for OTC derivatives activities should be integrated with the firm's overall management policies).

34. BIS Paper, *supra* note 15, at 6.

35. *See* John Plender, *The Box that Can Never Be Shut: The Collapse of Barings Leaves Eddie George with an Unsolved Derivatives Conundrum,* Fin. Times, Feb. 28, 1995, at 19.

36. DPG Report, *supra* note 20, at 14; G-30 Report, *supra* note 1, at 43–44; BIS Paper, *supra* note 15, at 14; IOSCO Paper, *supra* note 14, at 3–4.

37. An investment strategy has leverage if, with a given dollar of investment (either paid now or in the future upon settlement), a much larger dollar position in an instrument, or index of instruments, can be controlled.

38. For example, when interest rates rose in early 1994, many hedge funds were reported to have suffered losses ranging from 5% to 25% related to leveraged derivatives positions. Miriam Bensman, *Nine Risk Management Rules it Pays not to Forget,* Futures, June 1994, at 56.

39. Marking to market provides valuable information regarding a derivatives portfolio because it reflects the value of a portfolio's cashflows and provides information about market risk and how to hedge that risk. G-30 Report, *supra* note 1, app. I at 5 (Working Papers dated July 21, 1993). According to the Global Derivatives Study Group, valuation methodologies such as lower-of-cost-or-market and accrual accounting do not provide appropriate information for risk management. *Id.*

40. G-30 Report, *supra* note 1, at 9; IOSCO Paper, *supra* note 14, at 11–12.

41. In a survey of dealers conducted by the G-30 Global Derivatives Study Group, 85% of respondents stated that they mark to market all positions for management accounting of their trading and dealing activities. G-30 Report, *supra* note 1, app. III (Survey of Industry Practice dated Mar. 29, 1994).

42. OCC BC-277, *supra* note 3, at 13–14.

43. G-30 Report, *supra* note 1, at 9–10; *see also* DPG Report, *supra* note 20, at 20 (stating that the valuation policy should reflect fair market value and should include adjustments for credit quality, market liquidity, funding costs, and transaction costs, as appropriate); *cf.* OCC BC-277, *supra* note 3, at 31–32 (advocating that midmarket level valuation should be used over bid/offer levels).

44. G-30 REPORT, *supra* note 1, at 10, app. I at 8 (Working Papers dated July 21, 1993).

45. G-30 REPORT, *supra* note 1, at 10. In measuring market risk, the following risk elements should be considered across the time interval: price or rate change, convexity, volatility, time decay, basis or correlation, and discount rate. *Id.; see also Danger-Kids at Play*, EUROMONEY, Mar. 1995, at 43.

46. BIS PAPER, *supra* note 15, at 14; Alan Greenspan, Chairman, Board of Governors of the Federal Reserve, Remarks at the Financial Markets Conference of the Federal Reserve Bank of Atlanta (Feb. 23, 1996) (on file with the authors) [hereinafter Greenspan Speech] (noting also the importance of understanding how the risk measurements were calculated).

47. The Basle Committee on Banking Supervision has proposed that banks be allowed to use proprietary in-house models to calculate regulatory market risk capital requirements. CONSULTATIVE PROPOSAL BY THE BASLE COMMITTEE ON BANKING SUPERVISION, AN INTERNAL MODEL-BASED APPROACH TO MARKET RISK CAPITAL REQUIREMENTS (1995) [hereinafter BASLE PROPOSAL]; *see also Banking Supervision-Do-It-Yourself Regulation*, ECONOMIST, Apr. 15, 1995, at 70; John Gapper, *Basle Model for Banking Safeguards*, FIN.TIMES, Apr. 13, 1995, at 22.

IOSCO has noted that relying on firms' internal models poses certain issues, in that they implicitly assume that future events will track past ones, and that market participants may seek to rely on models that result in the lowest capital charges. REPORT BY THE TECHNICAL COMMITTEE OF IOSCO, THE IMPLICATIONS FOR SECURITIES REGULATORS OF THE INCREASED USE OF VALUE AT RISK MODELS 3 (1995) [hereinafter IOSCO VAR REPORT].

For a discussion of potential shortcomings of using internal models, *see* Paul Kupiec & James O'Brien, *Internal Affairs*, RISK, May 1995, at 43 (stating that one-day risk exposure estimates that in-house models typically generate cannot provide accurate measurements of risk over longer periods of time as are used to establish regulatory capital levels); *see also* Paul Kupiec & James O'Brien, *Model Alternative*, RISK, June 1995, at 37 (proposing alternatives to the Basle Proposal).

48. Greenspan Speech, *supra* note 46, at 9.

49. G-30 REPORT, *supra* note 1, at 10.

50. *Id.* at 12.

51. *Id.* at 10, 12-13.

52. *See, e.g.,* Paul H. Kupiec, *Techniques for Verifying the Accuracy of Risk Measurement Models* (Apr. 1995) (unpublished manuscript, on file with the authors) (stating that it is almost impossible to estimate potential losses associated with extremely unusual events).

53. *See* IOSCO VAR REPORT, *supra* note 47, at 6.

54. G-30 REPORT, *supra* note 1, at 11-12; DPG REPORT, *supra* note 20, at 20; *see also* IOSCO PAPER, *supra* note 14, at 10.

55. OCC BC-277, *supra* note 3, at 13.

56. G-30 REPORT, *supra* note 1, at 12-13; IOSCO PAPER, *supra* note 14, at 10.

57. G-30 REPORT, *supra* note 1, at 13; BIS PAPER, *supra* note 15, at 15, *cf.* OCC BC-277, *supra* note 3, at 15. Although an entity with limited derivatives activity may require less sophisticated risk measuring systems, material risks should be quantified, monitored, and controlled. *Id.*

58. G-30 REPORT, *supra* note 1, at 13; *see also* James McVay & Christor Turner, *Could Companies Use Value at Risk?*, EUROMONEY, Oct. 1995, at 84 (noting that risk management devices such as value at risk can play an important role in ensuring that internal funds are available for investment in such matters as research and investment).

59. BIS PAPER, *supra* note 15, at 15.

60. G-30 REPORT, *supra* note 1, at 47-49; DPG REPORT, *supra* note 20, at 14; IOSCO PAPER, *supra* note 14, at 3.

61. GREGORY R. DUFFEE, *On Measuring Credit Risks of Derivative Instruments, in* FINANCE AND ECONOMICS DISCUSSION SERIES 94-27, (Board of Governors of the Federal Reserve System). Even in the absence of a default, the value of a derivatives contract could fall if the credit quality of one of the counterparties were to decline. *Id.; see also* Robert M. McLaughlin, *Powerful Derivatives Involve Risks*, BUS. CREDIT, Feb. 1995, at 4.

62. IOSCO PAPER, *supra* note 14, at 4; G-30 REPORT, *supra* note 1, at 49-50. The risk that an asset underlying the derivatives instrument might default is another form of credit risk (e.g., imbedded options on corporate debt). Robert A. Jarrow & Stuart M. Turnbull, *Pricing Derivatives on Financial Securities Subject to Credit Risk*, 50 J. FIN. 53 (1995).

63. *Nightmare on Wall Street,* Euromoney, Feb. 1992, at 23, 24. As demonstrated by the 1987 market crash, the existence of a clearing agency is no guarantee against participant insolvency. For example, during the 1987 market crash, an Options Clearing Corporation clearing member, Shane, became insolvent and three other members faced severe liquidity problems. Division of Market Regulation, The October 1987 Market Break 10-44 to 10-48 (1988) [hereinafter Market Break Report]. The Options Clearing Corporation suffered an $8.5 million loss in connection with Shane's liquidation, and Options Clearing Corporation members were assessed pro rata for the loss. *Id.* at 10-45. The effect of the clearing agency's presence in the Shane liquidation was to spread the loss across all clearing members, rather than to limit that loss to Shane's counterparties. *Id.*

64. BIS Paper, *supra* note 15, at 13–14; G-30 Report, *supra* note 1, at 47. In the regulatory sphere, shortening the settlement cycle for securities transactions reduces the period of time a given transaction is exposed to settlement default risk. All things being equal, a shorter settlement cycle reduces the dollar value of all transactions outstanding. The settlement cycle in the United States securities markets recently was shortened from five business days to three. The SEC effected this change by adopting Rule 15c6-1 under the Securities Exchange Act of 1934. In adopting this rule, the SEC stated that Rule 15c6-1 is designed to reduce the inherent risk to clearing corporations, their members, and the investing public in settling securities transactions present in the clearance and settlement system at any given time. 58 Fed. Reg. 52,891-52,901 (1993) (to be codified at 17 C.F.R. pts. 200 & 240). Rule 15c6-1 became effective June 7, 1995. 17 C.F.R. 240.15c6-1 (1995).

65. G-30 Report, *supra* note 1, at 13–14; OCC BC-277, *supra* note 3, at 19 (also referring to current exposure as "mark-to-market").

66. G-30 Report, *supra* note 1, at 15.

67. Darryll Hendricks, *Netting Agreements and the Credit Exposures of OTC Derivatives Portfolios,* 19 FRBNY Q. Rev. 7, 9 (1994).

68. G-30 Report, *supra* note 1, at 13–14 (stating that potential exposure includes expected exposure and exposure under a worst case scenario); OCC BC-277, *supra* note 3, at 19–20 (referring to the inclusion of a credit risk "add-on" for market valuation).

69. Paul A. Schott, *Derivatives: A Primer on Bank Agency Actions for Managing Risks,* Banking Policy Report, Apr. 3, 1995, at 1.

70. G-30 Report, *supra* note 1, at 14–15.

71. G-30 Report, *supra* note 1, at 16; BIS Paper, *supra* note 15, at 13; IOSCO Paper, *supra* note 14, at 11–12.

72. *See* Consultative Proposal by the Basle Committee on Banking Supervision, The Supervisory Recognition of Netting for Capital Adequacy Purposes 1 (1993) [hereinafter Basle Committee Report]; Hendricks, *supra* note 67, at 10.

73. Basle Committee Report, *supra* note 72, at 2–3. Walk-away clauses are also known as "limited two-way payment provisions." Hendricks, *supra* note 67, at 8.

Walk-away clauses were prevalent prior to the 1992 ISDA Master Agreements because they constituted the default contractual provision under the 1987 ISDA Master Agreements. Christopher L. Culp & Barbara T. Kavanagh, *Methods of Resolving Over-the-Counter Derivatives Contracts in Failed Depository Institutions: Federal Banking Law Restrictions on Regulators,* Futures Int'l L. Letter, May/June 1994, at 1, 7. Although no longer widely used since the 1992 ISDA agreements, legacy transactions, and some transactions entered into after 1992, continue to contain walk-away clauses. The Office of the Comptroller of the Currency and the Board of Governors of the Federal Reserve System both have acted to prevent contracts with walk-away clauses from being included for purposes of risk-based capital computations. *Reining in Derivatives: Congress, Industry Examine Tighter Controls,* N.Y. L.J., May 19, 1994, at 5; *see also infra* notes 107–11 and accompanying text (discussing netting agreements and legal risk).

74. G-30 Report, *supra* note 1, at 17; *see also* Hu, *supra* note 4, at 1509. Hu states that entities may not evaluate legal risk because they may not be able to obtain the full benefit of such research. *Id.* If all firms were to aggregate their research, such information would be of great value to each firm. *Id.* To address this, Hu suggests that financial trade organizations and large law firms should undertake collective action. *Id.*

75. Robert C. Merton & Zvi Bodie, *On the Management of Financial Guarantees,* Fin. Mgmt., Winter 1992, at 87.

76. G-30 Report, *supra* note 1, at 17; BIS Paper, *supra* note 15, at 13–14; OCC BC-277, *supra* note 3, at 26; IOSCO Paper, *supra* note 14, at 11–12. It is essential, however, that a parent understand the nature and scope of a guarantee of its subsidiary. Parent companies are responsible for ensuring that adequate oversight of such subsidiaries is undertaken. *In re* MG Refining and Marketing, Inc. and MG Futures, Inc., No. 95-14, 1995 WL 447455, at *4, *7 (C.F.T.C. July 27, 1995).

77. OCC BC-277, *supra* note 3, at 26.

78. G-30 Report, *supra* note 1, at 15; IOSCO Paper, *supra* note 14, at 11; OCC BC-277, *supra* note 3, at 17–18.

79. BIS Paper, *supra* note 15, at 15.

80. IOSCO Paper, *supra* note 14, at 3; BIS Paper, *supra* note 15, at 15 (noting that a given product's market is susceptible to liquidity risk either because it is being disrupted or because it lacks depth). The liquidity of an instrument also can be viewed as a percentage of its fair market value that could be realized if the holder were forced to sell it immediately. Greenspan Speech, *supra* note 46, at 3.

81. G-30 Report, *supra* note 1, at 46.

82. BIS Paper, *supra* note 15, at 15 (describing funding liquidity risk as a type of liquidity risk); Promisel Report, *supra* note 5, at 17 (stating that funding (or cash) liquidity risk increases as an entity's involvement in derivatives increases, its reliance on short-term funding increases, its credit rating declines, and its ability to obtain access to central bank discount or borrowing facilities becomes more difficult).

83. BIS Paper, *supra* note 15, at 15. The DPG Report describes this form of risk as one that arises from a failure to match cash in-flows with cash out-flows. DPG Report, *supra* note 20, at 14.

84. *Id.;* G-30 Report, *supra* note 1, at 46 (noting that bid-ask spreads tend to be larger in illiquid markets).

85. Gerard Gennotte & Hayne Leland, *Market Liquidity, Hedging, and Crashes,* 80 Am. Econ. Rev. 999 (1990).

86. Brady Report, *supra* note 6, ch. 6.

87. *Id.*

88. Laura Jereski, *Mortgage Derivatives Claim Victims Big and Small,* Wall St. J., Apr. 20, 1994, at C15.

89. Abby Schultz & Gene Colter, *Credit Markets: Treasury Prices Rise, But Mortgage Sector Falters Due to Fallout from Sell-Off of Askin Holdings,* Wall St. J., Apr. 8, 1994, at C17.

90. BIS Paper, *supra* note 15, at 15; G-30 Report, *supra* note 1, at 46. The G-30 Report states that by relying on alternate markets, it is possible to move away from "product liquidity" to "risk liquidity." G-30 Report, *supra* note 1, at 46. Thus, even though a particular product (e.g., a U.S. dollar interest rate swap) or product category could be quite illiquid, the exposure it represents nevertheless could be hedged by using instruments such as other swaps, forward rate agreements, Eurodollar futures contracts, treasury notes, and other financial products. *Id.*

91. OCC BC-277, *supra* note 3, at 23–24.

92. DPG Report, *supra* note 20, at 19; G-30 Report, *supra* note 1, at 46–47 (referring to "funding liquidity risk" as "investing and funding risk"); *cf.* OCC BC-277, *supra* note 3, at 25–26. Diversifying cash inflows and out-flows in terms of sources, time, and currency also can reduce funding liquidity risk. *Id.*

93. IOSCO Paper, *supra* note 14, at 14.

94. BIS Paper, *supra* note 15, at 18; G-30 Report, *supra* note 1, at 51; IOSCO Paper, *supra* note 14, at 4; DPG Report, *supra* note 20, at 15.

95. G-30 Report, *supra* note 1, at 23. Bilateral collateral arrangements raise the risk that they may violate provisions in a counterparty's agreements with others, including negative pledge clauses and prohibitions against secured indebtedness. Anne Beroza & Robert M. McLaughlin, *What General Counsels Need to Know About Derivatives: Understanding Risks Can Protect Your Company,* Corp. Legal Times, Oct. 1994, at 14.

96. G-30 Report, *supra* note 1, at 23, 51; DPG Report, *supra* note 20, at 21; BIS Paper, *supra* note 15, at 18.

97. *See, e.g.,* Laurie Morse, *Survey of Derivatives,* Fin. Times, Oct. 20, 1993, at IV.

98. ISDA Master Agreements include the 1992 Multicurrency-Cross Border, and the 1992 Local Currency-Single Jurisdiction. Such master agreements contemplate being followed by one or more confirmations that describe the specific terms of a particular transaction. Examples of standard form

confirmations are the 1992 Confirmation for OTC Equity Index Option Transactions and the 1993 Confirmation of OTC Bond Option Transactions. *See also* ISDA, User's Guide to the 1992 ISDA Master Agreements (1993); David M. Lynn, *Enforceability of Over-the-Counter Financial Derivatives,* 50 Bus. Law. 291, 306-08 (1994).

99. *See* Beroza & McLaughlin, *supra* note 95; *see also* Florence D. Nolan, *Documentation: The Key to Containing Derivatives Risk,* Bankers Mag., May-June 1995, at 15. Nolan identifies the main categories of documentation as the confirmation (i.e., a written agreement that describes the terms of the specific transaction); the 1992 ISDA Master Agreements, to cover a series of transactions and to allow for their netting; ancillary documents that cover matters such as a counterparty's capacity to enter into a transaction; and credit support documents (e.g., guarantees and letters of credit). *Id.* at 18-19.

100. Lynn, *supra* note 98, at 301.

101. *Id.*

102. *See* Lynn, *supra* note 98, at 302.

103. N.Y. Gen Oblig. Law § 5-701(b)(2) (1994) defines a "qualified financial contract" as an agreement where neither party is a natural person and which relates to certain enumerated financial transactions. Such contracts include foreign exchange, foreign currency, bullion and commodities; currency, commodity, security and rate swaps; and options on such contracts and similar transactions. *See also* N.Y. U.C.C. Law § 1-206(3) (1994) (providing an exception to New York's statute of frauds for "qualified financial contracts").

104. Sufficient evidence that a contract exists includes: evidence of electronic communication; a written confirmation sent within a prescribed time, sufficient against the sender, and not objected to within a prescribed time; admission in court by a party against whom enforcement is sought that a contract has been made; or a writing sufficient to indicate that a contract has been made and signed by the party against whom enforcement is sought. N.Y. U.C.C. Law § 5-701(b)(1), (3) (1994).

105. N.Y. U.C.C. Law § 5-701(b)(1) (1994).

106. Aaron Pressman, *Oral Agreements, Common for Swaps, are Bolstered by New York Amendment,* Bond Buyer, Aug. 5, 1994, at 4.

107. BIS Paper, *supra* note 15, at 18; OCC BC-277, *supra* note 3, at 33-34; *see also* G-30 Report, *supra* note 1, at 51-52.

108. G-30 Report, *supra* note 1, at 52.

109. Under current law, the insolvency, receivership, or conservatorship of a counterparty that is a party to an ISDA Master Agreement is governed by the Bankruptcy Code, 11 U.S.C. § 101 (1988), or the Federal Deposit Insurance Act (FDIA), 12 U.S.C. § 1811 (1950), as amended by the Financial Institutions Reform, Recovery, and Enforcement Act of 1989 (FIRREA), Pub. L. No. 101-73, 103 Stat. 183 (1989), and the Federal Deposit Insurance Corporation Improvement Act of 1991 (FDICIA), Pub. L. No. 102-242, 105 Stat. 2236 (1991). Generally, FIRREA and FDICIA apply to failed depository institutions, while the Bankruptcy Code applies to failed non-depository institutions. Christopher L. Culp & Barbara T. Kavanagh, *Methods of Resolving Over-the-Counter Derivatives Contracts in Failed Depository Institutions: Federal Banking Law Restrictions on Regulators,* Futures Int'l L. Letter, May-June 1994, at 2; *see also* OCC BC-277, *supra* note 3, at 35-36. Lynn, *supra* note 98, at 332-33. The effect of these laws is to allow the exercise of termination rights and rights to collateral, and to recognize close-out netting agreements. *See* Robert M. McLaughlin, *Powerful Derivatives Involve Risks; Risk Management Methods; Credit Technique,* Bus. Credit, Feb. 1995, at 4.

110. Beroza & McLaughlin, *supra* note 95.

111. BIS Paper, *supra* note 15, at 18; OCC BC-277, *supra* note 3, at 35.

112. BIS Paper, *supra* note 15, at 16. These shortcomings include deficiencies in database management, trade entry, trade processing, trade confirmation, payment, delivery, receipt, collateral management, and valuation. DPG Report, *supra* note 20, at 15.

113. *Financial Terrorism,* Barron's, Mar. 6, 1995, at 10. For example, derivatives augment the possibility of human and computer errors because derivatives must be developed and priced through the use of sophisticated mathematical models. G-30 Report, *supra* note 1, at 50.

114. *Id.* app. I at 66; G-30 Report, *supra* note 1, at 50.

115. G-30 Report, *supra* note 1, at 18. Unfortunately, there may be a tendency among some firms to build up a derivatives practice on the trading side without devoting a commensurate degree of resources on the risk management side. Firms must give thought to the need for an appropriate derivatives in

frastructure and recognize the costs this will entail. *See* Carrie R. Smith, *Daily Departures,* Wall St. & Tech., Aug. 1994, at 34.

116. G-30 Report, *supra* note 1, at 18.

117. *Id.* at 19.

118. *Id.* at 12-13, 50; BIS Paper, *supra* note 15, at 17; IOSCO Paper, *supra* note 14, at 10-11, 13; *see also supra* notes 58, 78 and accompanying text.

119. *See* Nusbaum, *supra* note 30, at 63.

120. Levitt Stanford Speech, *supra* note 22, at 6.

121. Ludwig Speech, *supra* note 30; Donald D. Gallo, *How to Succeed in Business Without Betting the Bank,* N.Y. Times, Apr. 9, 1995, § 3, at 10.

122. Paul G. Barr, *Risk Management Gets New Respect,* Pensions & Investments, Mar. 20, 1995, at 26.

123. *Id.;* Levitt Stanford Speech, *supra* note 22, at 6; Levitt Testimony, *supra* note 6, 10 at 6.

124. Barr, *supra* note 122, at 26.

125. G-30 Report, *supra* note 1, at 50; OCC BC-277, *supra* note 3, at 11-12.

126. OCC BC-277, *supra* note 3, at 5-6.

127. Nusbaum, *supra* note 30, at 64.

128. BIS Paper, *supra* note 15, at 16. Part of the planning process is evaluating projections of current and future levels of derivative activities. *Id.* The resources to undertake derivatives activities should be considered by the board of directors and senior management. OCC BC-277, *supra* note 3, at 30; IOSCO Paper, *supra* note 14, at 13.

129. BIS Paper, *supra* note 15, at 16-18; OCC BC-277, *supra* note 3, at 30. The G-30 Report notes that while end-users need not invest in their systems to the degree that dealers do, at a minimum their systems should have the ability to evaluate the exposure and risk of their derivatives activities in a meaningful way. G-30 Report, *supra* note 1 at 18-19.

130. IOSCO Paper, *supra* note 14, at 13.

131. G-30 Report, *supra* note 1, at 18-19; *see also* Ellen Clarke, *Building an Integrated System to Control Derivatives Risk,* Am. Banker, Apr. 19, 1995, at 16; Patrick Harverson, *Survey of Derivatives,* Fin. Times, Oct. 20, 1993, at VI.

132. Deborah L. Williams, *Risk-Management Technology: What Banks Have . . . What They Need,* Mag. Bank Mgmt., Sept.-Oct. 1994, at 41.

133. *See* Brian Tracey, *In Derivatives Storm, Software Specialist Shines,* Am. Banker, May 1, 1995, at 23; Joshua Zecher, *Derivative Risk: An Uphill Struggle,* 12 Wall St. & Tech., Aug. 12, 1994, at 23-24.

134. Zecher, *supra* note 133, at 26.

135. For example, the SEC has proposed rule amendments that would allow broker dealers to use a theoretical pricing model when calculating capital charges for listed options and related positions so that haircuts reflect the inherent risk of such positions. Capital Requirements for Brokers or Dealers, 59 Fed. Reg. 13275 (1994) (proposed Mar. 21, 1994).

136. *See, e.g.,* Accounting Release, *supra* note 1.

137. The National Association of Securities Dealers recently filed a proposal with the SEC relating to its suitability rule. Self-Regulatory Organizations, 60 Fed. Reg. 54530 (1995) (proposed Oct. 17, 1995).

138. *Cf.* Greenspan Speech, *supra* note 46, at 1-2 (noting that both OTC derivatives and bank loans pose the same difficulties, given that they are both customized, privately negotiated agreements that can often lack transparency and liquidity).

10

The Board of Director's Role

CHARLES W. SMITHSON
JEFFREY L. SELTZER

Experts—like economists—are not known for agreeing with one another; nonetheless, we found a surprising degree of agreement on the role of the board of directors in the risk management process. There is essentially universal agreement that (1) the role of the board of directors is *crucial* and (2) the board of directors need to know the right questions to ask.

A former director of the Division of Market Regulation of the U.S. Securities and Exchange Commission provided insight into the way that the SEC might view the responsibilities of directors.[1] He said that the members of boards of directors must understand clearly the risks associated with the use of financial derivatives and must assume responsibility for making informed decisions about the company's investment and risk management policies. Moreover, directors must have a broad understanding of the credit, market, and operational risks involved and must establish clear guidelines about the way that the company will use derivative instruments. In addition, he noted that the board must ensure both that the company has adequate risk-management controls and qualified personnel in place to monitor the company's risk position and that the company's investments are in keeping with its overall objectives. He went on:

> When defining the company's fundamental risk-management policies, directors should consider its broader business strategies and management expertise and adopt policies consistent with the company's overall business objectives. Directors should require that the board be informed of the company's risk exposure and of the effect adverse market and interest-rate conditions may have on the company's derivatives portfolio. Directors should identify those individuals who will assume responsibility for managing risk as well as those who will have the authority to engage in derivative transactions. . . . Directors must fully understand the corporation's obligations to account for and publicly disclose information about derivatives activities.

Canadian Imperial Bank of Commerce (CIBC) is licensed to do business in the United States and is affiliated with CIBC Wood Gundy Corp., a New York Stock Exchange Member. The CIBC and Wood Gundy trademarks represent the corporate and investment banking businesses of CIBC and Wood Gundy Corp. Wood Gundy Corp. is solely responsible for its contractual obligations and commitments.

The authors wish to thank Greg Hayt, Lyle Minton, and Shang Song for their help in assembling this chapter.

The preceding provides the structure for our discussion by suggesting that the members of boards of directors have accepted four responsibilities: (1) The board must approve the firm's risk management policies and procedures. (2) The board must ensure that the operating management team possesses the requisite technical capabilities[2] (and is actively communicating with the people implementing the risk management program). (3) The directors must be able to evaluate the performance of the risk management activity. (4) The board must maintain oversight of the risk management activity. Once we have examined each of these four responsibilities, we will "operationalize" our discussion by providing some of the items that we think should be on a director's checklist. To date, much of the attention has been focused on the boards of directors of banks and securities firms (the derivatives *dealers*). While the discussion to follow is relevant to the boards of directors of both *dealers* and *end users,* our focus is more on *end-users.* However, for the directors of banks and securities firms, we include two appendices in which we summarize the detailed guidance issued by regulators and trade associations.

APPROVAL OF POLICIES

Every authority surveyed started with the board's responsibilities with respect to *policies.* In its report to the U.S. congress, the General Accounting Office (GAO) determined that the board of directors ". . . should be responsible for approving the risk management policies and controls. . ." The importance of this responsibility is evidenced by the fact that it was made Recommendation #1 in the report on derivatives produced by the Global Derivatives Project sponsored by the Group of Thirty:

> *G-30 Recommendation #1: Dealers and end-users should use derivatives in a manner consistent with the overall risk management and capital policies approved by their boards of directors. These policies should be reviewed as business and market circumstances change. Policies governing derivatives use should be clearly defined, including the purposes for which these transactions are to be undertaken . . .*

While effective risk management policies and procedures can take many different forms, the "risk management cycle" illustrated in Figure 10.1 has proven to be a useful organizing structure for a number of firms. In putting together policies and procedures, the firm must carefully consider four issues.

Goals for Risk Management

The firm must specify its goals—what it intends to accomplish with a risk management program. One goal is to seek additional profits by trading derivatives. If this is the firm's goal, the firm will need to decide how much of its capital it wishes to put at risk and how large a return it is attempting to earn. In October 1995, U.S. nonfinancial corporations were surveyed about their use of derivatives by the Wharton School at the University of Pennsylvania (see Bodnar/Marston, 1996); the survey was funded by CIBC Wood Gundy. Figure 10.2 suggests that a relatively small percentage of nonfinancial firms "frequently" actively take a position, but a more substantial percentage "sometimes" actively take a position.

FIGURE 10.1   The Risk Management Cycle

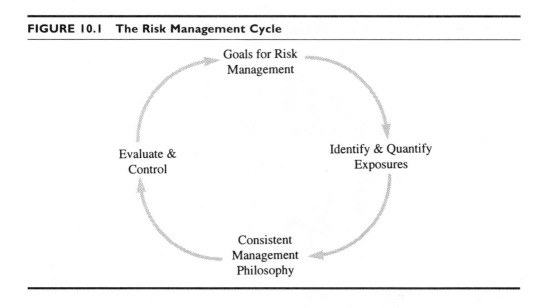

In many cases, firms specify the goal of their risk management program as the reduction in some form of volatility (e.g., the volatility of its cash flows, earnings, or market value). Figure 10.3 summarizes results from the 1995 Wharton/CIBC Wood Gundy Survey of U.S. Derivatives End-Users which indicate that firms are most likely to reduce cashflow or earnings volatility. However, if the goal is to reduce volatility, the directors and managers need to be clear about *why* they are doing so: they need to spell out how volatility reduction is going to increase the value of the firm.

FIGURE 10.2   Frequency with Which Derivatives Users Actively Take Positions

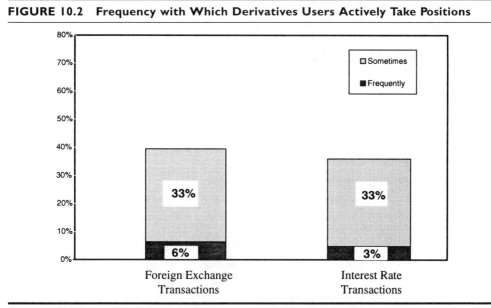

Source: 1995 Wharton/CIBC Wood Gundy Survey of U.S. Derivatives End-Users

FIGURE 10.3   "Most Important" Objective in Using Derivatives to Hedge

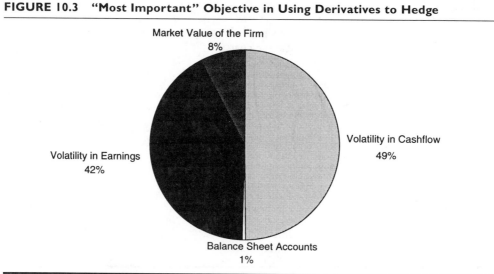

Source: 1995 Wharton/CIBC Wood Gundy Survey of U.S. Derivatives End-Users

More recently, we have witnessed something akin to "moral judgments" being made about the two goals. We have seen some people argue that volatility reduction (a.k.a., *hedging*) is "good" and trading for profit (a.k.a., *speculation*) is "evil."[3] We do not agree. First, on a philosophical level, there is nothing "evil" about trading for profit. Seeking additional profits from the use of derivatives may be an appropriate goal for a particular company; *but since it is a completely different objective from volatility reduction, it must be managed differently.* Second, on a more pragmatic level, our observation is that most firms act on their views about the future path of interest rates or foreign exchange rates or some other financial price. While Figure 10.2 suggested that relatively few U.S. nonfinancial firms are using derivatives to actively trade, Figure 10.4 suggests a substantial number *do* implement their views about future rates or prices by altering the timing or size of their "hedges." Do such changes in timing and/or size represent "hedging" or "speculation"? We would suggest that they are *both* and *neither.* Indeed, the recent use of the words "hedge" and "speculation" has been such that neither word has general meaning any more.[4]

Identify and Quantify Exposures

In order to manage risks, the firm must know what risks it faces and how big they are. Consequently, the firm must implement a "system" for measuring risk. It is essential for this system to be able to keep track of how big the risks were before the risk management program was implemented and how big they are after the program is put in place. Currently, much is being heard about Value at Risk (VaR).

VaR is not the only measure of market risk that is currently being used. Figure 10.5 summarizes the results obtained from the 1995 CIBC Wood Gundy/Wharton Survey of U.S. Derivatives End-Users when the respondents were asked what methods they used to evaluate market risk.[5]

Value at Risk

Value at Risk describes the risk of loss on a financial instrument or a portfolio of financial instruments resulting from changes in market-determined variables such as interest rates, foreign exchange rates, commodity prices, or volatility—what we will refer to collectively as *market factors*. Since changes in market factors over a given time period are not constrained (e.g., there is no limit on the magnitude of a one-day change in a foreign exchange rate), it is not possible to specify the *maximum* loss that could occur for a portfolio of financial instruments. However, it is possible to determine an amount of loss which one would not expect to be exceeded at some confidence level. In other words, we can make a probability statement about how much might be lost over a given period due to changes in market factors; and that is precisely what "value at risk" is.

For example, the following is a hypothetical distribution for one-day changes in the market value of a particular portfolio; for simplicity, we use a normal distribution. Suppose we want a 97.5% confidence level value-at-risk. The value change labeled VaR—a negative value change—is the loss that we would expect to be exceeded only on 2.5% of the trading days. VaR is located so that only 2.5% of the area of the distribution is to the left of VaR. (With our normal distribution, VaR would be 1.96 standard deviations below the mean.)

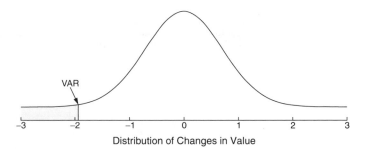

Distribution of Changes in Value

To calculate value-at-risk, one must determine the distribution of value changes for a specific portfolio of financial instruments contracts over a specific time period (e.g., one day). The three methods that are being used to do this are referred to as: *Historical Simulation, Monte Carlo Simulation,* and Analytic Variance/Covariance. (The most widely-publicized method for calculating value-at-risk, *RiskMetrics*™ (Trademark of Morgan Guaranty Trust Company), falls into the third category.)

Value-at-risk has proven to be an extremely useful concept among securities dealers because it captures the *total* market risk of a portfolio, expressing it as a "maximum" dollar loss at a given confidence level. For this reason VaR is a powerful tool for communicating risk to non-technical managers who are unfamiliar with traditional risk measures such as duration, the value of an "01," convexity, and the "Greek alphabet" of option pricing. Value-at-risk is also the starting point for determining how much capital is at risk in different business lines, making it valuable in the calculation of risk adjusted return measures.

FIGURE 10.4 Frequency with Which a "Market View" Impacts Foreign Exchange and Interest Rate Derivatives Transactions

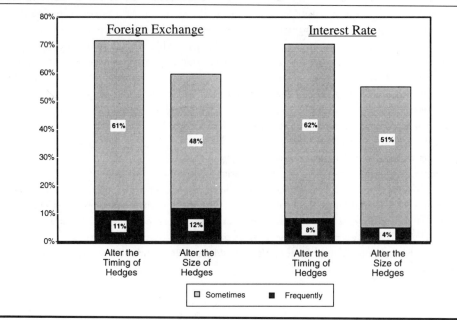

Source: 1995 Wharton CIBC Wood Gundy Survey of U.S. Derivatives End-Users

FIGURE 10.5 Methods Used for Evaluating Market Risk

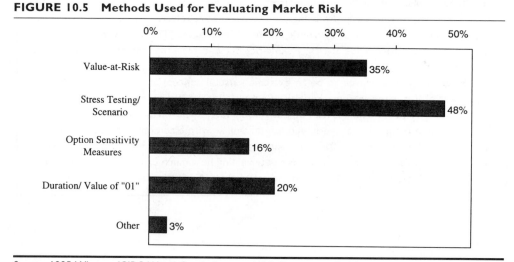

Source: 1995 Wharton/CIBC Wood Gundy Survey of U.S. Derivatives End-Users

And, we are not convinced that VaR or any of the other measures depicted in Figure 10.5 is the *right* one for a nonfinancial corporation. All of those measures are "stock" measures; they indicate how a change in the financial price will impact on the *present value* of an asset, a liability, or a portfolio. In contrast, most nonfinancial firms are managed to "flows"; the important measure is how changes in a financial price will impact on the firm's cash flows or earnings. We believe that, over the next few years, we will see a movement toward "cash flow-at-risk."[6]

Define a Risk Management Philosophy

To effectively manage financial price risks, the firm must have a risk management "philosophy"; and then it must turn this philosophy into an action plan via some careful operating rules. The philosophy should provide the firm's perspective on the markets, including the firm's beliefs about the degree to which financial prices can be forecasted. The decision concerning "active" versus "passive" hedging should follow directly from the firm's beliefs about market efficiency.

"Active" Hedging

Writing for the Association of Corporate Treasurers (U.K), Richard Cookson noted that there may be reasons for allowing treasuries some leeway. For example, a company might take a view that they can create value for their shareholders by locking in some of the company's debt at what it considers low interest rates or taking a view on what it thinks is an over or under valued currency. However, "active" risk management does involve taking a view. Is this hedging or speculation? As Arvind Sodhani (vice president and treasurer of Intel Corporation) put it in the *Harvard Business Review*, "[t]he board must be aware that, while risk management can be good and prudent business, it can turn into speculation."

The operating rules should define "what can be used" and "for what purposes." Different firms use different sets of financial instruments. Figure 10.6 summarizes the results obtained from the 1995 CIBC Wood Gundy/Wharton Survey of U.S. End-Users when the respondents were asked which derivatives were "most important" for the management of foreign exchange rate, interest rate, commodity price, and equity price exposures.

In addition to "what can be used" and "for what purposes," the operating rules should define "by whom," "in what amounts," and "with whom." The firm needs to be clear on what instruments are authorized for use for what application. Within the firm, it should be clear who is authorized to transact derivative contracts and what their transaction limits are. Since derivatives contracts involve promises of future performance, they are credit instruments; so, the firm must set the criteria of dealers with whom they are prepared to deal, review it frequently, and ration the amount of exposure that they have to any one dealer. Figure 10.7 summarizes the results obtained from the 1995 CIBC Wood Gundy/Wharton Survey of U.S. End-Users when the respondents were asked about the lowest counterparty rating they would accept for derivative transactions with maturities of one year or less and with maturities of more than one year.

FIGURE 10.6   "Most Important" Derivatives Used to Manage Underlying Financial Exposures

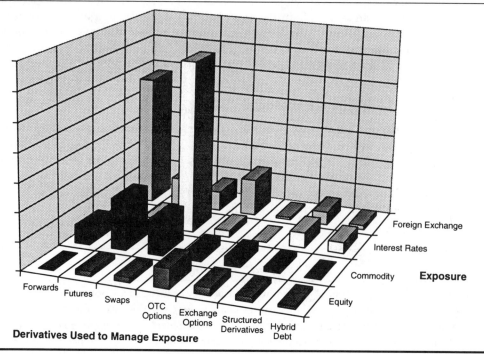

Source: Wharton/CIBC Wood Gundy Survey of U.S. Derivatives End-Users

FIGURE 10.7   Lowest Rated Counterparty for Derivative Transactions

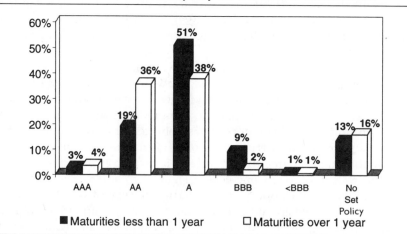

Source: Wharton/CIBC Wood Gundy Survey of U.S. Derivatives End-Users

Evaluate and Control

As with any other business activity, the risk management function must be evaluated (and the people involved must be compensated). The recent experiences of Barings, Sumitomo, and others highlight two things that are crucial to effective evaluation and control. First, the evaluation/control function must be *independent* from the activity itself.[7] Second, in order to avoid "surprises," the management of the firm must always know the value of the firm's portfolio of risk management instruments.[8]

To accomplish the evaluation/control function, the "system" for managing risk noted above must be expanded to reflect the impact of risk management on the firm's inherent exposures. The firm must have a common framework to report and evaluate compliance with the risk management plan. Measurement tools will have to be developed. If the firm is trying to reduce volatility in some financial measure (e.g., cash flow) in order to increase the value of the firm (e.g., by ensuring that funds are available to make investments at the most effective time), it will be necessary to measure (1) the degree to which volatility declined relative to what it would have been in the absence of any hedge, (2) the monetary cost paid to obtain this volatility reduction, and (3) the degree to which the *real* goal (e.g., accomplishing the firm's investment program) was attained. If the firm is going to employ active risk management, it will be necessary to design benchmarks that will tell the firm what a passive strategy would have achieved.

ENSURING CAPABILITY

The members of the board do not need to be aware of or understand the mechanics of each trade. However, their general duty of care requires that the board members be satisfied that management is adequate to implement board policy decisions. They should ask senior managers to verify that training and software systems are up to the job.[9] Writing in the *Harvard Business Review,* Cheryl Francis (treasurer of FMC Corporation) reinforced this view, "One of the keys to using derivatives properly is education and training. Managers must know how to identify risks and communicate them."

The problem is deciding what education to provide.[10] It's one thing to know that the people in treasury need to be "capable"; but it's quite another to know what it is they need to be capable *about.* To provide some insights into the issues that were concerning the people who were doing derivatives in 1995—issues that might merit additional education—we have summarized in Figure 10.8 the ranking of 12 issues thought to be of concern to derivatives users.

EVALUATION

The tools that will be used to evaluate the performance of the risk management function will be provided in the "evaluation" section of the firm's *Policies & Procedures.* If the "evaluation" section is *consistent* with the "goals" section, everything else will follow. However, this consistency is not as easy to attain as it might first seem. In the early 1990s, a number of firms had goals statements that talked about minimizing risk, while the evaluation of the risk management function was based on measuring

FIGURE 10.8   Significant Concerns about Derivative Transactions

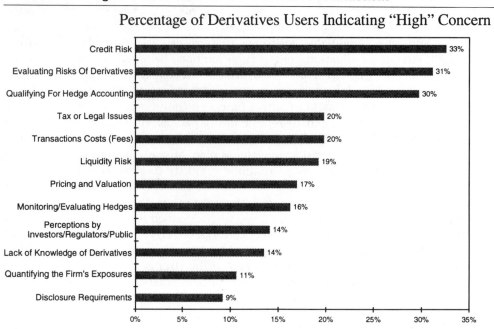

Percentage of Derivatives Users Indicating "High" Concern

Source: 1995 Wharton/CIBC Wood Gundy Survey of U.S. Derivatives End-Users

the performance of the treasury against investment or funding "bogeys" (e.g., LIBOR). The goal statement implied that the firm wanted the treasury to *reduce variance;* but, since beating the evaluation bogey required increasing expected returns, the evaluation section was actually implying that the firm wanted the treasury to *increase variance.*[11]

If the goal of the firm is to reduce volatility in cash flows or earnings or . . . , the members of the board must be convinced not only that the reduction in volatility occurred but also that the reduction in volatility actually led to the increase in firm value that was presupposed.

If the firm is using active risk management, the members of the board need to be convinced that, with the active management, the company ended up better off than it would have with a more mechanistic [passive] approach.

CONTINUING OVERSIGHT

The GAO report noted earlier also determined that the board of directors ". . . is ultimately accountable for risk assumed by the firm." Consequently, it is the responsibility of the board to make sure that the firm's risk management policy is fully explained and strictly enforced.

It may be useful for the board of directors to delegate the continuing oversight role to a committee of the board (which would then be accountable to the full board). It could be handled by an existing committee (e.g., the Audit Committee);

FIGURE 10.9   Frequency of Reporting Risk Management Activity to the Board

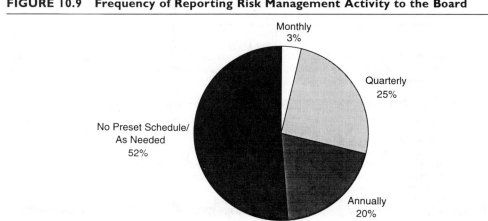

Source: 1995 Wharton/CIBC Wood Gundy Survey of Derivatives End-Users

or, if the firm's risk management activities are sufficiently complex, a Risk Management Committee of the board could be created.

To make sure that the firm's risk management policy is fully explained and strictly enforced, the members of the board—or the members of the oversight committee of the board—need to be in the loop. Figure 10.9 indicates how often users of derivatives in the United States were reporting risk management activity to the board in 1995.

The members of the board must remain alert for surprises of any kind. *Unanticipated* results are the most dangerous results for a risk management program. And unanticipated positive performance is as dangerous as unanticipated negative performance; both indicate that some aspect of the activity has not been properly understood. As David B. Weinberger, a managing director of Swiss Bank Corporation, wrote in the *Harvard Business Review,* "Used properly, derivative instruments don't create surprises. They help minimize them."

SOME ITEMS FOR A "DIRECTOR'S CHECKLIST"

As we noted at the outset, one of the most important things a member of a board should know is the right questions to ask. Former U.S. Securities and Exchange Commission Chairman Richard Breeden suggested a few questions:

- *Do we know what our risks are?*
- *Do we know what our positions are, right now?*
- *How effective are our controls?*
- *How much does our compensation system encourage perverse behavior?*
- *Who is responsible for making sure we know what we're doing?*

However, most of us are less comfortable with a list of questions than we are with a checklist. In Figure 10.10 we have provided some suggestions for items that

FIGURE 10.10   Some Items to Include on the Director's Checklist

RESPONSIBILITY #1 – APPROVAL OF POLICIES

Define Goals
- The firm intends to Trade for Profit ❏ -OR- Reduce Volatility in Cashflows ❏   Earnings ❏   Market Value ❏
- If the firm intends to reduce volatility, identify the benefits to be obtained from volatility reduction   ❏
- Determine the extent of "active" risk management to be permitted
    None ❏   Treasury Permitted to Trade in "Bands" ❏   Treasury to Operate as Profit Centre ❏

Identify & Quantify Exposures
- Identify the financial prices to which the firm is exposed   ❏
    - Determine volatility of relevant financial prices   ❏
    - Determine which of the financial prices have a material impact on the firm's performance   ❏
- Implement a technology for quantifying the firm's exposures ("risk quantification system")   ❏
    - Establish procedures for vetting models and assumptions   ❏
    - Establish procedures for stress testing the risk quantification system   ❏

Define a Risk Management Philosophy and Execution Plan
- If "active" risk management is permitted, define the market inefficiencies to be exploited   ❏
- Define the authorized instruments and the authorized uses for the instruments   ❏
- Implement and document Controls and Procedures
    - Determine who is authorized to enter into transact (and in what amounts)   ❏
    - Determine who is responsible for recording and confirming transactions   ❏
    - Determine limits for credit, market, liquidity, and operations risks   ❏
    - Determine acceptable counterparties and exposure limits for each   ❏

Evaluate and Control
- Ensure that the risk quantification system is capable of measuring pre/post impact of risk mgmt transactions   ❏
- Establish techniques for evaluating risk management transactions   ❏
    - If goal of program is to reduce volatility: Degree of reduction ❏ Impact of volatility reduction on performance ❏
    - If active risk management is permitted: Risk adjusted return measure ❏   Comparison to passive benchmark ❏

RESPONSIBILITY #2 – ENSURING CAPABILITY
- Verify that expertise exists within the firm to implement and control a risk management program   ❏
- Put in place education programs for staff and senior management   ❏
- Obtain external validation of models used to value risk management transactions   ❏

RESPONSIBILITY #3 – EVALUATION
- Confirm that the results of the risk management program are consistent with the firm's overall goals   ❏
- Confirm that the program did not impose undue regulatory costs and/or constraints on the firm   ❏
- Confirm that the market accurately perceives the intent and effect of the risk management program   ❏

RESPONSIBILITY #4 – CONTINUING OVERSIGHT
- Ensure that a risk management committee is established and is functioning   ❏
    - Risk management strategy in place   ❏
    - Risk management goal and strategy communicated throughout firm   ❏
    - Procedures in place for periodic review and evaluation of risk management activity   ❏
- Ensure implementation of independent monitor of risk management function   ❏

would be included on a director's checklist. These checklist items summarize—and operationalize—the preceding discussion.

CONCLUDING REMARKS

The dramatic growth of the markets for risk management products in the 1980s and early 1990s captured the attention of regulators, legislators, think tanks, and trade associations. A specific area of concern has been and remains the role of the board of directors with respect to the oversight and control of a financial risk management program.

We have characterized the directors as having four responsibilities: (1) The board must approve the firm's risk management policies and procedures; (2) the board must ensure that the operating management team possesses the requisite technical capabilities; (3) the directors must be able to evaluate the performance of the risk management activity; and (4) the board must maintain oversight of the risk management activity.

In addition, unhappy shareholders have also focused on derivatives. From time to time, shareholders have vented their anger through the judicial system with claims that their board breached its duty of care to shareholders through their corporation's use of derivatives, in some cases, or by their failure to use derivatives, in other cases. The knowledge that such suits have been filed should not paralyze directors. As with other complex issues that come before it, the board should consult its counsel on exactly what its role should be in light of the type of risks undertaken by the corporation and applicable law, regulation, and best practice. Our evaluation of the material available on this subject, leads us to conclude that there are two main themes for directors—*knowledge* and *accountability*. Directors should be able to fulfill their obligations by (1) becoming informed about risk management and how it relates to the firm's overall business strategies, (2) delegating the management, monitoring, and control functions to competent staff, and (3) establishing a periodic review process that enables them to understand and assess the risks facing the firm.

APPENDICES

Early in 1992, Gerald Corrigan, then president of the Federal Reserve Bank of New York, urged senior management of institutions using derivatives to understand and manage the risks inherent in these instruments. What seemed like such an obvious bit of advice started an avalanche of regulatory guidance from U.S. banking, securities, and commodities regulators as well as from those regulators responsible for global banking and securities matters. In the following material, we have tried to summarize this regulatory guidance. (Since what follows are excerpts, the reader should be aware that the original document should be examined for context.)

Guidance for Boards of Banks

In its *Risk Management Guidelines for Derivatives* (July 1994), the Basle Committee on Banking Supervision laid out the responsibilities of the Boards of Directors of banks:

The Board must approve and regularly re-evaluate the bank's policies related to the management of all risks throughout the institution. The risk management policies must be consistent with the bank's broader business strategies, capital strength, management expertise and overall willingness to take risk. The policies must identify risk tolerances of the Board and clearly delineate lines of authority and responsibility for managing the risk of these activities.

The Board must be informed regularly of the risk exposures. The reports to the Board should come via an independent reporting system, from the independent risk management function.

The Board must conduct and encourage discussions between it and senior management, as well as between senior management and the rest of the institution, regarding the bank's risk management process and risk exposure.

Once derivatives activities have commenced, any subsequent changes in such activities or any new activities should be approved by the Board or by an appropriate level of senior management as designated by the Board

The U.S. Office of the Comptroller of the Currency (OCC) added detail to the general guidance from the Basle Committee. The OCC reiterated that derivative activities must be subject to oversight by the Board and noted that, while the Board doesn't need operating expertise in derivatives, it must have sufficient understanding of the products and risks to approve the bank's derivatives business strategy, to limit the amount of earnings and capital at risk; and to review periodically the results of derivatives activity.

The OCC required that the Board review the bank's policies and procedures at least annually. In addition to the general items the Basle Committee required to be in the policies, the OCC also required that the policies (1) provide sufficient managerial and operational resources to conduct the activity in a safe and sound manner, (2) ensure appropriate structure and staffing of key risk control functions—including internal audit (where independence is paramount), (3) detail requirements for the evaluation and approval of new business or product initiatives, (4) establish guidelines for dealing with affiliates, (5) outline approved derivative products and authorized activity, (6) limit the aggregate level of risk exposure expressed as earnings or capital at risk and require review and approval of those limits by the Board, or committee thereof, at least annually, (7) provide a comprehensive limit structure that addresses key risk factors, (8) describe the limit exception approval process, (9) require stress testing of risk positions, and (10) require validation of risk measurement methodologies.

The OCC required the Board to review the performance of senior management on the following dimensions: (1) the consistency of performance against strategic and financial objectives over time, (2) internal and external audit results, (3) the level of compliance with policy, procedure, and limits, and (3) the quality and timeliness of communication to the Board.

The OCC required the Board to establish an independent risk control function which must: (1) report independently from those individuals directly responsible for trading decisions and trading management, (2) be adequately staffed with qualified individuals, (3) be fully supported by the Board and senior management and have sufficient stature within the organization to be effective, and (4) have been provided with the technical and financial resources, corporate visibility, and authority to ensure effective oversight.

The OCC required the Board to ensure that the bank has a strong audit function which evaluates internal controls, validates the integrity of data, and reviews new products.

The OCC required the Board to ensure that the bank complies with applicable federal, state, and foreign laws and regulations is periodically verified through a compliance function.

The OCC required the Board to ensure that the bank have mechanisms for effective assessment of capital, accounting and legal exposures.

The OCC required the Board to ensure that the bank establishes a mechanism through which new products are captured and reported. A uniform product assessment process should form part of the overall risk management function. Depending on the magnitude of the new product or activity and its impact on the risk profile of the bank, in some cases, the Board should provide the final approval.

To be sure that the Board understands the bank's derivatives activities, the OCC required the Board to review a number of documents including (1) a clear statement of derivatives strategy and the success thereof, (2) ongoing educational material and information regarding major activities, (3) reports indicating compliance with policies and law, (4) internal and external audit reports, (5) reports indicating level of risk, and (6) reports detailing performance of trading, positioning, and hedging activity.

The responsibilities of Boards of Directors of banks were further defined by the U.S. Federal Reserve Board. The Fed made it clear that board members are required to be aware of their responsibility and adequately perform their role in risk management. Moreover, the Fed added specificity to Basle's requirement of regular review of the risk level of the bank:

- *Market Risk.* The Board should approve market risk exposure limits in terms of specific percentage changes in the economic value of capital and in the projected earnings of the institution under various market scenarios. Similar and complimentary limits on the volatility of prices or fair value should be established at the appropriate instrument, product type and portfolio levels based on the institution's willingness to accept market risk. Market risk exposure should be reported to the Board no less than quarterly. Their evaluation should assess trends and performance in terms of established objectives and risk constraints and identify compliance with limits and exceptions.
- *Credit Risk.* The Board should be informed of the institution's total credit risk exposures no less frequently than quarterly. The Board, or a committee thereof, should set limits on the amounts and types of transactions authorized for each firm. They should also periodically review and reconfirm the list of authorized dealers, investment bankers and brokers.
- *Liquidity Risk.* The Board should be aware of liquidity risks and should address them in the institution's liquidity plan and the broader context of the institution's liquidity management process.

The Office of the Superintendent of Financial Institutions in Canada explicitly stated that financial institutions acting as a dealer of derivatives should implement the recommendations of the Group of Thirty's Global Derivatives Project.

OSFI required that each type of derivative product that an institution proposes to use should be subject to a product authorization signed off by senior management.

The product authorization should document which individuals or units are authorized to buy or sell the product, and the use(s) to which the product will be put—whether it will use a derivative product strictly to hedge positions or to actively take positions based on a market view, take advantage of arbitrage opportunities or to gain income from fulfilling customer orders.

Guidance on the Purchase of Structured Notes

With respect to the purchase of structured notes, the Federal Reserve, the OCC, and the FDIC issued specific guidance for banks. As with derivatives in general, the Board must approve policies that address the goals and objectives expected to be achieved and that set limits on the degree of acceptable price risk, as well as on the amount of funds that may be committed to them. However, the regulators went further, requiring bank management to be able to "understand the risks of structured notes and be able to explain how such securities accomplish strategic portfolio objectives." Indeed, the regulators required that "redemption linked notes" or notes that contain leverage specifically be authorized in written policy.

Guidance for Boards of Securities Firms

In 1994, the International Organization of Securities Commissions (IOSCO) provided some formal guidance for the boards of directors of securities firms that deal in derivatives.[12] IOSCO recommended that the board promulgate risk management policies and procedures and that these policies and procedures be reviewed as business and market circumstances change. The risk management policies and procedures and management controls should address (1) the measurement of market risk and credit risk including aggregate exposures against risk tolerance objectives, (2) the acceptability criteria for counterparties, strategies and products, (3) risk monitoring procedures and exception reporting criteria, (4) personnel policies (including expertise, training and compensation), (5) the separation of trading and risk management functions, and (6) the establishment of management control and checks over accounts, trades, operational staff and systems.

In March of 1995, the Derivatives Policy Group—CS First Boston, Goldman Sachs, Lehman Brothers, Merrill Lynch, Morgan Stanley, and Salomon Brothers—released the *Framework for Voluntary Oversight* which reaffirmed that, for securities firms that deal in derivatives, the board of directors must review and approve the firm's general authorizing guidelines. These guidelines should be written and should consider the firm's overall business strategies and product lines, its tolerance for risk and its general risk management philosophy, its past performance and experience, its financial condition and capital levels, its internal expertise and experience and the sophistication of its risk monitoring and management systems. The authorizing guidelines should address (1) the scope of authorized activity or any nonquantitative limitation on the scope of authorized activities, (2) quantitative guidelines for managing the firm's overall or constituent risk exposures, (3) the scope and frequency of reporting by management on risk exposures, and (4) mechanisms for reviewing the guidelines.

Guidance on Investments in Derivatives

In August of 1994, the Investment Company Institute (ICI) provided guidance for the boards of directors of those investment companies that use derivatives as investments.

The ICI recommended that the board not only review and approve policies developed by the investment advisor and other service providers but also oversee the performance of their duties. Moreover, depending upon the context and the particular circumstances of the fund (including the level, types and objectives of a fund's derivative instruments), the board should (1) understand generally the type of instruments and nature of associated risks, (2) request, receive and review information from the investment adviser about the adviser's overall strategy with respect to derivatives, (3) review the fund's valuation procedures, (4) consider the adequacy of disclosure, and (5) obtain assurances from the adviser as to the derivatives expertise of its portfolio managers and analysts, its operational capacities and its internal controls (including how risk management responsibilities are allocated and how risk management principles are applied).

REFERENCES

General References

American Institute of Certified Public Accountants Financial Instruments Task Force, *Detailed Questions About Derivatives* (June 1994).

Association of Corporate Treasurers (U.K.), *Guide to Risk Management and Control of Derivatives* (1994).

Breeden, Richard C. "Directors, Control Your Derivatives," *Wall Street Journal,* Monday, March 7, 1994.

Bodnar, Gordon and Richard Marston. *1995 Wharton/CIBC Wood Gundy Survey of Derivative Use by U.S. Nonfinancial Corporations.* The Wharton School, The University of Pennsylvania (April 1996). Another report on these survey results was provided by Charles Smithson in Chapter 9 of the *1996 Managing Financial Risk Yearbook,* CIBC Wood Gundy (February 1996).

Cookson, Richard. *Derivatives for Directors,* The Association of Corporate Treasurers.

Coopers & Lybrand, *Generally Accepted Risk Principles* (January 1996).

Global Derivatives Study Group, "Derivatives: Practices and Principles," *The Group of Thirty, Washington, DC,* July 1993.

Fitch, *Special Report on Managing Derivatives Risk* (February 1995).

Government Accounting Office, *Report on Financial Derivatives* (May 1994).

Hayt, Gregory and Shang Song. "Handle with Sensitivity," *Risk,* September 1995.

Keslar, Linda. "The View from the Boardroom: Under Control," *Derivatives Strategy,* March 1996.

Lacey, James. "The Consultants' Verdict: Still in Trouble," *Derivatives Strategy,* March 1996.

Lamoureux, Claude. "Derivatives: Beauty or the Beast?" The Role of Directors and Senior Management, University of Waterloo Conference, May 8, 1995.

Seltzer, Jeffrey L. "A View for the Top: The Role of the Board of Directors and Senior Management in the Derivatives Business," Chapter One in *Derivatives Risk and Responsibilities,* Robert A. Klein and Jess Lederman, editors (Irwin, 1995).

Treasury Management Association, *Voluntary Principles and Practices: Guidelines for End Users of Derivatives,* October 1995.

(No Author Listed) "Using Derivatives: What Senior Managers Must Know," *Harvard Business Review,* January-February 1995.

(No Author Listed) "The World According to Richard Breeden." *Derivatives Strategy,* March 1996.

Litigation Filed

Brane v. Roth 590 N.E. 2nd 587 (Ind.Ct.App.1992).
In re Compaq 848 F. Supp. 1307 (S.D. Houston 1991).
Drage v. Procter & Gamble (Hamilton County, Ohio 1994).
Markewich v. Beitzel et al. and Bankers Trust (New York 1995).

General Guidance from Bank Regulators

Basle Committee on Banking Supervision Risk Management Guidelines for Derivatives (July 1994).
Office of the Comptroller of the Currency, Circular on Risk Management for Financial Derivatives (BC-277, November 1993 and Q&A Supplement, May 1994)).
Office of the Comptroller of the Currency Examination Manual on Risk Management of Financial Derivatives (October 1994).
Federal Reserve Board, Examination Memo on Risk Management and Internal Controls for Trading Activities of Banking Organizations (December 1993).
Federal Reserve Board Letter on Evaluating the Risk Management and Internal Controls of Securities and Derivative Contracts Used in Non-Trading Activities (SR 95-17) (March 1995).
Federal Deposit Insurance Corporation, *Examination Guidance for Financial Derivatives* (May 1994).
Office of the Superintendent of Financial Institutions, Canada, *Derivatives Best Practices* (May 1995).
Bank of England, *Board of Banking Supervision Inquiry into the Collapse of Barings Bank* (July 1995).
Federal Supervisory Office of Banks (Germany), *Announcement of Minimum Requirements for the Carrying Out of Trading Transactions by the Banks* (October 1995).
Bank Negara Malaysia, *Statement on Applications by Commercial Banks to Offer or Trade in Derivative Instruments* (January 1995).
Hong Kong Monetary Authority, *Derivatives Trading Internal Control Review* (March 1995).
Bank Indonesia, *Decision of the Board of Executives of Bank Indonesia Concerning Derivatives Transactions*—No 128/119 (December 1995).

Guidance on "Structured Notes" from Bank Regulators

Office of the Comptroller of the Currency, *Advisory Letter on Purchases of Structured Notes* (August 1994).
Federal Deposit Insurance Corporation, *Examination Guidance for Structured Notes* (August 1994).
Federal Reserve Board, *Supervisory Memo on the Purchase of Structured Notes* (August 1994).

Specific Guidance for Securities Companies

SEC/CFTC/SIB, *Joint Statement on OTC Derivatives Oversight* (February 1994).

International Organization of Securities Commissions, *Operational Financial Risk Management Control Mechanisms for OTC Derivatives Activities of Regulated Securities Firms* (July 1994).

Derivatives Policy Group, *Framework for Voluntary Oversight* (March 1995).

See also Securities Industry Association Swap and OTC Derivatives Committee, Letter dated April 7, 1994 from Jeffrey L. Seltzer, Chairman, to Brandon Becker, Director, Market Regulation Division, Securities and Exchange Commission.

Guidance on Investments in Derivatives

Investment Company Institute, *Memorandum on Investments in Derivatives by Registered Investment Companies* (August 1994).

ENDNOTES

1. These comments by Brandon Becker, then the Director of the Division of Market Regulation of the U.S. Securities and Exchange Commission, were reported in the Jan.–Feb. 1995 issue of the *Harvard Business Review*. While the commissioners and the SEC staff make a point of noting at the outset of every speech and article that they are presenting their own views "and not necessarily those of the SEC or of other SEC staff members," the public pronouncements of SEC commissioners and staff provide us with at least some window on the thinking within the SEC.

2. Technical knowledge is *necessary,* but is not *sufficient;* technical knowledge will never replace good judgment.

3. Writing in *Derivatives for Directors,* Richard Cookson probably represents something very near an end-point with respect to trading for profit: "Any board considering using its treasury as a profit center should ask itself if its treasury really has an edge over banks and securities firms which speculate full time. Many companies that have come a-cropper with derivatives—Showa Shell, Kashima Oil, Volkswagen, and Allied Lyons (now Allied-Domecq) to name but a few—used their treasuries as profit centers."

4. Consequently, if a firm uses these words in its policies, we suggest that the firm carefully define what it means by "hedging" and "speculation."

5. This figure is intended to illustrate the range of market risk measurement methods currently being used. The question that the respondents were asked was: *Does your firm use any of the following methods for evaluating the riskiness of specific derivatives transactions or portfolios? (a) "Value at Risk," (b) Stress testing or scenario analysis, (c) Option sensitivity measures, (d) Price value of a basis point or duration, or (e) Other.*

6. For an introduction to "cash flow-at-risk," or what we call "cash flow sensitivity," *see* Hayt/Song (1995).

7. One way to put this is that you can have *player-coaches,* but *player-referees* are another matter altogether.

8. Regardless of whether the firm marks to market for accounting, the firm must know the value of the risk management instruments (and this valuation must be independent from the trader's valuation).

9. And, the more active the firm is—either in the *magnitude* of transactions or in the *complexity* of transactions—the more expertise the firm must possess.

10. And, once you have decided what to educate about, you have to decide how much of education to provide and in what format.

11. And, in some very well-publicized instances in 1994, that "increase variance" outcome is precisely what the firms got.

12. This guidance was also released in a joint statement from the SEC, the CFTC, and the SIB.

11

Risk Oversight for the Senior Manager: Controlling Risk in Dealers

ROBERT M. MARK

Senior management needs to encourage the implementation of best-practice risk management to control risk and provide the appropriate risk oversight for their dealing rooms. Accordingly, senior managers play a critical role in establishing the right corporate culture where best-practice risk management can flourish. Dealers and risk management personnel ultimately behave in a way that rewards them. A challenge for senior management is to harmonize the behavior patterns of dealers and risk managers into an environment where both sides "sink or swim" together and avoid an "us vs. them" mentality that fosters unnecessary political divisions between dealers and risk managers.

The trade-off between maximizing short-term revenue versus incurring incremental expense required to control risk is one that needs delicate balancing. For example, one often has to invest in longer term risk management projects whose benefits won't be apparent until several years out. Significant pressure to build revenue in lean years often discourages any long-term investment necessary to build a best-practice risk control infrastructure. In other words, short-term revenue maximization behavior is often diametrically opposite to the behavior required to encourage first-class risk management. The risk manager is typically asked to install the necessary risk controls at the least possible cost.

Senior management needs to ensure that risk managers are skilled with the requisite experience so that one can rationalize harmonizing compensation systems between dealers and risk managers. Risk managers need to be rewarded with fair and reasonable compensation in order to attract the best talent. Any organization that has dramatic disparities between dealer and risk management compensation is setting itself up for abject failure. One can easily forecast that the flow of talents will move from risk management to the deal side should compensation systems not be harmonized. In other words, these disparities can create a reverse sieve phenomenon. This classic failure to harmonize compensation systems can be placed squarely on the shoulders of senior management.

Many dealing organizations have neither invested in establishing the appropriate policies nor in developing the appropriate risk methodologies. To succeed, dealing organizations need to build a galvanizing organizational environment and the necessary infrastructure to measure, price, and control risk in a comprehensive manner.

The degree to which senior management has created best-practice risk management to control risk in their dealing operations can be benchmarked against best-practice policies, methodologies, and infrastructure.

The next section gives an overview of the organizational environment and its building blocks that should facilitate best-practice risk management. We then present the framework for risk management with its three pillars: best-practice policies, best-practice methodologies, and best-practice infrastructure. A detailed exposition of market risk and credit risk methodologies folllows. We end this chapter with some concluding thoughts.

DESIGN OF THE ORGANIZATIONAL FRAMEWORK

Senior management has to put building blocks into place to facilitate the penetration in the firm of a best-practice risk management culture. These building blocks are discussed next.

Integrated Risk Management

Senior managers need to encourage the development of integrated systems that aggregate the various risks (i.e., market, credit, liquidity, operational, etc.) generated by their businesses. An environment where the dealing units calculate their risk separately, with different rules, will not provide a meaningful oversight of the firmwide risk. The increasing complexity of products, linkages between markets, and the potential benefits offered by portfolio effects are pushing risk-literate organizations toward standardizing and integrating their risk management. Dealers and risk managers need an integrated risk management capability to ensure that they achieve an optimal return to risk tradeoff. Further, the implicit objectives of the dealer, risk manager, and the board are often not compatible with one another. For example, the board of directors is too often solely concerned about avoiding the big loss in contrast to encouraging a balanced book of businesses.

Some leading-edge dealing organizations have begun to improve their risk management capabilities through the creation of a highly integrated centralized risk management function. This approach allows one to measure and manage all of the firm's risk in terms of a common unit, as well as to analyze portfolios according to a wide variety of criteria. However, before integrated risk management can be truly effective, a common language has to be developed for measuring the different risks that dealers have to face. One should be able to compare and correlate every possible quantifiable risk, including market risk, credit risk, liquidity risk, operational risk, regulatory risk, and "human error" risk.

In this chapter we propose to measure all market risk according to a Risk Measurement Unit (RMU) methodology[1] which is somewhat similar to what is known as Value-at-Risk (VaR). Similarly, one can measure all credit risk according to a Credit Risk Measurement Unit (CRMU) methodology. The RMU and CRMU methodologies are described in detail later.

Corporate Culture

Dealing firms need to recognize that the firm's core values have a direct impact on the degree to which dealers and risk managers behave in mutually supportive ways.

A partnership between risk managers and their business counterparts is critical to the successful creation of a strong risk management culture. Each side needs to spend time seeking solutions in partnership, rather than avoiding each others' political minefields. Risk analysis should be used as an input to evaluate new businesses, determine dealer compensation, and to optimize one's investments. One should also take great care to integrate risk management requirements with business needs. When it is done well, integrated risk management permeates as organization's culture and underscores the importance of the "risk factor" when managers make any sort of strategic decision.

Integrated risk management means more than bundling together all the company's risks into a single variance-covariance matrix. More importantly, it means making sure the corporate culture embraces a "philosophy" of integrated risk management. For example, one needs to ensure that the risk management program is backed by the board, the firm's senior managers, as well as by the firm's top revenue generators. Furthermore, it means that risk is explicitly considered prior to making high-level strategic decisions.

Senior management needs to proactively create a corporate culture where best-practice risk management is considered crucial to the health of the organization. Leaders need to set the appropriate tone. All too often, senior management abrogate their leadership responsibilities to promote an appropriate culture. For example, senior management often delegates many responsibilities to subordinates in order to avoid dealing with classic conflicts between dealers and risk managers. The crafting and nurturing of the right culture, which includes having a healthy respect for best-practice risk management, is a necessary condition to facilitate a meaningful oversight of risk. In order to accomplish the genesis of a pro-active, risk-focused culture, it is important to hire the best people.

Tying Compensation to Risk

The single clearest way to make risk management tangible is by tying compensation to risk. Best-practice risk management provides the requisite tools that allow one to monitor the relationship between return and risk. In particular, businesses should be charged for the risks they incur, instead of using pure, unmodified returns as the sole guideline for determining bonuses.[2]

Dealers need to look at return-to-risk ratios, within the context of a Risk-Adjusted Return on Risk-Adjusted Capital (RAROraC or, more simply RAROC) framework, in order to make risk oversight meaningful. This sort of information has broad strategic implications. If two business opportunities have similar projected net returns, but one has much more (e.g., risk measured by the RMU and CRMU exposures) then one should prefer the less risky venture. One needs to calculate a risk-adjusted return on capital as the ratio of the expected net profit to the risk-adjusted capital, the later being in part a function of the RMU and CRMU exposures.

Risk Education

Providing first-class risk education is a key component of every successful integrated risk management program. Dealers and risk managers should understand why they have to change the way they do things. Staff are more comfortable if they know that new risk procedures exist for a good business reason. Risk education, moreover, can prevent human error by actively involving staff at all levels in the risk control process. Staff need to clearly understand more than basic limit monitoring techniques (Figure 11.1). For example, dealers and risk managers need to be educated on the analytics behind the risk measures.

Dealers and risk managers should also be educated on how risk can be used as the basis for allocating economic capital. Education should also be provided on how economic capital attribution techniques can be linked to pricing risk (i.e., to determining the cost of economic capital). For example, one very useful educational tool is to provide each dealer with an economic capital placemat that provides the spread required to cover the cost of economic capital for each deal type. One should educate dealers and risk managers on how to utilize the risk measurement tools to enhance their portfolio management skills (Figure 11.1).

Prototype Risk Management Organization

The prototype organization for a risk management division is shown Figure 11.2 with seven distinct but related risk units, each one corresponding to a key risk management function: Trading Room Market Risk Management (TrMr), Trading Room Credit Risk Management (TrCr), Risk Management Information Systems (RiskMIS), Advanced Analytics, Risk Advisory, RAROC (i.e., capital attribution) and Corporate Treasury.

The TrMr, TrCr, RAROC, Risk Advisory and Corporate Treasury units have the responsibility to work with RiskMIS and Advanced Analytics in rolling out risk reporting systems. Best practice calls for the TrCr unit to be separate from the corporate credit unit and linked tightly with the TrMr unit. The Advanced Analytics unit typically develops the mathematics required in the implementation of RMU and CRMU methodologies; vets all models developed by the dealer; proposes, when possible, more robust, accurate and computationally efficient models to price and hedge complex securities; and conducts research to develop the appropriate tools for the next generation of

---

FIGURE 11.1   Risk Education

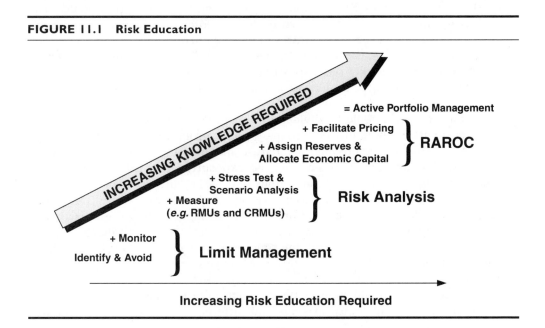

FIGURE 11.2   Organization Chart

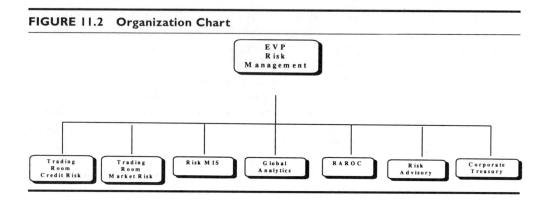

securities and risk management problems. The RAROC unit is responsible for ensuring that economic capital is properly allocated as a function of risk. Dealers need, however, to be already comfortable with using the RMU and CRMU reports prior to generating risk-adjusted returns on risk-adjusted capital for the dealing room. The Corporate Treasury function actively manages the residual risk. For example, the Corporate Treasury unit actively manages the gap created by interest rate mismatching on their balance sheet through executing in the market place. The Risk Advisory unit focuses on operational risk and provides both internal and fee-based external risk advisory services.

One needs to clarify roles and responsibilities among the risk management organization and the other units. For example, how should the TrCr unit interact with the overall institutionwide credit process. Should the Advanced Analytics unit develop as well as vet models? How does the Risk Advisory unit interact with the audit/inspection unit? How does the TrMr unit relate to risk managers within a business unit, and so on.

Each of the distinct units should have their infrastructure geared to satisfy specific risk-related objectives. For example, each morning the head of TrMr could chair a meeting of senior managers and global dealers in order to review and debate the previous end-of-day market risk exposures in light of current market conditions. For the rest of the trading day, the head of TrMr would keep abreast of ongoing developments and changes in market risk exposures. The head of TrMr will spend the day following markets, talking to traders, as well as trying to stay on top of situations as they develop.

The TrMr unit itself could be divided into distinct but related sections. For example, one can create three distinct groups: a policy group responsible for developing risk management methods and standards, an operating group charged with continuously monitoring the firm's market risk exposures, and a third group of market risk managers who cover specific regions (e.g., Asia, Europe) or products (e.g., commodity derivatives, high yield bonds). Product specialists within TrMr could provide direct risk management support to each product manager. Similarly, the TrCr unit needs to have its infrastructure geared to satisfy specific credit risk-related objectives. The objective is to shrink the time from an idea occurring in a trader's head to management review of the resulting market risk or credit risk exposures and approval of a trade.

The RiskMIS unit should support the production of the market risk and credit risk exposures. Different legacy systems and different local back-end processing

FIGURE 11.3   Risk System Infrastructure

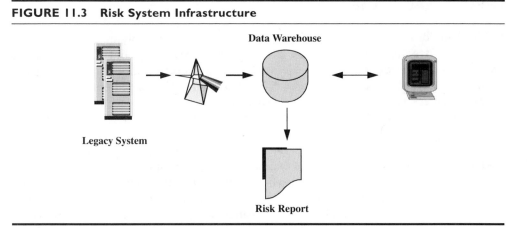

systems can transmit raw transaction-level data from the legacy systems to a central-ized data warehouse (Figure 11.3). Transaction data should be transferred at the end of each trading day, with the risk reports being made available early the next morn-ing. A market rate feed, comprising a broad range of automated market data feeds, and manual market data inputs as well as broker-dealer quotes for Over-the-Counter (OTC) products, should supply necessary information to the warehouse. Relatively static data, such as market volatilities and correlations, should also be resident in the warehouse.

The risk reports produced by the RiskMIS function are to be used by senior dealer and risk management personnel for monitoring risk, reporting on capital ade-quacy levels and allocating risk capital among global product lines. For example, RiskMIS should generate a report which displays the risk taken against limits within a consolidated authority, for each of say four main risk classes, with uniform mea-sures (Figure 11.4.).

FIGURE 11.4   Market Risk Authorities

MARKET RISK CLASS	Limits (RMUs)	Exposures (RMUs)	Usage (%)
Interest Rate	200	150	75%
Foreign Exchange	100	50	50%
Commodity	25	15	60%
Equity	75	25	33%
Grand total	300	150	50%

THREE PILLAR FRAMEWORK

Today, many dealing organizations have a structure that can only manage their current level of trading activities to the bare minimum standard, and risk assessment stays under the direct control of dealers. There is a need to establish a risk management function independent of direct risk takers. Senior management needs to encourage dealers and risk managers to work together in order to accelerate their efforts toward establishing a more uniform and sophisticated risk management framework.

The framework can be benchmarked in terms of policies, methodologies, and infrastructure. It also needs to include establishing an environment that is philosophically and culturally attuned to promote best-practice risk management. One needs to develop best-practice policies (e.g., trading authorities) as well as best-practice methodologies (e.g., RMU and CRMU measures) that protect against losses while supporting a profitable business. One also needs to build a best-practice infrastructure (Figure 11.5). An independent first-class active management of risk includes the capability to attribute capital, appropriately price risk, and to actively manage the portfolio of residual risks. Further, utilizing a sports analogy, first-class risk management should include not only having an outstanding goal keeper but also the ability to move up the field and help the team score.

Establishing the appropriate policies, methodologies, and infrastructure, as illustrated in Figure 11.6, are the "necessary" three pillars for building a first-class risk management function. However, the function is only as strong as its weakest pillar.

Best-Practice Policies

Best-practice policies, as illustrated in Figure 11.7, should follow directly from business strategies. From a risk perspective, one needs to set reasonable risk tolerances regarding how much risk the firm is willing to assume. Unambiguous and measurable

FIGURE 11.5   Risk Management Framework

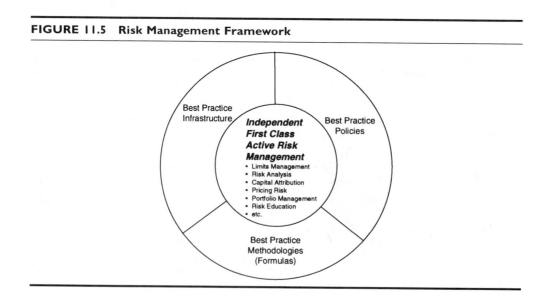

FIGURE 11.6   Necessary Three Pillars

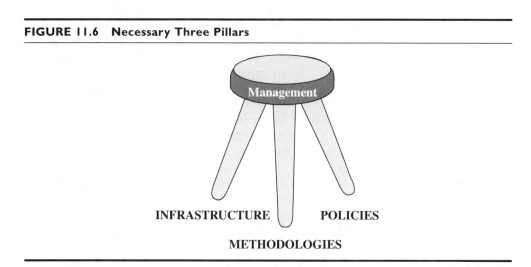

authorities need to be set within the risk tolerances established by policy. Also, one needs to review the internal and external disclosure of a business unit's risk profile (e.g., display performance on an economic capital at risk basis).

Market Risk Policy

Dealers and risk managers should establish a policy that explicitly states their risk appetite in terms of a statistically defined *worst case* loss. In other words, dealers need to have a policy that states how much they are willing to put at risk. Most major financial institutions are moving toward measuring risk according to a VaR framework that calculates risk based on a statistically derived worst case loss.

Going forward, banks with sophisticated risk measurement systems will be able to utilize their own internal risk methodology to calculate the required amount of

FIGURE 11.7   Best-Practice Policies

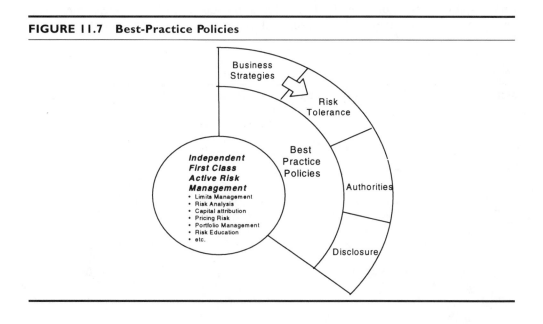

market risk regulatory capital in lieu of the more onerous standardized regulatory approach. For example, one could develop a policy that conservatively defines a statistically defined *worst case* loss in "normal markets," as an amount such that there is less than ⅕th of 1% probability of losing more than the worst case amount in one day. In other words, one can expect to exceed the statistically defined worst case loss in 1 out of every 500 business days.

A simple example illustrates what we mean by a statistically defined worst case market risk policy for a bond (e.g., a short position in a five-year Treasury note). Typical old-style risk methodologies are based on a simple parallel shift in the yield curve. One then calculates the amount at risk by assuming that every point along the yield curve shifts downwards in a parallel fashion by some arbitrary amount (say 1 bp^3 or 25 bp). For example, assume the five-year yield to maturity is 6.75% (Figure 11.8a). One can arbitrarily assume that the five-year yield to maturity declines overnight by 25 bp from 6.75% to 6.50%. One could also further assume, as illustrated in Figure 11.8b, that every point on the yield curve declines in parallel by the same amount (i.e., 25 bp). This is a simplistic approach since the yield curve rarely shifts in a parallel fashion.

A more realistic approach is to calculate a statistically defined worst case risk which should correspond to a more complicated nonparallel shift in the yield curve. For example, the yield curve could flatten, steepen, or invert (Figure 11.9). Accordingly, the market risk policy should state that one will measure market risk in terms of a statistically defined worst case loss, where the statistically defined worst case loss considers both parallel and nonparallel shifts in the yield curve.

The RMU methodology captures both parallel and complex nonparallel shifts in the yield curve based on actual historical changes in the yield curve.

Credit Risk Policy

Senior management should adopt a credit risk measurement policy that calls for measuring credit risk for off-balance sheet products, such as an interest rate swap, according to an analytic approach that is consistent with the one implemented for RMU. The CRMU approach is an outgrowth of the RMU approach. The CRMU approach enables one to measure off-balance sheet credit risk based on calculating a mark-to-market

---

FIGURE 11.8   Yield Curve (a) and Parallel Shift (b)

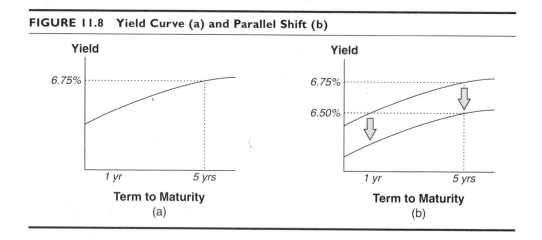

FIGURE 11.9

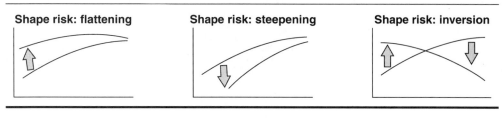

Shape risk: flattening | Shape risk: steepening | Shape risk: inversion

(i.e., current market risk exposure) and adding future exposure. This technique will be discussed later in the chapter.

Dealers should have a policy which calls for calculating and reporting their off-balance sheet credit risk on a daily basis.

Operational Risk Policy

All trading authorities should include a full review of operational risks which implies policies to review the introduction of all new products, and vet all pricing models used to value positions by an independent risk management function.

One needs to have confidence that the appropriate mathematical model is being used to value any product. All product valuation models need to be vetted prior to the start of a business when these models are used to mark-to-model a position of illiquid instruments. Operational risk can be reduced if one adopts a policy which calls for enhancing, consolidating, and integrating existing market and credit risk authorities with disparate measures, into new authorities.

It was the ability of the traders at Barings to act without authority and detection that allowed such large losses. The Bank of England report on Barings revealed some general operational risk lessons. First, management teams have the duty to understand *fully* the businesses they manage. Second, responsibility for each business activity has to be *clearly* established and communicated. Third, relevant internal controls, including independent risk management, *must* be established for all business activities. Fourth, top management and the Audit Committee must ensure that significant weaknesses are resolved *quickly*. Senior management needs to ensure that policies are established to ensure transparency in their dealing operations. It was operational risk that motivated and exacerbated the initial trading losses. Internal risk control structure should be designed to ensure existence, completeness and accuracy for all transactions via appropriate segregation of duties.

Best-Practice Methodologies

The best-practice methodologies, as illustrated in Figure 11.10, refer to applying the appropriate analytic models to measure market risk, credit risk, operational risk, and so on. The objective is not solely to measure risk, but also to ensure that the pricing and valuation methodologies are appropriate.

For example, leading practitioners such as the Group of Thirty (G30) recommend that dealers value derivatives at market prices, and that market and credit risk be measured according to a Value-at-Risk framework. Specifically, the G30 recommends explicitly that credit risk should be measured based on current plus potential exposures.

FIGURE 11.10   Best-Practice Methodologies

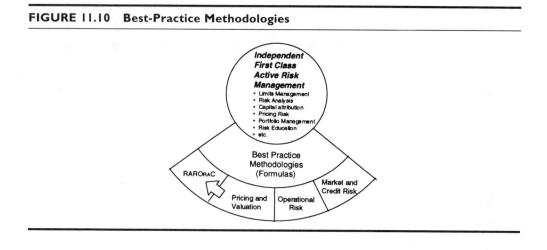

Finally, measurement tools should be developed to ensure that one is on the efficient frontier of the risk/reward trade-off. Toward this end, implementing a RAROraC approach is a particularly important priority. Simply put, what you can't measure well, you can't manage or price well.

Risk Measurement Methodology

Dealers and risk managers need to jointly continually upgrade their risk measurement capabilities. For example, assume last year that one utilized a market risk measurement approach based on a simple one basis point parallel shift in the yield curve. The sensitivity is equal to the value of the portfolio after the shift less the original value of the portfolio.

Consider now the same example as in the previous section (i.e., a short position in a five-year Treasury note, with a yield of 6.75%). If interest rates were to rise, then the portfolio would gain value. The value of the position at the current yield of 6.75% is $43.764 million. Assume now that interest rates decline by one basis point from 6.75% to 6.74%, then the value of the short position declines to $43.744 million. Accordingly, the sensitivity of the portfolio is the difference between the values at 6.75% and 6.74%, which represents a loss of $20,000.

One could easily upgrade to a more sophisticated approach, say at the third level, in order to capture level and shape risk. Ultimately, one needs to expand the third level measurement approach toward a full RMU measurement methodology that encompasses more intricate risk types (e.g., credit spread, vega related option risk). This permits a consistent measurement of market risk across all businesses. Detailed descriptions of the RMU and CRMU methodologies are provided later in this chapter.

Pricing and Valuation Methodologies

A valuation adjustment refers to the degree to which one fails to properly adjust the valuation of a position for going forward risk. The G30 recommends that one should take the mid-market price of the trade less the sum of the expected credit loss and the going forward administrative cost when valuing a perfectly matched derivative transaction. Accordingly, one needs to analyze the reasonableness of one's approach to estimating an expected credit loss. The G30 also suggests additional adjustments for close out costs (i.e., "eliminating" market risk) as well as investing and funding cost.

One needs to develop the appropriate techniques to value derivatives in a highly illiquid market. In other words, one needs to differentiate valuing a transaction where one has only limited price discovery from valuing a transaction where one has reasonable price discovery. For example, one would observe limited price discovery for long tenor (e.g., a 10-year option on a 20-year swap) and highly structured derivative transactions. This necessitates assumption-driven valuation methodologies (e.g., constructing the term structure of interest rates beyond 10 years) that normally require use of mark-to-model techniques. The need to make assumptions for illiquid transactions typically forces one to accept a wider range of reasonable valuations. The attributes of the selected model become highly important in terms of the ultimate value placed upon an illiquid derivative position. A wider range of values impacts the calculation of the average expected and average unexpected credit risk exposure levels (which in turn is utilized to establish the projected level of loss) and implies higher capital attribution for those wider ranges.

Accounting for Portfolio Effects

If one prices risk at the transaction level, without considering portfolio effects across the entire organization, then one would price in more risk than is necessary. Accordingly, one needs to consider the practical difficulties of the more complicated task of pricing in risk at the portfolio level (versus the relatively simpler task of pricing in risk at the transaction level).

If portfolio effects are taken into account, one can calculate the required economic capital for the entire organization. Economic capital is attributed as a function of risk. The economic capital required at higher organization levels, as illustrated in Figure 11.11, is less than the sum of the economic capital across organizational units required at lower levels. In other words, benefits arise from diversification effects such that the whole is less then the sum of the parts. Economic capital should be compared across organizational levels and within each level (e.g., across products). A portfolio-based risk measurement system incorporating correlations can assist an

FIGURE 11.11   Capital Allocation Portfolio Effects

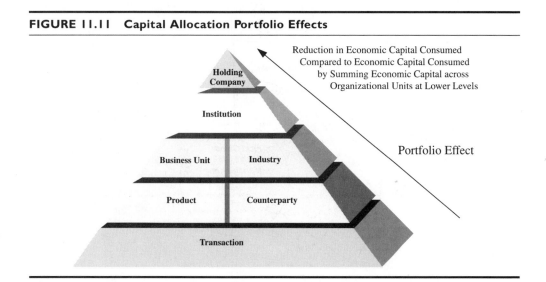

organization in understanding its risk profile not only by counterparty, but also for the organization as a whole. For example, a well-designed portfolio risk measurement approach enables one to slice and dice risk (the vegematic approach) vertically and horizontally across an organization to facilitate the pricing of risk.

Best-Practice Infrastructure

The importance of infrastructure can be appreciated by considering a situation where policies and methodology have been developed, but there is no infrastructure to make them work. Infrastructure is expensive and time consuming to construct.

The first and most important component of one's infrastructure, as illustrated in Figure 11.12, is people. One needs people with great skills, rewarded with fair and reasonable compensation, who have to be trained (or recruited), managed and motivated. Given the right environment and support, it is people who will make everything else happen. Pricing decisions will not be derived solely from a complex analytical black box—management judgment will always be a significant input.

Data integrity is an important competitive advantage. One needs to translate market data into risk management information for both transaction makers and policy makers. Finally, a key goal (critical to the successful management of risk) is to integrate one's risk management operations and technology.

Integrated, Goal-Congruent Risk Management Process

An integrated, goal-congruent risk management process which puts all the elements together, as illustrated in Figure 11.13, is the key which opens the door to a best practice assessment, management, and understanding of the return to risk tradeoffs (whose efforts are consistent with one's business strategies). Integrated refers to the need to ensure that one avoids having a fragmented approach to risk management.

FIGURE 11.12   Best-Practice Infrastructure

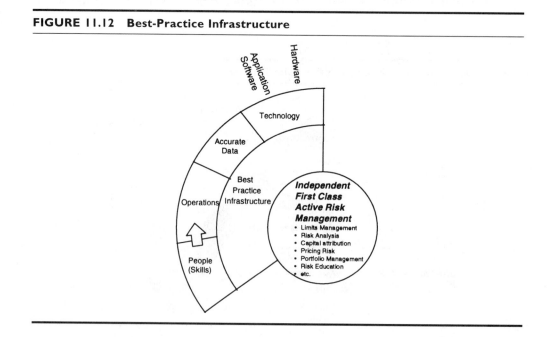

FIGURE 11.13   Integrated, Goal Congruent Risk Management Process

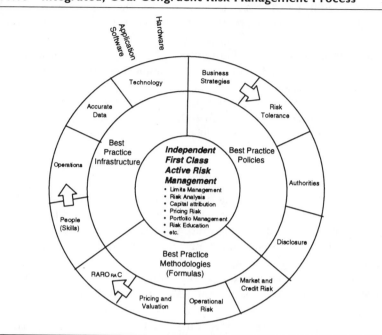

Risk management is only as strong as the weakest link. Goal-congruent refers to the need to ensure that one's policies and methodologies are consistent with one another. For example, one goal is to have an apple-to-apple risk measurement scheme so that one can compare risk across all products and aggregate risk at any level. This is a one-firm one-view approach that also recognizes the specific risk dynamics of each business.

MARKET RISK

The complexity and variety of today's financial instruments in an increasingly volatile environment have made the need to measure and control market risk an important task. In this section, an analytic framework is presented with the objective of measuring and controlling risk via the RMU approach which was mentioned in the introduction. The proposed framework enables dealers to consider the degree of risk that all trades have relative to each other, and to the portfolio as a whole. An RMU system can be designed where risk limits for lower-level organizational units can be dynamically shared within one overall limit. Risk can be added both horizontally and vertically across an organization under an RMU-based system.

Risk Management Basics

A well-designed, clearly articulated strategic plan calls for the implementation of increasingly sophisticated analytical tools. The plan should be designed to recognize that most of the major risks can be handled in the first twenty percent of the effort. The evolution of market risk measurement, as shown in Figure 11.14, normally proceeds from a crude assessment of risk based on the nominal amount traded, to higher levels of sophistication where risk is controlled based on an RMU system.

The next step beyond nominal amounts for an interest rate product is a system based on Basis Point Value (BPV). This is also sometimes referred to as a *duration-based* or *risk-equivalent system.*

The BPV approach measures the risk arising from a one-basis-point change in yield. One can compute the BPV for an individual security based on specifications such as its coupon, maturity, and market price (or yield to maturity). Two positions with different nominal amounts and different characteristics are risk equivalent if they have the same BPVs. Risk equivalent confidence levels can be constructed. They are sometimes referred to as duration-based confidence bands on change in price.[4] The third level of sophistication combines BPV with volatility.

The last step generalizes the approach at the portfolio level by taking into consideration the composition of the portfolio, volatilities and correlations between the yield changes. Then, the risks of the long and short positions partially net out according to their degree of correlation. The volatility of the changes in yields are combined with their correlations across key points on the yield curve, to produce a portfolio RMU. This approach enables the RMU measure to capture nonparallel yield curve shifts.

Similarly, a well-formulated approach for a foreign currency portfolio would incorporate volatility and correlation parameters in the RMU computation. For example, the risk associated with simultaneously buying and selling two highly correlated currencies is less than the risk associated with simultaneously buying and selling two negligibly correlated currencies. Furthermore, options risk can be calculated utilizing RMU matrix techniques which capture the delta, gamma, vega, and theta risks.

FIGURE 11.14   Market Risk-Evolutionary Steps

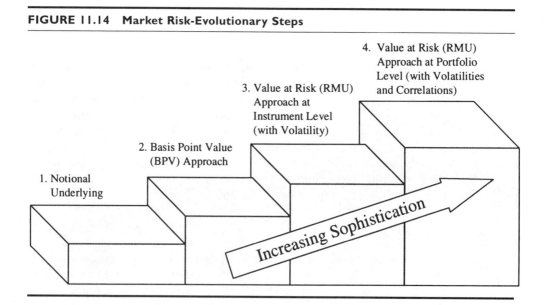

The Notional Approach

A notional system is deficient in that it simply adds the notional values of the securities in the portfolio, irrespective of their sensitivities. It does not differentiate between a long and short position, and ignores actual interest rate volatility as well as correlations between yield changes. For example, if a trader's limit equals $100 million notional, or if portfolio limit equals $200 million notional, then one does not explicitly know how much one is at risk over a given time period.

Basis Point Value (BPV) or Duration-Based Approach

The essence of the BPV approach, as illustrated in Figure 11.15, is to calculate the change in the price of a security that arises from a one basis point change in the yield of some benchmark security. One then compares this BPV with the impact of that same one basis point change in yield on the price of other securities. For example, assume that a one basis point rise in yield results in a $312 decline in the price of a one million dollar long four-year Treasury note . Accordingly, the amount of market risk exposure generated by a one basis point rise in yield is $312 per million dollars; that is, one could expect to lose $312 per million dollars given that the yield rises by one basis point.

Similarly, if there is a one basis point rise in yield then a one million dollar long 10-year Treasury note would decrease in price by $654. Accordingly, the 10-year Treasury note is over twice (2.1) as sensitive as the four-year Treasury note to each one basis point move. From these BPV calculations, it is possible to establish risk equivalents to some benchmark—say, the four-year Treasury note. Lowering the coupon and increasing the maturity raises the *BPV*. This is also sometimes referred to as a duration-based or risk equivalent system.

The BPV approach makes it much simpler to set meaningful limits with regard to exposure. For example, assume that the market risk exposure limit is equivalent to a

FIGURE 11.15   Basis Point Value Approach

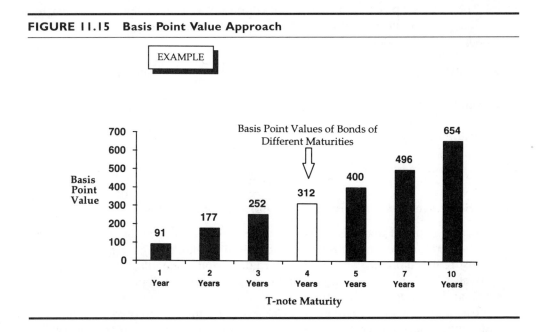

FIGURE 11.16   Sensitivity of Treasury Note Relative to Benchmark

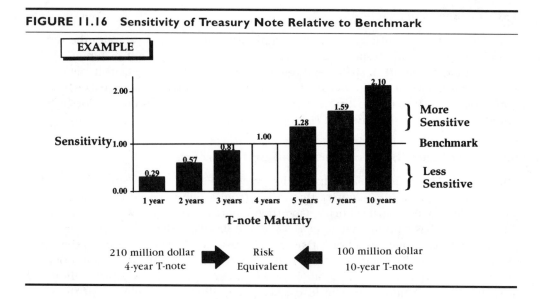

210 million dollar four-year Treasury note. The manager, as illustrated in Figure 11.16, has the choice of purchasing 210 million dollar four-year Treasury notes, or purchasing 100 million dollar 10-year Treasury Notes. These two positions are said to be *risk equivalent.*

The use of risk equivalent is directionally correct, but not very robust. The key weakness of the risk equivalent approach lies in its assumption of a parallel one basis point shift in the yield curve. According to duration analysis:

$$dP/P = -D \, di/(1 + i)$$

where P denotes the price of the bond, D its duration, and i the yield to maturity for a bond that pays a *coupon annually, dP* the price variation of the bond consecutive to a change di in its yield. It then follows:

$$dP = -D/(1 + i) \, P \, di$$

which can be rewritten as:

$$dP = -BPV \, di$$

if di is expressed in *bp.*

Transaction-Level RMU Approach Incorporating Volatilities

It is typically assumed that the statistical distribution of percentage price changes (i.e., rates of return) is approximately normally distributed. A worst case, market risk exposure based on two or three standard deviations then allows one to capture respectively 97.7% or 99.9% of all market configurations These percentages (97.7% or 99.9%) are called *levels of confidence.*

An easy way to approximate market risk exposure for a fixed-income security is by multiplying the security's BPV by a multiple of the volatility of the change in yield, for a given level of confidence. This approach only provides a reasonable approximation for small changes in yield, since the calculations ignore bond convexity, and only assume a linear relationship between price variations and changes in yield (Figure 11.17).

Figure 11.17 summarizes the transaction-level RMU approach where we assume for convenience that one RMU is equal to $1,000 of market risk exposure.

If K equals 2 then one RMU is the basic measure of market risk exposure such that actual exposure will exceed the number of RMUs on only one day in 43.5 (based on a risk tolerance of two standard deviations, i.e., a confidence level of 97.7%). If a position's VaR equals 10 RMUs then only 2.3% of the time will the market risk exposure exceed 10 times $1,000; that is, 97.7% of the time our market risk exposure will not exceed $10,000.

We can look at this from another perspective. Assume that an instrument has an overnight price risk of 1% at the 97.7% confidence level. If a transactor assumes a one million dollar position, the potential overnight market risk exposure equals 10,000 or 10 RMUs.

Typically, one calculates the volatility of the change in yield and the BPV by means of well-defined maturity buckets. In other words, the volatility of the change in yield does not need to be uniquely calculated for each individual security. It can be calculated by maturity bucket. For example, assume as before that the four-year Treasury note has a BPV of $312 per million, as illustrated in Table 11.1, and the volatility of the change in yield is five basis points. If a 1 million dollar position is assumed then the RMU total is 3.1 RMUs ($312 \times 2 \times 5bp = $3,120$).

The rationale behind the RMU system is straightforward. From the dealer's point of view, the market risk exposure for his individual position is assessed in terms of the overnight volatility of the value of the underlying securities and is quantified by the RMU approach. The exposure of an individual position will need to be determined as a function of the time required to close a position, which itself varies as a function of liquidity.

Observe that RMUs can be added up across a portfolio of products to compute a conservative estimate of portfolio exposure. The estimate is conservative because,

---

FIGURE 11.17   VAR Formula

$$\text{Value-at-Risk (VAR)} \approx \text{BPV} * K * \sigma$$

where:

Basis Point Value (BPV) = Price movement due to a one basis point change in yield

σ = Standard deviation of the change in yield in basis points

K = Number of standard deviations

$$\text{RMUs} \approx \frac{\text{VAR}}{1000}$$

TABLE 11.1   Calculating RMUs

Instrument	One Basis Point Value (per million)		"Worst Case" Movement (bp)		Total Value at Risk	RMUs
1 year T-note	91		12		1,092	1.1
2 year T-note	177		11		1,947	1.9
3 year T-note	252	*	10	≅	2,520	2.5
4 year T-note	312		10		3,120	3.1
5 year T-note	400		9		3,600	3.6
7 year T-note	496		9		4,464	4.5
10 year T-note	654		8		5,232	5.2

where:

2σ offers 97.7% coverage = "Worst Case" movement

unlike the methodology described in the next section, it does not take account of any portfolio effects caused by the degree of correlation between instruments.

Portfolio-Level RMU Approach Incorporating Volatilities and Correlations

Dealers need to take into account both volatility and correlation data in order to compute accurately the market risk exposure for an entire portfolio. Correlation looks at the degree to which two variables move with, or against, one another. Table 11.2 illustrates a situation in which a dealer has sold short A and purchased B. We will assume that the worst case market risk for both A and B is 2 million dollars. We will further assume that the current market value of instruments A and B each equal 100 million dollars.

The portfolio manager needs to know what will be the effect on the value of instrument B if the value of instrument A changes overnight. The market risk exposure of the portfolio, as illustrated in Table 11.3, clearly depends on the correlation between positions A and B.

TABLE 11.2   Calculating RMUs: Example Scenario

Action	Amount (Millions)	Worst Case Market Risk (RMU)
A	100	2000
B	100	2000
Total	200	?

TABLE 11.3   Portfolio Exposure and Correlation

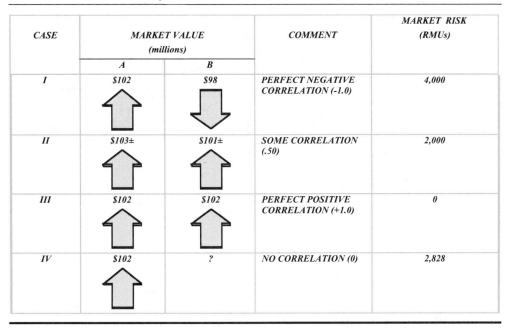

CASE	MARKET VALUE (millions)		COMMENT	MARKET RISK (RMUs)
	A	B		
I	$102	$98	PERFECT NEGATIVE CORRELATION (-1.0)	4,000
II	$103±	$101±	SOME CORRELATION (.50)	2,000
III	$102	$102	PERFECT POSITIVE CORRELATION (+1.0)	0
IV	$102	?	NO CORRELATION (0)	2,828

Table 11.3 displays four possibilities. In Case I where the price movements of A and B are perfectly negatively correlated, the RMUs are additive. If the price change for A and B has a 0.5 correlation , as illustrated in Case II, then the portfolio RMUs are the same as the RMUs of either the short or long position, If there is a perfect positive correlation, as in Case III, then any increase in market risk exposure generated by one instrument will be completely offset by a decrease in the market risk exposure generated by the other. Note that the numbers chosen for Case II are hypothetical and chosen to illustrate that market risk exposure, when correlation is .5, should fall most of the time half way between market risk exposures for Cases I and III. If there is a zero correlation, as in Case IV, then the portfolio RMU is moderately larger than the RMUs of either the short or the long position.

Generic RMU Examples

Portfolio 1 (Table 11.4) consists of $5 million long D, $10 million short E, and $5 million long F. Portfolio 2 (Table 11.5) consists of the same portfolio as portfolio 1 without the position E. Portfolio 3 (Table 11.6) consists of a $10 million short E and $10 million long F.

Assume that twice the overnight volatility of the percentage change in price (two standard deviations) for D, E, and F equals 1.87%, 1.56%, and 1.54%, respectively. Assume also that the correlation between E and F equals .97. Similarly, the correlation between F and D equals .08, and between D and E equals .06 (Table 11.4)

RMU exposure for position D in portfolio 1 is computed by multiplying 1.87 percent times $5 million, which equals $93,500 or 93.5 RMUs. Similarly, RMU exposure

TABLE 11.4   RMU Example 1

Item in Portfolio	Dollar Position	Item RMUs	Overnight Volatility (2σ)
D	5,000,000	93.5	1.87%
E	-10,000,000	156.0	1.56%
F	5,000,000	77.0	1.54%
Gross Position	20,000,000	326.5	
Net Position	0	122.9	

	Correlations		
	D	E	F
F	0.08	0.97	1.00
E	0.06	1.00	
D	1.00		

for positions E and F are, respectively, 1.56 percent × $10 million, i.e., 156 RMUs and 1.54 percent × $5 million, i.e., 77 RMUs. The gross position item RMUs of 326.5 is simply the sum of the RMU exposures. The net position of 122.9 RMUs is computed based on an RMU algorithm that allows offsets between positions based on their correlation. The algorithm to compute RMUs for a portfolio is described in the next section. The portfolio RMU is much lower than the gross position RMUs derived by simply adding the individual RMUs due to the high correlation between the short E and long F positions.

Assume that the $10 million short E position has been closed. Then portfolio 1 becomes portfolio 2. One can observe that the gross position in Example 2 ($10 million) is less than that in Example 1 ($20 million), yet the market risk exposure (VaR) in Example 2 (125.8 RMUs) is higher than in Example 1 (122.9 RMUs).

Consider next the position in Example 3. The gross position in Example 3 (i.e., $20 million) is higher than that in Example 2 (i.e., $10 million), yet the market risk exposure (VaR) in Example 3 (i.e., 38 RMUs) is lower. The VaR in Example 2 (i.e., 125.8 RMUs), due to the low correlation between D and F, is about the same if we were long D and short F, or were short both D and F. Observe that neither gross nor net notional amount by itself is a good indicator of market risk.

TABLE 11.5   RMU Example 2

Item in Portfolio	Dollar Position	RMU	Overnight Volatility (2σ)
D	5,000,000	93.5	1.87%
F	5,000,000	77.0	1.54%
Gross Position	10,000,000	170.5	
Net Position	10,000,000	125.8	

TABLE 11.6 RMU Example 3

Item in Portfolio	Dollar Position	RMU	Overnight Volatility (2σ)
E	-10,000,000	156.0	1.56%
F	10,000,000	154.0	1.54%
Gross Position	20,000,000	310.0	
Net Position	0	38.0	

RMU Algorithm

Consider the following portfolio composition N_x of security X and N_y of security Y, where N_x and N_y denote the dollar amount invested in each security, this value being positive or negative whether the position is long or short.

The portfolio total volatility (σ) expressed in dollars is:

$$\sigma^2 = N_x^2\sigma_x^2 + N_y^2\sigma_y^2 + 2\rho_{x,y}N_x N_y \sigma_x \sigma_y$$

If one defines the portfolio RMUs as equal to k standard deviations, where k represents the number of standard deviations associated with a desired confidence level, then:

$$\text{RMU}_p = \sqrt{\text{RMU}_x^2 + \text{RMU}_y^2 + 2\rho_{x,y}\text{RMU}_x\,\text{RMU}_y}$$

One should be clear that the RMUs are equal to or greater than zero. Accordingly, to be strictly correct, one should define an RMU = $\sqrt{N^2}\,K\sigma$ where N is positive or negative as a function of whether one is long or short. Nevertheless, for simplicity of presentation we show RMU = $NK\,\sigma$.

The RMU calculations for the portfolios in Examples 2 and 3 are:
Example 2:

$$\text{RMU}_p = \text{SQRT}\left(\text{RMU}_D^2 + \text{RMU}_F^2 + 2\times p_{DF}\times\text{RMU}_D\times\text{RMU}_F\right)$$

$$= \text{SQRT}\left[(93.5)^2 + (77.0)^2 + 2(.08)(93.5)(77.0)\right]$$

$$= 125.8$$

Example 3:

$$\text{RMU}_p = \text{SQRT}\left(\text{RMU}_{E_2}^2 + \text{RMU}_F^2 + 2\times p_{EF}\times\text{RMU}_E\times\text{RMU}_F\right)$$

$$= \text{SQRT}\left[(156.0)^2 + (154.0)^2 + 2(-0.97)(156)(154)\right]$$

$$= 38.0$$

Stress Testing Assumptions

The worst case assumption (Figure 11.18) depends on the risk coverage one chooses. The assumption that the percentage price change is derived from a stable, normally distributed probability density function (pdf) implies that the correlation is constant over time and that the volatility grows proportionately with the square root of time. These assumptions need to be stress tested.[4] A more realistic alternative to the normal pdf assumption (e.g., a jump process or a fat tail distribution) may require that volatility and correlation estimates be augmented by additional statistics.

Fat tail distributions do not necessarily imply a nonstable statistical process. For example, the underlying process may be a simple mixed diffusion-jump process whereby the percentage price change is normally distributed until interrupted by a price jump. The price discontinuities may come from structural breaks in the market. The frequency of the price jumps may be described by a Poisson distribution, whereby the expected number of jumps in a time interval T is a function of the jump parameter λ. In other words, the time interval between jumps is governed by an exponential pdf, and the number of expected jumps in time interval T can be determined from the jump parameter λ (Figure 11.19).

Further, the size of price jump may be normally distributed with volatility σ_2. The complex mixed diffusion-jump process may consist of varying per period volatilities where each period is defined by the time between jumps (Figure 11.20).

The appropriate (e.g., exponential) weighting of data, to provide one single estimate of volatility, may provide a reasonable alternative to the more complex task of estimating multiple volatility parameters.[5]

BPV versus RMU Based Hedge

Assume one needed to compute the number of liability instruments (N) to hedge an asset. Let P_A and P_L denote the price of the asset and liability, respectively. Further,

---

FIGURE 11.18 Choosing Risk Coverage and Worst-Case Assumptions

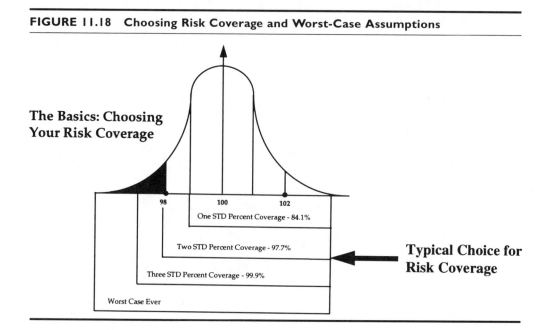

FIGURE 11.19 Jump Intervals and the Probability Density Function

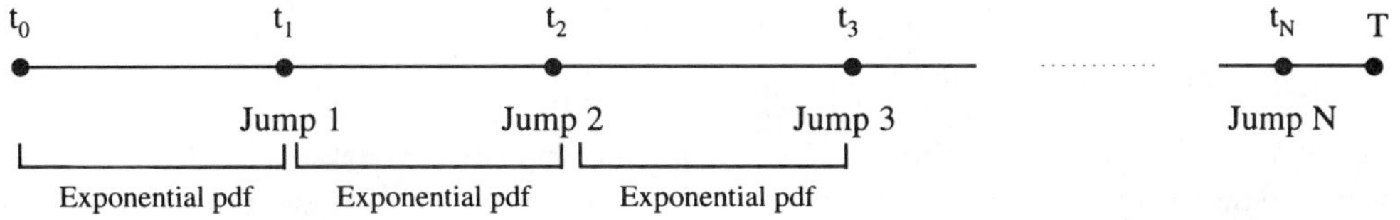
t_0
t_1
t_2
t_3
t_N
T
Jump 1
Jump 2
Jump 3
Jump N
Exponential pdf
Exponential pdf
Exponential pdf

let D_A and D_L equal the duration of the asset and liability, respectively. Also let dP_A and dP_L equal the change in price of the asset and liability, respectively; di_A and di_L equal the change in the yield of the asset and the change in the yield of the liability, respectively; and, N equals dP_A/dP_L.

As mentioned previously, the price changes are given by:

$$dP_A = -D_A/(1+i_A)\times P_A \times di_A = -\text{BPV}_\text{A} \times di_A$$

$$dP_l = -D_L/(1+i_L)\times P_L \times di_L = -\text{BPV}_L \times di_L$$

$$\text{then } N \text{ equals } \left(D_A/(1+i_A)\times P_A \times di_A\right)/\left(D_L/(1+i_L)\times P_L \times di_L\right) = \text{BPV}_L di_A/di_L$$

BPV matching assumes a flat yield curve $(i_A = i_L)$ and parallel yield curve shifts $(di_A = di_L)$ so that $N = (D_AP_A)/D_LP_L) = \text{BPV}_A/\text{BPV}_L$. If these strong assumptions are violated then one should not adopt a BPV based hedge approach.

The RMU hedging approach is superior to the BPV approach since it accounts for the correlation in the yield changes in the computation of the optimal hedge ratio. If one uses an amount N_y of security Y to hedge N_x of security X, the optimal hedge ratio is derived by solving for N_y which minimizes the total volatility σ^2 of the portfolio. This leads to an optimal hedge ratio of $N_y/N_x = \sigma_x/\sigma_y \times \rho_{xy}$. The residual risk, given an optimal hedge, is such that its variance is $\sigma^2 = N_x^2\sigma_x^2\,(1-\rho_{x,y}^2)$.[6]

A simple example illustrates why the BPV hedging approach is not as good as the RMU hedging approach. Assume we used the BPV matching technique to hedge a \$100 million in a long position 30-year T-bond. One would short \$536 million of the two-year T-note according to the BPV approach.[7] The resultant VaR is 889.7 RMUs. Optimal matching via an RMU approach, which looks at volatility and correlation, would be to hedge \$100 million long position in a 30-year bond through shorting \$327 million of the two-year T-note.[8] The resultant VaR is 760.8 RMUs, which shows

FIGURE 11.20 Complex Jump Process

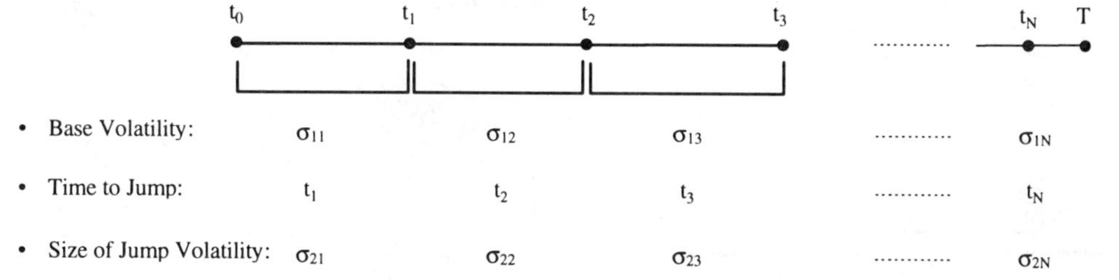
t_0
t_1
t_2
t_3
t_N
T
• Base Volatility: σ_{11} σ_{12} σ_{13} .... σ_{1N}
• Time to Jump: t_1 t_2 t_3 .... t_N
• Size of Jump Volatility: σ_{21} σ_{22} σ_{23} .... σ_{2N}

that the RMU based hedge reduced the risk over the BPV hedge by 128.9 RMUs (and saves transaction costs on $209 million of two-year T-notes).

RMUs for Options

Figure 11.21 shows the methodologies for measuring option risk divided into evolutionary stages, just as was done for the fixed income securities we considered earlier. One can measure option risk utilizing a delta equivalent approach,[9] or one can incorporate higher order derivatives (e.g., gamma). The more sophisticated approaches measure risk based on a portfolio value-at-risk basis.

However, each of these approaches depends on applying the appropriate models. The choice of a model will affect the valuation of the option and consequently the calculation of the market risk exposure, since it is related to the market value of the option. A number of risks exist within any mark-to-model process. These risks are more complicated for certain products such as long-dated options on long-dated swaps (e.g., 10-year option on a 20-year swap), and errors may also be introduced from the input data (e.g., inappropriate term structure data).

The valuation of individual derivatives positions can also vary widely as a function of the treatment of items such as credit reserves, close-out costs, and so on. One also needs to analyze the structure of the transaction, the liquidity of the underlying market, the availability of hedges, and so on when determining the risk present within a derivatives position.

To minimize input risk, one needs to check the "reasonableness" of any approach or assumptions. For example, if one were valuing a long-dated option on a swap then one would need to examine how the swap rate curve is constructed. This would include examining the current shape of the curve (e.g., risk-free term structure and swap spreads) as well as the trends in swap spreads, to ensure that the shape of the curve is consistent with the currently observed general shape (e.g., the degree of

---

FIGURE 11.21   Risk Measurement Methodologies for Options

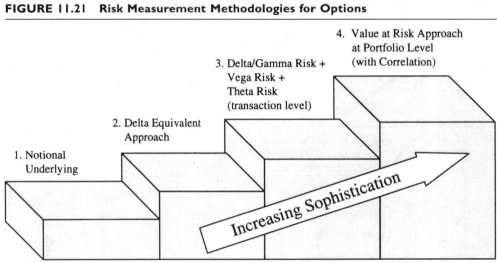

bowing). One would also need to pay particular attention to the interpolation techniques used to determine illiquid points on the curve. In the case of a swaption, one would also need to determine the implied volatilities. Often, reliable market-provided implied volatilities are not available and one needs to use historical volatilities in the valuation calculation.

The "traditional" approach to measuring an option's market risk is based upon delta equivalents. However, delta equivalents are not good enough; one needs also to account for convexity as well as volatility and interest rate risks to appropriately hedge the risk of the option.

Example 1: Gamma Risk

Assume in this first example that one wrote a call option on the nearby eurodollar futures contract with a 96 strike price, a 96.14 futures price, 3.875% risk-free rate, a 19.3% implied volatility, and 27 days to expiration.

The option's delta derived from Black's model equals 0.74 and the price is 425.[10] If we assume, as described above, that entity A wrote 100 call option contracts on the nearby futures (short position) and bought 74 nearby futures (long position) then the position delta is zero, but it shows a negative gamma exposure. Indeed, if the futures price drops to 96 (and the implied volatility is held constant at 19.3%) then the option price drops to 200. The resulting loss on the long futures position is equal to:

$$(\text{Futures price} - \text{Current price}) \times 25 \times \text{Number of futures contracts} = \$25,900$$

The gain on the short position is the original price minus the current price multiplied by the number of options contracts. In our case, this equals $22,500. The net loss is $3,400. The net loss is the loss arising from gamma risk or convexity exposure.

In the above example, we held implied volatility constant and ignored vega risk. Vega risk is the risk that changes in the volatility of the underlying security adversely affect the value of an options contract.

Example 2: Calculating RMUs

Assume that a straddle is created by entity A through a simultaneous purchase of 100 calls at $375 and 100 puts at $625 on the next nearby futures contract month. If the futures price declined by two standard deviations (holding volatility constant), then the call price would move to $215 (a loss of $16,000) and the put price would move to $955 (a gain of $33,000). The net position gain is $17,000. An upward two standard deviation move in futures price would lead to a call price of $610 (a 23,500 gain), while the put would fall to $362.50 (a 26,250 loss). The net position loss is $2,750. Accordingly, our delta/gamma risk arises from an upward two standard deviation movement in futures price, is thus $2,750 or 2.8 RMUs.

Let us now examine vega risk within this portfolio. The vega risk is computed by observing that the call price changes from $375 to $330 for a downward two standard deviation move in implied volatility (a loss of $4,500), and the put price moves from $625 to $577.50 (a loss of $4,750). The vega risk for the straddle created by a two standard deviation downward movement in implied volatility is therefore $9,250 or 9.25 RMUs. If one repeated the analysis, assuming a simultaneous change in the price of the underlying, then one would find that the vega risk is greatest when there is no change in the underlying futures price.

In order to examine theta risk, we hold implied volatility and the underlying price movement constant. As pointed out earlier, purchased options lose value with the passage of time. Accordingly, the one-day theta risk is a $250 incremental loss for the calls and a $500 incremental loss for the puts (for a total of $750), which equates to a theta risk of 0.75 RMUs.

The worst case risk for this example arises from no change in the price of the underlying, and is equal to 10 RMUs.

Vega risk is the major source of risk within this worst case scenario. Observe that the put at the time of purchase was slightly in-the-money, with a delta equal to 0.6, and the call was slightly out-of-the-money. A key point is that the individual worst case delta/gamma, vega and theta risks across scenarios should not be summed to determine the total worst case risk, since their individual values were determined while holding the others risk sources constant. For example, observe that in this example the worst case delta/gamma market risk (−$2,750) occurs when the underlying future price moves up two standard deviations. The worst case vega and theta risk occurs when there is no change in the underlying futures price—resulting in 10 RMUs. This is different from summing the worst case risks (i.e., 12,750 = 2,750 + 9,250 + 750) for each category of risk across three futures price scenarios.

Conclusion

The RMU system is easily understood at the trader level without the need for significant analytical insight or complex algorithms. RMUs cut across all levels of the organization and can be summarized vertically or horizontally to provide a picture of the total risk in one's portfolio. The RMU approach clearly measures the value-at-risk whereas other commonly used approaches (such as BPVs) fail to measure true risk. Finally, the RMU system can be used to construct optimal hedges.

CREDIT RISK

Contingent credit risk exposure was once measured in notional terms. The credit risk exposure of a transaction was simply defined in terms of the notional amount upon which the transaction was based. As an illustration, assume one were to repo a $210 million four-year T-note (Position A) and reverse repo a $100 million 10-year T-note (Position B) with a single counterparty. The credit risk exposure for the reverse repo (Position B), using the notional approach, would be considered less than 50% of the credit risk exposure of the repo (Position A). The credit risk exposure for the sum of both the repo and reverse repo positions would be calculated as $310 million in notional terms,[11] or $110 million if measured on a net basis.

This is a simple but misleading approach. From a credit risk perspective, it simply adds (or subtracts) the notional amounts and ignores both the mark-to-market value of the instruments, and projected potential risk. One of the most fundamental flaws in this approach is that it cannot reflect the way in which the credit risk profile of a portfolio of derivatives depends on the structure and maturity of the constituent instruments.

The next level of evolution treats the credit risk exposure generated by a transaction as a constant percentage of the notional amount over the life of the transaction. The idea is to estimate a credit risk exposure at the inception of the transaction, and then to treat that exposure just like a loan equivalent. The percentage varies as a function of the declining maturity of the transaction in a more advanced version of the static approach. The credit risk exposure for a portfolio of transactions is simply the sum of the individual static exposures.

The third evolutionary stage adopts a "dynamic" approach. It recognizes that credit exposures of derivative instruments fluctuate in value, and estimates exposures in terms of current mark-to-market value plus a simple measure of the projected future exposure. This is the approach followed by the Bank for International Settlements (BIS) to determine "risk weighted" amounts, from which the minimum required regulatory capital is determined. The BIS approach depicted in Figure 11.22 refers to the projected future exposure as the *add-on factor*. The credit equivalent exposure is calculated as the sum of the current replacement cost plus the add-on factor. The credit equivalent amount multiplied by a counterparty risk weight (which reflects the actual risk of the counterparty) equals the risk weighted amount. It offers a better rule of thumb than the two methods outlined above, but cannot predict future credit risk exposures with any accuracy.

Today, virtually all institutions have graduated to at least the second evolutionary level outlined in Figure 11.23, and most measure their credit risk exposures using methodologies based on a mixture of the second and third evolutionary levels. The third and fourth evolutionary levels require one to explicitly estimate future exposure, and later in this chapter we describe how this is best accomplished. But first we define a common language for credit risk exposure measurement.

Measuring Exposures

The crucial problem in developing an accurate measure of credit risk is to properly quantify future credit risk exposure. This is a complex problem because it is the outcome of multiple variables, including the structure of the instrument and changes in the value of' the underlying over time.

The amount of money one can reasonably expect to lose as a result of default (net of recoveries) over a given period is called the "expected credit risk exposure." The expected credit exposure varies over the life of the position. At any point in time the "average expected credit exposure" denotes the average of the expected credit exposures since the inception of the trade. The maximum amount of money that could be lost as a result of default, at a given confidence level, is called the

FIGURE 11.22 Calculating BIS Risk-Weighted Amounts

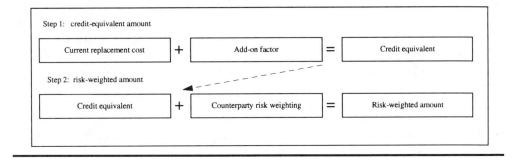

FIGURE 11.23   Evolution of Credit Risk Exposure Measurement Techniques

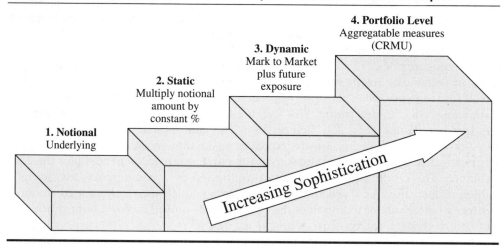

"worst case credit risk exposure" and it is sometimes called the "maximum potential credit risk exposure." The "average worst case credit risk exposure" is the average of the worst case exposures over the past period.

The worst case exposure is particularly important in terms of allocating credit risk limits and deciding how much economic and regulatory capital should be set aside for a transaction or portfolio. One needs to pay attention to the amount of regulatory capital consumed on each transaction since one needs to maintain key regulatory ratios. One can use either the worst case, or average worst case credit risk exposure, as a measure when setting limits to credit risk exposure—one simply needs to be consistent.

The amount of economic capital set aside for a portfolio, and for incremental transactions added to that portfolio, are vital factors in determining the profitability of lines of business and of individual transactions. The cost of the economic capital set aside for a single transaction is also a vital factor in calculating a fair price for these transactions.

For example, if one uses the worst case credit risk exposure to measure credit risk, then limits should obviously be set in terms of worst case credit risk exposures, in contrast to the average worst case credit risk exposures. The average worst case credit risk exposure, sometimes called the *fractional exposure* (FE), is a particularly important concept in this chapter as it forms the basis of the standard credit risk measurement unit that we describe next.

For a typical single cash flow product (e.g., an FRA), the worst case credit risk exposure at time t, W_t, grows as a function of time and peaks at the maturity of the transaction. Figure 11.24 illustrates the worst case credit risk exposure for such an instrument, and illustrates some typical relationships between this and the other measures mentioned above.

Let us examine the relationship between the worst case credit risk exposure and the average worst case credit risk exposure. The worst case credit risk exposure is defined as the maximum credit risk exposure likely to arise from a given position within the bounds of a predefined confidence interval. Many dealers define the

FIGURE 11.24   Credit Exposure of an Instrument Expressed as Different Exposure Functions

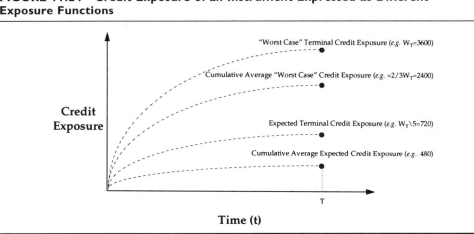

worst case credit risk exposure at a two standard deviation level, or a one-sided 97.7% confidence level. Let us assume, for illustrative purposes, that the worst case credit risk exposure at time t is equal to $(K \times \sigma \times t^{1/2})$ where K is a function of the desired confidence interval, σ is the overnight volatility of the position's percentage change in price, and t varies from 0 to T. For simplicity assume that the standard deviation is constant and comes from a stable stochastic process, where the risk grows as a function of the square root of time. For illustrative purposes, we will also assume that the probability of default is uniformly distributed over the time period. If we integrate the worst case function over the time period, and divide this result by the time period T, we obtain the average worst case credit risk exposure (Figure 11.24):[12]

Average worst case credit exposure = $\frac{2}{3} W_T$

Now let us look at how one can compute the *expected terminal credit exposure*— sometimes referred to as the *expected terminal replacement cost, $E[R_T]$*. At maturity the exposure is either 0 or positive. Assume that the distribution of returns is normally distributed, with a zero mean and a standard deviation which grows as a function of the square root of time, then using the option pricing framework we obtain:[13]

$$E[R_T] = \frac{FE}{3.33}$$

where FE, the fractional exposure, is shown to be equal to $\frac{2}{3} W_T$.

When estimating credit risk and other risks incurred across a dealer, defining a common unit of measurement is just as important as defining common market risk concepts. In this section, we outline the Credit Risk Measurement Unit (CRMU) methodology and relate it to the Risk Measurement Unit (RMU) methodology described earlier. We define CRMUs (similar to RMUs) as the worst case risk exposure for a position at a specific point in time, at a preset specified level of statistical confidence (e.g., 97.7%). Thus, the CMRU measurement can be traced along the worst case (W_T) path curve as in Figure 11.24. We describe how to calculate CRMUs more precisely later in this section.

Together the RMU and the CRMU approaches offer a standardized approach to quantifying the reward/risk trade-offs across products and investments.

From Exposure to Loss

In a "nightmare" scenario, an institution might suddenly realize that it is virtually certain to lose the total amount exposed to loss. More typically, the probable loss on any transaction, or portfolio of transactions, depends on three variables:

- Amount exposed to credit risk;
- Probability of the counterparty defaulting; and
- The amount that is likely to be recovered, i.e., the recovery rate, if the counterparty does indeed default.

The problem of measuring potential credit losses can thus be restated as finding the best way of estimating each of these variables, and the appropriate way of combining them to calculate the loss given default.

With regard to default rates, an institution needs to develop techniques to calculate the default rate path (i.e., current and future probabilities of default). A key challenge for a dealer is to develop techniques to properly assess the risk grade of a counterparty. The default rate distributions at specific points over the life of a transaction can be modeled through analyses of Standard & Poor's or Moody's data concerning the default rates of publicly rated institutions. Most institutions combine information gathered from agency data with their own proprietary default rate data (e.g., loan-default data). They also analyze the credit spreads of securities (e.g., yields of specific securities over duration-equivalent risk-free securities) to generate a default rate distribution.

These estimates of future default rate distributions are calculated for each credit grade. Just like the credit risk exposure measures described above, the distribution of future default rates can be usefully characterized in terms of an expected default rate (e.g., 1%) or a worst case default rate (e.g., 3%). The difference between the worst case default rate and the expected default rate is often termed the *unexpected default rate* (i.e., 2% = 3% − 1%). Typically, as illustrated in Figure 11.25, the distribution is highly asymmetric. A worst case default rate (e.g., the aforementioned 3%) may be structured so that one can say that there is a prespecified probability (e.g., 2.3% = 100% − 97.7%) of exceeding the worst case default rate. The probability density function describes how the probability of default varies over time. Clearly, the longer the maturity of the financial instrument, the greater the default rate. The widening tails in Figure 11.25 reflect the higher probabilities of a declining credit, as an increasing function of the maturity of the transaction.

The third factor needed to calculate counterparty credit loss is the recovery rate path. The distribution around the recovery rate path needs to be estimated at specific points in the future. Just like the other two variables, one can use the recovery rate distribution to determine an expected recovery rate or a worst case recovery rate. The recovery rate distributions may be modeled by means of Standard & Poor's or Moody's recovery rate data. Surveys on the recovery rate of senior corporate bonds that have defaulted indicate that they vary as a function of the pecking

FIGURE 11.25   Distribution of Default Rates

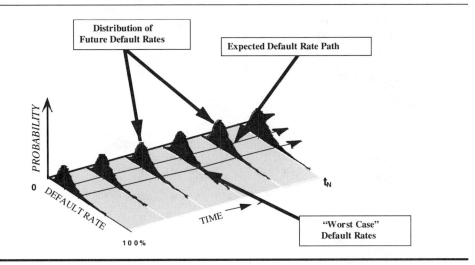

order (e.g., lien position) of the debt. For example, senior debt has a higher recovery rate than junior (subordinated) debt. As with default data, institutions normally combine information gathered from agency recovery rate data with their own recovery rate data—some institutions also obtain input from specialized legal counsel or insolvency practitioners—in order to provide a recovery rate distribution for each credit grade.

These analyses produce estimates of future recovery rate distributions which vary as a function of time (Figure 11.26). Just like default rate distributions, recovery rate distributions do not typically follow a normal probability density function.

FIGURE 11.26   Distribution of Recovery Rates

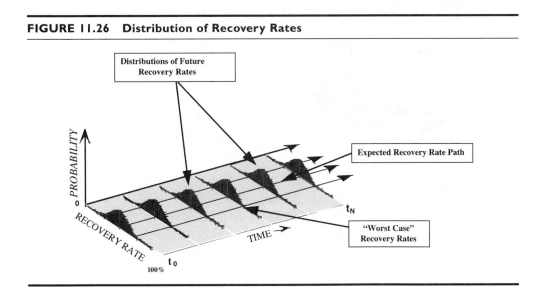

FIGURE 11.27   Combining Variables to Produce Credit Loss Distributions

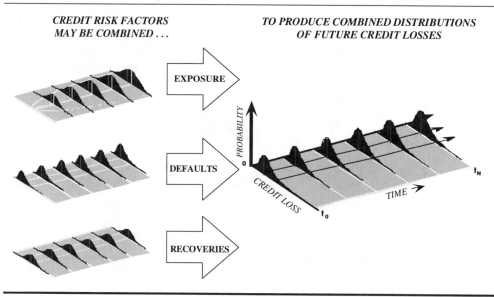

Having analyzed the distributions of the three credit risk variables—credit risk exposure, default, and recovery data—these can be combined (Figure 11.27) to produce future credit loss distributions. One would use the option pricing framework described earlier, and perform the necessary integration, in order to generate the expected credit loss. Theoretically, these three distributions can be combined by integrating across the combined function.[14]

FIGURE 11.28   Creating a Credit Risk Loss Distribution Summary

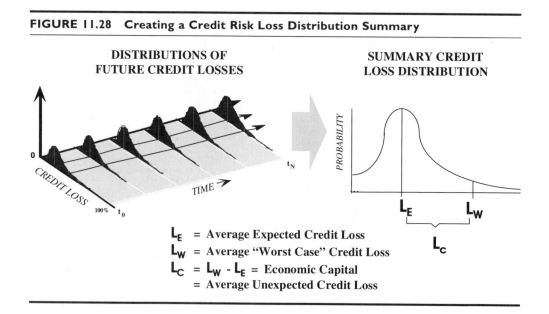

If a Monte Carlo simulation approach is adopted then one first simulates an exposure value from a credit risk exposure distribution given default, at a particular point in time. Second, one simulates a default distribution-typically a binomial probability function with a single probability of default—to discover whether or not the counterparty defaulted. Finally, assuming some recovery rate, one then summarizes the credit losses which occur across all points in time. Future credit loss distributions at various points over the life of the instrument may be combined. as illustrated in Figure 11.28 to produce a single summary-credit loss distribution.

Observe that the graph in Figure 11.28 does not pass through the origin as there is a positive probability of a nonzero loss. The summary credit loss distribution can be characterized as an average expected credit loss (L_E) and an average worst case credit loss (L_W). Ideally. one needs to construct a cumulative probability density loss function by integrating the multivariate probability density function, such that the worst case credit loss over the time period is set to the desired worst case probability of loss. The difference between L_W and L_E can be described as the average unexpected credit loss L_C (that is, $L_C = L_W - L_E$).

As pointed out earlier, combining credit risk exposure with the distribution of default rates, net of recovery, yields the distribution of credit risk losses. The distribution of credit loss needs to be translated into a provision (expected loss) and economic capital (unexpected loss). Under the loan equivalent approach:

Loan equivalent = Average expected exposure

We assume (Figure 11.29) that the average expected credit risk exposure for the derivative is 480, and the expected probability of default is 1%. Then, the expected loss is calculated by multiplying the expected probability of default, net of recoveries, by the average expected credit risk exposure to arrive at an expected loss of 11.8. Further, since the worst case probability of default is 3%, then the worst case loss is 14.4. Therefore, one would assign an unexpected loss (economic capital) of 9.6 derived from the difference between the worst case loss and the expected loss.

FIGURE 11.29 Calculating Risk-Adjusted Capital Requirements

Note: Assumes Capital = Unexpected Loss

The loan equivalent approach utilizes the same default factors for contingent credit products as for loans.

The potential unexpected loss, as illustrated in Figure 11.30, is clearly a function of the confidence level set by policy. For example, a confidence level of 97.7% would call for less economic capital than a confidence level of 99%. This loan-equivalent approach to calculating the average expected exposure is a proxy for more sophisticated approaches; it has the virtue of facilitating comparison to a more conventional loan product.

Another approach would be to generate—using analytical, empirical, or simulation techniques—the full distribution of losses, and then to select the appropriate confidence interval percentile. A third approach would be to multiply a binary probability of default by the difference between the average worst case credit risk exposure and the average expected credit risk exposure to compute L_C. This third approach may not provide the same answer as the earlier two approaches.

In any event, the amount of risk capital should be based on a preset confidence level (e.g., 97.7%). The amount of unexpected credit loss (L_C) should be used to establish the projected amount of risk capital. The dynamic economic capital assigned is typically the sum of the current replacement cost plus the projected L_C. In order to understand how contingent credit products generate credit risk exposure, and how the different risks to which a contingent credit product is exposed are interrelated, it is necessary to examine in more detail the relationship between credit risk and market risk.

Credit risk and market risk exposure are derived from the same market value distributions. However, they have an inverse relationship: Market risk is the risk that the market value of the position will decline; credit risk is the risk that a counterparty will default when the market value of the position is positive. Because of their inverse relationship, there are many similarities in the way that credit and market risk are measured. Both are computed from market value distributions taken at selected points in time over the life of the instrument.

FIGURE 11.30   Contingent Credit Risk Loss Distribution

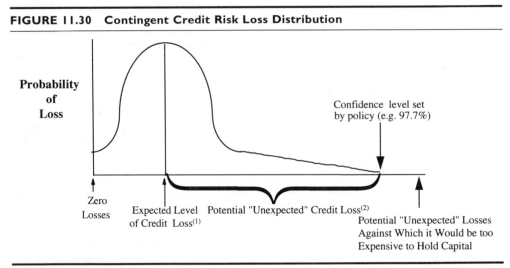

Note: [1] For which reserves should be held
[2] For which capital should be held

Measurements must be awarded a level of statistical confidence; and both must be measured over a specific time period. It is usually possible to offset or hedge market risk quite quickly, but it is usually impossible to do this in the case of credit risk. Therefore, there is a major difference in the time-scales related to market risk and credit risk analyses. For example, credit risk (e.g., an expected credit loss) is often expressed on a per annum basis (e.g., provision is a per annum estimation of expected credit loss), whereas market risk is typically measured in relation to much shorter periods, depending on the time it would most likely take to close out the position (overnight, two weeks, etc.).

Exposure at a Particular Point in Time

Calculating the credit risk exposure at a particular point in time requires one to construct a distribution of "replacement costs," these being defined as the amount that it would cost to replace the position if the counterparty defaulted on its obligation at that time. Replacement cost exposure distributions are derived from the market value distributions. But how do we arrive at these market value distributions?

One way of approaching the problem is to calculate probability distributions of market price movements around an expected average market value path, extending over the life of the instrument. As illustrated in Figure 11.31, one can determine a range of future market values around an average within a specified level of statistical confidence.

Market risk can be defined as the difference between the value of an instrument at the beginning of a specified market risk period, and the projected worst case market value over the period. One can connect the worst case exposures of each of these distributions to derive a worst case exposure path over time (Figure 11.32). Observe that the worst case market risk value increases as one projects potential worst case market values further out in time.

The properties of the distribution used to describe market risk create the range of market values which can be expected over the holding period. The market risk for individual positions may be combined (Figure 11.33) to calculate the market risk for

FIGURE 11.31   Probability Distributions of Market Price Movements

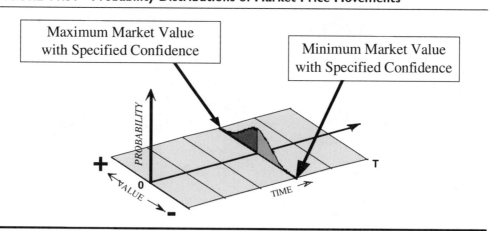

FIGURE 11.32   Market Risk Defined as Projected "Worst Case" Market Value

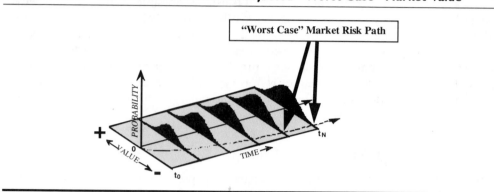

a portfolio of positions. This is accomplished by incorporating volatilities for each of the positions, the correlations between positions and other factors (e.g., convexity for fixed-income securities) to capture portfolio effects; in the case of options, one also needs to incorporate the dynamics of option effects (such as delta, gamma, vega, kappa, theta, and rho).

How does this approach to evaluating market risk relate to "market-induced" credit risk? Turning back to the example of a single transaction, worst case credit risk exposure can be described as the difference between the value at the beginning of credit risk period and the projected "best case" market value over the life of the transaction (Figure 11.34). However, the expected credit risk exposure (or the replacement cost), is greater over time than the expected market risk exposure. The

FIGURE 11.33   Combining Market Risk of Individual Positions to Produce Market Risk for a Portfolio of Positions

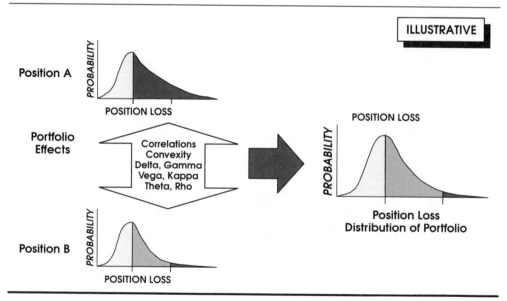

FIGURE 11.34 "Best Case" Market Risk Exposure Path Is Equivalent to "Worst Case" Credit Risk Exposure Path

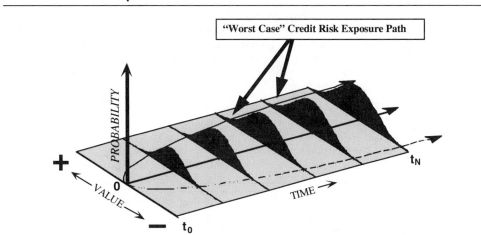

logic behind this relationship is straightforward: the magnitude of movements up and down in market value of one's derivative portfolio are both relevant in the calculation of expected market risk, while only positive market values are relevant for expected credit risk exposure.

Assume that a normal distribution describes the probabilities associated with the percentage change in the market value. If one assumes that the expected percentage change in market value is zero then one can expect an equal probability of either a percentage increase or a percentage decrease in market value. Accordingly, this set of assumptions would lead an expected zero change in market value, but an expected credit risk exposure which is positive.

One can illustrate the computation of credit risk exposure, as well as the difference between credit and market risk exposure, through a simple binomial example. Assume that a party agrees to pay $10 million for an asset in the future (Figure 11.35). Further, assume that the asset's value will be $9 million or $11 million, with equal probability on the agreed date. The expected change in market value is 50% × $1 million plus 50% × (−$1 million). which equals zero. The expected credit exposure is 50% × $1 million plus 50% × 0, which equals $0.5 million. In other words, there exists an expected credit risk exposure even though the expected change in market value is zero.

Evolution of Exposure over Time

Different types of instruments generate different credit risk exposure profiles because they are affected to quite different degrees by effects of the passage of time: the diffusion effect and the amortization effect. The diffusion effect describes how, as time lengthens, there is an increasing probability that the value of a position will travel further away from its initial value, tending to increase the amount exposed to default. The amortization effect describes how, as time progresses, cash tends to flow to a transacting party from its counterparty (e.g., in the form of

FIGURE 11.35   Credit Loss Given Default: Period 1

A One-Period Illustration				
Initial Asset Value	Period One Asset Value	Market Value Change	Credit Loss Given Default	Expected Credit Loss
$10 — 50% Probability → $11	$11	$1	$1	$0.5
$10 — 50% Probability → $9	$9	($1)	0	0
			Total Expected Credit Loss	$0.5

swap payments) reducing the value remaining exposed to default (often called the *pull-to-par* effect).

Let's examine in greater detail how the worst case market and credit risk exposures of a plain vanilla interest rate swap evolve over time. In order to calculate the worst case risk, one needs to first project the incoming and outgoing cash flows over the life of the interest rate swap. Second, one needs to project the potential worst case change in interest rates. And third, we need to input the projected cash flows and potential worst case change in interest rates into a mathematical model to project the effect of these on the exposure profile.

Assume Counterparty A enters into a fixed-rate receive swap with Counterparty B, that is, B pays fixed and receives floating. In our example, assume the notional amount is $100 million, the maturity is five years and the payment frequency is semiannual. The first step is to project the incoming and outgoing cashflows over the life of the swap. The second step is to determine how the value of the cash flows change with a change in interest rates, in order to quantify the worst case risk. However, only the first outgoing floating rate that Counterparty A has contracted to pay to Counterparty B in six months is known. The remaining floating rate cash flows are not known since they depend on future interest rates. Accordingly, one needs to forecast potential shifts in interest rates.

Let us move on to look at how the market value of the swap evolves over time. The future market value of a plain vanilla interest rate swap is affected by the interaction of two factors: potential changes in interest rates, and the remaining term to maturity of the swap. As one looks further out into the future one would observe a larger range of possible interest rates (the diffusion effect, mentioned earlier). For example, the range of potential interest rates over a one-year time horizon is less than the range of potential interest rates over a five-year time horizon (Figure 11.36).

A larger range of possible interest rates generates a larger range of possible market values. Typically, the range of possible values for a plain vanilla interest rate swap will grow throughout the first third or so of the transaction. After this, the range in

FIGURE 11.36   Range of Interest Rates over Time (Interest Rate Diffusion)

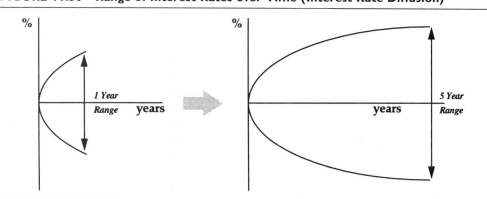

market value peaks because the decreasing term to maturity (the amortization effect) begins to dominate the effect of the larger range in interest rates (Figure 11.37).

More technically, let us assume for illustrative purposes that one has T payment exchanges of an amount A to make from time 0. Further, for simplicity, assume that the risk (defined at K standard deviations) of each payment exchange grows proportional to the square root of time (i.e., $K\sigma T^{1\backslash2}$). One has T-1 exchanges remaining at the end of the first period, T-2 exchanges remaining at end of the second period, and so on. Assume also that we ignore present-value considerations, one can show that the peak worst case exposure occurs after approximately one third of the life of the transaction, quite independently of how the worst case is defined[15] (in terms of K standard deviations). The range in market value continues to decline as the remaining term to maturity shortens. The market value must drop to zero at maturity, sometimes called the pull to *par effect* (Figure 11.38), since there are no more cash flows to be exchanged.

FIGURE 11.37   Peak in Contract Exposure (Caused by Amortization Effect)

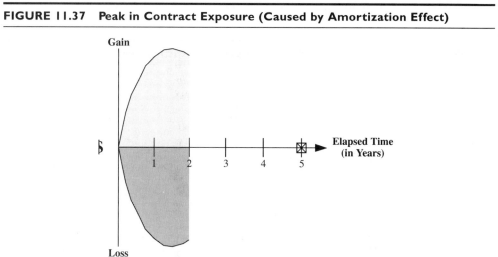

FIGURE 11.38   Exposure Generated Up to Contract Maturity

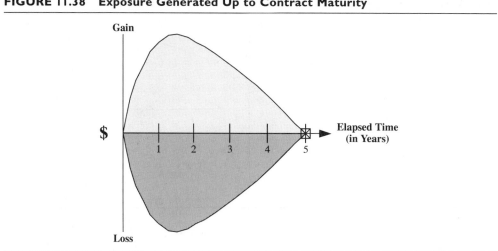

The market value of the swap, and how it evolves over time, has clear implications for contingent credit risk exposure. As pointed out earlier, the evolution of credit risk exposure of a swap is contingent because it is dependent on the value of the swap. If the value of a swap is negative then there can be no credit risk. Conversely, if the value of a swap is positive—as illustrated by the lighter shaded exposure in Figure 11.38—and the counterparty defaults, then the positive value, or replacement cost, may be lost.

The description given above of how credit risk exposure develops is necessarily schematic. Because of the interaction of the diffusion and amortization effects, the same principles applied to different instruments reveal a set of very different exposure profiles over the life of the instruments. For example, the profile of a single-currency swap which does not involve an exchange of principal is humpbacked, but the exposure of a cross-currency swap rises as a function of time (Figure 11.39) because of the exchange of principal amounts at the termination of the swap.

FIGURE 11.39   Credit Exposure Profiles of Differing Instruments

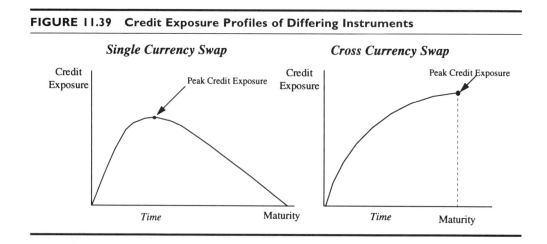

Earlier in this chapter, we identified the measurement of future credit risk exposure as the essential challenge in devising sophisticated credit risk exposure measurement, and in the previous section we looked at how future exposures grow and how they are related to market risk. How can we move on from this to develop practical methodologies? Figure 11.40 identifies four typical evolutionary levels with regard to sophisticated measures of future credit risk exposures. The four levels are the basis point value (BPV) approach, transaction level CRMU approach (which incorporates volatilities), portfolio CRMU approach (incorporating both volatilities and correlations), and, finally, a portfolio approach which combines CRMUs with stress testing.

This section examines each of these approaches as they build toward a CMRU-based approach to measuring the true amount of credit value at risk. The Value-at-Risk (VaR) approach, typically used to measure market risk, can easily be extended to measure credit risk exposure in terms of a Credit-Value-at-Risk (CVaR).

Basis Point Value (BPV) Approach

As pointed out earlier, the essence of the BPV approach (Figure 11.41) is to calculate the change in the price of a security that arises from a one basis point change in the yield of some benchmark security. For example, as assumed earlier, say a one basis point decline in yield results in a $312 increase in price on a 1 million dollar four-year Treasury note repo position. One then compares the impact of that same one basis point change in yield on the price of other securities. Accordingly, amount of credit risk exposure generated by a one basis point decline in yield is $312 per million dollars: that is, one could expect to lose $312 per million given that the yield declines by one basis point and the counterparty defaults.

Similarly, if there is a one basis point decline in yield, 1 million dollars of the 10-year Treasury note would increase in price by $654. Accordingly, the 10-year Treasury note repo is over twice as sensitive as the four-year Treasury note repo to each one basis point move. From these basis point calculations it is possible to establish credit risk equivalents to some benchmark, for example, the four-year Treasury note.

The BPV approach makes it much simpler to set meaningful limits with regard to counterparty exposure. For example, assume that, with regard to a particular

---

FIGURE 11.40   Evolution of Future Credit Risk Exposure Methodologies

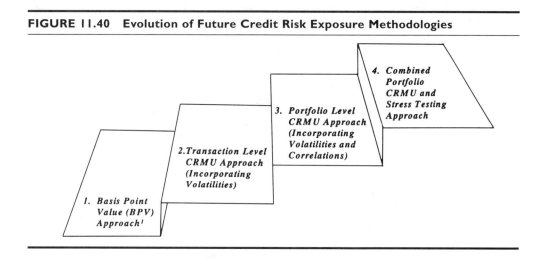

FIGURE 11.41   Basis Point Value Approach

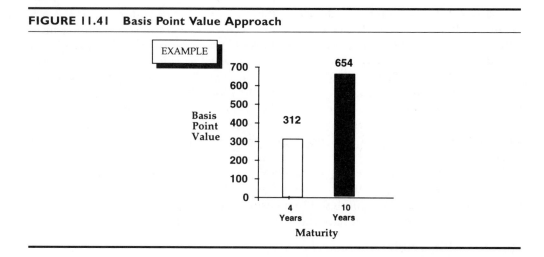

counterparty, the manager of a repo book is given a credit risk exposure limit equivalent to a 210 million dollar four-year Treasury note. The manager, as illustrated in Figure 11.42, has a choice of repoing $210 million dollars of four-year Treasury notes, or repoing 100 million dollars of ten-year Treasury notes. These two positions are said to be *credit risk equivalent.*

Transaction-Level CRMU Approach Incorporating Volatilities

We need to develop a CRMU methodology in order to move beyond a BPV or duration-based approach. Before presenting this approach, let us review certain fundamental concepts. Assume that counterparty RR reverse repoed a security with repo counterparty R. Assume further that the market value of the security is 100 million dollars and has an overnight volatility (or standard deviation) of 1% (or 1 million dollars). As pointed out earlier, the worst case credit risk for RR occurs when the value of the security declines to 98 million dollars and the credit counterparty defaults. In short, if the repo counterparty defaults then the counterparty

FIGURE 11.42   Sensitivity of Treasury Note Repo Relative to Benchmark

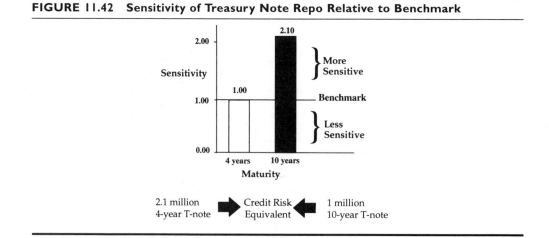

FIGURE 11.43   CRMU Formula

$$CRMUs \approx (BPV * K * \sigma)/1000$$

where:

Basis Point Value (BPV) = Price movement due to a one basis point change in yield

σ = Standard deviation of the change in yield in basis points

K = Number of standard deviations

executing the reverse repo is liable to be worse off by 2 million dollars than they would have been had they not executed that reverse repo in the first place.

The fixed-income security's credit exposure, similar to our earlier market risk calculation, can be determined by multiplying the security's change in yield volatility by the security's BPV The approximation provided by the CRMU formula in Figure 11.43 will be close to the actual risk for small changes in yield. We define one CRMU to be equal to 1,000 CVaR in a worst case scenario. In this way, we can express risk in terms of CRMUs.

For example, as before, assume the four-year Treasury note has a BPV of $312 per million dollars, (as illustrated in Table 11.7) and the volatility of the change in yield is five basis points. If a 1 million dollar position is assumed, then the CRMU for the repo is 3.1 CRMUs. From our repo manager's point of view, the credit risk exposure for his individual repo position is measured by a multiple of the overnight volatility of the value of the underlying securities.

TABLE 11.7   Calculating CRMUs

Instrument	One Basis Point Value per Million		"Worst Case" Movement (bp) overnight		Total Value at Risk $	CRMUs
4 year T-note	312	*	10	≅	3,120	3.1
10 year T-note	654		8		5,232	5.2

where:

2σ offers 97.7% coverage = "Worst Case" movement

TABLE 11.8   Calculating CRMUs: Example Scenario

Action	Amount (Millions)	Worst Case Credit Risk (CRMUs)
Repo A	100	2000
Reverse Repo B	100	2000

Portfolio-Level CRMU Approach Incorporating Volatilities and Correlations

Dealers need to take account of both volatility and correlation data in order to compute accurately the credit risk exposure for an entire derivative portfolio with a single counterparty (assuming netting). The CRMU calculation is clearly affected by correlation. Table 11.8 illustrates a situation in which a dealer has repoed instrument A and reverse repoed instrument B with a single counterparty. We will assume that A and B have a valid netting agreement and that the worst case credit risk for both the reverse repo and the repo is 2 million dollars.

We will further assume that the current market value of instruments A and B equals 100 million dollars and that the current replacement value for either A or B is zero. The credit risk exposure of the portfolio, as illustrated in Table 11.9, is a function of the degree of correlation between positions A and B. (Note that as in

TABLE 11.9   Portfolio Exposure and Correlation

CASE	MARKET VALUE (millions)		COMMENT	CREDIT VALUE AT RISK (CRMUs)
	A	B		
I	$102 ⬆	$98 ⬇	PERFECT NEGATIVE CORRELATION (-1.0)	4,000
II	$103± ⬆	$101± ⬆	SOME CORRELATION (.50)	2,000
III	$102 ⬆	$102 ⬆	PERFECT POSITIVE CORRELATION (+1.0)	0
IV	$102 ⬆	?	NO CORRELATION (0)	2,828

Table 11.3, the numbers given for Case II are hypothetical and chosen to illustrate that the credit risk exposure (when the correlation is .5) should fall most of the time half way between the credit risk exposure for Cases I and III.)

Given our stated aim of creating integratable measurement methodologies that can be used across organizations, it is important to note that a CRMU formula with the same structure as the Risk Measurement Unit (RMU) formula can be used to measure credit risk. The CRMU formula (Figure 11.44) for our two-position example, can easily be generalized and automated.

Stress Testing

As Mark Twain pointed out, "Forecasting is very difficult . . . especially when it concerns the future!" The analysis of credit risk described so far in this chapter has been based on a VaR (at K standard deviations framework) in normal markets. But measures such as variance and correlation can be highly unstable. Furthermore, chaos theory reveals that major price movements can cluster together more closely than anticipated by first-order methods. By means of stress testing institutions can incorporate into their credit risk predictions an element of reasonable paranoia about what can go wrong.

Correlation and Volatility Assumptions

The example used earlier in this chapter, where a dealer repoed security A and reverse repoed security B, assumed that A and B have the same volatility. As a first step in stress testing the exposures generated by this position one should examine CRMU values for potential normal shifts in price and the correlation between A and B. For example, a confidence band on the correlation between securities A and B may range

FIGURE 11.44   CRMU Formula

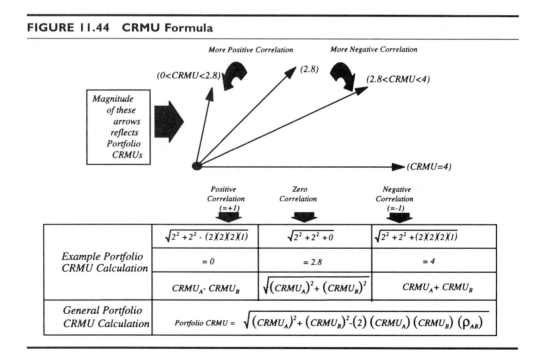

from 0.3 to 0.7. Similarly, the volatility in normal markets of both securities A and B may range from 0.5% to 1.5%. Observe that the most likely exposure is a CRMU of 2. Nevertheless, if the correlation declines from 0.5 to 0.3, and volatility rises from 1% to 1.5%, then the CRMU rises to 3.55. One should perform stress tests in order to examine the CRMU calculations for extreme shifts in more than one variable at the same time. For example, as illustrated in Table 11.10, if the correlation declines from plus 0.5 to minus 1 and, simultaneously, the volatility rises from 1% to 2%, then the CRMU quadruples from 2 to 8.

CONCLUSION

Any dealing organization that attempts to set up a truly integrated program will face several major challenges. Most risk management initiatives are fragmented and contradictory. The failure to integrate one's risk management approach will lead to virtually meaningless risk measures and a false sense of security. One can look forward to a considerable advance on the techniques used by much of the industry at the present. Measuring integrated risk is an extremely complicated process. Dealing organizations need to develop mathematical shortcuts without sacrificing accuracy in order to break down all risk into generic risk measurement units (e.g., RMUs and CRMUs). Dealers need to analyze the different risk types across diverse geographies, asset classes and time dimensions (including the correlations that may exist between

TABLE 11.10 Stress-Testing Exposures: Potential Extreme Shifts

Volatility [1] *(σ)*	*CRMUs* [2]			
0.5%	2.0	1.4	1.0	0
1.0%	4.0	2.8	2.0	0
2.0%	8.0	5.6	4.0	0
Correlation (ρ)	-1.0	0	0.5	1.0

0	1	2	2.8	4	8
	1σ	2σ	2σ	2σ	4σ
ρ=1	ρ=0.5	ρ=0.5	ρ=0	ρ=-1	ρ=-1

Note: (1) Assumes $\sigma_A = \sigma_B$
             (2) Table assumes CRMUs set at 2σ

these elements). For example, the next generation of credit-risk measurement techniques will be based on credit-risk gap exposure analysis (essentially, the management of credit risk using maturity time buckets) which will allow a much greater sensitivity to portfolio makeup and evolution.

The mathematical complexity described above will produce copious amounts of data. For example, one must create a huge matrix with perhaps hundreds of thousands of statistically based points. One needs a combination of very sophisticated hardware and data management technology to make your integrated risk management initiative work. One needs to adopt a "buy the best and build the rest" philosophy.[16] These new VaR systems are typically developed by specialized risk management personnel in cooperation with market knowledgeable deal personnel.

If sophisticated risk measurement systems are not carefully integrated with the abilities and ambitions of the institution then they will not be effectively utilized. A common language of risk must accurately describe the multiple dimensions of risk in a way that relates to the practical day-to-day activities of risk-takers. The risk management infrastructure needs to be both independent of, and a partner to, direct risk-takers. In other words, the risk management personnel need to function as an independent group charged with measuring, monitoring and managing the bank's overall market credit and operations risk exposure. For example, risk managers need to appreciate the impact that the measurement of risk will have on the ability of direct risk takers to compete on price (Figure 11.45). Institutions must also ensure that incentive compensation schemes are tied in with the institutional approach to recovering the cost of capital. Using a RMU and CRMU framework will allow management to quantify clearly their risk appetite, set profitability targets and decide on priority lines of business.

FIGURE 11.45   Risk Management Framework

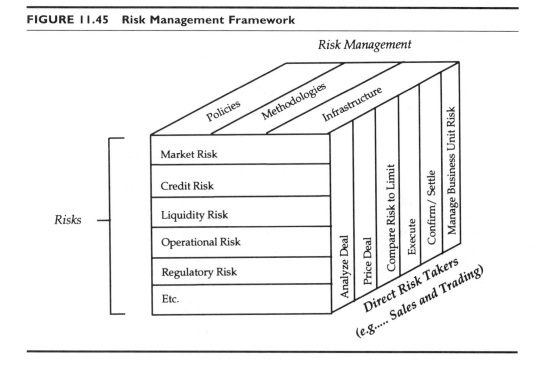

The RMU and CRMU measures (which form the basis of a general value-at-risk measure) allow the aggregation of market risk and credit risk exposures which in turn facilitate the efficient attribution of economic capital. For example, they facilitate the measurement of an institution's performance in terms of Risk Adjusted Return on Risk Adjusted Capital (RAROraC). The calculation of expected and unexpected loss which drives the RAROraC calculation should be based on the use of RMU and CRMU measures. Thus, a portfolio RMU and CRMU system incorporating correlations can assist an organization in understanding and managing its overall risk profile. If portfolio effects across an institution can be taken into account, then the amount of capital allocated to cover potential losses is reduced—the effect of diversification. Consequently, the cost of capital required at higher levels of the organization can be reduced.

The framework outlined in this chapter acts as the foundation for the development of product-specific risk measurement methodologies, procedures, and controls, including the implementation of risk information systems which can aggregate (or disaggregate) risks in a coherent manner. Risk can then be "sliced and diced" vertically and horizontally across an organization, making risk reporting much more flexible and informative for global risk managers. In order to produce actionable risk information, risk managers need to see the world from the point of view of the dealer. Conversely, in order to produce meaningful risk control information, dealers need to see the world from the point of view of the risk manager. One should plan to raise the Risk IQ, as well as keep the board of directors and the appropriate regulators informed with full disclosure so that they can exercise their responsibilities.

REFERENCES

Allen, S. L., and A. D. Kleinstein. (1991). *Valuing Fixed Income Investments and Derivative Securities: Cash Flow Analysis and Calculations.* New York: Simon & Schuster.

Binder, B., and R. Mark. (1988). "Technical ALCO in the New Marketplace." *Bankers Treasury Handbook.*

Brickley, J., C. Smith, and J. Zimmermon. (1995). "The Economic of Organizational Architecture." Bradley Policy Research Centre.

Fabozzi, F. J. (1993). *Fixed Income Mathematics.* Chicago, IL: Probus Publishing Company.

Hentschel, L., and C. Smith. "Control Risk Derivatives Market." *The Journal of Financial Engineering,* Vol. 4, No. 2-7, pp. 101–125.

Hull, J. C. (1993). *Options, Futures and Other Derivative Securities.* Englewood Cliffs, NJ: Prentice-Hall.

Leeson, N. (1996). *Rogue Trader.* Boston, MA: Little Brown.

Mark, R. (1991). "Risk Management." *International Derivative Review,* March, pp. 12-14.

Mark, R. (1991). "Units of Management." *Risk Magazine,* June, pp. 3-7.

Mark, R. (1991). "Risk According to Garp." *Wall Street Computer Review.* December.

Mark, R. (1995). "Integrated Credit Risk Measurement." *Risk Magazine,* London, England.

Markowitz, H. M. (1952). "Portfolio Selection." *Journal of Finance,* 7(March), pp. 77-91.

Marshall, J. F., and K. R. Kapner. (1993). *Understanding Swaps.* New York: John Wiley & Sons, Inc.

Miller, M. H. (1991). *Financial Innovation and Market Volatility* (pp. 24–31). Cambridge, MA: Blackwell.

Ray, C. (1993). *The Bond Market: Trading and Risk Management.* Homewood, IL: Business One Irwin.

Rubinstein, Mark, and John C. Cox (1985). *Options Markets.* Englewood Cliffs, NJ: Prentice-Hall.

Schiller, R. J. (1990). *Market Volatility.* Cambridge, MA: MIT Press.

Schwartz, R. J., and C. W. Smith, Jr. (1990). *The Handbook of Currency and Interest Rate Risk Management.* New York: New York Institute of Finance.

Schwartz, R. J., and C. W. Smith, Jr. (1993). *Advanced Strategies in Financial Risk Management.* New York: New York Institute of Finance.

Smith, C. W., and C. W. Smithson. (1990). *The Handbook of Financial Engineering.* New York: Harper & Row.

Weston, J. F., and T. E. Copeland. (1989). *Managerial Finance.* Chicago, IL: The Dryden Press.

Wunnicke, D., D. Wilson, and B. Wunnicke. (1992). *Corporate Financial Risk Management: Practical Techniques of Financial Engineering.* New York: John Wiley & Sons, Inc.

ENDNOTES

1. One RMU reflects a predetermined (say .15%) percentage that you will lose $1,000 on a particular investment. (Two RMUs imply a 0.15% chance that you will lose $2,000, etc.). It is important, however, to remember that risks may offset and be correlated across businesses. If you have, say, ten traders in a room, and each trader has one RMU of risk, then you rarely have ten RMUs of risk. Some of these risk positions typically partially offset each others or even cancel out others.

2. For example, a bonus driven culture which encourages an eat what you kill (here and now) behaviour has the virtue that one gets paid according to what one produces. Nevertheless, an eat what you kill culture, typical at some dealers, needs to be harmonized with the longer term focus of a typical risk management function.

3. A *bp* denotes a basis point, i.e., 1/100th of 1% or 0.0001.

4. For example, a one-day risk confidence band on the change in price equals ABS (D') [ABS (di) + $K\sigma$ (di)], where *di* is the one-day change in yield, σ (di) is the standard deviation of *di,* and ABS is the absolute value of the item shown. A two-day risk confidence band equals ABS (D') [2 ABS (di) + 1.414 $K \times \sigma$ (di)], where *K* is the confidence interval factor. For example, a 95% confidence band (*K* = 2) is equal to {2 ABS (D') [ABS (di) + 1.414 × σ (di)]}.

5. One needs to examine continually the trade-offs between erroneously rejecting the hypothesis that the underlying price distribution is lognormal (Type I error), and erroneously accepting that the price distributions are lognormal (Type II error).

6. It can be shown, by solving for the value of N_y such that

$$\frac{\delta\sigma}{\delta N_y} = 0$$

that the optimal hedge ratio N_y/N_x which minimizes σ is

$$\frac{N_y}{N_x} = \frac{\sigma_x}{\sigma_y}\rho_{x,y}$$

Plugging this ratio into the equation for variance gives:

$$\sigma^2 = N_x^2 \sigma_x^2 + N_x^2 \sigma_x^2 \rho_{x,y}^2 - 2\rho_{x,y}^2 N_x^2 \sigma_x^2$$

$$= N_x^2 \sigma_x^2 \left(1 + \rho_{x,y}^2 - 2\rho_{x,y}^2\right)$$

$$= N_x^2 \sigma_x^2 \left(1 - \rho_{x,y}^2\right)$$

7. Hedge ratio

$$= \frac{\text{BPV (30 year)}}{\text{BPV (2 year)}} = \frac{\$949.8}{\$177.1} = 5.36$$

8. Optimal Hedge ratio

$$= \frac{\text{BPV (30 year)} \times \sigma(\text{Change in 30 year yield}}{\text{BPV (2 year)} \times \sigma(\text{Change in 2 year yield})} \times \text{Correlation } (30Y, 2Y)$$

$$= \frac{\$949.8 \times 5.64 BP}{\$177.1 \times 7.12 BP} \times 0.77$$

$$= 3.27$$

9. Delta measures the degree to which small changes in the price of the underlying affect the price of the option. A delta-equivalent position would be a position taken in the underlying which, theoretically, could be used to continuously hedge an option. If, for instance, entity A wrote 100 call options on eurodollar futures (a short position) with a delta of 0.74, then a typical market risk hedge for the option contracts would be to purchase 74 futures contracts (in order to restore delta neutrality).

10. The price of a *call* on a eurodollar futures contract is given by Black's model as

$$e^{-rT}\left[(100 - X)N(-d_2) - (100 - F)N(-d_1)\right]$$

Where r is the risk-free rate, X is the option strike price, F is the futures price, T is the time to maturity

$$d_1 = \frac{\log\left(\dfrac{100 - F}{100 - X}\right) + \dfrac{1}{2}\sigma^2 T}{\sigma\sqrt{T}}$$

$$d_2 = d_1 - \sigma\sqrt{T}$$

and σ is the volatility of the underlying futures contract. The formula yields a value which is in units of basis points. We scale by $25 per basis point to obtain the call option price in dollars. Accordingly,

$$\text{price} = 25 \times 100 \times \left\{e^{-rT}\left[(100 - X)N(-d_2) - (100 - F)N(-d_1)\right]\right\}$$

Applying the Black call formula with $r = .03875$, $\sigma = .193$, $T = 27/365$, $F = 96.14$, and $X = 96$, leads to a price of $425. Futhermore, the call option's delta is .74.

The price of a put on a eurodollar futures contract is similarly given by Black's model as

$$e^{-rT}\left[(100 - F)N(d_1) - (100 - X)N(d_2)\right]$$

Applying the Black put formula (with the parameter values above) leads to a price of $76.14. The put option's delta is .256.

11. Similarly, from a market risk perspective, assume one held a portfolio that consisted of being long the 100 million 10-year note and long 210 million four-year notes. The market risk exposure would be calculated as 310 million in notional terms.

12. The "average worst case credit risk" exposure, at any time t, $0 < t < T$, is:

$$\left(\int_0^t K \times \sigma \times t^{1/2}\, dt / T\ dt\right)/T = \left(K \times \sigma \times T^{3/2}\right)/(3/2)\times(1/T) = 2/3 \times \left[K \times \sigma \times T^{1/2}\right] = 2/3 \times W_T$$

13. $E\left[R_T^*\right] = \int_{-\infty}^{\infty} \max(0, X) f(x)\,dx = \int_0^{\infty} x f(x)\,dx$ where $f(x) = \dfrac{1}{\sqrt{2\pi}\sigma^*}\ \exp\left(-\dfrac{x^2}{2\sigma^{*2}}\right)$

is the terminal univariate normal probability density function and $\sigma^* = \sigma\sqrt{T}$ provided the volatility is σ at time 0. Accordingly,

$$E\left[R_T^*\right] = \frac{1}{\sqrt{2\pi}\sigma^*}\left[-\int_0^{\infty}\frac{d}{dx}\left(\exp\left(\frac{-x^2}{2\sigma^{*2}}\right)\right)dx\right]\left[\sigma^{*2}\right]$$

$$E\left[R_T^*\right] = \frac{\sigma^*}{\sqrt{2\pi}}\left[-\exp\left(\frac{-x^2}{2\sigma^{*2}}\right)\right]\Big|_0^{\infty}$$

$$E\left[R_T^*\right] = \frac{\sigma^*}{\sqrt{2\pi}} = \frac{2\sigma^*}{2\sqrt{2\pi}} = \frac{1}{2\sqrt{2\pi}}\left[2\sigma\sqrt{T}\right]$$

If one sets the worst case terminal credit risk at a 97.7% (or a 2σ one-sided level of confidence) then $W_T^* = 2\sigma\sqrt{T}$. Accordingly: $E[R_T^*] = 1/2\sqrt{2\pi} \times W_T^*$. Further, if the notional amount (N) is then multiplied by $E[R_T^*]$ and $W_{T^*} = W_T^* \times N$ then $E[R_T]$ = Expected terminal replacement cost = $E[R_T^*] \times N = W_T/5 \times N = W_T/5$ since $5 = 2\sqrt{2\pi} = 5.013$. Accordingly, $E[R_T] = FE/3.33$ where FE, called the fractional exposure, is defined in this application as $2/3\ W_T^*$. Observe that

$$\frac{W_T^* \times N}{5} = \frac{3/2 \times \left[\dfrac{2}{3}W_T^* \times N\right]}{5} = \frac{3/2 \times FE}{5} = \frac{FE}{10/3} = \frac{FE}{3.33}$$

14. For example, the expected credit loss at a given point in time equals:

$\iiint CE \times DR \times (1 - RR) \times f(CE, DR, RR)\ dCEdDRdRR$ where CE denotes credit risk exposure, DR the default rate, RR the recovery rate, and f(CE, DR, RR) the multivariate probability density function. Observe, for illustrative purposes, that if one assumes *statistical independence* between CE, DR and RR, as well as a zero per cent recovery rate, then one can multiply the average expected credit risk exposure by the expected default rate to determine an expected credit loss. If one then assumes that a certain percentage of the expected loss can be recovered, one can multiply the result by 1 minus the expected recovery rate to obtain the expected loss.

15. If one defaults immediately before time period i then one has $(T - i + 1)AK_i^{1\backslash 2}$ at risk.

For example, if one defaults immediately before the second time period, then one has

$$(T - 1)AK\sigma\sqrt{2}\ \text{at risk.}$$

If one lets V equal $(T - i + 1)\ AK\sigma i^{1\backslash 2}$ and sets T^* equal to $T + 1$ and $V^* = V/Ak\sigma$

then, in order to find the peak, one needs to find the value of i that maximizes

$$V^* = (T^* - i)\ i^{\frac{1}{2}}$$

Solving $\dfrac{dr^*}{di} = (T^* - i)\dfrac{1^{1/2}}{2} - i^{1/2}$ reveals that i is equal to $\dfrac{T^*}{3}$

16. For example, Canadian Imperial Bank of Commerce (CIBC) utilizes a risk management information platform which incorporates internally and externally developed analytic tools (such as provided by CATS), a purchased relational database (such as Sybase) using an internally developed data model and sophisticated workstations (such as Hewlett-Packard).

12

Firmwide Risk Management: An Integrated Approach to Risk Management and Internal Control

James C. Lam

Recently, it seems as if every six months or so the front pages of newspapers reminds us of the perils of improper risk management. These headlines include, among many others, Barings, Daiwa, Kidder, Metallgesellschaft, Orange County, and Sumitomo. Unfortunately, major losses due to lax controls are not new in the financial services industry. In the more distant past, the headlines ranged from companies such as Bank of New England, BCCI, Continental Illinois, and Drexel, to entire industries and market segments such as the thrift crises, LDC lending, junk bonds, HLT lending, commercial real estate lending, and mortgage derivatives. While some benefit might result from the heightened awareness caused by these highly publicized stories, business managers should strive to gain "lessons learned" to ensure that past mistakes are not repeated in their organizations.

Some people reading these stories look for simple answers and are quick to blame specific financial products for these losses, such as junk bonds and real estate loans in the 1980s or financial derivatives in the 1990s. However, it may be much more valuable for management to assess the underlying root causes for these debacles (and their own internal control problems) and to make real changes that will minimize the possibility that risk management lapses will result in embarrassing headlines, financial losses, or even the ultimate demise of the firms that they are responsible to oversee. With this objective in mind, the focus of this chapter is to discuss the answers to three basic questions:

I would like to thank Jerry Lieberman, CFO of Fidelity Investments, for providing me with the leadership, opportunity, and resources to significantly increase the scope of my risk management work. I would also like to thank Kelly Smith, an associate at the Global Risk Management Department, for her excellent research and production support. While my views on risk management have benefited greatly from working with my colleagues at Fidelity Investments, any errors or omissions are strictly my own.

- *What are the key lessons learned from the headlines?* We will look beneath the headlines and assess the key lessons learned. Rather than reviewing individual case studies of events leading to the headlines just mentioned, we will discuss seven key lessons drawn from the common themes underlying these events.
- *How can management establish an integrated approach to risk management?* In the major section of this chapter, we will discuss the various components of a comprehensive and integrated risk management framework (i.e., firmwide risk management). We will then discuss the rationale and best practices for integrating financial risk management and internal control, as well as the challenges facing management in establishing an integrated risk management framework.
- *What are the "quick hits" that management can implement?* Last, we will discuss some of the immediate steps management can take in establishing better risk management and controls at their companies. While many aspects of an integrated risk management framework may take months, or even years, to fully implement (e.g., an integrated risk system), there are a number of key steps that management can take in the short term that may represent quick pay-back opportunities.

LESSONS LEARNED

Collectively, the headline stories serve as a strong wake-up call for management regarding the dangerous consequences of improper risk management and control. Lapses in risk management have resulted in significant losses for companies in different industries and countries around the world. A number of these companies—some once considered the pillars of their industries—are no longer in existence because they couldn't survive the financial and reputational loss they suffered. The players and circumstances surrounding each story are unique, with the culprit(s) ranging from a single rogue trader involved in unauthorized trading to groups of individuals involved in unsound business practices that were once accepted (or even encouraged) by management. Some events occurred over days or months while others happened over a decade or longer. While there are many differences in these cases, there are important common themes from which the following seven lessons can be derived:

Lesson 1: Know Your Business

Perhaps the most important lesson one can learn is the obligation of managers to know your business. This responsibility is shared among everyone involved in the business, ranging from the board of directors to front-line supervisors and employees. In fact, the requirement to know your customer (which is an integral part of knowing your business) is not only widely recognized as a tenet of a sound risk management process, but also has been adopted as a requirement by various regulatory agencies. While this requirement is critical for managers with oversight and approval authority, it is also important for all employees to understand how their individual accountabilities can impact the risks of the organization, and how their functions and responsibilities relate to others within the company. Business managers should be knowledgeable about all aspects of the business, including business processes and interfaces, key drivers of revenue and cost, and the major risks and exposures embedded in their operations and products (i.e., know your risks).

Lesson 2: Establish Checks and Balances

Establishing the appropriate checks and balances, or segregation of duties, can be thought of as applying the principle of portfolio diversification to managing people and processes. From a risk diversification perspective, it is not desirable to have a concentration of market risk exposure to a specific segment (e.g., emerging markets) or a large concentration of credit exposure to a counterparty or industry. Likewise, it is not desirable to have a concentration of power and authority in any individual or group of individuals who can commit the company's capital to a specific risk taking activity. A clear danger of various re-engineering efforts is that some important checks and balances (which are often, by definition, redundant processes) have been re-engineered out of the business. Appropriate checks and balances, or segregation of duties, are not only safeguards to errors in people, process, and systems, they are also fundamental to sound business practices (examples range from independent boards of directors and audit committees to something as simple as having someone proofread an important document).

Lesson 3: Set Limits and Boundaries

As business strategies and product plans tell a business "where to go," risk limits and boundaries tell a business "when to stop." It is widely accepted that risk limits are an integral part of a sound risk management program. For *market risk,* these risk limits may include trading limits, product limits, duration and other sensitivity limits (otherwise known as the "Greeks"), value-at-risk limits, and stop-loss limits. For *credit risk,* these risk limits may include mark-to-market and risk-adjusted limits by counterparty, risk grade, industry, and country. For *operational risk,* risk limits may include minimum quality standards (or maximum error rates) by operation, system, or process. They may also include internal and external audit reviews and findings. In addition to limits for financial and operational risks, boundaries should be established to control *business risk* such as the acceptable level of business activity that represent exceptions to business or operational guidelines. Boundaries should also be established to control *organizational risk* such as the company's hiring policies vis-à-vis a prospective employee's background check or its termination policies when an employee violates company policies. Without clear limits and boundaries, a fast-growing company is analogous to a race car without brakes.

Lesson 4: Keep Your Eye on the Cash

When a famous bank robber was asked why he robbed banks, his answer was "because that's where the cash is." Embedded in this simple answer lies an important lesson for all financial institutions regarding the appropriate safeguards for managing cash positions and cash flows. These safeguards range from basic controls such as authorized signatures to initiate, approve, and move cash, to internal processes to measure, monitor, reconcile, and document when appropriate, all cash and security transactions and positions. Actual cash flows and positions can also provide management with valuable reasonableness checks against the company's trading systems and profitability models. New and emerging technologies such as Internet/Intranet, electronic banking, and smart cards will provide financial institutions with new challenges in this important function. Inadequate cash management and accounting systems represent opportunities for potential fraud, as well as blind spots for trading and operational errors to go undetected.

Lesson 5: Use the Right Yardstick

The measures of success used (and not used) by a company to track individual and group performance is a key driver of behavior and, by extension, a key driver of risk. Most companies establish performance goals for sales, revenue, and profitability. Some companies have also augmented their financial measures with performance measures regarding quality, customer satisfaction, and internal processes. In order to provide management with a risk/return perspective on the business, it is important that risk measures (similar to those alluded to in Lesson 3 above) are incorporated in the management reporting and performance measurement processes. An integrated set of risk measures should provide management with timely information on all types of risks faced by the company, including actual (ex-post) and early warning (ex-ante) risk indicators.

Lesson 6: Pay for the Performance You Want

Closely related to performance measurement is how compensation and incentives are designed and implemented, and whether or not they reinforce desired behavior and performance. The combination of performance measurement and incentive compensation is probably one of the most powerful drivers of human behavior and organizational change, which can work for or against the company's risk management objectives. For example, if the performance of managers and employees is measured by, and rewarded for, strictly sales or revenue-based results with no consideration given to risk exposures or losses, then it should be expected that the company will be exposed to higher and higher levels of potential risk that may become inconsistent with the company's risk appetite and capital. Therefore, management should pay careful attention to the signals that performance measurement and incentive compensation systems provide to ensure that they are consistent with the company's business and risk management objectives.

Lesson 7: Balance the Yin and the Yang

Discussions of risk management and control tend to focus on infrastructure, or the hard side (the Yang) of risk management, including independent risk functions and oversight committees, risk assessments and audits, risk management policies and procedures, systems and models, measures and reporting, and risk limits and exception processes. However, it is equally if not more important for companies to focus on the soft side (the Yin) of risk management. This would include (a) setting the tone from the top and building awareness by communicating and demonstrating senior management commitment; (b) establishing the principles that will guide the company's risk culture and values; (c) developing communication channels for discussing risk issues, escalating exposures, and sharing lessons learned and best practices; (d) providing training and development programs; and (e) reinforcing desired behavior and results through performance measurement and incentives. While the hard side is focused on the processes, systems, and reporting, the soft side is focused on the people, skills, culture, values, and incentives. In many respects, the soft side components are the key drivers of risk taking activities while the hard side components are enablers to support risk management activities. Therefore, business managers should take a balanced approach to managing risk at their companies.

INTEGRATED APPROACH TO RISK MANAGEMENT

The focus of this section is to discuss a top-down framework for risk management, and the components that financial institutions[1] need to integrate to effectively manage global risks. As a whole, these components represent a new organizational model for firmwide risk management: the *integrated risk management organization.* A number of major trends and developments establish the case for integrated risk management:

- Globalization and integration of financial markets have broken down the boundaries between countries, and strengthened the linkages and interdependencies between markets and economies around the world. Today, a policy change by the Bundesbank in Germany may have a direct and immediate effect on the returns of a domestic fixed income investor in the United States. Institutions with international investments and operations need to measure and manage global risks on an integrated basis.

- The breathtaking growth and innovation in financial and derivative products have broken down the boundaries between various risks and various industries. For example, a bank can choose to eliminate traditional banking risks by exchanging credit risk for market risk through an interest rate swap, or mitigate both credit and market risk through a contingent option. On the other hand, an industrial corporation that hedges with swaps may find itself in the business of lending to financial institutions because a swap, in effect, is a two-way loan.[2] Derivatives offer flexible solutions to manage risk, but institutions involved in derivatives need to manage the multiple and dynamic risks associated with derivative products.

- The same technologies that help fuel the growth in financial and derivative products are also helping institutions measure and manage risk. The reduced cost of client/server networks, object-oriented software, and powerful database applications has enabled a larger number of institutions to gain access to valuable information and state-of-the-art risk management technologies. A regional bank can develop similar financial engineering and risk simulation capabilities that are used by large investment banks by leasing vendor models or through outsourcing arrangements. However, the use of advanced technologies also comes with higher levels of model risks.[3] Nonetheless, more institutions have gained access to advanced technologies for measuring and managing financial risks. The dependency on computer systems in all aspects of business operations has provided complex challenges associated with technology and information security risks, such as solving the millennium problem[4] and maintaining security over the Internet or Intranet.

- The combination of the above forces has increased the complexity of risk management because risks can easily be transformed from one form to another (from market risk to credit risk or from spot risk to forward risk), and they can freely roam across counterparties, industries, markets, and countries. Traditional organizational structures and incentives, generally accepted accounting principles, and outdated systems are simply inadequate in the new world of risk management. Therefore, to effectively manage risks that are now more complex and interrelated, financial institutions must rethink their approaches to risk management. In short, they need to be an integrated risk management organization.

To manage risk on an integrated basis, financial institutions must ensure that each component of risk management is effective, and that these components are functioning as an integrated whole to optimize risk/return for the institution. The rest of this section will discuss the three major components of an integrated risk management framework:

1. *Organizational effectiveness.* Risk management policies and processes must be fully integrated with the organization's business strategy, organizational structure and culture, and incentive compensation programs.
2. *Risk and performance measurement.* The key objective of risk management is to optimize the relationship between risk and return: monitoring and controlling global risks on the one hand, while maximizing risk-adjusted returns (i.e., shareholder value) on the other.
3. *Systems and technology.* The underlying foundation of integrated risk management is a seamless and integrated systems and technology platform, including advanced modeling and database capabilities.

Organizational Effectiveness

Organizational effectiveness can be defined as the soft side of risk management, or the fabric that holds all of the other business and risk management components together. This involves an organization's people (Who is in a position to put the firm at risk?), skills (What are their experiences and competencies?), culture and values (What are their beliefs?), organizational structure (How do they work together?), and incentives (How are they recognized and rewarded for their performance?). While many aspects of organizational effectiveness are intangible, they probably play an even more important role than the hard side of risk management (e.g., systems, methodologies, measures and reporting, risk limits). An integrated risk management organization excels at, and balances, both the hard and soft side of risk management.

From an overall organizational perspective, risk management is more than the methodologies and systems used to measure financial risks. It is more than the day-to-day tactics used to control financial risks. While measurement and control techniques are key components of risk management, the overall risk management framework is underpinned by three fundamental aspects of the organization, including (1) the business strategy that defines how the organization will compete in its target business segments, (2) the organizational structure and people that provide management oversight and control for business and risk management activities, and (3) the incentive compensation system that provides rewards for key personnel.

Business Strategy and Risk Management

Organizations can increase their effectiveness in risk management by integrating risk management controls into their business processes and operations, especially in the business strategy development process. Organizations that have linked business strategy and risk management are characterized by effective teamwork and communication between business units and risk management. First, line managers involve risk managers in the business strategy development process. Risk managers provide independent assessments of new business and product opportunities and raise risk management concerns at an early stage. For example, risk management may have serious concerns about an industry that a business unit is planning for rapid expansion. The involvement of risk managers in developing business strategies and formulating relationship/product plans ensures that business initiatives are consistent with risk management policies. It also facilitates the discussion of business and risk management issues in a rational and strategic context, and encourages teamwork in the development of business strategies, target market and relationship plans, and new business and product initiatives. This contrasts with debating key issues for the first time in the middle of a transaction, and the mistrust and miscommunication that can be found between business units and risk management at some organizations.

Similarly, risk managers involve line managers in the development of risk management policies. Line managers provide timely information on factors that should be incorporated in risk management policies, such as market and competitive trends, and insights on customer needs. For example, new underwriting procedures being developed by risk management may not be competitive given new customer service initiatives undertaken by direct competitors. The involvement of line managers in the development of risk management policies ensures wider acceptance, and more importantly, greater understanding and compliance by the line units. It also ensures that emerging risk management issues, such as credit risk concentrations or market price volatility, are communicated at an early stage. This contrasts with the "roll out" of risk management policies that simply don't work because they have not been fully discussed from a business, market, or customer perspective.

Organizations that have successfully linked business strategy and risk management take a proactive approach to business and risk management, while maintaining independence and appropriate checks and balances. They avoid the offense-versus-defense (which, by the way, have opposite goals) mentalities that exist in other organizations where (1) the line units are viewed as unfocused in their business efforts and/or uncertain on risk management standards, and (2) the risk management units are viewed as a barrier to business development and are in a reactive mode to the transactions being proposed by the line units. Instead, they are proactive in defining the businesses that they should target and the risks that they should accept or mitigate. From a strategic perspective, these organizations are better positioned to achieve a balance between originating business and managing risk.

Organizational Structure and Corporate Governance

Financial institutions are generally organized by line units, risk management, and support functions. Typically, the line units are organized by region or market (North America, Europe, Asia), customer (wholesale vs. retail), product (equities, fixed income, foreign exchange, commodities at investment banks, or loans, deposits, and operating services at commercial banks), or a combination thereof (e.g., product within market). Risk management is usually organized by market risk and credit risk functions. Central support functions include finance, credit, human resources, and other administrative units. From a risk management perspective, the typical organization structure and risk management responsibilities for a financial institution are shown in Figure 12.1.

FIGURE 12.1   Risk Organizational Structure

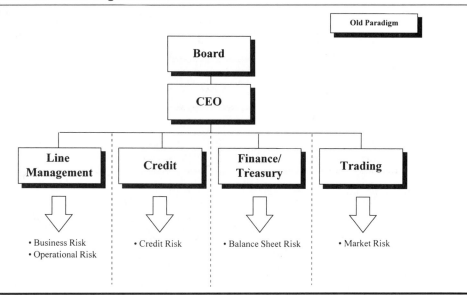

An examination of the U.S. banking industry shows how this functional organization structure has evolved over time as a result of the risks that banks needed to manage. Prior to the 1980s, the chief risk faced by commercial banks (and thrifts) was credit risk. Banks were not concerned about market risk because (1) interest rates were more stable than they are today, (2) bank rates were regulated by Regulation Q, and (3) banks were not involved in securities underwriting and capital market activities due to Glass-Steagall restrictions. In the start of the 1980s, the elimination of Regulation Q combined with volatile interest rate movements exposed banks to significant interest rate risk. By the end of the decade, the breakdown of Glass-Steagall (e.g., Section 20 subsidiaries) and new ventures in derivatives trading and other capital market businesses exposed banks to significant market risk. In order to manage their new risks, banks have set up Asset/Liability Management Committees (ALCOs) to manage interest rate risk, as well as trading desks to manage market risk. Today, this functional organization structure is how most U.S. financial institutions are organized and managed.

Disconnected Risk Management

Organization structures based on functional areas and/or product groups are often ineffective in managing risks because of one key reason: many risks are multidimensional and interrelated, and therefore they should not be segregated and managed by separate functions or departments. As shown in Figure 12.2, the management decisions, models/methodologies, and databases are generally the responsibilities of the various functions involved in risk management within a functional organizational structure. This is a flawed approach because:

1. *Senior managers responsible for each business or support function may come from different professional backgrounds and they may have different, and*

FIGURE 12.2   Risk Organizational Structure

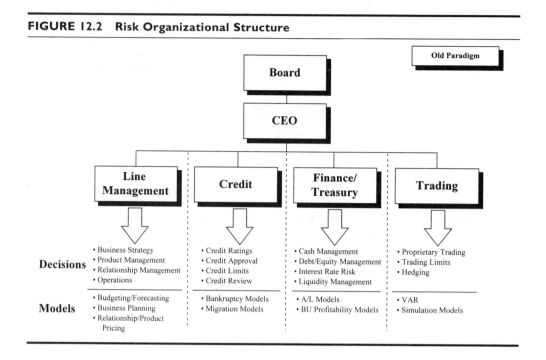

sometimes conflicting, objectives and initiatives. As a result, they often have different perspectives on risks, and how risks should be managed within their functional area and the organization overall. At some organizations, these functions operate as separate and independent units, as opposed to parts of an integrated whole, with ineffective communication and coordination of risk management activities.

2. *Risk management policies are not established with a top-down perspective, and may be inconsistent with each other and the risk/return tradeoff preference of senior management.* While each business or support function is responsible for key risk management decisions—such as credit limits, credit ratings, reserve levels, interest rate risk limits, trading limits, and product pricing—the policies established to guide these decisions may vary in terms of overall philosophy, risk tolerance, and approach. For example, credit ratings might be based on expected loss while trading limits are based on the volatility of loss (value-at-risk). Some policies might be conservative while others are aggressive. These inconsistencies may lead suboptimal economic performance, such as higher transaction and hedging costs (e.g., one unit is executing hedging transactions that are offset by another unit's trading strategies).

3. *Models and methodologies used to support risk management within the business or support functions are inconsistently developed and applied.* The definition of risk or loss may be inconsistent, where some functions might use accounting models that estimate the probability and severity of annual accounting losses, while other functions might use economic models that estimate the probability and severity of mark-to-market losses. The assumptions used by models might also be different, where some models might estimate future losses based on historical data (average actual losses), while others use

market price data (security price volatilities and credit spreads) or stochastic loss estimation techniques (e.g., Monte Carlo simulations).

4. *Databases and data models are developed independently and fail to measure the correlations of various risk factors.* These databases and data models are usually designed to provide input to the analytical models used by the specific business or support function. They do not communicate with each other nor support the analytical models used by other functions. However, from a capital management and diversification perspective, it is important for management to assess how risks throughout the organization correlate with each other. For example, management needs to know not only how credit losses in one industry correlate with losses in other industries, but also how credit losses in general correlate with interest rate movements. Such insights are difficult to develop if models and databases are scattered throughout the organization.

The end result is a risk management organization that is disconnected with respect to key decision makers, risk management policies and strategies, models and methodologies, and databases. A key question is where do these disconnected risk management activities converge? At most financial institutions they converge at the chief executive's office. While the chief executive and the board of directors should bear the ultimate responsibility for ensuring that a sound risk management program is in place, few chief executives would include directing day-to-day risk management activities as part of their job descriptions. Many financial institutions lack a central function that monitors and coordinates global risk management activities.

The Chief Risk Officer or Global Risk Management Committee

A growing number of financial institutions have recognized the need for a central and independent risk management function.[5] While most of these initiatives are efforts to centralize credit risk management or market risk management, several financial institutions have organized central risk functions that deal with all aspects of financial risks, including credit, market, liquidity, technology, and operational risks.

Financial institutions that have set up a centralized risk management function generally appoint a chief risk officer and/or establish of a central risk committee. Examples of these functions or committees can be found at large commercial banks, investment banks, and investment management companies. Examples of well integrated risk management functions can be found at the derivative product companies (DPCs). These companies face the business, operational, market, credit, and organizational risks associated with dealing in complex derivative instruments. To obtain their triple-A ratings, these companies go through an exhaustive rating agency and legal process, ensuring that the appropriate organizational structure, management controls, systems, and compliance and reporting processes are in place to manage all of their risks on an integrated basis. This process is required to ensure that, at inception and on an ongoing basis, the capital to risk ratio is at a triple-A level.

Regardless of the organization or approach, the central risk management function typically has the following key responsibilities:

- Establish risk management policies and procedures, including management reporting requirements.

- Coordinate or direct[6] day-to-day risk management activities through risk limits, capital allocation, and transaction approval processes.
- Measure global risks on a consistent and integrated basis, as well as monitor financial markets and other economic developments that may impact the organization's risk exposures.
- Review and approve risk management methodologies and models, in particular those used for pricing and valuation.
- Work with the audit and compliance functions to ensure that business activities are in compliance with laws, regulations, and internal policies and procedures.
- Communicate risk management results to executive management and the board of directors, as well as investors, rating agencies, stock analysts and regulators.

Financial institutions that adopt a centralized and integrated risk management approach should improve their organizational effectiveness in risk management. Over time, these financial institutions will develop a uniform risk culture with consistent policies, processes, and technologies. They will be more effective in managing global risks that are multi-dimensional and interrelated.

Incentive Compensation

If incentive compensation is a key driver of human behavior, then by extension it is a key driver of risk management. A financial institution with the best organizational structure, risk management processes, and systems will still be doomed for failure if the right people are not in place and/or incentive compensation motivates adverse behavior. The effectiveness of a financial institution in managing its risks is ultimately dependent on the collective decisions made, and actions taken, by its people. All other aspects of risk management are simply tools designed to guide human behavior through organizational hierarchy and information. Despite the importance of incentive compensation programs, many are simply linked to revenue or business volume, and not directly tied to shareholder interests such as risk-adjusted returns and shareholder value added.[7]

On Wall Street, a typical incentive compensation program would set aside, say 20%, of revenue as a bonus pool for senior management and traders. Such an incentive program, when combined with accounting standards that often inflate current profits (e.g., swaps accounting provides for the present-valuing of future income but no uniform standards for reserving for future credit costs, operating costs and capital costs), motivates traders to focus on longer-term and more capital intensive (i.e., more risky) transactions. These transactions may not be in the best interests of shareholders. The signals created by the typical incentive compensation system is illustrated by the example in Figure 12.3. In this example, the trader may opt to focus on executing a long-term plain vanilla swap (transaction A) instead of a short-term structured transaction (transaction B) if transaction A generates greater revenues (and hence a greater bonus) even though transaction B creates greater shareholder value. It would be in the best interest of the shareholders and the long-term success of the business if the trader's bonus is 50% of the shareholder value created, instead of 20% of revenue generated. While revenue-linked bonuses are ingrained in Wall Street's compensation scheme, firms have a number of options to link incentives with risk-adjusted return. These options include (1) linking a trader's bonus to both revenue and shareholder value created, (2) increasing the portion of the trader's total compensation that is made up of stocks and/or stock options, and (3) linking

FIGURE 12.3   Incentive Compensation

	Transaction A	Transaction B
Amount:	$25 million	$25 million
Tenor:	20 years	5 years
Spread:	5 bps	10 bps
Revenue:	$125,000	$100,000
Bonus @ 20% Revenue:	$25,000	$20,000
ROE:	15%	25%
Shareholder Value Created:	$0	$50,000
Bonus @ 50% Shareholder Value Created:	$0	$25,000

compensation and promotions to longer term risk/return performance. The key point is that firms can remain competitive in their compensation programs while establishing congruence between trader incentives and shareholder interests.

The averse behavior that may be motivated by inappropriate incentive programs should be of paramount concern to senior management. A large number of financial institutions have made significant changes in how they reward their senior managers and traders.[8] In fact, the important role that incentive compensation plays in managing risk is also recognized by the rating agencies and regulators, and has recently become a key topic during their reviews of risk management programs. To directly link the incentives for the traders (and other personnel) to the interest of shareholders, senior management should establish incentive compensation formulas that are based on risk-adjusted returns (the measurement of which is discussed in the next section).

Risk and Performance Measurement

Since the beginning of management science, the P&L represents a key management tool. The central objective of any performance measurement system is to establish a benchmark to evaluate the economic return of business activities. Such a benchmark would enable management to evaluate and compare economic performance of business activities at various levels of the organization, from specific transactions to the individual products or customers. It would also enable management to evaluate the trend in performance of business units and the overall organization over time. In order to properly measure the profitability of any transaction, whether it is a mortgage loan or a currency swap, the economic risks and costs of that transaction must be fully incorporated into the performance measurement.

History Lesson from Banking Crises

The importance of risk-adjusted performance measurement and pricing cannot be overstated. In fact, failures in performance measurement represent a key underlying factor in every major banking crisis since the 1980s: LDC lending, junk bonds, the U.S. thrift crisis, commercial real estate, and HLT lending. In each of these market crashes, there was a common chain of events that lead to market dislocation:

1. The risks of, and thus the required capital for, these business were understated. In addition, profits were often overstated due to accounting deficiencies

(e.g., loan fee accounting in commercial real estate lending). As a result, the return on capital of these businesses was grossly inflated.

2. Organizations attracted by the inflated returns committed significant financial and human capital, and other resources in building up their investments in these businesses, often increasing market share at the expense of margins.
3. The combination of increased suppliers and aggressive pricing helped fuel the growth in these markets.
4. Eventually, the disconnect between risk and return is recognized by the market leading to a correction or market crash.

Participants in the derivatives industry should be concerned about the issues relating to flawed performance measurement because the derivative products industry exhibits some of the common characteristics of these market crashes. First, swaps accounting recognizes as income the present value of future revenue streams, while no uniform reserving practices are established for future administrative, credit, and capital costs. This can result in grossly overstated profitability. Second, organizations around the world have committed significant financial and human capital,[9] and other resources in building up their derivatives capabilities. Last, the industry has experienced exponential growth for over a decade. While the derivatives industry has experienced significant market volatility in 1994 without any major market dislocations, and the derivative products business is fundamentally attractive because of the value added to end users, the industry is not exempt from the consequences and potential dangers of flawed performance measurement.

Risk-Adjusted Capital Allocation

The key to measuring risk-adjusted performance of a business activity is to clearly establish a linkage between risk and return. One of the most effective ways to link risk and return is by allocating risk capital and measuring return on risk capital. Risk-adjusted performance measurement involves three interrelated processes:

1. *Risk Measurement.* The first process is to measure financial risk throughout the organization. Any risk, whether it is a market risk or credit risk (parallels with operational risk can also be made), is driven by four key factors: (a) the *risk position* such as a long position on U.S. Treasury securities, a short position on Japanese equities, or a credit exposure (i.e., long position)

FIGURE 12.4   Calculating Risk-Adjusted Capital—Simplified Example

Risk-Adjusted Capital =	f (Position,		Volatility, Liquidity,		Covariance)
Market Risk Example:	Value of .01	×	98% Probability Move	×	Covariance
	$1mm	×	25bp	×	.8
=	$20mm				
Credit Risk Example:	Credit Exposure	×	98% Credit Loss	×	Covariance
	250mm	×	10.0%	×	.8
=	$20mm				

to ABC counterparty, (b) the *volatility* of risk or how quickly market or credit conditions can move against the risk position, as measured by the variability of potential outcomes in terms of market prices or credit losses, (c) the *liquidity* or holding period of the risk position (e.g., a good indicator for market liquidity may be the bid/ask spread), and (d) the *correlation* of the risk position to other risk positions in the organization. These four factors are used to determine the "capital at risk"[10] or the amount of money that the institution can lose in an adverse scenario.

2. *Capital Allocation.* The second process is to allocate risk capital to each business unit based on its risk positions. For each risk position, capital needs to be allocated to cover a certain level of unexpected loss. The appropriate level of risk-adjusted capital (or capital-at-risk) should be a function of the target leverage and loss coverage that management wants to achieve. For example, a triple-A rated company may need to allocate sufficient capital to cover, say 99.9% of unexpected loss, whereas a single-A company may need to allocate capital to cover, say 98% of unexpected loss. Figure 12.4 shows two simplified examples of calculating risk-adjusted capital for both market and credit risk. In these examples, $20 million of risk-adjusted capital is allocated to the market risk position, and $20 million is allocated to the credit risk position.

3. *Performance Measurement.* The final process is to measure the performance of each risk position relative to the capital that is required to support that risk position. To calculate the risk-adjusted return on any financial product, methodologies need to be developed to adjust revenues for market risk, credit risk, and other economic costs (see Figure 12.5 for a description of these methodologies). Two key performance measures are ROE and shareholder value added.

By allocating capital to cover a consistent level of risk, management can monitor how efficiently capital is used throughout the organization. For example, an organizational risk/return matrix (see Figure 12.6) can be developed for management to measure for each organizational unit (e.g., segmented by business units, customers, or products), the types and levels of risk being taken and the risk-adjusted returns being achieved. Risk-adjusted performance measurement represents a powerful management tool for (1) shareholder value-based business strategy development, (2) product development and pricing or relationship planning, (3) profitability and risk measurement, (4) incentive compensation, and (5) capital and other resource allocation.

Risk-Adjusted Pricing

The same methodologies used for risk-adjusted performance measurement can be reverse engineered to support risk-adjusted pricing. The schematic in Figure 12.7a shows how these methodologies represent the building blocks needed to calculate the required net revenue on any financial product.[11] In Figure 12.7b, a numerical example is shown for calculating risk-adjusted ROE (i.e., 30% ROE given a 2.50% margin) and calculating risk-adjusted margin (i.e., 1.50% margin given a target 20% ROE).

Example: Risk-Adjusted Pricing for Derivatives

While risk-adjusted performance measurement and pricing can be performed for any product, we will use derivative products as an example. To accurately measure

Figure 12.5   Risk-Adjusted Return Methodologies

Methodology	Description
1. Gross Product Yield	Gross product yield and fees
2. Matched Funding/Hedging Cost	Less: Matched maturity funds transfer rate and hedging costs (i.e., risk adjustment for interest rate risk)
3. Net Product Yield (1-2)	Equals: Product yield net of interest rate risk (e.g., matched net interest margin on loans, bid/ask spread on swaps)
4. Credit Provision	Less: Credit costs (i.e., risk adjustment for expected credit loss)
5. Operating Expense	Less: Fully allocated expenses (i.e., direct, indirect, and overhead expenses)
6. Tax Provision	Less: Tax expenses
7. Risk-Adjusted Net Income (3-4-5-6)	Equals: Risk-adjusted net income available to shareholders
8. ROE (7 ÷ Risk-Adjusted Capital)	Risk-adjusted net income divided by risk-adjusted capital (i.e., measure of return in relation to risk taken by shareholders)
9. Shareholder Value Created PV [7 − (Risk-Adjusted Capital × Cost of Capital)]	Present value of the difference between risk-adjusted net income and cost of risk-adjusted capital (i.e., measure of shareholder value creation—is positive if ROE is above cost of capital and vice versa)

Figure 12.6   Risk/Return Matrix

Organizational Unit	Credit Risk	Market Risk	Operational Risk	Other	Total
Business Unit A	Capital-At Risk / ROE	$ / %	$ / %	$ / %	$ / %
Business Unit B					
. .					
Business Unit N					
Total	$ / %	$ / %	$ / %	$ / %	$ / %

FIGURE 12.7a Risk-Adjusted Pricing

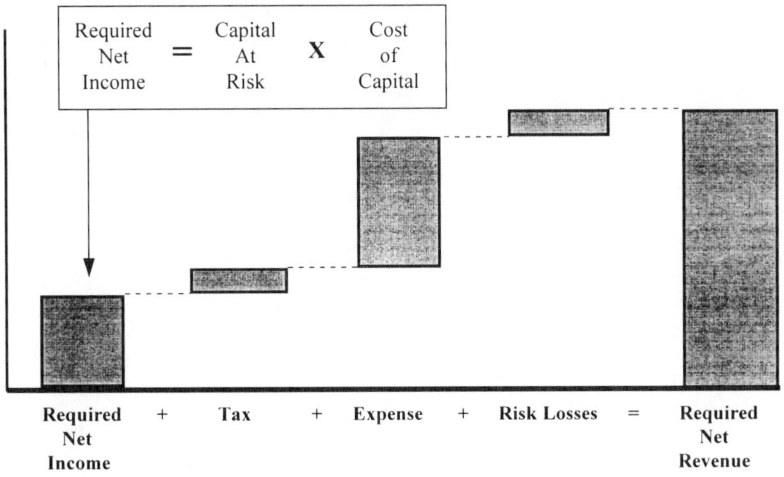

the risk-adjusted returns of derivative products, the appropriate reserves for future credit, administrative expense, and hedging/capital costs must be fully incorporated. These reserves should be established by dealers because they recognize as revenue the present value of the bid/ask or bid/mid spread while multi-year transactions require multi-year management and capital resources. Therefore, future period risk and other economic costs should be fully reserved against. To a lesser extent, these reserves should also be established by end users because the benefits of using derivatives (e.g., risk reduction, yield enhancement) should be measured against their economic risks and costs throughout the life of the transactions.

The application of risk-adjusted return measurement to derivative products is shown in Figure 12.8. Figure 12.9 shows a pricing model for a $25 million five-year interest rate swap for counterparties with ratings ranging from Aaa/AAA to

FIGURE 12.7b Risk-Adjusted Pricing

	Calculate ROE	*Calculate Pricing*
Volume	$100 mm	$100 mm
Margin	2.50%	150%
Revenue	$2.5 mm	$1.5 mm
Risk Losses	<0.5 mm>	<0.5 mm>
Expense	<1.0 mm>	<1.0 mm>
Pre-Tax Net Income	$1.0 mm	0.7 mm
Tax	<0.4 mm>	<0.3 mm>
Net Income	$0.6 mm	$0.4 mm
Risk-Adjusted Capital	$2.0 mm	$2.0 mm
Risk-Adjusted ROE	30%	20%

FIGURE 12.8 Measuring Risk-Adjusted ROE

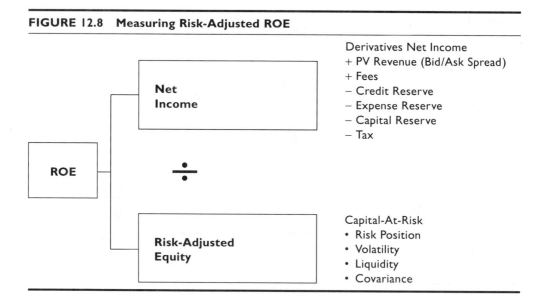

Baa/BBB. *The assumption for the net cost of capital is 7%, which is based on a 15% gross cost of capital minus an 8% capital funding credit.*[12] *For the purpose of this example, capital-at-risk is assumed to range from 4 basis points of notional for a Aaa/AAA counterparty to 25 basis points for a Baa/BBB. Next, the capital-at-risk ratios are multiplied by the net cost of capital to obtain the required net income. The required pretax income is based on a 40% marginal tax rate assumption. Last, the required revenue is calculated by adding various expense, credit, and funding/hedging cost assumptions to the required pretax income. In this example, the required revenue for a five-year swap range from 2.25 basis points for a Aaa/AAA counterparty to 8.5 basis points for a Baa/BBB counterparty. Pricing levels above these required revenue numbers would result in ROEs above the organization's cost of capital, and vice versa.*

FIGURE 12.9 Swaps Pricing Example

Notional Amount:	$25 Million
Product:	5-Year Interest Rate Swap
Net Cost of Capital:	7.00%

(BP of Notional)	Aaa/AAA	Aa/AA	A/A	Baa/BBB
Required Revenue	2.25	3.50	5.30	8.50
− Funding/Hedging Costs	0.50	0.50	0.50	0.50
− Credit Provision	0.29	0.56	1.05	2.58
− Expenses	1.00	1.50	2.00	2.50
= Required Pretax Income	0.47	0.93	1.75	2.92
− Tax	0.19	0.37	0.70	1.17
= Required Net Income	0.28	0.56	1.05	1.75
Capital-at-Risk	4.00	8.00	15.00	25.00

The risk-adjusted performance measurement methodologies discussed above represent the building blocks of an economic model of the business. Such a model can be used to address some of the key decisions faced by any business manager or trader:

- How should I price a transaction or relationship based on its underlying risks (risk-adjusted pricing)?
- What is the financial performance of my book of business, in aggregate and by various segments such as transaction, product, relationship, trader, or business unit (performance measurement)?
- How should I reward my business managers and traders for their contributions (incentive compensation)?

To optimize financial performance and ensure consistency in decision making, the same set of methodologies should be used for pricing, performance measurement, and incentive compensation.

Risk Measurement and Management

While performance measurement provides management with an economic assessment of risk-adjusted profitability, the primary risk control tools are the people, systems, limits, and processes that are in place to measure and manage risks. Some of the key components of risk measurement and management include:

- *Description of risk categories and components.* As a first step, management should describe all of the major categories of risk exposures as well as the components (and, as appropriate, sub-components) of each category. For example, the major categories of risk may be described as business risk, operational risk, market risk, credit risk, and organizational risk. Market risk can further be disaggregated by risk exposures associated with interest rates,[13] foreign exchange rates, equities, commodities, and real estate. Credit risk can be disaggregated by single obligor, product, industry, risk grade, country, and so on. Operational risk can include trading errors, pricing errors, failed trades, systems failures, unreconciled items and other operational exceptions, etc. The key is to be able to disaggregate (or slice and dice) the overall risk portfolio with sufficient granularity so that meaningful components of risk can be measured and managed. This process should be interactive and reflect the dynamic and changing nature of the business.[14]
- *Development of stop-loss limits.* For each category and component of risk, stop-loss limits should be established to ensure that *actual* economic losses do not exceed management's threshold levels. Stop-loss limits control the amount of losses the institution has incurred due to its risk positions. While the stop-loss limit is a well adopted practice for controlling market risk, such as the stop-loss limits established for traders and business units at the trading operation of an investment bank, the same concept can be extended to other types of risk. For example, a stop-loss limit can be established for credit risk with actual credit losses being measured by the combination of charge-offs (i.e., realized losses) and the mark-to-market losses based on credit spreads[15] (i.e., unrealized losses). Also, the stop-loss limit concept can be extended to operational risk such as requiring an operational review and assessment if error rates exceed a certain

threshold. Risk limits should be consistent with management's risk appetite, the institution's strategies and financial resources (assets, earnings, capital), and the capabilities and track records of those involved in taking such risks.

- *Development of sensitivity limits.* For each category and component of risk, sensitivity limits should be established to ensure that *prospective* economic losses do not exceed management's threshold levels. Sensitivity limits control an institution's exposure to various adverse economic scenarios. These scenarios can be developed using (1) historical or implied volatility stressed to some confidence level (i.e., capital-at-risk approach), (2) pre-defined stress tests, such as rates moving up 100 to 400 basis points, October 1987 equity price declines, or depression level default rates, and (3) simulation models that are driven by probabilistic models for the key stochastic variables. The objective is to limit the amount of loss potential for the institution's risk positions to ensure appropriate diversification (i.e., avoiding excessive risk concentrations).
- *Development of risk measurement systems and limit management processes.* This includes (1) processes for setting and allocating risk limits to business units, (2) methodologies and systems used to measure the institution's risk exposures, (3) processes for reporting on risk exposures and limit usage, and (4) policies and procedures for resolving limit excesses, including individual accountabilities, decision-making processes, and documentation requirements. The systems, databases, and overall technology that are required to support integrated risk management are discussed in the following section.

Systems and Technology

A seamless and integrated systems environment is a key component of an integrated risk management framework. Ideally, the inputs to the system include global risk positions, real-time market data feeds, and key assumptions about market variables and behavior. These inputs feed into a system that would stress-test the risk portfolio under a wide range of possible scenarios. The outputs from the system are reports and graphics that support risk measurement and management. To ensure the accuracy and integrity of the system, auditing and independent review processes are established to verify the assumptions and results of the system.

While it is straightforward to specify, developing the appropriate systems and technology for risk management is one of the biggest challenges and risks facing financial institutions. Commercially available vendor systems may offer appropriate solutions for certain products and applications (e.g., asset/liability models for interest rate risk or credit grade migration models for credit risk), but they do not represent a full and integrated technology solution for the user. On the other hand, developing proprietary models is often too daunting and costly a task for most small- to medium-sized institutions, and represents significant development and maintenance costs even for the largest of institutions. Although a fully integrated systems and technology platform that meets all user requirements may always be a goal to reach for, it is nonetheless important to develop a vision of such a platform so as to guide systems development and/or vendor selection.

Integrated Database and Systems

The ideal systems and technology platform would be supported by an integrated database. The old computer axiom "garbage in garbage out" speaks to the point that the quality of the output can only be as good as the quality of the input. An integrated database would capture all of the institution's risk positions (e.g., trades, market positions, credit exposures) as well as external market variables that impact these risk positions (e.g., interest rates, foreign exchange rates, default rates). Ideally, this information is captured on a real-time basis, and the data are stored in a time series structure so that analyses on trends, volatilities, and correlations can be performed. A number of powerful database programs are now commercially available that can store and manage very large data files. The key is defining the required data elements, and establishing the process and discipline to capture and verify the data over time. The integrated database would feed into a system(s) that is integrated across three key dimensions: (1) business applications in the front office (e.g., pricing, structuring, product development), middle office (e.g., risk management, performance measurement), and back office (e.g., trade processing, operations, accounting), (2) risk factors, such as business, operational, market, credit, and organizational risks, and (3) products including all asset, liability, and derivative categories.

Scenario Analysis

An integrated database and systems capability enables management to perform scenario analysis on the overall risk portfolio. Most risk management systems are capable of analyzing the impact of a user-defined scenario on a specific risk exposure. For example, the system can quantify how a 300 basis point rise in rates would impact the institution's trading positions. However, this analysis does not quantify how the same rate change would impact the institution's credit and liquidity risks. An integrated database and systems capability would be able to measure how one or more user-defined scenarios can simultaneously impact all of the institution's risk positions. For example, suppose interest rates move up by 300 basis points and 20% of the institution's counterparties are downgraded by 2 risk ratings. An integrated database and systems capability would then quantify for management (1) how this scenario would impact the institution's trading positions, (2) how derivatives gains and losses, along with the counterparty downgrades, would affect the institution's counterparty exposure and risk, and (3) how this scenario would impact the institution's liquidity positions given trading gains and losses as well as downgrade triggers and cash settlements that would occur. Such a capability would allow management to develop appropriate contingency plans for any adverse scenario.

However, the usefulness of scenario analysis is heavily dependent on the expertise and experience of those responsible for defining the scenarios. The appropriate number, range, and paths of scenarios would need to be defined and tested to fully measure an institution's risk exposure. For example, the worst case scenario for an institution that is hedging discounted POs (principle-only mortgage strips) with premium IOs (interest-only mortgage strips) may be a fall in interest rates, resulting in significant prepayments on the IOs, followed by a rise in rates, resulting in large losses on the POs with no or partial offset from the IOs. The point of this example is that this unique scenario must be defined and tested to truly measure the risk exposure of the hedge. In a highly complex portfolio with multiple contingent-payout instruments, the required number, range, and alternative paths of scenarios can be quite high, especially in an environment where risks must be measured on a real-time or daily basis. The need to stress test many scenarios is the key reason why simulation modeling has become an important risk management tool.

Simulation Modeling

A simulation modeling approach utilizes the increasingly powerful and cost effective computer technologies to test a position or portfolio against a full range of possible scenarios. An integrated simulation capability includes the following:

- *Databases.* Feeding into the simulation model would be a database of the institution's risk positions and information on how these positions are managed (e.g., limits, holding periods), as well as real-time data feeds of market prices/rates and credit spreads and default rates.
- *Key factor calculators.* These calculators would measure the volatilities and correlations of the key stochastic variables, including market variables such as interest rates, foreign exchange rates, and default rates.
- *Market behavior models.* These models contain assumptions of how financial markets would behave given observed relationships between market variables. Examples include interest rate parity and other arbitrage models, and mean reversion patterns for interest rate movements.
- *Simulation model.* The simulation model is the main analytical engine that generates hundreds or thousands of rate/price paths and calculates the expected values and losses under each path. These outcomes can then be used to determine expected profitability and losses, as well as worst-case losses.[16] Further analysis can reveal the market factors, assumptions, and scenarios that the institution is most exposed to, as well as the key levers that management has to reduce risk.

Grounding Models to Reality

A major technology risk faced by financial institutions is that the prices produced by their models (mark to model) may be very different from actual market prices (mark to market). The differences are caused by the fact that all models and assumptions are best estimates of an unpredictable market and these models and assumptions may be invalid during periods of market stresses. In some instances, the models and assumptions used are simply incorrect.

There are a number of ways in which management can mitigate technology risk, including:

1. Comparing the model prices with market prices on a regular basis, and equilibrating the model to market pricing as appropriate.
2. Updating the models and assumptions on a regular basis and performing sensitivity analysis on key models and assumptions.
3. Testing the models against historical prices and/or price benchmarks (i.e., back testing), especially during periods with high market volatility.
4. Hiring a independent expert, with strong academic and professional credentials, to review the methodologies and assumptions used by the models.
5. Linking the accounting and auditing functions with the financial modeling process to ensure that projected cash flows, in terms of timing and size, are consistent with actual cash flows.

While the above discussion was focused on financial simulation, and many financial institutions have developed simulation models for financial products and risks, there is an opportunity to apply dynamic simulation techniques to analyze all of the major risks faced by a business enterprise. In addition to financial risk, a simulation model can be used to analyze (1) business risk such as how pricing decisions can impact competitor behavior, (2) operational risk such as how volume spikes can impact the firm's operational and system constraints, or (3) organizational risk such as how hiring plans can impact training and development requirements. More importantly, a dynamic simulation model can be used to analyze the interdependencies of the risks faced by management, and therefore improve the quality of business and risk management decisions.

QUICK HITS

While many of the best practices for integrated risk management discussed in the previous section would take months, or even years, to establish, business managers can take a number of immediate steps to move toward an integrated approach to risk management. These steps may include:

1. *Provide leadership.* The CEO or another senior executive (e.g., CFO) should take the leadership role to sponsor the overall program for integrated risk management. This individual should also set the tone from the top and increase overall awareness through internal communication channels.
2. *Allocate resources.* Designate an individual and a cross-functional team with the responsibility and resources to provide ongoing focus, share best practices, and develop policies and measures for all types of risk across the company. This would include a firmwide risk assessment and the development of standard risk categories and definitions (e.g., a common language for risk).
3. *Establish a plan.* An overall business plan should be developed, which may include defining scope, long-term vision and plans, and overall framework for integrated risk management. This may also include guiding principles that best describe the desired risk culture, as well as the roles and responsibilities of line and staff units.
4. *Set milestones.* In addition to the long-term vision and overall framework, the business plan should establish clear milestones, say, over the next 12 months, that will move the company forward. Individual accountabilities, timing, and prototype deliverables should be organized and reviewed regularly with the sponsor.
5. *Track losses.* While financial institutions are in the business of taking risks, and therefore risk minimization is not always the appropriate objective, companies do want to minimize the losses in relationship to revenue and risk exposures. Thus, it is important for business managers to develop a disciplined process to track all categories of losses, as well as a loss review process to understand root causes so that appropriate controls can be established.
6. *Prototype risk measures.* In addition to losses, it is important for management to measure the exposures and early warning indicators for all types of risk across the company. While it may take months or years to develop an automated risk measurement system, management should "start with the end" by prototyping the appropriate set of risk measures and reports.

These prototypes will then drive the data collection, reporting, and systems development efforts.

7. *Link risk to compensation.* Perhaps the greatest lever to influence behavior and culture is the combination of performance measurement and incentive compensation. This initiative can be implemented through a top-down process of explicitly assigning individual, functional, business unit, and firm-wide accountabilities for risk management and control, reinforced by risk performance measures and incentives.

SUMMARY

As financial intermediaries, financial institutions exist to manage risk. That is, to originate, assess, price, diversify, hedge, monitor, and distribute risks more effectively and efficiently than their customers and competitors. The overall strength of a company's risk management program is, like the strength of a chain, based on its weakest link. A weak component or linkage will likely result in the mismanagement of risks that are becoming more complex, more global, and more interdependent. Financial institutions are well advised to take a hard look at their risk management program from the vantage point of an integrated risk management organization.

ENDNOTES

1. The concepts and practices for integrated risk management described in this chapter may be applied to any institution involved in the capital markets, including investment banks, commercial banks, thrifts, insurance companies, mutual funds, and treasury operations of corporations.

2. In a swap transaction, either side of the transaction may become in-the-money based on market changes. The counterparty that is in-the-money is, in effect, a lender to the counterparty that is out-of-the-money because if the latter defaults, the former will suffer a credit loss that is equal to the replacement cost of the swap.

3. A key model risk is whether or not prices produced by the model truly reflect market prices, especially with highly complex and illiquid positions. There is growing support for establishing reserves for model risk.

4. Most computers and software programs cannot correctly handle the year 2000.

5. Independent risk management was one of the common recommendations coming out of the Group of Thirty, CFTC, OCC, GAO, and other studies on risk management practices.

6. For organizations with a centralized and integrated risk management function, one of the key issues is should the risk management function be responsible for managing risk through a central hedge book of capital markets and derivative transactions, or should the function strictly be responsible for policy development and risk measurement.

7. Shareholder value added is the difference between shareholder value (market value or M) and invested capital (book value or B). A short-hand formula known as the one-stage capital asset pricing model can be used to calculate shareholder value added (M − B):

$$M/B = (ROE - g)/(Ke - g)$$

where M = market value; B = book value; ROE = return on equity capital; g = long-term growth rate; and Ke = cost of equity capital

8. For example, in an interview with *Investment Dealer's Digest,* Allen Wheat, president of CS First Boston, discussed the shift in the firm's compensation program from a "cash culture to much more of an [stock] ownership culture."

9. In the case of the triple-A special purpose companies established for derivative businesses, over $1.5 billion of initial capital have been committed (and legally separated from the parent company) to the derivative products business.

10. The measurement of capital-at-risk, also known as "value at risk," for market risk is one of the recommendations (#5) from the Group of Thirty study. The same principles can be applied to measure credit and operational risks.

11. In a typical income statement (or performance measurement), the sequence of calculations shown in Figure 12.7 would go from the right side (actual revenue) to the left side (actual net income and ROE). In a pricing model, the sequence is reversed, starting from the left side (required ROE, or cost of capital) to the right side (required net revenue).

12. The cost of capital represents the firm's cost of equity capital based on, for example, the Capital Asset Pricing Model. The capital funding credit is the marginal yield on financial assets funded by equity capital, and therefore represents an offset in cost.

13. Interest rate risk can be further disaggregated into exposures to parallel shifts (delta), changes in delta (gamma), volatility (vega), time value (theta), yield curve twists, prepayment/convexity and basis risk.

14. In addition to risks associated with current operations, management may wish to include business risks as part of their risk management program, such as the potential adverse impact of market price changes to the institution's business volume and market share relative to its key competitors.

15. For example, a loan or security that is downgraded (widening in credit spread) would incur a mark-to-market loss even though no defaults or charge-offs have occurred. Marking the credit portfolio to market using credit spreads provides an economic assessment of credit losses. Institutions are also using credit ratings migration techniques to estimate portfolio ratings and related mark-to-market losses under expected and adverse economic scenarios, as a basis for determining required reserve and capital for credit risk.

16. The simulation approach is used by the DPCs (derivative product companies) and rating agencies to determine the appropriate capital levels for their standalone triple-A ratings.

PART FIVE

Regulation

13

Ready—Fire—Aim: An Antidote to Derivatives Regulation by Anecdote

WENDY LEE GRAMM
GERALD D. GAY

I n Washington, the saying goes, "one anecdote makes a regulation, two anecdotes make a law." While incidents sometimes expose flaws or gaps in a system, all too often they just serve as an excuse for regulators and legislators to show that they are doing "something." This results in too many unnecessary and job-killing regulations and laws. An excellent case in point was the flurry of regulatory and legislative activity following the many reported incidents (i.e., "anecdotes") of organizations having lost money during the volatile 1993-1994 market period, reportedly in OTC derivatives.[1] But legislation in response to incidents is hardly a desirable way to govern and it can produce inefficient results. Unfortunately, with respect to derivatives, this seems to describe the modus operandi in this country dating back to the 1800s. In fact, much of the historical evolution of derivatives regulation, as reflected in the Commodity Exchange Act, has been in response to market incidents.[2] It seems inevitable that a new round of incidents will once again prompt calls for additional regulation.

Before any new regulation or law is enacted, there are basic questions that should be answered. These questions are too often overlooked or quickly dismissed during the rush to regulate. These fundamental questions include:

1. What is the market failure that justifies government intervention in the workings of markets—in other words—what conditions exist that prevent this industry and its participants from working out a market-based or contractual solution to the problem themselves?
2. Will the proposed remedy indeed address the problem?
3. Have the benefits and costs of the proposed action been evaluated properly and do the benefits exceed the costs?
4. What are the alternatives and which is the most cost effective?

We focus primarily on the first question—the rationale for regulation—because this most basic issue is often addressed inadequately if at all in the rush to regulation. We provide a simple framework for assisting future debates on the necessity of additional regulatory controls on OTC derivatives instruments. This framework is

433

also useful for assessing the relevance and appropriateness of existing regulations (including the regulations of exchange-traded futures), many of which were imposed under different times and circumstances (and in response to incidents). We begin by providing some of the more popularly argued reasons for enhancing government's hand in regulating this market. We then provide additional and countervailing analysis and evidence that should be seriously considered and addressed by officials before regulating.

ALLEGED JUSTIFICATIONS FOR GOVERNMENT INTERVENTION

In the case of OTC derivatives, what are the areas of concern for regulators and policymakers? The reasons for financial market regulation traditionally include: (1) providing for adequate levels of customer and investor protection; (2) maintaining market or price integrity; (3) protecting the financial integrity of the system.

One objective of financial regulation is to provide for appropriate levels of consumer and investor protection. With respect to OTC derivatives, an alleged market imperfection often cited is an asymmetry of information between "sophisticated" sellers and "naive" purchasers. That is, offerors of derivatives are alleged to possess more information than their counterparties and they may have incentives to withhold certain damaging information from customers—problems rectified through suitability requirements and the establishment of fiduciary duties that place the interest of customers ahead of their own. A related concern pertains to protection of the claimholders or investors of the derivatives-using firm. Here, regulators are concerned that firms will not provide adequate levels of information regarding their derivatives activity, which causes investors to make less-than-informed investment decisions.

A second rationale frequently offered for government intervention is to protect the integrity of prices and to prevent manipulation. Some maintain that OTC derivatives markets are not sufficiently transparent and that derivatives (because of the ease of leverage) permit traders to unfairly distort or control values of both derivatives and the underlying assets. It is further argued that such price manipulation impairs the price discovery function of these markets, thus harming those individuals and businesses who rely on prices as basing points for other transactions and for planning business activity. This latter concern is predicated on the assumption of a readily available and informationally efficient derivatives price being a public good.

Regulators use two arguments to justify their interest in protecting the integrity of the financial system. First, government has a role in protecting the taxpayers' interest with regard to the deposit insurance fund. In the case of derivatives, this would arise if an inappropriate use of derivatives causes a federally insured institution to fail and expose taxpayers to covering the cost of an exhausted deposit insurance fund. Second, concerns have been expressed over "systemic" or spillover risk. It is argued that a default by a major player could cause a domino effect, affecting not only the well-being of immediate counterparties, but spreading and ultimately bringing down the entire financial system. The alleged market failure is that firms will expend only those resources sufficient to protect themselves individually from failing rather than the socially optimal amount to protect the system.

While these concerns may justify government intervention, regulators and legislators generally make little effort to verify their validity. Even less attention is paid to whether market forces are or can be an effective substitute for government intervention. In the following section, we discuss reasons why these concerns may not make a good case for regulatory action.

ARE CONCERNS ABOUT DERIVATIVES JUSTIFIED?

Customer Protection

There are two types of customers that policy makers and regulators want to protect. The traditional notion of a customer is the purchaser of a derivatives product or the counterparty of the derivatives dealer, typically, the corporate end-user. The second group that securities regulators protect are the claimholders or investors of the derivatives-using firm.

The appropriate levels of protection for customers of derivatives dealers, particularly end-users, received prominent attention following reports during 1993 and 1994 that several entities incurred significant losses attributable to derivatives. These losses provoked calls to establish and enhance suitability rules that govern derivatives transactions. Those calling for higher suitability standards disregarded some very important considerations, especially the market forces that mitigate the need for additional regulations.

Historically, transactions in the market for swaps and other OTC derivatives have been arm's-length or principal-to-principal transactions with neither party being viewed as having entered into an advisory capacity that would have established a fiduciary relationship.[3] Rather, terms of the transaction and other understandings between counterparties are typically delineated under a bilaterally negotiated master agreement.[4] As discussed in Overdahl and Schachter (1995), it is not practical for every contingency to be covered in the master agreement because of transactions costs including those associated with negotiating, monitoring, and enforcing the contract. It is efficient for the legal system to resolve many of the issues that fall into these so-called gaps. These authors also point out that both common law and statute allow arm's-length contracts to be voided under certain instances including willful deception, the failure to disclose material information, and the possession of information that would give one party an "unconscionable" bargaining advantage.[5] Thus, any proposed change to existing suitability requirements would alter currently understood practices and relationships between parties and would likely have significant economic consequences.

As Overdahl and Schachter discuss, the potential benefit from any change in existing requirements is reduced investment losses by uninformed investors. However, there are several potential costs of such a change. There is likely to be higher compliance and litigation expenses. As a result, dealers may decide to withhold valuable risk-shifting products from marginally sophisticated users. This in turn could lower liquidity in the market and raise bid-ask spreads as certain customers withdraw. In addition, dealers may feel compelled to share information with clients regarding proprietary pricing models.[6] If so, this could lower dealer returns on investment in such technology, thus reducing the incentive to develop better models.

It is important to recognize that these costs will be borne not only by the less sophisticated customer, but by all customers including those not requiring the same levels of protection. One should also consider whether market forces can alleviate the need for government intervention. As suggested, derivatives dealers face enormous entry costs in the form of technology, personnel, and capital, among others. As a consequence, derivatives dealers have strong incentives to protect their investment. Dealing with any counterparty in an inappropriate manner would risk future business opportunities and would also damage their reputation capital.[7]

There is little reason to believe that market participants cannot reach contractual solutions to customer protection problems. Following the losses by Gibson Greetings, the Commodity Futures Trading Commission (CFTC) brought an enforcement action against Bankers Trust alleging that they had an advisory relationship with Gibson. Dealers also responded by amending their master agreements with clients to include explicit language that the firms have not entered into an advisory capacity. On March 6, 1996, the International Swaps and Derivatives Association (ISDA) released wording that could be used in master agreements documenting each counterparties' understanding of the nature of their relationship. Included is language pertaining to (1) nonreliance (e.g., each party is acting for its own account, is making its own independent decision as to the merits of the transaction and is not relying on the other party for investment advice); (2) assessment and understanding (e.g., each party is capable of assessing the merits of and understanding the risks of the transaction); and (3) status of parties (the other party is not acting as a fiduciary for or an advisor to it in respect of the transaction). The language is both optional and negotiable.

With respect to the second group of customers—the firm's investors—it is frequently argued that inadequate accounting rules have resulted in an insufficient level of financial reporting of derivatives activities. In response, regulatory bodies in recent years have taken action to enhance derivatives disclosure. For example, beginning in 1986, the Financial Accounting Standards Board (FASB), an industry accounting rule-making body, initiated a review of the treatment of financial instruments and off-balance sheet financing in financial statements. FASB published a series of guidelines including Statement 105 issued in 1990 titled "Disclosure of Information About Financial Instruments with Off-Balance Sheet Risk and Financial Instruments with Concentrations of Credit Risk," Statement 107 issued in 1991 titled "Disclosures About Fair Value of Financial Instruments," and Statement 119 issued in 1994 titled "Disclosure about Derivative Financial Instruments and Fair Value of Financial Instruments." More recently, the Securities and Exchange Commission (SEC) has proposed amendments to Regulations S-X and S-K, and to various forms, in an attempt to clarify and substantially expand requirements concerning financial statement disclosures regarding derivatives.[8] Despite these initiatives, there are claims that these measures do not go far enough.

Policy makers' views toward derivatives disclosure often ignore many of the basic tenets of finance and the economics of disclosure. In order to attract and to keep shareholders and as their agent, corporate managers should promote the interest of shareholders and maximize shareholder value. Other investor groups such as creditors and bondholders have explicit contractual means for specifying the scope and extent of a firm's activities (e.g., loan agreements, master agreements, and indentures). To maximize share price, managers should provide disclosures to the market concerning its derivatives activities up to the point where the marginal cost of its provision equals the marginal benefit.

On the benefit side, greater disclosure can lead to a higher share price. As investors are generally risk averse, the market will discount uncertainty regarding a firm's activities and this will be reflected in a lower share price. Thus, firms have a positive incentive to disclose in order to maximize shareholder wealth. Indeed, over the past few years, as the value investors place on derivatives disclosure has increased, firms have responded voluntarily with greater and better disclosures regarding their derivatives activities. And as expected, to the extent that disclosure is valued by the market, firms can and will use it as a basis on which to compete for investor funds.

Regulators tend to gloss over the fact that there is a cost to derivatives disclosure. First, disclosure is costly to physically produce. Second, firms run the risk of disclosing proprietary information regarding their hedging activities that may be highly valued by competitors. A third related point is that mandated disclosure can create incentives for firms to alter their behavior in a nonwealth maximizing manner. For example, to protect against disclosure of the details of a hedge of a particular risk or exposure, a firm may initiate an additional derivatives position so that the combined reported disclosure disguises the intended hedge.[9] Thus, to maximize share value, firms must find the appropriate balance between these costs and the benefits of additional disclosure.

Evidence that firms view current and proposed derivatives rules as costly measures can be gleaned from the 1995 survey of nonfinancial U.S. corporations conducted by the Wharton School in conjunction with CIBC Wood Gundy. The survey reported that for respondent firms that did not use derivatives, 13% cited FASB Statement 119 disclosure as the reason. Also, for firms reporting using derivatives, 9% expressed a "high degree of concern" regarding disclosure requirements. Additional evidence of the cost of derivatives disclosure is the many negative comment letters filed in response to the proposed SEC regulations covering derivatives disclosure (see above).[10]

Price Integrity

Financial market regulators have traditionally tried to maintain market integrity, that is, to ensure that prices are "true prices" and are not manipulated or readily susceptible to manipulation. Some allege that these efforts should be extended to the market for OTC derivatives. Among the regulatory measures recommended are enhanced levels of market oversight, including specific requirements for record keeping, filing, and reporting.

It is argued that such reporting requirements are needed because of the levels of transparency in these markets. Transparency refers to the degree to which real-time trading information regarding prices, order flow, and quotations are publicly disseminated. It is argued that greater transparency in the market for OTC derivatives is necessary for several reasons. First, traders are attracted by liquid markets and transparency contributes to liquidity. This in turn attracts more traders and orderflow to the market, and leads to lower spreads and execution times. Also, a market's price discovery function is enhanced when markets are liquid and active. Thus, many people believe that transparency, because it contributes to liquidity and price discovery, is a public good that will be underproduced by the market without regulatory intervention.[11]

Second, it is argued that greater transparency reduces the potential for manipulation, because the ease of leverage coupled with low transparency may encourage traders to distort values of both the derivatives and the underlying assets. By increasing transparency, and hence visibility and liquidity, an instrument's susceptibility to manipulation is reduced. Third, greater transparency is said to promote intermarket arbitrage that helps to keep the prices of assets that are traded in different markets aligned. A fourth reason offered is that transparency increases customer protection as investors are able to better monitor trading and the quality of their trade executions.

Many of the concerns are the result of attempts to compare the economic purpose and regulatory regime for exchange-traded futures contracts with that for OTC derivatives contracts. However, such comparisons fail to distinguish important differences in market structure between OTC derivatives and a traditional price discovery market like futures.

Futures markets, in addition to their use for hedging, facilitate price discovery by providing a centralized, open, and competitive forum for the assimilation of important market information about an underlying commodity (or asset, currency, index, rate, etc.) held by market participants. No single trader possesses complete information related to the pricing of a particular commodity. However, as futures traders exploit their private information through their trades, the sum of information held by traders about a particular commodity is largely, if not entirely, revealed to the marketplace through the commodity price. This produces two benefits for society. First, it leads to more efficient resource allocation within the economy. Producing observable and readily disseminated prices allows individuals and firms to plan more effectively. Second, these prices provide valuable reference points on which many other transactions are based.

By contrast, OTC derivatives do not trade in a centralized, exchange environment as do futures. OTC derivatives transactions are privately negotiated, bilateral arrangements between institutional counterparties, the terms of which are largely customized. In fact, swaps and related instruments must *not* be standardized as to their "material economic terms" in order to be exempt from Commodity Exchange Act (CEA) requirements.[12] This phrase is intended to encompass terms that define the rights and obligations of the parties and would include variables such as notional amounts, amortization schedules, maturities, payment dates, and payment computation methodologies.

Further, those who would invoke the price discovery role as a justification for regulatory intervention should recognize the use of nonprice components appearing in many OTC derivatives arrangements. Evidence of customization is the number of nonprice components in OTC contracts, such as a variety of credit enhancement measures including collateral that are often employed. These measures are tailored to the perceived level of counterparty credit risk.

An additional requirement that swaps and related instruments must satisfy for CEA exemption is that "the creditworthiness of any party . . . be a material consideration in entering into or determining the terms of the swap agreement." This is in sharp contrast with futures market practices where the financial integrity of the exchange's clearinghouse is substituted for the individual creditworthiness of market participants or counterparties. Further, futures markets require all traders to post similar prescribed levels of performance bonds (margin) prior to trading.

We must also address the fundamental question as to what "price" is actually being discovered by an OTC derivatives transaction that would be useful in price-basing for other transactions. On occasion, we will see a structured note or perhaps a swap whose pricing terms incorporate reference to a quoted swap spread, a price-basing use. However, most swap transactions are themselves priced off other instruments, such as Treasury instruments and Eurodollar futures.

Those who argue that more regulations are necessary to enhance transparency and price discovery in OTC markets first must address these differences between the markets. They should also consider the alternative of establishing property rights for those who produce prices and quotes.

Some have argued that the OTC market has impaired the liquidity and price discovery of the established futures exchanges. Others have argued that the OTC market has enhanced futures exchange volume rather than reduced it as dealers have used futures markets to hedge residual risks in their books. Indeed, much of the growth in volume and open interest of the Chicago Mercantile Exchange's Eurodollar futures contract and the New York Mercantile Exchange's energy futures contracts has been attributed to the swaps market. Also, the OTC market can serve as a proving ground or incubator for many new products that may not succeed if traded first in an exchange environment. Innovation is enhanced when new products and trading structures are flexible enough to adapt to global challenges easily.

Recent concerns of futures exchanges regarding competition from the OTC market reflect the great regulatory burden that they face—regulations that have accumulated over the decades (including requirements that have been added in response to incidents) but which are rarely eliminated if they are unnecessary or obsolete. While some of the regulatory burden on futures exchanges is attributable to participation by the general public,[13] regulators and legislators can level the playing field by eliminating unnecessary and obsolete regulations rather than increasing the regulation of the OTC market.[14]

Finally, it is occasionally argued that greater regulatory attention is needed because derivatives trading exacerbates volatility in underlying markets. Voluminous research by academics and various government agency staffs indicates that derivatives have either no effect on underlying prices or actually tend to stabilize prices.

Financial Integrity

The third and perhaps most important role of financial regulators is to protect the integrity of the financial system. As mentioned, regulators wish to protect taxpayers from the cost of an exhausted deposit insurance fund due to derivatives losses. In addition, regulators wish to prevent "systemic" or spillover risk from a major default caused by the use of derivatives. Regulators are concerned that firms will not take adequate precautions or spend necessary resources to control risks and prevent default, thus creating externalities for taxpayers and those dependent on the viability of the financial system. The first issue to address is the reality of the risk. The second issue is the ability of market forces to address the risk.

First, we note that banks' use of derivatives is subject to extensive federal oversight with capital requirements and regulatory examinations. To justify further controls beyond existing measures, regulators must articulate why they believe derivatives add risks that are unique when compared to banks' other activities. For example, some refer to money center banks with derivatives exposures that sometimes exceed their capital. However, little mention is made of their loan exposures which are commonly several times greater than capital.[15] Further, these loan portfolios are typically less liquid and have lower credit quality and higher default rates than derivatives portfolios.

Second, some have asserted that nonbank derivatives dealers pose the same risk to the financial system as dealers which are banks and should be subjected to comparable capital adequacy standards and federal oversight. Comparisons with banks is puzzling since deposit insurance and taxpayer funds are not involved if a nonbank dealer fails. If the concern is rather to protect equity holders and creditors, this would represent an unprecedented intrusion into corporate affairs.

Third, despite the frequent invocation of systemic risk as a justification for regulatory initiatives, there is little analysis of the causes of or even descriptions of the underlying conditions for systemic risk.[16] Hentschel and Smith (1995) offer a reasoned analysis that suggests that systemic risk concerns attributable to derivatives have been overstated. They argue that a firm's probability of defaulting on a derivatives transaction such as a swap is much lower than for its debt. With debt, the firm has borrowed funds and must always make payments. The firm will default whenever it becomes insolvent. On the other hand, two conditions most hold for a firm to default on a swap. Not only must the solvency of the firm be sufficiently impaired so that the firm cannot make payment, but it must also be the paying party. The probability that both conditions will hold simultaneously is further reduced if the firm is using derivatives as a hedge since if it must make a payment, the market conditions are likely to put the firm in a good position to do so.

Hentschel and Smith further examine the likelihood that systemic problems would result from widespread, correlated default across dealers. In conducting the analysis, they assume that defaults on derivatives contracts are approximately independent across dealers and over time. Reasons given for this assumption include current risk management practices of dealers, the idiosyncratic nature of derivatives defaults, and other risk-reducing arrangements, such as the maintenance of balanced books and substantial capital reserves. They offer several estimates of the likelihood of multiple dealers defaulting simultaneously. For example, they show that if there are 50 dealers, the odds of five or more defaulting during the same year are one in 650 billion. Even if the assumption of independence is too strong, the probability of widespread default is much smaller than most discussions of systemic risk suggest.

With regard to claims that dealers are undercapitalized and take inadequate precautions against default, we first note the strong incentives for dealers to back their operations with high levels of capital. Counterparties generally seek dealers with high credit standings which implies more capital. In fact, the demand by many market participants for dealers with high credit ratings (notably, triple-A) prompted the formation of special financial intermediaries known as derivative products companies (DPCs), also referred to as special purpose derivative vehicles or triple-A subs.[17] These entities are typically subsidiaries set up by larger dealer firms to provide enhanced levels of credit protections for the products they offer. The first of the structured DPCs appeared in 1991 with Merrill Lynch Derivatives Products. Today, there are approximately 12 such entities with others under consideration. An increasing volume of trade is reported to be conducted by these highly capitalized subsidiaries.

A large portion of the end-user and counterparty market is comprised of firms having investment grade ratings. In 1994, the GAO reported that 94% of dealers' derivatives contracts were with investment grade counterparties. The GAO also found that 97.5% of 200 firms with more than $1 billion in swaps outstanding had investment grade ratings. These ratings are prepared by major independent rating agencies that have access to substantial nonpublic firm specific information.

Another important market innovation is the development of counterparty ratings by the major rating agencies. For example, in 1994 Standard & Poor's began assigning counterparty ratings to approximately 400 financial institutions. These and corporate credit ratings (for nonfinancial institutions) are somewhat distinct from traditional debt ratings because they address a firm's overall creditworthiness, not just its willingness to repay debt. The ratings are useful for entities wishing to sign contracts with counterparties who may not have a senior debt rating or who are a subsidiary of a rated company. Similarly, Moody's Investors Service also assigns counterparty ratings that indicate the ability of a company to meet its obligations stemming from OTC derivatives contracts.

Another example highlighting the ability of the market to develop contractual solutions to mitigate risk, notably credit and legal risk, is the evolution of standardized master agreements. Before standardized master agreements were developed, participants often used their own forms. A lack of uniformity in definitions and terminology made negotiations difficult and time consuming. This often resulted in significant delays in completing the documentation for transactions that had already taken place which increased legal and credit risk.

Efforts to develop master agreements for derivatives transactions have been led largely by the industry organization ISDA.[18] Currently, several standardized master agreements are available which differ mainly in the underlying product of the transaction. For example, there are master agreements for foreign currency, energy derivatives, and single and multicurrency swaps. There are also efforts to develop multiproduct masters. The current most widely used master is the ISDA Multicurrency-Cross Border agreement.

In addition to lowering the cost of transactions, the increased use of standardized master agreements has increased market transparency, facilitated assignability, and increased liquidity. For dealer banks, it has facilitated netting and contributed to a more efficient use of capital and credit lines.

Many provisions of the ISDA master agreement are aimed specifically at mitigating credit and legal risk. Broadly speaking, the agreements address these risks by allowing for up-front risk assessment. For example, counterparties may assess the riskiness of the other prior to the initiation of a transaction by requiring both representations and documents concerning credit risk as well as representations concerning enforceability. Also, the agreements may facilitate "ongoing" risk assessment following the initiation of the transaction by requiring, for example, the periodic provision of documents, the maintenance of covenants, and the use of collateral and mark-to-market margining. These provisions help alleviate potential information asymmetries between counterparties and facilitate monitoring.

In addition, the ISDA master agreement contains "ex-post" risk control mechanisms such as provisions for early termination to limit exposure caused by the occurrence or discovery of specific events. Early termination protects parties from the risk of significant credit and legal developments arising from factors that may or may not be within the control or the fault of the counterparty (event risk protection) or that may result from ex-post opportunism by counterparties (moral hazard). In addition, it may serve as an additional mechanism to help address problems with information asymmetries and to deter parties from making false or misleading representations.[19] The industry has also led efforts to have these agreements legally recognized in a large number of jurisdictions.

Many other market initiatives have evolved to prevent default. Dealer risk management practices generally conform to the Group of Thirty (1993) recommendations as well as guidances established by bank regulators. Firms regularly employ independent credit risk-management groups that analyze counterparty creditworthiness, set limits on exposures, and monitor compliance with these limits. Also, dealers increasingly use sophisticated models for assessing credit and market risks, mark-to-market the value of their positions at least daily, use credit enhancement mechanisms such as collateral arrangements, and mark-to-market margining, compute estimates of potential risk exposures such as daily earnings at risk (DEaR) and value at risk (VaR), and conduct stress testing of their portfolios under various market scenarios.

Acceptance of VaR, defined as the estimated maximum expected loss in market value over a specified time period with a specified probability, is becoming increasingly widespread.[20] VaR has the added benefit that it can be easily understood even by those members of management who are not derivatives experts as it pulls together into a single number sources of risk from different activities under normal market risk conditions. When coupled with stress testing and other risk measurement techniques to overcome its limitations (e.g., normality assumptions and convexity risk), VaR is a powerful tool for quantifying risk.

To further simplify firms' use of VaR, in 1994, J.P. Morgan began making their vast daily estimates of the volatility and correlations of key interest rates, exchange rates, and equity indices, that was part of its RiskMetrics risk measurement system, freely available.[21] This development spawned other industry initiatives to improve risk management practices. For example, many of the industry's systems suppliers quickly developed supporting software packages to use with the RiskMetrics data. Also, as one would expect in a competitive market environment, new systems are emerging that claim to offer broader coverage of markets and more accurate volatility and correlation estimates and with more frequent updating.[22]

Another rapidly emerging industry initiative to control credit risk is credit derivatives. Credit derivatives offer risk managers new opportunities to isolate, trade, diversify, and otherwise reduce the credit risk of their portfolios. Currently, credit derivatives can be found in a variety of forms, including credit swaps, options on credit spreads, and credit-linked structured notes.[23]

Finally, another type of industry response to market problems that we have not explored is self-regulation. One recent example would be the formation in 1994 of the "Derivatives Policy Group" (DPG). The DPG, a group of six dealer firms, was organized to address regulators' concerns regarding the derivatives activities of unregulated affiliates of SEC-registered broker-dealers and CFTC-registered futures commission merchants. In March 1995, the DPG released their report "Framework for Voluntary Oversight" that set forth standards and practices to be undertaken in four major areas: management controls, regulatory reporting, evaluation of risk in relation to capital, and counterparty relationships.

A second self-regulatory initiative was an August 1995 agreement released by the Federal Reserve Bank of New York in conjunction with various industry trade associations titled "Principles and Practices for Wholesale Financial Market Transactions." This agreement contained a "voluntary" code of conduct that provided guidance to market participants regarding expectations that counterparties should have of each other. In addition, the agreement also intended to set "best practice" standards for derivatives dealers and end-users.

These initiatives should also be considered seriously by regulators. We question, however, the extent to which such measures are indeed "voluntary," but rather are the response to pressure applied by regulators. If the latter, these initiatives may serve as *de facto* rule-making without giving others the opportunity to comment on the proposals. In addition, the standards may not have been subjected to the basic framework we have set forth and could provide a means for anti-competitive behavior.

CONCLUSION

Officials responsible for the oversight of the market for OTC derivatives should address fundamental questions before proposing any new regulation or law, especially in such a rapidly changing market and where international competition is strong. An important question is what is the market failure or contractual impediment that prevents affected parties from resolving the problem on their own. We have noted many of the industry's own initiatives to develop market-based solutions including providing for customer and investor protection, maintaining market integrity and protecting the integrity of the financial system. It is not too surprising that an industry where product innovation has been a hallmark has the ability to develop a host of market mechanisms to solve contractual problems. Whether these are sufficient is subject to debate, but they should at least be acknowledged by policy makers in future discussions over the appropriate regulation of derivatives markets.

REFERENCES

Das, Satyajit (1994), *Swap & Derivative Financing*, Probus, Chicago.

Derivatives: Practices and Principles, The Group of Thirty (Washington, DC: July 1993).

Eisenberg, Laurence (1995), "Connectivity and Financial Network Shutdown," Santa Fe Institute Working Paper No. 95-04-041.

Epstein, Richard (1975), "Unconscionability: A Critical Reappraisal," *Journal of Law and Economics, 18*, p. 293.

Figlewski, Stephen (1994), "The Birth of the AAA Derivatives Subsidiary," *Journal of Derivatives, 1*, pp. 80-84.

Financial Derivatives: Actions Needed to Protect the Financial System, U.S. General Accounting Office (Washington, DC: May 1994).

Gay, Gerald and Joanne Medero (1996), "The Economics of Derivatives Documentation: Private Contracting as a Substitute for Government Regulation," *Journal of Derivatives, 3*, pp. 78-89.

Gramm, Wendy and Gerald Gay (1994), "Scams, Scoundrels, and Scapegoats: A Taxonomy of CEA Regulation over Derivative Instruments," *Journal of Derivatives, 1*, pp. 6-24.

Hentschel, Ludger and Clifford W. Smith, Jr. (1995), "Controlling Risks in Derivatives Markets," *Journal of Financial Engineering, 4*, pp. 101-125.

Howard, Kerrin (1995), "An Introduction to Credit Derivatives," *Derivatives Quarterly, 2*, pp. 28-37.

Longstaff, Francis and Eduardo Schwartz (1995), "Valuing Credit Derivatives," *Journal of Fixed Income, 5*, pp. 6-12.

Marshall, John and Kenneth Kapner (1993), *The Swaps Market*, 2nd ed. Kolb, Miami.

Miller, Merton and Christopher Culp (1996), "The SEC's Costly Disclosure Rules," *Wall Street Journal*, June 25, A14.

O'Hara, Maureen (1993), "Real Bills Revisited: Market Value Accounting and Loan Maturity," *Journal of Financial Intermediation, 3*, pp. 51-76.

Overdahl, James and Barry Schachter (1995), "Derivatives Regulation and Financial Management: Lessons from Gibson Greetings," *Financial Management, 24*, pp. 68-78.

Remolona, E., W. Basset and I. S. Geoum (1996), "Risk Management by Structured Derivative Product Companies," *FRBNY Economic Policy Review, 2,* pp. 17–37.

Schachter, Barry (1995), "Suitability, Legal Risk, and Derivatives Regulation," *Journal of Financial Engineering, 4,* pp. 147–156.

Schneck, Leonard (1995), "Systemic Risk in Off-Exchange Derivatives Markets," working paper, University of Kentucky.

Smithson, Charles (1995), *Managing Financial Risk: 1995 Yearbook,* CIBC Wood Gundy.

Smithson, Charles (1996), *Managing Financial Risk: 1996 Yearbook,* CIBC Wood Gundy.

ENDNOTES

1. Smithson (1995, 1996) discusses several incidents involving derivatives losses by corporations and investment groups during this period.

2. *See,* for example, Gramm and Gay (1994) for a discussion of these developments.

3. Schachter (1995) reviews existing suitability rules and standards of various market regulators and provides a discussion of the economics of suitability requirements.

4. Later, we explore in greater detail the use of master agreements as a contractual tool for controlling especially credit and legal risks.

5. *See* Epstein (1975) for a discussion of unconscionability in contract law.

6. Indeed, as part of the "Written Agreement" entered by Bankers Trust New York Corporation and its subsidiaries with the Federal Reserve Bank of New York on December 4, 1994, Bankers Trust was requested to develop and submit written policies and procedures that would, among other things, "ensure reasonable transparency of LDT (leveraged derivative transaction) pricing and valuation to its customers."

7. We note, for example, the market reaction to BT Securities Corporation following the reported incidents with Gibson Greetings and Procter & Gamble.

8. *See* "Proposed Amendments to Require Disclosure of Accounting Policies for Derivative Financial Instruments and Derivative Commodity Instruments and Disclosure of Qualitative and Quantitative Information About Market Risk Inherent in Derivative Financial Instruments, Other Financial Instruments, and Derivative Commodity Instruments," Release Nos. 33-7250, 34-36643, IC-21625, File No. S7-35-95.

9. For a discussion of this point, *see* Miller and Culp (1996). Also, *see* O'Hara (1993) for a related discussion on perverse incentives created by accounting regulations.

10. For a discussion of the many comment letters received, *see* Miller and Culp (1996).

11. A strong case could be made that if it was indeed true that dealers produced a level of price transparency lower than demanded by the market, it could be attributable to an inadequate assignment of property rights to producers of prices.

12. A fuller discussion of the swap exemption can be found in the CFTC's "Exemption for Certain Swap Agreements" 58 FR 5587 (January 22, 1993).

13. An additional requirement for swaps to be exempt from CEA regulation is that they be entered into solely between "eligible swap participants" which in essence precludes participation by the general public.

14. Indeed, exemptions from some provisions of the Commodity Exchange Act used by the OTC market are also available to futures exchanges under certain circumstances.

15. In their 1994 report to Congress, the General Accounting Office (GAO) did report that the derivatives-related credit exposure for the seven U.S. bank dealers included in its survey were, with one exception, much lower than those from their "traditional" loan portfolios.

16. Theoretical attempts to model systemic risk in terms of correlated bankruptcies of derivatives dealers can be found in Eisenberg (1995) and Schneck (1995).

17. For a discussion of these entities and their different forms of structure *see,* for example, Figlewski (1994) and Remolona, Bassett, and Geoum (1996).

18. *See* Das (1994) and Marshall and Kapner (1993) for a chronology of the development of "standardized" master agreements.

19. For further discussion of the economics of master agreements, *see* Gay and Medero (1996).

20. Calculation of VaR was one of the Group of Thirty's "best practice" recommendations in their 1993 report.

21. Published estimates can be found, for example, on the Internet, CompuServe, and Telerate.

22. This would include, for example, CS First Boston's PrimeClear.

23. For a more detailed discussion of credit derivatives *see,* for example, Howard (1995), Longstaff and Schwartz (1995) and Smithson (1996).

14

Functional Regulation

I have the luxury of being an *academic* specialist on financial regulation. Physicians often say that the best medical specialty is dermatology, skin diseases. Your patients never die; they never get well; and they never call you in the middle of the night. My specialty, financial regulation, is equally blessed. Complaints about financial regulation are chronic everywhere. The pains are often intense (and sometimes embarrassing), but never fatal. And the experts on regulatory reform can usually delay their house-calls until after the academic year is over.

That our regulatory patients seem neither to die nor get well is not surprising. The modern theory of regulation, properly understood, predicts exactly that. To explain why, I propose first to review the theory, illustrating it with examples drawn from current regulation of financial markets in Japan; and from that vantagepoint, to move on to appraise one new approach to financial regulatory structure in the United States, the "functional regulation" noted in my title, advanced recently by a major player in the financial services industry.

GEORGE STIGLER AND THE POSITIVE THEORY OF REGULATION

The birth of the modern theory of regulation can be dated precisely to the year 1971 when my late colleague George Stigler published his pathbreaking paper entitled "The Theory of Economic Regulation." That paper moved the theory of regulation from its traditional home in normative economics (concerned exclusively with what regulation ought to be) to a new and very exciting home in positive or descriptive economics (concerned with what regulation actually is). Specifically, Stigler assigned his new theory of regulation the task of explaining "who will receive the benefits or burdens of regulation, what form the regulations will take, and the effects of regulation on the allocation of resources" (p. 5). And he takes as the central insight of his positive theory of regulation "that as a rule, regulation is acquired by the industry regulated" and—and this is the key—"is designed and operated primarily for its benefit" even though the regulation might initially have been thrust on the industry against its opposition (p. 5).

Reprinted from *Pacific Basin Finance Journal: Vol. 2* (1994), pp. 91–106, with kind permission from Elsevier Science—NL, Sara Burgerhartstraat 25, 1055 KV Amsterdam, the Netherlands. My thanks to Christopher Culp for helpful comments on an earlier draft. Copyright © 1994 Elsevier Science B.V. All rights reserved.

That may seem a very cynical way perhaps of looking at regulation and is certainly not how the regulators see themselves or how the general public sees them. The commonly held "alternative view of regulation" as Stigler dubs it is that "Regulation is instituted primarily for the protection and benefit of the public at large or some large subclass of the public" (p. 3). And surely some of it *does* protect and benefit the public. But if so, Stigler suggests you treat that as a bonus. Sometimes, the producer interests that dominate the regulatory process really can do well by doing good.

Stigler's oft-dubbed "capture theory of regulation," though departing from the high-minded tone in which so much discussion of regulation is normally carried out, has proved enormously fruitful as a research agenda. The original 1971 paper, emphasizing mainly the demand for regulation, has been much enriched and extended since 1971, notably by James Buchanan and other public-choice theorists who brought a supply side into the model. I will get to that side in due course. But Stigler's simple demand model still remains the best way to begin—and I emphasize to begin—any discussion of regulation in practice.

How Regulators Benefit Their Industry

Stigler identifies four main channels by which the regulatory authorities exert the power of the state to benefit the industries they regulate: subsidies, price fixing, entry controls, and restriction of substitute products. The Ministry of Finance in Japan—which I will call hereafter by its familiar nickname MOF—provides in its regulation of the Japanese stock brokerage industry an almost perfect illustration of Stigler's model—an uncanny case of out-of-sample predictive power, since, to my knowledge Stigler never actually visited Japan and certainly could not have had MOF in mind when he was writing his 1971 paper.

Subsidies and Price Supports

Governments have long subsidized agricultural producers and processors by purchasing their output to support farm prices and incomes. MOF in Japan has adapted this ancient form of subsidy to the stock market, hoping to make stocks more attractive to the customers of the brokerage industry. MOF does not actually warehouse the shares directly like the Ministry of Agriculture warehouses rice. MOF's price support operations—known derisively in Japan as PKOs, or Price Keeping Operations in a word play on the U.N.'s Peace Keeping Operations—are usually done indirectly by exercising MOF's *de jure* control over the portfolio decisions of the huge Japanese postal savings system and its considerable *de facto* control over the portfolios of Japanese insurance companies that also fall under its regulatory jurisdiction.

Supporting stock prices differ in at least one critical way, however, from supporting agricultural prices, as MOF has lately been learning to its sorrow. Support of stock prices gets built into the public's expectations. The conspicuous success, in fact, of MOF's price-support policies in cushioning the impact in Japan of the worldwide October 1987 crash led many to believe that MOF could and would intervene again whenever the market weakened. That perception, by seeming to eliminate major downside risk in owning Japanese shares, effectively transformed the Japanese stock market to a call option market, or better, to a market where everyone had (or thought they had) a free put to MOF. Talk about portfolio insurance!

Not surprisingly, the months after the crash saw Japanese share prices surging, propelled further in 1988 and 1989 by the easy credit policies the Bank of Japan instituted after the Louvre accords. During those golden days of ever-rising stock prices, MOF was hailed for its genius. *Everyone* praised MOF's benevolent and intelligent management, not just MOF's primary constituents in the brokerage cartel and their customers. Japanese firms got cheap equity capital; Japanese banks, as big holders of that equity, got huge cushions of regulatory capital to support their commercial loan activities at home and around the world; and Japanese politicians got payoffs from sweetheart deals on new issues.

By the end of 1989, however, prices on the Tokyo Stock Exchange, with no downside risk to worry about, had spiraled upward until they lost all contact with the underlying economic reality of sustainable earnings growth. At that point, the newly appointed head of the Bank of Japan intervened to halt what he saw as an out-of-control speculative frenzy. (The BOJ is technically under MOF, but occasionally, and usually to MOF's chagrin, acts independently.) By slamming on the monetary brakes in early 1990 he soon ended the market's euphoria. Over the next two years, MOF could do little more than slow the massive price deflation that followed—a deflation that did not end until more than 50 percent of the market's capitalization had been blown away.

The huge losses suffered by investors who felt betrayed by MOF, and rightly so, has had obvious adverse consequences for the regulators and their political sponsors, on which subject more below. The collapse on the way down also undermined everything for which MOF had been so praised in the good old days. No new equity issues now for Japanese firms. They were forbidden by MOF for fear of further depressing stock prices. And the banks, so heavily into equities, saw their reserves of regulatory capital evaporate and at a time, moreover, when they were facing big loan losses. You would have thought that by then even MOF would have seen the folly of attempting to support share prices. But because of the banks, it cannot stop. Were Japanese stock prices to fall much below current levels, the Japanese banking industry, for which MOF is responsible, would no longer meet international capital requirements. MOF, in sum, has a tiger by the tail.

Control over Entry, Price-Cutting, and Substitute Products

For its mastery of the second of Stigler's channels of regulatory influence, entry restriction, MOF, of course, has long been famous. To enter the brokerage industry in Japan you must get a license from MOF and, needless to say, those licenses are not easy to come by. Until the recent limited deregulation of banking, which permits a few banks to sell a few kinds of debt securities to the public, there hasn't been a new Japanese entrant to the brokerage industry since the 1960s. U.S. brokerage firms and investment banks were finally allowed to join the Tokyo Stock Exchange in 1988 but only after years of unrelenting pressure from U.S. trade negotiators. Control over entry is especially critical, as Stigler notes, whenever the industry and its regulators seek to maintain prices, in this case minimum brokerage commissions, at far above competitive levels. That MOF has, in fact, set commission rates well above competitive levels, at least for institutional customers, is indicated, among other things, by the frequency of kick-backs and other under-the-table payments to favored customers, including, of course, the notorious compensation for losses on their trading accounts managed by the brokerage firms.

Which brings me to the last of Stigler's four regulatory mechanisms, the control over competing products. The specific example Stigler used to illustrate this mechanism in his 1971 paper was the effort by the U.S. dairy industry and its regulators in the 1930s to suppress the production of margarine, then, as now, the leading substitute for butter. Compelling as that challenge was to the butter regulators, it pales in comparison to the competition from substitute products faced by the retail stock brokerage industry and its regulatory protectors. To produce margarine, after all, you need oil, labor, and factories. But, thanks to the derivatives revolution, you can produce unlimited quantities of synthetic stocks and bonds almost out of thin air, as it were, by nothing more than a stroke of the pen once the necessary underlying legal structure has been put in place.

MOF's War against Index Futures

The difficulties financial regulators face in keeping newly created substitutes from undermining the cozy cartel arrangements of their clients are nowhere better illustrated than by MOF's long struggle against stock index futures. By fixing commissions on stocks substantially higher than those on index futures, MOF had unwittingly created an intermarket arbitrage opportunity that the foreign brokerage firms and investment banks, so recently and so reluctantly allowed to join the Tokyo Stock Exchange were uniquely positioned to exploit. And exploit it they did, by buying stock as Tokyo Exchange members and selling futures at retail commissions to the tune of several hundreds of millions of dollars annually—money, of course, MOF saw as coming out of the pockets of its domestic cartel constituents.

MOF had still another reason for hostility to index futures: They weakened, or at least MOF thought they weakened, MOF's efforts to keep stock prices up. Before index futures, insurance companies or large corporate holders, anxious to reduce their equity exposure, could only sell their shares. MOF would hear about that, of course, and so would the companies whose shares had been dumped. Keep in mind that the quaint Japanese custom of universal cross-holding of corporate shares, intended in part to discourage raiders, also amounts to a mutual exchange of hostages. With an impersonal futures market available, however, equities could be effectively converted to cash merely by taking a short position in futures. The share themselves never left the vault. To maintain intermarket equilibrium, *someone* had to go long the futures and short the shares. And who else but those foreign arbitragers, already deep on MOF's hit list?

The story of MOF's futile attempts to shore up its regulatory structure against the onslaught of the U.S. arbitragers was recounted in my paper, "The Economics and Politics of Index Arbitrage in the U.S. and Japan," and I won't repeat it again here. Let me just bring you up to date on some of the latest new moves instituted or threatened by MOF to end the competition from index futures once and for all.

When the story left off, you may recall, MOF's efforts to raise the cost of trading futures in Osaka had simply served to move a big chunk of the futures volume offshore to Simex in Singapore, in much the same way MOF had earlier driven the Japanese corporate bond markets and especially the convertible bond market to Europe. MOF's efforts to browbeat the Simex people into accepting MOF's guidelines were an embarrassing failure as were MOF's subsequent efforts to enlist IOSCO—the International Organization of Securities Commissions, or the regulators cartel as I sometimes teasingly like to call it. How then to get Simex to stop trading the Nikkei 225 index futures? Answer: eliminate the Nikkei 225 index! MOF (via its surrogate the Tokyo Stock Exchange) threatened to replace the Nikkei 225 with a totally new index. The proposed new index is to be a value-weighted index, like the S&P 500 in the U.S. rather than a price-weighted index like the Dow Jones Index or the Nikkei 225. Value-weighting, or better yet, value-weighting adjusted for cross-holdings would surely give a more accurate reading on real equity values in Japan. But all technical talk of index construction by MOF and the TSE is just window dressing. The real point was that the old index would die and any new index would be copyrighted by Nikkei. MOF could thus arm-twist Nikkei into refusing to enter into a licensing agreement with Simex for the new index unless Simex agrees to play by MOF's rules.

But even a new index could still be traded in Japan and hence would divert profits from MOF's clients to the foreign arbitrage firms. So MOF now proposes to make life even harder for the foreign arbitrage firms. MOF had long used its rules for daily disclosure of arbitrage positions to tip off its Japanese constituents to the strategic moves of the foreign arbitragers. But currently, according to recent complaints by U.S. firms, MOF is leaking proprietary information to their Japanese competitors on virtually a real-time basis. Surely, however, the prize for ingenuity must go to MOF's proposed (threatened?) new rules forbidding all proprietary arbitrage activities whenever the market is "overheated." When is a market overheated? Answer: whenever MOF says it is!

I can't resist adding one final note of irony to these latest attempts by MOF to drive a stake through the heart of index arbitrage. Arbitrage, and derivative trading generally was originally almost exclusively the province of the foreign firms. After all, they had no comparative advantage in the retail Japanese market; and the resident Japanese firms initially had little expertise in derivatives. But they learned. Nomura, in fact, has become the largest index arbitrager on the New York Stock Exchange. Many other Japanese brokerage firms are now active in derivatives both abroad and at home. MOF, in others words, lagging behind events as usual, is killing a formerly competitive business just as its traditional constituents are getting ready to enjoy that business in a big way. And, of course, since Nomura and others are arbitraging profitably in the United States, MOF's policies expose them to retaliation from the U.S. trade negotiators.

THE OBSTACLES TO REGULATORY REFORM

That MOF has been slower than its constituents to adjust to the new market realities of derivatives is by no means unusual in regulation. Regulatory structures often linger on, doing business in the same old way, long after the disappearance of the landscape that gave rise to them initially. A classic example, of course, is the U.S. Rural Electrification Administration created in the 1930s when less than 10 percent of U.S. farms had electrical service, but still running strong in the 1990s when less than 10 percent of U.S. farms didn't have electricity.

Financial Crises and Regulatory Reform

As a practical matter, a major crisis or scandal of some kind must occur—the analog of a bankruptcy filing by a private firm—before obsolete, and even counterproductive, regulatory arrangements can actually be restructured. A conspicuous crisis may be necessary for major regulatory changes, but is surely not sufficient, as the case of MOF makes plain. The scandals and failures occurring almost daily in MOF-regulated markets would long since have discredited the regulatory regime in any country but Japan.

Some may think I'm being unduly harsh on MOF. After all, MOF has maintained a tight rein on government spending (except perhaps for the huge construction contracts directed to its political patrons). And, just look at the tremendous success of the Japanese economy under MOF's stewardship. But to credit MOF with that success is to confuse association with causality—a fallacy so ancient it even has a Latin name, *post hoc, ergo propter hoc.* A compelling case can be made, in fact, for the counter-proposition that the Japanese economy has succeeded *despite* policies of MOF that have spread waste, corruption and inefficiencies throughout Japan's capital markets (and driven much capital market activity abroad). The real credit for Japan's economic success belongs not to its bureaucrats but to its people—to their talent, their energy, their work-ethic and not least their willingness to save. An admirer, like me, can only hope that someday the Japanese people will have a government worthy of their best achievements in art and technology.[1]

That political change usually precedes major regulatory change is well illustrated by the U.S. experience. Much of the current regulatory structure of the U.S. traces to the early and middle 1930s when a crusading Roosevelt Administration under the slogan of a New Deal for America, overhauled and greatly expanded government regulation in virtually every area of economic life, not least in financial markets and banking. The stock market collapse of 1929 and the banking collapse of 1930–32 had completely discredited the existing vested interests in those industries and left them politically powerless.

The Roosevelt Reforms and the Stigler Model

The New Deal regulatory "reforms," however, restrictive as they may appear to be should not be taken as evidence against George Stigler's view that regulation serves primarily to benefit the industry regulated. Some of the new securities regulations, especially in matters of corporate disclosure and of prospectuses for securities offerings were basically codifications into Federal law of existing rules and practices of the major exchanges and investment banking firms, benefiting them at the expense of their smaller competitors. Other regulations, especially, the strong new penalties and enforcement activities against fraud and market manipulation were also welcomed by the brokerage industry establishment. When the U.S. Securities and Exchange Commission was created in the early 1930s, the volume of business of the brokerage industry was near total collapse. The public was widely believed to be shunning the stock market because confidence was lacking in the honesty and integrity of a market dominated by Wall Street professionals—professionals whose unfair and manipulative tactics were widely, if erroneously, believed to have brought on the great stock market crash of 1929. The industry hoped that a tough-cop, nononsense regulator like the SEC would restore its tarnished image and entice investors back, even if a few victims, like the Chairman of the New York Stock Exchange had to be ritually slaughtered in the process.

That the SEC in the United States, unlike MOF in Japan, has chosen the tough-cop image for itself is clear enough—perhaps even too clear. Though enforcement is only a small part of the total SEC activity, a recent opinion poll found that most think of the SEC not as an independent economic regulatory agency (dealing as it does with such unglamorous matters as accounting conventions, proxy rules, or capital requirements, to name just a few), but as part of the criminal justice system—a unit of our Justice Department, much like our fabled Federal Bureau of Investigation. In fact, the main contribution of the SEC was seen to be prosecuting insider trading—

which is particularly ironic because insider trading issues played virtually no role in the original establishment of the SEC. Insider trading achieved its current prominence only in the 1960s, when improvements in computer technology made it possible routinely to detect "unusual" patterns of trading activity. In regulation as elsewhere in life, what can be done inevitably will be done. And the SEC was quick to see the value to its reputation capital in Congress and among the voting public from its high-profile prosecutions of insider trading.

The U.S. experience in the 1930s suggests that those seeking new regulatory accommodations should try to do so in the early days of an administration when problems (and there will always be problems) can still plausibly be blamed on the previous administration. Hence many have been anticipating proposals from the Clinton Administration—always harping on the evils of 12 years of supposed financial excesses under Reagan and Bush—for major regulatory change in the financial area somewhat in the spirit of its calls for reform of medical care in the United States. And, in fact, though it has received relatively little publicity until recently, the Administration *has* set up a task force, chaired by Vice President Gore, to review the entire regulatory structure of the United States and to bring in, by early September 1993, a blueprint for "streamlining it"—what else?

Of the grand reform schemes submitted to the Gore Commission, one of the most interesting is the Model for Financial Regulation along functional rather than departmental lines proposed by John F. Sandner, Chairman of the Chicago Mercantile Exchange on whose board I currently serve as an outside governor.

FUNCTIONAL REGULATION

To see what Sandner's proposal hopes to accomplish, turn first to a schematic map of the current Federal financial regulatory system (Figure 14.1). The contrast with the centralized MOF system in Japan could hardly be more striking. Not only are three separate cabinet departments (Treasury, Commerce, and Labor) directly involved in financial regulation, but so are three entirely independent agencies (the Federal Reserve System, the SEC, and the Commodity Futures Trading Commission)—independent of the Executive branch, that is, but not from Congressional oversight. Note also that banks, always a key part of any financial system, are regulated by no less than four separate agencies (the Office of Thrift Supervision, the Comptroller of the Currency, the Fed, and the Federal Deposit Insurance Corporation), not always consistently; and that a fifth agency, the SEC is struggling to gain control over bank accounting statements.

Remember also that the Figure shows only the tip of the iceberg. Not pictured are the so-called Self-Regulatory Organizations (the SROs), that is, the exchanges and trade associations like the National Futures Association which levy user fees and which promulgate rules and regulations subject to the approval and oversight of the various governmental agencies. Most of the 50 states have financial regulatory functions especially in the area of insurance, and still, though to a declining extent, in banking. Corporate law is also a preserve of the states, though so many corporations are registered in Delaware as to make it the *de facto* national jurisdiction. And, finally, there are the additional checks on the rulings of the regulators and the SROs by the courts. All in all, an enormous bureaucratic regulatory apparatus, and this, mind you, even after the 12 years of supposed deregulation under the Reagan and Bush Administrations!

FIGURE 14.1 Current Federal Financial Regulatory System

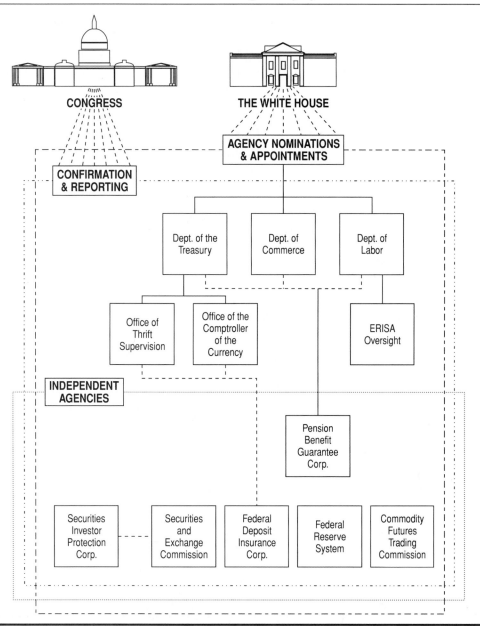

Source: Chicago Mercantile Exchange, *Model for Financial Regulation.*

The Sandner Proposal for Functional Regulation

The contrasting proposal for functional regulation is shown in Figure 14.2. The essence is to be a newly created, single, cabinet-level Department of Financial Regulatory Service with 8 separate commissioners, each to be appointed by the President and confirmed by Congress to maintain political accountability. Each commission covers one clearly-specified functional area; and the eight commissioners serve as a

FIGURE 14.2   Proposed Federal Financial Regulatory Service

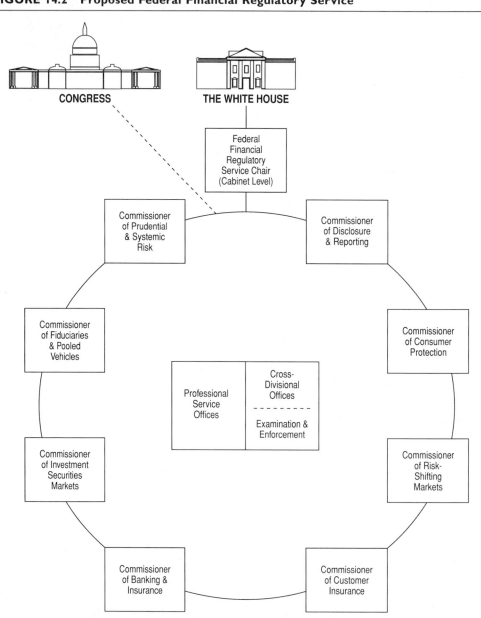

Source: Chicago Mercantile Exchange, *Model for Financial Regulation.*

governing and coordinating board for the agency along with a separate 9th appointee to serve as chairman and tie-breaker.

I won't go over the functional breakdown in detail beyond noting its similarity to some academic work on the subject, notably a recent and characteristically thoughtful paper by Robert C. Merton, though there are also some important differences. The Sandner plan, for example, has a single commissioner of banking and insurance, while Merton would even distinguish between the function of loan activities by banks and their deposit function as part of the payment system. But rather than speculate about functional breakdowns, let me focus instead on why the prospects for this or any other sweeping reorganization of the current U.S. regulatory landscape are so remote.

Extensions of the Stigler Model: The Regulators' Stake in Regulation

For appraising the prospects of plans like Sandner's Model of Financial Regulation, Stigler's theory of regulation can take us only part way. Stigler's basic capture-model treats the regulated industry as if it were the sole stockholder in a firm supplying regulatory services for its benefit. In Japan, as has been seen, that is, indeed, a good approximation. But not so in the United States where at least two other major stakeholders in the regulatory enterprise must be reckoned with.

One group, of course, are the regulators themselves. True, their interests are normally aligned with those of the industry by a process of executive recruitment similar in all essential respects, though less blatant, than in Japan where the arrival of a retired senior MOF bureaucrat to a sinecure in top management ranks has come to be known, derisively, as "the descent from heaven." The current chairman of the SEC is a former chairman of the American Stock Exchange; and the former head of the SEC's key Market Regulation Division is now chief executive officer of the National Association of Securities Dealers. That sort of back-and-forth flow of personnel between the regulators and the industry exists everywhere. Regulators in the United States are unusual only in the substantial salaries and perks they can earn while still in office.

Not bribes particularly. That happens, of course, but much more so in third-world countries where bureaucrats are often poorly paid (or not paid at all). U.S. government salaries, by contrast, are comparable to those for equivalent skills in the private sector. Comparable *on average,* that is. The top-echelon jobs are underpaid relative to the private sector; hence their high rate of turnover. The lower echelons are overpaid relative to private industry; hence the high frequency of recent university graduates among lawyers, economists, accountants and others in the professional grades. The good ones eventually move on to higher-paying careers outside government; the others stay behind and collect economic rent.

This stake in the regulatory enterprise held by the regulators themselves explains why industry sources, in seeming contradiction to Stigler's capture model, seem to be complaining so often these days about the harshness or over-obtrusiveness of government regulation. To preserve their agency budgets, and hence their career rents, the regulators must continually find new "problems" in the industry—problems which the agency can claim unique qualifications to solve. Just such an explosion of regulatory, micromanaging zeal by the CFTC, hoping to restore its tarnished reputation after the FBI sting of the trading floors, may well have triggered Sandner's call for a radically new approach to regulation.

The Congressional Stake in Regulation

The U.S. Congress also has a stake in the regulatory enterprise, less direct perhaps than that of the bureaucrats themselves, but no less real. The Political Action Committees (PACs) of the regulated industry and of its member firms and executives, are major sources of campaign contributions for the members, and especially for the chairmen of the relevant Congressional oversight committees. Congressmen can also use their powers over an industry and its regulators to leverage up their political standing with other constituency blocs. The CFTC again offers a neat illustration.

Regulatory oversight of the CFTC rests currently with the Agriculture Committees of the U.S. House and Senate, even though the CFTC-regulated futures exchanges now trade mainly financial products (interest rates, foreign exchange, stock indexes) not farm products; and even though their customers are now mainly financial institutions (pension funds, banks, insurance companies), not individuals and certainly not farmers. But major segments of the farmer constituents of the Agriculture barons in the House and Senate retain strong prejudices against the futures exchanges. Piling more restrictions on the Chicago exchanges can thus be a popular, vote-getting strategy for the congressional agriculture overseers of the CFTC, even though those restrictions hurt the industry stakeholders by weakening their competitive posture against other sectors of the financial services industry.

Sandner's Proposal and Stigler's Model

Interpreted in the light of Stigler's extended model, the Sandner proposal to reorganize U.S. financial regulation along functional rather than departmental lines can thus be interpreted, at least, in part as an attempt by the futures exchanges to recapture their regulation from bureaucrats and congressional overseers claiming too large a share of the industry's economic rents. Under the conventions of American politics, of course, such an objective cannot be acknowledged openly. All proposals for regulatory reform must be framed for public discussion in terms of general social, rather than narrow specific benefits. And the enormous overlapping and duplication in U.S. regulation can make almost any rational scheme of reorganization, such as the Sandner plan, look like (and almost certainly be) a net gain to society (or at least to its taxpayers).

The Sandner plan would freeze out the current congressional agriculture overseers of the futures industry—the group whose own private agendas have driven so many of the recent and costly regulatory restrictions piled on the industry. Setting up the proposed new stand-alone Commission on Risk-Shifting Markets would free the industry of the agriculture barons in congress, but it would still leave the industry subject to a CFTC-style regulator—a regulatory body almost certain to be recruited from the current staff of the CFTC. The hope, presumably, was that the staff would become less overbearing once their long-cultivated links to their congressional agriculture protectors had been severed. And since the CFTC, to broaden congressional support for its reauthorization as an independent agency, had to renounce regulating swaps, any new, functionally organized Risk-Shifting Market Commission covering both on and off-exchange derivative products would support efforts by the exchanges to "level the playing field" against their less-strictly regulated competitors in the swap industry.

CONCLUSION: THE PROSPECTS FOR FUNCTIONAL REGULATION

The Sandner plan, though conceived originally with the special problems of the futures exchanges in mind, is typical of a wider class of proposals for reducing the current dead-weight costs of regulation and regulatory compliance in the United States by redrawing regulatory jurisdictions along more logical functional lines. But benefits promised to the taxpaying public from such restructurings cannot, by themselves, assure enactment. Consolidations of long-established regulatory agencies will be resisted by at least two key stakeholders in the affected regulatory enterprises, the regulators and their congressional overseers. And who can blame them, since they face the loss of significant "property rights" (in the form of career rents, perks and political leverage). Admittedly, restructurings of comparable scope are routinely observed these days for private-sector enterprises. But the stakes in those firms are typically represented by securities, which can be freely bought or sold; and even where not, buyout deals for cash can normally be made. The efficiency gains from reorganizations or restructurings can then provide the means for inducing the losers to abandon their opposition. The restructuring of regulatory enterprises, however, generates no such pool of transferable resources—nothing, alas, that can be used to compensate the regulators and congressional overseers displaced.

If we were looking for a single word to epitomize U.S. regulation in the future, it won't be Functional. How about Dysfunctional?

REFERENCES

Miller, M. H., 1993, The economics and politics of index arbitrage in the U.S. and Japan, *Pacific-Basin Finance Journal 1*, 3–11.

Chicago Mercantile Exchange, 1993, Model for financial regulation (Chicago, IL) February.

Stigler, G.J., 1971, The theory of economic regulation, *Bell Journal of Economics and Management Science 2*, 2–19.

Merton, R.C., 1992, Operation and regulation in financial intermediation: A functional perspective, Working Paper 93-020 (Harvard Business School).

ENDNOTE

1. When this passage was first written in early June 1993, the "someday" seemed far in the distant future. Since then, however, the Liberal Democratic Party has lost the firm electoral majority it had maintained for 40 years and new governments have raised the prospect of fundamental change and deregulation. We shall see.

15

Functional and Institutional Interaction, Regulatory Uncertainty, and the Economics of Derivatives Regulation

CHRISTOPHER L. CULP

U ncertain regulation can increase the costs of doing business, stifle financial innovation, and result in resource misallocations toward regulatory compliance and avoidance. For these reasons, uncertain regulation may be demanded by some market participants to try and secure an advantage over their competitors (Stigler, 1971). Regulators, in turn, are sometimes willing to supply costly and uncertain regulations when it suits their interests (Niskanen, 1971).

The next section of this chapter presents a summary of the economic forces that affect regulation, including those underlying the theory of economic regulation and the theory of public choice. In the following section, derivatives and their risks are introduced. The means by which market participants confront regulatory uncertainty are examined, with particular emphasis placed on how regulatory uncertainty can be used in the political process. The current framework for the regulation of derivatives activity in the United States, both institutional and functional is then summarized. Some specific sources of regulatory uncertainty in the current regime are analyzed. Examples are given that relate some sources of regulatory uncertainty to the forces of *political* supply and demand. In the spirit of Friedman (1953), no attempt is made to explain whether the current system is "bad." The examples in this chapter merely help explain why the current system has evolved into its current form. (See also Miller, 1993a, 1993b, 1994a, 1994b, 1995.)

This paper first appeared in *The Financier:* ACMT Vol. 2, No. 5, 1995. http://www.the_financier.com. Earlier versions of this chapter were presented at the 25th Annual Meeting of the Financial Management Association in New York (October 1995) and the 10th Annual General Meeting of the International Swaps and Derivatives Association in Barcelona (March 1995). The author is grateful to Mark Brickell, Steve Hanke, Robert Mackay, Merton Miller, and Todd Petzel for numerous conversations on this subject.

THE ECONOMICS OF REGULATION

Two sharply distinct perspectives of regulation compete to explain why certain institutions and markets are subject to government supervision. This section provides an overview of these two explanations for regulatory policy.

Market Failure

The justification for regulation typically given by politicians and public commentators is the "benevolent despot" view that regulation should promote competition, ensure market integrity, and/or facilitate the provision of public goods. Even advocates of government intervention by a benevolent despot are quick to agree that the free market works and often makes regulation unnecessary. Regulation is thus usually predicated on the assumption that the market fails and government is needed to correct those market failures.

A market failure is presumed to occur when market participants do not take into consideration all the costs of their decisions. A firm's *private* cost, or the cost that governs its private behavior, is presumed to diverge from the true *social* cost of the firm's decisions, thus resulting in an "externality" and hence a failure of the market to allocate resources most efficiently (Bator, 1958; Pigou, 1932).[1] A factory that pollutes as part of a production process, for example, is typically thought to produce a negative externality. In other words, the firm does not consider the *social* costs of pollution when it engages in its normal production decisions, and it therefore produces too much. Regulation is presumed an appropriate means of correcting this and other market failures.[2]

Regulation and Rent Seeking

George Stigler, James Buchanan, and Ronald Coase each received the Nobel Prize in Economic Science (in 1982, 1986, and 1991, respectively) for helping to discredit the market failure paradigm as an explanation for regulation. They argued that market failure is more of a *normative* rationalization offered by some for why we *need* regulation. Market failure does not, however, often explain why we *get* regulation.

The Nobel laureates have been instrumental in proposing alternative explanations for actual regulatory policies. These explanations are perhaps best understood by separately exploring the demand and supply sides.

Demand: The Theory of Economic Regulation

The theory of economic regulation, pioneered by George Stigler (1971), explains that market participants will demand regulation when the expected marginal benefits of such regulation exceed the expected marginal costs. Regulation thus is often demanded, not surprisingly, as a means by which one firm or industry can raise the costs of its competitors *or* reduce that firm or industry's costs while leaving the costs of its competitors unchanged.[3]

When companies demand regulatory policies that are designed to increase their market share at the expense of their competitors' market share, they are engaged in "rent-seeking" behavior (Krueger, 1974; Tullock, 1967). An economic rent is the supranormal profit a firm can earn when its market power is increased. Rent seeking thus is the process by which firms allocate real resources to lobbying and the use of pressure groups to try and generate rents from regulation. (See, e.g., Becker, 1985; Mueller, 1989.)

To visualize rent seeking most clearly, consider a firm that wants to secure for itself a monopoly in its industry—say, securities underwriting.[4] To accomplish this, suppose the underwriter attempts to promote a policy that calls into question the legality of underwriting for every firm but itself. If the firm succeeds in even calling into question the legality of underwriting, competitors may exit the underwriting industry. If all competitors exit, the rent seeker will adjust its optimal level of underwriting services to a level consistent with the demand for those services. According to standard microeconomic analyses of monopoly, total underwriting services will decline, say from competitive level Q_c to monopolistic level Q_m. The marginal price of underwriting, furthermore, will rise, say from competitive price P_c to monopoly price P_m. The higher price at the new level of output generates a loss for consumers exactly equal to $(P_m - P_c)Q_m$, and that loss is the monopolist's gain. (See, e.g., Stigler, 1987.) Quantity $(P_m - P_c)Q_m$ is thus the "rent" the monopolist is extracting by heightening the uncertainty facing its competitors.

Rent seeking need not involve such a preposterous example. It need not even involve a monopoly. When a group of large broker/dealer underwriters argues for higher licensing fees on new entrants into underwriting, for example, the effect is similar. The existing underwriters have engaged in rent seeking by using licensing regulations to erect a barrier to entry against competition, thereby increasing their own market power.[5]

Supply: The Theory of Public Choice

Some would argue that rent-seeking behavior is sensible on the industry side but could never actually affect regulatory policy because benevolent regulators would simply oppose such policies. The "theory of public choice" says otherwise. (See, e.g., Buchanan and Tullock, 1962; Niskanen, 1971.)[6] Public choice theory begins with a simple axiom: Whereas the objective function facing corporations is to maximize the value of the firm, the objective function typically facing regulatory agencies is to maximize their budgets. That, after all, is more often than not what leaves the employees of the agency better off, and employees of a regulatory agency, like other economic agents, do prefer to be better off than not (Niskanen, 1971).[7]

Several patterns of observed regulatory agency behavior can be explained by recognizing that regulatory agencies often pursue policies of budget maximization. First, budget-maximizing agencies tend to aggressively promulgate new regulations and take actions designed to draw the attention of their paymasters, congress.[8] Any regulatory action that appears to evidence the *perceived* benefits of regulation (e.g., "top cop" posturing in enforcement actions), *ceteris paribus,* will help the agency justify its budget. One can hardly imagine, after all, an agency chairperson approaching a congressional appropriations committee and receiving a budget increase after announcing "All is well, and we didn't do anything last year."

Second, regulatory agencies tend to favor policies that promote certain types of uncertainty. If the efficacy and/or impact of a particular regulation over a product or activity is uncertain, the agency has an easy justification for proposing additional regulations requiring a bigger budget. A self-fulfilling feedback loop thus develops in which regulators like to keep regulation a little uncertain to justify the need for continued regulation. In addition, uncertain regulation is less apt to be judged "ineffective" by congress than certain regulation that actually did fail to accomplish its supposed benevolent regulatory objectives. Otherwise known as the "not-on-my-watch" syndrome, agencies often promulgate slightly uncertain policies so that mistakes can be blamed on the uncertainty rather than an actual error for which the whole agency or a specific regulatory policy would be held accountable.[9]

Consider, for example, a commercial bank engaged in a perfectly legitimate hedging strategy comprised of complex, hard-to-value financial transactions. Preferring to err on the side of conservatism, an over-zealous bank examiner might prefer to discourage the hedging strategy at the bank rather than engage in the costly and complex analysis of the strategy required to determine its validity. If the examiner acts precipitously, even with the best intentions, the bank may be forced to abandon the strategy, thereby unexpectedly incurring higher costs. If taken to task, the examining agency's out is simply that bank regulation relies on examiner discretion. At most, the single examiner will be held responsible, and that is not even likely.

Third, regulations designed principally to secure a greater budgetary allocation for an agency often have the secondary purpose of serving the interests of the regulated industry. The public choice factors affecting the *supply* of regulation thus interact with the factors affecting the *demand* for regulation in a Stiglerian world. Regulators often respond favorably to demands for regulation from certain market participants to ingratiate themselves to those seeking the regulation. Especially in areas like derivatives, the specialized knowledge acquired as (and sometimes required to be) a regulator is often most useful in the regulated industry. Bureaucrats with specialized knowledge, training, and experience about the industry they are regulating thus rarely wish to alienate themselves from that industry, as it holds the most promising prospects for future employment. This tendency to avoid alienating *all* parts of industry is especially pronounced for politically-appointed officials whose tenures in regulation may be quite short.

When regulatory agencies become hostages to the demands of the regulated industry, the agencies are said to be captured. Capture, moreover, need not involve an *entire* industry. A futures regulator, for example, may ingratiate himself to the retail segment of the futures industry by supporting regulations designed to benefit retail participants in futures at the expense of their wholesale competitors. Or a futures regulator may try to defend the futures industry at the expense of the swaps industry. And so on.

The Efficiency Consequences of Rent-Seeking Behavior

The theories of economic regulation and public choice generally are viewed as highly critical of regulation. In fact, the theories are in themselves entirely positive—that is, they seek to explain why regulation is, not what it should be. At the same time, the empirical work that has given so much support to these two theories paints a critical picture of regulation for two reasons. (1) The obvious one is that regulation does not usually accomplish what it is ostensibly intended to accomplish (see, e.g., Stigler, 1964). (2) A second criticism is that the rent seeking behavior associated with regulation can be quite inefficient.[10] Returning to the earlier monopoly example, the creation of a monopoly from regulation does not merely transfer wealth from consumers to the monopolist. Because output falls from its optimum competitive level Q_c to the private optimum of the monopolist Q_m, too little will be produced. In other words, given some demand curve, the price increase will cause some customers who were purchasing it before at the higher level of production to *stop purchasing the product.* This is called the *deadweight loss* of a monopoly because the resource misallocation that occurs represents a net loss to all of society.[11] The creation of monopoly *rents* is thus a wealth *transfer*, whereas the deadweight loss is actually a net social welfare reduction.

As Posner (1975) explains, moreover, the social cost of monopoly does not stop with the deadweight loss. Because the monopoly profits are perceived as valuable to the would-be monopolist, the firm will be willing to spend real money to try and secure the monopoly. In fact, the company will spend *up to the amount of additional profits it expects to get from the monopoly.* Because the resources being spent on rent seeking are *not* being put to productive use, however, the expenditure on rent seeking is thus also a misallocation of resources. In other words, rent seekers will spend in advance up to all the expected rents from regulation on lawyers, lobbyists, and so forth instead of putting that capital into productive activities like paying people to flip hamburgers (Miller, 1995).[12] This opportunity cost of the resources dedicated to rent seeking is thus an additional cost of regulatory uncertainty (see, e.g., Posner, 1975; Tullock, 1967).

RISK, UNCERTAINTY, AND DERIVATIVES

The theories of economic regulation and public choice are usually discussed in terms of *known* costs that market participants may demand and regulators supply. The theories are most clear, for example, when taxes or barriers to entry are the instruments of policy used to secure rents. The use of known costs and regulations for rent seeking is no less pronounced in derivatives than in other industries (Miller, 1994a). In this section, we discuss the means by which *unknown costs* can also be used as an instrument of policy. That *uncertain regulation* can be deliberately supplied and demanded is shown.

Risk and Uncertainty

Knight (1921) defined risk as a situation in which the randomness facing an economic agent can be expressed in terms of specific, numerical probabilities. These probabilities may be objective (as in a lottery) or subjective (as in a horse race), but they must be quantifiable (Machina and Rothschild, 1987). Unlike risk, uncertainty exists when an economic agent faces some randomness that *cannot* be expressed in terms of the probabilities of alternative outcomes (Knight, 1921). Measurable uncertainty is often called *Knightian risk,* whereas unmeasurable uncertainty is known as *Knightian uncertainty* (Ellsberg, 1961).

Knight (1921) maintained that true uncertainty exists in limited circumstances: The economic agent is ignorant of the statistical (i.e., historical) frequency of events relevant to his decision; economic agents cannot formulate a priori beliefs about subjective probabilities; the situation confronting the decision maker is somehow completely unique; or an important, irreversible, once-and-for-all decision faces the economic agent. The standard approach in economics and finance for addressing such uncertainty is the state preference approach (Arrow, 1964; Debreu, 1959; Hirshleifer, 1965, 1966; Machina and Rothschild, 1987). In that approach, uncertainty is expressed by specifying a set of exhaustive and mutually exclusive states of nature with which are coupled particular outcomes. In many situations, analysis of the uncertainty is limited to stating "preferences" for one state-dependent outcome relative to another.

When confronting risk, by contrast, a richer set of analytical tools is available because the consequences of agents' actions can be expressed using well-defined probability distributions. Analysis usually begins with the expected utility model in which economic agents are presumed to maximize the expected utility of their wealth. From this, the consequences of decisions for both individuals and firms can be thoroughly analyzed. And as far as practical finance goes, this approach is sufficiently rich to generate most interesting analyses of financial decision making (Fama and Miller, 1972).[13]

At many levels, the Knightian distinction between risk and uncertainty seems not particularly useful. Arrow (1951, pp. 417, 426) concluded that "Knight's uncertainties seem to have surprisingly many of the properties of ordinary probabilities, and it is not clear how much is gained by the distinction. . . . Actually, his uncertainties produce about the same reactions in individuals as other writers ascribe to risk." The distinction between risk and uncertainty, however, does have some pedagogical value. The usefulness of Knight's perspective becomes especially evident when addressing the practical question of how government agencies and market participants manage risk and uncertainty, a subject to which we now turn.

Derivatives and Risk

A derivatives contract is a zero net supply, bilateral contract that derives most of its value from some underlying asset, reference rate, or index. (Culp, 1995; Culp, Furbush, and Kavanagh, 1994; Culp and Overdahl, 1995.) Common types include futures, forwards, options, and swaps.

Types of derivatives are often distinguished based on the manner in which they are negotiated. "Privately negotiated derivatives," such as swaps and forwards, are contracts that are negotiated in an opaque, decentralized environment *off* the floor of any organized financial exchange. "Exchange-traded derivatives," as their name implies, are negotiated on an organized financial exchange, such as the Chicago Mercantile Exchange (CME) or the Chicago Board Options Exchange (CBOE). Exchange-traded derivatives include futures, options on futures, and certain options on securities.

The Global Derivatives Study Group for the Group of Thirty (G30) identified in 1993 four principal types of risk facing participants in derivatives activity—and in most other activities, too, for that matter. Market risk is the risk of a loss due to changes in market prices or interest rates; credit risk is the risk of a loss due to a counterparty default; and operational risk is the risk of a loss due to failures in internal controls, systems, disaster-planning contingencies, or personnel. The fourth type of risk, called "legal risk," the Study Group defined as "[t]he risk of loss because a contract cannot be enforced" (G30, 1993, p. 51).

The Enforceability Subcommittee of the Global Derivatives Study Group identified five sources of legal risk for many derivatives negotiated privately (G30, Appendix 1, 1993).[14] First, legal risk can result because oral transactions are not always properly and promptly documented. In the event that an oral transaction is *not* documented properly, the losing counterparty to the transaction may try to "walk away" from the contract, claiming it is unenforceable. As a related concern, some locations that have specific laws pertaining to written documentation, such as the state of New York, may present legal risks to derivatives participants if the contract formation standards are unclear.[15]

Second, legal risk can arise over questions about the capacity of certain types of institutions to engage in derivatives transactions. In a famous case decided by the House of Lords in the United Kingdom in 1991, for example, the Law Lords held that a number of swaps entered into by the London boroughs of Hammersmith and Fulham were void because the municipality had no legal capacity to engage in the transactions. That decision invalidated otherwise legitimate contracts between over 130 government councils and over 75 commercial banks around the world (G30, Appendix 1, pp. 46–47).[16]

Third, the treatment of certain derivatives contracts under alternative bankruptcy laws is often considered a source of legal risk (see, e.g., Culp and Kavanagh, 1994; Cunningham and Casper, 1993). Of particular concern is the enforceability of "bilateral netting" following the early termination of a swap contract. Netting involves the replacement of two gross cash flows between swap counterparties with a single net cash flow from one party to the other. If Bank A owes Bank B $10 and B owes A $3, the exchange of *gross* cash flows would require two payments: one by A to B of $10, and the other by B to A of $3. Bilateral netting, by contrast, requires only a single payment by B to A of the difference, or $7. If netting is unenforceable in bankruptcy, the solvent counterparty may face a situation in which it is forced to make a gross payment without receiving anything from the bankrupt counterparty. If Bank A goes bankrupt and "close-out" netting is *not* enforceable, Bank B may have to pay Bank A its $3 without receiving its $10 in turn, resulting in a $13 loss as compared to the $7 loss that would have resulted if netting was enforceable.

Fourth, the G30 (1993) expressed concern about the enforceability of multibranch netting agreements under bankruptcy and solvency laws. If such agreements are enforceable, a solvent counterparty to the insolvent institution may, if it has documented its transactions with multiple branches under a single multibranch master agreement, treat the branches of the institution as a "single entity" and net across branches to a single payment. Otherwise, the solvent counterparty can be faced with treating separate branches as separate legal entities following an insolvency of the institution, thus giving rise to some of the same problems noted in the previous paragraph (Cravath, Swaine, and Moore, 1994). Finally, legal risk can result if certain statutes can render particular types of derivatives transactions illegal.

In addition to the G30's legal risks, a broader source of uncertainty sometimes confronts market participants that is "regulatory" in nature. Whereas legal risk pertains only to enforceability, regulatory uncertainty also concerns the *costs* of regulation. All regulation is costly, so what separates regulatory *uncertainty* from regulatory *cost* is that the former involves some source of randomness about the latter.[17]

Confronting Regulatory Uncertainty

That market and credit risk can be treated as risks in the Knightian sense is uncontroversial. Risk can be measured in some way and therefore can be managed (Arrow, 1964; Hammond, 1987). But is it appropriate to treat *legal* and *regulatory* risks as risks in the Knightian sense—as measurable uncertainties?

If the uncertainty confronting derivatives participants about legal and regulatory issues is viewed as *Knightian uncertainty,* one of two assumptions must be made: Data that can be used for inference about the probabilities of regulatory actions is lacking; or market participants cannot form *prior* probabilities about regulatory actions.

The track records of congress and many regulatory agencies are well-known, suggesting that perhaps some measure of probability could be deduced from history to estimate regulatory *risk.* This data, however, is dependent on a variety of circumstances that are hardly stable over time, not the least of which is who happens to be legislating and regulating when the policies are formulated. In regards to prior beliefs, the assumption that some market participants consider the actions of regulators and legislators to be so unpredictable as to defy the assignment of subjective probabilities is perhaps unlikely, but at least plausible.

This chapter thus treats legal and regulatory risk as uncertainty in Knight's sense. Although this characterization is plausible anyway, the pedagogical value will become clear when the implications of treating regulatory uncertainty as Knightian uncertainty on the responses of market participants to the uncertainty are considered.

Hedging and Information Acquisition

When risks can be measured, they can almost always be managed or "hedged."[18] If the assumptions underlying Modigliani and Miller's (1958) capital structure propositions do not hold and a value-maximizing company wishes to reduce its risk, the ability of the company to formulate risk in a probabilistic context makes risk reduction feasible.[19]

Managing uncertainty, however, can be more problematic. When the number of assets available to market participants is exactly equal to the number of exhaustive and mutually exclusive "states of nature," markets are said to be "complete." When contracts *cannot* be written at a reasonable cost that "insures" market participants against the outcomes of all states of nature, however, markets are said to be "incomplete" (Duffie, 1992). Lack of knowledge about the probabilities for states of nature coupled with market incompleteness and uncertainty make hedging next to impossible.

That market participants cannot write insurance contracts at a reasonable cost to protect themselves against unexpected and adverse regulatory changes is quite plausible. So, regulation can give rise to a situation in which financial contracting is not a viable means of managing the uncertainties of regulation. In Knight's (1921) world, the means by which market participants typically manage uncertainty is to get more and better information about the nature of the uncertainty and then make discrete choices about their preferences concerning those states of nature.

Consider, for example, a company that is concerned about the enforceability of its swap contracts in a particular legal jurisdiction. Few explicit contracts can be written at low cost that protect the company against the losses it might incur if its contracts do, in fact, prove to be unenforceable.[20] The states of nature as seen by the company thus are that the contracts are enforceable or they are not. Some companies will manage such uncertainty by simply refusing to transact in jurisdictions where the latter is even among possible states of the world.

About the only other thing a company can do directly to "hedge" such uncertainty about jurisdictional enforceability is to acquire information so that its decision about transacting in the uncertain jurisdiction is based on the best information available and then take "discrete" actions like those noted above (i.e., choose not to transact at all in uncertain jurisdictions).[21] But that is not very comforting for most market participants.

Shareholder Diversification

As the assumptions underlying the Modigliani-Miller (1958) propositions imply, *any* form of diversifiable *risk* can be reduced in the portfolio selection decisions made by shareholders. If risk cannot be quantified in a meaningful sense, however, shareholder diversification decisions become complicated. Faced with "unmeasurable uncertainty," a shareholder in a company threatened with unexpectedly high regulatory costs or contract unenforceability might not have the necessary information to decide *how* to diversify. In other words, just knowing that the stock of one company may be adversely affected by changes in regulation and that the stock of another company is positively affected by such changes does not help the shareholder decide how much of each stock to hold. More information about the precise manner in which uncertainty impacts the stocks is required.[22] Without information about the nature of the uncertainty, shareholder diversification probably will *not* be a viable means for companies to manage regulatory uncertainty.[23]

Financial Innovation

Financial innovation is often associated with uncertain regulation. Miller (1986, 1992) argues that unexpected changes in regulation account for a large amount of financial innovation. Allen and Gale (1990), Duffie (1992), and others explain that when markets are "incomplete," profit-maximizing economic agents have a strong incentive to engage in financial innovation to provide "market-completing" securities. These associations between innovation and regulation, however, do not explain the *causality*.

Financial innovation, in fact, is rarely used to address regulatory uncertainty *ex ante*. Instead, market participants respond to unexpected changes in regulation by engaging in financial innovation. Innovation thus may be viewed as a means of managing uncertainty *ex post,* or uncertainty that has been realized. Innovation, however, is probably not an effective means of managing regulatory uncertainty *ex ante*.

Rent Seeking and the Use of Uncertainty in the Political Process

Knight (1921) emphasized that most opportunities for profits and losses trace to *uncertainty* rather than risk. Uncertainty is what allows firms to acquire information and become specialized, thereby allowing some firms to become "better" than others in an entrepreneurial sense. Uncertainty is thus a source of competitive advantage for some firms (Hammond, 1987). Regulatory uncertainty can be viewed as a potential instrument by which some companies attempt to profit at the expense of their competitors.

Uncertainty in regulation complicates and sometimes inhibits decision making. This is perhaps most clear for legal uncertainty when the enforceability of a contract is in question. Some firms thus will demand regulations that reduce their own regulatory uncertainty but leave the regulatory uncertainty confronting other participants unchanged. Alternatively, some firms may actually argue for policies that increase the uncertainty facing their competitors.

Rarely would any market participant or regulator say that they "like" uncertainty in regulation. The fact remains, however, that regulatory uncertainty for one segment of an industry can significantly inhibit the ability of those firms to conduct normal business. Stigler's theory thus suggests that some positive amount of regulatory uncertainty *will be* demanded. On the supply side, the public choice theory likewise implies that uncertainty will also be supplied, as well. (As will become clearer later, evidence that regulatory uncertainty is supplied abounds in current derivatives regulations.)

Regulatory uncertainty, it also should be noted, can arise with no deliberate design on the part either of market participants or regulators. Distinguishing between intended regulatory uncertainty and unintended uncertainty is thus largely an empirical problem. In the 1993 Omnibus Budget Reconciliation Act, for example, congress enacted a "federal depositor preference" statute that reorders the priority of claimants on a failed insured depository institution.[24] Under the statute, any amounts realized from the liquidation or resolution of a failed institution are paid in the following order: the administrative expenses of the receiver, any domestic deposit liability of the bank (insured *or* uninsured), other senior liabilities, subordinated liabilities, and equity. Congress intended in enacting national deposit preference legislation to place insured and uninsured depositors ahead of other general creditors in the event of a bank failure, thus theoretically allowing the Federal Deposit Insurance Corporation (FDIC) as insurer to recoup as much as it can on payments to insured depositors of the institution. The legislation, however, had the consequence of placing derivatives participants *behind* depositors.

Although perhaps unintended by congress, the adoption of the 1993 Budget Reconciliation Act had the *immediate* effect of increasing the credit risk facing any derivatives counterparties dealing with insured depository institutions.[25] The heightened credit risk facing derivatives counterparties to U.S. commercial banks could have been an unintended consequence or a deliberate effort of competitors, such as investment bank swap dealers. The answer is far from clear.

DERIVATIVES REGULATION IN THE UNITED STATES

Before analyzing the extent to which the theories of public choice and economic regulation explain the presence of legal and regulatory uncertainty in the current derivatives regulatory regime, that regime must first be explained. A brief history of current regulation is instructive for illustrating the extent to which regulatory uncertainty has affected the regulatory landscape and market participants over time.

Financial regulation comes in two types. "Functional regulation" is the regulation of economic functions that the financial system provides, such as spatial and intertemporal resource allocation (Chicago Mercantile Exchange, 1993; Merton, 1993, 1995; Scholes, 1995). "Institutional regulation," by contrast, is the regulation of specific types of institutions (e.g., commercial banks). An institutional regulator regulates all the activities in which an organization is engaged without respect to their economic functions.

Perhaps the best way to view the two types of regulation is by asking what institution or function the regulation treats as "special" or evidencing a possible market failure. Institutional regulation is based on the premise that externalities trace to the nature of certain "special" institutions. Active derivatives participants, for example, are presumed not to consider the costs of "systemic risk" when making their trading and risk management decisions, thus implying the perceived need for the regulation of "systemically important" institutions.[26] Alternatively, the extension of a "safety net" under insured depository institutions is often presumed to be a source of market failure, as insured banks and thrifts make decisions without considering the full implications on the taxpayer-backed bank insurance fund. Regulation is thus presumed necessary to prevent excessive risk-taking by insured depository institutions.[27]

Functional regulation, by contrast, is presumed necessary to correct market failures involving the functions of the financial system. Merton (1993, 1995) defines these functions of the financial system as follows: (1) the provision of a payments system; (2) the provision of a mechanism that facilitates capital pooling; (3) a means by which resources can be allocated spatially and across time; (4) a means by which risk can be controlled and uncertainty managed; (5) the provision of information that facilitates coordination and resource allocation; and (6) a means by which information asymmetries and incentive problems can be mitigated across market participants. When a market failure is presumed to occur in the provision of one of these functions, regulation is deemed appropriate. As in the institutional approach, for example, the risk that the failure of a "systemically important" institution could disrupt the payments mechanism might warrant the regulation of the process by which the payments system is provided.

Viewed from another perspective, Merton (1995) distinguishes the objectives of regulation and public policy under the two distinct approaches as follows:

> There are two fundamentally different frames of reference for analysis of financial intermediation. One perspective takes as given the existing institutional structure of financial intermediaries and views the objective of public policy as helping the institutions currently in place to survive and flourish. . . . The functional perspective takes as given the economic functions performed by financial intermediaries and asks what is the best institutional structure to perform those functions. (Merton, 1995, p. 23)

As Merton's quote makes clear, *both* institutional and functional regulation involve *both* financial products and institutions. In other words, institutional regulation inevitably engenders the regulation of financial products used by the regulated enterprise. Similarly, functional regulation necessarily involves the regulation of institutions involved in providing the function. The critical difference between the two types of regulation is thus whether institutions or functions are presumed to be "special." If institutions are presumed "special" (Macey and Miller, 1992), any regulation of the institutions' products and activities is *secondary* to the regulation of the institution itself. If functions are instead presumed to be "special" (Merton, 1993, 1995; Scholes, 1995), any regulation of the institutions that provide those functions is *secondary* to the regulation of the function itself. This distinction may seem semantic, but it is actually quite important, as will become clearer below.

Institutional Regulation of Derivatives Activity

The institutional regulation of derivatives activity is not separable from institutional financial regulation more generally. In *no present case* is the justification for institutional regulation that a firm is engaged in derivatives activity, per se. Rather, certain institutions are regulated because they are perceived as "special" for some other reason, and the derivatives activities of those firms is then subject to regulation *because* those activities are being conducted by already-regulated enterprises.[28]

Institutions currently involved in derivatives activity that are regulated institutionally include commercial banks, thrifts, insurance companies, and pension funds.

Other firms that are also regulated institutionally are involved in derivatives activity (e.g., credit unions), but their activity is sufficiently small to eliminate any discussion of them here. Derivatives at these institutions are subject to three types of institutional regulation. First, regulators of these institutions may specify "permissible" activities. This allows some firms to engage in derivatives activity while prohibiting others. Second, the derivatives activities in which regulated institutions are permitted to engage are subject to prudential supervisory oversight. Finally, regulators must determine the adequacy of derivatives participants' capital relative to the risks of their derivatives activities.

Because institutions are regulated based on their type (e.g., a bank, thrift, and so forth), little uncertainty exists about the regulations to which a particular firm is subject. What the institution must do to comply with those regulations, however, is a different story.

Commercial Banks

Commercial bank regulation in the United States is based on the type of charter held by the bank. A commercial bank may be either nationally or state-chartered. If the bank is state-chartered, it may apply for membership in the Federal Reserve System, hence submitting itself to the Federal Reserve Board (Fed) as its primary federal regulator. State-chartered banks that are not members of the Federal Reserve System are regulated by the FDIC. National banks, by contrast, are all regulated by the Office of the Comptroller of the Currency (OCC). State-chartered banks are also regulated by state banking commissioners *in addition* to the FDIC or Fed. All bank holding companies (BHCs) are regulated by the Federal Reserve. Capatides (1993) reviews the regulations of derivatives activities at banks and BHCs in detail.

Banking regulations are numerous and complex. Regulation, moreover, relies heavily on a "discretionary" approach. Entities like the Federal Reserve Board have discretion in approving permissible activities, and examiners have discretion in supervision. As will be explained later, discretion and judgment always give rise to some regulatory uncertainty.

Thrifts

U.S. savings and loan associations are regulated by the Office of Thrift Supervision (OTS). The OTS quite specifically defines permissible derivatives activities for thrifts. Thrifts may only participate in derivatives activity as end users, and they may only hold derivatives as hedges to reduce their overall *interest rate* risk. All swaps are permissible, but the supervisory monitoring of the correlations between swaps and the assets or liabilities being hedged is still mandated so the OTS can regularly ensure the contracts held are actually hedges.[29] For reasons similar to those explained in the previous section, agency discretion is perhaps the main source of uncertainty in thrift regulation.

Insurance Companies

Insurance companies are subject to regulation entirely at the state level. The National Association of Insurance Commissioners, in an effort to coordinate state regulations on insurance companies, has drafted a model regulation for adoption by state regulators that specifies requirements on derivatives users, including regulations concerning prudential risk management, stress testing, and maximum size of derivatives activities. The regulation of insurance companies, and hence their derivatives activities, does *not* translate into the regulation of insurance company *affiliates.*

Because insurance companies are subject to exclusive regulation by states, uncertainty can arise based on differences in state regulatory statutes and authorities, as well as confusion about the state regulations to which a particular company may be primarily subject.

Pension Funds

Pension funds are regulated under the Employment Retirement Income Security Act (ERISA) by the Department of Labor (DOL). DOL regulations on pension fund participants in derivatives activity are principally concerned with permissible activities. In addition, pension fund users of derivatives are also subject to disclosure and reporting requirements.

Functional Regulation of Derivatives Activity

Two primary types of functional regulation exist in the U.S. financial system today. These regulatory regimes include securities regulation by the Securities and Exchange Commission (SEC) and futures regulation by the Commodity Futures Trading Commission (CFTC). Judge Frank Easterbrook of the Seventh Circuit has characterized SEC/CFTC functional regulation as follows: "Securities usually arise out of capital formation and aggregation (entrusting funds to an entrepreneur), while futures are means of hedging, speculation, and price revelation without the transfer of capital. So one could think of the distinction between the jurisdiction of the SEC and that of the CFTC as the difference between regulating capital formation and regulating hedging."[30]

Futures

In 1936, Congress amended the Grain Futures Act of 1922 and adopted the Commodity Exchange Act (CEA), which remains the primary statute underlying futures regulation today. Congress' primary objective was to protect the integrity of a trading market whose primary perceived functions were the facilitation of risk shifting and the provision of information from the price discovery process. As part of these functional desires to regulate price discovery and risk shifting, congress considered important the prevention of fraud, manipulation, and sales abuses. To carry out the provisions of the CEA, congress created the Commodity Exchange Commission, which delegated day-to-day regulatory authority to the Secretary of Agriculture who, in turn, formed the Commodity Exchange Administration (later re-named the Commodity Exchange Authority) (Markham, 1987).

Congress believed that by facilitating public price dissemination and risk-shifting opportunities, organized futures exchanges produced a positive externality (i.e., the marginal social benefits of production exceed its marginal private benefits). Beyond just ensuring that prices and the trading environment were stable and free from manipulation, congress thus also considered it important to establish incentives for exchanges to reap the benefits of designing and listing futures contracts for trading—a costly activity.[31] Congress thus also sought in the CEA to eliminate "bucket shops," or companies that "free ride" on exchange-determined prices and exchange-traded contracts.

To achieve its functional objectives of regulation, congress relied heavily on a provision of the CEA known as the exchange trading requirement (Stein, 1988). This clause of the CEA requires that unless specifically exempted by the CFTC, a futures contract is illegal unless it is traded on an organized commodity exchange. The term *futures contract* is not, however, explicitly defined in the CEA. Instead, futures contracts are defined by allusion using phrases like "any transaction in, or in connection with, a contract for the purchase or sale of a commodity for future delivery."[32] The statute thus rests heavily on terms like *commodity* and *future delivery,* but those definitions, too, are far from straightforward.

In 1974, congress significantly revised the CEA in the Commodity Futures Trading Commission Act of 1974 (CFTC Act). Among other things, the CFTC Act ceded responsibility for futures regulation from the Secretary of Agriculture to the CFTC, which was created in the 1974 Act. The CFTC Act also broadened the definition of the term *commodity.* Previously, commodities were limited to a list of enumerated agricultural products, but the 1974 Act broadened the definition to include a variety of other products, including financial assets. Because futures are not defined but *must* involve commodities to fall under the CEA, this broader definition of commodities implied an equally broader nondefinition of futures.

Armed with the exchange-trading requirement, the CEA aims to regulate the functions of price discovery and risk-shifting in futures by regulating futures as financial products. In addition, the CEA also regulates futures markets, as well as certain institutions involved in those markets. The CFTC regulates four types of institutions in particular: futures exchanges, or the organized exchanges where futures trading occurs; exchange clearinghouses, or those entities that clear and settle the transactions executed on futures exchanges; futures commission merchants (FCMs), or firms that execute futures transactions on behalf of customers; and commodity trading advisors (CTAs), or companies that render professional advice pertaining to futures transactions. Although such institutions are subject to institutional-like regulations (e.g., disclosure, reporting, and capital requirements), their regulation is *entirely* a result of their involvement in futures transactions.

As noted earlier, institutions regulated under the CEA are not themselves special; they are regulated *as if* they were special only because they are involved with futures, which are deemed special. The artificiality of this framework can only be appreciated by recognizing its self-fulfilling nature. Futures, after all, are economically exchange-traded forwards (Culp, 1995; Culp and Overdahl, 1995). Although in 1922 and 1936 they may have been special, the only reason futures are special now is because of the CEA.

There are multiple sources of regulatory uncertainty in futures regulation. At the forefront is uncertainty over exactly what products fall under the scope of the CEA. Related to that is uncertainty about what institutions are regulated under the CEA; if futures cannot be defined, users of futures must be equally hard to legally identify.

Securities

Like futures, Congress also deemed securities to be special. Securities regulation was established to facilitate the function of capital formation. More than that, however, securities regulation treats as special capital formation *in public markets.* (Bank loans, after all, are also a type of capital formation.)

Congress viewed securities as special in providing the function of capital formation for several reasons (Rattner, 1992). First, like futures and unlike physical assets, securities are created when they are issued rather than produced. Because securities represent an interest in the issuer of the instrument (or a "right" in the underlying), Congress deemed regulations appropriate to ensure that purchasers of securities have adequate information about the issuer and about the exact rights that the securities convey regarding the security purchasers' interest in the underlying firm. Second, because securities are actively traded in secondary markets, congress deemed it appropriate to establish regulations concerning the regular and accurate flow of information about the issuers of securities. Third, like futures, nonexempt securities are traded on organized exchanges, so congress deemed it appropriate to regulate securities markets to prevent fraud and manipulation. Securities laws were also adopted to regulate institutions involved in securities markets, including securities broker/dealers, investment companies, and public issuers of securities, for similar reasons.

Various laws establish the functional regulatory framework for securities, securities markets, and participants in securities markets. The Securities Act of 1933 (33 Act) was enacted to regulate the public offering of securities. Unlike the CEA for futures, the 33 Act explicitly defines securities, including exempt securities. The 33 Act also prohibits fraud in the public sale of securities and requires that any public security offering of a nonexempt security be conducted through a firm registered with and regulated by the appropriate federal regulator.

The Securities Exchange Act of 1934 (34 Act) elaborated on and broadened much of what was behind the 33 Act. The 34 Act accomplished three primary objectives in securities regulation. First, it established the SEC as a formal regulator of securities, securities markets, and security market participants.[33] Second, the 34 Act established new regulations on the trading of securities in secondary markets. Third, the 34 Act expanded on the regulatory framework set forth in the 33 Act. Some of the regulations promulgated pursuant to the 34 Act include the following: disclosure and reporting requirements on publicly held companies; prohibitions on market manipulation and fraud; restrictions on credit extended for security purchases; broker/dealer registration requirements; regulations on broker/dealer activities; and the registration and regulation of securities exchanges, clearing associations, and transfer agents.

The 33 and 34 Acts established much of what is now the securities regulatory infrastructure. Other laws subsequently adopted by congress that elaborate on the functional securities regulatory framework include the Public Utility Holding Company Act of 1935, the Trust Indenture Act of 1939, the Investment Company Act of 1940, the Investment Advisors Act of 1940, and the Securities Investor Protection Act of 1970.[34]

Several similarities between securities and futures regulation should be immediately obvious. First, the justifications for both regulatory regimes are functional in their underlying purpose. In their implementation, however, the regulations end up being regulations primarily on products and markets. Second, although the protection of retail investors from fraud and sales abuses was an ostensible justification for both regulatory regimes, the protection of such investors is *generally unrelated* to the provision of the economic functions about which the regulations are principally concerned. Protections of retail participants came about partly because the futures and securities markets that provided the functions deemed special by congress were characterized at that time by significant retail participation.[35] Third, both regulatory regimes involve some institutional regulation, but such regulation occurs only because the regulated enterprises are using regulated products, not because they were viewed by congress as important in and of themselves.

Like futures, uncertainty in securities regulation traces to ambiguities in jurisdictional boundaries concerning products and institutions. Even though securities are defined explicitly, the distinction between exempt and nonexempt securities is not always clear. The role of state securities laws also adds to regulatory uncertainty for securities participants.

Overlaps

As the discussion in the preceding sections has suggested, derivatives activity in the United States is actually subject to *both* institutional and functional regulation. Depending on the particular product and institution, regulation may be exclusively functional or institutional, or it may be both. Overlaps are sources of additional uncertainty in both types of regulation.

Three types of regulatory overlap are reviewed in this section. Institutional-institutional and functional-functional overlaps occur when regulators of the same type are faced with the potential regulation of the same business enterprise or product, respectively. Institutional-functional overlap results when a regulated institution also happens to be using a functionally-regulated product.

Institutional-Institutional

Several types of institutions that are subject to institutional regulation are supervised by more than one institutional regulator. State-chartered banks are a classic example. They are regulated both by the state that charters them and by either the Federal Reserve (for state-member banks) or the FDIC (for state nonmember banks). Such overlaps can engender some uncertainty about an institution's primary regulator, especially when multiple regulators disagree on an important matter affecting the institution.

Institutional-Functional

When a business enterprise is a regulated institution *and* is engaged in activities that deal with regulated futures and/or securities transactions, the firm is technically subject to *both* types of regulation. In practice, however, the institutional regulator often delegates regulatory authority to the functional regulator *when such regulation pertains to a regulated product.* The primary regulator is usually the institutional regulator.

Consider, for example, a bank holding company with three subsidiaries: a state-member bank, an FCM, and a securities broker/dealer (i.e., a Section 20 subsidiary).[36] As the regulator of BHCs, the Federal Reserve has the ultimate authority for the holding company, any activities undertaken directly by the BHC, and the ultimate safety and soundness of the consolidated enterprise. The Fed also regulates the bank affiliate because it is state-chartered and a member of the Federal Reserve System. Technically, the Federal Reserve also has the responsibility for regulating the non-bank affiliates of the BHC, including the FCM and broker/dealer. In the case of the FCM, the Fed is likely to delegate regulatory responsibilities to the CFTC, although it will still require regular reports from the affiliate pertaining to issues like capital adequacy. Bank-affiliated FCMs, moreover, are still examined routinely by banking supervisors, although day-to-day regulation of such enterprises pertaining to their futures activities is carried out by the CFTC. The Fed would take a more active role in supervising the Section 20 subsidiary, but as a registered broker/dealer the subsidiary would also be accountable to the SEC.

As in the previous case, institutional-functional overlaps can engender uncertainty principally by raising questions about the primary regulator. As will become clearer later, competition between regulators in a public choice context sometimes exacerbates this source of uncertainty for institutional-functional overlaps.[37]

Functional-Functional

More problematic than the above two cases of overlap is the case in which a particular financial *product* is regulated (or perceived to be regulated) by both the SEC and CFTC. Few would disagree that regulatory uncertainty in these cases is significant.

Problems arise here for two reasons. First, the Commodity Exchange Act gives the CFTC *exclusive* jurisdiction over products that fall under the scope of the CEA.[38] Second, although *security* is a term defined in the 33 Act, the term *futures contract* is not defined in statute law. As a consequence, any product that has the attributes of *both* a security *and* a futures contract can become the subject of a bitter jurisdictional dispute (Culp, 1991; Russo and Vinceguerra, 1991).

The exclusivity clause granting the CFTC exclusive jurisdiction over futures was adopted in the CFTC Act of 1974 (i.e., in the same act that broadened the definition of commodities). The SEC thus demanded during debate over the CFTC Act that congress add a savings clause to preserve its jurisdiction over securities that might also be deemed futures contracts. The SEC savings clause provides that

> . . . *nothing in this section shall (I) supersede or limit the jurisdiction at any time conferred on the Securities and Exchange Commission or other regulatory authorities under the laws of the United States or of any State, or (II) restrict the Securities and Exchange Commission and other such authorities from carrying out their duties and responsibilities in accordance with such laws.*[39]

Among other things, the inclusion of the SEC savings clause in the CFTC Act was thought to secure the SEC's jurisdiction over options on securities, including options on individual stocks and debt securities.

Only a year after the CFTC Act, conflict arose between the SEC and CFTC over the SEC savings clause (Culp, 1991; Gilberg, 1986; Markham and Gilberg, 1983; Russo and Vinceguerra, 1991). Based upon a determination that Government National Mortgage Association (GNMA) certificates were commodities under the amended CEA, the CFTC approved the trading of futures on GNMAs at the Chicago Board of Trade. Soon thereafter, the CBOT and other futures exchanges began trading futures on other types of financial instruments, including futures on U.S. Treasury securities. The SEC challenged the CFTC's approval of those products, arguing that "GNMA certificates and Treasury bills are securities, as that term is defined in the federal securities laws. [The SEC] also believe[s] it to be quite clear that contracts for future delivery of those securities are also 'securities.'"[40] The CFTC had already approved those products and claimed the exclusivity clause gave it the right to do so. For the time, the disagreement between the SEC and CFTC thus remained confined to a series of unpleasant letters exchanged by the agencies.

In 1978, the jurisdictional disagreements between the SEC and the CFTC flared up again in the hearings regarding the Futures Trading Act of 1978.[41] In those hearings, the SEC and the CBOE stressed that futures contracts on securities and options on securities were functionally indistinguishable, and because the SEC had jurisdiction over the latter it should also have jurisdiction over the former.[42]

Congress disagreed and left the CFTC's exclusive jurisdiction in tact, attempting to assuage the SEC by requiring the CFTC to "maintain communications" with the SEC in areas of potential jurisdictional dispute and to "take into consideration" the SEC's view on the approval of futures on government securities.[43]

The burgeoning jurisdictional dispute between the SEC and the CFTC was finally litigated in *Board of Trade of the City of Chicago v. SEC* (hereinafter *GNMA Options*).[44] This case arose after the SEC approved, in February 1981, a proposal by the CBOE to trade options on GNMA certificates. The SEC repeated its earlier claim that those options on securities were securities and hence were protected by the SEC saving clause. The CFTC and the CBOT, on the other hand, claimed that GNMA options were options on commodities and hence fell under the CEA. By extension, the CFTC and CBOT were arguing that not only did the CFTC have exclusive jurisdiction over such products, but also that their classification under the CEA required them to be traded on a designated contract market. As the CBOE is a securities exchange and not a CFTC-regulated board of trade, the CFTC and CBOT effectively claimed that GNMA options were illegal as long as they continued to trade on the CBOE.

In November 1981, the Seventh Circuit Court of Appeals granted a motion by the CBOT for a stay pending review and blocked the CBOE from trading GNMA options. The Court of Appeals determined that because GNMA certificates had previously been determined to be commodities, GNMA options were *commodity options* that are regulated under the CEA.[45] The court also explicitly noted that its same line of reasoning could be applied to options on corporate and Treasury debt securities, however, which would have negated the congressional intent behind the SEC savings clause.

To protect the SEC's jurisdiction over options on securities without contradicting its determination that GNMA options were commodity options and that commodity options were under the jurisdiction of the CFTC, the court undertook an analysis of scope for the CFTC's jurisdiction over transactions involving futures contracts. The court stated, "Since GNMAs are not traditional stocks and GNMA options have the character of a legitimate commodity derivative, we hold that the proposed GNMA options 'involve' the pre-existing GNMA futures and therefore are within the exclusive jurisdiction of the CFTC."[46]

Further complicating matters, the SEC and CFTC tried to take jurisdictional matters in their own hands while the *GNMA Options* case was pending before the circuit court. In December 1981, the CFTC and SEC reached a mutual agreement regarding their disputes over innovative financial instruments, including options. This agreement, called the Shad-Johnson Accord after the two agency chairmen at the time, provided four basic ground rules:

1. The CFTC would regulate *futures* and *options on futures* based on government securities and based on broad stock indexes.
2. The SEC would regulate all *options on securities* (including GNMAs) and *options on stock indexes* (as opposed to options on stock index futures).
3. Futures on individual securities, such as stocks, were prohibited.
4. The SEC would play a formal role in the CFTC's approval of then-evolving stock index futures contracts.

Only a few months after the adoption of the Shad-Johnson Accord, *GNMA Options* called the Accord into question when the appellate court ruled that "the CFTC and SEC [cannot be allowed] to reapportion their jurisdiction[s] in the face of a clear, contrary statutory mandate."[47] Congress decided to give force to the Accord, however, and enacted it into law almost verbatim in the Futures Trading Act of 1982. The Shad-Johnson Accord was incorporated into the CEA as new § 2(a)(1)(B), and the exclusivity clause was amended to read,

> *The Commission shall have exclusive jurisdiction, except to the extent otherwise provided in subparagraph (B) of this paragraph, with respect to accounts, agreements. . . , and transactions involving contracts of sale of a commodity for future delivery. . . .*[48]

The adoption of the Accord thus left in place the central premise on which the Seventh Circuit based its decision in *GNMA Options: the CFTC has exclusive jurisdiction over any transaction that is both a security and a futures contract.* In consequence, every transaction that has attributes of both a security and futures contract is subject to the same legal questions that arose concerning options on GNMA certificates. As Judge Easterbrook described the dilemma:

> *[T]he question a court must decide is the same as in GNMA Options: is the instrument a futures contract? If yes, then the CFTC's jurisdiction is exclusive, unless it is an option on a security, in which case the SEC's jurisdiction is exclusive. So long as an instrument is a futures contract (and not an option), whether it is also a "security" is neither here nor there.*[49]

REGULATORY ECONOMICS AND UNCERTAINTY IN THE CURRENT SYSTEM

The previous section's review of current regulation should have been instructive for identifying some of the sources of regulatory uncertainty in the present system. In this section, some of the demand and supply forces affecting regulatory uncertainty are considered. To facilitate this analysis, alternative means by which regulatory uncertainty can be affected are examined. Examples are given of how these sources can affect the supply of and demand for uncertainty.

Statute Law

One of the most obvious sources of regulatory uncertainty stems from the potential for changes in the statutes—federal or state—that either establish regulations directly or empower an agency to adopt its own regulations. Such statutory changes can involve legislation that either codifies new statutes or amends existing ones.

Opportunities for rent seeking in the legislative process abound (Downs, 1957). Lobbyists, pressure groups, direct industry contact, and the selective use of campaign contributions can give market participants a surprisingly powerful degree of influence over legislation. Regulators, moreover, often take a very active behind-the-scenes role in ensuring that their interests, too, are represented in the legislative process. The statutes underlying the derivatives regulatory infrastructure are thus primary vehicles by which different groups can attempt to influence the degree of regulatory uncertainty in the market.

Among the most significant statutes underlying institutional regulation include statutes pertaining to banking regulation, many of which appear in Chapter 12 of the United States Code.[50] The Banking Act of 1933 (i.e., the Glass-Steagall Act) established this chapter of the U.S.C., and it has since been amended numerous times by such laws as the Bank Holding Company Act of 1956, the Financial Institutions Reform, Recovery, and Enforcement Act of 1989 (FIRREA), and the Federal Deposit Insurance Corporation Improvement Act of 1991 (FDICIA).

Chapter 11 of the U.S. Code, pertaining to bankruptcy, is also relevant for institutional regulation. Although the Bankruptcy Code does not establish any regulatory body for a particular set of institutions, it establishes the legal framework in which many commercial bankruptcies occur. Changes in the Bankruptcy Code can affect the enforceability of derivatives contracts through their terms concerning matters such as close-out netting. The 1990 amendments to the Bankruptcy Code actually represented a significant *reduction* in legal uncertainty by establishing clearly the enforceability of bilateral netting in bankruptcy. Insolvencies of banking institutions, however, fall under the Banking Act and thus do not receive the same legal protections. FIRREA and FDICIA, in turn, eliminated a large amount of uncertainty about the enforceability of netting involving depository institution failures (Cunningham and Casper, 1993).[51]

Not surprisingly, in light of Stigler's model, the International Swaps and Derivatives Association (ISDA) expended tremendous efforts to secure the netting provisions in the 1990 Bankruptcy Code Amendments, in FIRREA, and in FDICIA.

The primary statutes that affect functional regulation include the CEA and the statutes underlying securities regulation. Changes in state anti-gambling laws and state securities laws may also affect functional regulation. The former, for example, may affect the legality of genuine financial contracts even when the laws are intended only to eliminate actual gambling.

An oft-cited example of a statutory change that served to *reduce* functional regulatory and legal uncertainty was the Futures Trading Practices Act of 1992 (FTPA), in which Congress gave the CFTC the authority to exempt certain products or classes of products from most sections of the CEA.[52] Believing this to provide some relief from regulatory uncertainty, ISDA was again instrumental in pushing the FTPA through Congress. Granting the CFTC the authority to exempt certain products did not, however, reduce regulatory uncertainty in itself. The effects of this statutory change on regulatory risk depend totally on how the CFTC uses its new authority, some examples of which are discussed next.

Federal and State Regulations

Beyond the statutes that underlie regulation, regulations themselves may also be changed. Corresponding to virtually all federal and state statutes are implementing regulations. Sometimes such regulations do little more than echo the intent of congress to provide for specific regulations, whereas statutes also often give regulatory agencies the discretion to adopt their own regulations to discharge their responsibilities.

New regulations are usually promulgated only after a lengthy period of public comment. An agency first issues an advanced notice for proposed rulemaking in the *Federal Register,* and then receives and considers comments on the proposal. If it decides to proceed, the agency publishes the proposed new regulations in the *Federal*

Register and again solicits comments from other agencies, market participants, and interested observers. This process continues until a rule is finally reached. Like legislation, explicit regulations provide market participants, public policy analysts, pressure groups, and other regulators numerous opportunities to influence future regulatory policies. The public and visible nature of the regulatory approval process, moreover, does not necessarily limit the extent to which Stiglerian and public choice forces come into play.

An example of a regulation *thought* to decrease regulatory uncertainty but which actually did *not* occurred with the 1993 adoption by the CFTC of regulations pursuant to its exemptive authority under the FTPA. The CFTC adopted a new regulation as Part 35 of Chapter 17 of the Code of Federal Regulations that is commonly referred to as the "Swaps Exemption." Under the Swaps Exemption, certain types of swap agreements are exempt from most of the CEA. An agreement can be exempt if it is negotiated between "eligible swap participants," non-standardized, reflects counterparty creditworthiness as a material consideration, and is not executed on a "multilateral transaction execution facility."[53]

The Swaps Exemption was initially viewed as having decreased the regulatory and legal uncertainty of swaps owing to the risk that the CFTC could try and regulate swaps as futures, possibly subjecting them to the exchange-trading requirement of the CEA and hence declaring swaps illegal off-exchange futures. ISDA, in fact, lobbied strongly for the Swaps Exemption in an effort to abrogate this uncertainty. As Stigler's model predicts, moreover, the exemption received significant opposition from futures exchanges (Donovan, Brodsky, and Halperin, 1992). Although futures and swaps exhibit important *complementarities,* the futures exchanges must have then viewed the competitive similarities in swaps and futures as more important, likely pushing for continued regulatory uncertainty as a means of preserving a competitive advantage over swaps through Stiglerian means.

The effects of the Swaps Exemption, however, have been far from certainty-enhancing (Stassen and Young, 1995). Even setting aside definitional ambiguities arising from terms like "swap agreement," two sources of regulatory risk were created by the Swaps Exemption. First, although the CFTC granted the swaps exemption without making a determination that swaps *were in fact* futures, the exemption should not have been necessary were swaps actually *not* futures under the CEA (Stassen and Young, 1995). The mere adoption of the exemption does not create any real legal uncertainty, but an exemption can be subsequently reversed by an agency in a later regulation. The initial adoption of the Swaps Exemption thus raises the spectre of future changes in the exemption that could significantly affect the legality and regulation of swaps.

The CFTC, in fact, did propose in 1994 a revision to the Swaps Exemption that would have substantially narrowed the definition of eligible swap participants for whom the exemption was available. Perversely, the uncertainty about such *changes* to the exemption would not have existed in the absence of the exemption itself—an example of the uncertainty-begets-uncertainty feedback loop noted earlier.

Second, the Swaps Exemption specifically reserved the right for the CFTC to enforce the anti-fraud and anti-manipulation provisions of the CEA on participants in swap contracts. This reservation of authority clearly fed the belief that although the CFTC did not say it, the agency did view swaps as futures. This part of the exemption, moreover, is subject to interpretational confusion. On the one hand, it is possible the CFTC intended to reserve anti-fraud and anti-manipulation enforcement authority over swaps *regardless* of whether swaps are or are not futures contracts. Given the phrasing adopted, however, equally plausible is that the CFTC only intended to subject swaps to the fraud and manipulation rules *to the extent such swaps are actually found to be futures.* Because no one knows what the exemption actually implies, the exemption created the uncertainty that swap participants could be subject to regulations to which they had previously not been subject.

Case Law

In contrast to changes in statutes and implementing regulations, which tend to occur in a highly public forum and over a relatively long period of time, case law that results in a reinterpretation of statute law or regulations often takes market participants by surprise. A court, after all, is an unpredictable entity, with both juries and judges sometimes making rulings that many observers do not expect. Any regulatory or legal uncertainty that results from case law is virtually always unintended, given the virtual impossibility of exerting political pressure on jurists and juries.

Numerous examples of regulatory uncertainty arising from case law can be identified. Some of the most significant uncertainty concerns a part of the CEA known as the Treasury Amendment. When the CFTC Act broadened the definition of commodities, the Treasury Department, like the SEC, was concerned that the new definition might include certain types of transactions that were off-exchange and under the purview of the Treasury, such as foreign exchange interbank transactions and transactions involving U.S. government debt. To allay the Treasury's concerns, congress included the Treasury Amendment to the CEA in the CFTC Act, which excludes from the CEA transactions in foreign currency, government securities, and several other products "unless such transactions are conducted on a board of trade." As with much of the CEA, however, the terms "transactions in" and "board of trade" are not well-defined in the statute.

The CFTC has historically tried to interpret the Treasury Amendment as concerning only relatively "sophisticated" market participants. The Commission's justification is the legislative history of the CFTC Act of 1974. During the debate over that legislation, the Department of Treasury expressed the following concerns:

> *The Department feels strongly that foreign currency futures trading, other than on organized exchanges, should not be regulated by [the CFTC]. Virtually all futures trading in the United States is carried out through an informal network of banks and dealers. . . . The participants in this market are sophisticated and informed institutions, unlike the participants on organized exchanges, which, in some cases, include individuals and small traders who may need to be protected by some form of government regulation.*[54]

The CFTC thus usually takes the position that the Treasury Amendment was intended only to exclude "transactions in" the enumerated products if those transactions are negotiated among relatively sophisticated investors, such as banks. The CFTC claims that retail "transactions in" products like foreign currency futures were meant to be regulated as futures under the CEA, including its exchange-trading requirement.

Several recent court cases have called this interpretation of the Treasury Amendment into question.[55] Although the courts have been deferential to the

CFTC's position in recent years, few have agreed with it. In *Salomon Forex v. Tauber,* the Fourth Circuit acknowledged that it might in the future adopt a different construction for a board of trade if the enterprise in question is "mass marketing to small investors . . . [that] would appear to require trading through an exchange."[56] The Fourth Circuit did, nonetheless, disagree with the CFTC's argument, as did the District Court that first heard the CFTC's argument in the same case.[57] The Fourth Circuit stated plainly that "[t]he statute distinguishes only between on-exchange and off-exchange trading," *not* between sophisticated and unsophisticated investors.

In *CFTC v. Frankwell Bullion Ltd.* (hereinafter *Frankwell Bullion*), the Commission again suggested its interpretation of the Treasury Amendment as excluding only transactions negotiated with relatively sophisticated investors.[58] The Commission argued that if the literal interpretation of board of trade in the Act is used, "any association of persons buying or selling currency would be covered, such that the very purpose of the exemption might be rendered meaningless by the subsequent 'unless' clause."

In his ruling, Judge Jensen of the Northern California District Court was highly critical of the CFTC's position on the Treasury Amendment, arguing that "[t]he Treasury Amendment makes no distinction based on the identity or character of the participants."[59] He stated,

> *Because the language of the Amendment conclusively reveals Congress' intent that off-exchange transactions in foreign currency are exempted from the Act, the analysis is complete. Even if the legislative history underlying the Amendment is examined, the same result is reached. As the legislative history does not evidence a clearly established intention to the contrary, the language of the statute must be regarded as conclusive.*[60]

Since the *Frankwell Bullion* and *Salmon Forex* rulings, numerous commercial banks have reportedly started routinely marketing foreign exchange contracts to retail investors. Those and other cases thus demonstrate the extent to which case law can blindside the market with a significant and rapid change in legal interpretation of already-ambiguous statutes.

Because jurists are not often subject to the same forces that can sway legislators and regulators, case law can provide interesting insights into the forces of supply and demand at play in the regulatory arena elsewhere. Looking at *amicus curiae* and other briefs filed for certain cases, for example, reveals much about the Stiglerian model and the theory of public choice. To take an obvious example, the cases that have involved the Treasury Amendment generally always evoked briefs from the CFTC and futures exchanges arguing for the interpretation of the Treasury Amendment that would see retail transactions in foreign currency subjected to the exchange-trading requirement.

Settlements and Administrative Orders

Administrative law is the body of law created by regulatory agencies through their discharge of regulations, orders, and decisions. Governed by the Administrative Procedures Act (60 Stat. 237, 5 USCA), administrative law usually involves a process in which disputes concerning federal agencies are presented in an administrative hearing supervised by an administrative law judge. Final dispositions of administrative proceedings are called administrative orders and may either be declaratory or contain some positive or negative command. Actions by agencies against market participants that are settled prior to the initiation of any administrative proceeding are still considered part of administrative law but have more limited precedential value.

As the three examples below illustrate, settlements and administrative law proceedings embody the economics of regulation quite well. All the incentives of agencies to be budget maximizers can come to bear on an administrative proceeding. The public choice calculus thus dictates the direction of administrative law more often than not.

The FRBNY/Bankers Trust Written Agreement

On December 4, 1994, the Federal Reserve Bank of New York (FRBNY) reached a written agreement with Bankers Trust New York Corp. and its affiliates BT Co. and BT Securities.[61] The written agreement pertains to BT's use of what the parties called leveraged derivatives transactions. In the agreement, BT and its affiliates agreed to undertake activities involving leveraged derivatives only if they met certain requirements concerning client selection and suitability, marketing, valuation, management and internal controls, staff training, credit administration, reporting, and other related requirements (Horwitz, 1995; Klejna and Walsh, 1995).

The written agreement was not the by-product of any enforcement action by the FRBNY against BT or its affiliates and thus has no significant precedential value. In the context of public choice theory, the agreement thus might be viewed as a preemptive measure by the FRBNY to protect against any allegation that the agency was "asleep at the wheel."

The agreement, moreover, signalled a possible change in *future* Federal Reserve policy toward risk-taking and risk management, thus creating new uncertainties for regulated state-member banks and BHCs. The agreement indicated a variety of considerations the FRBNY expects BT to take into account when conducting its derivatives business. Many market participants have interpreted these expectations by the FRBNY of BT as applying more generally to a broad cross-section of banking participants in derivatives activity. Horwitz (1995) provides a more detailed analysis.

The SEC/CFTC Bankers Trust Settlements

On December 22, 1994, Bankers Trust Securities Corp. settled with the CFTC concerning an enforcement action the CFTC filed charging BT with violations of the sections of the CEA pertaining to fraud.[62] The action concerned a number of swaps and other contracts entered into by BT with Gibson Greetings in 1993 and 1994. In the settlement, BT agreed to pay a fine of $10 million to the CFTC and to cease and desist from violating the section of the CEA pertaining to fraud. The particular section of the CEA that BT was charged with violating concerned fraud perpetrated by commodity trading advisors. Recall that CTAs are one type of institution regulated by the CFTC because they render professional advice concerning futures and contracts that fall under the scope of the CEA.

BT Securities Corp. also was a registered broker/dealer with the SEC. The SEC also brought fraud charges against BT, which BT also settled on December 22, 1994.[63] The regulatory authority of the SEC in the case was based on two facts. First, BT Securities Corp. was a registered broker/dealer and hence subject to regulation under the 33 and 34 Acts. Second, the SEC order claimed that some of BT's transactions were securities as defined in the 33 Act. Whether or not the contracts in question actually *were* securities is debatable, however. One of the transactions was a swap linked to Treasury securities, which are exempt securities. By calling the swap a security, the SEC created some regulatory uncertainty by implying that such contracts are securities and should be regulated as such (Hanley and Moser, 1995).

If the SEC's explicit claim that BT's contracts were securities is accepted *by assumption,* the remainder of the SEC order is not controversial and does not represent a new posture for the SEC. The order is a straightforward application of the anti-fraud portions of the 33 Act and 34 Act once the definition of securities has been accepted. Right or wrong, the SEC order thus produced minimal regulatory uncertainty.

The clarity of purpose in the SEC order cannot be found in the CFTC order, and the questions surrounding the CFTC's very authority to bring the case have resulted in significant regulatory risk. The CFTC argued in its complaint that by entering into an advisory relationship with Gibson Greetings, BT had become a CTA.[64] As such, the CFTC charged BT with the sections of the CEA that pertain to fraud committed by CTAs.

Problematic is the CFTC's lack of explanation about *why* BT's provision of advisory services made BT a CTA. To be a CTA under the CEA, after all, a firm must not simply render professional advisory services, but it must render professional advice *pertaining to futures contracts or contracts under the scope of the CEA.* Unlike the SEC, which specifically noted the transactions in which BT engaged were securities under the 33 Act, the CFTC merely included an appendix in its complaint with a list of *all* BT's significant contracts, including interest rate swaps and swaps on securities.

Two interpretations of the CFTC/BT settlement are possible. The first is that among BT's contracts was at least one contract viewed by the CFTC as a futures contract. BT's offering of that contract would have made them a CTA. The second interpretation is that the CFTC utilized the authority it reserved for itself to enforce the anti-fraud provisions of the CEA under the Swaps Exemption. Although perhaps exempt from other parts of the CEA, the CFTC could still enforce the anti-fraud portions of the CEA on BT under the Swaps Exemption as adopted. Even in that case, the CFTC must have implicitly believed that the exempt swaps were *futures,* thereby enabling them to go further than just applying the generic anti-fraud rules of the CEA and instead to apply the anti-fraud rules of the CEA that pertain *specifically to CTAs.*

The BT/CFTC settlement thus created regulatory and legal uncertainty in large part because it suggested to many market participants that the CFTC believes swaps to be futures. Under the Shad-Johnson Accord as codified, swaps on securities, such as those BT entered with Gibson, cannot be exempted by the CFTC from the CEA *unless* such swaps are first found to be futures.[65] Because the CFTC did not indicate whether its actions were directed at BT's swaps on securities that it viewed as *nonexempt futures* or at BT's interest rate swaps that it viewed as *exempt futures but still subject to the anti-fraud rules,* market participants have a heightened sense of legal uncertainty concerning numerous types of swaps.

Aside from legal uncertainty, the BT/CFTC settlement also created regulatory uncertainty inasmuch as market participants are still speculating on what exactly gave the CFTC cause to call BT a CTA and thus subject to the relevant portions of the CEA.

Note also that *both* the SEC and CFTC settlements can be interpreted from the public choice perspective as efforts to demonstrate clearly to congress their "tough cop" approach to derivatives and to violations of the relevant regulations.

The CFTC/MGRM Settlement

On July 27, 1995, MG Refining and Marketing, Inc. (MGRM) and MG Futures, Inc. (MGFI) settled an enforcement claim with the CFTC.[66] In the action, the CFTC fined

MGRM and MGFI $2.25 million for negotiating illegal off-exchange futures contracts, failing to notify the CFTC of material inadequacies in its internal risk management systems, and failing to file certified financial statements with the CFTC in 1993.[67]

The CFTC settlement with MGRM and MGFI created regulatory risk in two ways. First, the settlement created legal uncertainty about the enforceability of a large class of commercial derivatives contracts. Prior to the MGRM settlement, the CFTC had avoided offering a rigid definition of futures under the CEA, choosing instead to emphasize certain conditions it perceived as *necessary* for a contract to be a futures contract. In the MGRM settlement, however, the CFTC defined "*all* the essential elements of a futures contract [emphasis added]," suggesting a list of *sufficient* conditions for the first time.[68] After the MGRM ruling, a contract is now a futures contract subject to the CEA if (1) it contains a price or pricing formula specified at the contract's inception; (2) it can be honored either by physical delivery or an offsetting transaction (presumably including cash settlement, given that MGRM's contracts were accordingly defined); and (3) it is used either to speculate or hedge.

All derivatives and many other financial contract types, of course, satisfy the first and third criteria, and numerous derivatives satisfy the second due to elements of optionality and cash-settlement provisions. Especially for nonexempt contracts like swaps on securities, legal uncertainty now abounds in the marketplace. Even if the settlement proves to have no precedential value, the *perception* that it represents new law may be sufficient to lead some losing counterparties in derivatives deals to perceive a free option of walking away from their loss, claiming their contracts, too, are now illegal (Miller and Culp, 1995).

Second, the CFTC's ruling that MGRM and MGFI failed to notify the CFTC of inadequacies in its internal controls creates significant regulatory risk. MGFI was an FCM, and the CFTC thus held MGFI responsible for notifying the CFTC of any perceived inadequacies in its internal controls. This insistence raises a number of questions about the CFTC's regulation of FCMs. Because MGRM was the real source of concern to the CFTC and was merely a *customer* of MGFI, does the CFTC intend all FCMs to know about the risk management systems in place at their customers? Are FCMs expected to know the financial condition of their *parent,* which was also a point of contention in the CFTC/MGRM settlement? Does the CFTC intend to dictate what are and are not "reasonable" and "adequate" internal controls and risk management systems? These questions and more have given many market participants cause for concern about the future of FCM regulation by the CFTC (Cadwalader, Wickersham, and Taft, 1995).

A particularly noteworthy feature of the CFTC action against MGRM and MGFI is that although it was negotiated between the parties to the settlement exclusively, the implications of the settlement affect virtually all market participants. As noted above, this is the manner in which settlements and administrative proceedings can be used to circumvent the policy-making process and try to establish new policy in disguise. Miller and Culp (1995) argue, for example, that the CFTC settlement with MGRM was a very deliberate effort on the part of the CFTC to broaden its regulatory jurisdiction over privately negotiated derivatives *without* facing the public scrutiny that would have accompanied the adoption of a new regulation.

Also notable in the MGRM settlement is the extent to which "regulatory ambulance chasing" appears to have been a principal motivation of the agency.[69] Those employees of MGRM accused of committing the regulatory violations have long since gone from the firm; the company is plagued by litigation; and the enforcement came well over a year and a half after events at MGRM supposedly almost led to the firm's downfall. The most compelling justification for the severity of the action brought against MGRM is thus again "muscle flexing" by the CFTC, at that time attempting to push its proposed budget through congressional appropriations. This justification, of course, is precisely what public choice theory predicts.

"Guidance" to Agency Personnel

Especially in institutional regulation, "guidance" issued to examiners by regulatory agencies often has a strong effect on market perceptions of regulatory risk. Guidances issued by both the Federal Reserve and the OCC to bank examiners, for example, are generally interpreted as implicit rules that the banks must follow. Likewise, when a regulatory agency issues a "manual" to examiners, the guidance to examiners generally is interpreted by market participants as no different from a regulation. Examples of such "guidance" that affects derivatives participants include *OCC Banking Circular 277,* Federal Reserve *SR Letter 93-69,* the Federal Reserve's *Commercial Bank Examination Manual* and *Trading Activities Manual,* and the OCC's *Risk Management of Financial Institutions Comptroller's Handbook.*

The absence of any specific regulation backing guidance to agency personnel ensures that in the case of a dispute, the agency cannot rely on a specific regulation but usually must point to general regulations that led to the particular guidance issued. In other words, guidance itself is not enforceable on market participants. Guidance documents are, nonetheless, typically public domain. Regulated institutions thus are usually expected to adhere to the principles set forth therein. In this sense, guidance to agency personnel almost acts like a type of moral suasion on market participants. Were guidances *not* intended to have such public choice effects, they probably would not be in the public domain.

Agency Statements and Moral Suasion

Some regulatory agencies can create regulatory uncertainty simply by making formal or informal statements. Formal statements may include documents published in the *Federal Register,* such as policy statements or statutory interpretations. Informal statements can range from publicly accessible letters sent from agency chairmen to members of Congress, congressional testimony, statements of agency personnel to the media, and direct contact between agency personnel and market participants. The latter, of course, have limited (if any) precedential value in legal proceedings, but they can sometimes be effective in persuading market participants of the agency's views on some particular policy or legal matter.

Transnor and the CFTC Statutory Interpretation on Forwards

A good example of the political forces often lying behind formal statements by agencies is the CFTC's 1990 Statutory Interpretation Concerning Forward Transactions.[70] The Statutory Interpretation was a response to a case decided by a U.S. District Court in April of 1990 called *Transnor (Bermuda) Ltd. v. BP North American Petroleum* (hereinafter *Transnor*).[71] In *Transnor,* the court ruled that certain transactions involving the future purchase and sale of Brent oil off-shore were futures under the CEA. The court relied heavily on the fact that those contracts were cash-settled and routinely "offset" like futures.

The implications of *Transnor* were immediate. The market for forward purchases and sales of Brent oil is quite large, and participants in the Brent market feared that losing counterparties would try to walk away from their payment obligations in light of the *Transnor* decision. ISDA and other swap participants, moreover, were seriously concerned that *Transnor* might have adverse legal implications for *any* such cash-settled contracts, such as interest rate swaps.[72]

In response to so-called concerns about uncertainty created by *Transnor*, the CFTC issued its Statutory Interpretation, in which the agency effectively stated that it viewed the Brent contracts as forward contracts excluded from the CEA and *not* as futures. The Interpretation also set forth several criteria that the agency viewed as necessary (but not sufficient) to exclude certain contracts from the CEA.

Regulatory and legal uncertainty following *Transnor* was quite real, as any of the participants in the Brent market can attest. At the same time, the broad response of the CFTC to eliminate this uncertainty for both the Brent contracts *and* other types of swaps can be viewed as an effort by the agency to respond to the demands of the swaps industry for greater legal certainty. Not surprisingly, the futures industry was opposed to the broadness of the Interpretation for exactly this reason (Stassen and Young, 1995).

The Statutory Interpretation is an instructive example because it shows that regulatory responses to market participants' demands can often appear quite reasonable and consistent with public policy. The agency's action also shows, however, the manner in which uncertainty is a driving force politically. Even if the CFTC did not explicitly intend to "choose" off-exchange products over futures, its actions helped the former at the expense of the latter.[73]

If asked, the futures industry in this case would certainly *not* claim that it "supported" uncertainty for its off-exchange cousins. Instead, the industry would simply argue that it wanted to maintain consistency in the law (Stassen and Young, 1995). That, too, is probably right. But just because that argument is legitimate does not mean it is not *also* intended to serve Stiglerian ends. Part of the difficulty in analyzing regulation, in fact, is distinguishing between such motives. That is no easy task, and, as is true for all the examples in this chapter, "true" incentives are next to impossible for outsiders to do more than hypothesize about based on patterns of observed behavior.

Informal Public Statements on the CFTC/MGRM Settlement

In some cases, public statements by agency officials actually exacerbate regulatory risk. Following the CFTC's enforcement action against MGRM and MGFI, for example, the CFTC made a number of statements indicating that the settlement did not have implications for market participants other than those named in the settlement (i.e., MGRM and MGFI). CFTC Chairman Schapiro stated, for example, that "the commission has been charged [by bringing this case] of signalling a change in its view of what constitutes an unlawful off-exchange futures contract or a permissible swap agreement. Nothing, however, could be further from the truth" (Schapiro, 1995, p. A9). Such statements carry no probative weight in a court of law, however. Schapiro's statement thus does nothing but exacerbate the regulatory uncertainty created by the original ruling, as is so often the case with attempts at moral suasion.

At the same time, public statements and moral suasion are one of the "lowest cost" means by which an agency can assert its "usefulness" on the public scene. As with the other examples noted, such actions thus are completely consistent with the theory of public choice.

Also noteworthy is that Schapiro's (1995) public statements were accompanied by a similar statement from two top officials at the CME. The officials state, "Off-exchange futures peddled through seedy bucket shops or respectable broker-dealers cannot be tolerated by the CFTC" (Sandner and Brodsky, 1995). By using the MGRM/CFTC settlement as an opportunity to remind the public of the need for the CFTC to punish those who peddle "off-exchange futures," even at legitimate broker-dealers, the exchange is simply confirming its longstanding support of the exchange-trading requirement, which establishes regulatory uncertainty for off-exchange participants to the benefit of organized exchanges.[74]

Judgment Calls

The discretion and judgment of agency personnel is often a primary source of regulatory uncertainty. In institutional regulation, this source of regulatory uncertainty manifests itself mainly in examiner determinations about the adequacy of certain activities in which a regulated institution is engaged. An examiner that confronts a complex valuation model or hedging strategy, for example, may opt to conservatively conclude that the strategy is risky and order the institution to rely less heavily on it. Because such judgment calls can be quite wrong and are totally unpredictable, regulated institutions thus bear ever-present uncertainty due to potentially poor examiner oversight. Common reasons for failures at the examiner level include inadequate training and the "not-on-my-watch" mentality.

The judgment and discretion of agency personnel can also fuel opportunities for regulatory capture. In the case of bank regulation, for example, the job satisfaction of "resident examiners" often depends heavily on the quality of their interactions with the regulated institution. OCC resident examiners, for example, usually even have offices at the regulated banks, and everyone likes to eat lunch with other people sometimes! The not-on-my-watch incentives of some bank examiners is thus sometimes attenuated by partial capture of the examiners by the institutions they supervise.[75]

Functional regulation is also dependent on the judgment of agency personnel, especially when the statutes underlying the regulations are ambiguous. CFTC staff, for example, have considerable latitude in choosing how to interpret the CEA's non-definition of futures. Depending on the particular objectives of the personnel, this discretion can also give rise to significant uncertainty among market participants about the nature and objectives of CFTC regulation.

SUMMARY AND CONCLUSIONS

The use of regulatory uncertainty as an instrument of policy is perhaps more common in derivatives than elsewhere. In large part this is true because those who demand derivatives regulation are often those tapped for public service, hence moving them to the supply side. The suppliers of derivatives regulation, moreover, often end up working in the industry that demands regulation. The high degree of specialization involved in derivatives thus exacerbates the extent to which Stiglerian demand and public choice supply forces determine the look of the regulatory landscape.

From a normative perspective, most market participants and regulators involved in derivatives would agree that the current system is unusual and riddled with complexity, especially when compared to the regulation of other industries. But the system is what it is for a reason. The system looks like it does because rational economic agents on both the demand and supply sides want it that way (Miller, 1993a, 1993b, 1994a, 1994b, 1995).

REFERENCES

Allen, F., and D. Gale, 1990, "Incomplete Markets and Incentives to Set Up an Options Exchange," *Geneva Papers on Risk and Insurance Theory, 15*(1), March, 17-46.

Anscombe, F., and P. Aumann, 1963, "A Definition of Subjective Probability," *Annals of Mathematical Statistics, 34,* 199-205.

Arrow, K. J., 1951, "Alternative Approaches to the Theory of Choice in Risk-Taking Situations," *Econometrica, 19,* 404-437.

Arrow, K. J., 1964, "The Role of Securities in the Optimal Allocation of Risk-Bearing," *Review of Economic Studies, 31,* 91-96.

Bator, F. M., 1958, "The Anatomy of Market Failure," *Quarterly Journal of Economics, 72,* August, 351-379.

Becker, G. S., 1985, "Public Policies, Pressure Groups, and Dead Weight Costs," *Journal of Public Economics, 28,* 329-347.

Black, F., 1995, "Systemic Risk in Derivatives," *Journal of Derivatives, 3*(2), Winter.

Buchanan, J. M., and G. Tullock, 1962, *The Calculus of Consent* (University of Michigan Press, Ann Arbor).

Cadwalader, Wickersham & Taft, 1995, *Memorandum to Clients and Friends in RE OTC Futures Contracts and FCM Reporting Requirements,* August 1.

Capatides, M. G., 1993, *A Guide to the Capital Markets Activities of Banks and Bank Holding Companies* (Mayer, Brown & Platt and Bowne Publishing, New York).

CCH Business Law Editors, 1994a, *Bank Compliance Laws and Regulations* (CCH, Chicago).

CCH Business Law Editors, 1994b, *Federal Deposit Insurance Corporation Laws and Regulations* (CCH, Chicago).

CCH Business Law Editors, 1994c, *Federal Reserve Board Laws and Regulations* (CCH, Chicago).

CCH Business Law Editors, 1994d, *Office of the Comptroller of the Currency Laws and Regulations* (CCH, Chicago).

Chicago Mercantile Exchange, 1993, *Model for Financial Regulation,* White Paper.

Coase, R. H., 1960, "The Problem of Social Cost," *Journal of Law and Economics, 3,* October, 1-44.

Cochrane, J. H., 1994, *Discrete-Time Empirical Finance,* Forthcoming.

Cravath, Swaine & Moore, 1994, "Enforceability of Multibranch Close-Out Netting in ISDA Master Agreements," *Memorandum of Law for the International Swaps and Derivatives Association, Inc.* (November 29).

Culp, C. L., 1991, "Stock Index Futures and Financial Market Reform: Regulatory Failure or Regulatory Imperialism?" *George Mason University Law Review, 13*(3), Summer, 517-605.

Culp, C. L., 1995, *A Primer on Derivatives: Their Mechanics, Benefits, and Risks* (Competitive Enterprise Institute, Washington, D.C.).

Culp, C. L., and B. T. Kavanagh, 1994, "Methods of Resolving Over-the-Counter Derivatives Contracts in Failed Depository Institutions: Federal Banking Law Restrictions on Regulators," *Futures International Law Letter, 14*(3-4), May/June, 1-19.

Culp, C. L., and M. H. Miller, 1994, "Hedging a Flow of Commodity Deliveries with Futures: Lessons from Metallgesellschaft," *Derivatives Quarterly, 1*(1), Fall, 7-15.

Culp, C. L., and M. H. Miller, 1995a, "Auditing the Auditors," *Risk, 8*(4), April, 36-39.

Culp, C. L., and M. H. Miller, 1995b, "Basis Risk and Hedging Strategies: Reply to Mello and Parsons," *Derivatives Quarterly, 1*(4), Summer, 20-26.

Culp, C. L., and M. H. Miller, 1995c, "Hedging in the Theory of Corporate Finance: A Reply to Our Critics," *Journal of Applied Corporate Finance, 8*(1), Spring, 121-127.

Culp, C. L., and M. H. Miller, 1995d, "Metallgesellschaft and the Economics of Synthetic Storage," *Journal of Applied Corporate Finance, 7*(4), Winter, 62-76.

Culp, C. L., and J. A. Overdahl, 1995, "An Overview of Derivatives: Their Mechanics, Participants, Scope of Activity, and Benefits," in C. E. Kirsch, ed., *Financial Services, 2000 A.D.: The Dissolving Barriers Among Banks, Mutual Funds and Insurance Companies* (Irwin Professional Publishing, Burr Ridge, Ill.).

Culp, C. L., D. Furbush, and B. T. Kavanagh, 1994, "Structured Debt and Corporate Risk Management," *Journal of Applied Corporate Finance, 7*(3), Fall, 73-84.

Cunningham, D. P., and R. Y. Casper, 1993, "Over-the-Counter Derivatives Transactions: Netting Under the U.S. Bankruptcy Code, FIRREA, and FDICIA," *Memorandum of Law,* Cravath, Swaine & Moore (July 9).

Debreu, G., 1959, *Theory of Value: An Axiomatic Analysis of General Equilibrium* (Yale University Press, New Haven, Conn.).

Donovan, T. R., W. J. Brodsky, and D. Halperin, 1992, *Letter to the CFTC in Re: Proposed Exemption for Swap Agreements,* December 28.

Downs, A., 1957, *An Economic Theory of Democracy* (Harper & Row, New York).

Duffie, D., 1992, "The Nature of Incomplete Security Markets," Laffont, J. J., ed., *Advances in Economic Theory: Sixth World Congress, Volume II,* Econometric Society Monograph (Cambridge University Press, Cambridge).

Ellsberg, D., 1961, "Risk, Ambiguity, and the Savage Axioms," *Quarterly Journal of Economics, 75,* 643-669.

Fama, E. F., and M. H. Miller, 1972, *The Theory of Finance* (Dryden Press, Hinsdale, Ill.).

Fite, D., and P. Pfleiderer, 1995, "Should Firms Use Derivatives to Manage Risk?" in Beaver, W. H., and G. Parker, eds., *Risk Management: Problems & Solutions* (McGraw-Hill, Inc., New York).

Friedman, M., 1953, "The Methodology of Positive Economics," in his *Essays in Positive Economics* (The University of Chicago Press, Chicago).

General Accounting Office, 1994, *Financial Derivatives: Actions Needed to Protect the Financial System,* GAO Report GAO/GGD-94-133, May.

Gilberg, D. J., 1986, "Regulation of New Financial Instruments Under the Federal Securities and Commodities Laws," *Vanderbilt Law Review, 39,* 1599.

Global Derivatives Study Group, 1993, *Derivatives: Practices and Principles* (The Group of Thirty, Washington, D.C.).

Gooch, A. C., and L. B. Klein, 1993, "A Review of International and U.S. Case Law Affecting Swaps and Related Derivative Products," in Schwartz, R. J., and C. W. Smith, eds., *Advanced Strategies in Financial Risk Management* (New York Institute of Finance, New York), 387–438.

Hammond, P. J., 1987, "Uncertainty," in Eatwell, J., M. Milgate, and P. Newman, eds., *The New Palgrave: A Dictionary of Economics* (Macmillan, London).

Hanley, W. J., and J. T. Moser, 1995, "The Policy Implications of the Bankers Trust Settlement," *Derivatives Quarterly, 1*(3), Spring, 24–28.

Hansen, L. P., and S. F. Richard, 1987, "The Role of Conditioning Information in Deducing Testable Restrictions Implied by Dynamic Asset Pricing Models," *Econometrica, 55*(2), May, 587–613.

Hirshleifer, J., 1965, "Investment Decision Under Uncertainty: Choice-Theoretic Approaches," *Quarterly Journal of Economics, 79,* 509–536.

Hirshleifer, J., 1966, "Investment Decision Under Uncertainty: Applications of the State-Preference Approach," *Quarterly Journal of Economics, 80,* 252–277.

Horwitz, D. L., 1995, "The Bankers Trust Settlement with the Federal Reserve Bank: A Precedent for the OTC Derivatives Industry?" *Futures International Law Letter, 14*(11–12), January/February, 1–8.

Klejna, D., and N. L. Walsh, 1995, "Bankers Trust Settlements and Regulatory Policy," Manuscript, CFTC Division of Enforcement, April 6.

Knight, F. H., 1921, *Risk, Uncertainty, and Profit* (Houghton Mifflin Company, New York).

Krueger, A. O., 1974, "The Political Economy of the Rent-Seeking Society," *American Economic Review, 64,* June, 291–303.

Macey, J. R., and G. P. Miller, 1992, *Banking Law and Regulation* (Little, Brown and Company, London).

Machina, M. J., and M. Rothschild, 1987, "Risk," in Eatwell, J., M. Milgate, and P. Newman, eds., *The New Palgrave: A Dictionary of Economics* (Macmillan, London).

Markham, J. W., 1987, *The History of Commodity Futures Trading and its Regulation* (Praeger, New York).

Markham, J. W., and D. J. Gilberg, 1983, "Stock and Commodity Options-Two Regulatory Approaches and Their Conflicts," *Albany Law Review, 47.*

Merton, R. C., 1993, "Operation and Regulation in Financial Intermediation, A Functional Perspective," in Englund, P., ed., *Operation and Regulation of Financial Markets* (The Economic Council, Stockholm).

Merton, R. C., 1995, "A Functional Perspective of Financial Intermediation," *Financial Management, 24*(2), Summer, 23–41.

Miller, M. H., 1986, "Financial Innovation: The Last Twenty Years and the Next," *Journal of Financial and Quantitative Analysis, 21*(4), December, 459–471.

Miller, M. H., 1992, "Financial Innovation: Achievements and Prospects," *Journal of Applied Corporate Finance, 4*(4), Fall, 4–11.

Miller, M. H., 1993a, "Financial Market Regulation in Practice," Speech before the National University of Singapore's Conference on Asian-Pacific Financial Markets, September 9.

Miller, M. H., 1993b, "Positive and Normative Aspects of Regulation in Financial Markets," Speech before the Universidad Torcuato di Tella (Buenos Aires), August 2.

Miller, M. H., 1994a, "Functional Regulation," *Pacific-Basin Finance Journal, 2,* 91–106.

Miller, M. H., 1994b, "Inside Financial Derivatives," *Taxes,* December, 1027–1030.

Miller, M. H., 1994c, "Systemic Risk," Speech presented to the 9th Annual Meeting of the International Swaps and Derivatives Association, Chicago, March.

Miller, M. H., 1995, "The Social Costs of Some Derivatives Disasters," *Pacific-Basin Finance Journal, 3,* forthcoming.

Miller, M. H., and C. L. Culp, 1995, "Rein in the CFTC," *Wall Street Journal,* August 17.

Modigliani, F., and M. H. Miller, 1958, "The Cost of Capital, Corporation Finance, and the Theory of Investment," *American Economic Review, 48,* June, 261–297.

Mueller, D. C., 1989, *Public Choice II* (Cambridge University Press, New York).

Niskanen, W. A., 1971, *Bureaucracy and Representative Government* (Aldine-Atherton, Chicago).

Pashigian, B. P., 1985, "Environmental Regulation: Whose Self-Interests Are Being Protected?" *Economic Inquiry, 23,* October, 551–584.

Peltzman, S., 1980, "The Growth of Government," *Journal of Law and Economics, 23,* October, 209–287.

Pigou, A. C., 1932, *The Economics of Welfare,* 4th ed. (Macmillan & Co., London).

Posner, R. A., 1975, "The Social Costs of Monopoly and Regulation," *Journal of Political Economy, 83*(4), August, 807–827.

Ramsey, F. P., 1931, *The Foundations of Mathematics* (Routledge & Kegan Paul, London).

Rattner, D. L., 1992, *Securities Regulation in a Nutshell* (West, St. Paul).

Russo, T. A., and M. Vinceguerra, 1991, "Financial Innovation and Uncertain Regulation: Selected Issues Regarding New Product Development," *Texas Law Review, 69*(6), May, 1431–1538.

Sandner, J. F., and W. J. Brodsky, 1995, "CFTC Must Protect Individual Investors," *Wall Street Journal,* August 25, A9.

Savage, L., 1954, *The Foundations of Statistics* (John Wiley and Sons, New York).

Schapiro, M. L., 1995, "A Prescription for Disaster," *Wall Street Journal,* August 25, A9.

Scholes, M. S., 1995, "The Future of Futures," in Beaver, W. H., and G. Parker, eds., *Risk Management: Problems & Solutions* (McGraw-Hill, Inc., New York).

Stassen, J. H., and M. D. Young, 1995, *Memorandum Submitted to Senator Richard G. Lugar,* Kirkland & Ellis, August.

Stein, W. L., 1988, "The Exchange-Trading Requirement of the Commodity Exchange Act," *Vanderbilt Law Review, 41,* 473–505.

Stigler, G. J., 1964, "Public Regulation of the Securities market," *Journal of Business, 37*(2), April.

Stigler, G. J., 1971, "The Theory of Economic Regulation," *Bell Journal of Economics and Management Science, 2,* Spring, 1–21.

Stigler, G. J., 1987, *The Theory of Price,* 4th ed. (Macmillan Publishing Company, New York).

Stigler, G. J., ed., 1988, *Chicago Studies in Political Economy* (The University of Chicago Press, Chicago).

Tullock, G., 1967, "The Welfare Costs of Tariffs, Monopolies, and Theft," *Western Economic Journal, 5,* June, 224–232.

ENDNOTES

1. In addition to the criticisms of market failure theory implicit in the work of Stigler (1971), Buchanan and Tullock (1962), and others, Coase (1960) also attacked—many would say *successfully*—the notion that market failures necessitate government intervention.

2. *See* Coase (1960) for an alternative argument.

3. Evidence supporting Stigler's theory can be found in a variety of industries, including, to name just a few, U.S. securities regulation (Stigler, 1964), Japanese securities and futures regulation (Miller, 1994a), and environmental regulation (Pashigian, 1985).

4. Ignore for this example antitrust laws.

5. Through the Glass-Steagall Act, investment banks were long able to keep commercial banks out of underwriting. Limited underwriting powers can now be granted to such banks, however, even without Glass-Steagall reform.

6. For a survey, *see* Mueller (1989).

7. For a corporation, maximizing shareholder wealth is the same as maximizing firm value under most circumstances. For a government agency, the nominal "owners" are taxpayers whose incentives to monitor the agency are too small to have any practical effect. No "market value" rule governs the actions of agency employees, furthermore, as there is no market value of a government agency.

8. The classic model of legislators' economic behavior is presented in Downs (1957).

9. That examiner discretion can sometimes result in such unintended consequences is not a *prima facie* case for selecting a rule-bound regulatory regime in lieu of a discretionary one.

10. *See* Coase (1960) for a critique of this concept.

11. The loss is equal to $\frac{1}{2}(P_m - P_c)(Q_c - Q_m)$.

12. As Posner (1975) explains, the degree to which rent seeking has the additional social waste depends on the degree to which rent-seeking behavior itself leads to external benefits. More overtime for lawyers and lobbyists could itself lead to longer hours and more "flipped hamburgers," thereby reducing the misallocation and replacing it with a simple wealth transfer. The answer is, of course, empirical. *See* Posner (1975) for a more detailed discussion. The author thanks the editors for urging clarification of this point.

13. Hansen and Richard (1987) and Cochrane (1994), for example, explain how the expected utility and state-preference approaches are related. *See also* Ramsey (1931), Arrow (1951), Savage (1954), Anscombe and Aumann (1963), and Machina and Rothschild (1987).

14. The economic distinction between privately negotiated derivatives and exchange-traded derivatives is simply that the latter are negotiated on a financial exchange, whereas the former are not. For all that implies, *see* the discussion in Culp and Overdahl (1995).

15. For a discussion of the multiple statutes of frauds provisions in New York, *see* G30 (1993, Appendix 1, pp. 45–46).

16. For a more detailed discussion, *see* Gooch and Klein (1993, pp. 403–412).

17. Miller (1986,1992) explains that many of the financial innovations of the last three decades trace to unexpected changes in regulation.

18. "Systematic risk," such as β risk in the single-factor Capital Asset Pricing Model, cannot be hedged, even though it can be measured (subject, of course, to measurement error).

19. Under the assumptions of the Modigliani-Miller (1958) capital structure irrelevance propositions, companies should be indifferent to policies that reduce their financial risks. Models of corporate hedging thus traditionally rely on violations of one or more of the M&M assumptions. *See, e.g.,* Fite and Pleiderer (1995) for a summary. Note also that postulating probabilities is sufficient to allow hedging, but it is not always necessary. *See, e.g.,* Hirschleifer (1965,1966).

20. Some types of swap credit enhancements allow for "third-party guarantees" of contractual performance. Most master agreements (i.e., the documentation governing swap transactions), however, stipulate that unexpected legal changes are *force majeur* in the contracts, and even third-party guarantors are often unwilling to guarantee against events considered *force majeur*.

21. Lending further support to the treatment of legal risk and Knightian uncertainty is the fact that many swap dealers *do*, in fact, simply avoid transacting in jurisdictions where enforceability questions

are pronounced. When a group of dealers surveyed by the G30 were asked if any countries caused them concern about enforceability, 53% of the respondents said there were such countries, but only 5% and 2.5% cited the United States and United Kingdom, respectively, as uncertain legal environments for swaps. Not surprisingly, the same survey showed that 53% of the surveyed dealers negotiate their swaps most frequently under English law, and 31% under U.S. law. *See* G30 (1993, Appendix 1, pp. 43–61).

22. Knowledge of the covariance between stocks is often enough to dictate a simple diversification decision. If regulatory uncertainty is treated as leading to potentially "catastrophic" events, such as contract nullifications, however, one can argue that statistical estimates of covariances are unreliable. In other words, estimated covariances may dictate a diversification decision that proves unhelpful when a catastrophic event occurs, because that is when the historical covariance will break down.

23. *N.B.* This is equivalent to saying that the symmetric information assumption underlying the M&M propositions does not hold.

24. Prior to the adoption of national depositor preference legislation, all depositors were treated as general unsecured creditors to the failed institution. After paying the administrative expenses of the receiver, the cash proceeds from the liquidation of the institutions' assets or from its sale were distributed on a *pro rata* basis to all general unsecured creditors, whether depositors or "in-the-money" counterparties to swap contracts. For a more detailed discussion of banking insolvency before and after depositor preference, *see* Culp and Kavanagh (1994, pp. 16–18).

25. *See* Culp and Kavanagh (1994) for a more detailed discussion.

26. That "systemic risk" is never actually defined by regulators and legislators complicates any critical analysis of this particular presumed source of market failure. *See, e.g.,* Miller (1994b) and Black (1995).

27. Regulation is also viewed as necessary because banks sometimes *do* consider the consequences of deposit insurance in the sense that they take greater risks than they otherwise would if only their private capital were at risk.

28. The General Accounting Office has proposed the regulation of currently-unregulated dealers in privately negotiated derivatives on the grounds that those institutions (i) are "systemically important" and (ii) are currently unregulated. (General Accounting Office, 1994.) Although these proposals have gone unheeded, they represent one move to regulate institutions simply because of their involvement in derivatives activity.

29. Numerous problems may arise in defining what is and is not a hedge. For an example, *see* Culp and Miller (1995c).

30. *Chicago Mercantile Exchange v. SEC,* 883 F.2d 537 (7th Cir. 1989), at 543 (hereinafter *CME v. SEC*).

31. Because futures trading was viewed as producing a positive externality, giving exchanges incentives to facilitate such trading was viewed as "socially beneficial."

32. 7 U.S.C. § 6.

33. The SEC's authority included not only the regulations adopted pursuant to the 34 Act, but also those adopted pursuant to the 33 Act that had previously been enforced by the Federal Trade Commission.

34. For a summary of these acts, *see, e.g.,* Rattner (1992).

35. Merton (1995) and Scholes (1995) argue that a benefit of functional regulation is avoiding regulations tailored to a specific institutional structure that may or may not be efficient. Because U.S. securities and commodities regulation seek to protect retail investors, however, these regulations already fail to remain "participant-neutral," thus reducing the benefit for which functional regulation is often praised.

36. Section 20 subsidiaries are affiliates of commercial banks that have been granted limited securities underwriting powers. The name comes from Section 20 of The Banking Act that prohibits state-member banks from being affiliated with an entity that is "engaged principally" in securities underwriting.

37. By contrast, regulatory competition is often deemed desirable for reducing institutional-institutional overlaps. When only institutional regulators are involved, regulated firms can alter their regulation by changing the type of firm they are. A national bank, for example, can renounce its federal charter and apply for a state charter. When functional *and* institutional regulation is involved, however, competition does not so much come into play. To avoid the functional regulation, the institution

would have to stop using the regulated product, but that might simply mean switching to *another* functional regulator and thus perpetuating the problem.

38. *See* 7 U.S.C. § 2. This "exclusivity clause" only applies to products. As the earlier example of a bank-affiliated FCM shows, an institution *using* futures may be regulated by a primary regulator other than the CFTC.

39. *See* CEA § 2(a)(1)(A)(i).

40. *See* Securities Exchange Commission-Commodity Futures Trading Commission Jurisdictional Correspondence, *compiled at* [1975–1977 Transfer Binder] COMMODITY FUTURES LAW REPORTER (CCH) ¶ 20204 (N.D. Ill. 1975), at 20829.

41. *Hearings on* H.R. 10285 *Before the House Subcommittee on Conservation and Credit of the House Committee on Agriculture,* 95th Cong., 2d Sess. (1978) (hereinafter *1978 Hearings*).

42. *1978 Hearings,* pp. 182–219. Joseph Sullivan, then-president of the CBOE, argued that "because the SEC has historically regulated securities and securities markets in general, it is appropriate and necessary that the SEC's jurisdiction extend to futures contracts and options with respect to securities." *Id.* at 216. *See generally* Markham and Gilberg (1983).

43. Prior to enactment of the legislation, the Treasury Department had also submitted to Congress that it had some authority over futures contracts on government securities. In addition, the General Accounting Office supported the SEC's position. As such, the CFTC was also urged to "maintain communications" with the Treasury Department and the Federal Reserve Board. *See* Pub. L. No. 95-405, 92 Stat. 865, *H.R. Rep. No. 1181,* 95th Cong., 2d Sess. 13 (1978), and *H.R. Conf. Rep. No. 1628,* 95th Cong., 2d Sess. 17 (1978). For a more general discussion of jurisdictional issues concerning the Treasury Department, *see* Stassen and Young (1995).

44. *Board of Trade of the City of Chicago v. SEC,* 677 F.2d 1137 (7th Cir.), *vacated* 459 U.S. 1026 (1982).

45. Section 2(a) of the CEA gives the CFTC jurisdiction over agreements including "any transaction which is of the character of, or is commonly known to the trade as, an 'option' . . . involving contracts of sale of a commodity for future delivery. . ."

46. *GNMA Options,* pp. 1152-53.

47. *GNMA Options,* p. 1142 n.8.

48. 7 U.S.C. § 2.

49. *CME v. SEC,* at 545.

50. Other sections of the U.S. Code are also relevant but are not discussed. For a summary of banking regulations, *see* Macey and Miller (1992), Capatides (1993), and CCH Business Law Editors (1994a,b,c,d).

51. *See* Culp and Kavanagh (1994) for a more complete discussion.

52. Notably, the CFTC does *not* have the power to exempt products from the section of the CEA that codified the Shad-Johnson Accord.

53. Because the CFTC cannot exempt products that fall under Shad-Johnson, the CFTC cannot exempt swaps on securities from the CEA because such instruments do not clearly fall under the CEA.

54. *S. Rep. No. 1131,* 93d Cong., 2d Sess. (1974), at 49–50.

55. *See, e.g., Salomon Forex, Inc. v. Tauber,* 8 F.3d 966 (4th Cir. 1993) (hereinafter *"Salamon Forex"*), and *CFTC v. William C. Dunn and Delta Options,* 2 COMM. FUT. L. REP. ¶ 26,429 (2d Cir. June 23, 1995).

56. *Salomon Forex,* at 978.

57. *See Tauber v. Salomon Forex, Inc.,* 795 F. Supp. 768 (E.D. Va. 1992), at 775 n.15, *aff'd Salomon Forex.*

58. *CFTC v. Frankwell Bullion,* No. C-94-2166 DLJ, 1995 LEXIS 12716 (N. D. Cal. August 14, 1995), at *10.

59. *Frankwell Bullion,* at *12.

60. *Frankwell Bullion,* at *12-*13.

61. "Written Agreement By and Among Bankers Trust New York Corporation and Bankers Trust Company and BT Securities Corporation and Federal Reserve Bank of New York," Federal Reserve System Docket Nos. 94-082-WA/RB-HC, 94-082-WA/RB-SM, 94-092-WA/RB-HCS (December 5, 1994) (hereafter "FRBNY Written Agreement").

62. "Complaint Pursuant to Sections 6(c) and 6(d) of the Commodity Exchange Act and Opinion and Order Accepting Offer of Settlement, Making Findings and Imposing Remedial Sanctions," *In re BT Securities Corp.,* CFTC Docket 95-3 (December 22, 1994) (hereinafter "CFTC Complaint and Order").

63. "Order Instituting Proceedings Pursuant to Section 8A of the Securities Act of 1933 and Sections 15(b) and 21C of the Securities Exchange Act of 1934, and Findings and Order Imposing Remedial Sanctions" (December 22, 1994) (hereinafter "SEC Complaint and Order").

64. CFTC Complaint and Order, p. 8, ¶¶ 28-29.

65. Under *GNMA Options,* if swaps on securities *are* found to be futures, they are regulated by the CFTC under the CEA *whether or not* they are also securities.

66. "Order Instituting Proceedings Pursuant to Sections 6(c) and 8a of the Commodity Exchange Act and Findings and Order Imposing Remedial Sanctions," *In re MGRM and MGFI,* CFTC Docket 95-14 (July 27, 1995) (hereinafter "MG Settlement").

67. For a general discussion of MGRM's program, *see* Culp and Miller (1994,1995a,b,c,d).

68. MG Settlement, p. 4.

69. Merton Miller deserves credit for using this phrase to describe the MGRM/CFTC settlement.

70. [1990–1992 Transfer Binder] COMM. FUT. L. REP. (CCH) ¶ 24,925 (Sept. 25, 1990).

71. 738 F. Supp. 1472 (S.D.N.Y. 1990).

72. *Transnor* predated the Swaps Exemption.

73. Especially in discussions of "swaps versus futures," that the products are more often than not *complementary* is extremely important to keep in mind. Policies are thus often supported by both groups or opposed by both groups for obvious reasons. But this is not *always* true.

74. Sandner and Brodsky (1995) actually were concerned in their letter about the Treasury Amendment. Emphasizing retail investors in that connection, however, subjects their letter to same criticism leveled against the CFTC in *Frankwell Bullion.*

75. Examiner capture is almost certainly less problematic when examiners are rotated across institutions or are not forced to work on-site all the time.

PART SIX

Transparency and Disclosure

16

Derivatives Address

ALAN GREENSPAN

I n my remarks I shall attempt to set the stage for the sessions that follow. I shall begin by clarifying the characteristics of OTC derivatives that determine their transparency and liquidity and that tend to make a significant portion of these instruments opaque and illiquid. Then I shall identify some of the challenges that are created by the use of opaque and illiquid financial instruments. I shall conclude by offering some suggestions on how to meet them.

Before beginning I want to emphasize that by discussing these difficulties and challenges I do not mean to call into question the benefits of OTC derivatives or the utility of the risk management techniques that derivatives dealers have developed. I would note that bank loans pose essentially the same difficulties. Like OTC derivatives, bank loans are customized, privately negotiated agreements that, despite increases in availability of price information and in trading activity, still quite often lack transparency and liquidity. This unquestionably makes the risks of many bank loans rather difficult to quantify and to manage. Yet no one seriously questions the public benefits of bank loans, and most would agree that efforts to apply modern risk management techniques to bank loans should be supported and encouraged. Indeed, it is my hope and expectation that by addressing the challenges posed by the lack of transparency and liquidity of the more customized OTC derivatives, the way will be paved for significant and parallel advances in the management of the risks of bank loans and the many other relatively opaque and illiquid instruments.

The intermediation and unbundling of credit risks and market risks are critical functions of a financial system. These functions can be achieved only partially through standardized instruments and organized exchanges. Hence, more opaque and illiquid financial instruments serve an invaluable function in our economy. The use of such instruments entails higher risks which, of necessity, are reflected in higher intermediation costs. As advances in risk management are achieved, however, these risks and related costs can be expected to decline.

TRANSPARENCY AND LIQUIDITY OF OTC DERIVATIVES AND OTHER FINANCIAL INSTRUMENTS

At the outset I should clarify what I mean by transparency and liquidity. By the transparency of a financial instrument I mean the degree of certainty with which one can

---

This article is adapted from a speech by Alan Greenspan, delivered at the Federal Reserve Bank of Atlanta's Financial Markets Conference, February 1996. Reprinted with permission.

determine its "fair value," which the Financial Accounting Standards Board (FASB) defines as "the amount at which the instrument could be exchanged in a current transaction between willing parties, other than in a forced or liquidation sale." Thus, fair values are a matter of conjecture rather than fact; they cannot be known, but must be estimated. FASB has noted that quoted market prices, when available, are the best indicators of fair values. As I shall note later, however, even quoted market prices are not always reliable indicators of the values at which transactions could be executed. Moreover, quoted market prices simply are not available for many financial instruments, despite a rapid expansion of sources of price information, such as broker screens. When quoted market prices are unavailable, fair values typically are estimated on the basis of quoted market prices for related instruments. Such estimates require assumptions about relationships between fair values of different instruments. Inaccurate or outdated assumptions inevitably heighten uncertainty about potential transactions prices.

By the liquidity of a financial instrument, I mean the percentage of its fair value that could be realized in a forced or liquidation sale. A perfectly liquid financial instrument is one whose fair value could, if necessary, be realized instantaneously. Few financial instruments, however, are perfectly liquid. For most instruments, time is required to search out a counterparty who is willing to transact at the fair value of the instrument. In general, the less time that is available to complete the transaction, the smaller is the percentage of fair value that can be realized. Also, the percentage of fair value that can be realized tends to decrease with the size of the transaction.

By these definitions, many OTC derivatives are neither highly transparent nor highly liquid. The defining characteristic of OTC derivatives is the customization of terms through private negotiations between counterparties. To be sure, broker screens provide market quotations for the more standardized or "plain vanilla" OTC derivatives, and these account for a large portion of outstanding contracts. Even for plain vanilla derivatives, however, the estimation of fair values generally involves adjustments to market quotations to reflect operating, hedging, and other potential costs. For more customized OTC derivatives, the estimation of fair values often involves use of a mathematical model that relates fair values of the customized instruments to available market quotations for more standardized products. For example, the fair values of OTC options often are estimated using pricing models that utilize market quotations for the underlying asset and implied price volatilities from exchange-traded or plain vanilla OTC options as inputs.

Especially for more complex options, the choice of a pricing model and of certain inputs to the model includes important elements of art as well as science. Assumptions must be made, for example, about the shape of the sampling distributions of prices and price volatilities of the underlying assets. The growing availability of independent valuation services allows users of complex instruments to assess whether or not their price estimates are consistent with other estimates. But for many instruments the range of estimates can be quite wide. Moreover, estimates are estimates. Without timely transactions prices for very similar instruments, the accuracy of the estimates remains questionable.

In principle, the value of an OTC derivative can be promptly realized either by terminating the contract or by transferring it to another counterparty. In practice, however, either procedure is likely to be time-consuming and may require the counterparty seeking to liquidate the contract to accept something less than the fair value. In either case, the prior consent of the original counterparty usually must be obtained. Counterparties typically require prior consent for termination because termination would require them to bear the costs of replacing the terminated contract with a new contract. In general, the more customized the contract, the greater will be the cost of replacement, for which the counterparty will expect compensation. Prior consent typically is also required for a transfer, so as to protect the other counterparty against the possibility of a transfer to a less creditworthy counterparty. Although accommodating a transfer request generally would be less costly than the cost of accommodating a termination request, the counterparty may nonetheless seek compensation.

This discussion suggests that the opaqueness and illiquidity of many OTC derivatives stems from both the customization of contract terms and differences in creditworthiness across counterparties. Users of the more customized OTC derivatives, in particular, are forced to accept a trade-off between the benefits of individually tailored contract terms and credit relationships and the costs of opaqueness and illiquidity. This trade-off can perhaps be seen more clearly by comparing the benefits and costs of exchange-traded derivatives and OTC derivatives.

Exchange-traded derivatives are highly transparent and liquid, but these advantages are not achieved costlessly. The terms of contracts traded on exchanges are very standardized. In addition, credit risk is standardized by substitution of the exchange's clearing house as the central counterparty to every trade. The standardization of contract terms limits the precision with which users can manage their risk exposures. The standardization of credit risk requires the clearing house to impose costly margin requirements that are not yet routinely imposed in OTC transactions. Users of highly customized OTC derivatives evidently perceive the benefits of tailoring contract terms and counterparty credit relationships as exceeding the costs associated with less transparency and liquidity. Otherwise, they would choose more standardized contracts, either of the plain vanilla OTC or exchange-traded variety.

Over time, the terms of this trade-off between the benefits of customization of contract terms and credit relationships and the costs of opaqueness and illiquidity are likely to improve. In recent years, futures and options exchanges have successfully introduced so-called "flex" products that allow for greater tailoring of terms than traditional exchange offerings. At the same time, the use of bilateral margining agreements for OTC derivatives has been spreading. Existing proposals to create facilities for the centralized administration of such bilateral margining agreements may prove to be the first step toward the creation of clearing houses for OTC derivatives. In general, I expect that we shall see further convergence between the characteristics of OTC and exchange-traded derivatives. But I believe that it would be a mistake for policymakers to attempt to force this process. Economic forces will ensure that market participants will seek to implement exchange or clearing house arrangements if they can enhance liquidity and transparency while maintaining most of the benefits of customized contracts.

IMPLICATIONS FOR RISK MANAGEMENT

The development of OTC derivatives unquestionably has stimulated very significant improvements in financial risk management practices. In particular, concerns about the risks associated with use of OTC derivatives prompted the Group of Thirty (G-30) to sponsor development and publication in July 1993 of a set of recommended risk management practices that have been extremely effective in fostering improvements. Critical elements of the G-30 risk management framework are accurate assessments of the fair values of financial instruments and portfolios and the use of risk measures that presume significant portfolio liquidity. The authors of the G-30 study recognized that a series of difficulties arise in applying this framework to financial instruments that are relatively opaque and illiquid, including the more customized OTC derivatives. But the study's discussion of practices and procedures necessary to address these difficulties was rather vague. Our banking supervisors report that at the most sophisticated U.S. banks the relevant practices have been rapidly evolving but remain diverse. In part, the diversity reflects differences in risk profiles and business strategies, but varying levels of refinement also are apparent.

Opaqueness and illiquidity affect each of the critical elements of risk management—valuation, risk measurement, and risk control. The critical first step in risk management is determining the current market value of the portfolio. Earlier I noted that market quotations simply are not available for many financial instruments. I should emphasize that these include not only the more customized OTC derivatives but also thinly traded securities, as many investors in mortgage-backed securities discovered in early 1994. Values of these instruments must be estimated on the basis of market quotations for other, more standardized instruments. This requires use of mathematical or economic models that relate the values of the customized instrument to the values of more standardized instruments.

Sophisticated risk managers recognize the uncertainty and the potential for error in valuation methods for opaque instruments and seek to compensate for various sources of error by creating reserves. Among the reserves that institutions often create are reserves for additional hedging costs, for uncertainty about the accuracy of models, especially in valuing new or especially complex products, and, quite explicitly, for illiquidity. The values of these reserves can be quite significant, especially in the aggregate. In addition, some institutions establish a credit risk reserve that is intended to incorporate credit quality into fair values. While these reserving practices can be described within a broad common framework, there appears to be no common understanding within the industry of the circumstances in which many of these reserves should be created or on their appropriate size.

Risk measurement is the assessment of potential future changes in portfolio values. Opaqueness affects the measurement of both market risk and credit risk. Consistent with the recommendations of the G-30, sophisticated managers typically measure market risk by value-at-risk (VaR), often defined as the amount of losses over one day that would be expected to occur only one day out of a hundred. In practice, VaR measures typically assume that the values of all instruments in a portfolio are determined by a common set of underlying risk factors—interest rates, exchange rates, commodity prices, and stock indexes—most of which are readily hedgeable. But the sensitivity of customized instruments to these factors sometimes is difficult to assess. Furthermore, the values of such instruments may be influenced importantly by risk factors other than common hedgeable factors recognized in VaR measures. One can hope that these residual risks are well diversified, but, absent a means of measuring them, this may be nothing more than wishful thinking. Unfortunately, the measurement of these risks requires accurate measures of fair values which, by definition, are problematic in the case of opaque instruments.

The difficulties in valuing some financial instruments also make accurate measurement of credit risk quite difficult. In the case of OTC derivatives, much progress has been made in modeling potential future claims on counterparties, which often are termed potential future credit exposures. However, as is the case for any financial instrument, the credit risk of an OTC derivative depends on the creditworthiness of the counterparty. If the holder seeks to transfer an OTC derivative, the amount that a transferee will be willing to pay for the contract will depend on market discount rates then applying to claims on the counterparty. Likewise, the amount that the counterparty will be willing to pay in a negotiated termination will depend on the cost at which the counterparty could replace the terminated contract, which will depend on these same future discount rates. The development of techniques for estimating potential future discount rates remains at the frontier of risk measurement. Even in the best of circumstances—in which the counterparty has issued actively traded corporate bonds—techniques extracting estimates of the relevant discount factors remain at an early stage of development.

Assessments of the liquidity of financial instruments are critical to efforts to control risks. VaR measurements often are translated into position limits for traders, which are a critical element of internal risk controls. When VaR is measured using a one-day horizon, it is implicitly assumed that risk exposures in the portfolio can, if necessary, be offset within a day. This assumption does not require that all of the financial instruments in the portfolio can be liquidated within a day. Rather, it merely assumes that the hedgeable risk exposures that are the focus of VaR measures can be offset that quickly, presumably through use of highly liquid instruments such as exchange-traded derivatives. Still, even the most liquid markets may experience periods of illiquidity. As noted in the title of today's first session, one needs to consider the consequences if everyone can't get into the lifeboat at the same time. Furthermore, as I have suggested, the unhedgeable instrument-specific risks of illiquid instruments cannot be ignored. Losses stemming from an inability to offset or close out portfolios promptly are among the risks that sophisticated risk managers seek to assess through so-called stress tests. However, stress testing is another area in which our bank supervisors observe considerable diversity of practice. Consensus has not yet emerged on how to identify scenarios that pose the greatest risk of loss or, as important, on appropriate responses to test results. As I have noted, some banks establish reserves to cover the potential costs of illiquidity. Others supplement VaR-based risk limits with instrument-specific position limits. In principle, stress tests could be used to evaluate the size of such reserves and limits.

IMPLICATIONS FOR PUBLIC DISCLOSURE

The opaqueness and illiquidity of customized OTC derivatives and other financial instruments create uncertainty about the financial position and performance—the net worth, earnings, and risk profile—of users of such instruments. Concerns about such uncertainty often are termed concerns about the transparency of financial statements, a concept that is broader than the concept of transparency I have been using thus far. These concerns have prompted issuance in recent years of a series of new accounting standards and proposals by the FASB and the Securities and Exchange Commission. The most recent changes have required disclosure of accounting policies for derivatives, of the purposes (trading or hedging) for which derivatives are used, and of fair values of derivatives, either carried on the balance sheet or in supplemental schedules. FASB has encouraged disclosures of quantitative information on market risk, and the SEC recently has proposed to require such disclosures.

I have discussed the difficulties involved in determining fair values for the most customized OTC derivatives and the diversity of valuation practices actually employed. An implication of this discussion is that market participants could better assess the financial position of users if more information were disclosed on valuation policies, including the size of the various reserves, if material, and how those reserves are determined. Fuller disclosure would reduce not only uncertainty but also the danger that reserves could be manipulated to reduce the volatility of reported earnings.

My discussion of risk measurement issues suggests that disclosure of quantitative measures of market risk, such as value-at-risk, is enlightening only when accompanied by a thorough discussion of how the risk measures were calculated and how they related to actual performance. Moreover, no single quantitative measure can summarize all aspects of such a complex concept as market risk. These conclusions are fully consistent with an analysis of appropriate public disclosures of market and credit risks (the Fisher Report) that was released in September 1994 by the Euro-currency Standing Committee of the Group of Ten central banks.

IMPLICATIONS FOR COUNTERPARTY RELATIONSHIPS

The opaqueness and illiquidity of some OTC derivatives also have contributed to tensions between counterparties, tensions that in some instances have produced litigation or threats of litigation. As I noted earlier, even when a market quotation is available, there may be uncertainty and confusion about what the quotation is intended to convey and how it should be interpreted. In particular, there may be confusion about whether a quotation represents an estimate of the fair market value of an instrument or a firm offer to transact in the instrument at the quoted price.

By definition, transaction prices of illiquid instruments can be different, possibly significantly different from fair market values. A fair market value is an estimate of the price at which a transaction might be executed with a willing counterparty. As I have emphasized, estimation errors are to be expected, especially for more customized, illiquid contracts. Moreover, a price concession may be necessary to produce a willing counterparty. Consequently, the price at which a transaction can be executed cannot be inferred from estimates of fair market value.

Transactions prices can be determined only by contacting potential counterparties and soliciting offers to transact. Moreover, when soliciting quotations it is essential that it be made clear to potential counterparties that a transactions price, rather than a fair market value estimate or a nonbinding "indicative" price quotation is desired. Likewise, counterparties that receive requests for quotations should determine clearly what type of quotation is desired before responding.

ADDRESSING THE CHALLENGES POSED BY OPAQUENESS AND ILLIQUIDITY

Before concluding, I would like to offer a few brief suggestions for addressing the challenges I have identified. On the risk management front, there should be more public discussion of valuation difficulties and best practices for addressing those difficulties. This would appear to be an area in which an industry initiative by derivatives dealers or by accounting or consulting firms would be quite useful. Regarding public disclosure, I remain convinced of the usefulness of the central recommendation of the aforementioned Fisher Report, which called for financial intermediaries to move in the direction of disclosing to the public the quantitative measures of market risk and credit risk that the firm's management relies upon. A November 1995 review of the Basle Supervisors Committee and the Technical Committee of IOSCO found that internationally active banks and securities firms had made progress in implementing the Fisher Report's recommendations, but the Report also concluded that further efforts were needed by intermediaries in many G-10 countries. Finally, I believe the problems that opaqueness can create for counterparty relationships can best be addressed by heightening awareness of potential ambiguities associated with market quotations and encouraging clarity in communications between counterparties. The initiative on valuation that I have suggested would clearly contribute to an understanding of the differences between fair value estimates and transactions prices.

CONCLUSION

In my remarks I have tried to identify the challenges posed by the opaqueness and illiquidity of some OTC derivatives and of many other financial instruments as well. I have done so on the assumption that the long debate on derivatives has reached a stage of maturity at which we can openly discuss difficulties and challenges without running the risk of a legislative or regulatory overreaction. In any event, I am confident that, in the long run, frank discussions most effectively hedge against that risk.

17

Position Transparency—What Do We Need to Know and When Do We Need to Know It?

DOUGLAS E. HARRIS

T he information age continues to change the nature and scope of transactions such that financial opportunities are available almost anywhere on the globe, at any time, and in ways that can be tailored and customized to meet specific funding or investment objectives. The speed with which technology can make such transactions possible also continues to increase at a rapid pace. From this perspective, one may question whether it is possible to keep up with an institution's changing financial risk profile, or for that matter, whether anyone can fully understand the nature of an institution's risks. The question—what do we need to know and when do we need to know it?—has seldom been more important. But the question itself is instructive, so before we attempt to answer the question, it may be helpful to consider the question more carefully.

WHO, WHY, AND WHAT

It is first necessary to identify *who* needs to know, *why* they need to know, in order to assess, *what* they need to know. For example, the nature and detail of information needed by a trader may not be the same as information needed by an institution's senior managers or the board, or an institution's counterparties, or regulators, or the investing public.

Much of the recent attention has centered on a need for *more information* and for information to be made available on a *more frequent basis*. But this may lead to information overload. Specifically, there can be too much information to make sense of it all.

To make good policy, we must focus on why information is needed. In most cases, that can be answered by considering whether *appropriate* parties have *sufficient* information to identify, measure, monitor, and control the risk—the risk which

This article is adapted from a speech by Douglas Harris, delivered at the Federal Reserve Bank of Atlanta's Financial Markets Conference, February 1996. Reprinted with permission.

can result from their decisions. Or do they have sufficient information to assure themselves that those responsible for controlling risk are appropriately doing so. Thus, a trader may require frequent access to detailed information about a narrow component of a financial market or markets. Alternatively, a senior manager may require less detail, but should receive information at a similar frequency and for a wider variety of financial markets. Financial regulators may also be interested in a more aggregated view of an institution's health. Analysts and the investing public are generally interested in institution-wide information, but may also have very specific information requirements. Collection and presentation of information, therefore, is critical, but it is by no means an exact science.

The difficulty lies in determining the appropriate level of information aggregation. Some have even suggested that institutions should simply publicly release raw data and allow the users of that information to process it as they see fit. This approach, however, may fail to protect proprietary information and may not be cost effective for the information users who may find it difficult to sift through the volume of information in order to answer specific questions. Moreover, there are benefits to processing of data prior to its release. Information can be presented in a consistent manner and there can be come degree of assurance about the integrity of that information.

As bank supervisors, we are primarily concerned with how information is generated and used within a bank and whether we have sufficient information to ensure banks' safety and soundness.

Example: OCC's Data Filters

The Office of the Comptroller of the Currency (OCC) collects its supervisory information through the examination process, which contains nonpublic information, and through quarterly Call Reports filed by banks, which primarily contain publicly available information.

Call Reports allow us to receive a consistent and regular picture of a bank's condition and income. However, as market circumstances change, Call Report information often does not provide sufficient detail to allow specific assessments of a bank's safety and soundness. While on-site examinations allow us to obtain more detailed information, such information is generally gathered on a less-frequent basis than Call Report information.

To bridge that gap, the OCC combines Call Report information with macroeconomic and regional economic data. These complementary information sources provide insights about banks' conditions that might not otherwise be apparent through regular reviews of Call Reports. For example, following the thrift crisis, regulators and market participants alike began to focus more attention on interest rate risk. However, the Call Report was primarily designed to convey a bank's financial health according to credit risk. It is generally not amenable to making inferences about price and interest rate risk. Quite obviously it is not cost effective for the OCC to be inside every bank on a continuous basis. The OCC has, therefore, been using "Data Filters" over the last several quarters to identify banks that *might* have material exposures to interest rate risk.

The Data Filters combine economic assumptions and current information about the financial environment together with selected Call Report items to provide an indicator which is suggestive of the presence of interest rate risk. The OCC then uses the examination process to determine whether high levels of interest rate risk are, in fact, present at the particular institutions and, if so, whether it is first, known by the institution, and second, appropriately managed. This form of off-site monitoring has allowed the OCC to utilize information in more cost-effective manners, as well as to deploy examination resources more efficiently.

In most cases, follow-up reviews of the banks that have been identified by these Data Filters have shown that examiners were already aware of problems and that bank management had developed or put into place a strategy for corrective action. In some cases, follow-up reviews revealed additional information that indicated that problems did not exist—in other words, the filters had produced "false positives." However, in a few cases, the filters identified banks which had not yet identified their potential problems or had not yet developed strategies to correct the problems. In those instances, examiners were able to work with the banks to pursue corrective measures.

Like the OCC, many institutions are also looking at the efficiency of their utilization of information in decision-making processes.

INFORMATION FLOW AND INFORMATION PROCESSING

When considering information needs, two phenomena appear to be occurring at the same time. First, information in financial markets, especially in the area of financial derivatives transactions and products, is becoming *more specialized* as a result of newer and more complex instruments. These instruments often require a high level of expertise to understand and/or proprietary models to price. This can have the unfortunate effect of, at times, creating a reliance on a relatively small number of individuals within an institution who establish standards to determine what information is appropriate or relevant. As a risk management matter, this can create a form of "intellectual risk" for an institution—a risk which should be identified and addressed by senior managers. Information specialization issues are usually more pronounced during turning points in market trends or times of market stress.

Second, information is being *organized and aggregated in new and different forms.* Market participants are moving away from a product-oriented view of the financial world and have begun to view their business in terms of specific types of risk. This raises new questions regarding whether "apples are being combined with apples" when risks are aggregated at successively higher levels within institutions. For example, market risks are usually reduced to a common denominator—generally, the amount of loss associated with a prespecified likelihood of occurrence over a prespecified time period. Likewise, credit risks are reduced to loan equivalents or some other common denominator. In both of these efforts, "risk" is defined in terms of earnings and/or capital exposures. However, market risks and credit risks are generally not consistent with each other.

These problems can be further complicated when the separateness between the risk categories becomes blurred. For example, a change in an institution's measured market risk might also result in a change in that institution's measured counterparty credit risk exposure. This can occur when cash flows between the institution and its counterparty are indexed to the affected market factors. Complicating matters still further, the market change may have also broadly affected the business conditions of the counterparty and thereby changed the default likelihood of the counterparty. If the original institution had focused only on changes in counterparty credit *exposure,* and not the potential for changes in default probability, it would not have captured changes to credit risk.

Information organization and aggregation issues are receiving a great deal of attention as institutions attempt to identify and measure such interconnection risks—including both cross-price and cross-risk correlations—to develop enterprise-based measures of risk.

It is useful to note that the evaluation of risk, as it generally pertains to an institution's earnings and capital stability, involves determining the effects of tail events—and strange things can happen in the tails. Markets can become less liquid or traditional counterparties may change their behaviors rapidly. And, since by definition tail events are rare, market participants and others have had few opportunities to learn about them.

INFORMATION COSTS

The popular view is that more information is needed by everyone or that more information is better. Granted, much of what I have said would support such a view. But it is important to note that information is generally costly to collect, analyze, and present in an understandable manner. The more an institution's proprietary information is made freely available, the less incentive there is for other institutions to develop new products or trading strategies. This is particularly relevant in a competitive market place where institutions might view information about trading positions and strategies as revealing the fruits of a competitor's research. In the aggregate, this might lead to a decrease in innovation and an increase in the extent to which institutions might piggy-back off of one anothers' positions. Such herding among institutions may ultimately lead to undesirable consequences.

It is, nevertheless, important for regulators to find an appropriate balance between proprietary information and information that is necessary so that other interested parties, including financial supervisors and the public, have sufficient information to make informed decisions regarding the issues that they face.

In addressing the needs of outside parties for meaningful and timely information, we must also remain sensitive to the additional costs that institutions would likely face if new reporting and disclosure requirements require significant systems changes.

RISK MEASUREMENT SYSTEMS

Banks use a number of complementary methods to identify, measure, monitor, and control risk. Sophisticated risk measurement and reporting systems have been implemented, or are currently being developed, at the major trading banks. For example, in order to measure market risk, systems have been designed that project probable changes in market factors over a predefined holding period in order to determine the likelihood of specific reductions in the value of a bank's positions (i.e., value-at-risk), or the likelihood of specific reductions in the bank's future revenues (i.e., earnings-at-risk). (Note: In a mark-to-market accounting environment, value-at-risk and earnings-at-risk are essentially equivalent measures.) Similarly, measurement systems have been designed to project the potential credit exposure over the term of a transaction.

While the methods used by risk measurement systems are similar, banks tend to employ slightly different market and mathematical assumptions in their measurements based on their experience, their portfolio construction, and theoretical perspectives. Such differences typically reflect differences in the level of technical sophistication among institutions and/or genuine differences of opinion about the underlying nature of financial markets. The existence of these differences, however, tends to become evident only when market factors experience sudden and extreme changes—in other words, when a tail event occurs. This is because it is easy to disagree about something that we know so little about. That is, of course, until it occurs. It is important, therefore, that banks select, monitor, and adjust their assumptions in order to maintain valid systems. Among the most common assumptions are the length of the historical time horizon for calibrating measurement parameters, the degree and extent of correlation among various market factors, and the length position liquidation periods. These assumptions are validated at inception and verified thereafter by independent parties. An additional layer of control is added through bank management's comparison of actual performance versus model projections.

For many banks with small or matched-book trading operations, the cost of sophisticated systems that quantify value-at-risk on a consistent basis across the organization currently may outweigh the benefits to be achieved. That may change as vendor value-at-risk systems are developed. As a result, most end-user banks, and some major banks, measure exposure by setting and monitoring compliance against notional or par limits. These can be used to control the type of instrument, maturity, or market that may be traded. Also, most banks do not currently have true "real-time" information systems for their global trading networks that can be used to measure intraday exposures. However, the need to establish real-time measures is largely based on the nature of the bank's activities, historical experience, and expectations regarding the future volatility in a certain position size, tenor, or market.

Virtually all banks supplement these risk measurement and control mechanisms with both risk limits and loss control limits and/or management action triggers. A loss control limit requires specific management action if a defined level of loss is approached or breached. Exceptions may require that a position be closed or that an additional level of management be contacted for approval of the exposure. In many cases, limits are established to foster communication rather than to limit management's ability to maintain a position. At this point, decisions are made regarding the desirability of maintaining or reducing the position. As a consequence, risk measures that are based upon the effects of statistically simulated market changes on a static portfolio may not properly capture the extent to which management may take action to mitigate potential losses before they materialize.

The precision and accuracy of risk measurement methods, and the timeliness of reports, will vary according to the types, volumes, and the riskiness of the activities undertaken. For example, most of the larger trading banks currently utilize "near real-time" position and scenario information covering specific traders, products, and geographic locations. In contrast, managers at smaller banks with considerably less turnover and less complex transactions may successfully measure and monitor positions by physically reviewing traders' written ledgers and daily trade summaries generated by the operations area.

The level of detail required for effective communication of risk levels, profitability results, and related trends will increase as the business focus moves from senior management to the specific line areas. For example, management directly responsible for a trading area should receive detailed reports with adequate information to assess risk, return, and the ability to meet stated business objectives. In contrast, information provided to senior management and the board of directors at large trading banks will likely illustrate consolidated exposures, trends, compliance with policies and risk limits, and performance compared to risk assumed.

A critical aspect of risk measurement and reporting is the implementation of systems that provide for information independent of trading personnel. The valuation of positions, as well as formal reports comparing positions relative to policy limits, should be constructed and validated by areas that are not associated with trading decisions. This speaks to the need to ensure that the incentives of the people who generate the data are consistent with a desire to see the accurate reporting of that information. This is a fundamental internal control practice that should not be compromised.

In sum, risks are quantified in a variety of ways. Risks are aggregated at many different levels and these measures are subjective to the extent that they are ultimately based upon personal judgment. Information must also be gathered and processed with diligence to ensure its integrity. In short, risk measurement is as much an art as it is a science.

CONCLUSION

Ultimately, the informational issues associated with the question, "What do we need to know and when do we need to know it?", speak as much to the management of information and how it is used as to the specific information items themselves. It is currently popular to call for more information. However, more does not always mean better. Regulators have always had access to bank-specific information, but have worked to use information more creatively and to balance their information needs against the costs and burdens to the institutions providing such information.

Nevertheless, surveys continue to show that the principles of financial disclosure are improving as institutions are finding more effective means of providing information while protecting proprietary interests. Regulators, too, are disseminating more information specifically related to current areas of public interest (e.g., the quarterly derivatives data releases from the OCC). Institutions should be encouraged to go beyond regulatory filing requirements and to find more innovative ways of disclosing information and bank management should take it upon themselves to provide high quality information to help demystify current discussions about trading activities and derivatives. Such information should be both quantitative and qualitative.

The public outcry for more information has been framed by debacles where one party had superior information. However, many of those situations involved fraud, which is related to, but different than concerns about risks and risk management. It is important to maintain perspective when answering the who, the why, and the what, of the information question.

18

Hedge Accounting: An Exploratory Study of the Underlying Issues

Harold Bierman, Jr.

Hedge accounting is the process of linking the accounting for the hedge security and the hedged item so that the gains and losses of the two hedge components are reported in the same period. The basic accounting issues associated with hedging are the valuations of the hedging instrument and the hedged item and the determination of when changes in the value of the hedging instrument and the hedged item should affect income.[1] The primary issue is whether the accounting for the hedging instrument should be affected because there is a special economic relationship between two items involved in the hedge. The income of a period is directly affected by the decision to allow or not to allow hedge accounting for a specific situation. The issues as to which transactions, if any, qualify as hedges and also qualify for hedge accounting are important. If hedge accounting is accepted in principle, then having determined the existence of a hedge transaction, the next step is to determine the necessary conditions for a hedging relationship to affect the accounting for the hedge instrument or the hedged item. If the necessary conditions are met, how should the items involved be measured in the balance sheet and how should the income statement be affected by changes in the values of the items involved in the hedging? The managerial decision to hedge creates accounting issues. Normal accounting practice, as distinguished from hedge accounting, can result in gains or losses being reported in different accounting periods when there are zero net economic gains or losses because of the hedge (the gain or loss on the hedge is exactly balanced by a loss or gain on the hedged item). But attempts to eliminate this timing problem create their own measurement problems.

Four major issues of accounting for hedges are as follows:

1. Should the hedging process receive special accounting treatment?
2. How is hedge accounting to be defined and to be implemented?
3. Under what conditions should the existence of a hedge lead to the use of hedge accounting?
4. Can anticipated transactions qualify for hedge accounting?

DISCUSSION OF THE FOUR ISSUES

The first issue to be discussed is whether hedge accounting should be used at all. Should accounting transactions be linked in the presence of hedging or should each transaction be accounted for independently?

Issue 1: Should the Hedging Process Receive Special Accounting Treatment?

Should both components of a hedging transaction be tied together for accounting purposes? Or should each transaction be accounted for independent of linked transactions? It will be necessary to evaluate the advantages and disadvantages that would result from the choice. If it is decided that components of hedging transactions should not be linked for accounting purposes, then the specific hedge accounting issues are not relevant.

There are advantages in not allowing hedge accounting. All the problems of defining which transactions qualify for hedge accounting and how hedge accounting is to be implemented (including the disposition of loss and gain accruals) are eliminated. Hedge accounting adds complexities to financial accounting that are bypassed if hedge accounting is not allowed under any circumstances. This position has strong support among accountants and little support among operating managers.

There are several arguments for not allowing the deferred loss and gain variation of hedge accounting. For example, if a gain or loss has occurred and would be recognized following normal accounting, it is argued that it should affect income and not be deferred. Even if there is an effective hedge, the events involving the hedge and the hedged item are separate transactions and should be accounted for separately. Whether or not there is a hedge (the existence of a hedge is difficult to determine) should not affect the accounting. Also, if hedge accounting is used, the financial statements for a hedged firm tend not to be comparable to the financial statements for an otherwise identical firm that did not hedge. The hedged firm will have gains and losses on the hedge that the unhedged firm does not have, but these gains and losses do not affect the income of the interim period. Thus using hedge accounting two firms can have the same operating income but one of the firms has large deferred losses (or gains) on the hedge and these losses (or gains) do not affect income, even though they have occurred.

For example, assume two otherwise identical firms but one hedges and loses $100 million on the hedge, but the second firm does not hedge. The $100 million loss is deferred if the firm that is hedging. To show the same income and the same stock equity for the two firms is misleading. The firm that is hedging lost $100 million that the other firm did not lose. The primary argument in favor of hedge accounting is that with a perfect hedge the loss on the hedging instrument is exactly balanced by the gain on the hedged item and that just reporting the loss (or gain) on one component of the hedge in an accounting period and not the other gain (or loss) is misleading. Some believe that managements will be reluctant to use economic hedges if the accounting incomes are going to be affected adversely, not by economic events, but by the accounting convention applied to hedges (not allowing hedge accounting). If all free standing derivatives are recorded at their fair value, then a form of hedge accounting takes place. But the disposition of gains and losses of the instrument used to hedge still remains as an issue, as do other accounting issues associated with hedges (e.g., anticipated transactions). Not allowing hedge accounting can be criticized as moving financial statements away from accurately reporting the underlying economic events and the effects of managerial decisions. Should the reporting of accounting transactions be independent of the economic linkages between the transactions? If each item is accounted for individually without considering the fact that a hedge exists, then the gains and losses of the hedge security and the hedged item will frequently be reported in different time periods. This occurs if the hedge securities are marked to fair value while the hedged items are not, or alternatively the life of the hedge security is different than the life of the hedged item (thus, the gain and losses of the hedge are realized and recognized but the gains and losses of the hedged item are not recognized).

The June 1996 exposure draft of the FASB on hedging allows the use of hedge accounting for designated hedges. Under what conditions should the existence of an economic hedge lead to the use of hedge accounting? To answer this question we first need to define hedge accounting.

Issue 2: How Is Hedge Accounting to Be Defined and to Be Implemented?

Pure hedge accounting is the process whereby changes in the values of the hedged item and the hedge security, from the date of the hedge, are reported and affect income in the same period. If the gain or loss of the hedged item is deferred (recognized), the loss or gain of the hedge security is also deferred (recognized). One side of the hedge transaction (the security used to implement the hedge) normally involves a comparatively liquid security (either readily marketable or with a relatively short maturity) that does not require an initial cash outlay (a zero investment security). If an option is used, there is an initial premium and with futures contracts there are margin requirements. With all the securities used in hedging, fees are likely.

The two basic hedge accounting alternatives are:

1. Recognition of the gains or losses on the hedged item to match the recognition of gains or losses on the hedge. (Mark both the hedge and hedged item to fair value and have the gains and losses affect income.)
2. Defer the recognition of the gains or losses on the one component to match the deferral of the gains or losses on the other hedge component.

Fair value accounting for the hedge process recognizes the gains or losses on the hedged item to match the early recognition of the gains or losses on the hedge. We will refer to this as the fair value accounting for hedges method or the immediate recognition of gains and losses method. It is an alternative to a method of hedge accounting which defers gains and losses.

Fair value accounting for hedges is a form of hedge accounting, and departs from conventional accounting which would not adjust all hedged items to fair value and have the value changes affect income. For purposes of illustration assume all hedged financial instrument assets and liabilities are adjusted to their fair values as would be any hedge instrument. With a perfect hedge any gain or loss on the hedge instrument would be balanced by a loss or gain on the hedged asset in the same period. However, the anticipatory hedge accounting issues still remain as well as the issues involving the hedging of real assets (not normally marked to fair value).

Also, the problem of comparability between firms (those hedging and those not hedging) would still remain. It should be noted that any method of hedge accounting that accelerates or defers gains and losses creates comparability problems between firms that hedge and firms that do not hedge.

The immediate recognition of gains and losses on the hedged items has several complexities. One is that the fair value of the hedged item might not be easily obtained. A second is that with extensive hedging, many assets and liabilities (maybe all) would have to be adjusted to fair value, and the comparability of firms using and firms not using hedging would be reduced further. The hedging firm would be largely adjusted to fair values and the firm not hedging would be at historical cost or proceeds. A third complexity is that some assets would be carried at cost, some at fair value, and some at a hybrid (a fair value that no longer applies).

With immediate recognition of gains and losses for hedged items there is a problem involving gains and losses that are unrecognized and that have occurred prior to the start of the hedge. Would the gain and losses that have already taken place affect income? In general, it is not desirable to have a decision (such as the decision to start to hedge) affect the amount of gains and losses reported. That would occur if past gains and losses are recognized because a hedge is started. One solution is to require that fair value hedge accounting only be allowed to start at the time of acquisition of the hedged item. A second solution is to record only the gains and losses since the beginning of the hedge. That has the disadvantage of adding to the record keeping complexity.

If the hedge is terminated, the recorded adjustments to cost for hedge-balanced gains and losses would become the new basis for the historical-cost-based accounting. The new carrying amount would be different from the initial cost basis.

Hedge accounting with deferral of gains and losses is now widely used where hedge accounting is allowed. No gain or loss is recognized until both components of the hedge mature. But hedge accounting, with the deferral of gains or losses, and no control of the amounts of deferral opens up the possibility of abuse. The June 1996 exposure draft of the FASB would report all gains and losses as affecting either earnings or comprehensive income (outside of earnings). The hedges of forecasted transactions and foreign currency transaction would only affect comprehensive income.

Issue 3: Under What Conditions Should the Existence of a Hedge Lead to the Use of Hedge Accounting?

In the following sections we will consider the necessary conditions for determining whether an economic hedge should be accounted for using hedge accounting. The subissues that must be resolved are:

1. Should an enterprise approach or a transaction approach be used to evaluate risk reduction? Should risk reduction be required?
2. Should a correlation coefficient requirement be specified?
3. Is designation of a transaction by management necessary for a situation to be eligible for hedge accounting?

Transaction versus Entity

We start with the concept that the hedging transaction should be expected to reduce the firm's exposure to risk to qualify for hedge accounting. However, there is disagreement as to how to determine whether or not there is risk reduction. Should the test be whether the hedged item for the transaction can be identified or whether the effect of the transaction on the enterprise's risk can be identified? Given the difficulty of determining if entity risk has been reduced, some conclude that risk reduction should not be a requirement.

Some believe the test should be whether the risk to the firm from an identified hedged item is reduced by the hedge. Others believe the test should be whether the hedge reduces the entity's overall risk or, alternatively, the overall risk of one of the entity's business units. Still others believe that both tests must be met.

FASB Statement No. 52, *Foreign Currency Translation,* provides for a transaction approach:

> *A gain or loss on a forward contract or other foreign currency transaction that is intended to hedge an identifiable foreign currency commitment (for example, an agreement to purchase or sell equipment) shall be deferred and included in the measurement of the related foreign currency transaction (for example, the purchase or the sale of the equipment). [paragraph 21]*

FASB Statement No. 80, Accounting for Futures Contracts, provides for an entity approach:

> a. *The item to be hedged exposes the enterprise to price (or interest rate) risk. In this Statement, risk refers to the sensitivity of an enterprise's income for one or more future periods to changes in market prices or yields of existing assets, liabilities, firm commitments, or anticipated transactions. To meet this condition, the item or group of items intended to be hedged must contribute to the price or interest rate risk of the enterprise. In determining if this condition is met, the enterprise shall consider whether other assets, liabilities, firm commitments, and anticipated transactions already offset or reduce the exposure. An enterprise that cannot assess risk by considering other relevant positions and transactions for the enterprise as a whole because it conducts its risk management activities on a decentralized basis can meet this condition if the item intended to be hedged exposes the particular business unit that enters into the contract. [Paragraph 4, footnote references omitted.]*

The last sentence of this paragraph gives the accountant an opportunity to shift from the entity basis to a business unit basis. Some organizations hedge on a departmental basis rather than on an entity basis. This does not preclude a firm having an overall risk manager, but it is consistent with the fact that frequently risk management on a micro (a transaction) basis is much more feasible to implement than risk management from a firm's perspective.

The primary advantage of a transaction (or business unit) approach to hedging is feasibility of tracing the hedge. If a bank is engaged in swap transactions as a Principal, the risk manager can invest in interest rate futures to hedge interest rate risk of the swap portfolio. At another level, one could include all the bank's operations to determine whether the purchase of the interest rate futures decreases or increases risk. This latter process is a much more difficult evaluation task. On the other hand, only applying the risk-reduction test on either a business unit or a transaction basis could result in hedge accounting treatment for a transaction that increases the entity's overall risk.

The economic evaluation of risk from an entity point of view is the theoretically correct approach if costs and complexities of implementation are ignored. A transaction that increases the entity's overall risk is not an effective hedge. However, it is very difficult to determine how a specific transaction affects the entity's risk if the organization is complex. Statement 80 allows the use of a business unit basis in substitution for the entity point of view.

The evaluation of risk (and the hedging transaction) on a transaction basis would be the equivalent to the evaluation of risk management on an entity basis *if* all transactions are effectively hedged. Also, the transaction approach has the advantage of making it easier to evaluate each individual hedging transaction. One may be able to cope with an analysis of the risk of an individual transaction much more easily than evaluating the effect of a transaction, described as a hedge, on the overall entity's risk.

A compromise solution is the business unit approach allowed by Statement 80. If the business unit is small enough, the results would be approximately the same as the transaction approach. One possibility is that a transaction approach would be acceptable *unless* analysis of a broader nature makes it apparent that the hedge transaction actually increases the entity's risk. In a complex organization in which the entity approach is not economically feasible, the business unit approach of Statement 80 may be useful. In some cases (in which the business unit is not complex) a business unit approach will give approximately the same results as the transaction approach.

If hedge accounting were to require identification of the item or items being hedged (a type of transaction approach that does not preclude many transactions being grouped together), it would still be desirable that there not be known (with reasonable expectation) increases in enterprise risk as a result of the transaction (an enterprise approach). Thus there may be a double hurdle to be overcome before hedge accounting can be used.

The June 1996 exposure draft of the FASB would eliminate the requirement to assess the effect on enterprise risk of hedges. Instead the proposal focuses on the specific risks of the individual transaction, rather than the risks of a group of items or the risk at the entity-wide level of analysis.

Correlation Coefficient

Many hedging transactions can be expected to be less than perfect, varying as to the degree of effectiveness. The best hedges will involve a hedge security that is highly correlated with the hedged asset or liability. Even if the hedge security has a zero correlation (or positive correlation), there can be risk reduction. But this may not be hedging but rather an investment strategy that leads to risk reduction. How do we distinguish between risk-reducing investments and hedges? With a hedge the primary purpose of the transaction is to reduce risk. A risk-reducing investment, as distinguished from a hedge, will tend to have expected return (profit) possibilities. For example, a steel corporation that invests in an oil corporation (or vice versa) may be reducing risk (with the correct investment allocation) but this is not considered a hedge for financial reporting purposes since the transaction is being arranged to increase the firm's expected profits as well as to decrease risk.

The fact is that it is not possible to define a hedge so that there is a clear-cut distinction between a hedge and a risk reducing investment that is not a hedge. At the margin this could be interpreted to argue for common accounting treatment for both types of transactions. Given the wide range of transactions that qualify as being risk-reducing, using hedge accounting for all types of risk-reducing transactions would effectively rewrite the rules of accounting. The alternative is to rely on the definition that a hedge is a transaction to reduce price, interest rate, and exchange rate risk that is entered into with the expectation of reducing risk and not to earn expected profit.

Management might want to hedge a foreign currency but is unable to find a suitable financial instrument denominated in the same currency. If a second currency were expected to be highly correlated with the first, then a hedge might be deemed to exist. But for hedge accounting to be allowed, there should be an economic explanation for the high correlation rather than merely a historical correlation. The dollar and yen may be highly correlated for a period of time, but there may be no valid economic explanation for the two currencies to be highly correlated in the future. While the two currencies may be used to hedge each other, it is not obvious that hedge accounting should be allowed. What conditions should be necessary for a transaction involving a "tandem currency" to be a hedge eligible for hedge accounting? Is it necessary that there be a valid economic justification for expecting a high correlation of the currencies in the future? For example, if the United States and Canada were to agree to accept the other country's dollars at face value (they would be exchangeable at face value with no restrictions), we would have tandem currencies. There would be risks, but for the short run they would be tandem, and hedge accounting would be allowed. Would hedge accounting be allowed if there were a weaker linkage between currencies? Is the control of the amount of deferrals an effective substitute for a strict hedge accounting qualification rule?

For a hedge to exist, it is not necessary that the value change for the hedge security and the hedged item be identical (and opposite) for all possible changes in prices, interest rates, and exchange rates. In fact, it is likely the value elasticities will be different. Hedge securities will rarely exactly mimic the value changes of the hedged item, and less than perfect correlation should not disqualify a transaction for being eligible for hedge accounting. Because of the rareness of perfect hedges, requiring near perfect correlation would be effectively equivalent to the choice of not allowing hedge accounting in any circumstances.

We can define a high positive correlation between two items or a high negative correlation as the requirement for hedge accounting as long as we structure the transaction correctly. It may be necessary that one component of the hedge be the selling short of one of the two items in order to have equal and opposite outcomes. Thus, the relationship necessary for hedging to qualify for hedge accounting may be a high positive correlation (with selling short allowed) or a high negative correlation. These are two equivalent ways of saying the same thing.

The Emerging Issues Task Force considered the issue of correlation (proposed EITF Issue No. 88-7, "Hedging Correlation Issues Under FASB Statement No. 80") and attempted to resolve issues concerning correlation (for example, to define high correlation and to determine how often the correlation should be measured). The working group of the EITF recommended that the issue be dropped from the EITF agenda, and it was dropped without resolution.

One could define the necessary (but not sufficient) conditions for a hedge to be either or both of the following:

   a. The likelihood of a high correlation of value changes based on the economic characteristics of the item being hedged and the hedge item.
   b. Empirical evidence through time that substantiates (a). A correlation analysis could be a significant part of the evidence.

The June 1996 exposure draft does not attempt to define a required amount of correlation for a transaction to be a hedge.

Statement 80 defines high correlation as being required for a hedge to exist, but does not define high nor does it define the frequency or timing of the correlation analysis (paragraphs 4 and 11). Are paragraphs 4 and 11 of Statement 80 adequate descriptions of the statistical requirements to determine if a hedge exists?

Each transaction must be analyzed to determine if the linkages between the hedge instrument and the hedged item are sufficient to qualify for hedge accounting. It is possible that a well-structured hedge may prove not to be effective. For example, an investment in long-term bonds may be hedged by the short sale of short-term securities. But assume the one-period rate goes down (the firm loses on the short sale) and the long-term rate goes up (the firm loses on the long-term bonds). The hedge turns out to be ineffective. In this situation, in which there is not a matching of gains and losses but only two losses, it is difficult to justify deferring the loss on the hedge.

On the other hand, the hedging process was reasonable based on an ex ante conventional analysis of the expected results, and if the process were to be used again, hedge accounting might be allowed. If this pattern of interest rate changes became common, then the hedging technique would become suspect and the use of hedge accounting might be prohibited. Thus, a change from high to low correlation does not necessarily negate the existence of a hedge. A valid hedge might have existed on an expected basis, but relatively unusual events might occur that cause the hedge to be ineffective.

As either a substitute or a test of the degree of correlation, the amount of deferrals of the hedge's gain or losses can be compared with the unrealized gains or losses of the hedged item. Assume that hedge accounting leads to a deferral of losses. Theoretically, (with a perfect hedge) those losses will be balanced by gains on the hedged items. But what if the hedge is imperfect?

The size of the deferred gains or losses on hedges could be evaluated to determine if some of the losses or gains should be recognized as affecting income. Deferral of gains and losses would be limited to the unrecognized gains and losses of the items on the other side of the hedge. The accounting for the loss and gain deferrals is as important an issue as deciding initially whether a transaction is a hedge. With immediate recognition of gains and losses, a net gain or loss would be reported if the other hedge component does not have a gain or loss to match the gain or loss of the hedge.

Risk Management

Given the difficulty of determining if a transaction leads to risk reduction, the FASB considered (as of December 1996) risk management as the requirement for a hedge. Unfortunately, speculation and other forms of risk increasing actions are forms of risk management, thus any transaction would be eligible for hedge accounting. If hedge accounting and the deferral of gains and losses is to be allowed, then the expectation of risk reduction must be required of the transaction before hedge accounting is permitted.

Designation

Statement 80 establishes standards of financial accounting and reporting for futures contracts (except for foreign currencies). A futures contract qualifies as a hedge if it is designated as a hedge (paragraph 4(b)) and satisfies other conditions. The fact that a firm can choose to designate or not designate a futures contract to be a hedge means that the hedging accounting is optional from the viewpoint of the reporting firm. Both Statements 52 and 80 require that a transaction be designated a hedge before hedge accounting can be used.

If hedge accounting is optional under proposed standards (a hedge must be designated), it is important that the decision to "designate" a hedge be made before any gains or losses occur. If this is not required, management can determine which transactions are hedges after the fact based on the desired income effects. If management could affect income by merely designating or not designating a transaction to be a hedge after the gain or loss has occurred, this would be undesirable. Designations should be made in writing when the hedge is initiated, so that the intentions are not ambiguous. Also, a system for managing the hedges should be in place and fully described.

Not all items designated to be hedges by management would be accepted as being hedges by an impartial observer. Thus, designation by management may be a necessary, but not sufficient condition, for an item to be a hedge for accounting purposes. Should the economic nature of the transaction or management's designation be the final determining factor if the other conditions are satisfied? Should hedge accounting be required for a hedging transaction even though management has not designated the transaction to be a hedge? Is designation by management necessary if hedged accounting is to be allowed? The 1996 exposure draft requires designation, if hedge accounting is to be used.

There is a tendency to view the hedging process to be the result of a specific hedging strategy that is separate from the operational activities. Assume a firm has a hedging strategy that qualifies for hedge accounting. But a second firm with no well-defined hedging activity may perform the same actions with the same results. Is the fact that the hedging was or was not done with a purposeful act relevant to the accounting? Does management have to designate the act to be a hedge for the transaction to qualify for hedge accounting? The 1996 proposal says "yes."

One attractive solution is to modify normal accounting so that the normal accounting achieves the essential objectives of hedge accounting (mark all financial instruments to fair value) thus removes the necessity of determining whether or not a hedge exists. But the problems of hedge accounting for anticipated transactions and the hedging of real assets would still exist.

Issue 4: Can Anticipated Transactions Qualify for Hedge Accounting?

Should hedge accounting be allowed for anticipated transactions? Statement 52 requires a firm commitment, but Statement 80 allows anticipated transactions to qualify for hedge accounting (if futures are used and if the transaction does not involve foreign currencies) even if they are not firm commitments.

Statement 52 states:

A foreign currency transaction shall be considered a hedge of an identifiable foreign currency commitment provided both of the following conditions are met:

a. the foreign currency transactions is designated as, and is effective as, a hedge of a foreign currency commitment.
b. The foreign currency commitment is firm. [paragraph 21].

This precludes designating an accounting hedge for an anticipated foreign currency transaction in which the foreign currency commitment is not firm. Statement 80 allows hedge accounting for transactions that are anticipated.

Statement 80 states:

A futures contract may relate to transactions (other than transactions involving existing assets or liabilities, or transactions necessitated by existing firm commitments) an enterprise expects, but is not obligated, to carry out in the normal course of business. A change in the market value of a futures contract that hedges the price or interest rate of such an anticipated transaction shall be included in the measurement of the subsequent transaction if the two conditions in paragraph 4 and both of the following conditions are met:

a. The significant characteristics and expected terms of the anticipated transaction are identified. The significant characteristics and expected terms included the expected date of the transaction, the commodity or type of financial instrument involves, and the expected quantity to be purchased or sold. For transactions involving interest-bearing financial instruments, the expected maturity of the instrument is also a significant term.
b. It is probable that the anticipated transaction will occur. Considerations in assessing the likelihood that a transaction will occur include the frequency of similar transactions in the past . . . [paragraph 9].

Hedging existing firm commitments qualifies under Statement 52 for hedge accounting. If an entity has contracted to buy inventory and to pay 1 million francs payable in 30 days, it can buy a forward or futures contract now to supply 1 million francs in 30 days at a given price. The firm commitment is being hedged, and following Statement 52 hedge accounting is allowed.

If the foreign currency transaction is merely expected rather than a firm commitment, then a futures or forward contract is no longer a hedge that qualifies for hedge accounting. For example, if the probability of buying the inventory and paying francs is judged to be high, but there is not a firm commitment, then the transaction does not currently qualify for hedge accounting. It can be argued that the transaction is essentially certain and hedge accounting is appropriate. But Statement 52 precludes hedge accounting unless there is a firm commitment. Is the firm commitment requirement of Statement 52 a desirable necessary condition? In a situation in which there is significant probability that the transaction might not take place, then hedge accounting with loss deferral would introduce an amount of subjectivity into the accounting process. There would be situations in which hedge accounting leads to misleading reports (excessive deferrals). But there can also be situations in which not using hedge accounting can be misleading (reporting a loss in one period followed by a gain in the next period, when the gain merely balances the loss).

Should hedge accounting be allowed for hedges of anticipated transactions? If hedge accounting can be used for anticipated transactions, what guidelines can be established for determining the cut-off amount of uncertainty? Should a firm commitment always be required? Is it desirable to shift the criterion to a level of probability rather than require a firm commitment? How far into the future can the anticipated hedged transaction be?

If there is some element of uncertainty (including whether the transaction will take place and the amount of foreign currency), then any general recommendation regarding hedge accounting will be faulty for some types of economic situations.

If with anticipated transactions firm commitments (with no element of uncertainty) are required for hedge accounting (as with Statement 52), then companies that hedge an anticipated transaction that is not firm will show gains or losses in the interim period even though management thinks there is a good economic hedge and acted accordingly. This rule would discourage management from engaging in economic hedging practices that management perceives to be desirable; thus, this rule would not be neutral to decision making for hedges.

On the other hand, permissive rules for hedge accounting could result in speculative gains and losses being deferred. If hedge accounting is allowed for expected but uncertain anticipated transactions (as with Statement 80), there will be deferred gains and losses. These deferrals may take place even when the transaction does not take place or does not require a hedge; thus, the hedge security losses are not balanced by hedged item gains (and gains are not balanced by losses).

A permissive use of hedge accounting will facilitate the use of economic hedging where management thinks it desirable, even though the anticipated event might not occur. Faulty accounting practices will not be blamed for preventing hedging thought to be desirable by management. Some losses (and gains) would be deferred. These losses (and gains) could be revealed in a footnote of the following type:

> *There are currently deferred losses of $_____ associated with hedging operations. These losses have not been recorded in the income statement since it is expected that they will be balanced by deferred gains to be realized on the hedged items.*

A user of the financial statements would have the information for adjusting the period's income if that is thought to be appropriate.

A restrictive use of hedge accounting would require the reporting of the hedge security's gains and losses through time, thus, would tend to reduce the use of the economic hedging process. Interim accounting gains and losses on the hedge security would be reported even though the net economic gains and losses might be zero if the changes in the value of the anticipated hedged items were also included.

What types of anticipatory transactions, if hedged, are appropriately eligible for hedge accounting? Protecting revenue, expense, and future income of foreign subsidiaries from exchange rate changes is a different type of a hedge than the hedge of net investments in a foreign subsidiary. One position would be to allow hedge accounting for assets and liabilities (cash, receivables, and payables) but disallow hedge accounting for all anticipated transactions. With anticipated transactions this would result in the hedge security's gains and losses being reported as they occur rather than being deferred. The advantage of this process would be the elimination of ambiguity as to what accounting procedure is appropriate. The disadvantage would be that management would feel they were being constrained by accounting conventions from using economic hedges, and even more importantly the accounting is further removed from being consistent with the economic transactions and changes taking place.

In summary, one alternative is to allow hedge accounting for transactions in which there is a firm commitment (legally enforceable) or generally accepted accounting principles have led to a transaction having been recorded. A second alternative is to allow hedge accounting for likely anticipated transactions but to limit the time of deferral. A third alternative is to allow hedge accounting for likely anticipated transactions and not specifically limit the time of deferral. A fourth alternative is not to allow hedge accounting for any anticipatory hedges.

Consider two consequences:

a. Not allowing hedge accounting: Results in an effective economic hedge incorrectly showing a loss (or gain) in a period to be followed by a gain (or loss) in a subsequent period.

b. Allowing hedge accounting: Results in two otherwise identical firms incorrectly showing the same income when one firm lost on a hedge that has not yet expired and the second firm did not hedge (thus did not lose).

The 1996 proposal allows hedge accounting for anticipated transactions and firm commitments.

FASB Statement No. 119 (October 1994)

FAS 119 deals with disclosure about derivative financial instruments and other financial instruments. The statement concludes that additional disclosures are required for financial instruments that are being used to hedge anticipated transactions (para. 63):

> The Board concluded that four additional disclosures should be required for derivative financial instruments that are held or issued for the purpose of hedging anticipated transactions (both firm commitments and forecasted transactions for which there is no firm commitment): (a) a description of the anticipated transactions whose risks are hedged with derivative financial instruments, including the period of time until the anticipated transactions are expected to occur, (b) a description of the classes of derivative financial instruments used to hedge the anticipated transactions, (c) the amount of hedging gains and losses explicitly deferred, and (d) a description of the transactions or other events that result in the recognition in earnings of gains or losses deferred by hedge accounting.

Para. 64 indicates that the Board concluded "that it should not require entities to provide information about gains and losses deferred as a result of hedge accounting of existing assets and liabilities." Thus the requirements for anticipated transactions as defined in para. 63 is different from the requirements of hedging existing assets and liabilities. The Board also concluded that it would require disclosure of hedging gains and losses that are implicitly deferred because of changes in value of the hedging instrument (para. 65).

A Proposal by the FASB

As of December 1995 the FASB was considering an approach where an enterprise would choose to either:[2]

1. Classify derivatives in one of two categories (the November 1994 approach). Classification would be fairly discretionary. Derivatives classified in the "trading" category would be measured at fair value and changes in fair value would be recognized in earnings in the period in which they occur. Derivatives classified as "other than trading" also would be measured at fair value, but the changes in fair value would be reported as a separate component of equity until realized. All realized gains and losses would be recognized in earnings. No gains or losses would adjust the basis of assets or liabilities, or

2. Mark all financial instruments to market. At a minimum, changes in fair value of "trading" instruments would be recognized in earnings. Changes in fair value of all other financial instruments would be reported as a separate component of equity until realized. All realized gains and losses would be recognized in earnings.

Alternative 1 deals with the accounting for derivatives. The derivatives would be measured at fair value. The gains and losses of derivatives in the "trading" category would be recognized in earnings in the period in which they occur. If the gain on the hedged item has not yet been realized, this would not be consistent with hedge accounting.

The changes in value of derivatives classified as "other than trading" would be reported as part of equity until they are realized, at which time they would be recognized in earnings. Since a gain on the hedge can be realized before the gain on the hedged item this would also not be consistent with hedge accounting.

Alternative 2 would recognize all changes in fair value of all financial "trading" instruments in earnings. Changes in fair value of all other financial instruments would be part of equal until the gains and losses are realized at which time the gains and losses would be recognized in earnings. This would not be consistent with hedge accounting.

The FASB's Proposal (1996)

The FASB's 1996 proposal requires that all derivatives be reported at fair (or market) value on the balance sheet. Changes in fair value would depend on the derivatives' designation. If a derivative is designated as a hedge there are three choices.

1. A hedge of the cash flow of a forecasted transaction.
2. A hedge of the market value of an existing asset, liability, or forecasted transaction with a firm commitment.
3. A hedge of the foreign currency exposure.

If foreign currency or a forecasted transaction is hedged (and there is designation) any gain or loss would be deferred. It would affect comprehensive income currently. It would affect earnings when the transaction is scheduled to occur.

Any other change in fair value of a derivative would affect earnings of the period in which the gain or loss occurs. The gain or loss of the hedged item would also be recognized. If the hedge is perfectly effective there would be no net effect on earnings. The gain loss on the hedged item would be recognized only to the extent of the gain or loss on the hedge.

For a derivative to qualify for hedge accounting, there must be formal documentation of the hedge including a description of the risk being hedged and the specific item being hedged.

The hedging derivative cannot be a written option. Also, hedge accounting cannot be applied to a portfolio of items (a "macro" hedge).

CONCLUSIONS

The FASB has set a high priority on establishing reasonable methods of accounting for financial instruments. When the financial instruments are used for hedging, special accounting rules are needed if the accounting is to be consistent with the economic motivations behind the hedge. In the past, there was a wide gulf between the financial managers who use financial instruments to hedge risk and the FASB as it attempted to proscribe rules for accounting for these hedges. Just as there are few perfect hedges, there is not a set of accounting rules for hedges that will not be subject to criticism.

A special report titled *Major Issues Related to Hedge Accounting* (Jane B. Adams and Crliss J. Montesi, 1995) was published in the names of the Australian Accounting Standards Board, Canadian Accounting Standards Board, International Accounting Standards Committee, United Kingdom Accounting Standards Board, and the United States Financial Accounting Standards Board. The issues were adequately defined.

Any rule relative to the use of hedge accounting directly affects managerial decision making. The method of accounting for a hedge is likely to affect the willingness of a firm to hedge. If all assets and liabilities were marked-to-market, the magnitude of the issue would be greatly reduced. But with cost-based accounting, the prevention or allowance of the use of hedge accounting is a major factor in managerial decisions whether to hedge. Thus, a characteristic of accounting (cost-based information) contributes to the need for hedge accounting, and the rules for allowing hedge accounting affects managerial decisions. Given the acceptance of economic hedging as a legitimate business activity, it is desirable to control the amount of distortion in decision making likely to be caused by the accounting rules for hedging. On the other hand, the extent to which gains and losses can be deferred also has to be controlled so that the hedge accounting privilege is not misused. The proposals of the FASB aim to achieve this.

Any accounting rule for hedging will have flaws, but not having consistent rules is also flawed. The FASB is to be commended for its efforts.

ENDNOTES

1. *See* the FASB Research Report, *Hedge Accounting: An Exploratory Study of the Underlying Issues,* H. Bierman, L. T. Johnson, and D. S. Peterson, FASB, Norwalk, Ct., 1991. Also relevant for hedge accounting are FASB Statements No. 52, *Foreign Currency Translation* and No. 80, *Accounting for Futures Contracts,* and FASB Technical Bulletin No. 88-2, *Definition of a Right of Setoff.* The 1986 AICPA Issues Paper, *Accounting for Options,* is also relevant as are numerous EITF issue statements. In June 1996 the Board issued an Exposure Draft of a proposed statement, "Accounting for Derivatives and Similar Financial Instruments and for Hedging Activities."

2. Report to Financial Instruments Task Force dated December 12, 1995, p. 1.

PART SEVEN

Case Study: Metallgesellschaft

19

Metallgesellschaft and the Economics of Synthetic Storage

CHRISTOPHER L. CULP
MERTON H. MILLER

A U.S. subsidiary of the German industrial conglomerate Metallgesellschaft AG (MG AG), MG Refining & Marketing, Inc. (MGRM) is a contender for the world's record in derivatives-related losses—$1.3 billion at year-end 1993. Unlike many of its rivals for that record, however, MGRM was not using derivatives as part of a treasury function, with a view to enhancing the return on an investment portfolio or to lowering the firm's interest expense.

MGRM's derivatives were part and parcel of its *marketing* program, under which it offered long-term customers firm price guarantees for up to ten years on gasoline, heating oil, and diesel fuel purchased from MGRM. The firm hedged its resulting exposure to spot price increases to a considerable extent with futures contracts. Because futures contracts must be marked to market daily, cash drains must be incurred to meet variation margin payments when futures prices fall. After several consecutive months of falling prices in the autumn of 1993, MGRM's German parent reacted to the substantial margin calls by liquidating the hedge.

The top management of the parent corporation has yet to make clear why it chose to unwind the futures leg of the hedge while the fixed-price contracts were still in force. That MGRM had no way of financing the margin payments, except on distress terms, cannot be the explanation. Even if MGRM had been locked out of public capital markets, it hardly needed to go hat-in-hand to strangers unfamiliar with its strategy. Over 100 of the world's leading banks were *already* creditors to MG AG; and Deutsche Bank, one of the world's largest financial institutions, was both a major creditor *and* a major stockholder of MGRM's parent. If new sources of outside credit had to be tapped, the program should have been "self-financing"

Originally published in the *Journal of Applied Corporate Finance* 7(4), Winter. Reprinted with permission. For comments on earlier drafts (under various titles), we owe thanks to Malcolm Basing, Halsey Bullen, Don Chew, George Constantinides, Kent Daniel, Dean Furbush, Ken French, Steve Hanke, Steve Kaplan, Randy Kroszner, Bill Margrabe, Mark Mitchell, Todd Petzel, Richard Roll, José Scheinkman, Charles Smithson, and to a number of industry and derivatives specialists, many of whom prefer to remain anonymous (even those who agree with us!). Special thanks are due to Barbara Kavanagh for helpful discussions on credit risk and funding risk.

because the flow contracts increased in expected value as oil prices fell. Other ways of staunching the cash drains on the futures, while still remaining hedged, were also available had the firm really been facing a binding cash constraint.

Perhaps the supervisory board of the parent believed that MGRM was not hedging, but "speculating" on oil prices. The team the supervisory board called in to liquidate the futures positions, after all, had resolved an earlier oil derivatives fiasco for Deutsche Bank—the notorious Klöckner speculative episode of some six years before.[1] Possibly the supervisory board of the parent misinterpreted the appeals by its MGRM subsidiary for more cash as "doubling-up" or, at the least, as the telltale sign of a business failure in the making. Or perhaps the supervisory board had other corporate motives of its own for ending the program.[2]

Whatever the reason, the decision to liquidate the futures leg proved unfortunate on several counts, turning paper losses into realized losses, sending a distress signal to MGRM's over-the-counter (OTC) derivatives counterparties, and leaving MGRM exposed to rising prices on its remaining fixed-price contracts.

In this chapter, we explore in more detail the economics of MGRM's delivery/hedging program, a strategy aptly dubbed "synthetic storage."[3] But despite the frequent references throughout to MGRM, this article is not a case study in the usual sense. Too many essential facts about the program and its liquidation have still not been made public and perhaps never will be, given that one of the key lawsuits in the case has been sent to private arbitration.[4] Our focus here will be mainly on the economic logic underlying a synthetic storage program like MGRM's. In particular, we show such a strategy is neither inherently unprofitable nor fatally flawed, *provided* top management understands the program and the long-term funding commitments necessary to make it work.

DID MGRM'S MARKETING/HEDGING PROGRAM MAKE ECONOMIC SENSE?

MG's Marketing Program

MG AG is a 112-year-old enterprise owned largely by institutional investors, including Deutsche Bank AG, Dresdner Bank AG, Daimler-Benz, Allianz, and the Kuwait Investment Authority. At the end of 1992, MG AG had 251 subsidiaries with activities ranging over trade, engineering, and financial services. Its subsidiary responsible for U.S. petroleum marketing was MGRM.

In December 1991, MGRM recruited from Louis Dreyfus Energy Corporation Arthur Benson and his management team, whose key marketing strategy was to offer long-term customers firm price guarantees for five, and in some cases up to ten, years on gasoline, heating oil, and diesel fuel purchased from MGRM. So successful, apparently, were these marketing efforts that by September 1993 MGRM had sold forward the equivalent of over 150 million barrels (bbls.) of petroleum products in its flagship, long-term "flow delivery" contracts.[5] In conjunction with those forward short positions, MGRM entered long into futures and OTC derivatives, such as commodity swaps.

MGRM's derivatives positions protected the firm and its creditors against the *principal* risk the program faced—that is, the risk that rising spot prices would erode the gross profit margins on its fixed-price forward sales. Price protection per se, however, need not be presumed the primary motivation for the hedging. The combined delivery/hedging strategy was intended to maximize the expected profits from marketing and storing oil products, a field in which MGRM possessed special expertise and superior information, without having to gamble on directional movements in spot prices, an activity in which MGRM had no such comparative advantage.[6]

The bulk of MGRM's futures positions were on the New York Mercantile Exchange (NYMEX) in the most liquid contracts of between one and three months to maturity based on New York harbor regular unleaded gasoline, New York harbor No. 2 heating oil, and West Texas Intermediate (WTI) grade light, sweet crude oil.[7,8] Liquidity was an important consideration in MGRM's overall strategy, because it lowered the cost of managing its positions to meet seasonal changes in the demand and supply of heating oil and gasoline.[9]

Most of MGRM's fixed-price contracts also contained an "option" clause allowing counterparties to terminate their contracts early if market prices surged above the fixed price at which MGRM was selling the oil product. Why MGRM included these sell-back options in the first place will become clearer later. But because contingent liabilities of that kind can raise the specter of "runs" on a supplier, MGRM sought to reassure its customers by contractually agreeing to remain fully hedged[10]—a policy it was prepared to follow for the separate reasons already noted.

Hedging Long-Dated Obligations with Short-Dated Futures[11]

Borrowing short and lending long is an oft-cited recipe for financial disaster. But for MGRM, unlike, say, the S&Ls of the 1980s, or the more recent episode in Orange County, California—an episode purportedly surpassing even MGRM in losses incurred—maturity mismatch was not the real culprit.

Counter-intuitive as it may seem, a firm *can* use short-dated futures to hedge its long-term delivery commitments against spot oil price increases simply by purchasing a "stack" of short-dated futures equivalent to its remaining delivery obligations. Note, in this connection, that we are not here saying (nor have we ever said) that such a stacked hedge is a *perfect* hedge, whatever that may mean.[12] The strategy involves risks other than the principal one of market price risk, and those additional risks will be considered in due course later.

The mechanics of a stacked hedging strategy are straightforward. On the first delivery date, the firm buys in the spot market for delivery, offsets all its maturing futures contracts, and re-establishes a long position in the new front-month (i.e., one-month) futures contract—this time, though, with its long futures positions reduced by the amount delivered on its flow contracts. On the next settlement date, the hedger again decreases the size of its futures position by the amount delivered and rolls the rest forward to the next maturing one-month futures contract. And so on, month by month.[13,14]

A Three-Period Example

To convince yourself that such a stacked hedging strategy can protect a firm's gross profit margin, consider the following three-period example in which a firm enters fixed-price flow contracts to sell 1,000X bbls. of oil monthly for $20/bbl.[15] Suppose prices happen to rise over time as follows:

$$S_0 = \$17 \quad S_1 = \$18 \quad S_2 = \$19 \quad S_3 = \$20$$

where S_t denotes the spot price at time t. Given those prices, we can approximate the time t prices of the futures contract in the stack by invoking the familiar cost-of-carry formula:[16]

$$F_{t,t+1} = S_t[1 + b_{t,t+1}] = S_t[1 + r_{t,t+1} + z_{t,t+1} - d_{t,t+1}]$$

where the one-period basis, $b_{t,t+1}$, includes the interest cost of physical storage $r_{t,t+1}$, the physical cost of storage $z_{t,t+1}$, and the convenience yield of having physical inventories on hand $d_{t,t+1}$—all assumed known at the start of period t and all expressed as a fraction of the time t spot price.

Suppose further that the current one-period interest rate, storage cost, and convenience yield are

$$r_{0,1} = 0.005 \quad z_{0,1} = 0.01 \quad d_{0,1} = 0.015$$

and that those values happen to change over time as follows:

$$r_{1,2} = 0.008 \quad r_{2,3} = 0.01$$

$$z_{1,2} = 0.015 \quad z_{2,3} = 0.02$$

$$d_{1,2} = d_{2,3} = 0.007$$

Given these values for the above variables and the assumed path for spot prices, the one-period futures prices and bases will evolve as follows:

$$F_{0,1} = \$17.00 \quad F_{1,2} = \$18.29 \quad F_{2,3} = \$19.44$$

$$b_{0,1} = 0.0 \quad\quad b_{1,2} = 0.016 \quad b_{2,3} = 0.023$$

When the basis is positive and thus the current futures price is higher than the current spot price, the market is said to be in "contango" for that period. Although not typical of oil markets, we are assuming in this example, to make the role of storage costs stand out most sharply, that the market moves unexpectedly into contango at time 1 and stays there.

Table 19.1 shows the cash flow and income statements over the three periods for a firm selling 1000X bbls. of oil each period for $20/bbl. The firm holds initially three futures maturing at month 1, then rolls into two contracts maturing at month 2, and finally into one contract maturing at month 3.

In month 1, for example, the firm delivers 1000X bbls. at $20/bbl. on its flow contract, obtaining that oil by buying in the spot market at $18/bbl. Its spot cash flow (Column (1)) thus is $2,000X. At the same time, the firm offsets the three futures it had previously initiated in month 0 at a price of $17.00/bbl., re-establishing at $18.29/bbl. two new long positions maturing in month 2. Because spot and futures prices must be equal at maturity, its month 1 futures cash flow (Column (2)) is $3,000X = 3X × 1000 × [18-17].

Column (4) shows the gross margin on the flow contract. Because the firm hedged when the spot price was $17/bbl., it "locks in" a gross margin per period of $3,000X. The net cost of carry (Column (5)) reflects the storage costs the firm effectively pays each month when it rolls over its stack of futures. At the end of month 1, for example, the firm offsets its three futures at $18/bbl. and re-establishes a

TABLE 19.1   Hedging Long-Dated Obligations with Short-Dated Futures

Month	Cash Flows		Income			
	(1) Spot[a]	(2) Futures[b]	(3) Net Cash Flow	(4) Gross Flow Contract Income[c]	(5) Net Cost of Carry[d]	(6) Net Income
1	$2,000X	$3,000X	$5,000X	$3,000X	0X	$3,000X
2	$1,000X	$1,420X	$2,420X	$3,000X	($580X)	$2,420X
3	$0X	$560X	$560X	$3,000X	($440X)	$2,560X
TOTAL	$3,000X	$4,980X	$7,980X	$9,000X	($1,020X)	$7,980X

a. $1000X (20 - S_t)$
b. (# contracts) $\times 1000 \ (F_{t,t} - F_{t-1,t})$
c. $1000X (20 - S_0)$
d. (# contracts) $\times 1000 \ (S_{t-1} - F_{t-1,t})$

position of two futures at \$18.29/bbl. Its implicit storage cost for the second month thus is $580X = 2X \times 1000 \times [18\text{-}18.29]$. The *net* margin for the hedger (Column (6)) is thus its gross margin from the fixed-price deliveries less the implicit cost of storing oil using futures.

Note also that while the hedger's monthly net margin over the entire period need not equal its monthly net cash flow, the firm's *total* net margin equals the *total* net cash flow, regardless of spot price movements. In this sense, the firm's net worth is indeed fully hedged against spot price risk.

The Benefits and Costs of Synthetic Storage

Our example above has been constructed deliberately with the basis positive and rising. In oil markets, however, unlike most commodity markets, the basis is typically *negative;* that is, the spot price is greater than the futures price because the convenience yield often exceeds the cost of physical storage plus the interest cost of storage. In the case of crude oil, for example, the front-month basis, defined as $F_{t,t+1} - S_t / S_t$, averaged $-.0082$ over the period May 1983 to September 1994; and for heating oil, the proportional basis averaged $-.0096$ from January 1980 to September 1994.[17]

The negative basis, usually referred to as "backwardation," occurs when the current demand for oil is high relative to current supply. Because firms may need physical oil on hand to avoid inventory stock-outs, spot prices rise above futures prices to reward firms for "lending" their inventory to the current spot market, as it were.[18] When the market is in backwardation, a stacked hedger remains hedged against spot price changes, but its net margin is *higher* than the gross margin to reflect the negative net cost of carry. The firm is still paying the cost of storage, of course, but the presence of those costs is masked by the high convenience yield.

The stacked hedging strategy of synthetic oil storage does differ from actual physical storage in some important respects, however. In the physical storage strategy, the firm pays its own marginal costs of storage and receives its own marginal convenience yield. By contrast, under the synthetic storage strategy, the firm pays the marginal storage cost net of the convenience yield for the marginal physical storer. A firm expecting its own marginal cost of storage to be higher than the marginal cost of storage in the futures price would thus be better off *ex ante* hedging with futures rather than physical storage. By the same token, fully-integrated producing firms with lower marginal costs of storage—such as Exxon with tank farms around the world—typically find it more efficient to store physically rather than synthetically.

Were "Rollover Costs" a Basic Flaw in the Strategy?

Critics have argued that "the crushing impact of [MGRM's] monthly rollover costs"[19] made MGRM's hedging method a "basically flawed trading strategy."[20] The rollover cost is the difference between the price of the maturing futures contract and the price at which the new futures position is established times the size of the stack. As long as the rollovers are in front-month contracts and occur near the maturity date, the price of the expiring futures contract is essentially the spot price because the two must converge at maturity. The rollover cost is thus just the basis expressed as a lump-sum dollar value. In our previous illustration, for example, the time 1 rollover cost per contract would be $F_{1,1} - F_{1,2} = S_1 - F_{1,2} = \$18 - \$18.29$, or a cost of \$0.29. (Adjusted for the size of the stack, this total rollover cost of \$580X appears in Column (5) of Table 19.1 in the row corresponding to Month 2.)

Because the front-month rollover cost per contract is simply the basis in another form, expected rollover costs are quite literally the marginal expected implicit costs of interest and physical storage less the convenience yield built into futures prices. As noted earlier, the one-month net cost of storage and interest *averaged* less than zero over the last ten years. Even so, some critics believe the decision to liquidate MGRM's futures hedge was justified because those costs were becoming excessive in the autumn of 1993.[21] And indeed, by historical standards, the rollover costs then may well have been perceived as unusually high. For crude oil, the November 1993 mid-month rollover cost was \$0.33/bbl. compared to a mean over the entire sample of −\$0.2091/bbl., placing that month in the 86th percentile of the historical sample. For heating oil, the corresponding values were \$0.0021/gal., −\$.0076/gal., and the 56th percentile; and for gasoline, \$.0187/gal., −\$.0082/gal., and the 89th percentile.[22] (See Appendix 2.)

Remember, however, that the liquidation of the hedge, though relieving MGRM of the net costs of oil storage, exposed it instead to spot price risk on its still-outstanding flow contracts. And spot price risk is huge relative to basis risk. In a regression of front-month futures prices ($F_{t,t+1}$) on the contemporaneous spot price S_t, the value of R^2 will measure the fraction of the variance in futures prices explained by the variation in spot prices. For crude oil (May 1983 to February 1994), the R^2 was .99, for heating oil (January 1980 to September 1994) the value was .96, and for gasoline (December 1984 to September 1994) the value was .95. Or, to put it the other way around, no more than one to five per cent of the historical variation in futures prices can be traced to variations over time in the basis.[23]

Not only do variations in the basis thus account for little of the intertemporal variation in futures prices, but we also know that the lump-sum dollar basis (i.e., the rollover cost) varies inversely with spot prices. For WTI crude, heating oil, and gasoline, the simple correlation coefficients of each basis with spot prices were −0.359, −0.091, and −0.453, respectively, for the sample periods noted above. If, therefore, the supervisory board's decision to liquidate the hedge in mid-December 1993 was done to avoid rollover costs, that decision turned out to be doubly-cursed when crude and heating oil prices rose *and* rollover costs fell in early 1994—triply-cursed, in fact, because the futures positions were unwound in mid-December 1993 *after* the December rollovers had already occurred.

Finally, critics of MGRM rarely seem to recognize that rollover costs by themselves tell us nothing about the profitability of a *combined* delivery/hedging strategy. A combined delivery/hedging program of the kind MGRM was following must not be judged by the storage or related costs it happens to incur *over any short interval of time.* What counts, rather, is the program's profit potential over the long haul or, as finance specialists might prefer to put it, its expected net present value. How to compute the requisite net present value for a *hedged* delivery program is far from obvious, but we sketch out the method for doing so in the next section, leaving the mathematical details to a separate paper.[24]

The Marketing/Hedging Decision as a Capital Budgeting Problem

Calculating the net present value of a combined delivery/hedging program would be simplicity itself, of course, in a futures market with a complete set of contracts covering every maturity for which the flow commitments had been made. As long as the fixed price for deliveries in period T exceeds the current T-period futures price, the locked-in *net* profit on the period T delivery is precisely the difference between the two prices. By going long X T-period futures contracts for each 1,000X bbls. of period T delivery commitments, MGRM would both have hedged the delivery commitments *and* reduced basis or rollover risk (but, by the same token, also giving up any rollover gains). The set of futures contracts actually available, however, is *not* rich enough to support such a strategy—a pure "strip," as it is called in the trade. The NYMEX has no liquid contracts for crude beyond 18 months to maturity and a year to maturity in heating oil.[25]

Though futures contracts are not available for all maturities, their prices can be approximated by repeated application of the cost of carry formula. In particular, the presumptive basis for a T-period futures contract would be the *expected* value of the storage and interest cost net of convenience yield over T periods. If the cash receipt on a period-T fixed-price delivery discounted at that expected basis exceeds the current price of oil, the program has a positive *expected* net present value.[26] Stated more formally, a firm will enter into a hedged N-period fixed-price delivery program to sell one unit of oil each period if the program has a positive expected NPV at time t = 0—that is, if

$$E_t(NPV_t) = \sum_{j=t+1}^{N} \frac{K_j}{1 + E_t(b_{t,j})} - (N - t) \times S_t > 0 \tag{1}$$

where K_j is the fixed price of a time j delivery, S_t is the time-t spot price, and $E_t(b_{t,j})$ is the basis expected to prevail from time t to j evaluated with information available at time t.

Although different hedging strategies may have different values for the $E_t(b_{t,j})$ terms in equation (1), we show elsewhere that under plausible assumptions about equilibrium futures pricing, MGRM's strategy must have the same *expected* NPV at time 0 as a pure strip.[27] *Realized* outcomes may differ from their expectations, however. Some strategies may thus have higher or lower net profits *ex post,* depending on how the bases happen to evolve over time relative to initial conditional expectations.

That the expected NPV might be positive for MGRM does not mean, of course, that the expected NPV is necessarily negative for MGRM's customers. MGRM's customers, almost by definition, have very high marginal storage costs and place a high value on security of delivery.[28] Those customers might have opted for synthetic storage themselves, of course, but as episodic do-it-yourself users of derivatives have come to recognize, risk management professionals have a considerable comparative advantage in those matters.

The Economic Function of the Sell-Back Options

The expected value of the program can be re-calculated each period to reflect the arrival of new information. In the example above, we assumed that the market moved at time 1 unexpectedly into contango, which would change the discount rates used in expected NPV calculations *after* time 0. Using the value of $b_{1,2}$ realized at time 1 for $E_1(b_{1,2})$, 0.016, and assuming $E_1(b_{1,3}) = 0.032 = 2 \times 0.016$, the expected NPV of the program *conditional* on information available at time 1 is

$$E_1(NPV_1) = \left[\left(\frac{20}{1.016} + \frac{20}{1.032} \right) - 18 \times 2 \right] \times 1.000X = 53065X$$

The conditional expected NPV at time 2 using the still-higher one-period basis prevailing then is $550X. Despite the two unexpected increases in the basis, the conditional expected NPV of the program is positive at the beginning of all three periods.

Now suppose instead that spot prices beyond period 0 were to increase more rapidly than before, say, as

$$S_0 = \$17 \quad S_1 = \$19 \quad S_2 = \$21 \quad S_3 = \$23$$

The initial expected NPV of the program would still be positive ($9,000X), and hence a rational corporation would again accept the policy at time 0. The conditional expected NPV is also positive at time 1 ($1,065X). But now the conditional expected NPV of the program would be negative at time 2 (−$1,550X). A firm committed to the combined delivery/hedging program at time 0, though still technically hedged, would then seem to be profiting handsomely on the stack of futures but "losing money" on the flow contracts. If the firm could possibly end the program by "buying out its customers" for *less* than it expects to pay for servicing them, it would.

Bilaterally-negotiated contracts cannot be unwound at zero cost, however, especially on favorable terms. Getting out of such contracts means negotiating their unwinding with customers on a case-by-case basis. The Master Agreements of the International Swaps and Derivatives Association (ISDA), for example, allow counterparties to choose a method of calculating "close-out settlement values" in the event OTC derivatives terminate early. In the absence of an "event of termination or default," the unwinding counterparty must obtain the consent of the other party and negotiate the terms of the unwind, not always an easy or inexpensive task.[29,30]

As a substitute for negotiated unwinds under a master agreement, MGRM chose to add the early exercise options to its flow contracts. These options take effect when the front-month futures price rises above the fixed delivery price in the flow contract. On exercising their options, customers receive a pre-specified monetary payment equal to one-half the difference between the front-month futures price and the fixed price in the flow contract times the total volume remaining on the flow contract. The sell-back options thus not only specify in advance the method of calculating a "close-out price," but also eliminate the need for negotiating the close-out itself.

Although customers might wish to exercise their sell-back options if they expect spot prices in the future to fall, they might well wish to do so even if they regarded a surge in spot prices as permanent. Remember that they must compare the immediate cash payment on exercise with the *present value* of expected future differences between spot prices and the delivery prices over the remaining life of the contract. And if the customers, unlike MGRM, are neither hedged nor otherwise well-diversified corporations, their discount rates must reflect the risk of changing spot prices as well as their own time-value of money. In any event, the likelihood that customers will exercise their buy-back options at some time in the life of their contracts cannot be ignored in appraising MGRM's synthetic storage program. Computing the exact present value to MGRM of those embedded "reverse options" is a task of great technical difficulty, but whether the exercise rights rested with MGRM or its customers, the value of those options would clearly be substantial in a world in which spot prices are highly volatile. By the same token, the presence of the options substantially reduces the effective tenor of the flow delivery contracts.[31]

The Expected Net Present Value When Prices Fall

When prices fall, a repeat of the previous calculations holding the expected bases constant would find the conditional expected net present value for MGRM actually rising, suggesting that a company in MGRM's position should be even more anxious to continue the program. This may seem paradoxical because of cash drains on the futures stack and management's possible reaction to them. Those cash drains, however, are essentially *sunk costs* at this point and, as such, should have no effect on current decisions about whether to *continue* the program. And because the firm is still hedged, those costs are not even sunk irrevocably but will eventually be recovered by the fixed-price deliveries over time.

Calculating the conditional expected NPV for MGRM when prices fall *and* the bases change is more difficult, because the effects are at least partially offsetting. To separate the effects, suppose first the term structure undergoes a uniform, parallel downward shift as spot prices fall. The discount rate in equation (1) would be unaffected, and the expected net present value would rise one-for-one with the fall in the spot price. When prices fall, however, prices of short-term futures typically will fall by more than deferred prices, giving rise to the "horizontal tornadoes" or "diving boards" about which oil derivatives specialists never cease to prattle. But precisely because these effects are concentrated at the short end, their impact on the conditional expected NPV is limited. They show up essentially as a temporary rise in *expected* rollover costs, thus reducing the gross present value of *near-term* deliveries. If the basis were assumed to remain at its high throughout the life of the contracts, the discounting effect would eventually overwhelm the spot-price effect for deliveries as well. But more reasonable estimates of the expected bases for deferred deliveries, calculated from historical market norms, would leave the expected NPV for the deferred deliveries and the program as a whole positive.[32]

Customer Incentives and Credit Risk

Though MGRM would have no obvious incentive to terminate its flow contracts early when prices fall, its *customers* might. The sell-back options, however, specify no termination rights in the event of price *declines*. Customers could unwind their contracts after a price decline only by buying their way out; but they would have no positive incentive to do so unless MGRM offered to settle for less than the present value of the customers' purchase obligations. And indeed, that appears exactly what MGRM did in January 1994 when a new management awakened only belatedly to its naked price exposure following the futures liquidation. Despite the positive gross present value of the flow contracts to MGRM, it offered customers the right to terminate their contracts *with no close-out payment to MGRM*—"leaving money on the table," as they say on Wall Street.[33] How much money new management effectively burned in this fashion was still unknown at the time of this writing, but the cancelled contracts could have been for as much as 60 million bbls.[34]

Although some customers not released from their contracts might well have had incentives to walk away when prices fell, we remain unconvinced that customer credit risk could justify the draconian relief strategy of liquidating the futures hedge. Even in the face of price declines in 1993, no customer defaults have been documented. MGRM had stipulated in its flow contracts that none of its smaller customers could rely on MGRM for more than 20%—usually only 5-10%—of their annual required input purchases. Because MGRM was the only firm selling long-dated fixed-price delivery contracts, this ensured that at least 80% of the input purchases by those firms were being made at *variable* prices. Many of these smaller firms, moreover, were selling oil products at retail prices—far slower to adjust to market conditions than their wholesale input purchase prices.[35] Consequently, the smaller customers would be losing money on and thus might want to exit their flow contracts precisely when they are *making* money from the more than 80% of variable inputs purchased at the lower spot price. Nor should it be assumed in assessing the credit risks in MGRM's strategy that MGRM's customers were all of the mom-and-pop variety. MGRM's customer base also included large firms, Chrysler Corp., Browning-Ferris Industries Corp., and Thornton Oil Corp. among them.

Should MGRM Have Used Long-Dated Futures?

Exactly as in the short-dated stacked hedging strategy, MGRM could have held an amount of futures always equal to its remaining delivery obligations, but this time in contract months with deferred maturity dates. As before, MGRM would have to roll over its hedge every month. This time, however, the current position would be rolled into the new *deferred* contract. This strategy, like MGRM's, would have protected the firm against the risk of rising spot prices.[36]

But the long-dated futures strategy was not obviously a superior alternative for a program as large as MGRM's. Volume and open interest are lower for longer-dated commodity futures contracts, so longer-dated futures would have had substantially higher transaction costs. Lower relative liquidity would also have made it difficult and much costlier for MGRM to switch its hedge between heating oil, gasoline, and crude as seasonal conditions dictated. A long-dated stack would also still have to be rolled each month, often a costly and challenging task in a relatively illiquid contract.

Because long-dated futures prices are imperfectly correlated with front-month prices, moreover, using long-dated futures would have exposed MGRM to basis risk on its customer sell-back options—that is, when the customers exercised their options, the long-dated contract price might not have risen as much as the front-month price on which the options were written. One might imagine that MGRM might then have based the settlement value of the sell-back options on the deferred futures contract, but that would be to miss the point of those options. As with other options, the sell-back options are most valuable when prices are more volatile. In one sense, the spot price itself would have been the ideal asset on which to write the sell-back options, if indeed the concept of the spot price were better defined. Given the complexities of delivery grades, geography, liquidity, and the like, however, using the front-month futures contract here, as elsewhere in commodity markets, is the best approach to defining the "spot commodity."

WAS FUNDING RISK TO BLAME?

Funding risk, or liquidity risk, has been defined as "[t]he inability to meet cash flow obligations at an acceptable price as they become due. . ."[37] Funding risk is a natural suspect for MGRM's problems because futures hedging programs can require substantial infusions of cash to meet variation margin calls when prices are falling. In 1993, oil and oil product prices fell precipitously after OPEC failed to reach agreements on its production quotas, and substantial margin payments were due from MGRM to the NYMEX.

The Funding Risk of a Marketing Program Hedged with Futures

In Figure 19.1 we illustrate the funding risk that a stacked hedger faces when prices fall in a 12-month example (with a zero basis for simplicity). Assume the price of oil

FIGURE 19.1   Funding Risk with a Downward Price Trend (1-Year Fixed-Price Delivery Contract Hedged with Stacked Futures)*

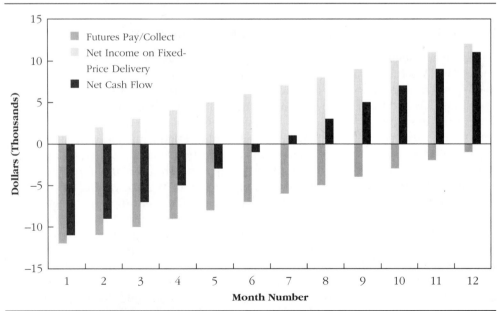

Source: Assume an initial price of $20/bbl. and a $1 price decline each month. The fixed-price delivery involves the monthly sale of 1000 bbls. of oil at $20/bbl. for 12 months. The futures position is a stacked hedge beginning with 12,000 bbls. and declining by 1000 bbls. each month.

falls steadily from \$20/bbl. by \$1 every month, and that margin calls are monthly. The cash flows are for a single flow contract to sell 1,000 bbls. of WTI crude each month at \$20/bbl, and for a futures hedge of 12 contracts in the first month declining by one contract each subsequent month.

Note first that stacking creates a cash flow asymmetry over time between futures pays and collects and the net income on the fixed-price contract. Each \$1 oil price decrease (increase) between settlement dates triggers a pay (collect) on the futures position that is 12-t+1 times larger than the net inflow (outflow) on the 12-month fixed-price contract, where t is the settlement month number. Thus, the cash requirements are largest in the early part of the program when the stack is large and reverse later as deliveries occur.

Although Figure 19.1 is designed to depict the funding risk of stacked futures, it is important to keep in mind that cash flows of the same order of magnitude would be required on *any* futures strategy in which the entire remaining delivery commitment is hedged. The only difference is the less than perfect correlation between futures prices of all maturities. Because short-dated futures are more volatile than long-dated futures, the cash inflows and outflows on a short-dated stack may be larger than those on a long-dated stack, but only marginally so.

The large cash infusions the stacked hedging program would require if prices fell can hardly have come as a surprise to the original management team at MGRM. You don't have to be a rocket scientist, after all, to prepare something like Figure 19.1. Given those likely cash drains, the team at MGRM would presumably not have maintained or expanded its program in the summer and autumn of 1993 unless it thought it had firm assurances from its parent and bank creditors that a secure line of credit was there on which to draw. As things turned out, MGRM had no such firm commitment, though the reasons why are still in dispute (and in litigation).

How Might the Cash Needs Have Been Financed at the Time?

The evidence suggests that funding risk alone was not responsible for the untimely end of MGRM's futures hedge; alternatives *were* available. That MGRM had no access to external financing, except on ruinous, distress terms, cannot be taken seriously. Even if MGRM had been locked out of public capital markets, it hardly needed to go hat-in-hand to strangers unfamiliar with its strategy. Over 100 of the world's leading banks were *already* creditors to MG AG; and Deutsche Bank and Dresdner Bank, two of the world's largest financial institutions, were both major creditors *and* major stockholders of MGRM's parent. And those very same creditors did agree, after all, on January 15, 1994, to a \$1.9 billion capital infusion to MG AG, raising the perplexing question of why that step was taken to cover the liquidation of the hedge rather than to continue financing it.[38]

If the expected net present value of the program was positive and substantial, moreover, the program as a whole should have been viewed as an asset by *any* would-be lenders.[39] Indeed, because the intrinsic asset value of the combined program was locked-in, the program was self-financing in the sense that the accreting gains on the flow contracts as oil prices fell should, in principle, have provided the economic equivalent of at least partial collateral to finance margin calls on the futures leg. Press accounts indicate that several banking institutions, including Chemical Bank and J.P. Morgan, made just such an offer to MGRM but were rebuffed by the new management team.[40] The puzzle thus remains as to why alternative sources of financing could not have been arranged.

Several authorities with whom we have discussed the possibility of collateralizing the margin loan have expressed concerns that the flow contracts alone might not have been usable as collateral because of the inability to "perfect a lien" on forward contracts. If the contracts could not serve directly as collateral, an obvious alternative for firms like MGRM (assuming existing debt covenants allowed it) would be to sell the program as a whole, as was done when the Development Finance Corp. of New Zealand failed;[41] or, to spin off the *combined* delivery/hedging program into a new subsidiary, as is routinely done with accounts receivable subsidiaries or issuers of "securitized products."[42] The stock of the new subsidiary could then be posted as collateral for the loan, with the additional covenant that the subsidiary remain hedged at all times.[43]

If the new affiliate remained hedged, it could continue to service its obligations to the bank no matter how much prices rose. Both firms would benefit from this arrangement; the new subsidiary obtains the funding it needs to continue its hedging/delivery program, thus earning the gross profit locked-in by hedging, and the bank earns interest on its loan.

Note in this connection that under these circumstances, the bank has no need to insist on a variance-minimizing hedge. The function of the variance-minimizing hedge is usually taken to be reducing a firm's reliance on the capital market for external financing by lowering the variance of the firm's cash flows. But what sense does a variance-minimizing hedge at the new subsidiary make for a bank that is *supplying* (at a price) the external financing the variance-minimizing hedge is intended to reduce?

MGRM might also have been able to staunch the cash drains on its futures positions if prices fell further by purchasing futures puts. Such an emergency strategy was in fact suggested by Benson and his team to the new MGRM management but was rejected. To the new team, still concerned about MGRM's cash drain on its futures position, Benson's suggestion must have seemed a classic "hair of the dog" remedy—in which a badly hung-over drunk proposes to start off the day with a double shot of whisky.[44]

Managing Funding Risk *Ex Ante*

Admittedly, arrangements like those above can be difficult to negotiate quickly and under duress, even when not embittered by managerial feuds and finger-pointing. Firms hoping to initiate potentially cash-intensive combined delivery/hedging programs like MGRM's might be well advised, therefore, to do an unsecured borrowing *up front* (in presumably calmer waters) equal to the initial face value of its total futures position—a so-called "pure synthetic" strategy. Rather than depositing only the required minimum initial margin with a futures exchange clearinghouse, such firms could give this *total amount* to the clearinghouse in T-bills thus ensuring that no further cash outlays would be required over the life of the hedge, regardless of price movements.[45] It can be argued, of course, that no lender could have assurance that the unsecured loan would in fact be used to purchase T-bills and posted as margin. But this potential agency problem could be solved by requiring the borrower to keep the funds on deposit at the lender bank. The lender bank would then pay all variation margin calls of the borrower by drawing down its margin-equivalent deposit account.[46]

THE REAL CULPRIT

The forced liquidation of MGRM's futures highlights an ill-defined, catch-all risk category dubbed "operational risk" by the Group of Thirty's Global Derivatives Study Group.[47] In the Group's open-ended definition, operational risk is associated with systems failures, natural disasters, or personnel problems. But operational risk also covers unapproved speculative activities by subordinates not detected by the senior management and board until serious losses have occurred.[48] In referring to MGRM, for example, the General Accounting Office states that "[p]oor operations controls were reportedly responsible for allowing losses at this firm to grow to such levels."[49]

A Failure of Understanding?

MGRM faced operational risk, to be sure, but the opposite of that assumed by the GAO and many others: the supervisory board may not have understood that MGRM was hedging and not speculating. As noted earlier, the team the supervisory board called in to liquidate the futures positions had also been used to resolve the Klöckner speculative episode for Deutsche Bank.[50] The supervisory board may have interpreted MGRM's appeals for more cash as doubling-up or, at the least, as the all-too-typical symptom of an imminent business failure. Or perhaps the supervisory board, in light of the power struggles then going on within MG AG,[51] may have deliberately chosen not to understand MGRM's program.

In any case, unwinding MGRM's futures positions, though widely applauded in some parts of the press then and now, proved unfortunate on several counts.[52] By the time MGRM began to unwind its positions in mid-December, the price of oil had fallen to its low of roughly $14/bbl. The precipitous liquidation of MGRM's futures hedge thus turned paper losses on that leg into realized losses and left MGRM exposed to rising spot prices on its still-outstanding flow delivery contracts. And indeed, as noted earlier, when the new management awakened to its naked price exposure following the liquidation, it began negotiating unwinds of its flow contracts without demanding *any* compensation for its positive expected future cash flows.

In fairness to MG AG, however, ending a combined delivery/hedging program is never costless. As noted earlier, unwinding bilateral contracts may require concessions from the party initiating the unwind. The supervisory board increased the cost of ending the program both by giving *full* concessions to its counterparties and by not following the common practice of unwinding both legs of a hedged transaction as close to simultaneously as possible.

If MGRM had not unwound its futures, the positive daily pays received when prices recovered in 1994 would have given it a substantial positive cash inflow. MGRM's forced liquidation, moreover, sent a signal to MGRM's OTC derivatives counterparties that its credit standing might be in jeopardy, thereby increasing calls for collateral to keep its OTC positions open and making it virtually impossible to establish new OTC positions. (See Appendix 1.)

Accounting and Disclosure

Operational risk can also arise from the accounting and auditing process.[53] Under German accounting rules, assets normally are valued at the lower of historical cost or market value, LOCOM. The U.S. Generally Accepted Accounting Principles

(GAAP), by contrast, allow for "hedge accounting" if a specific hedge transaction can be linked to a specific obligation.[54] Hedge accounting under GAAP then allows the firm to account for the hedge transaction in the same manner as the underlying transaction using either mark-to-market or deferral accounting.

The more conservative German accounting rules thus tend to exaggerate economic losses in hedge operations. In the typical hedge transaction, the profitable leg of the hedge will be valued at cost, thus deferring the gain, while the losing leg of the trade is accounted for at its lower market value, thus recording the loss. By contrast, GAAP would allow both transactions to be deferred or both marked-to-market. Accounting losses under German accounting rules can thus exceed those losses under GAAP for a legitimate hedge transaction.

Whether this difference in accounting treatments was significant in MGRM's case is difficult for outsiders to judge. We do know that Arthur Andersen & Co. had audited MG Corp. and its affiliates through September 30, 1993, and showed a $61 million *profit* under U.S. GAAP before special reserves for MGRM.[55] By contrast, MG's German auditor Klynveld Peat Marwick Goerdeler Deutsche Treuhand Gesellschaft (KPMG) showed an accounting loss of $291 million for the same period for MGRM under German accounting rules, though press accounts suggest that these losses may have been deliberately inflated to discredit the previous management.[56] The discrepancy in the two audits may well have had an unfortunate consequence for MGRM if the accounting loss under German accounting conventions had been perceived as a *real* loss on the combined delivery/hedging program.

That the almost universally cited figure of $1.3 billion for MGRM's loss on oil derivatives might contain "big bath" write-offs seemed likely to us from the publicly available information on the company's positions. But the $1.3 billion figure for *gross* cash losses has since been confirmed in an auditors' report commissioned last year by the shareholders of MG AG.[57] The auditors put the *net* loss at $1.0 billion, but only because they grossly underestimate the appreciation in the value of the flow contracts as prices fell. We have estimated the real 1993 net loss in the combined delivery/hedging program to be about $200 million.[58]

CONCLUSION

Why did MGRM's synthetic storage program come to such grief? Was it fatally flawed—an accident waiting to happen? Or was it killed off prematurely? Although we lean to the latter view, we recognize that the deeper issue of the long-run viability of synthetic storage programs like MGRM's cannot yet be settled definitively. The identification problem is insuperable: many contending theories, but only a single observation! We can only hope that other firms, in the petroleum industry or elsewhere, adopt programs similar to MGRM's. If indeed any are willing to follow MGRM's pioneering path, perhaps our account here may at least help show them where they are most likely to run into trouble along the way.

To avoid being ambushed, top managers and directors of those firms need not become derivatives experts—as some legislators and regulators at the moment seem to be urging—but they must understand the essential logic behind their firms' marketing and hedging strategies and the long-term commitments needed to make the programs work. Otherwise, their firms may encounter not the classical gambler's ruin problem—they will be hedging and not gambling, after all—but an insidious new phenomenon of the derivatives age: an economically sound hedging program may be liquidated prematurely because highly visible rollover costs and temporary cash drains may be construed by top management as gambling losses. Perhaps we might call this new phenomenon "hedger's ruin."

APPENDIX I: OVER-THE-COUNTER DERIVATIVES

MGRM negotiated OTC derivatives contracts largely maturing in three months or less to mimic its futures stack. The OTC positions thus were for all practical purposes indistinguishable from futures—setting credit risk aside. But the OTC products subjected MGRM to some risks that the futures did not, and the premature liquidation of MGRM's hedge transformed these risks into reality. OTC derivatives do not utilize margin explicitly and usually do not involve cash flows other than those occurring on settlement dates. Adverse price movements thus do not *always* precipitate cash flows between OTC derivatives counterparties. But sometimes they do.

Cash flow needs could have arisen on OTC derivatives if MGRM's perceived credit risk changed. "Credit enhancements" are often demanded by counterparties to reduce their credit exposure to institutions with increased default potential. The three most common forms of credit enhancements accepted by dealers are cash collateral, securities collateral, and third-party guarantees of performance. Of the dealers using collateral surveyed by the Group of Thirty, over 70% vary the amount of collateral depending on their exposure to the counterparty. Specifically, at least 55% of those dealers demand additional collateral if their counterparty receives a credit downgrade.[59]

For short-dated OTC contracts, counterparties would use collateral much as exchanges use margin. OTC dealers would simply require advance posting of collateral before rolling into a new OTC contract. MGRM would thus have faced potential funding needs on its OTC contracts if it or its parent experienced a perceived credit deterioration. When the supervisory board of MG began liquidating the futures hedge in full public view, it became apparent that the flow contracts were being "unhedged." This prompted calls for collateral from OTC counterparties and impaired MGRM's ability to roll over the short-dated OTC contracts.

MGRM might have avoided concentrating its OTC hedge in longer-dated OTC derivatives because they can be difficult to liquidate. Master agreements governing most OTC derivatives usually do not allow firms in MGRM's position simply to decide to terminate. On the contrary, adverse credit events give the *non*defaulting counterparties the right to terminate the swap early but do *not* usually give that right to the defaulting counterparty.[60] If, therefore, MGRM's counterparties chose to demand collateral in accordance with negotiated master agreements rather than terminate the contracts, MGRM would either have had to post the collateral, default on the contracts, sell them to another party, or negotiate close outs with the original counterparties—all expensive choices.

Long-term OTC derivatives subject their users to counterparty credit risk. On ten-year commodity swaps, *any* corporation is likely to be perceived as a potential credit risk, making costly credit enhancements or collateral requirements possible. Perhaps more importantly, few OTC derivatives dealers would enter into such a long-dated commodity swap without in turn also hedging that risk.

Dealers virtually always either hedge their exposures directly or enter into off-setting transactions when negotiating a transaction. If a dealer hedges its exposure from entering 10-year commodity swaps, it loads the cost of hedging that contract into the price of the transaction paid by its counterparty. Because a dealer would have to use a strategy such as stacking and rolling, it would in turn presumably pass along those costs (and perhaps add a risk premium) to MGRM. As a large corporation already involved in derivatives, there is no reason to believe MGRM's cost of hedging directly with futures would have been higher than those of an OTC dealer.

APPENDIX 2: DATA

We obtained daily settlement prices for futures contracts of all maturities on NYMEX light, sweet crude oil, New York habor regular unleaded gasoline, and No. 2 New York harbor heating oil from the Futures Industry Institute in Washington, D.C. Spot data were also obtained from FII for crude oil and heating oil but were unavailable for gasoline.

A monthly time series of front-month futures prices was constructed for each commodity based on an assumed rollover date. For light, sweet crude, rollovers are assumed to occur on the 15th of the month or on the first business day preceding the 15th when the 15th is not a business day. For heating oil and gasoline, the front-month contract is rolled over on the last business day of the month.

We define the relation between spot and futures prices in the text in two ways. When we refer to the "basis," we define it as a fraction of the spot price, or

$$b_{t,t+1} = F_{t,t+1} - S_t/S_t$$

measured on the first business day *following* an assumed rollover. The December 1993 heating oil basis, for example, is measured on December 1, 1993, corresponding to the rollover initiated on November 30, 1993.

Because spot prices were unavailable for gasoline, we define the gasoline basis as $F_{t,t+1} - F_{t,t}/F_{t,t}$, or the proportional difference between the one-month futures price and the maturing futures contract price. Spot and futures prices must converge at futures maturity, so this is a reasonable approximation to the actual gasoline spot-futures basis.

Our second measure for the relation between spot and futures prices is the "lump-sum basis," defined as $F_{t,t+1} - S_t$. Like the proportional basis, we measure the lump-sum basis on the first business day following a rollover.

We define "rollover costs" as the difference between the maturing futures contract price and the price of a new one-month futures contract one day hence $(F_{t,t+1} - F_{t,t})$. Because we measure rollover costs near the expiration date of the maturing futures contract, the convergence of spot and futures prices at maturity ensures that the lump-sum basis is closely related to per contract rollover costs. We make the simplifying assumption that rollovers are non-synchronous, so the rollover cost is the difference in the price of the futures contract being offset on the rollover date and the price of the new contract into which the firm rolls *on the next business day.* Rollover costs are thus assumed realized when the new front-month contract price is sampled. As with the basis, the observation for the December 1993 rollover is thus dated December 1, 1993.

In the absence of spot data for gasoline, we assume the lump-sum basis and per contract rollover costs are the same.

ENDNOTES

1. *See* Kenneth Gilpin, "Trying to Rescue a Soured Oil Bet," *New York Times* (March 9, 1994):D1.

2. For an account of the internal politics behind the liquidation decision, *see* Jens Eckhardt and Thomas Knipp, "Das Protokoll einer vermeidbaren Krise," *Handelsblatt* (November 4, 1994):28–29. We thank our colleague Rudi Schadt for his help in translating this very revealing article. *See also Heinz Schimmelbusch v. Ronaldo Schmitz, Deutsche Bank AG, and Metallgesellschaft AG,* Civ. Act. No. 94-134662, Supreme Court of the State of New York (December 16, 1994).

3. MGRM also engaged in "synthetic refining" by going long crude oil and short refined oil product futures (or vice versa)—in industry parlance, trading the "crack spread." (*See* Robert C. Merton, "Financial Innovation and the Management and Regulation of Financial Institutions," *Journal of Banking and Finance,* Vol. 19, No. 1 (1995 forthcoming).) To keep the story uncluttered, however, we will focus here mainly on MGRM's long-term flow contract and synthetic storage program.

4. Press accounts and statements from the new management of MG AG, possibly self-serving, have raised questions about the role MGRM's "offtake agreements" with Castle Energy might have played in the decision to liquidate MGRM's futures hedge. Because the public record on this matter is far from complete, however, we shall here and throughout be treating MGRM's combined delivery/hedging program as independent of the Castle Energy program.

5. *W. Arthur Benson v. Metallgesellschaft Corp. et. al.,* Civ. Act. No. JFM-94-484, U.S.D.C.D. Md. (1994):5.

6. MGRM's program is squarely in the tradition of Holbrook Working rather than in the these-days more familiar context of "variance-minimizing hedging." Stated differently, MGRM might be considered as effectively "risk-neutral" with little concern for the expected costs of bankruptcy given the financing commitments it believed it had from its parent and deep-pocketed shareholder/creditors. Much of the discussion of hedging in the finance and trade literatures is thus applicable only peripherally to our analysis of MGRM.

7. Under NYMEX rules, MGRM had been granted a "hedging exemption," allowing it to hold total futures positions of 55 million bbls. (25 million bbls. of WTI crude, 15 million bbls. of gasoline, and 15 million bbls. of heating oil). NYMEX rules also limit substantially the amount held in the front or delivery month contract. For simplicity of exposition, however, we assume throughout that the entire position was in the front-month futures contract even though, as will become clearer later, this assumption exaggerates some of the costs of managing the program.

8. The major portion of MGRM's hedge was actually in "over-the-counter" (OTC) derivatives, including commodity swaps and forwards. If it hedged a total of 150 million bbls., its OTC position would have been on the order of 95 million bbls. These OTC positions, rarely more than three months to maturity, were functionally equivalent to the futures MGRM held, so that, for simplicity, we proceed as if MGRM's entire hedge was in futures. MGRM's OTC position is discussed in Appendix 1.

9. For an account of how futures may be used in seasonal inventory management, *see* Holbrook Working, "Futures Trading and Hedging," *American Economic Review* (June 1953):314–43, and Holbrook Working, "New Concepts Concerning Futures Markets and Prices," *American Economic Review* (June 1962):432–59.

10. Just how to interpret that contractual obligation to remain hedged is precisely the issue in one prominent and highly contentious court case. *See Thornton Oil Corp. v. MG Refining and Marketing, Inc.* Civ. Act. No. 94-CI-01653, Jefferson Circuit Court Div. Five, Ky. (March 29, 1994).

11. Portions of this section are based on Christopher L. Culp and Merton H. Miller, "Hedging a Flow of Commodity Deliveries with Futures: Lessons from Metallgesellschaft," *Derivatives Quarterly* Vol. 1, No. 1 (Fall 1994).

12. The only perfect hedge can be found in a Japanese garden, as accountants often quip. Certainly the so-called "variance-minimizing hedge," which would presumably involve a smaller stack, does not meet the test of perfection in this context for a variety of reasons. The key coefficients underlying the "optimal" hedge ratio can only be estimated from past data subject to considerable error. A hedge designed solely to minimize the variance of net cash flows in the face of price changes, moreover, need not be maximizing expected returns to the firm. Important managerial and control motivations for corporate hedging also exist that are not always well-captured by a variance-minimizing approach. We will deal with some of these issues in a subsequent paper.

13. Because futures contracts, unlike forward contracts, are marked to market daily, normal market practice is to reduce the size of a hedge by "tailing." (*See, for example,* Ira G. Kawaller, "Comparing

Eurodollar Strips to Interest Rate Swaps," *Journal of Derivatives* Vol. 2, No. 1 (Fall 1994):67–79, and the references therein.) We ignore this adjustment in our examples for simplicity.

14. Note that while the policy is dynamic in the sense that the number of contracts in the stack changes over time, the policy is not appropriately described as "dynamic hedging." Unlike true dynamic hedging, the synthetic storage stack adjusts not to changes in *prices,* but only to the quantities actually delivered. MGRM, it is true, might well have increased its expected long-run profits by dynamic hedging—increasing the stack as prices rise, and decreasing it as prices fall. But there are no free lunches. Catastrophic losses can result if prices gap unexpectedly and adversely while the futures portfolio is being rebalanced—as dynamic hedgers in a variety of contexts have learned to their sorrow over the years.

15. Crude oil is used in the examples because prices and the quantities for crude are denominated in more tractable units than heating oil and gasoline.

16. For a succinct explanation of the cost of carry formula, *see* Merton H. Miller, "Equilibrium Relations Between Cash and Futures Markets," in *Financial Innovations and Market Volatility* (Cambridge: Blackwell, 1991).

17. Past results, of course, are no guarantee of future performance—a phrase familiar enough from mutual fund prospectuses—but ample theoretical grounds exist for believing that the numbers above are not just sample-dependent flukes. *See* Robert H. Litzenberger and Nir Rabinowitz, "Backwardation in Oil Futures Markets: Theory and Empirical Evidence," Working Paper, The Wharton School (April 11, 1994).

18. *See* Jeffrey Williams, *The Economic Function of Futures Markets* (Cambridge: Cambridge University Press, 1986), and the references therein.

19. Michael J. Hutchinson, "The Metallgesellschaft Affair: Risk Management in the Real World," Memorandum (October 10, 1994):3. Hutchinson was a member of the management team that took over in December 1993 and unwound MGRM's futures positions.

20. William Falloon, "The Market Responds," *Risk* Vol.7, No. 10 (October 1994):29.

21. *See, for example,* Hutchinson, cited previously, and Falloon, cited previously.

22. Some critics of MGRM have argued that MGRM's position in the oil market was so large by November that its very presence kept the market in contango, presumably because prices were bid up by other traders on the contracts into which they knew MGRM had to roll each month and bid down on the contracts MGRM was offsetting. Assuming MGRM held as many futures contracts as the NYMEX allowed firms with a hedge exemption, MGRM would have held 25,000 WTI crude futures, 15,000 gasoline futures, and 15,000 heating oil futures. Those amounts would have constituted 6.32%, 11.06%, and 7.88% of the total NYMEX open interest in December 1993 in those products—hardly numbers to suggest MGRM was driving the market. Note also that crude oil, at least, remained in contango as late as March, long after MGRM's futures liquidation.

23. No evidence of which we are aware supports the notion that a structural change in market conditions occurred in 1993. Although realized rollover costs were high, the coefficients of determination of futures prices regressed on spot prices in 1993 are virtually the same as those for the full sample.

24. *See* Christopher L. Culp and Merton H. Miller, "The Net Present Value of Hedged Commodity Contracts," mimeo, The University of Chicago, Graduate School of Business (forthcoming, 1995).

25. WTI crude futures are also listed for maturities of 21, 24, 30, and 36 months to maturity, but those contracts are relatively illiquid.

26. For a detailed proof, *see* Culp and Miller, mimeo, cited previously.

27. Culp and Miller, mimeo, cited previously.

28. The Chrysler Corp., for example, had a policy of putting five gallons of gasoline into every completed car coming off its assembly lines. Failure to have gasoline on-hand could mean shutting down the whole assembly line.

29. For a discussion of the costs of unwinding, *see* Christopher L. Culp and Barbara T. Kavanagh, "Methods of Unwinding Over-the-Counter Derivatives Contracts in Failed Depository Institutions: Federal Banking Law Restrictions on Regulators," *Futures International Law Letter* 14(3–4) (May/June 1994):1–19.

30. *See* the ISDA Master Agreements (1992), § 5–6 (events which trigger terminations of the Agreements), § 7 (restrictions on transfers), and § 6(e)(i)-(ii) (method of payment for close-out netting after a default or early termination). The ISDA Master Agreements are not the only master agreements, but they are the most widely used for common OTC derivatives contracts.

31. The uncertainty about the true tenor of the flow contracts will also seriously complicate the calculation of the size of the appropriate tail. *See* our earlier reference to tailing.

32. An upward-sloping term structure, moreover, implies a market expectation of rising spot prices and, hence, a declining basis. *See, for example,* Eugene F. Fama and Kenneth R. French, "Commodity Futures Prices: Some Evidence on Forecast Power, Premiums, and the Theory of Storage," *Journal of Business,* Vol. 60 (January 1987):55–74.

33. Plaintiff W. Arthur Benson's Reply to Defendants MG Corp. and MGR&M's Memorandum in Opposition to Plaintiff's *Motion for Permission to Depose MG Corp.'s Former General Counsel, W. Arthur Benson v. Metallgesellschaft Corp. et. al.,* Civ. Act. No. JFM-94-484, U.S.D.C.D. Md. (October 1994):3.

34. *See* Christopher L. Culp and Merton H. Miller, "Auditing the MG Shareholders' Audit," mimeo, The University of Chicago, Graduate School of Business (March 1995).

35. Note that the sluggishness of retail price adjustment works in the opposite way when wholesale prices rise. As retail prices rise more slowly, MGRM's customers might well welcome the immediate cash payment from MGRM in return for terminating their long-term flow contracts.

36. MGRM also might have employed several variations of this strategy, such as combining it with a strip for listed contract months—that is, matching futures maturities to flow contract deliveries for the listed futures contracts and stacking in the most deferred futures contract to hedge deliveries beyond that maturity. For a flow contract with five or 10 years to maturity, however, this strip and stack would be closer to a long-dated stack than a strip for most of the contract's tenor.

37. Office of the Comptroller of the Currency, "Risk Management of Financial Derivatives," *Banking Circular No. 277* (October 27, 1993).

38. Some believe that the liquidation of MGRM's program was inevitable once press reports of liquidity problems at MGRM appeared in early December, 1993. It is hard to believe, however, that a reassuring statement from Deutsche Bank at that point would not have quieted those concerns.

39. If lenders perceived, however, that MGRM itself as a company had a negative present value (as some have suggested because of the offtake agreements with Castle Energy mentioned earlier), even secured lending might have been problematic.

40. *See* Eckhardt and Knipp, cited previously, and *Schimmelbusch v. Schmitz et. al.,* cited previously. The precise details of those offers, however, have not been made clear.

41. *See* Culp and Kavanagh, cited previously.

42. For an example, *see* Barbara Kavanagh, Thomas R. Boemio, and Gerald A. Edwards, Jr., "Asset-Backed Commercial Paper Programs," *Federal Reserve Bulletin,* Vol. 78, No. 2 (February 1992):107–118.

43. If existing covenants preclude splitting off the delivery/hedging program, the funds would have to be provided by an equity infusion or additional subordinated debt. When MG AG was restructured in January 1994, additional equity and subordinated debt were indeed added.

44. For an account of the new team's views on liquidation strategy, *see* Gilpin, cited previously.

45. Not the least of the advantages in the notion of a pure synthetic strategy is its putting to rest, once and for all, the widely-held view that the "maturity mismatch" in a long-term delivery program hedged with short-term futures must inevitably give rise to financial distress when prices fall.

46. Either form of the pure synthetic strategy would allow the firm to earn interest on its margin or margin-equivalent deposit. Thus, despite the seemingly large numbers of the *principal* values involved, the total *interest* cost would only be the net difference in interest paid on the loan and the interest earned. If prices fall, of course, the amount of funds on deposit earning interest will fall below the principal on the loan. In this sense, when prices fall there is an additional interest cost to the firm over and above the interest cost built into the basis, but the opposite is also true when prices rise.

47. Global Derivatives Study Group, *Derivatives: Practices and Principles* (Washington, DC: The Group of Thirty, July 1993).

48. *See* Global Derivatives Study Group, cited previously:50–51.

49. General Accounting Office, *Financial Derivatives: Actions Needed to Protect the Financial System,* GAO/GGD-94-133 (May 1994):4.

50. *See* Gilpin, cited previously.

51. *See* Eckhardt and Knipp, cited previously.

52. Contrary to many press accounts, the unwinding was *not* undertaken in response to the removal of MGRM's hedging exemption by the NYMEX. In fact, the hedging exemption expired at the end of December 1993, by which time the liquidation of MGRM's hedge was well underway.

53. For another account of how MGRM's problems trace in part to accounting and disclosure rules, *see* Franklin R. Edwards, "Systemic Risk in OTC Derivatives Markets: Much Ado About Not Too Much," presented before the conference on Coping with Financial Fragility: A Global Perspective (Maastricht: September 7-9, 1994):28-29.

54. This is called a "micro hedge." If a hedge transaction cannot be associated with a specific balance sheet entry, it does not necessarily receive hedge accounting treatment under GAAP. *See, for example,* Jennifer Francis, "Accounting for Futures Contracts and the Effect on Earnings Variability," *The Accounting Review* 65(4) (October 1990).

55. *See* Benson, cited previously: 8-9.

56. *See* Eckhardt and Knipp, cited previously.

57. Coopers & Lybrand Treuarbeit Deutsche Revision and Wollert-Elmendorff Treuhand, *Report No. 4011742 RE: The Special Audit in Accordance with Paragraph 142 Section 1 AktG of Metallgesellschaft Aktiengesellschaft Frankfurt am Main* (February 1995).

58. *See* Culp and Miller, "Auditing. . . ," cited previously.

59. Group of Thirty Global Derivatives Study Group, *Appendix III: Survey of Industry Practice,* in *Derivatives: Practices and Principles* (Washington, D.C.: The Group of Thirty, March 1994).

60. *See* Culp and Kavanagh, cited previously.

20

The Collapse of Metallgesellschaft: Unhedgeable Risks, Poor Hedging Strategy, or Just Bad Luck?

FRANKLIN R. EDWARDS
MICHAEL S. CANTER

I n late 1993 and early 1994, MG Corporation, the U.S. subsidiary of Germany's 14th largest industrial firm, Metallgesellschaft A.G. (MG), reported staggering losses on its positions in energy futures and swaps. Only a massive $1.9 billion rescue operation by 150 German and international banks kept Metallgesellschaft A.G. from going into bankruptcy, an event that could have had far-reaching consequences for MG's creditors, suppliers, and its 58,000 employees.

During 1993, MG's U.S oil trading subsidiary, MG Refining and Marketing (MGRM), established very large derivatives positions in energy futures and swaps (equivalent to about 160 million barrels of oil), from which it would profit handsomely if energy prices were to rise. But instead of rising, energy prices (crude oil, heating oil, and gasoline) fell sharply during the latter part of 1993, causing MGRM to incur unrealized losses and margin calls on these derivatives positions in excess of $900 million.

Initial press reports indicated that MG's predicament was the result of massive speculation in energy futures and off-exchange (OTC) energy swaps by MGRM. Some members of Metallgesellschaft A.G.'s Supervisory Board also characterized MGRM's oil trading activities as "a game of roulette." And when MG's Supervisory Board installed new management at MGRM near the end of 1993, the new management team declared that "speculative oil deals . . . had plunged Metallgesellschaft into the crisis."[1]

Originally published in the *Journal of Applied Corporate Finance* 8(1), Spring. This chapter is an abbreviated version of an earlier article in the *Journal of Futures Market* (Vol. 15, No. 3) May 1995. Reprinted with permission. For a complete set of citations, references, and figures, see the earlier article.

Not all press reports, however, have held to this view. Some have suggested that MGRM's derivatives activities were in fact part of a complex oil marketing and hedging strategy that it was pursuing. In particular, MGRM reportedly was using its derivatives positions to hedge price exposure on forward-supply contracts that committed it to supply approximately 160 million barrels of gasoline and heating oil to end-users over the next ten years at fixed prices. The fixed supply prices in these contracts, negotiated at the time that the contracts were established, were typically three to five dollars a barrel higher than prevailing spot prices when the contracts were negotiated (and were MGRM's profit margins or mark-ups).[2]

The forward delivery contracts also contained a cash-out option for MGRM's counterparties. If energy prices were to rise above the contractually fixed price, MGRM's counterparties could choose to sell the remainder of its forward obligations back to MGRM for a cash payment of one-half the difference between the prevailing near-month futures price and the contractually fixed supply price times the total volume remaining on the contract.

Most of the forward delivery contracts were negotiated during the summer of 1993, when energy prices were low and falling. Energy end-users apparently saw an attractive opportunity to lock in low energy prices, and MGRM apparently saw an equally attractive opportunity to develop long-term profitable customer relationships that it could build on in pursuing its long-run strategy of developing a fully-integrated oil business in the United States.[3] MGRM's counterparties in these forward contracts were retail gasoline suppliers, large manufacturing firms, and some government entities. Although many of the end-users were small, some were substantial firms: Chrysler Corporation, Browning-Ferris Industries Corporation, and Comcar Industries (which uses 60 million gallons of diesel fuel a year).

In 1989, as part of its efforts to develop a fully-integrated oil business in the United States, MGRM also acquired a 49% interest in Castle Energy, a U.S. oil exploration company, which it then helped to become an oil refiner. In order to assure a supply of energy products in the future, MGRM agreed to purchase Castle's entire output of refined products (estimated to be about 126,000 barrels a day) at guaranteed margins for up to ten years into the future. In addition, MGRM set about to develop an infrastructure to support the storage and transportation of various oil products.

MGRM's fixed-price forward delivery contracts exposed it to the risk of rising energy prices. If energy prices were to rise in the future, it could find itself in the unprofitable position of having to supply energy products to customers at prices below prevailing spot prices. More important, if prices rose high enough and remained high, the profit margins in the contracts would be eroded and MGRM could end up taking substantial losses for years to come.

MGRM hedged this price risk with energy futures and OTC swaps. Not to have hedged would have put MGRM (and therefore MG) in the position of making a substantial bet that energy prices would either fall or at least not rise in the future. Had MGRM been able to hedge its price risk successfully, it stood to make substantial profits. By locking in an average contractual mark-up of $4 a barrel on its forward energy sales over ten years, it would have earned profits of approximately $640 million.

The controversy surrounding MG's fate is whether MGRM's hedging strategy was in fact ever capable of locking in these profits. Critics contend that its hedging strategy was fatally flawed, and exposed the firm to unacceptable risks. The objective in this chapter is to examine the risks that MGRM was taking and to clarify the risk trade-offs that it was making. In addition, the chapter provides as many facts as are available so that readers can judge for themselves whether MGRM's hedging strategy exposed the firm to an unreasonable risk.

A complicating factor in evaluating a hedger's risk exposure is that all hedgers take some risk. As every student of futures markets knows, hedgers are "speculators on the basis," trading a greater price risk for a lessor basis risk.[4] To determine whether a particular hedger's strategy is sound, the risk assumed by the firm must be evaluated in the context of the firm's objectives. The objective of MGRM's hedging strategy was to protect the profit margins in its forward delivery contracts by insulating them from increases in energy prices. The overall strategic objective of MG, however, was to develop a fully-integrated oil business in the United States. MGRM's role in this strategy was to market and supply petroleum products to end-users, which it did through its forward-delivery program. The soundness of MGRM's hedging strategy, therefore, should be judged against both its specific hedging objective as well as the firm's overall strategic objective.

MGRM'S SHORT-DATED STACK HEDGING STRATEGY

MGRM hedged the risk of rising energy prices with both short-dated energy futures contracts and OTC swaps. It acquired long futures positions on the New York Mercantile Exchange (NYMEX), and entered into OTC energy swaps entitling it to receive payments based upon floating energy prices while making fixed payments. MGRM's counterparties in these swaps were large OTC swap dealers such as banks. By the fourth quarter of 1993, MGRM held long futures positions on the NYMEX equivalent to 55 million barrels of gasoline, heating oil, and crude oil (55,000 contracts), and had swap positions of 100 to 110 million barrels—substantial positions by any measure. MGRM's total derivatives position was virtually identical to its forward-supply commitments: 160 million barrels. Thus, MGRM hedged its forward-supply commitments "barrel for barrel" (or with a hedge ratio of one).[5]

An important aspect of MGRM's hedging strategy was that its derivatives positions were concentrated (or "stacked") in short-dated futures and swaps that had to be "rolled forward" continuously to maintain the position.[6] In general, its futures and swap positions were in contracts with maturities of at most a few months from the current date. It therefore had to roll these contracts forward periodically (probably monthly) to maintain its hedge. As MGRM rolled its derivatives positions forward each month, it reduced the size of its derivatives positions by the amount of the product delivered to customers that month, maintaining a one-to-one hedge.

This stack-and-roll strategy can be profitable when markets are in *backwardation*—that is, loosely speaking, when spot prices are higher than futures prices. But when markets are in *contango*—futures prices are higher than spot prices—the strategy will result in losses. In a backwardation market, a strategy of continually rolling short-dated positions forward yields "rollover gains" because oil for immediate delivery ("nearby" oil) gets a higher price than does, say, three-month oil ("deferred-month" oil). In a contango market, however, MGRM would incur rollover losses; it would be forced to purchase deferred-month futures at higher prices than the prices it could sell these contracts for as they neared expiration. Thus, the success of MGRM's stack-and-roll strategy partially depended on whether energy markets were going to be in contango or backwardation.

WHAT WENT WRONG?

MGRM's problems surfaced in late 1993 when energy spot prices tumbled. As a result, it experienced large unrealized losses on its stacked long futures and swap positions and incurred huge margin calls.[7] MGRM's problems were compounded by the fact that energy futures markets went into a contango price relationship for almost the entire year of 1993, causing it to incur substantial costs each time it rolled its derivatives positions forward.

If energy prices had risen rather than fallen, MGRM would not have had a problem. It would have had unrealized gains on its derivatives positions, and positive margin flows (or cash in-flows). Although it would also have had unrealized losses on its forward delivery obligations, no one would have cared. But energy prices did fall, from around $19 a barrel of crude oil in June of 1993 to less than $15 a barrel in December 1993, causing MGRM to have to come up with enormous amounts of money to fund margin calls. In December 1993, at the height of what to many seemed like a liquidity crisis, MG's Supervisory Board fired MGRM's management and brought in new management, which quickly made the decision to liquidate the bulk of MGRM's derivatives and forward delivery positions.

Was MGRM's short-dated, stack, hedging strategy fatally flawed? Critics assert that this strategy exposed it to three significant and related risks: *rollover risk, funding risk,* and *credit risk.* It was exposed to rollover risk because of uncertainty about whether it would sustain gains or losses when rolling its derivatives positions forward. Critics also believe that MGRM was exposed to funding risk because of the mark-to-market conventions that applied to its short-dated derivatives positions. Finally, they claim that MGRM was exposed to credit risk because its forward delivery counterparties might default on their long-dated obligations to purchase oil at fixed prices. Each of these risks is examined in the sections of the paper which follow.

PHYSICAL STORAGE AS AN ALTERNATIVE HEDGING STRATEGY

To better understand MGRM's rationale for choosing to hedge with short-dated derivatives, it is instructive to examine why it did not hedge by physical storage.[8] MGRM clearly could have hedged the price risk on its forward delivery contracts by purchasing and storing the amount of physical oil (or other energy products) needed to meet its forward-supply commitments, thereby locking in today's energy prices. This strategy, however, while assuring that MGRM would have the oil it needed in the future, would have locked in a *loss* rather than a profit.

Physical storage is not costless. Funds must be committed to the immediate purchase of oil ("financing" costs), and there are "storage" costs—storage tanks, insurance, and so forth. In MGRM's case, these costs would have exceeded the profit margins built into its forward-supply contracts, so that it would have ended up losing money on its forward delivery contracts. In fact, if total storage costs were to exceed 7.33 cents per barrel per month, a strategy of physical storage would have resulted in a net loss for MGRM. (See our *JFM* article cited earlier.) The actual cost of physical storage is considerably higher.[9] Thus, while a strategy of physical storage could have successfully eliminated MGRM's price risk, it also would have eliminated the profits on its forward sales.[10]

By using short-dated derivatives, or a "synthetic" storage strategy, MGRM believed that it could successfully hedge its price risk while having to pay what was in effect a lower cost of storage.[11] More specifically, it believed that, because energy futures markets are often in "backwardation," when it rolled its short-dated derivatives positions forward through time it would receive a "convenience yield" that would offset or reduce the implicit costs of storing oil. The success of MGRM's hedging strategy, therefore, depended on the belief that it would profit from rolling forward its short-dated derivatives positions.

MGRM'S BELIEF THAT ROLLOVERS WOULD BE PROFITABLE

Some idea of what MGRM believed its rollover gain was likely to be can be obtained from data on historical price relationships in energy markets. To estimate likely rollover gains and losses, however, two assumptions must be made about exactly how MGRM went about rolling its positions forward.[12] First, we assumed that each month MGRM purchased the futures contract with the second closest delivery date (hereafter referred to as the "second-month" futures), requiring delivery in approximately one month from the purchase date. Second, we assumed that four days prior to the end of trading on these contracts (or three days prior to the last day of trading on the contracts), MGRM sold these contracts and again purchased second-month futures contracts.[13] This rolling-forward trading strategy is referred to as the "three-day rollover rule." The rollover gains and losses that result from this rule are calculated as the near-month futures price minus the second-month futures price on the third day prior to the last day of trading.[14] (Other rollover rules were also analyzed with similar results.[15]) Closing (or settlement) prices are used for all calculations.

Table 20.1 shows how MGRM would have fared using the three-day rollover rule during the nearly 11-year period from April 1983 to December 1992.[16] These results are based on daily data for crude oil, heating oil, and gasoline, using closing (or settlement) prices. Several results in Table 20.1 are noteworthy. First, energy markets show a high *frequency of backwardation,* or a high frequency of rollover gains. For example, in the case of crude oil futures, on about 67% of the rollover dates the price of the second-month futures contract was below the price of the "spot" futures contract (or the contract closest to delivery). Thus, in crude oil futures MGRM would have made a positive return, or had a rollover gain, on two-thirds of its rollovers. The corresponding figures for heating oil and gasoline futures are 45% and 70%, respectively. (Monthly rollover gains and losses are shown in Figure 20.1 for crude oil.[17])

Second, dividing all rollover dates into two categories based on whether the market was in contango or backwardation on that date, the *average monthly rollover gain far exceeds the average monthly rollover loss.* The average monthly rollover losses and gains in crude oil, heating oil, and gasoline are, respectively, -0.24/barrel vs. 0.48/barrel; -0.33/barrel vs. 1.10/barrel; and -0.51/barrel vs. 0.86/barrel. Given these disparities in the magnitude of average rollover gains and losses, rollovers would have produced a net loss only if the frequency of contango in these markets were to far exceed the frequency of backwardation, which, as we have seen, is not the case.

TABLE 20.1 Summary of Rollover Gains and Losses Using Three-Day Rollover Rule* April 1983–December 1992

		Crude Oil	Heating Oil	Gasoline
Summary Statistics	Mean Rollover	0.25	0.32	0.45
(April 1983–	Mean of All Rollover Gains	0.48	1.10	0.86
December 1992)**	Mean of All Rollover Losses	−0.24	−0.33	−0.51
	Cumulative Rollover Gain	29.63	37.69	43.58
	Frequency of a Rollover Gain	67%	45%	70%
Frequency of a	Jan	67%	89%	50%
Rollover Gain	Feb	78%	78%	13%
	Mar	67%	100%	38%
	Apr	80%	100%	75%
	May	40%	70%	88%
	Jun	50%	10%	88%
	Jul	70%	0%	88%
	Aug	60%	0%	100%
	Sep	80%	0%	88%
	Oct	70%	0%	88%
	Nov	80%	50%	75%
	Dec	70%	60%	56%
Cumulative Rollover	Jan	3.70	13.20	0.02
Gains by Month**	Feb	3.80	10.68	−2.75
	Mar	1.99	9.77	−3.18
	Apr	2.09	8.41	5.95
	May	2.03	1.71	5.59
	Jun	2.24	−1.46	6.17
	Jul	1.82	−3.76	5.63
	Aug	0.71	−3.89	6.88
	Sep	3.17	−3.74	7.00
	Oct	2.39	−3.29	8.94
	Nov	2.66	−1.02	3.10
	Dec	3.03	11.09	0.23
Cumulative Rollover	1983	1.14	−0.60	
Gains by Year**	1984	−0.55	6.18	−0.25
	1985	9.50	6.75	11.75
	1986	1.53	5.32	3.36
	1987	3.64	0.70	0.17
	1988	1.42	2.83	8.58
	1989	7.96	12.15	6.35
	1990	1.15	2.33	7.47
	1991	4.23	3.97	7.56
	1992	−0.39	−1.94	−1.41

*All rollovers are calculated using a three-day rollover rule: on the third day prior to the last day of trading we sell the near month contract and buy the contract month which is the second closest to delivery. The rollover gain or loss is calculated as the near month price minus the second month price. Data for gasoline begins in December 1984. We have also calculated these statistics after excluding the extreme observations in late 1989. The results do not change appreciably, except for heating oil, where the mean rollover becomes .20 and the mean of all rollover gains becomes .85.

**All rollover gains, losses, and means are reported in $/barrel. Heating oil and gasoline are traded on a $/gallon basis. There are 42 gallons per barrel.

Data Source: Knight-Ridder Futures Markets Database

**FIGURE 20.1   Crude Oil Monthly Rollover Gains and Losses
(April 1983–September 1994)**

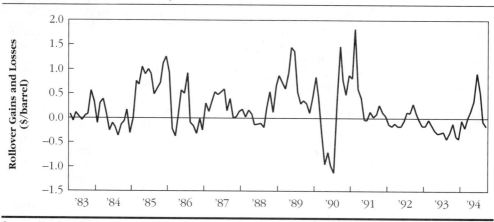

Source: Knight-Ridder

In markets prone to backwardation, as are energy futures markets, it is not surprising to find that average price backwardation exceeds average price contango. The amount of contango is limited by arbitrage to the "full cost-of-carry" (cash-and-carry arbitrage). In contrast, when markets are in backwardation, there is no arbitrage-limiting boundary to restrict the amount of backwardation.[18] This asymmetrical characteristic can be seen in Figure 20.1, which plots monthly rollover gains and losses for crude oil from 1983 to 1994.

Finally, aggregating all rollover gains and losses produces a *net average monthly rollover gain* for all three energy futures: $0.25/barrel for crude oil; $0.32/barrel for heating oil; and $0.45/barrel for gasoline (see Table 20.1). Thus, if past price relationships in energy futures markets are a good predictor of future price relationships, MGRM could have expected to make a profit by rolling its short-dated derivatives position forward through time. Stated another way, the price characteristics of energy futures markets appear to reward a "synthetic" storage hedging strategy by permitting hedgers in effect to avoid the full costs (or any cost) of storage.

The intuition behind this result is that energy markets are characterized by frequent, seasonal shortages of the physical commodity, and at these times there is a substantial "convenience yield" embedded in futures prices. For commercial reasons, energy-supplying firms are willing to hold the physical commodity even though expected spot prices are considerably below current spot prices, providing an opportunity for others to purchase forward oil at prices that do not reflect storage costs for physical product.

These results need to be qualified in two ways. First, in reality MGRM need not have been so inflexible about when it rolled its positions forward. It could, for example, have rolled on days when particularly favorable price relationships existed, in which case our findings would understate the potential benefits to MGRM in holding short-dated futures and rolling these forward through time. On the other hand, our analysis implicitly assumes that MGRM would have been able to execute at the observed prices, which may not always have been possible.

The seasonality of price relationships in energy markets is also evident. Table 20.1 provides data on "rollover frequencies" for each calendar month and on "cumulative" rollover gains or losses by both calendar month and year. In general, heating oil is in backwardation and exhibits rollover gains from December through March; gasoline is in backwardation and exhibits rollover gains from April through November. Further, backwardation in heating oil and gasoline markets coincides with the approach of the end of the heating oil and gasoline "high-demand" seasons, when energy suppliers are reducing their inventories in anticipation of falling demand. Backwardation appears to be a general characteristic of crude oil futures.

Given this seasonality, it is possible that MGRM could have further increased its net rollover gain by moving its futures and swap positions from one commodity to another depending on the time of year and the expected backwardation in the respective markets.[19] Though such a strategy would have entailed more (cross-hedging) basis risk, the high correlations among the different energy prices suggest that this added risk would not have been large.[20]

Thus, at least on the basis of past price relationships, it does not seem unreasonable for MGRM to have expected that over a long period of time (such as ten years) its hedging strategy would have produced a net rollover gain.

DID MGRM HAVE A ROLLOVER RISK?

A key issue is whether MGRM was exposed to a significant rollover risk. If markets were to experience an unusually long period of contango, MGRM could have been exposed to significant rollover losses; it would consistently have been forced to buy high and sell low in rolling its positions forward. We estimate that had a typical contango market occurred at the beginning of MGRM's hedging program and lasted for a period of only one year and two months, its entire profit mark-up could have been wiped out.[21]

Some idea of the likelihood of MGRM's experiencing rollover losses for extensive periods of time can be gleaned from past data on the volatility of the "second-month" basis.[22] The standard deviations of the daily second-month basis for the 1983 to 1992 period for heating oil and gasoline are, respectively, $.89/barrel and $0.85/barrel.[23] Thus, given a mean rollover gain in the range of $.25 to $.45/barrel per month, the possibility of rollover losses occurring is not insignificant.

It is revealing, however, to compare this rollover risk to the price risk that MGRM had on its forward-supply commitments. MGRM's price risk depended on the expected volatility of spot prices for heating oil and gasoline over the ten-year contractual period. Using data from the 1983–1992 period, the respective standard deviations of daily heating oil and gasoline prices were $5.96 and $5.17/barrel.[24] Thus, if the respective basis and price standard deviations are used to measure MGRM's respective risk exposures, its short-dated hedging strategy exposed it to rollover risk on the order of 15% of its price risk.

Despite these statistics, 1993 turned out to be a disaster for MGRM. In 1993 crude oil was in contango every month, heating oil was in contango every month except March and April, and gasoline was in contango every month except August. Thus, virtually every time that MGRM rolled its positions forward, it sustained losses. If it is assumed that MGRM had positions on for the entire year and had to roll these forward every month, its cumulative roll *losses* for the year would have been $1.86/barrel for heating oil, $4.87/barrel for gasoline, and $3.10/barrel for crude oil. (See Table 20.2.) Had MGRM sustained roll losses of this magnitude for very long, its profit margins of $3 to $5 would have been quickly eroded.

TABLE 20.2   Rollover Gains and Losses Using a Three-Day Rollover Rule and Changes in Spot Prices 1993*

	Rollover Date	Rollover Gain or Loss	Changes in Spot Prices
Crude Oil	01/15/93	−0.16	−0.54
	02/17/93	−0.03	0.46
	03/17/93	−0.13	0.84
	04/16/93	−0.24	−0.03
	05/17/93	−0.32	−0.63
	06/17/93	−0.30	−0.81
	07/16/93	−0.28	−1.49
	08/17/93	−0.43	0.71
	09/17/93	−0.30	−0.85
	10/15/93	−0.11	1.20
	11/17/93	−0.38	−1.23
	12/16/93	−0.42	−2.81
	Total	−3.10	−5.18
Heating Oil	01/26/93	−0.12	−1.09
	02/23/93	−0.03	0.85
	03/26/93	0.44	0.17
	04/27/93	0.01	−0.97
	05/25/93	−0.11	−0.46
	06/25/93	−0.24	−0.83
	07/27/93	−0.33	−0.27
	08/26/93	−0.42	0.51
	09/27/93	−0.43	0.09
	10/26/93	−0.30	−0.38
	11/23/93	−0.30	−0.77
	12/27/93	−0.03	−2.52
	Total	−1.86	−5.67
Gasoline	01/26/93	−0.58	0.20
	02/23/93	−1.71	−0.14
	03/26/93	−0.43	1.86
	04/27/93	−0.26	0.17
	05/25/93	−0.07	−0.21
	06/25/93	−0.16	−1.64
	07/27/93	−0.23	−0.87
	08/26/93	0.32	0.17
	09/27/93	−0.34	−2.00
	10/26/93	−0.09	−0.07
	11/23/93	−0.50	−1.62
	12/27/93	−0.81	−3.21
	Total	−4.87	−7.34

*All rollovers are calculated using a three-day rollover rule: on the third day prior to the last day of trading we sell the near month contract and buy the contract which is the second closest to delivery. The rollover gain or loss is the near-month price minus the second-month price. To proxy for changes in spot prices we use changes in near-month futures prices. Spot price changes are from one rollover date to the next. All prices are reported in $/barrel. Total figures may differ from the sum of the monthly figures because of rounding.

Data Source: Knight-Ridder Futures Markets Database

How predictable were the contango markets that occurred in 1993? The monthly rollover gain and loss frequencies reported in Table 20.2 suggest that the probability of a string of contango months occurring in the particular months in which they occurred in 1993 is extremely small—in fact, close to zero.[25] Nevertheless, there have been unusual strings of contango months in the fairly recent past. In particular, for the 12-month period from May 1991 through May 1992, heating oil was in contango 10 out of 12 months; from July, 1986 through June, 1987, gasoline was in contango 9 out of 12 months; and from January, 1992 through December, 1992, crude oil was in contango 8 out of 12 months. Thus, the string of contango months in 1993, though unusual, was not without some precedent.

Alternatively, 1993 can be compared to a "worst-case" scenario constructed with past data. Figure 20.2 plots the rollover losses for crude oil that occurred in each month during 1993 against the *maximum* (or "worst-case") rollover losses (or contango) that occurred in the past in *each* of the calendar months (using data from the period April 1983, to December 1992).[26] In other words, the *maximum* calendar-month rollover losses consist of the worst January rollover loss that occurred in any of the previous ten years, the worst February rollover loss in any previous year, and so forth, for every calendar month. As shown in Figure 20.2, the monthly rollover losses that occurred in 1993 were generally quite similar, though with some exceptions, to the maximum rollover losses that occurred in earlier years.

Critics also contend that MGRM's rollover strategy was fatally flawed because of the size of its derivatives positions. They argue, first, that its derivatives positions were large enough to move the market from backwardation into contango; and second, that MGRM's counterparties (or traders) were in a position to extract from MGRM a monopoly price when it rolled positions forward, forcing it to sell at a lower price and buy at a higher price because of their market power vis-à-vis MGRM.

MGRM's positions, however, were not large relative to total open interest. Its total futures positions constituted only about 6.7 percent of total open interest, and its combined futures and swaps positions constituted about 20 percent of total open interest.[27] In addition, it seems unlikely that traders would have had monopoly power

FIGURE 20.2 Crude Oil Monthly Rollover Gains and Losses in 1993–1994 versus Maximum Rollover Gains and Losses Prior to 1993

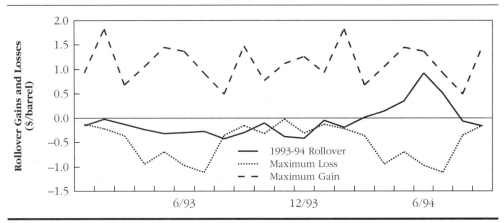

Source: Knight-Ridder

relative to MGRM. There are no significant barriers to entry into trading futures on an exchange, and in OTC swap markets there are a large number of potential counterparties. MGRM could have moved positions from one energy market to another, and from exchange to off-exchange positions, and could have rolled positions forward on many different dates.

In summary, past data provide reasonable support for MGRM's presumption that it could expect to earn a net rollover gain. But in relying on past data to predict future rollover gains, MGRM was implicitly making two critical assumptions: that the structure of energy futures markets would not change significantly in the future (that history would repeat itself), and that a history of only ten years is long enough to provide accurate long-term forecasts of rollover returns. While such assumptions may seem "heroic" to many observers, there is some reason to believe that periodic price backwardation is a permanent feature of energy markets. Seasonal spikes in demand coupled with a shortage of storage facilities appear to assure that backwardation will continue to exist. On the other hand, institutional speculators in commodity markets (such as commodity pools), which have been growing rapidly in recent years, may in the future compete away the positive roll returns on which MGRM's strategy depended.[28]

Finally, although hedgers commonly assume a stable market structure in formulating their hedging policies,[29] a characteristic that may distinguish MGRM from other hedgers is that its strategy required an assumption that the market structure would be stable for a very long period of time. Further, even with a stable market structure, MGRM could only be assured of a net rollover gain if it were able to continue its hedging program for a long period of time. In the short run almost any outcome was a possibility, as MGRM's experience in 1993 clearly revealed. In addition, the early cash-out options in MGRM's forward delivery contracts could have caused it to end its hedging strategy unexpectedly.[30] In particular, had its customers exercised their options subsequent to a period during which MGRM incurred rollover losses, it would have had to end its hedging program before being able to offset these losses with rollover gains. Finally, to reap the expected long-term rollover gains, MGRM implicitly assumed that it could fund whatever rollover losses it sustained in the short run. The soundness of MGRM's short-dated hedging strategy, therefore, must be judged on the basis of the reasonableness of these assumptions.

ROLLOVER RISK: LESSONS FROM OTHER COMMODITIES

To get some idea of the reliability of using past price data to predict future rollover returns, we examine two commodity futures with longer price histories than energy futures: soybeans and copper. These commodity futures are similar to energy futures in that they also exhibit periods of recurring contango and backwardation price relationships. Daily data for soybean and copper futures are available for the 30-year period 1965 to 1994, permitting an analysis of three separate ten-year periods.

Tables 20.3 and 20.4 provide, for each of these periods, various statistics for soybean and copper futures on the frequency of contango and backwardation price relationships as well as summary statistics on the size of rollover gains and losses (similar statistics were provided earlier in Table 20.1 for crude oil, heating oil, and gasoline futures).[31] In the first period, 1965 to 1974, both soybeans and copper were in backwardation much of the time (44% and 62%, respectively) so that the average rollover

TABLE 20.3   Summary of Rollover Gains and Losses Using Three-Day Rollover Rule for Soybeans and Copper* 1965–1994

Soybeans		1965–74	1975–84	1985–94
Summary Statistics for Soybeans (1965–1994)	Mean Rollover	5.52	−4.56	−0.50
	Mean of All Rollover Gains	16.74	10.14	9.59
	Mean of All Rollover Losses	−3.50	−8.91	−6.86
	Cumulative Rollover Gain	386.12	−319.00	−34.75
	Frequency of a Rollover Gain	44%	23%	36%
Frequency of a Rollover Gain for Soybeans	Jan	20%	0%	10%
	Mar	20%	0%	0%
	May	10%	30%	50%
	Jul	80%	70%	70%
	Aug	90%	50%	60%
	Sep	70%	10%	60%
	Nov	20%	0%	0%
Cumulative Rollover Gains by Month for Soybeans	Jan	−21.25	−110.00	−58.00
	Mar	−0.88	−107.50	−57.75
	May	25.13	−13.75	−15.75
	Jul	161.25	26.25	62.25
	Aug	197.75	47.00	92.75
	Sep	53.13	−44.50	2.50
	Nov	−29.01	−116.50	−60.75
Copper		1965–74	1975–84	1985–94
Summary Statistics for Copper (1965–1994)	Mean Rollover	1.47	−0.94	1.65
	Mean of All Rollover Gains	2.64	1.15	3.87
	Mean of All Rollover Losses	−0.48	−1.03	−0.53
	Cumulative Rollover Gain	88.03	−56.60	97.60
	Frequency of a Rollover Gain	62%	3%	49%
Frequency of a Rollover Gain for Copper	Jan	70%	10%	40%
	Mar	70%	0%	60%
	May	80%	0%	50%
	Jul	50%	0%	30%
	Sep	60%	0%	60%
	Dec	40%	10%	56%
Cumulative Rollover Gains by Month for Copper	Jan	12.80	−16.30	16.25
	Mar	25.02	−8.70	22.80
	May	16.51	−9.15	13.20
	Jul	9.85	−8.55	3.40
	Sep	15.40	−14.10	33.30
	Dec	8.45	0.20	8.65

*All rollovers are calculated using a three-day rollover rule: on the third day prior to the last day of trading we sell the near-month contract and buy the contract month which is the second closest to delivery. The rollover gain or loss is calcluted as the near month price minus the second month price. For soybeans all rollover gains, losses, and means are reported in cents per bushel, for copper they are reported in cents per pound. Our data ends in September, 1994.

Data Source: Knight Ridder

TABLE 20.4   Cumulative Rollover Gains by Year for Soybeans and Copper*

Year	Soybeans	Copper
1965	31.14	21.67
1966	42.37	5.85
1967	16.24	3.66
1968	9.25	13.50
1969	18.12	10.60
1970	−17.62	8.05
1971	−14.50	−1.30
1972	23.87	−2.80
1973	297.75	19.80
1974	−20.50	9.00
1975	−9.25	−3.50
1976	−29.00	−1.90
1977	54.25	−2.90
1978	−1.75	−4.20
1979	−58.50	−2.05
1980	−94.75	−16.35
1981	−69.25	−9.45
1982	−27.75	−6.50
1983	−63.50	−5.35
1984	−19.50	−4.40
1985	−2.25	−3.30
1986	56.75	−2.60
1987	12.00	5.45
1988	−53.25	46.40
1989	29.25	16.05
1990	−61.75	29.25
1991	−29.00	7.35
1992	−12.25	−2.10
1993	3.25	−2.55
1994	22.50	3.65

*All rollovers are calculated using a three-day rollover rule: on the third day prior to the last day of trading we sell the near-month contract and buy the contract month which is the second closest to delivery. The rollover gain or loss is calculated as the near-month price minus the second month price. For soybeans all rollover gains, losses, and means are reported in cents per bushel, for copper they are reported in cents per pound. Our data ends in September, 1994.

Data Source: Knight Ridder

gains were 5.52 cents per bushel and 1.47 cents per pound.[32] During the second period (1975-1984), however, rollover returns for soybeans and copper were quite different. Rather than rollover gains, both soybeans and copper experienced rollover losses on average. Further, the frequency of backwardation dropped precipitously, to 23% for soybeans and 3% for copper. In the third period (1985-1994), rollover gains and losses were again quite different than they were in the second period. Thus, these data suggest that in commodity futures markets it would not be surprising to find that average rollover returns during any ten-year period would not be a good predictor of average rollover returns during any successive ten-year period.

A striking parallel to what happened to MGRM in 1992 and 1993 also can be seen in the soybeans and copper data. During the last year of the first time period (1974) and the first year of the second time period (1975), rollover returns for soybeans and copper turned sharply negative, similar to what happened to rollover returns for energy futures in 1992 and 1993. If one were standing in 1974 or 1975, would one have concluded that rollover returns for soybeans and copper would soon revert to being positive, or that they would remain negative for an indefinite period of time? As it turned out, rollover returns remained negative for most of the next ten years, finally reverting to being positive in 1986 and 1987. Thus, in 1975 a bet that rollover returns would soon turn positive again would have gone sadly awry.

There are several possible explanations for the unreliability of past price data in predicting future rollover returns. First, a period of ten years may simply not be long enough to identify the true (structural) price relationship, or to infer long-run equilibrium rollover returns. Second, markets and structural price relationships can change from one period to the next, as fundamental economic events occur. If this happens, equilibrium rollover returns can be quite different in different time periods. Finally, because the distribution of rollover returns in commodity futures tends to be characterized by relatively high variances (relative to mean rollover returns), relying solely on past mean rollover returns for any finite period of time can result in large prediction errors. MGRM's hedging strategy, which depended on positive rollover returns, was vulnerable to any one (or to all) of these possibilities.

MG'S ALLEGED FUNDING PROBLEM

A combination of falling energy prices and a contango market caused MGRM to have to fund sizeable cash outflows in 1993. Between June and December in 1993 crude oil prices declined by nearly $6/barrel, forcing MGRM to post nearly $900 million to maintain its hedge positions. In response, MG's Supervisory Board replaced MG's top management and liquidated MGRM's derivatives and forward-supply contracts positions, ending MG's foray into the U.S. oil market.

MG's funding needs in 1993 can be decomposed into two components: funds to finance margin calls (or unrealized losses) on its derivatives positions due to declines in energy prices and funds to finance rollover losses due to contango markets (discussed earlier). Falling energy prices and contango markets, of course, may not be unrelated phenomena: falling energy prices are usually an indication that there are no product shortages, and in the absence of such shortages contango price relationships are normal. The bulk of MGRM's funding needs in 1993 arose, however, from having to meet margin calls due to price declines and not from rollover losses (see Table 20.2).

It is not obvious why MGRM would have had a problem funding these margin calls. Consider, for example, the following hypothetical situation. Suppose that MGRM's hedge was such that falling energy prices, although resulting in unrealized losses on its derivatives positions, also resulted in equal and offsetting unrealized *gains* on its fixed-price, forward-supply contracts. Since MGRM's forward-supply contracts locked in a fixed sale price for future deliveries, these contracts could be expected to increase in value as energy prices fell because MGRM's expected cost of supplying oil in the future also would fall, making the contracts more profitable. Given equal and offsetting gains and losses on its derivatives and forward delivery contracts, it is not clear why MGRM would have had a funding problem. Arguably, it should have been able to borrow against the collateral of its now more valuable forward delivery contracts.

There are two potential "economic" explanations for why MGRM may have encountered difficulty in using its forward delivery contracts as collateral to fully fund its margin outflows.[33] First, it may not in fact have had equal and offsetting unrealized gains on its forward delivery contracts. In that event it would have had to increase its general debt obligations to obtain the necessary funding, and its creditors may have balked if MG was already heavily indebted. Second, MGRM's forward delivery contracts may have lacked the necessary "transparency" for creditors to lend against them, or at least for creditors to lend an amount necessary to cover its margin needs. In particular, it may have been difficult for MG's creditors to evaluate the counterparty credit risk embedded in MGRM's forward delivery contracts.

The Funding Risks Implicit in MGRM's Hedging Strategy

MGRM's hedging strategy had two features that, as it turned out, may have had important funding implications. First, it used a one-to-one hedge instead of a "minimum-variance" hedge.[34] Second, it did not take into consideration the mismatch that existed in the timing of its expected cash flows (or, it did not "tail" its hedge).

MGRM's One-to-One Hedging Strategy

MGRM's strategy of using a one-to-one hedge could have caused a potential funding problem because it did not result in equal and offsetting unrealized gains in its forward delivery contracts when energy prices fell. Alternatively stated, when energy prices fell, the value of MGRM's forward contracts did not increase by as much as the value of its derivatives positions would have declined, creating an imbalance in unrealized gains and losses.

MGRM's one-to-one hedge strategy had this consequence for two reasons. First, for this strategy to produce equal and offsetting changes in the value of MGRM's forward delivery contracts, there would have to be a one-to-one price relationship between "forward" and spot energy prices, which is not the case in energy markets. More specifically, changes in the value of its forward delivery contracts depended on changes in *forward* energy prices, while changes in the value of its short-dated derivatives positions depended on changes in *spot* energy prices. Because MGRM's forward-supply contracts called for it to deliver energy products over many years in the future, changes in the value of these contracts should have reflected expectations about what spot prices were likely to be at the various times when MGRM was expected to make deliveries. A reasonable procedure for valuing these forward delivery contracts would thus have been to use forward prices as predictors of future spot prices. In contrast, MGRM's derivatives positions were short-dated and their value depended solely on current spot prices. Thus, since the valuation of MGRM's derivatives and forward delivery contracts depended on different prices, a one-to-one hedge strategy would result in equal and offsetting unrealized gains and losses on its forward and derivatives positions only if there were also a one-to-one relationship between spot and forward prices.

There is good reason to believe that a one-to-one relationship between spot and forward prices does not exist in energy markets. Theoretically, we would expect a $1 change in spot prices to cause a less than $1 change in forward prices. Changes in contemporary demand and supply conditions, which cause changes in current spot prices, can be expected to have less of an effect on prices five or ten years from now, and therefore to generate smaller changes in forward prices than spot prices.

The evidence confirms this intuition. As shown in Table 20.5, the volatility of more distant futures prices is considerably less than the volatility of spot energy prices.[35] (See also Figure 20.3, which plots forward price curves for selected dates using available energy futures prices.[36]) It is clear that the volatility of forward prices is considerably less than that of spot prices, and that the price volatility of distant-month futures declines sharply even over a period as short as a year.[37]

A reasonable estimate of the price relationship between spot and forward energy prices over a ten-year period is 0.50; that is, a $1 increase (decrease) in the current spot price will on average result in only a $0.50 increase (decrease) in forward prices over a ten-year period. (See the regression estimates reported in Table 20.6.[38]) Given this estimate, when spot energy prices fell in 1993, MGRM's one-to-one hedge ratio would have resulted in an increase in the value of its forward delivery contracts that was only half as large as the unrealized loss that it sustained on its short-dated derivatives contracts.

The second reason that MGRM's one-to-one hedging strategy would not have resulted in equal and offsetting gains on its forward-supply contracts is that it did not account for the mismatch that existed in the timing of the expected cash flows on its forward-supply contracts and its hedge positions. Even assuming a one-to-one relationship between spot and forward prices, the later realization of the cash flows on MGRM's forward delivery contracts would have resulted in a smaller change in the

TABLE 20.5   Price Volatilities of Different Contract Months and Volatilities of Intertemporal Bases* 1990–1992

Contract Maturity	Heating Oil Futures Standard Deviation	Gasoline Futures Standard Deviation
One Month	4.91	4.03
Two Months	4.91	3.53
Three Months	4.70	3.19
Six Months	3.36	3.23
Nine Months	2.48	3.19

Intertemporal Basis	Heating Oil Intertemporal Bases Standard Deviation	Gasoline Intertemporal Bases Standard Deviation
One Month—Two Month	0.84	1.01
One Month—Three Month	1.39	1.68
One Month—Six Month	2.69	2.48
One Month—Nine Month	3.07	2.44

*All volatilities are calculated using daily closing futures prices on the New York Mercantile Exchange. The volatilities are calculated using price levels. To create continuous time series for the different contract months all contracts are rolled into the next month three days prior to the last trading day of the near-month contract.

Data Source: Knight-Ridder Futures Markets Database

FIGURE 20.3   Crude Oil Forward Price Curves for Selected Dates

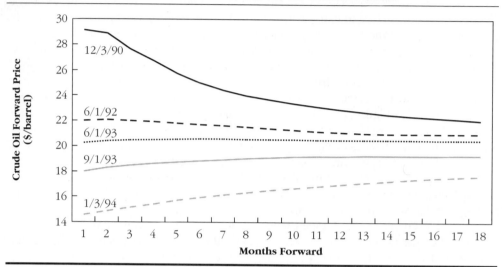

Source: Wall Street Journal

TABLE 20.6   Regression Estimates of Relationship between Spot and Forward Prices* 1990–1992

Time to Expiration	Heating Oil Futures		Gasoline Futures	
	β	R^2	β	R^2
Two month futures	.735	.84	.740	.80
Three month futures	.625	.79	.650	.75
Six month futures	.513	.80	.562	.76
Nine month futures	.492	.79	.520	.72

*$\Delta F(t,T) = \alpha + \beta \, \Delta F(t, t+1) + e$, where $F(t,T)$ is the futures price at time t for delivery at time T. Δ signifies the daily change in price. Separate regressions are run for the cases where $T = t+2, t+3, t+6, t+9$. Thus for t+2, changes in two-month futures prices are regressed on changes in near-month futures prices, for t+3 changes in three-month futures prices are regressed on changes in near-month futures prices, etc. To create continuous time series for the different contract months all contracts are rolled into the next contract month three days prior to the last day of trading of the near-month contract. The β coefficients reported in the table are the regression coefficients and represent the minimum-variance hedge ratio that should be used to hedge a forward obligation in month T. All of the regression coefficients reported below are statistically significant at the one percent level. A Durbin-Watson test showed little serial correlation in the error terms in all cases. We obtained similar estimates after excluding Gulf War observations.

net present value of these contracts than on its derivatives contracts for *a given change in price*. In contrast to MGRM's short-dated derivatives, most of the cash flows (or revenues) from its forward-supply contracts would not have occurred until many years later. Consequently, to produce equal and offsetting unrealized gains and losses, MGRM would have had to adjust (or "tail") its hedge in order to put the expected cash flows from its forward delivery contracts on an equivalent footing to the cash flows generated by its derivatives positions.[39] The use of a one-to-one hedge ratio did not accomplish this.

Taking both the likely price relationship between spot and forward energy prices and the "tailing" factor into consideration (and for the moment ignoring the options embedded in the forward delivery contracts), it is estimated that MGRM would have needed a derivatives position of less than half of the position that it actually held in order to equate changes in the net present value of its forward-supply contracts to changes in the net present value of its derivatives positions.[40] More specifically, it would have needed a derivatives position of about 61 million barrels to hedge forward commitments of 160 million barrels. (See our *JFM* article.)

Had MGRM used this smaller hedge position, its funding situation in 1993 when energy prices fell would have been significantly altered. First, with a derivatives position less than half as large as it actually held, its *net* unrealized losses (on both its forward delivery contracts and derivatives positions) would have been virtually zero. Second, its margin calls would have been less than half of what they were. Finally, while not exclusively a funding problem, had MGRM held a smaller short-dated derivatives position in 1993, its rollover losses also would have been reduced substantially. If prices had risen instead of falling as they did in 1993, and had markets remained in backwardation, MGRM's one-to-one hedge would have worked out beautifully, producing substantial cash (or margin) inflows and large rollover profits.

The Customer Cash-Out Option

An argument has been made that MGRM, nevertheless, needed a one-to-one hedge ratio because of the customer "cash-out" options embedded in its forward-supply contracts. Specifically, in the event of an increase in spot energy prices, its customers had an option to "cash-out," or to liquidate their forward obligations to purchase oil and receive a cash payment from MGRM based on the future value of these contracts to customers.[41]

Two aspects of these contracts are noteworthy. First, the cash payment depends on near-month (or spot) energy prices, and not on forward energy prices (or expected spot prices). Second, MGRM and the customer shared equally in the customer's prospective gains due to higher energy prices. Thus, these options would be in-the-money for a customer only if the cash-out payment were greater than the net present value of the remaining forward deliveries on the contract. This could occur, for example, if near-month futures prices rose much faster than forward prices. Alternatively, even if the forward delivery contracts were not in-the-money for MGRM's customers (or even though the net present value of the forward contracts exceeded the option's value), they may nevertheless have exercised their cash-out options if they needed liquidity.

In either case, MGRM had to be prepared to make such up-front, lump-sum payments. Notwithstanding this possibility, it still did not need a one-to-one hedge. Suppose, for example, that a $10/barrel increase occurred in spot energy prices within a year of MGRM writing the forward delivery contracts, and that for whatever reason all of its customers opted to exercise their early cash-out options. What futures position would MGRM have needed to generate gains sufficient to cover its option payouts? Clearly, it would not have needed a one-to-one hedge because the maximum that customers could receive was 50% of the gain from the $10 increase in spot prices. In the more general case, where the probability of exercise is less than one, a hedge ratio of .5 would more than cover MGRM's potential option payments. Thus, the customer "cash-out" options embedded in MGRM's forward delivery contracts did not require use of a one-to-one hedging strategy.

For all of the reasons discussed above, MGRM's one-to-one hedge exposed the firm to funding risk that it could have avoided had it used a "minimum-variance" hedge ratio. In particular, a derivatives position about half as large as the one it actually used would have substantially reduced its funding needs in 1993 while at the same time providing reasonable protection against unpredictable fluctuations in energy prices. Further, had MGRM held a smaller short-dated derivatives position in 1993, its rollover losses would have been less.

Why a One-to-One Hedge Ratio?

It is not known why MGRM chose to use a one-to-one hedge, but the following is a feasible rationale. To see the logic of using a one-to-one hedge, suppose that MGRM had been able to hedge with a "strip" (or a series) of forward contracts, where the contractual amounts and the expiration dates exactly matched the dates and the amounts of MGRM's forward-delivery obligations. In this case it is clear that a one-to-one hedge would have locked in all future delivery prices, and as such would have locked in the profit margins on MGRM's forward delivery contracts. This hedging strategy also would not have been exposed to rollover risk and possibly not to funding risk as well (assuming an absence of "settling-up" provisions in the forward contracts).

The point of this "strip hedge" example is to show that ultimately MGRM would have needed a one-to-one hedge against all of its forward-supply obligations to insulate itself completely from rising energy prices. Thus, had it used a hedge ratio of less than one, it would have had to increase this ratio to one as the dates of its forward delivery commitments drew near—or to adjust its hedge "dynamically" over time. Such adjustments could have imposed significant costs on MGRM had energy prices risen, and this may have deterred it from using a hedge ratio of less than one. (For an example of such dynamic hedging costs, see our *JFM* article cited earlier.)

Thus, in choosing a one-to-one hedging strategy, MGRM consciously made a risk trade-off: in exchange for better protection against rising energy prices, it exposed itself to both greater funding risk and to greater rollover risk. Presumably, it had reasons to believe that the latter risks were less significant than were the potential consequences of rising energy prices.

Nontransparency and Credit Risk

A second potential funding obstacle for MGRM was that its forward delivery contracts may have lacked the transparency necessary for creditors to be willing to accept them as collateral. In particular, the enhanced value of its forward delivery contracts due to falling energy prices was dependent on the willingness and the ability of its counterparties to meet their future obligations. Critics argue that MGRM was exposed to substantial non-performance risk because of the long-duration of its forward-supply contracts. Further, as energy prices fell, this risk could be expected to increase because of the growing disparity between the contractually-fixed sales prices and prevailing spot prices. Thus, without concrete information about the characteristics of MGRM's counterparties, its creditors might have been reluctant to lend against the collateral of its forward delivery contracts.

It is well-known that the probability of a firm defaulting rises with time—or that "cumulative" default rates rise with time. Studies of bond defaults by Moody's suggest the probability of an issuer defaulting by the tenth year after issuance is much larger than the probability of its defaulting during the first year. For a B-rated issuer, for example, the probability of default during the first year is 8.31%, but rises to an impressive 39.96% by the 10th year.[42]

MGRM apparently recognized this default risk and sought to mitigate it by contracting to supply only a fraction of a customer's energy needs. If energy prices fell, customers would still be able to purchase most of the product they needed at the lower market prices. Further, when energy prices are falling, end-users typically have higher-than-normal profits for some time because retail prices commonly lag wholesale prices in energy markets.

Whatever the validity of these arguments, the key issues are whether MGRM's non-performance exposure was such that it could have reasonably predicted its losses arising from non-performance, and, if so, whether its profit markups were sufficiently high to cover the expected credit losses. Well-diversified credit risks are insurable risks. The fundamental question, therefore, is whether MGRM charged a "self-insurance" risk premium that was high enough to cover its expected credit losses.

Given the available information, it is difficult to answer either of these questions. For example, without knowing how many customers MGRM had, or what businesses its customers were in, it is not possible to determine whether MGRM was sufficiently diversified. Further, without information about the balance sheets and income statements of MGRM's customers, it is impossible to attach a likelihood of default to them as a group. Until such information becomes available, therefore, there is no way of judging MGRM's credit exposure. Nevertheless, if MGRM's creditors did not have the necessary information to evaluate the nature and size of MGRM's credit exposure, they may have been reluctant to lend against the collateral of its forward delivery contracts.

DID MGRM REALLY HAVE A FUNDING PROBLEM?

Numerous press reports suggested that MGRM's hedging strategy unraveled because of a "liquidity" problem, an inability to raise the necessary funds to meet its margin calls. But this view is questionable. While MGRM's need to raise substantial funds clearly resulted in a complete reassessment of its strategy, it seems highly unlikely that MG's Supervisory Board would have jettisoned an otherwise sound strategy simply because of a short-term liquidity need. This view is based upon two considerations: the particular ownership structure of MG, and the fact that MG did not avail itself of funding that *was* available to it.

MG's ownership structure makes it highly unlikely that a simple liquidity problem would cause its owners to abandon an otherwise sound and profitable long-run investment strategy. MG is a classic German firm; ownership is concentrated in the hands of a few large owners with easy access to credit. Seven institutional investors hold just over 65% of the its stock. Deutsche Bank and Dresdner Bank, Germany's largest and second largest commercial banks, together directly own 33.82% of the stock. This does not include MG stock that these banks hold (or control) through mutual funds or as a custodian. Thus, the ownership and control of MG rests squarely in the hands of Germany's two largest banks: Deutsche Bank and Dresdner Bank. Not surprisingly, the Chairman of MG's Supervisory Board also is a prominent member of the Management Board of Deutsche Bank.

MG's ownership and debt structure also makes it unlikely that its problem was that of a "liquidity-constrained" firm. If its owners—some of which are among the largest financial institutions in the world—viewed its business and hedging strategies as sound, they clearly had the "deep-pockets" to finance it through short-run reversals. Further, potential conflicts between the equity and debt holders were greatly mitigated by the ownership and debt structure of MG. Deutsche Bank and Dresdner Bank are both major stockholders and creditors of MG.

Finally, the non-transparency of MGRM's forward delivery contracts should not have been a critical factor for a closely-held firm such as MG. While such nontransparency may be a severe obstacle to raising external funds, MG's owners were in a position to obtain complete information without compromising the propriety of the firm's operations.

There is also evidence that in late 1993 funding was in fact available to MG. First, it had an unrestricted DM 1.5 billion Euro-credit line with 48 banks that it chose not to draw on. This credit line, arranged in May, 1992, by Dresdner Bank, was never used. Second, on December 7, 1993, Chemical Bank (and possibly other banks) reportedly approached MGRM about the possibility of providing financing on the basis of securitizing its forward-supply contracts. The precise terms offered by these banks, of course, are unknown. But the fact that MG did not avail itself of these financing opportunities suggests that its Supervisory Board believed that the real problems lay elsewhere.

CONCLUSIONS

Our view is that MG's fate was decided not by its inability to deal with a short-term liquidity need but by a sharp disagreement between its Supervisory Board and its "old" management about the fundamental soundness of MGRM's forward-delivery program. MGRM's losses in 1993 undoubtedly caused MG's Supervisory Board to change its assessment of the potential risks involved in its forward-delivery program. This reassessment probably focused on two basic risks: rollover risk and credit risk. The unusual contango price relationships that occurred in energy markets in 1993 made clear that sustained rollover losses were not only theoretically possible but could in fact occur. In addition, the sharp fall in energy prices in 1993 brought into sharper relief the potential non-performance risk that MGRM had on its forward delivery contracts. Thus, although there is no way of knowing exactly what motivated MG's Supervisory Board's actions to end MGRM's forward-delivery program, it appears that it acted on the belief that MGRM's strategy was fatally flawed—that its exposure to either or both rollover risk and credit risk did not justify the expected returns on its forward-delivery program.[43]

This chapter has examined both of these risks, and has provided statistical information where possible for readers to judge for themselves whether MGRM's judgments with respect to these risks were flawed. With respect to rollover risk, the reasonableness of MGRM's judgment that this risk was neither excessive nor unmanageable comes down to the reasonableness of its assumption that the last ten years of price history in energy markets can be relied on to make predictions about what price relationships will be for the indefinite future. With respect to credit risk, the issue is whether MGRM correctly evaluated its exposure and priced this risk accordingly. While MGRM's credit risk was not insignificant, we have no information which suggests that its exposure in this regard was excessive.

A central controversy surrounding the MG case is whether MG's Supervisory Board took the right action when it ordered the liquidation of MGRM's positions in December, 1993. This action implicitly reflects two key decisions that the Board had to make: *whether* to abandon MGRM's program; and, if it decided to abandon the program, *when* to liquidate MGRM's positions. With respect to its decision to abandon MGRM's program entirely, the reasonableness of this decision is not clear cut. In particular, in December, 1993, there was no way to be certain that the price structure in energy markets had not already changed or would not change in the future, imposing higher rollover costs on MGRM. With respect to the Board's decision about when to liquidate MGRM's derivatives position, this decision clearly seems ill-timed, at least in retrospect. When the bulk of the liquidation occurred, between December 20 and December 31, 1993, energy prices were at their lowest in many years, resulting in substantial losses on MGRM's derivatives positions when they were sold. In addition, in order to eliminate exposure on its forward-supply contracts due to rising prices, MGRM liquidated many of these contracts as well, apparently waiving cancellation penalties on the contracts, thereby giving up potential unrealized gains that could have offset its derivatives losses.

Had MG's Supervisory Board not ordered the liquidation until sometime later, the situation would be far different today. From December 17, 1993, when the new management took control, to August 8, 1994, crude oil prices increased from $13.91 to $19.42 a barrel, heating oil prices increased from $18.51 to $20.94 a barrel, and gasoline prices increased from $16.88 to $24.54 a barrel. Given these price increases, MGRM would have had a massive inflow of margin funds on its derivatives positions. Nevertheless, it must also be recognized that if energy prices had continued to fall, say to $10 a barrel, rather than rising, MGRM would have sustained even greater losses than it did.[44] It is not clear, therefore, how much weight should be given to retrospective criticisms in judging the timing of the Supervisory Board's decision to liquidate MGRM's positions.

Regardless of whether MG's Supervisory Board's decision to abandon MGRM's hedging strategy was the correct one, it is clear that at some point a lack of understanding at the Supervisory Board level played an important role in MGRM's fate. In particular, on November 19, 1993, the Supervisory Board decided to extend the contract of its then Management Board chairman, Heinz Schimmelbusch, for another five years. But just four weeks later, the same Supervisory Board fired Schimmelbusch. Why the sudden turnaround? Did the Board not understand MGRM's hedging strategy prior to December, 1993? And if it did not, should it have? Alternatively, did the Board initially assess the risks that MGRM was taking and find them acceptable, but later change its collective mind and decide that these risks were unacceptable? Still another possibility is that the Board simply did not understand MGRM's strategy and panicked in the face of huge margin calls.

EDWARDS AND CANTER VERSUS CULP AND MILLER: WHAT ARE THE CRITICAL DIFFERENCES?

To clarify the debate surrounding the MG case, it may be useful to contrast our views with those expressed by Christopher Culp and Merton Miller in Chapter 19. First, we agree with Culp and Miller that it is possible to hedge long-dated obligations with short-dated futures (or derivatives), but we believe that this strategy entails more risk than Culp and Miller appear to acknowledge. Hedging long-dated obligations with short-dated derivatives involves a potentially significant "rollover risk" because of the difficulty of predicting the term structure of forward energy prices over long periods of time. Culp and Miller, in contrast, argue that all that counts "is the program's profit potential over the long haul or, as finance specialists might prefer to put it, its expected net present value." They minimize the importance of rollover risk, noting that "the one-month net cost of storage and interest *averaged* less than zero over the last ten years." Thus, Culp and Miller have greater faith than we in the efficacy of using past price relationships to predict future forward price relationships (or to predict future rollover returns). Although hardly definitive, we provide evidence from other commodity markets (soybeans and copper) that reliance on past price relationships to infer future "rollover returns" can be quite dangerous.

Second, we believe that a sound hedging strategy should not require the hedger to "stay in the game" until its long-run strategy pays off. A hedger should be able to unwind its positions at any time without sustaining substantial (or life-threatening) losses. Culp and Miller, by their use of the terms "gambler's ruin" and "hedger's ruin," suggest that MGRM should have been allowed to continue to operate until the long-run profit potential of its combined delivery/hedging program was realized. In particular, they appear to argue that MGRM should have been allowed to stay in the game long enough to realize the anticipated rollover gains. In our view such a strategy would have entailed a significant bet that contango markets would not prevail over any significant period of time in the future. In any case, as MGRM's experience in 1993 clearly shows, MGRM's hedging program turned out to be quite vulnerable to early exit. Further, because of the early cash-out options in MGRM's forward delivery contracts, it should not have come as a surprise to MGRM that it might have to unwind its hedged delivery program much sooner than the lengthy contractual periods stated in its forward delivery contracts (such as ten years).

Third, in contrast to Culp and Miller, we do not believe that MGRM's hedge was "self-financing": that the value of its forward delivery contracts increased in value by the same amount as its short-dated derivatives contracts decreased in value as energy prices declined. The difference here with Culp and Miller turns primarily on our different methods for calculating the net present value of MGRM's combined delivery and hedging program. We argue that, in valuing MGRM's positions at a given moment in time (say "t"), it makes sense to use the information contained in the term structure of forward energy prices at time t. Specifically, our methodology uses forward energy prices and current interest rates at time t to calculate net present values at time t. In contrast, Culp and Miller use an "expected basis" as the critical discount factor in their net present value formula, where this "expected basis" is not obtained from the term structure at time t. Rather, they use as their expected basis an average basis obtained from historical data. We are dubious about a procedure which uses such an average (or constant) basis to determine net present values at different times. In addition, neither our procedure for calculating net present values nor theirs takes into consideration the uncertain term (maturity) of MGRM's forward delivery contracts due both to the early cash-out options and to the "firm-flexible" provisions included in some of these contracts.[45]

Fourth, while we agree with Culp and Miller that MGRM's "funding problem" was probably not the critical factor in bringing down the firm, we argue that this is true because of MG's ownership structure, rather than because MGRM's hedged delivery program was self-financing. Both Culp and Miller and we contend that because MG was owned and controlled by "deep-pocket" investors—some of the largest financial institutions in the world, it should have had access to sufficient funding. Nevertheless, it is difficult to draw definitive conclusions about this issue because neither Culp and Miller nor we have all of the facts with respect to MG's funding situation.

Fifth, given our method of calculating the net present value of MGRM's hedged delivery program, we argue that MGRM could have substantially reduced its funding needs as well as its rollover losses by using a minimum-variance hedging strategy instead of a one-to-one hedge. But we show that in doing so MGRM would have exposed itself to potential dynamic hedging costs. In addition, we agree that if funding were no obstacle, as Culp and Miller believe, the case for MGRM using a minimum-variance hedging strategy is considerably weaker.

Finally, although we are uncertain about exactly what Culp and Miller's overall view of MGRM's hedged delivery program is, they seem to "lean to" the view that its program was "economically sound" but was "killed off prematurely" by the "unfortunate" and "precipitous liquidation of MGRM's futures hedge" in December, 1993. With respect to this liquidation decision, we are more agnostic than they. Succinctly stated, we believe that MGRM's rollover and credit exposures at that time were such that a reasonable case could have been made for the unwinding of its positions. However, we agree with Culp and Miller that "too many essential facts about [MGRM's] program and its liquidation have still not been made public" for us to evaluate definitively the correctness of MG's liquidation decision.

ENDNOTES

1. *See* W. Arthur Benson v. Metallgesellschaft Corp (and others), Civil Action No. JFM-94-484, Supplemental Memorandum of W. Arthur Benson Relative to Judicial Estoppel, 1994.

2. *See* affidavit of W. Arthur Benson v. Metallgesellschaft Corp. (and others), U.S.D.C Maryland, Civil Action No. JFM-94-484 (October 13, 1994). MGRM's mark-ups were the same regardless of the length of the contracts. Critics have argued that higher mark-ups should have been used for longer-term contracts, perhaps because of increasing credit risk. *See* Special Audit Report of MG A.G. prepared by C&L Treuarbeit and Deutsche Revision and Wollert-Elmendorff, Frankfurt, Germany (January 20, 1995).

3. Alternatively, it has been contended that MGRM entered into these contracts in order to book unrealized profits against the futures losses it had at that time. *See* Special Audit Report (1995), cited previously.

4. The "basis" is the difference between the price of the instrument that is being used to hedge (in the case of MGRM, near-month futures and swaps) and the price of the instrument or commitment that is being hedged (forward sales in the case of MGRM.) "Basis risk" is the volatility of the basis. All hedgers, by definition, choose to assume basis risk as a trade-off for eliminating the price risk they would have if they did not hedge, presumably because the basis risk is less than the price risk. *See* Franklin R. Edwards and Cindy W. Ma, *Futures & Options*, New York: McGraw-Hill, 1992.

5. *See* Exhibit C in affidavit of Benson (1994). This exhibit shows that as of October 1, 1993, MGRM had sold forward approximately 93 million barrels of heating oil and 67 million barrels of gasoline,

and that it had hedged these commitments by buying futures and swaps in the approximate amount of 39 million barrels of heating oil, 16 million of gas-oil, 58 million of gasoline, and 47 million of crude.

6. A "stack" hedge refers to a futures position being "stacked" or concentrated in a particular delivery month (or months) rather than being spread over many delivery months. In MGRM's case, it placed the entire 160 million barrel hedge in short-dated delivery months, rather than spreading this amount over many, longer-dated, delivery months. "Rolling over" this stacked position refers to the process of rolling it forward: selling contract months which will soon expire and purchasing (or replacing these contracts with) deferred-month contracts. Common reasons for using short-dated stack hedges are that liquidity is much better in near-month contracts, that longer-dated derivatives may not be available on reasonable terms, and that hedgers hold certain expectations about how the term structure of forward prices will change in the future. In a recent article, MGRM's short-dated, stack, hedging strategy is referred to as a "textbook" hedging strategy. *See* Christopher L. Culp and Merton H. Miller, "Hedging a Flow of Commodity Deliveries with Futures: Lesson from Metallgesellschaft," *Derivatives Quarterly*, Vol. 1, No. 1 (Fall 1994).

7. Futures contracts are marked-to-market daily by exchanges, and traders are required to post with the exchange any losses they incur. While swap contracts usually are not formally marked-to-market, it is not uncommon for counterparties in swap agreements to call for additional collateral from losing counterparties as losses mount. In addition, swap contracts entail cash flows on settlement dates. Thus, in terms of cash flows, short-dated OTC swaps are very similar to futures contracts.

8. Physical storage is defined simply as purchasing and storing oil, and not physical storage in conjunction with "reverse cash-and-carry" arbitrage to take advantage of backwardation. The latter would involve continually making and taking delivery of oil.

9. The statistics in Table 20.1 suggest that carrying costs would be in the order of $.24/barrel per month. Further, a recent study of energy markets reported that storage space for oil above ground is limited and entails an "extremely high cost per unit value." *See* Robert H. Litzenberger and Nir Rabinowitz, "Backwardation in Oil Futures Markets: Theory and Empirical Evidence," Rodney L. White Center for Financial Research, Wharton School of the University of Pennsylvania, 1993.

10. A strategy of physical storage would also have exposed MGRM to some risk. First, there would have been some "funding risk" because of uncertainty about future carrying costs (such as interest rates). Second, because of the customer "cash-out" options in MGRM's forward delivery contracts, MGRM was exposed to "market risk." Had customers exercised their options, MGRM would have had to sell a large volume of physical oil at short notice to produce the cash needed to meet its cash-out obligations.

11. Christopher L. Culp and Merton H. Miller refer to MGRM's hedging program as "synthetic storage" in their article "Metallgesellschaft and The Economics of Synthetic Storage," *Journal of Applied Corporate Finance*, Vol. 7, No. 4 (Winter 1995).

12. No information is available on exactly how MGRM conducted its rollovers.

13. The last day of trading for heating oil and gasoline is the last business day of the month preceding the delivery month; for crude oil it is the third business day prior to the 25th calendar day of the month preceding the delivery month.

14. Alternatively, roll gains (losses) can be calculated as the change in the second-month futures price minus the change in the spot price over the same period. This methodology yielded nearly identical results during the 1983–92 period.

15. Specifically, we analyzed (1) a ten-day rollover rule using a near-month stack and (2) a three-day rule using a stack in six-month futures. The results of this analysis appear in the original *Journal of Futures Markets* article and can be obtained from the authors.

16. The period from April, 1983, to December, 1992, was chosen because trading in crude oil futures did not begin until 1983. Also, gasoline futures did not start trading until December, 1984. The period of analysis ends in December, 1992, in order to make the results comparable with what happened to MGRM in 1993. Data are from the Knight-Ridder futures markets database.

17. Similar graphs for heating oil and gasoline can be obtained from the authors.

18. The ability to do reverse cash-and-carry arbitrage is limited because a shortage of the physical commodity makes it difficult and costly to borrow the physical commodity in order to short it. For a discussion of arbitrage bounds when there are restrictions on short-selling, *see* Da-Hsiang Donald Lien, "Asymmetric Arbitrage in Futures Markets: An Empirical Study," *The Journal of Futures Markets*, Vol. 6 (1986).

19. MGRM apparently did do this. *See* affidavit of Benson (1994), cited previously.

20. The simple correlation coefficients for daily changes in near-month futures prices are: .84 between crude oil and gasoline, and .88 between crude oil and heating oil.

21. *See* Appendix 1.B of our *JFM* article cited earlier. This calculation assumes an average contractual markup of $4, a constant interest rate of 6%, and an average monthly rollover cost of $.24—the average monthly rollover loss in crude oil during the 1983–92 period when crude oil was in contango. (See Table 20.1) In addition, it assumes that MGRM rolled forward its entire position every month.

22. The daily "second-month" basis is calculated by subtracting daily "nearby" closing futures prices from daily closing "second-month" futures prices.

23. Daily settlement prices are used for over 2,400 trading days, from April, 1983, to September, 1994. In calculating *daily* basis volatilities, a random rollover date is implicitly assumed. The standard deviations of the "second-month" basis are calculated using only the roll dates generated by the three-day rollover rule. These are $1.25/barrel for heating oil, and $.89 for gasoline, which are higher than the volatilities calculated assuming a random rollover date.

24. Near-month futures prices are used as proxies for spot prices because data on spot prices are notoriously bad.

25. This assumes that monthly rollover gains and losses are independent of one another. If this were not true, the probability of MGRM's experiencing a string of contango months would be higher.

26. Similar graphs for heating oil and gasoline can be obtained from the authors.

27. Taking only MGRM's futures positions, MGRM constituted about 6.7% (55,000/(160,000 + 200,000 + 450,000)) of the combined highest total open interest of gasoline, heating oil, and crude oil during December, 1993. If MGRM's swap positions are also included (because its swap counterparties would have been hedging with futures), these combined positions would have constituted about 20% (160,000/810,000) of total open interest in December, 1993.

28. An example of a recent institutional investment product aimed directly at taking advantage of the well-known price backwardation in energy futures markets is Goldman, Sachs' "commodity index." Petroleum products have a heavy weight in this index, and a substantial portion of the "advertised" return on this index is predicated on the continued existence of price backwardation in energy futures markets.

29. For example, when hedgers rely on regression analysis to choose both the commodities to hedge with and the hedge ratio to use, they are relying on historical data being a good predictor of future price relationships. *See* Edwards and Ma (1992) Chapters 5 and 6, cited previously.

30. According to the Special Auditor Report (1995), cited previously, MGRM believed that the average life of a typical forward delivery contract that included the cash-out option was between 2.5 and 3 years.

31. Similar to the earlier procedure for energy futures, a three-day rollover rule is used to calculate rollover gains and losses. The last day of trading in the soybean futures contract is seven days prior to the last business day of the delivery month. The last day of trading in copper futures is the third-to-last business day of the month. Rollovers occur in the main contract months for each of the commodities: January, March, May, July, August, September, and November for soybeans; and, January, March, May, July, September, and December for copper.

32. In order to compare these rollover gains with the earlier findings for energy futures, they can be restated as average percentage returns by dividing the average rollover gains by the respective average prices during the period. Thus, in the 1965–74 period, the average rollover returns were 1.48 percent and 2.4 percent for soybeans and copper while for crude oil, heating oil, and gasoline the average rollover returns during the 1983–92 period were, respectively, 1.12 percent, 1.24 percent, and 1.80 percent.

33. "Economic" obstacles should be distinguished from "legal" obstacles. It is possible, for example, that there may have been some difficulty in creditors' perfecting legal title to MGRM's forward delivery contracts in the event of a default by MG.

34. A "minimum-variance" hedge attempts to minimize the variance in the firm's per-unit hedged revenues due to changes in price levels.

35. Distant futures prices are used as proxies for forward energy prices.

36. Reliable price data for futures contracts more distant than nine months are not available. There is little trading in many distant months, so that settlement prices are often not realistic prices. They may, for example, be "interpolated" prices.

37. The volatility of nine-month futures is from 50 to 65 percent of the volatility of spot futures prices.

38. The forward price curves plotted in Figure 20.3 also suggest that forward prices quickly flatten out, so that price volatility for more distant forward prices may not be much different than that reflected in nine-month futures prices. Our presumption, therefore, is that the price relationship reflected in the regression of spot prices on nine-month futures (shown in Table 20.6) would hold for more distant forward prices as well.

39. Adjusting the hedge ratio for differences in the timing of cash flows is known as "tailing" the hedge. It is well-known that failure to tail the hedge ". . . could force the premature liquidation and seriously disrupt a well-considered hedging or trading strategy." Ira G. Kawaller and Timothy W. Koch, "Managing Cash Flow Risk in Stock Index Futures: The Tail Hedge," *Journal of Portfolio Management,* Vol. 14 (1988) p. 41. *See also* S. Figlewski, Y. Landskroner, and W. Silber, "Tailing the Hedge: Why and How," *The Journal of Futures Markets,* Vol 11. (1991) pp. 200–212.

40. There are other ways to derive the appropriate hedge ratio. Gibson and Schwartz (1990) use a two-factor contingent claims pricing model to estimate hedge ratios for oil deliverable in the future. They find, for example, a hedge ratio of about .5 would be appropriate for hedging oil deliverable in five years and a ratio of about .25 would be appropriate for oil deliverable in ten years. *See* "Stochastic Convenience Yield and the Pricing of Oil contingent Claims," *The Journal of Finance,* Vol. 45 (1990) pp. 959–976. The authors wish to thank John Parsons for bringing this paper to their attention.

41. There were no customer options that could be triggered by a decline in energy prices.

42. Jerome S. Fons, "Using Default Rates to Model the Term Structure of Credit Risk," *Financial Analysts Journal* (September/October 1994) pp. 25–32.

43. MG's Supervisory Board's rejection in December of alternative actions that could have protected MGRM against further margin outflows also is evidence that it did not believe that MGRM's forward-delivery strategy was fundamentally sound. For example, MGRM could have protected itself against further margin outflows due to price declines by purchasing put options on energy products, which were available in December 1993. This strategy would have neutralized further margin outflows on MGRM's long futures and swap positions and may have been able to lock-in the net gains that MGRM had as of that time. In addition, the characterization of MGRM's hedging strategy as "a game of roulette" by members of MG's supervisory board certainly suggests that the board believed that MGRM's strategy was fatally flawed.

44. Culp and Miller (1995) argue that MG should not have liquidated in December 1993 because at that time the term structure of oil prices was upward sloping (contango). (p. 12) However, it should be noted that the term structure was also upward sloping for virtually all of 1993, during which time spot oil prices fell sharply.

45. Approximately one-third of MGRM's forward delivery contracts gave customers the right to request that deliveries be deferred until the last day of the contract. Thus, the timing of futures cash flows from these contracts was highly uncertain. *See* Special Audit Report (1995), cited previously.

21

Maturity Structure of a Hedge Matters: Lessons from the Metallgesellschaft Debacle

Antonio S. Mello
John E. Parsons

A t the start of 1994, Metallgesellschaft A.G., the 14th largest corporation in Germany, stood on the brink of bankruptcy as a result of more than $1 billion in losses from trading in oil futures. The futures trades were part of a sophisticated strategy ostensibly conceived by its New York subsidiary to hedge against dangerous swings in the price of oil and oil-related products. How could a set of transactions that purportedly "locked in" profits, making the firm safer, in fact lead the firm to bankruptcy? Understanding the mistakes made by Metallgesellschaft is critical if other firms are to avoid a similar fate without forsaking the significant benefits available from a correctly planned hedging strategy.

The parent corporation Metallgesellschaft A.G. is a large conglomerate with interests in a wide variety of metal, mining, and engineering businesses, including 15 major subsidiaries. Total sales in 1993 topped DM 26 billion ($16 billion) on assets of DM 17.8 billion ($10 billion) and with total employment of 43,292. Metallgesellschaft is closely held with over 65% of its stock owned by seven institutional investors, including the Emir of Kuwait, Dresdner Bank, Deutsche Bank, Allianz, Daimler-Benz, the Australian Mutual Provident Society, and M.I.M. Holdings Ltd. of Australia. Some of these are also important creditors to the firm.

Metallgesellschaft's U.S. subsidiary (MG Corp.) was reorganized in 1986 with equity capital of $50 million and net sales of $1.7 billion from trading in U.S. government bonds, foreign currency, emerging market instruments, and various commodities. The U.S. subsidiary's oil business, organized under MG Refining and Marketing (MGRM), grew significantly between 1989 and 1993. In 1989 the company obtained a 49% stake in Castle Energy, a U.S. oil exploration company, whose transformation into a refiner MGRM helped finance. MGRM contracted with Castle Energy to purchase their output of refined products—approximately 46 million bbl. per year—at guaranteed margins for up to 10 years, and assembled a large network of infrastructure necessary for the storage and transport of oil products. During 1992 and 1993, MGRM succeeded in signing a large number of long-term contracts for delivery of gasoline, heating oil, and

Originally published in the *Journal of Applied Corporate Finance* 8(1), Spring. Reprinted with permission.

jet fuel oil to independent retailers. By late 1993 MGRM had become an important supplier. In addition MGRM ran large trades in energy-related derivatives. Its portfolio included a wide variety of over-the-counter forwards, swaps, and puts, and it did large amounts of trading in futures contracts on crude oil, heating oil, and gasoline on a number of exchanges and markets.

MGRM AS A FINANCIAL INTERMEDIARY

MGRM had no competitive advantage in its cost of supply. It did not own significant amounts of oil in the ground and the refineries run by Castle were old and inefficient. Instead, MGRM's business plan laid out a marketing strategy based on long-term pricing.[1] MGRM's management believed that independent retailers required protection against temporarily high spot prices for their supplies. According to MGRM, spot price movements quickly impacted the wholesale price of refined oil products but not the retail price. While retailers attached to large integrated oil companies were able to ride out the temporary squeezes on margins, independent retailers often faced a severe liquidity crunch. And while retailers could buy products under contracts protecting them against these temporary price surges, MGRM believed these contract price terms were unnecessarily high given the recent history of spot prices.

This was the central premise of MGRM's strategy. MGRM believed it possible to arbitrage between the spot oil market and the long-term contract market. This arbitrage required skilled use of the futures markets in oil products, and this was to be MGRM's stock in trade.

MGRM developed several novel contract programs. First, MGRM offered a "firm-fixed" program, under which the customer would agree to a fixed monthly delivery of oil products at a set price. By September of 1993, MGRM was obligated for a total of 102 million barrels under this type of contract. About 95.5 million barrels were covered by contracts running for ten years, with most of the remainder covered by contracts running for five years.[2]

A second program, called "firm-flexible" contracts, included a set price and a specified total volume of deliveries over the life of the contract, but gave the customer extensive rights to set the delivery schedule—up to a maximum of 20% of its needs in any year—and with 45 days notice. By September of 1993, MGRM was obligated for a total of 52 million barrels under this type of contract. About 47.5 million barrels were covered by contracts running for ten years and 10.5 million barrels were covered by contracts running for five years.

MGRM also ran a third program of "guaranteed margin" contracts, under which it agreed to make deliveries at a price that would assure the independent operator a fixed margin relative to the retail price offered by its geographical competitors. The contract could be extended annually for a defined period and at MGRM's discretion. By September of 1993, MGRM was obligated for a total of 54 million barrels under this type of contract, although MGRM's renewal option meant that these volumes were not firm obligations. It is the first two programs involving 154 million barrels of obligations for periods up to ten years that constituted MGRM's designated short position in oil.

Although the contracts appear to deliver price protection in a straightforward manner, in fact the advantage to MGRM's customers was more roundabout. A familiar problem with long-term fixed-price contracts is that the protection offered on one side of the contract creates its own financial squeeze on the other side; that is, when the contract is deep in the money for the seller, the buyer may in fact be forced into default or at least a renegotiation of the terms. To minimize this danger, MGRM limited the annual volume supplied under contract to no more than 20% of the customer's needs. Of course, this also minimized the degree to which MGRM's contract would resolve the squeeze on a retailer during a period of high spot prices.

In order to both minimize the default risk in times of low spot prices and meet the customer's liquidity needs in times of high spot prices, MGRM included in its contracts a cash-out option. In times of high spot prices, customers could call for cash settlement on the full volume of outstanding deliveries over the life of the contract, thus receiving a cash infusion exactly when they were otherwise liquidity constrained. Under the *firm-fixed* contracts, the customer would receive *one-half* the difference between the current nearby futures price and the contract price, multiplied by the entire remaining quantity of deliveries. Under the *firm-flexible* contracts, the customer would receive the full difference between the second-nearest futures price and the contract price, multiplied by the portion of deliveries called.[3]

Through its pricing terms and these options, MGRM had assumed a good deal of its customers' oil price risk. To hedge this risk, MGRM used a strategy known as the rolling stack. At the peril of some oversimplification, the strategy worked as follows. MGRM opened a long position in futures stacked in the near month contract. Each month MGRM would roll the stack over into the next near month contract, gradually decreasing the size of the position. Under this plan, the total long position in the stack would always match the short position remaining due under the supply contracts. As of September 1993, the stack consisted of some 55 million barrels in futures on crude oil, heating oil, and gasoline, primarily in the near or next month contract, and a portfolio of similarly short-dated over-the-counter swap contracts bringing the total hedge to the full 154 million barrels of delivery obligated under the supply contracts. MGRM thus had a hedge ratio of one-to-one.[4]

MISMATCHED MATURITY IN THE HEDGE

The distinctive characteristic of this strategy is that MGRM was running a hedge with a maturity structure that did not match that of its delivery contracts. This had two critical consequences. First, it significantly *increased* the variance of the firm's cash flow at the outset of the strategy, making it vulnerable to an enormous liquidity crisis—exactly the opposite of what one would expect from a well-designed hedging strategy. Second, it exposed the firm to an excessive amount of basis risk—variations in the value of the short-dated futures positions not compensated by equal and opposite variations in the value of the long-dated delivery obligations—so that the rolling stack had not actually succeeded in locking-in the value of the delivery contracts. We illustrate these two problems in turn.

Cash Flow Trouble with a Short-Dated Hedge

A rolling stack of short-dated futures initially increases the variance of cash flow because movements in the price of oil within the month create losses or gains on the entire stack of contracts—losses or gains that must be settled by the end of the month—while compensating gains or losses on deliveries are realized only gradually over the remaining ten years of the delivery contract. We illustrate this danger with an example in Table 21.1.[5]

TABLE 21.1   Cash Flow Deficit Created by a Maturity Mismatched Hedge

			Supply Contracts		Futures Stack		Net Position	
Month (A)	Near Month Futures Price ($/bbl) (B)	Next Month Futures Price ($/bbl) (C)	Deliveries (million bbl) (D)	Net Receipts ($ million) (E)	Size of Stack (million bbl) (F)	Monthly Settlement ($ million) (G)	Net Cash Flow ($ million) (H)	Accumulated Net Cash Flow ($ million) (I)
March	20.16	20.30	0.00	0.0	154.0	0.0	0.0	0.0
April	20.22	20.42	1.28	1.0	152.7	(12.3)	(11.3)	(11.3)
May	19.51	19.83	1.28	1.9	151.4	(139.0)	(137.1)	(148.4)
June	18.58	18.90	1.28	3.1	150.2	(189.3)	(186.2)	(334.6)
July	17.67	17.92	1.28	4.3	148.9	(184.7)	(180.4)	(515.0)
August	17.86	18.30	1.28	4.0	147.6	(8.9)	(4.9)	(519.9)
September	16.86	17.24	1.28	5.3	146.3	(212.5)	(207.2)	(727.1)
October	18.27	18.38	1.28	3.5	145.0	150.7	154.2	(572.9)
November	16.76	17.06	1.28	5.4	143.7	(234.9)	(229.5)	(802.4)
December	14.41	14.80	1.28	8.5	142.5	(380.9)	(372.4)	(1,174.8)

(B) As the maturity of the near month futures price approaches, this price becomes a proxy for the prevailing spot price. This is the price it will cost to supply monthly delivery requirements and the price at which the stack of futures will be closed out.

(C) This is the price at which the stack of futures contracts will be rolled over into the next month.

(D) Monthly deliveries equal the total initial position divided by 120 months, 154m.bbl./120 months.

(E) Monthly profit on the supply contract equals the difference between the contract delivery price—constant at $21/bbl—and the prevailing settlement price on the near month futures contract shown in column (B), multiplied by the volume of deliveries shown in column (D): $E = [21 - B]*D$.

(F) The initial long position is 154 million barrels. It declines monthly by the volume of deliveries under the supply contract.

(G) Settlement on the futures position equals the price on the near month futures contract shown in column (B) less the price prevailing the month before when the position was opened and shown in column (C), multiplied by the number of contracts held at the start of the month shown in column F: $G = [B_t - C_{t-1}]*F_{t-1}$.

(H) Net cash flow is the sum of profits on the deliveries under the supply contract and settlement of the futures contracts: $H = E + G$.

(I) Accumulated net cash flow is the sum of all the net cash flow for prior months: $I_t = I_{t-1} + H_t$.

To see the effect of an oil price decrease on current cash flow, look at May, the second month of the contract. A $0.71/bbl. drop in the price of oil from $20.22 to $19.51/bbl. creates realized losses of $139 million on the more than 152 million barrels of futures contracts outstanding going into the month, while only raising realized gains on the month's deliveries of oil by $900,000, a 154-to-1 ratio of losses to gains.[6] In November and December, the eighth and ninth months of the contracts, the consecutive oil price drops create realized losses on the futures portfolio of $235 and $381 million, respectively, while raising realized gains on the monthly deliveries by only $2 and $3.1 million. The cash flow deficit grows monthly, so that at the end of the year it is just over $1.17 billion.[7]

The danger of this type of cash flow problem is all too often overlooked. Recommendations for designing a good hedge too often focus exclusively on reducing variance in the total value of the firm's projects and underplay the consequences that different hedges have for variability and timing of cash flow. But often the firm's very reason for hedging is to assure a positive cash flow so that it can fund upcoming investments without turning to external sources for additional financing.[8] The strategic motivation for hedging should determine the choice of tactics, the choice of hedging instruments, but this simple fact is too often overlooked.[9] Even if a rolling stack of short-dated futures could help to lock in the total value of the long-term delivery contracts, the fact that it increases the initial variability of the firm's cash flow so significantly can make it a worse than useless hedging strategy.

Metallgesellschaft needed to pay attention to cash flow. MGRM's parent corporation was facing a long-term liquidity crisis of its own and could not afford to finance cash shortfalls at its subsidiary. A series of expansions in the late 1980s and early 1990s had cost the company dearly and had not yet paid off as expected. Between 1989 and 1992, the company's fixed assets rose from DM 2.124 billion to DM 6.617 billion. During the same period, its reported return on capital fell from 13.1% to 6.7%, and its actual return had probably fallen further still. MG's accumulated cash flow deficit between 1988 and 1993 ran to DM 5.65 billion and was financed with a DM 4.44 billion increase in net debt and three equity issues yielding DM 1.21 billion. The U.S. subsidiary had also been forced to raise capital through a public sale of stock in Castle Energy. By 1993, the parent corporation was forced to turn to asset sales as a tool for continued financing of its central lines of business. Employment fell between 1992 and 1993 from 62,547 to 43,292. The company had already cut its dividend and was considering omitting the next dividend entirely. In light of these circumstances, the parent corporation had recently announced that its subsidiaries were to be independent profit centers and could not expect to be easily financed by the parent company.

MGRM's foray into the oil trading business emerges, then, as a singularly bad fit for the parent corporation in its current circumstances. Just when the parent corporation was faced with low cash flow and a weak balance sheet, its U.S. subsidiary embarked on a business plan that involved functioning as a financial intermediary to independent oil retailers. MGRM's strategy was based upon its readiness to assume the oil price risk that independent operators would otherwise be forced to bear, but MG itself could not afford to shoulder the risk. MGRM might have tried to offload this risk in a number of ways—for example, by selling the contracts and taking its profit in the form of an origination fee. Or it might have managed the risk using a hedge that was the mirror image of its short obligation.[10] By choosing a hedge of short-dated futures contracts, however, MGRM actually exacerbated the problem, increasing the total risk of a large negative cash flow in the near term.

When cash flows matter, the rolling stack may be worse than no hedge at all, as we now illustrate. To evaluate the full effects of the rolling stack hedge under a wide variety of possible spot price paths, not just the extremely unfavorable one occurring in 1993, we constructed a simulation model of MGRM's financial condition for the life of the delivery contracts.

The inputs to the model are displayed in Table 21.2 along with the results. MGRM is assumed to have a contract obligation to deliver 150 million barrels of oil products over a period of 10 years, or 1.25 million barrels a month. The contract delivery price is $20/bbl, and MGRM has a cost of making delivery equal to $2/bbl, yielding a net price of $18/bbl. MGRM buys oil at the prevailing spot price, which starts at $17/bbl and which for any horizon is expected to be 17/bbl, but which may vary from month to month with an annual variance of 12%. The rate of interest is 7%. Under these assumptions, the contract for long-term delivery of oil has a value of $10 million.

The contract is, however, very risky. For example, should the price of oil rise to $21, then MGRM would have a monthly cash flow deficit of $3.25 million.

Our assumption about the cost paid by MGRM if it has a sudden cash shortfall requiring external financing is also detailed in Table 21.2. The cost increases with the amount of financing required. Because of this cost, a constant low-risk cash flow is

TABLE 21.2   Ex Ante Valuation of Contracts Unhedged and Hedged with a Running Stack*

Inputs to Simulation Model:	
Duration of contract	10 years
Total delivery obligation	150 million bbl.
Monthly delivery	1.25 million bbl.
Fixed contract delivery price	$20/bbl
Cost of delivery	$2/bbl.
Initial spot price of oil	$17/bbl
Annual interest rate	7%
Annual convenience yield less cost of storage	7%
Cost of external financing:	
$1 million/month	0 basis points
$10 million/month	0.2 basis points
$50 million/month	2.2 basis points
Results:	
Present value of contract	$63.6 million
Cost of financing, unhedged	$ 4.4 million
Net value of contract, unhedged	$59.2 million
Cost of financing, rolling stack	$28.5 million
Net value of contract, rolling stack	$35.1 million

*Value estimates are derived using a standard contingent claims model to price commodity-related assets and related hedges: see M. Brennan and E. Schwartz, 1985, "Evaluating Natural Resource Investments," *Journal of Business*, 58:135–157.

more beneficial to MGRM than the risky cash flow. Running our simulation model with this cost incorporated, we find that the value to MGRM of the unhedged contract declines to $9.86 million. The cost of external financing reduces the value of the contract by $0.74 million.

When a rolling stack with a one-to-one hedge ratio is included in our simulation model, the results are striking. The costs of external financing *increase* dramatically, to $4.75 million, so that the value of the contract hedged with a rolling stack is actually less than the value of the contract unhedged!

It was exactly a liquidity crisis like the one described in Table 21.1 that precipitated Metallgesellschaft's brush with bankruptcy. MGRM had been losing money on its futures position throughout 1993. The consequences had already been felt within the U.S. subsidiary by the end of the summer as the firm's credit lines were used up and, for example, traders in the emerging markets group were unable to find counterparties for some of their swap transactions. When the oil price fell yet more precipitously at the end of the year, the company did not have sufficient cash to continue rolling over its stack of oil futures contracts as planned and could not meet a large number of its other obligations until it received an emergency line of credit from its bankers.

Losses eventually totaled nearly $1.3 billion. By January the firm was close to declaring bankruptcy and its future was not clear. MG eventually negotiated a $1.9 billion bailout from its bankers in tandem with a plan to shed assets such as its auto parts manufacturing business, its tin mining operations, its recently acquired heating equipment, stainless steel, and boiler making lines, and others. MG was also forced to scale back a number of its central businesses, cutting employment in these businesses by more than 7,500 and reducing planned capital outlays by one-half, to a level below depreciation. The company has also since withdrawn from its lead position in the construction of a new copper smelter in Indonesia.

In short, the cumulative effect of the original trading losses and the firm's bankruptcy has been severe. The price of a share fell by half, from a high of DM 427 ($246) in November 1993, prior to news of the oil trading losses, to DM 216 ($125) in February 1994, after the rescue plan was organized.

Was the Firm Value-Hedged?

MGRM's management tried to downplay the significance of the liquidity crisis, arguing that it was *merely* a liquidity crisis and that the cash losses on the stack of futures were matched by an increase in the value of the supply contracts: the drop in oil prices that created losses on the stack of futures would mean a lower cost of meeting future delivery requirements under the long-term supply contracts. Summed over the life of the contract, the extra profits earned on future deliveries would exactly match the initial losses on the stack of futures. So although the firm faced a short-run liquidity crisis like the one illustrated in Table 21.1, the value of its total assets, they claimed, had not actually declined and so the firm was solvent.[11] MG's financial crisis, however, was more than just a liquidity crisis. The losses on its future contracts were real; it is simply not true that these losses were matched by an equivalent increase in the value of the supply contracts.

MGRM hedged its long-run delivery commitments with an equal number of futures contracts. While this one-to-one hedge portfolio appears sensible, it was not. This brings us to the second problem with a hedge portfolio of mismatched maturity structure: basis risk. One barrel of oil for delivery in one month is simply not equal in present value to one barrel of oil for delivery in ten years, and the value of the two differently dated obligations do not move in lock step. In general, spot prices are more variable than futures prices, and a one dollar fall in the current spot price of oil implies a smaller change in the expected price of oil anytime in the future. As a result, it is unlikely that a drop in the current price of oil creates gains on the delivery contracts that match in present value terms the losses incurred on the stack of short-dated futures.[12]

To illustrate the effect that this has on MGRM's net position, we have provided in Table 21.3 some reasonable estimates for the present value factors relating a $1 movement in the prevailing spot price of oil with the change in expected value of forward contracts for oil at different dates. While a $1 increase in the spot price of oil would increase the expected value of a 6-month forward contract by $0.941, it would increase the expected value of a 5-year forward obligation by only $0.520 or approximately one-half. A ten-year forward obligation would increase by only $0.266. These estimates make clear that there may be variation in the spot price that changes the value of the stack of short-dated futures without a comparable offsetting movement in the expected value of the long-dated delivery contracts.[13]

In Table 21.4 we calculate how the value of the outstanding contracts may have changed as the spot price fell during 1993: calculations are based on the factor estimates given in Table 21.3. In May, with 151.4 million barrels of oil to be delivered over a little less than ten years, and with a $0.71 drop in the price of oil, the present value of the outstanding delivery obligation increases by 56% of the changed cost of

TABLE 21.3   Relationship between the Changing Oil Price and the Value of Forward Delivery Commitments

Time Forward to Delivery	First Derivative of Present Value with Respect to Spot Price	Time Forward to Delivery	First Derivative of Present Value with Respect to Spot Price
1 month	0.991	5 years	0.520
6 months	0.941	6 years	0.454
12 months	0.884	7 years	0.398
2 years	0.776	8 years	0.348
3 years	0.678	9 years	0.304
4 years	0.594	10 years	0.266

Based on data in Rajna Gibson and Eduardo Schwartz, 1990, "Stochastic Convenience Yield and the Pricing of Oil Contingent Claims," *Journal of Finance*, 45:959–976.

supply—that is, by $60.24 million, an amount far less than the $139 million loss on the futures portfolio in the same month. The cumulative increase in the value of the delivery contracts during 1993 was $479 million, less than one-half the losses on the futures portfolio.

A comparison of the monthly losses on the futures portfolio in 1993 against the monthly realized and unrealized income on the delivery contracts is shown in Figure 21.1. The cumulative loss for 1993, net of unrealized increases in the value of the delivery contracts, is more than $695 million.

The situation described in these tables is a generous picture of what actually befell MGRM. Oil prices dropped in late 1993 due to conflicts within OPEC that temporarily added supplies onto the market. The expectation of the long-term spot price 3, 4, and 5 years out was largely unchanged so that the losses on the stack of futures were actually matched by little if any change in the capitalized value of the supply contracts.

TABLE 21.4   Unrealized Gains on the Delivery Contracts Based on Monthly Price Changes in 1993

Month	Outstanding Delivery Obligation (million bbl.)	Monthly Price Change ($/bbl.)	Present Value Factor for Remaining Deliveries	Total Change in Contract Value ($ million)
March	154.0	0.00	0.56	0.00
April	152.7	0.06	0.56	(5.11)
May	151.4	(0.71)	0.56	60.24
June	150.2	(0.93)	0.56	78.59
July	148.9	(0.91)	0.57	76.57
August	147.6	0.19	0.57	(15.92)
September	146.3	(1.00)	0.57	83.43
October	145.0	1.41	0.57	(117.12)
November	143.7	(1.51)	0.58	124.87
December	142.5	(2.35)	0.58	193.45
Total				478.99

FIGURE 21.1   Monthly Income for Ten Year Delivery Contracts Hedged with a Rolling Stack of Futures and for the Oil Price Structure Realized in 1993*

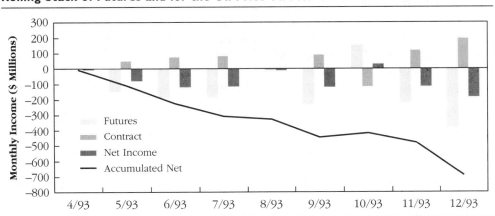

*Income on the futures portfolio is realized profits or losses. Income on the contracts is the sum of realized income on deliveries plus unrealized capital gains on outstanding deliveries as calculated in Table 21.4.

Because of basis risk, if one is committed to using a stack of short-dated futures contracts, then it is necessary to use a hedge ratio much smaller than MGRM's one-to-one hedge. A comparison of the minimum variance hedge against the one-to-one hedge run by MGRM over the ten years of the program is presented in Table 21.5. Two alternative minimum variance hedge calculations are shown, corresponding to alternative assumptions about the underlying delivery contracts being hedged. Using the present value factors shown in Table 21.3, the minimum variance hedge ratio (A) for a ten-year monthly annuity of oil deliveries is about .56; and, so, to cover 154 million barrels in delivery over 10 years would initially require a stack of only about 86 million barrels.

TABLE 21.5   A Comparison of the One-for-One Hedge with the Minimum Variance Hedge under Alternative Assumptions

	One-for-one Hedge	Minimum Variance Hedge of a Ten-year Annuity of Forward Deliveries		Minimum Variance Hedge Assuming Option Exercise at Year 3	
0	154.0	85.5	0.56	87.3	0.57
1	138.6	81.2	0.59	83.1	0.60
2	123.2	76.2	0.62	78.2	0.63
3	107.8	70.5	0.65	72.2	0.67
4	92.4	64.0	0.69		
5	77.0	56.5	0.73		
6	61.6	48.0	0.78		
7	46.2	38.3	0.83		
8	30.8	27.1	0.88		
9	15.4	14.4	0.94		
10	0.0	0.0	1.00		

Revising the minimum variance hedge ratio to incorporate the effect of the cash-out options is technically quite difficult, but we have made an illustrative calculation based on the assumption that the contracts were all to be cashed out at the end of the third year, the horizon assumed by MGRM's management. This calculation yields the second minimum variance hedge ratio, ratio B, in which the firm's optimal stack is still only 87.3 million bbl at the outset.[14]

There are additional reasons to believe that the long-term contracts had not increased in value as much as the stack of futures had lost value. The risk of default by some of the independent operators was great and naturally increasing as the price of oil fell. In valuing the supply contracts it is necessary to take into account the high probability of default or renegotiation in the shadow of possible future defaults. Renegotiation is a very common event for fixed-price delivery contracts, as distinguished from the sort of financial forward contracts financial economists are used to valuing and as opposed to the futures contracts used to hedge the supply obligation.

MGRM's management was aware of the danger that fixed-price terms designed to benefit the retailers on one side of spot price movements could hurt those same retailers on the other side, and it had placed limits on the quantity of oil products provided to each retailer under the contract specifically to minimize the danger of just this sort of default or renegotiation problem. But however intelligently the program was designed, some significant risk of renegotiation or non-performance remained, and it is essential to factor this in when estimating the true value of MGRM's short exposure.[15] This extra default risk on the supply contracts means that a drop in oil prices does not create a one-to-one increase in the value of the contracts to match the drop in the value of the futures.

MGRM's choice of maturity structure for its hedge produced enormous deadweight costs on the firm. These costs could have been avoided with a smaller hedge ratio or using a hedge with a better matched maturity structure. But is the issue here really the right hedge for the delivery contracts? In fact, analyzing the stack of futures as a hedge has been a little misleading as we shall now see.

HEDGING OR SPECULATION

If our preceding analysis is correct, it leaves us with some puzzling questions. Why did management choose a hedge with a mismatched maturity structure? And why did management run such a large stack? The answers are revealing of the depth of the problems at MGRM, and they give us some insight to the questions raised above about the valuation of the delivery contracts themselves.

Far from being simply a hedge meant to lock in profits generated by the long-term delivery contracts, the rolling stack itself was intended by MGRM management to be a source of profits. The company's business plan reads:

As is well documented in standard textbooks, a hedge is said to be perfect when the gain (or loss) in the cash market is totally offset by the loss (or gain) in the futures market. However, it is important to recognize that if a hedge program is carefully designed to "lock in" a favorable basis between spot and futures prices at the most advantageous time, hedging can generate trading profits which can substantially enhance the operating margin. Our proposed risk management program, discussed below, not only protects the pump profit margins with a

*minimum amount of risk from the spot market, but also offers us an opportunity
for extraordinary upside profit with no additional risk. (2, p. 2)*

Locking in return was clearly only one part of MGRM's motivation for buying the
futures contracts. The second part was speculation. Management believed that
prices on a wide variety of oil-related derivatives often deviated from fundamentals
and that profits could be made with the right trades. MGRM's management had identified a long list of mispricings, and a large part of their time was spent analyzing
market data in order to quickly recognize others as they might arise. Far from being
simply a subordinate element of MGRM's general business strategy, we believe that
MGRM's overall position in oil-related derivatives was driven more by its own belief
that these financial instruments were mispriced than by a need for hedging its underlying activity in the cash markets—the tail wagging the dog, so to speak.

In evaluating a portfolio of futures contracts as a hedge, one should generally assume that the prevailing price structure is "fair," so that the contracts themselves
have zero net present value. The benefit of the contracts should not be in the value
they yield directly to the company, but in whether they succeed in locking in the
value of the company's underlying business. One hedge is better than another, not
because the particular instruments used are priced more favorably, but because the
instruments provide a better lock on profits being earned elsewhere.

MGRM did not make the key assumption of fair market prices in choosing its
hedge. As the previous quote indicates, MGRM's management believed that a good
hedge can create value because the prevailing market prices are not fair. The prevailing prices for long-dated oil instruments, they believed, were too high relative to
the prevailing pattern of prices for short-dated oil. According to their estimates, the
second component of the business as described above, the speculation on the basis,
had a positive value. Moreover, MGRM chose not to hedge the delivery contracts
with long-dated instruments precisely because management felt that the prevailing
price structure for those instruments was too high: i.e., the first component of the
business as described above, the delivery contracts cum long-dated hedge, had a negative net present value.

In sum, MGRM's management wanted to sell the long-dated instruments and buy
the short-dated ones. Thinking of the short-dated contracts as MGRM's hedge of its
delivery contracts has the situation turned on its head. In fact, it was the favorable
returns MGRM imagined to be available on short-dated futures that gave a value to a
business of signing up customers for long-term delivery contracts. The following
passage from its business plan illustrates how this way of thinking worked at MGRM:

*Even if we do not have a 10-year forward product in place, we still should take ad-
vantage of the pricing inefficiency between the spot crude market and the crude
oil reserves market. Using the data from the previous section, when the spot crude
oil prices rose to $44, the 18-month forward was only at $28, and the reserves
were valued at $6.25. With this kind of price scenario, we should look into buying
crude oil reserves and selling crude oil swaps. (1, p. 7)*

Backwardation and Profiting from the Roll

What was the source of the favorable returns on short-dated oil futures? The rolling
stack was a bet placed by MGRM management on the persistent backwardation that

arises in the oil market. Buying a near-month futures contract when the market is in backwardation means buying at a price low relative to the prevailing spot. Assuming that the prevailing spot price remains constant, then as the contract matures and the futures price increases to the spot the position makes a profit.

MGRM's front-to-back hedging strategy was designed to reap this anticipated "roll return." It is because MGRM viewed this anticipated monthly return as an extra profit, unrelated to the need to hedge its delivery commitments, that it was not reluctant to run an excessively large stack. MGRM planned to maximize the return from backwardation by timing the placement of its hedges in different months and commodities. During the winter months, approximately November through March, the futures price for heating oil is generally below the spot price and the market exhibits backwardation, moving closer to a cost-of-carry relationship during the summer months. The opposite seasonal pattern arises for gasoline. MGRM believed it could make extra profit by exploiting the cyclical nature of the backwardation:

> It is during these off-seasons or weak periods that we have to secure this negative
> refinery economics. With the existence of the energy futures market, we can create
> a "paper refinery" which can produce oil products from $1.25 to $1.50 per barrel
> cheaper than a standard $800 million oil company refinery, by taking advantage
> of the inefficiencies created in the illiquid distant contract months in the futures
> market. (2, pp. 2–3) This profit is made possible as the 12-month spreads are es
> tablished at the most advantageous level (i.e., taking advantage of the narrow
> backwardation when the gasoline market is weak) and continuously rolling for
> ward to capture the market inefficiency whenever it occurs. (2, p. 19)

It needs to be emphasized at this point that there may be good reasons why markets for oil products move into backwardation and of course why they do so in a cyclical fashion. If the seasonal swing in gasoline and heating oil prices is an equilibrium reflective of the underlying fundamentals of supply and demand in the heating oil and gasoline markets, then it offers no special profit opportunities and no reason to run a front-to-back hedging strategy. The same is true for backwardation in oil in general.[16]

Although MGRM's management never did any appropriate estimations of the size of the basis risk, MGRM's management implicitly believed that the amount of backwardation was often too much to be accounted for by fundamentals and that a strategy of purchasing the near-month futures contract and rolling them over in each market during its period of backwardation would produce a profit on average. They based this belief on a simple simulation of the returns to a strategy of purchasing a one-month oil futures contract and rolling it over. Using the recent historical data, they found, the strategy would have made money.[17]

But such data have very little to do with identifying a good hedge and everything to do with identifying a good speculative investment strategy. The two are not at all the same thing! The fact that this strategy is open to any and all investors only serves to reinforce the point that it is an essentially speculative bet, not an argument for a hedging strategy being driven by MGRM's business in supplying the long-term market. In fact, a good number of Wall Street houses market their own commodity investment vehicles using return data on just such a strategy run over the same period of time.[18]

The profitability of the rolling stack of near-month contracts was central to MGRM's entire set of profit calculations. Had the long-term contracts been evaluated based upon a hedge with a longer maturity structure, their profitability would have disappeared. This fact helps to highlight the extent to which MGRM's very choice of business line was essentially a bet on the basis.

A rolling stack of near-month futures can be run for either hedging or for speculative purposes. Unravelling these two distinct motives is the key to drawing the right lessons from MG's financial crisis. We do not wish to argue with the speculative motive for rolling oil futures—although the mere fact that the strategy was good in the past is for us a rather weak argument. We are not taking a stand that this speculative investment was a bad one for any investor. MGRM's management took a position that the prevailing price structure in oil was not an equilibrium structure. There is clearly room for disagreement. Differences of opinion make a horse race and there will always be some investors willing to take either side of such a bet.

But while there is room for one to argue that a rolling stack of short-dated contracts is a good speculative investment, we think it is important to make a clear distinction between a good speculative investment and a sound hedge. The short-dated contracts were not a sound hedge. In a very important sense they were not meant to be. The very fact that MGRM's management believed the short-dated stack was a good speculative investment undermines the argument that it was a good hedge. A speculative investment is a risky undertaking. But the hedge is supposed to reduce the corporation's risk. MG cannot be both hedging and speculating in the oil futures business. As MGRM added to its stack of near-month futures it was not trying to decrease its risk, contract by contract; it was trying to multiply its bet on backwardation; it was increasing the corporation's capital at risk, a different matter entirely.

MGRM's strategy document makes clear that the mechanical rolling stack described earlier is a stark oversimplification of MGRM's trading in the futures markets. MGRM planned from the beginning to shift its position among contract months for a given commodity as well as from commodity to commodity—gasoline to heating oil to crude—according to management's own beliefs about where profits were to be had. It was MGRM's readiness to speculate on a variety of perceived mispricings in oil derivatives that explains the many variations in their positions. MGRM's management had identified a long list of mispricings, and a large part of their time was spent analyzing market data in order to quickly recognize others as they might arise. MGRM was to operate as any other speculator in the financial markets, buying low and selling high.

How would management know which prices were "low" and which were "high"? MGRM developed what amounted to a traditional technician's trading system. For a first approximation, they modeled the historical experience in each of the markets and operated on the standard assumption that the price patterns of the past would mechanically extend into the future. Then, for improved profit performance they developed some mathematical signals to anticipate the peaks of cyclical price movements:

> If we can take advantage of the market weakness in establishing the hedges, we should also make use of the strength of the market in taking off the hedges. For example, the maximum values for the inter-month spread are, respectively, 19.36, 21.84, 25.35 and 21.58 cents per gallon in 1986, 1987, 1988 and 1989. Therefore, instead of taking off the hedges ratably, it may be possible to take off the hedges at a much higher level, thus improving the profit margins. . . . By liquidating the spreads at their peak or close to the peak, we are capturing the positive refinery economics in lifting our hedges without giving back any of the profit margin that a normal refinery would lose during its off-season low-demand period. Therefore,

we need some reliable exit indicators to suggest an optimal time to take off the hedges. (2, p. 19)

The exit indicators chosen are embarrassingly old fashioned: they are the standard computational techniques for identifying a local maximum in a function and therefore rely heavily upon very questionable assumptions about the smoothly cyclical structure of commodity futures prices. In addition to modifying its basic running stack, MGRM's management conducted a number of so-called arbitrages otherwise completely unrelated to its basic delivery contracts. Members of the management team claimed that at least $25 million a month were made exploiting such transient arbitrage opportunities in addition to the longer-term mispricings that formed the core of MGRM's speculative strategy.

Once one investigates MGRM's actual transactions in futures and takes note of management's very clearly articulated belief that there were speculative profits to be had, the decision of the creditors to bring the operation under control is thrown into a different light. A speculation with one's own money is one thing, a speculation with the creditors' several billion dollars is another thing entirely. And while a speculation may properly be put onto the balance sheet of an appropriately capitalized investment house, the very same speculation does real damage on the balance sheet of an industrial corporation, especially one with a weak balance sheet. Adding a speculative financial investment to the balance sheet is the simplest, most obvious example of what is politely known as "the risk shifting game." Creditors quite wisely make great efforts to prevent such actions by the management.[19]

CONCLUSION

The case of Metallgesellschaft provides a wide array of lessons for businesses interested in properly hedging their exposure to various risks.

Taking MGRM's decision to provide long-term contracts for granted and focusing instead on the design of the hedge used to manage the risk of the business, one can use the Metallgesellschaft case to elucidate the importance of maturity structure in hedging as in every other product line of finance. A hedge with a mismatched maturity structure can create enormous funding risks. The case of Metallgesellschaft only reinforces the recommendations of the Group of Thirty that a corporation's position needs to be stress tested and evaluated against worst case scenarios. It is folly to put in place a seemingly innocuous hedge without careful regard for the possibly temporary but nevertheless large amount of financing it may require in the event of unfavorable price movements. If, as is often the case, the original reason for hedging is to avoid funding problems arising in the course of the firm's normal operations, then cash flow patterns ought to be the starting point and not an afterthought in the choice of hedging instruments. The maturity structure of a hedge is also central to the degree to which the firm's value is actually hedged; a mismatch in maturity structure means that the firm has assumed important risks.

The Metallgesellschaft case also illuminates the fine line that sometimes exists between hedging and speculating. The lingo of the derivatives industry and its relative novelty has allowed a number of speculative activities to be passed off as "risk management." MGRM's losses in late 1993 made this pretense no longer possible, and Metallgesellschaft's shareholders and creditors took the necessary remedial actions to limit the sorry consequences. MGRM's use of a one-for-one hedge of near-month futures looks superficially to be a straightforward purchase of insurance against capital gains and losses on its delivery contracts. In reality, the entire line of business was a bet on the basis, a bet on the roll return earned by the futures contracts in a backwardated market. Adding this bet onto the balance sheet of a major industrial corporation was a disastrous mistake. Recognizing the bets implicit in a variety of hedging strategies requires careful attention. As the Metallgesellschaft case illustrates, the stakes can be high.

REPLY TO CULP AND MILLER

MGRM's strategy has received support in Chapter 19 by Christopher Culp and Merton Miller, "Metallgesellschaft and the Economics of Synthetic Storage." Since our analysis of Metallgesellschaft's debacle differs significantly from theirs, we sketch here the main points of agreement and differences between the two papers. The areas of agreement are much greater than might be supposed, given the large degree of public controversy surrounding the case.

First, there is agreement that using a rolling stack to hedge a flow of deliveries may produce temporarily large negative cash flows. The warnings of the Group of Thirty regarding potential funding risks and the need for thorough stress tests of any derivative strategy should be kept in mind when considering the rolling stack. There is also agreement that the cash flow losses in the case of Metallgesellschaft were quite large. Culp and Miller estimate $650 million from price declines and another $250 million due to rollover costs, for a total cash flow loss on the futures leg of the transaction of $900 million. In our Table 21.1 we estimated $1.17 billion. The special auditors calculated losses on the futures and OTC swaps portfolios at $413 million by the end of September 1993 and at over $1.276 billion by the end of December. MGRM's original management had estimated losses on the rolling stack of $434 million through September, prior to the spectacular price drop in November and December. The differences among all of these estimates is small relative to the range in which all of the estimates lie and given the assumptions buried in each of the calculations. $900 million is a large cash flow deficit to finance in a single calendar year.

Second, there is agreement that the rolling stack with a one-to-one hedge ratio leaves a firm exposed to basis risk. This shows up in Culp and Miller's Table 19.1 as an increase in the net cost of carry (the rollover costs) and therefore a divergence between the anticipated contract income and the realized cash flow or income. Culp and Miller break the firm's risks down into two components, spot price risk and rollover risk, and they emphasize that the rolling stack fully hedges the firm against the spot price risk. We, on the other hand, emphasize that in hedging the firm fully against spot price risk, the rolling stack leaves the firm very exposed to rollover risk.

There also appears to be growing agreement that this basis risk was large for MGRM. Elsewhere Culp and Miller recently estimated that oil price movements in 1993 increased rollover costs by $620 million—an increase of $250 million in realized rollover costs in 1993 and of $370 million in expected future rollover costs.[20] This $620 million figure is very close to our own estimate of a $695 net loss on MGRM's contract and futures positions.[21]

Both the firm's exposure to funding risk and its exposure to basis risk are a result of its choice of a hedge with a mismatched maturity structure. In another paper we have used Culp and Miller's own illustrative example of "synthetic storage" and shown that a firm that had hedged using a maturity matched strip of futures instead of a stack would have been exposed to less variation in the timing of its cash flows, and would have completely hedged the basis risk.[22] The contrast between the strip and the stack makes clear that it was MGRM's use of a stack of short-dated futures contracts to hedge a set of long-dated delivery obligations that opened the door to the losses incurred in 1993.

Although both sides seem to agree that MGRM was exposed to significant funding and basis risk, there is disagreement about whether these risks undermined the business plan from the start. Naturally this disagreement carries over to a different assessment about how the parent corporation responded when these risks became apparent at the end of 1993. We believe that the business plan and hedging strategy were essentially and significantly flawed. Culp and Miller, on the other hand, believe the delivery contracts were valuable and that the funding risk and basis risk mentioned above were worth the bet. Correspondingly, we believe it was appropriate to try and close down as much of MGRM's activities as possible in December 1993, even at certain costs, while Culp and Miller believe it was still valuable and closing it down merely dissipated this value. Since we have already made our case, we turn to a few particulars of this dispute.

We think Culp and Miller play down the funding risk too much and lean far too much on the idea that MG's creditors and shareholders should have readily coughed up extra cash. Culp and Miller have argued in the abstract that MG *could not* have really faced a liquidity constraint, except as Deutsche Bank and others foolishly chose not to continue financing the oil business. But we have documented in fact that Metallgesellschaft faced a liquidity crunch *prior* to MGRM's huge losses at the end of 1993, and that it took a variety of actions consistent with this fact both before the futures trading crisis and afterwards: for example, it was forced both times to sell other assets in order to improve liquidity. Speaking of Deutsche Bank as if it had unlimited pockets is simply not facing up to the real-world constraints that had already been evidenced. We believe that cash flow mattered for Metallgesellscaft and MGRM management should have paid attention to funding risks in its choice of maturity structure of its hedge or, alternatively, in its decision to pursue the entire strategy of operating as a financial intermediary.

Culp and Miller believe that MG's pre-existing relationships with many banks should have made it possible to survive a brief liquidity crisis had the company remained behind the basic strategy. We note, on the other hand, that a plethora of creditors, each with a different stake in the firm and different circumstances of its own, can in some cases ensure deadlock should the firm have to negotiate additional financing or a restructuring of debt. It is management's job to design a hedge precisely to avoid the dangers inherent in such a process.

Culp and Miller believe that the funding risks at hand were obvious, that "you don't have to be a rocket scientist" to see the possible cash drains. But if one assumes away the possibility that management made a mistake—as this argument does—then one can never learn from the mistakes management actually makes. We think that the possible cash flow drains were ignored, rocket scientists or not. We have seen nothing in the documentary record at MGRM to suggest that they had done any "worst case" simulation. On the contrary, only after experiencing large losses partway through 1993 did they consider the use of put options to place a floor on the possible cash losses from their hedging. The opportunity of using puts had always been available but had never been considered until *after* enormous losses had been incurred. As Culp and Miller themselves note, there were a large variety of alternative corporate and financial structures that could have been used, including spinning off a subsidiary with the delivery contracts and the hedge: many of these might have been viable had they been pursued *before* the firm faced its liquidity crisis. That they were only entertained in the midst of a crisis highlights the failure of forethought at MGRM.

Our own review of MGRM's strategy documents and other materials suggests that they were fixated on the historical record of regular profits from their proposed strategy: they made the classic mistake of devising a technical trading strategy based on past data without testing it out of sample. And they made another classic mistake of not "stress testing" their derivative trading strategy. MGRM's business plan includes a few scenario analyses of projected profits, but the worst outcomes displayed are "minimum profit" scenarios and do not reveal the possibility of any cash drain.

A good illustration of how easy it is to underestimate the problem of possibly negative cash flow is Culp and Miller's own suggestion for a pure synthetic strategy, a suggestion made with no number attached. Under this strategy MGRM deposits with the clearinghouse collateral in the form of T-bills equal to the initial face value of its total futures position, "thus ensuring that no further cash outlays would be required over the life of the hedge, regardless of price movements." Just how much in T-bills would have been required given MGRM's position? Assuming no basis risk, we estimate more than $3 billion, a hefty sum indeed! A calculation recognizing possible losses due to basis risk would raise the number higher still. Culp and Miller say that the notion of a pure synthetic strategy puts to rest once and for all the view that maturity mismatch gave rise to financial distress. We think, on the contrary, that the $3 billion figure illustrates perfectly the significance of the maturity mismatch problem: when that number is compared against the rest of the parent corporation's balance sheet, the idea that MGRM would have received funding becomes dubious to say the least.

A final point of difference we have with Culp and Miller is our claim that MGRM was actively speculating in oil derivatives. Although Culp and Miller downplay this possibility, we think their representation of MGRM's strategy as "synthetic storage" makes *our* point. The firm was not hedging any real storage activity. Rather it was constructing storage using the financial markets, betting that the prevailing cost of long-term deliveries relative to the implicit cost of storage reflected in the history of short-term oil futures prices. We have already pointed out above that this strategy is essentially a speculation on the basis risk. There seems to be agreement on the formal mathematical facts describing MGRM's strategy but some difference in how we each judge these facts.

We claim, moreover, that a careful examination of MGRM's actual business plan as well as the history of its trading activities and most especially the exaggerated size of its stack all lead one to the conclusion the MGRM's management was speculating. It was MGRM's management who justified the rolling stack using calculations of the historic profit an arbitrary investor would have made rolling over a one-month crude oil futures contract: these calculations did not include any careful analysis of the net present value of synthetic storage. The calculations in the business plan regarding synthetic storage are riddled with assumptions about mispriced contracts and the opportunity available to profit by buying in at highs and selling at lows. Nowhere in the business plan does MGRM's management do any accounting for basis risk and the appropriate discount to charge for it. Not only was MGRM's strategy speculative, but it exhibited all the features of classically mistaken speculations. MGRM's decision to run a "front-to-back" strategy is just the oil market equivalent of riding the yield curve in the bond market, with all the dangerous consequences that entails.

ENDNOTES

1. *Business Plan for MG Refining and Marketing, Inc., December 1, 1991 to May 31, 1992.*

2. A comprehensive overview of MGRM's programs and positions is available in the report of the special auditor requested by the extraordinary shareholders meeting of February 24, 1994, *Bericht über die Sonderprüfung nach 142 Abs. 1 AktG bei der Metallgesellschaft Aktiengesellschaft, gemäß Beschluß der außerordentlichen Hauptversammlung am 24. Februar 1994,* by C&L Treuarbeit and Wollert-Elmendorff, January 20, 1995.

3. Attention to the customer's particular circumstances is key in valuing these options. To see why, notice that under the terms of the *firm-fixed* contracts the customer would forgo half the amount by which the contract was in the money. Therefore the customer has a significant disincentive to exercising the option except as their own liquidity needs outweigh the capital loss involved. The actual duration of MGRM's forward obligation is therefore highly variable and, due to its dependence on the customer's circumstances, difficult to anticipate. Note, moreover, that the duration may be either shorter or *longer* than that of an annuity since under the flexible contracts the customer had the right to delay taking deliveries until it believed spot prices put its option in the money.

In mid-1993 MGRM succeeded in renegotiating the terms of the option in a little more than half of the *firm-fixed* contracts so that cash settlement would occur automatically once the near-month futures price reached a certain level. The customers received a concession on the delivery price in exchange for losing this option.

4. The full details of MGRM's trading were more complicated than this simple characterization. For example, since some customers could alter the delivery schedule and since the options in the supply contracts allowed the buyer to advance maturity of the contract it was envisioned that the quantity of futures contracts rolled over might change to match the changing quantity of short positions retired. Moreover, MGRM maintained a long position in a variety of contract months, not only the near-month contract, and had flexibility to alter the exact maturity structure of its stack. Finally, MGRM shifted its position among different oil products independently of the products shorted under the delivery contracts. For full details of the actual positions see the special auditors report previously cited and court documents in *W. Arthur Benson v. Metallgesellschaft Corp. et,* Civ. Act. No. JFM-94-484, U.S. District Court for the District of Maryland, 1994. Also relevant is MGRM's own *Policy and Procedures Manual,* 1992, although its trades were not always faithful to these guidelines.

5. The example is a simplified version of what happened to MGRM since we have assumed that all of the contracts were signed in March of 1993 and that the rolling stack consists entirely of near month crude oil futures contracts. The actual losses as reported by the special auditors differ modestly in timing.

6. It is not just the monthly variation in the spot price that determines MGRM's losses on its futures stack. What matters is the monthly realization of the spot price relative to the futures price at which the position was opened, i.e., how the entire term structure of oil prices moves from month to month. In 1993 this movement was characterized both by a marked fall in the spot price and a persistent contango. It is the combination that yields the exact cash flow consequences for MGRM.

7. The realized losses on the rolling stack detailed in Table 21.1 do not include the cash contributions necessary to meet margin calls and so significantly understate the cash flow deficit created by a rolling stack.

8. *See* Kenneth Froot, David Scharfstein, and Jeremy Stein, "Risk Management: Coordinating Corporate Investment and Financing Policies," *Journal of Finance,* December 1993.

9. We have made this point elsewhere in Antonio Mello, John Parsons, and Alexander Triantis, "An Integrated Model of Multinational Flexibility and Financial Hedging," forthcoming in the *Journal of International Economics.*

10. Constructing a mirror-image hedge of a forward contract can be difficult. The mark-to-market feature of futures makes it difficult to use them to exactly match the maturity of a forward delivery

obligation even when, as in the case of a strip, the nominal maturity is the same. Because settlement of the futures occurs continuously, cash flows resulting from price movements are paid out earlier than under a forward obligation with nominally identical maturity. In any case, due to the long maturity of MGRM's forward commitments an appropriate strip of exchange traded futures was not feasible. MGRM could have used the OTC market to construct an instrument with appropriate maturity. The OTC market makes it possible to custom design an instrument to mirror the maturity structure of the delivery obligations inclusive of the options.

11. MG's liquidity crisis was never *merely* a liquidity crisis. Even if the firm were solvent and merely needed a cash infusion, a liquidity crisis itself can create real costs. MG had a large number of bankers, and while this may seem advantageous, the question of who shall provide the extra financing and with what seniority relative to the preexisting debt obligations opens up a Pandora's box of maneuvering and negotiation, all of which may impose dead weight losses on the firm. And while one may be critical of the bankers for engaging in such conduct, one should also be critical of the management for not anticipating these kinds of problems in its design of the hedge. It is no use complaining about the costs that arise in going to the market for external funds when the very purpose of the hedge should be to avoid this necessity in the first place!

12. For data on oil see Rajna Gibson and Eduardo Schwartz, 1990, "Stochastic Convenience Yield and the Pricing of Oil Contingent Claims," *Journal of Finance,* 45:959–976, and Rajna Gibson and Eduardo Schwartz, "Valuation of Long Term Oil-Linked Assets," in *Stochastic Models and Option Values,* D. Lund and B. Kendal, eds., Amsterdam:North-Holland, 1991, 73–101, and also Franklin Edwards and Michael Canter, "The Collapse of Metallgesellschaft: Unhedgeable Risks, Poor Hedging Strategy, or Just Bad Luck?," forthcoming in *The Journal of Futures Markets,* 15(3), May 1995. For data on other commodities *see* E. Fama and K. French, "Business Cycles and the Behavior of Metals Prices," *Journal of Finance,* 43:1075–1094.

13. The present value factors shown in Table 21.3 provide only a rough order of magnitude for the relationship being estimated. The values shown were derived at a particular historical period and are only the local change in value for a small change in price. A detailed calculation is beyond the scope of this paper.

14. These two simple hedge ratio calculations have been made for ease of exposition. The proper ratio incorporating the options can be calculated using the appropriate differential equations as shown in Gibson and Schwartz (1990), previously cited. In recognizing the cash out option it is important to remember that customers holding the firm-fixed contracts would forego half of the profit on the contract should they call. MGRM's exposure, therefore, to the volume called is only one-half the nominal volume and it should hold maximally a one-to-two ratio of futures to deliveries to cover this exposure.

15. MGRM's accountants, Arthur Andersen, had always recognized the possibility of defaults, adding to reserves against this possibility. After the adverse price movements in 1993 KPMG suggested that this reserve might need to be increased. *See* "Draft Report on Handelsbilanz II Financial Statements," KPMG, January 14, 1994.

16. For an equilibrium model producing persistent backwardation, *see* Robert Litzenberger and Nir Rabinowitz, "Backwardation in Oil Futures Markets: Theory and Empirical Evidence," working paper, Wharton School, University of Pennsylvania, April 11, 1994. Of course, if futures prices are backwardated according to the predictions of this model, then a strategy of buying the futures contract does not yield a positive net present value when properly discounted to recognize its risk.

17. *See* especially the paper "MG Refining and Marketing Inc: Hedging Strategies Revisited" in *W. Arthur Benson v. Metallgesellschaft Corp. et al.,* Civ. Act. No. JFM-94-484, U.S. District Court for the District of Maryland, 1994.

18. *See,* for example, *The JPMCI—A Commodity Benchmark,* J.P. Morgan, September 20, 1994.

19. The agency problems to which we are referring here arise both between the shareholders and the creditors and between the subsidiary management and the shareholders. A good introduction to the problems of shareholder-creditor relations in general and the risk shifting game in particular is given in Brealey and Myers, *Principles of Corporate Finance,* Chapter 18, 4th edition, New York: McGraw Hill, 1991.

20. Christopher Culp and Merton Miller, "Auditing the MG Shareholders' Audit," *Risk,* v. 8, n. 4 (April 1995).

21. Curiously, in their paper that appeared in the *Journal of Applied Corporate Finance,* Culp and Miller give the impression that basis risk is a relatively minor issue, referencing their own estimates of

the high correlation between spot and front month futures prices. Despite the impression raised that these correlation figures are high, in fact, they are consistent with the data we referenced and used to construct Tables 21.3, 21.4 and 21.5. For example, Culp and Miller focus on the basis risk within one month and find R2 values of 0.99 for crude oil, 0.96 for heating oil, and 0.95 for gasoline, while the factor we used to relate a $1 change in the prevailing spot price to the change in the expected value of a one-month forward delivery obligation was 0.991, relatively close. And as the time to maturity of the forward obligation increases, the effect of imperfect correlation within any single month is compounded, yielding the other factors shown in Table 21.3 of our paper. The one month correlation data in Culp and Miller's paper therefore appear perfectly consistent with our estimates of $650 million net loss due to basis risk. This fact seems to be borne out by Culp and Miller's own later estimate of the total change in rollover costs, which appeared in their *Risk* magazine article.

22. Antonio Mello and John Parsons, "Hedging a Flow of Commodity Deliveries with Futures: Problems with a Rolling Stack," forthcoming in *Derivatives Quarterly,* Fall 1995.

22

Hedging in the Theory of Corporate Finance: A Reply to Our Critics

CHRISTOPHER L. CULP
MERTON H. MILLER

O n first reading the comments on our Metallgesellschaft papers[1] by Antonio Mello and John Parsons (hereafter M&P),[2] we had the eerie feeling that perhaps they were confusing our MGRM with another company of the same name. Surely M&P must have realized that for *our* MGRM, their standard finance models of corporate hedging were not appropriate. The standard models, focusing as they do on reducing costs of financial distress, *might* have been appropriate if our MGRM had been a stand-alone firm with independent, outside creditors. But it wasn't.

MG Refining and Marketing, Inc. (MGRM) was one subsidiary of a large German conglomerate, MG AG, in which Deutsche Bank, one of the world's biggest banks, was not only the leading creditor but, thanks to multiple cross-holdings with other stockholder firms like Allianz and Daimler Benz, also the controlling shareholder. True, the parent MG AG did undergo a major financial restructuring in January 1994, following a year of losses by MGRM and other subsidiaries; but some believe that this presumed near brush with "bankruptcy" was deliberately precipitated to provide cover for a change in management.

Rather than apply the standard finance model of hedging to a firm we saw as just the lengthened shadow of Deutsche Bank, we turned instead to the "carrying-charge hedging" model proposed long ago by Holbrook Working after years of studying the hedging policies of commercial grain merchants such as Cargill.[3] Although we gave citations in our paper to Working's analysis and its applicability to MGRM, M&P appear not to have bothered to check out those references. We begin here, therefore, by reproducing the relevant passages from the writings of Holbrook Working and by showing how Working's theory of hedging explains MGRM's strategy.

Originally published in the *Journal of Applied Corporate Finance* 8(1), Spring. Reprinted with permission. The authors acknowledge with thanks helpful discussions with Todd Petzel and José Scheinkman.

THE MOTIVATION FOR MGRM'S HEDGE

Holbrook Working categorizes standard finance models of hedging (including what is now called variance-minimizing hedging) as "pure risk-avoidance hedging."[4] Firms may hedge their value to reduce the expected costs of financial distress.[5] Or firms may hedge to reduce the variability of their net cash flows.[6] In either case, the hedging reflects some "concavity" in the firm's profit or value function that makes a value-maximizing corporation behave *as if* it were a risk-averse investor solving a traditional portfolio selection problem rather than a capital budgeting problem.

Carrying-Charge Hedging

Pure risk-avoidance hedging is only one of several types of real-world hedging Working identifies. MGRM's strategy represents what he would call "carrying-charge hedging" and what we called "synthetic storage." Working explains,

> *Whereas the traditional concept [of hedging] implies that hedging is merely a collateral operation that . . . would influence the stockholding only through making it a less risky business, the main effect of carrying-charge hedging is to transform the operation from one that seeks profit by anticipating changes in price level to one that seeks profit from anticipating changes in price relations.*[7]

Carrying-charge hedging, in other words, may be undertaken by value-maximizing corporations to exploit their superior information about price *relations,* like the basis, while remaining "market neutral" with respect to spot prices. MGRM, like other carrying-charge hedgers, was essentially in the business of "trading the basis" without exposing itself to spot price risk.

Pure risk-avoidance hedging typically assumes that firms enter into forward contracting *and then* decide how to manage the risk of the position. Working's contribution was to recognize that the cash transaction and the hedge were two parts of a joint decision-making process. When information is asymmetric, he explains that

> *[H]edging is not necessarily done for the sake of reducing risks. The role of risk-avoidance in most commercial hedging has been greatly overemphasized in most economic discussions. Most hedging is done largely, and may be done wholly, because the information on which the merchant or processor acts leads logically to hedging. . . . To put it briefly, we may say that hedging in commodity futures involves the* purchase or sale of futures in conjunction with another commitment, usually in the expectation of a favorable change in the relation between spot and futures prices.[8] (emphasis his)

Absent superior information, value-maximizing firms may not only avoid the hedging, but may well shun the underlying activity itself.[9]

That carrying-charge hedging may be undertaken by value-maximizing firms principally if not wholly to exploit a perceived informational advantage does *not* mean that carrying-charge hedging is "speculation." Working also argues that risks are, in fact, reduced by carrying-charge hedging, even though its primary motivation need not be risk reduction:

Hedging we found not to be primarily a sort of insurance, nor usually undertaken in the expectation that spot and futures prices would rise or fall equally. It is a form of arbitrage, undertaken most commonly in expectation of a favorable change in the relation between spot and futures prices. The fact that risks are less with hedging than without is often a secondary consideration.[10] (emphasis added)

Because a value-maximizing firm engaged in synthetic storage exchanges its natural exposure to the absolute price level for a net exposure to *relative prices,* synthetic storage virtually always reduces the variance of the value of the firm. Had MGRM undertaken its long-term marketing program *unhedged,* the volatility of its net income would have been proportional to the volatility of *spot* prices. Hedged, the volatility of MGRM's net income was proportional instead to the volatility of the bases reflected in the futures contracts MGRM held (i.e., contracts with one, two, and three months to maturity). As we have shown, the volatility of spot prices is huge relative to the volatility of the bases in those contracts.[11] Hence, MGRM chose to exploit its informational advantage by hedging rather than simply taking a position in the underlying commodity.

That MGRM saw itself as a carrying-charge hedger in the Working tradition is clear in this excerpt from MG AG's 1991/92 *Annual Report,* on which the supervisory board members of MG AG placed their signatures:

While the futures markets provide hedging vehicles that reflect the realities of the crude oil markets, petroleum products remain a different story. Regional supply-demand differences can introduce major basis risk. . . . A solid presence in the physical markets and the resulting awareness of local refinery economics enable the MG Energy Group to turn that difficulty into an advantage.[12]

Like Working, MGRM even referred to its hedging objective as a type of basis arbitrage:

At any given point in time, certain parts of the commodity market may be over-valued or under-valued relative to that commodity's own forward price curve, to other commodities, or to other markets. . . . That, in turn, provides attractive opportunities from an arbitrage standpoint.[13]

What about Expected Bankruptcy Costs?

MGRM's strategy of carrying-charge hedging rather than standard finance risk-avoidance hedging makes perfect sense under the assumption that *basis risk* exposed MGRM to no real threat of bankruptcy, whereas naked spot price exposure might well have.[14] M&P seem to believe that MGRM should have been much more concerned with bankruptcy, even in its core business of basis trading. Addressing bankruptcy concerns by reducing the size of the program as M&P and others have recommended can be a mixed blessing, however. As explained in Edwards and Ma, "Hedgers . . . may be willing to assume more risk in order to assume greater profits. Eliminating all . . . risk often means eliminating all profit, a condition that most businesses cannot tolerate for long."[15]

M&P's obsession with bankruptcy in this case rests heavily on their interpretation of the events of December 1993 in which the cash flow strains of MGRM's hedge supposedly did in the program. But the turn of events *ex post* does not estab-lish whether MGRM was correct in seeing itself as an effectively risk-neutral corpo-ration *ex ante*—particularly so in this case, because of the still unresolved doubts over whether that liquidity crisis was real or contrived.

As a stand-alone firm, MGRM and its outside creditors might well have been con-cerned with the costs of bankruptcy or depleted cash for investment expenditures, especially after the large margin calls of late 1993. But MGRM was *not* a stand-alone firm. Deutsche Bank was not only the principal *inside* creditor and principal share-holder of MG AG, but thanks to its cross-holdings, it was also effectively the *control-ling* shareholder. With Deutsche Bank thus standing *in loco parentis,* as it were, what sense does it make to assume that MGRM could be brought to ruin by the cash requirements of a *hedged* program? And does anyone seriously think that the NYMEX would have allowed MGRM to take positions as large as 55,000 contracts without an assurance that Deutsche Bank stood behind the firm? Or that swap deal-ers would have negotiated nearly 100 million additional barrels of contracts without requiring enormous collateral? As one swap dealer commented, "[T]here was a feel-ing in the market that [MGRM] was the Bundesbank: the Bundesbank would bail out Deutsche Bank, which stood behind MG. The ultimate risk was the country."[16,17]

Surely no controversy would have arisen about Deutsche Bank's ability to fi-nance MGRM's program without flinching had the program been for 15 million bbls. rather than 150 million bbls. The issue thus comes down to how big a commitment is "too big" for a Deutsche Bank; and if there was such a maximum that Deutsche Bank was prepared to back, why the supervisory board of MG AG had not communicated it as policy earlier.

As a further irony, Thornton Oil Corp. sued MG when the new management's boasts of having narrowly averted bankruptcy first surfaced.[18] Even though its deliv-ery contracts were "out-of-the-money," Thornton wanted its contracts to continue and demanded assurances from MG to that effect. The issue had not arisen earlier because the customers had been contractually assured MGRM would remain hedged, with Deutsche Bank believed to be standing behind the agreements through thick or thin.[19]

Why a One-for-One Hedge?

Because synthetic storage or carrying-charge hedging differs from pure risk avoidance hedging, so naturally does the "optimal" hedging strategy. For a carrying-charge hedger, that optimal strategy is "one-for-one" (subject, of course, to any tailing).[20] M&P's frequent stigmatizing as "speculation" any futures held in excess of the much smaller "optimal" hedge implied by their analysis is thus just a verbal trick.[21]

A firm entering into a carrying-charge hedge does so because of superior infor-mation it has on *relative* prices (i.e., the basis), not on *absolute* spot prices. M&P be-lieve this amounts to saying that futures are "mispriced." Not so. Futures prices reflect the equilibrium expected basis conditional on information possessed by the *marginal* market participant. That MGRM's conditioning information might be dif-ferent from that of the marginal participant does not imply a mispricing, though it does offer a sufficient rationale for carrying-charge hedging.

MGRM's simple one-for-one hedging strategy had a further important *organiza-tional* advantage for the shareholders of its German parent MG AG: it could easily be monitored at the end of every trading day.[22] By comparing the amount of futures and swaps to the underlying customer contracts, MG AG's management board could safely leave the details of the hedging program to MGRM without fear that someone might be covertly betting the ranch on price moves in Leeson/Barings fashion.

WHAT WAS THE INITIAL NET PRESENT VALUE OF THE PROGRAM?

Our quarrel with M&P is more than just the semantic issue of what constitutes "hedging" and what constitutes "speculation." By using inappropriate assumptions in their models, M&P have also been led to mis-estimate—by a *huge* amount—the true value of MGRM's combined hedging/delivery program.

M&P's Table 21.2 summarizes what they call *"ex ante"* estimates of the value of MGRM's customer contracts, both hedged and unhedged. Using an estimate of $3/bbl. for the initial gross profit margin, they put the gross present value of the contracts at $63.6 million for 150 million bbls. of customer contract sales. Their estimates of net value are $59.2 million for the unhedged contracts and $35.1 million for the hedged program.

M&P's simulated estimates of gross and net present values can only be described as weird. They assume, among other things, a $2/bbl. "cost of delivery." Actually, the prices in MGRM's contracts were FOB, making M&P's deduction of a $2/bbl. delivery cost totally absurd. But, we suppose, once M&P had made up their minds that the program was worthless, what was another two or three hundred million dollars?

M&P's adjustment from the gross present value of the program unhedged to the net present value of the program hedged is equally strange. The costs of financing the hedge are driven almost entirely by M&P's assumption that external financing costs rise exponentially as prices fall. But the issue of whether *any* external financing really was required is what the shouting is all about. And it is still very much a matter of dispute, currently being fought out in courtrooms around the world. Had Deutsche Bank stepped up to the plate in December the way MGRM's original management expected it to and the way it actually did two months later in the MG AG restructuring, no "external" financing would have been needed. In sum, rather than present a well-reasoned estimate of the value of the program, M&P simply *assume* the answer they wanted.

The correct approach for computing the initial value of MGRM's program was presented and illustrated in our earlier article, but we gave no precise calculations.[23] The numbers appear, however, in our recent article in *Risk* magazine.[24] We assume there that MGRM sold forward 150 million bbls. of oil in its flow contracts at a $3/bbl. gross margin. We take the *expected* basis as zero, which is actually a conservative assumption for early 1993 given the backwardation in the market at the time (as well as historically). Our estimate of the initial discounted expected net present value at the inception of MGRM's program was at least $450 million—an amount $414.9 million higher than M&P's!

WHAT WAS THE 1993 NET ECONOMIC LOSS?

In addition to their estimates of initial gross and net present values, M&P attempt to estimate MGRM's gross and net *losses* in 1993. They put the gross losses on MGRM's hedge in their Table 21.1 at about $1.174 billion. To get to their net loss estimate, they subtract the *change* in the value of MGRM's customer contracts in 1993 from their gross loss estimate. Using "present value factors" based on a paper by Gibson and Schwartz,[25] which M&P present in their Table 21.3, they estimate in Table 21.4 the gain on the customer contracts as about $479 million in 1993. (Curiously, M&P seem to sense no "cognitive dissonance" between their estimate that the contracts *gained* in value by nearly half a billion dollars in 1993, but were worth only $59 million to start with. Can it be that one of the co-authors did Table 21.2 and the other Table 21.4?) Subtracting that $479 million from the $1.174 billion gross loss gives them a net loss of $695 million for MGRM that year.

Gibson and Schwartz, on whom M&P rely so heavily, freely concede that their present value factors for oil delivered in the future turned out to be extremely low, surprisingly so even to them. Their model implies that prices of oil derivatives are determined at the margin by risk-averse investors who demand a premium over and above the riskless rate for bearing convenience yield (i.e., basis) risk.[26] Their reasoning is reminiscent of Keynes' classic discussion of the returns to speculators and hedgers.[27] Keynes believed that commodity futures risk premiums were positive and large, but his view commands little support.[28] Although Gibson and Schwartz assume the presence of a risk premium in oil, they recognize that it can be estimated only subject to substantial measurement error.[29] For that reason, they warn that their present value factors "must be interpreted with caution"—advice, alas, M&P ignored.[30]

Our valuation model, in contrast with Gibson and Schwartz (hence, also M&P), but in accordance with most discussions of commodity pricing these days, assumes that equilibrium prices for oil derivatives are determined by buyers and sellers who are effectively risk-neutral. We have presented our own method of calculating MGRM's 1993 net economic loss elsewhere and need not repeat the calculations in detail here.[31] Suffice it to say that when we put all the separate pieces together—and remembering that, thanks to the hedge, the pure spot price change (net of rollover costs) raises the capital value of the flow contracts by exactly as much as the cash loss on the futures—we calculate the net 1993 loss for MGRM as the *initial* capital asset value of the program less unexpected 1993 rollover costs and less the change in conditional expected rollover costs during the year, or

$$\$450 \text{ million} - \$250 \text{ million} - \$370 \text{ million} = -\$170 \text{ million}.$$

Thus, even after ruling out any future rollover gains from backwardation, we estimate MGRM's 1993 net loss at roughly $170 million, or just a fourth of M&P's $695 million net loss estimate.

Losing even $170 million is hardly pleasant, needless to say, but that figure by itself does not indicate that the program should have been ended in 1993. The $170 million is simply the cumulative loss through the year 1993—that is, after one year of operation. Those losses would be correspondingly reduced were we to recompute the cumulative losses on a program continued through the end of 1994, by which time the flattening of the term structure would have dramatically reduced realized and conditional expected future rollover costs. In fact, by April 1995, had the program been continued it would have shown a substantial *net profit*.

What Were the Alternatives in December 1993?

M&P argue that "[t]he lingo of the derivatives industry and its relative novelty has allowed a number of speculative activities to be passed off as 'risk management.'

MGRM's losses in late 1993 made this pretense no longer possible, and Metall-gesellschaft's shareholders and creditors took the necessary remedial actions to limit the sorry consequences." But to invoke past losses as a justification for ending the program is to be taken in by the sunk cost fallacy. Regardless of how big past losses may have been, the test for *continuing* a program is the same as for *initiating* it: Is the conditional expected net present value positive? After the spot price decline of $5.575/bbl in 1993, which widened the gross margin in the customer contracts to more than $8/bbl, the net present value at that point was surely positive.

Even if management wanted to end its participation in the program, the 1993 increase in the capital value of the customer contracts could, in principle at least, have been realized by selling the program to another firm. MGRM could not, of course, recover past losses simply by selling the program at market prices (any more than an investor can recover *past* losses by selling a stock), but at least selling the program would have staunched the cash drains with which MG AG's supervisory board had become so obsessed.[32] Whether to continue the program or sell it can be shown to depend almost entirely on whether prospective buyers' expectation of future rollover costs were less than MGRM's.[33]

MGRM also had a third alternative. Rather than continuing the program intact or selling the program as a whole, the company could have attempted to scale down the program by simultaneously reducing the hedge and unwinding its customer contracts at the best possible prices. And after a $5.575/bbl decline in spot prices in 1993, the "best possible price" for unwinds should have been substantial.[34] What MG AG's supervisory board actually did in December 1993 was none of the above. They liquidated much of MGRM's futures hedge and canceled valuable customer contracts *with no compensation required.*[35] As we have explained elsewhere, this decision cost shareholders dearly.[36]

POST-SCRIPT ON EDWARDS AND CANTER

We apologize to Messrs. Edwards and Canter (E&C) for neglecting their paper and concentrating exclusively on M&P.[37] E&C bring little to the party that has not already been covered by us—several times, actually—except their computation of "variance-minimizing" hedge ratios. We ignored variance-minimizing hedge ratios because, as explained earlier, they are irrelevant for MGRM. Anyway, E&C did not even calculate them correctly.[38] E&C do allow explicitly for "tailing," but we had ignored this adjustment only for simplicity of exposition.[39]

E&C also remind us that MGRM's program would have suffered even greater losses than the $170 million we estimated for 1993 had the market gone further into contango. We certainly have no quarrel with that, but E&C might have mentioned that the market did *not* slip further into contango in 1994. Quite the contrary. Nor do we disagree with their computations of rollover costs for beans and copper, although we are not sure what point E&C were trying to make with them. That virtually all markets for storable, non-petroleum commodities are normally in contango is well-known, after all. Perhaps they were simply cautioning firms proposing to offer MGRM-style long-term, fixed-price contracts in beans or copper to be sure and set their initial gross margins higher than might be appropriate for a chronically-backwardated market like crude oil.

ENDNOTES

1. *See* Christopher L. Culp and Merton H. Miller, "Metallgesellschaft and the Economics of Synthetic Storage," *Journal of Applied Corporate Finance, 7*(4) (Winter 1995):62–76. *See also* Christopher L. Culp and Merton H. Miller, "Hedging a Flow of Commodity Deliveries with Futures: Lessons from Metallgesellschaft," *Derivatives Quarterly, 1*(1) (Fall 1994):7–15, and Christopher L. Culp and Merton H. Miller, "Auditing the Auditors," *Risk, 8*(4) (April 1995).

2. Antonio S. Mello and John E. Parsons, "Maturity Structure of a Hedge Matters: Lessons from the Metallgesellschaft Debacle," *Journal of Applied Corporate Finance,* this issue. *See also* Antonio S. Mello and John E. Parsons, "Hedging a Flow of Commodity Deliveries with Futures: Problems with a Rolling Stack," *Derivatives Quarterly, 1*(4) (Fall 1995 forthcoming).

3. Working's contributions may perhaps have been overlooked in the corporate finance literature because he was addressing them essentially to an audience of agricultural economists. His contributions, however, include early formulations of the cost of carry model for futures prices and the "efficient markets hypothesis." *See* Holbrook Working, "Theory of the Inverse Carrying Charge in Futures Markets," *Journal of Farm Economics,* 30 (1948), Holbrook Working, "The Theory of Price of Storage," *American Economic Review* (December 1949), and Holbrook Working, "The Investigation of Economic Expectations," *American Economic Review* (1949). Working's analysis of hedging on the Chicago futures exchanges is highlighted in the papers contained in Anne E. Peck, ed., *Readings in Futures Markets Book I: Selected Writings of Holbrook Working* (Chicago: Board of Trade of the City of Chicago, 1977).

4. Holbrook Working, "New Concepts Concerning Futures Markets and Prices," *American Economic Review* (June 1962):248–53. Unless otherwise noted, all page references to Working's articles are from Peck, cited previously.

5. *See, for example,* Clifford W. Smith, Jr., Charles W. Smithson, and D. Sykes Wilford, "Financial Engineering: Why Hedge?" *Intermarket, 6*(7) (1989).

6. *See, for example,* Kenneth A. Froot, David S. Scharfstein, and Jeremy C. Stein, "Risk Management: Coordinating Corporate Investment and Financing Policies," *Journal of Finance, 48*(5) (December 1993):1629–1658.

7. Working (1962), cited previously:249.

8. Holbrook Working, "Futures Trading and Hedging," *American Economic Review* (June 1953), quoted from *Selected Readings of Holbrook Working,* cited previously:148–149.

9. We need hardly remind readers that most value-maximizing firms do not, in fact, hedge. Chase Manhattan Bank and The Wharton School recently surveyed 1,999 non-financial U.S. firms randomly selected from COMPUSTAT tapes. Of the 530 firms responding, only 35% answered "yes" when asked if their firms buy or sell futures, forwards, options, or swaps. *See* "The Wharton/Chase Derivatives Survey," in Charles W. Smithson, *Managing Financial Risk: 1995 Yearbook* (Princeton, NJ: The Chase Manhattan Bank, 1995):159.

10. Working (1953), cited previously:163.

11. *See* Culp and Miller (Winter 1995), cited previously:67. No more than 1 to 5% of the historical variation in front-month futures prices can be traced to variations over time in the basis.

12. Metallgesellschaft AG *Annual Report* (1991/92):40.

13. "MGRM: Hedging Strategies Revisited," Exhibit E in *W. Arthur Benson v. Metallgesellschaft Corp. et al.,* Civ. Act. No. JFM-94-484. U.S.C.D. Md. (October 3, 1994):E13.

14. Looking at the problem in this way is equivalent to seeing MGRM as "locally" risk-neutral. Positive bankruptcy costs, for example, might have led MGRM to hedge its spot price risk, but once hedged it behaved as an essentially risk-neutral basis trader. *See* Culp and Miller (Winter 1995):footnote 6.

15. Franklin R. Edwards and Cindy W. Ma, *Futures and Options* (New York: McGraw-Hill, Inc., 1992):141.

16. Quoted in David Shirreff "In the Line of Fire," *Euromoney* (March 1994):42–43.

17. Remember also that Deutsche Bank had earlier announced to all—in MG AG's 1992-93 company newsletter, no less—that it had increased MG's 5-year credit line to DM1.5 billion, a credit line intended, among other things, to serve as "a permanently available reserve of liquidity." *See* "DM1.5 Billion Credit Line Granted to MG," *MG UPDATE: Company News from Around the World* (2/92). MG officials now claim that the credit line was intended only as a back-up provision for the Commercial

Paper Program. But as even MG AG's Special Auditors note, no such restriction was mentioned in the documentation for the credit facility. *See* MG AG's Special Audit:3.3.3.5.

18. *See Thornton Oil Corp. v. MG Refining and Marketing, Inc.,* Civ. Act. No. 94CI101653, Circuit Court of Jefferson County, KY (1994).

19. Three related cases involve counter-claims by several customers against MGRM that it has not provided adequate assurances of its ability to honor its long-term customer contracts—assurances that were apparently sufficient *ex ante. See* Counterclaim, *MG Refining and Marketing, Inc. v. Knight Enterprises, Inc. v. MG Refining and Marketing, Inc., et al.,* Civ. Act. No. 94-2512, U.S.D.C.S.D.N.Y. (April 4, 1994); Counterclaim, *MG Refining and Marketing, Inc. v. R.L. Jordan Oil Company, Inc.,* Civ. Act. No. 94-7804, U.S.D.C.S.D.N.Y. (October 27, 1994); Counterclaim, *MG Refining and Marketing, Inc. v. A.T. Williams Oil Company v. MG Refining and Marketing, Inc., et al.,* Civ. Act. No. 94-7862, U.S.D.C.S.D.N.Y. (October 31, 1994).

20. Technically, the objective function is to maximize expected net present value subject to remaining market-neutral.

21. In this version of their paper, M&P now admit that MGRM *was* hedged against spot price risk, but they dismiss the hedging strategy as "rolling the dice" on the basis. That is like saying a market-neutral swap dealer is rolling the dice on credit risk.

22. The Group of Thirty has endorsed the notion of transparent exposure monitoring, though not necessarily daily. *See* Global Derivatives Study Group, *Derivatives: Practices and Principles* (Washington, DC: The Group of Thirty, July 1993).

23. *See* Culp and Miller (Winter 1995):equation (1). Strictly speaking, S_t in equation (1) is part of the summand, and the entire summand should be multiplied by $(1+E_t(w_{t,j}))$, the interest-adjusted basis. We omitted that term for simplicity, because our concern there was with sufficient conditions for profitability under worst-case assumptions (i.e., contango). Including this term only increases the number of situations for which the sufficiency test is satisfied.

24. Culp and Miller (April 1995), cited previously.

25. Rajna Gibson and Eduardo S. Schwartz, "Stochastic Convenience Yield and the Pricing of Oil Contingent Claims," *Journal of Finance, 45*(3) (July 1990).

26. Gibson and Schwartz rely on a general methodology developed by Michael J. Brennan and Eduardo S. Schwartz, "A Continuous Time Approach to the Pricing of Bonds," *Journal of Banking and Finance, 3* (1979).

27. John Maynard Keynes, *The Theory of Money: Volume II, The Applied Theory of Money* (London: Macmillan, 1950):Book VI, Chapter 29, (iii)–(v).

28. *See, for example,* Lester Telser, "Futures Trading and the Storage of Cotton and Wheat," *Journal of Political Economy, 66* (June 1958), and Katherine Dusak, "Futures Trading and Investor Returns: An Investigation of Commodity Market Risk Premiums," *Journal of Political Economy, 87*(6) (December 1973).

29. *See also* Eugene F. Fama and Kenneth R. French, "Commodity Futures Prices: Some Evidence on Forecast Power, Premiums, and the Theory of Storage," *Journal of Business, 60*(1) (January 1987).

30. Gibson and Schwartz, cited previously:972-73.

31. *See* Culp and Miller (April 1995), cited previously.

32. By purchasing puts, MGRM could have both limited its cash outlays and bought itself time to decide on the appropriate means for ending the program.

33. *See* Culp and Miller (April 1995), cited previously.

34. That customers might have been willing to pay less than another firm buying the whole program cannot be ruled out. Customers presumably would use a higher discount rate than MGRM or an outside bank in valuing the contracts. Once MGRM's troubles became public, moreover, customers would have possessed an unusual amount of leverage over MGRM in negotiating the prices for bilateral unwinds or transferring the contracts to another firm.

35. That MG's canceled contracts had *some* value is confirmed on the public record. On December 22, 1993, one of MGRM's biggest firm-flexible customers reportedly paid MGRM $2 million to terminate its firm-flexible contracts. New management accepted the offer. Two months later when most of the remaining firm-flexible contracts were canceled with no compensation required from customers, MG refunded the $2 million it had been paid earlier. *See* Cindy W. Ma, "Rebuttal to the Special Audit Report," manuscript sent to MG AG shareholders (March 7, 1995), 4.4.3.

36. Culp and Miller (April 1995), cited previously.

37. Franklin R. Edwards and Michael S. Canter, "The Collapse of Metallgesellschaft: Unhedgeable Risks, Poor Hedging Strategy, or Just Bad Luck?" *Journal of Applied Corporate Finance,* this issue. *See also* Franklin R. Edwards and Michael S. Canter, "The Collapse of Metallgesellschaft: Poor Hedging Strategy or Just Bad Luck?" *Journal of Futures Markets, 15*(3) (May 1995).

38. For an equally irrelevant but econometrically superior estimation method, *see* Stephen Craig Pirrong, "Metallgesellschaft: A Prudent Hedger Ruined, or A Wildcatter on NYMEX?" Manuscript (February 1995).

39. *See* Culp and Miller (Winter 1995):footnote 13.

23

Derivatives Debacles: Case Studies of Large Losses in Derivatives Markets

ANATOLI KUPRIANOV

To conduct great matters and never commit a fault is above the force of human nature; but to learn and improve by the faults we have committed, is that which becomes a good and sensible man.

—Fabius Maximus

Recent years have witnessed numerous accounts of derivatives-related losses on the part of established and reputable firms. These episodes have precipitated concern, and even alarm, over the recent rapid growth of derivatives markets and the dangers posed by the widespread use of such instruments. What lessons do these events hold for policymakers? Do they indicate the need for stricter government supervision of derivatives markets, or for new laws and regulations to limit the use of these instruments? A better understanding of the events surrounding recent derivatives debacles can help to answer such questions.

This chapter presents accounts of two of the costliest and most highly publicized derivatives-related losses to date. The episodes examined involve the firms of Metallgesellschaft AG and Barings PLC. Each account begins with a review of the events leading to the derivatives-related loss in question, followed by an analysis of the factors responsible for the debacle. Both incidents raise a number of public policy questions: Can government intervention stop such incidents from happening again? Is it appropriate for the government even to try? And if so, what reforms are indicated? These issues are addressed at the end of each case study, where the lessons and public policy concerns highlighted by each episode are discussed.

This chapter is an abridged version of a longer article that appeared in the Fall 1995 issue of the Federal Reserve Bank of Richmond's *Economic Quarterly*. Alex Mendoza assisted in the preparation of this article. Ned Prescott, John Walter, and John Weinberg provided valuable comments on earlier drafts. Any remaining errors or omissions are the responsibility of the author. The views expressed are those of the author, and do not necessarily represent those of the Federal Reserve Bank of Richmond or the Federal Reserve System.

RISK AND REGULATION IN DERIVATIVES MARKETS

Perhaps the most widely cited report on the risks associated with derivatives was published in 1993 by the Group of Thirty—a group consisting of prominent members of the international financial community and noted academics. The report identified four basic kinds of risks associated with the use of derivatives.[1] *Market risk* is defined as the risk to earnings from adverse movements in market prices. Press accounts of derivatives-related losses have tended to emphasize market risk; but the incidents examined in this chapter illustrate the importance of *operational risk*—the risk of losses occurring as a result of inadequate systems and control, human error, or management failure.

Counterparty credit risk is the risk that a party to a derivative contract will fail to perform on its obligation. Exposure to counterparty credit risk is determined by the cost of replacing a contract if a counterparty (as a party to a derivatives contract is known) were to default.

Legal risk is the risk of loss because a contract is found not to be legally enforceable. Derivatives are legal contracts. Like any other contract, they require a legal infrastructure to provide for the resolution of conflicts and the enforcement of contract provisions. Legal risk is a prime public policy concern, since it can interfere with the orderly functioning of markets.

These risks are not unique to derivative instruments. They are the same types of risks involved in more traditional types of financial intermediation, such as banking and securities underwriting. Legal risk does pose special problems for derivatives markets, however. The novelty of many derivatives makes them susceptible to legal risk because of the uncertainty that exists over the applicability of existing laws and regulations to such contracts.

Although the risks associated with derivatives are much the same as those in other areas of finance, there nonetheless seems to be a popular perception that the rapid growth of derivatives trading in recent years poses special problems for financial markets. Most of these concerns have centered on the growth of the over-the-counter (OTC) derivatives market. As Stoll (1995) notes, concern about the growth of OTC derivatives markets has arisen because these instruments are nonstandard contracts, without secondary trading and with limited public price information. Moreover, OTC markets lack some of the financial safeguards used by futures and options exchanges, such as margining systems and the daily marking to market of contracts, designed to ensure that all market participants settle any losses promptly. The absence of such safeguards, along with the complexity of many of the new generation of financial derivatives and the sheer size of the market, has given rise to concerns that the growth of derivatives trading might somehow contribute to financial instability. Finally, there is some concern among policymakers that the federal financial regulatory agencies have failed to keep pace with the rapid innovation in OTC derivatives markets.[2] Such concerns have only been reinforced by frequent reports of derivatives-related losses in recent years.

The traditional rationale for regulating financial markets stems from concerns that events in these markets can have a significant impact on the economy. Much of the present-day financial regulatory system in the United States evolved as a response to financial panics that accompanied widespread economic recessions and depressions. For example, the creation of the Federal Reserve System was prompted in large part by the Panic of 1907, while the advent of federal deposit insurance was a response to the thousands of bank failures that accompanied the Great Depression.

The present-day financial regulatory system has several goals. The most important is to maintain smoothly functioning financial markets. A prime responsibility of institutions like the Federal Reserve is to keep isolated events, such as the failure of a single bank, from disrupting the operation of financial markets generally. During the twentieth century, U.S. financial market regulation expanded to encompass at least two more goals. The creation of a system of federal deposit insurance in 1933 gave the federal government a stake in the financial condition of individual commercial banks, since a federal agency was now responsible for meeting a bank's obligations to its insured depositors in the event of insolvency. In addition, Congress enacted the Securities Exchange Act to help protect investors by requiring firms issuing publicly traded securities to provide accurate financial reports. The act created the Securities and Exchange Commission (SEC) to regulate the sales and trading practices of securities brokers, as well as to enforce the provisions of the law more generally.

Although financial market regulation deals largely with the problem of managing risk, it cannot eliminate all risk. Risk is inherent in all economic activity. Financial intermediaries such as commercial and investment banks specialize in managing financial risks. Regulation can seek to encourage such institutions to manage risks prudently, but it cannot eliminate the risks inherent in financial intermediation. There is a tension here. Regulators seek to reduce the risks taken on by the firms they regulate. At the same time, however, firms cannot earn profits without taking risks. Thus, an overzealous attempt to reduce risk could prove counterproductive—a firm will not survive if it cannot earn profits.

Conventional wisdom views derivatives markets as markets for risk transfer. According to this view, derivatives markets exist to facilitate the transfer of market risk from firms that wish to avoid such risks to others more willing or better suited to manage those risks. The important thing to note in this regard is that derivatives markets do not create new risks—they just facilitate risk management. Viewed from this perspective, the rapid growth of derivatives markets in recent years simply reflects advances in the technology of risk management. Used properly, derivatives can help organizations reduce financial risk. Although incidents involving large losses receive the most public attention, such incidents are the exception rather than the rule in derivatives markets.

Most public policy concerns center around the speculative use of derivatives. Speculation involves the voluntary assumption of market risk in the hope of realizing a financial gain. The existence of speculation need not concern policymakers as long as all speculative losses are borne privately, that is, only by those individuals or organizations that choose to engage in such activities. But many policymakers fear that large losses on the part of one firm may lead to a widespread disruption of financial markets—the collapse of Barings illustrates some of the foundations for such concerns. In the case of an insured bank, regulators discourage speculation because it can lead to losses that may ultimately become the burden of the government.[3]

A view implicit in many recent calls for more comprehensive regulation of derivatives markets is that these markets are subject only to minimal regulation at present. But exchange-traded derivatives, such as futures contracts, have long been subject to comprehensive government regulation. In the United States, the SEC regulates securities and options exchanges while the Commodity Futures Trading Commission (CFTC) regulates futures exchanges and futures brokers. Although OTC derivatives markets are not regulated by any single federal agency, most OTC dealers, such as commercial banks and brokerage firms, are subject to federal regulation.[4] As it happens, both incidents examined in this chapter involve instruments traded on regulated exchanges. Any judgment as to whether these incidents indicate a need for more comprehensive regulation of these markets requires some understanding of just what happened in each case.

METALLGESELLSCHAFT

Metallgesellschaft AG (hereafter, MG) is a large industrial conglomerate engaged in a wide range of activities, from mining and engineering to trade and financial services. In December 1993, the firm reported huge derivatives-related losses at its U.S. oil subsidiary, Metallgesellschaft Refining and Marketing (MGRM). These losses were later estimated at over $1 billion, the largest derivatives-related losses ever reported by any firm at the time. The incident helped bring MG—then Germany's fourteenth largest industrial corporation—to the brink of bankruptcy. After dismissing the firm's executive chairman, Heinz Schimmelbusch, and several other senior managers, MG's board of supervisors was forced to negotiate a $1.9 billion rescue package with the firm's 120 creditor banks (Roth 1994a, b).

MG's board blamed the firm's problems on lax operational control by senior management, charging that "speculative oil deals . . . had plunged Metallgesellschaft into the crisis."[5] Early press reports echoed this interpretation of events, but subsequent studies report that MGRM's use of energy derivatives was an integral part of a combined marketing and hedging program under which the firm offered customers long-term price guarantees on deliveries of petroleum products such as gasoline and heating oil. Reports that MG's losses were attributable to a hedging program have raised a host of new questions. Many analysts remain puzzled by the question of how a firm could lose over $1 billion by hedging.

The Metallgesellschaft debacle has sparked a lively debate on the shortcomings of the firm's hedging strategy and the lessons to be learned from the incident. The ensuing account draws from a number of recent articles, notably Culp and Hanke (1994); Culp and Miller (1994a, b, 1995a, b, c, d); Edwards and Canter (1995a, b); and Mello and Parsons (1995a, b).

MGRM's Marketing Program

In 1992, MGRM began implementing an aggressive marketing program in which it offered long-term price guarantees on deliveries of gasoline, heating oil, and diesel fuels for up to five or ten years. This program included several novel contracts, two of which are relevant to this study. The first was a "firm-fixed" program, under which a customer agreed to fixed monthly deliveries at fixed prices. The second, known as the "firm-flexible" contract, specified a fixed price and total volume of future deliveries but gave the customer some flexibility to set the delivery schedule. Under the second program, a customer could request 20 percent of its contracted volume for any one year with 45 days' notice. By September 1993, MGRM had committed to sell forward the equivalent of over 150 million barrels of oil for delivery at fixed prices, with most contracts for terms of ten years.

Both types of contracts included options for early termination. These cash-out provisions permitted customers to call for cash settlement on the full volume of outstanding deliveries if market prices for oil rose above the contracted price. The firm-fixed contract permitted a customer to receive one-half the difference between the current nearby futures price (that is, the price of the futures contract closest to expiration) and the contracted delivery price, multiplied by the entire remaining quantity of scheduled deliveries. The firm-flexible contract permitted a customer to receive the full difference between the second-nearest futures price and the contract price, multiplied by all remaining deliverable quantities.[6]

MGRM negotiated most of its contracts in the summer of 1993. Its contracted delivery prices reflected a premium of $3 to $5 per barrel over the prevailing spot price of oil. As is evident in Figure 23.1, energy prices were relatively low by recent historical standards during this period and were continuing to fall. As long as oil prices kept falling, or at least did not rise appreciably, MGRM stood to make a handsome profit from this marketing arrangement. But a significant increase in energy prices could have exposed the firm to massive losses unless it hedged its exposure.

MGRM sought to offset the exposure resulting from its delivery commitments by buying a combination of short-dated oil swaps and futures contracts as part of a strategy known as a "stack-and-roll" hedge. In its simplest form, a stack-and-roll hedge involves repeatedly buying a bundle, or "stack," of short-dated futures or forward contracts to hedge a longer term exposure. Each stack is "rolled over" just before expiration by selling the existing contracts while buying another stack of contracts for a more distant delivery date; hence the term stack-and-roll. MGRM implemented its hedging strategy by maintaining long positions in a wide variety of contract months, which it shifted between contracts for different oil products (crude oil, gasoline, and heating oil) in a manner intended to minimize the costs of rolling over its positions.

Had oil prices risen, the accompanying gain in the value of MGRM's hedge would have produced positive cash flows that would have offset losses stemming from its commitments to deliver oil at below-market prices. As it happened, however, oil prices fell even further in late 1993. Moreover, declines in spot and near-term oil futures and forward prices significantly exceeded declines in long-term forward prices. As a result, contemporaneous realized losses from the hedge appeared to exceed any potential offsetting gains accruing to MGRM's long-term forward commitments.

FIGURE 23.1   Crude Oil Prices (1985–1995)

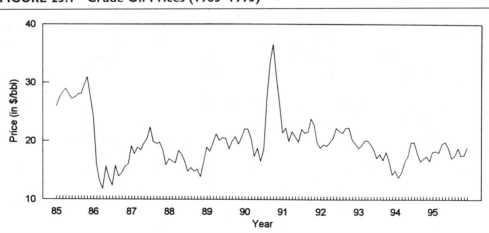

This precipitous decline in oil prices caused funding problems for MGRM. The practice in futures markets of marking futures contracts to market at the end of each trading session forced the firm to recognize its futures trading losses immediately, triggering huge margin calls. Normally, forward contracts have the advantage of permitting hedgers to defer recognition of losses on long-term commitments. But MGRM's stack-and-roll hedge substituted short-term forward contracts (in the form of short-term energy swaps maturing in late 1993) for long-term forward contracts. As these contracts matured, MGRM was forced to make large payments to its counterparties, putting further pressure on its cash flows. At the same time, most offsetting gains on its forward delivery commitments were deferred.

Rumors of MGRM's problems began to surface in early December. In response to these developments, the New York Mercantile Exchange (NYMEX), the exchange on which MGRM had been trading energy futures, raised its margin requirements for the firm. This action, which was intended to protect the exchange in case of a default, further exacerbated MGRM's funding problems. Rumors of the firm's financial difficulties led many of its OTC counterparties to begin terminating their contracts. Others began demanding that it post collateral to secure contract performance.

Upon learning of these circumstances, MG's board of supervisors fired the firm's chief executive and installed new management. The board instructed MG's new managers to begin liquidating MGRM's hedge and to enter into negotiations to cancel its long-term contracts with its customers. This action further complicated matters, however. NYMEX withdrew its hedging exemption once MGRM announced the end of its hedging program. Hedging exemptions permit firms to take on much larger positions in exchange-traded futures than those allowed for unhedged, speculative positions. The loss of its hedging exemption forced MGRM to reduce its positions in energy futures still further (Culp and Miller, 1994a).

The actions taken by MG's board of supervisors have spurred widespread debate and criticism, as well as several lawsuits. Some analysts argue that MGRM's hedging program was seriously flawed and that MG's board was right to terminate it. Others, including Nobel Prize-winning economist Merton Miller, argue that the hedging program was sound and that MG's board exacerbated any hedging-related losses by terminating the program prematurely.

The Debate over MGRM's Hedging Program

As Figure 23.1 shows, oil prices began rising in 1994, soon after MGRM's new management lifted the firm's hedge. It thus appears that MGRM could have recouped most if not all of its losses simply by sticking to its hedging program. Whether management should have been able to anticipate this outcome is the topic of an active debate, however.

Disagreements over the efficacy of MGRM's hedging program stem from differing assumptions about the goal of the hedging program (or, perhaps more accurately, what the goal should have been), and the feasibility of continuing the program in light of the large negative cash flows MGRM experienced in late 1993.

Culp and Miller (1994a, b, 1995a, b, c, d) and Culp and Hanke (1994) are critical of MG's board of supervisors for terminating MGRM's marketing and hedging program. To be sure, Culp and Miller do find that MGRM's hedging program had suffered losses, albeit much smaller losses than those calculated by MG's auditors. But they argue that those losses did not justify terminating MGRM's hedging program. According to Culp and Miller, most of MG's reported losses were attributable to the manner in which its new management chose to terminate its subsidiary's marketing program, not to defects in its hedging strategy. It is not unusual for the parties to such agreements to negotiate termination of a contract before it expires. The normal practice in such circumstances involves payment by one party to the other to compensate for any changes in the value of the contract. In contrast, it appears that MGRM's new management simply agreed to terminate its contracts with its customers without asking for any payment to reflect the increased value of those contracts. The hedge—however imperfect—effectively was transformed by this action into a huge speculative transaction after the fact.

Edwards and Canter (1995a, b) and Mello and Parsons (1995a, b) are more critical of MGRM's hedging strategy. These writers emphasize the difficulties that MGRM's large negative cash flows created for the parent company. They argue that MGRM's management could have—and should have—sought to avoid such difficulties by designing a hedge that would have minimized the volatility of its cash flows.

Although they are critical of MGRM's hedging strategy, Edwards and Canter offer no opinion as to whether MG's board was right to terminate the program. Like Culp and Miller, they are puzzled about the decision to terminate existing contracts with customers without negotiating some payment to compensate for the increase in the value of those contracts.[7]

Mello and Parsons' criticisms of MGRM's hedging strategy are unequivocal. They argue that MGRM's strategy was fatally flawed, and they defend the decision to terminate the hedging program as the only means of limiting even greater potential future losses. They also emphasize the difficulty that MG's new management would have had in securing the financing necessary to maintain MGRM's hedging program and argue that funding considerations should have led the subsidiary's managers to synthesize a hedge using long-dated forward contracts. In this context, Mello and Parsons note that the parent firm already had accumulated a cash flow deficit of DM 5.65 billion between 1988 and 1993. This deficit had been financed largely by bank loans. Considering these circumstances, they find the reluctance of MG's creditor banks to fund the continued operation of the oil marketing program understandable.

Reconciling Opposing Views

These disagreements over the efficacy of MGRM's hedging strategy seem unlikely ever to be resolved, based as they are on different assumptions about the goals management should have had for its strategy. The main issue, then, is whether MG's senior management and board of supervisors fully appreciated the risks the firm's U.S. oil subsidiary had assumed. If they did, the firm should have arranged for a line of credit to fund its short-term cash flows. Indeed, Culp and Miller (1995a, c, d) claim that MGRM had secured lines of credit with its banks just to prepare for such contingencies. Yet the subsequent behavior of MG's board suggests that its members had very little prior knowledge of MGRM's marketing program and were uncomfortable with its hedging strategy, despite the existence of a written strategic plan.

It is difficult for an outside observer to assign responsibility for any misunderstandings between MG's managers and its board of supervisors. MG's board ultimately held Heinz Schimmelbusch, the firm's executive chairman, responsible for the firm's losses, claiming that he and other senior managers had lost control over the activities of the firm and concealed evidence of losses.[8] In response, Schimmelbusch has filed suit against Ronaldo Schmitz and Deutsche Bank, seeking $10 million in general and punitive damages (Taylor, 1995b). Arthur Benson, former head of MGRM and architect of the firm's ill-fated hedging program, is suing MG's board for $1 billion on charges of defamation (Taylor, 1994). Thus, the issue of blame appears destined to be settled by the U.S. courts.

Response of the CFTC

The Metallgesellschaft debacle did not escape the attention of U.S. regulators. In July 1995, the U.S. Commodity Futures Trading Commission instituted administrative proceedings against MGRM and MG Futures, Inc. (MGFI), an affiliated Futures Commission Merchant that processed trades for MGRM and other MG subsidiaries.[9] The CFTC order charged both MGRM and MGFI with "material inadequacies in internal control systems" associated with MGRM's activity in energy and futures markets. In addition, MGFI was charged with failing to inform the CFTC of these material inadequacies, while MGRM was charged with selling illegal, off-exchange futures contracts. The two MG subsidiaries settled the CFTC action without admitting or denying the charges and agreed to pay the CFTC a $2.5 million settlement. They also agreed to implement a series of CFTC recommendations to reform their internal controls and to refrain from violating CFTC regulations. The CFTC's action rendered MGRM's firm-fixed agreements illegal and void.[10] Thus, the CFTC's action would have created legal risk for Metallgesellschaft and its customers except that the firm had already canceled most of the contracts in question.

The CFTC's actions in this case have proven somewhat controversial. Under the Commodity Exchange Act, the CFTC is charged with regulating exchange-traded futures contracts. At the same time, the act explicitly excludes ordinary commercial forward contracts from the jurisdiction of the CFTC. The legal definition of a futures contract is open to differing interpretations, however, leading to some uncertainty over the legal status of OTC derivatives under the Commodity Exchange Act. Most market participants felt that this uncertainty was resolved in 1993 when, at the behest of Congress, the CFTC agreed to exempt off-exchange forward and swaps contracts from regulations governing exchange-traded contracts. CFTC chairman Mary Schapiro maintains that the agency's action against MGRM does not represent a reversal of its policy on OTC contracts. According to Schapiro, the CFTC's order is worded narrowly so as to apply only to contracts such as the firm fixed (45-day) agreements sold by MGRM in this case.[11] Nonetheless, this action has prompted some critics to charge the agency with creating uncertainty about the legal status of commercial forward contracts. Critics of the action include Miller and Culp (1995) and Wendy Gramm, a former chairman of the CFTC.[12] The CFTC's action has also been criticized by at least two prominent members of Congress—Rep. Thomas J. Bliley, Jr., Chairman of the House Commerce Committee; and Rep. Pat Roberts, Chairman of the House Agricultural Committee.[13]

Since the CFTC's action against Metallgesellschaft is narrowly directed and involves somewhat esoteric legal arguments, it is too soon to know what its effect will be on OTC derivatives markets generally. Still, commodity dealers must now take extra care in designing long-term delivery contracts to avoid potential legal problems.[14]

An Overview of Policy Concerns

Considering the debate over the merits of MGRM's hedging strategy, it would seem naive simply to blame the firm's problems on its speculative use of derivatives. It is true that MGRM's hedging program was not without risks. But the firm's losses are attributable more to operational risk—the risk of loss caused by inadequate systems and control or management failure—than to market risk. If MG's supervisory board is to be believed, the firm's previous management lost control of the firm and then acted to conceal its losses from board members. If one sides with the firm's previous managers (as well as with Culp, Hanke, and Miller), then the supervisory board and its bankers misjudged the risks associated with MGRM's hedging program and panicked when faced with large, short-term funding demands. Either way, the loss was attributable to poor management.

Does this episode indicate the need for new government policies or more comprehensive regulation of derivatives markets? The answer appears to be no. MGRM's losses do not appear ever to have threatened the stability of financial markets. Moreover, those losses were due in large part to the firm's use of futures contracts, which trade in a market that is already subject to comprehensive regulation. The actions taken by the CFTC in this instance demonstrate clearly that U.S. regulators already have the authority to intervene when they deem it necessary. Unfortunately, the nature of those actions in this case may create added legal risk for other market participants.

To view the entire incident in its proper perspective, it must be remembered that MG's losses were incurred in connection with a marketing program aimed at providing long-term, fixed-price delivery contracts to customers, a type of arrangement common to many types of commercial activity. Systematic attempts to discourage such arrangements would seem to be poor public policy.

Finally, MG's financial difficulties were not attributable solely to its use of derivatives. As noted earlier, the firm's troubles stemmed in part from the heavy debt load it had accumulated in previous years. Moreover, MGRM's oil marketing program was not the only source of its parent company's losses during 1993. MG reported losses of DM 1.8 billion on its operations for the fiscal year ended September 30, 1993, in addition to the DM 1.5 billion loss auditors attributed to its hedging program as of the same date (Roth, 1994b). Simply stated, the MG debacle resulted from poor management. As a practical matter, government policy cannot prevent firms such as Metallgesellschaft from making mistakes. Nor should it attempt to do so.

BARINGS

At the time of its demise in February 1995, Barings PLC was the oldest merchant bank in Great Britain. Founded in 1762 by the sons of German immigrants, the bank had a long and distinguished history. Barings had helped a fledgling United States of America to arrange the financing of the Louisiana Purchase in 1803. It had also helped Britain finance the Napoleonic Wars, a feat that prompted the British government to bestow five noble titles on the Baring family.

Although it was once the largest merchant bank in Britain, Barings was no longer the powerhouse it had been in the nineteenth century. With total shareholder equity of £440 million, it was far from the largest or most important banking organization in

Great Britain. Nonetheless, it continued to rank among the nation's most prestigious institutions. Its clients included the Queen of England and other members of the royal family.

Barings had long enjoyed a reputation as a conservatively run institution. But that reputation was shattered on February 24, 1995, when Peter Baring, the bank's chairman, contacted the Bank of England to explain that a trader in the firm's Singapore futures subsidiary had lost huge sums of money speculating on Nikkei-225 stock index futures and options. In the days that followed, investigators found that the bank's total losses exceeded US$1 billion, a sum large enough to bankrupt the institution.

Barings had almost failed once before in 1890 after losing millions in loans to Argentina, but it was rescued on that occasion by a consortium led by the Bank of England. A similar effort was mounted in February 1995, but the attempt failed when no immediate buyer could be found and the Bank of England refused to assume liability for Barings' losses. On the evening of Sunday, February 26, the Bank of England took action to place Barings into administration, a legal proceeding resembling Chapter 11 bankruptcy-court proceedings in the United States. The crisis brought about by Barings' insolvency ended just over one week later when a large Dutch financial conglomerate, the Internationale Nederlanden Groep (ING), assumed the assets and liabilities of the failed merchant bank.

What has shocked most observers is that such a highly regarded institution could fall victim to such a fate. The ensuing account examines the events leading up to the failure of Barings, the factors responsible for the debacle, and the repercussions of that event on world financial markets.[15] This account is followed by an examination of the policy concerns arising from the episode and the lessons these events hold for market participants and policy makers.

Unauthorized Trading Activities

In 1992, Barings sent Nicholas Leeson, a clerk from its London office, to manage the back-office accounting and settlement operations at its Singapore futures subsidiary. Baring Futures (Singapore), hereafter BFS, was established to enable Barings to execute trades on the Singapore International Monetary Exchange (SIMEX). The subsidiary's profits were expected to come primarily from brokerage commissions for trades executed on behalf of customers and other Barings subsidiaries.[16]

Soon after arriving in Singapore, Leeson asked permission to take the SIMEX examinations that would permit him to trade on the floor of the exchange. He passed the examinations and began trading later that year. Some time during late 1992 or early 1993, Leeson was named general manager and head trader of BFS. Normally the functions of trading and settlements are kept separate within an organization, as the head of settlements is expected to provide independent verification of records of trading activity. But Leeson was never relieved of his authority over the subsidiary's back-office operations when his responsibilities were expanded to include trading.

Leeson soon began to engage in proprietary trading—that is, trading for the firm's own account. Barings' management understood that such trading involved arbitrage in Nikkei-225 stock index futures and ten-year Japanese Government Bond (JGB) futures. Both contracts trade on SIMEX and the Osaka Securities Exchange (OSE). At times price discrepancies can develop between the same contract on different exchanges, leaving room for an arbitrageur to earn profits by buying the lower-priced contract on one exchange while selling the higher-priced contract on the other. In theory this type of arbitrage involves only perfectly hedged positions, and so it is commonly regarded as a low-risk activity. Unbeknownst to the bank's management, however, Leeson soon embarked upon a much riskier trading strategy. Rather than engaging in arbitrage, as Barings' management believed, he began placing bets on the direction of price movements on the Tokyo stock exchange.

Leeson's reported trading profits were spectacular. His earnings soon came to account for a significant share of Barings' total profits; the bank's senior management regarded him as a star performer. After Barings failed, however, investigators found that Leeson's reported profits had been fictitious from the start. Because his duties included supervision of both trading and settlements for the Singapore subsidiary, Leeson was able to manufacture fictitious reports concerning his trading activities. He had set up a special account—account number 88888—in July 1992, and instructed his clerks to omit information on that account from their reports to the London head office. By manipulating information on his trading activity, Leeson was able to conceal his trading losses and report large profits instead.

Figure 23.2 shows Leeson's trading losses from 1992 through the end of February 1995. By the end of 1992—just a few months after he had begun trading—Leeson had accumulated a hidden loss of £2 million. That figure remained unchanged until October 1993, when his losses began to rise sharply. He lost another £21 million in 1993 and £185 million in 1994. Total cumulative losses at the end of 1994 stood at £208 million. That amount was slightly larger than the £205 million profit reported by the Barings Group as a whole before accounting for taxes and for £102 million in scheduled bonuses.

A major part of Leeson's trading strategy involved the sale of options on Nikkei-225 futures contracts. Figure 23.3a and 23.3b show the payoff at expiration accruing to the seller of a call or put option, respectively. The seller of an option earns a premium in return for accepting the obligation to buy or sell the underlying item at a stipulated strike price. If the option expires out-of-the-money, the option premium becomes the seller's profit. If prices turn out to be more volatile than expected, however, an option seller's potential losses are virtually unlimited.

FIGURE 23.2   Concealed Trading Losses

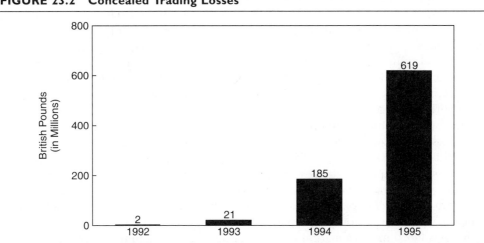

Source: Bank of England, Board of Banking Supervision

FIGURE 23.3   Payoffs to Selected Option Positions

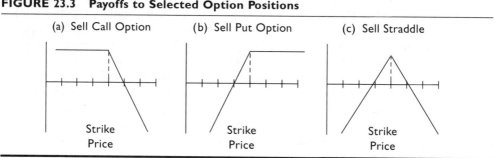

(a) Sell Call Option   (b) Sell Put Option   (c) Sell Straddle

Strike Price   Strike Price   Strike Price

Some time in 1994, Leeson began selling large numbers of option straddles, a strategy that involved the simultaneous sale of both calls and puts on Nikkei-225 futures. Figure 23.3c shows the payoff at expiration to a sold option straddle. Option prices reflect the market's expectation of the price volatility of the underlying item. The seller of an option straddle earns a profit only if the market proves less volatile than predicted by option prices. As is evident in Figure 23.3c, Leeson's strategy amounted to a bet that the Japanese stock market would neither fall nor increase by a great deal—any large movement in Japanese stock prices would result in losses. By January 1, 1995, Leeson was short 37,925 Nikkei calls and 32,967 Nikkei puts. He also held a long position of just over 1,000 contracts in Nikkei stock index futures, which would gain in value if the stock market were to rise.

Disaster struck on January 17 when news of a violent earthquake in Kobe, Japan, sent the Japanese stock market into a tailspin. Over the next five days, the Nikkei index fell over 1,500 points—Leeson's options positions sustained a loss of £68 million. As stock prices fell, he began buying massive amounts of Nikkei stock index futures. He also placed a side bet on Japanese interest rates, selling Japanese government bond futures by the thousands in the expectation of rising interest rates.

This strategy seemed to work for a short time. By February 6, the Japanese stock market had recovered by over 1,000 points, making it possible for Leeson to recoup most of the losses resulting from the market's reaction to the earthquake. His cumulative losses on that date totaled £253 million, about 20 percent higher than they had been at the start of the year. But within days the market began falling again—Leeson's losses began to multiply. He continued to increase his exposure as the market kept falling. By February 23, Leeson had bought over 61,000 Nikkei futures contracts, representing 49 percent of total open interest in the March 1995 Nikkei futures contract and 24 percent of the open interest in the June contract. His position in Japanese government bond futures totaled just over 26,000 contracts sold, representing 88 percent of the open interest in the June 1995 contract. Leeson also took on positions in Euroyen futures. He began 1995 with long positions in Euroyen contracts (a bet that Japanese interest rates would fall) but then switched to selling the contracts. By February 23 he had accumulated a short position in Euroyen futures equivalent to 5 percent of the open interest in the June 1995 contract and 1 percent of the open interest in both the September and December contracts.

Barings faced massive margin calls as Leeson's losses mounted. While these margin calls raised eyebrows at the bank's London and Tokyo offices, they did not prompt an immediate inquiry into Leeson's activities. It was not until February 6 that Barings' group treasurer, Tony Hawes, flew to Singapore to investigate irregularities with the accounts at BFS. Accompanying Hawes was Tony Railton, a settlements clerk from the London office.

While in Singapore, Hawes met with SIMEX officials, who had expressed concern over Barings' extraordinarily large positions. Hawes assured them that his firm was aware of these positions and stood ready to meet its obligations to the exchange. His assurances were predicated on the belief that the firm's exposure on the Singapore exchange had been hedged with offsetting positions on the Osaka exchange. He was soon to learn that this belief was incorrect.

Leeson's requests for additional funding continued during February, and Barings' London office continued to meet those requests—in all, Barings committed a total of £742 million to finance margin calls for BFS. Meanwhile Tony Railton, the clerk Hawes had dispatched to Singapore, found that he could not reconcile the accounts of BFS. Particularly disturbing was a US$190 million discrepancy in one of BFS' accounts. For over a week, Railton attempted to meet with Leeson to resolve these discrepancies. Leeson had become hard to find, however. Railton finally tracked him down on the floor of the Singapore exchange on Thursday, February 23, and persuaded Leeson to meet with him that evening. When the meeting began, Railton began asking a series of difficult questions. At that point, Leeson excused himself, stating that he would return shortly. But he never did return. Instead, he and his wife left Singapore that evening. The next day, Leeson faxed his resignation to Barings' London office from a hotel in Kuala Lumpur, stating in part, "My sincere apologies for the predicament I have left you in. It was neither my intention nor aim for this to happen."[17]

After Leeson failed to return, Railton and others at Barings' Singapore office began investigating his private records and quickly discovered evidence that he had lost astronomical sums of money. Peter Baring, the bank's chairman, did not learn of the bank's difficulties until the next day, when he was forced to call the Bank of England to ask for assistance. Ironically, this was the same day that Barings was to inform its staff of their bonuses. Leeson was to receive a £450,000 bonus, up from £130,000 the previous year, on the strength of his reported profits. Baring himself expected to receive £1 million.

The Bank of England's Board of Banking Supervision (1995) subsequently conducted an inquiry into the collapse of Barings. According to the Board's report, total losses attributable to Leeson's actions came to £927 million (approximately US$1.4 billion) including liquidation costs, an amount far in excess of Barings' total equity of £440 million. Most of the cost of the Barings' debacle was borne by its shareholders and by ING, the firm that bought Barings. Barings was a privately held firm; most of its equity was held by the Baring Foundation, a charity registered in the United Kingdom. Barings' executive committee held the firm's voting shares, which constituted a small fraction of the firm's total equity. Although ING was able to buy the failed merchant bank for a token amount of £1, it had to pay £660 million to recapitalize the firm. SIMEX subsequently reported that the funds Barings had on deposit with the exchange were sufficient to meet the costs incurred in liquidating its positions (Szala, Nusbaum, and Reerink, 1995). It is not known whether the OSE suffered any losses as a result of Barings' collapse.

Leeson was later detained by authorities at the airport in Frankfort, Germany, and was extradited to Singapore the following November. In Singapore, Leeson pleaded guilty to charges of fraud and was sentenced to a 6½-year prison term (Mark 1995).

Certain material facts regarding the entire incident are not yet known, as Leeson refused to cooperate with British authorities unless extradited to Great Britain. He later contested the findings of the Banking Board's inquiry, however. A letter to the board from his solicitors states,

> *These conclusions are inaccurate in various respects. Indeed, in relation to certain of the matters they betray a fundamental misunderstanding of the actual events. Unfortunately, given the uncertainty regarding Mr. Leeson's position we are not able to provide you with a detailed response to your letter.*[18]

Leeson has promised to write a book describing his own version of events while serving out his prison term in Singapore.

Market Aftershocks

Once the Singapore and Osaka exchanges learned that Barings would not be able to meet its margin calls, they took control of all the bank's open positions. The Nikkei index fell precipitously when market participants learned that the exchanges would be liquidating such large positions. Thus, in the days immediately following the announcement of Barings' collapse, it was not known whether the margin money the bank had deposited with the exchanges would cover the losses stemming from the liquidation of its positions.

Matters were further complicated when SIMEX announced it would double margin requirements on its Nikkei stock index futures contract effective Tuesday, February 28. Fearing that their margin money might be used to pay for Barings' losses, several of the exchange's U.S. clearing members threatened to withhold payment of the additional margin SIMEX was demanding of them unless given assurances that such margin payments would be used solely to collateralize their own accounts. A refusal to pay would have caused the affected dealers to forfeit their positions. If that had happened, SIMEX would have been faced with a series of defaults. According to CFTC chairman Schapiro, such an event could have "destroyed the ability of SIMEX to manage the situation."[19] Indeed, there are reports that many market participants feared that the very solvency of the SIMEX clearinghouse was in question. To complicate matters further, Japanese and Singaporean regulators were slow to inform market participants of the steps they were taking to insure the financial integrity of the exchange clearinghouses. This lack of communication served only to exacerbate the fears of market participants (Falloon, 1995; Irving, 1995; McGee, 1995a, b; Szala, Nusbaum, and Reerink, 1995).

Upon learning of the situation, Chairman Schapiro contacted the Monetary Authority of Singapore (MAS) to persuade the agency to assure SIMEX's clearing members that their margin deposits would not be used to offset Barings' proprietary losses. The MAS subsequently acceded to these requests and provided its assurance in a short statement released before the start of trading on Tuesday. SIMEX's margin calls were met and a potential crisis was avoided.

This was not the end of headaches for Barings' customers, however. BFS was one of the largest clearing member firms on SIMEX. As such, it handled clearing and settlement for 16 U.S. firms and held approximately $480 million in margin funds on their behalf when it went bankrupt.

U.S. futures exchanges typically arrange the immediate transfer to other firms of all customer accounts of a financially troubled clearing member. Laws in the United

States facilitate such transfers because they provide for strict segregation of customer accounts, which prevents the creditors of a broker or clearing member firm from attaching the assets of customers. That Japanese law contains no such provisions was not well known before the collapse of Barings. Although laws in Singapore do recognize the segregation of accounts, SIMEX had never before dealt with the insolvency of a clearing member firm. To complicate matters further, most of BFS' customer accounts had been booked through Baring Securities in London. Consequently, SIMEX did not have detailed information on individual customer positions. It had records only on a single commingled account for Baring Securities. Finally, much of the information that Leeson had provided to the exchange, as well as to Barings' other offices, was false. These circumstances made the task of sorting out the positions of individual customers extremely difficult.

During the next week, Barings' U.S. customers scrambled to reproduce documentation of their transactions with the bank and supplied this information to SIMEX and the OSE. But while this information made it possible for the exchanges to identify customer positions, Barings' bankruptcy administrator in London had asked the exchanges to block access to all Barings' margin deposits. The bankruptcy administrator had raised questions about whether U.K. laws on the segregation of customer accounts were applicable in an insolvency of this kind (Szala, Nusbaum, and Reerink, 1995).

It was not until ING took over Barings, on March 9, that the bank's customers were assured of access to their funds. Even then, access was delayed in many cases. By one account, several major clients waited more than three weeks before their funds were returned (Irving, 1995).

Policy Concerns Highlighted by Barings' Default

All futures exchanges maintain systems to prevent the accumulation of large speculative losses. But events surrounding the collapse of Barings have served to highlight weaknesses in risk management on the part of SIMEX and other futures exchanges. They also suggest a need for closer international cooperation among futures exchanges and their regulators, and for clearer laws on the status of customer accounts when a clearing member firm becomes insolvent.

Futures exchanges maintain stringent speculative position limits for individual firms and traders to prevent large losses and to limit their exposure. It appears that SIMEX relaxed some of these restrictions for BFS, however. It is not unusual for futures exchanges to grant exemptions to established position limits for hedged positions, such as those Leeson claimed to maintain. But it is normal for the exchange clearinghouse to monitor closely the activities of firms receiving such exemptions and to take steps to verify the existence of offsetting exposures. It now appears that SIMEX failed to pursue such precautions in its dealings with Barings.

The exchange's attitude toward Barings was influenced in part by the bank's strong international reputation, but its willingness to relax normal risk management guidelines also may have been attributable to its desire to attract business. Although the OSE was first to list Japanese government bond and Nikkei-225 stock index futures, SIMEX soon began listing similar contracts in direct competition with the Osaka exchange. Thereafter, the two exchanges battled each other for market share. Barings was one of the most active firms on SIMEX—and Leeson was responsible for much of the exchange's trading volume in Nikkei stock index futures and options. Thus, some observers believe that SIMEX may have been too willing to accommodate BFS (McGee, 1995a). Critics include representatives of U.S. futures exchanges, who maintain that their risk management standards are more stringent.[20] A report on the incident commissioned by the government of Singapore came to a similar conclusion, finding that the exchange may have been too liberal in granting increases in position limits.[21]

Communication between exchanges can be important for identifying and resolving potential problems. Communication between SIMEX and the OSE was minimal, however. This lack of communication not only helped make it possible for Leeson to accumulate large losses but also hampered efforts to contain the damage once Barings collapsed. Although the OSE routinely published a list of the positions of its most active traders, SIMEX did not make such disclosures. It now seems apparent that SIMEX officials never consulted the OSE's list to verify Leeson's claim that he was hedging his large positions in Singapore with offsetting exposures on the Osaka exchange.

Some observers blame this lack of communication on the rivalry between the two exchanges. Arrangements existing between U.S. exchanges suggest that competition need not preclude information sharing, however. In the United States, futures exchanges attempt to coordinate their activities with the CFTC and other futures exchanges. Each exchange maintains strict speculative position limits established under CFTC oversight. The CFTC monitors compliance through a comprehensive surveillance policy that includes a large-trader reporting system. Market participants are required to justify unusually large positions. This system enabled the CFTC to ascertain quickly that Barings had no significant positions on any U.S. futures exchange at the time of its collapse.[22]

While competitive concerns may sometimes give exchanges incentives to relax prudential standards, as many observers seem to think that SIMEX did, it does not follow that regulators should seek to discourage such competition. Competition among exchanges serves an important economic function by encouraging innovation. Securities and futures exchanges constantly compete with one another to provide new products to their customers. Thus, whereas futures exchanges once listed contracts only for agricultural and other commodities, a significant fraction of all futures trading today involves contracts for financial instruments. The growth of trading in such instruments has provided important benefits to international financial markets, helping to make them more efficient while facilitating risk management by financial intermediaries and commercial firms alike. Moreover, competition gives futures exchanges an incentive to maintain strong financial controls and risk management systems, as most market participants seek to avoid risks like those faced by SIMEX customers after the collapse of Barings. Finally, policymakers need not restrict competition to address the problems highlighted by the Barings debacle.

The events surrounding the collapse of Barings led futures industry regulators from 16 nations to meet in Windsor, England, in May 1995 to discuss the need for legal and regulatory reform. At that meeting, officials agreed on a plan of action now known as the Windsor Declaration. The declaration calls for regulators to promote, as appropriate, "national provisions and market procedures that facilitate the prompt liquidation and/or transfer of positions, funds and assets, from failing members of futures exchanges," and to support measures "to enhance emergency procedures at financial intermediaries, market members and markets and to improve existing mechanisms for international co-operation and communication among market authorities and regulators."[23] The International Organization of Securities Commissions (IOSCO) later endorsed the Windsor Declaration and pledged to study the issues it raised. IOSCO also asked its members to promote declaration measures in cross-border transactions.[24]

The Barings debacle has also spurred efforts by market participants to strengthen financial safeguards at futures and options exchanges. In March 1995, the Futures Industry Association (FIA) organized a task force to investigate measures to improve the financial integrity of futures and options exchanges. The association's Global Task Force on Financial Integrity (1995) subsequently published a report containing 60 recommendations, ranging from risk management practices to customer protection issues. The FIA report encourages all nations to review their bankruptcy laws to clarify the status of customer funds and to modify provisions that might conflict with the laws of other nations. It recommends that exchanges and their regulators establish procedures for the transfer of a troubled clearing member firm's customer assets *before* it is declared insolvent, as is now typically done in the United States. In addition, the report encourages exchange clearinghouses to monitor their clearing member firms closely and to perform periodic audits. Thus, the FIA's recommendations are broadly consistent with the principles espoused by the Windsor Declaration, especially in their emphasis on customer protection and the need for improved information sharing among exchanges and government authorities.

Subsequently, the clearing organizations for 19 U.S. stock, stock option, and futures exchanges announced their intent to begin pooling data on transactions of member firms (McGee, 1995c). In addition, CFTC Chairman Schapiro has announced that her staff will work with the futures industry to develop concrete customer protection proposals.[25]

The Barings debacle has served to galvanize an international effort—one that has been joined by government officials and market participants alike—to re-evaluate risk management systems, customer protection laws, and procedures for dealing with the failure of a large clearinghouse member. It also has prompted increased communication and pledges of greater cooperation among regulators from different nations. It is still too early to pass judgment on the ultimate success of such initiatives, however. While regulators have pledged increased international cooperation, recent press accounts have noted that officials in Britain, Japan, and Singapore have not always cooperated with one another in conducting their investigations of the Barings case.[26]

Lessons from the Barings Debacle

The losses suffered by Barings provide a good example of the market risk associated with derivatives. But, as with the case of Metallgesellschaft, the Barings debacle best illustrates operational risk and legal risk. In this regard, the Bank of England's Board of Banking Supervision inquiry concluded,

> *Barings' collapse was due to the unauthorized and ultimately catastrophic activities of, it appears, one individual (Leeson) that went undetected as a consequence of a failure of management and other internal controls of the most basic kind. Management failed at various levels and in a variety of ways . . . to institute a proper system of internal controls, to enforce accountability for all profits, risks and operations, and adequately to follow up on a number of warning signals over a prolonged period.*[27]

The board's inquiry found nine separate warning signs that should have alerted Barings' management to problems with its Singapore futures subsidiary. A partial list of those warning signs includes the following:

- *The lack of segregation of duties between front and back offices.* This lack was identified as a weakness and potential problem area in an internal audit report following a review of BFS' operations in the summer of 1994. Barings' management failed to act on the report's recommendations to remedy this situation.
- *The high level of funding requested by Leeson.* Between December 31, 1994, and February 24, 1995, Barings provided Leeson with £521 million to meet margin calls. Total funding of BFS stood at £742 million, more than twice the reported capital of the Barings Group, when Leeson's activities were finally discovered on February 24.[28]
- *The unreconciled balance of funds transferred to BFS to meet margin calls.* In his requests for additional funding, Leeson often claimed the money was needed for client accounts but never provided detailed information about these accounts as was the usual practice. Nonetheless, the bank's head office in London paid those funds without any independent check on the validity of Leeson's requests and with no attempt to reconcile those requests with known trading positions. Perhaps the most troubling aspect of Barings' behavior in this regard is that SIMEX rules prohibit its members from financing the margin accounts of customers. Barings' management apparently ignored evidence that the firm might be doing so in violation of SIMEX rules.
- *The apparent high profitability of Leeson's trading activities relative to the low level of risk as perceived and authorized by Barings' management in London.* High returns typically entail high risk. Yet no one in senior management seriously questioned how Leeson's strong reported profits could result from what was supposed to have been a low-risk activity. To be sure, at least one executive observed that "This guy must be busting his intraday limits or something."[29] But Leeson's reports were never challenged until too late, and management did little to restrain his trading activities. According to interviews with Barings' staff, Leeson was regarded as "almost a miracle worker," and there was "a concern not to do anything which might upset him."[30]
- *The discovery of discrepancies in Leeson's accounts by outside auditors.* Barings' auditors, the firm of Coopers & Lybrand, informed the bank's management of a £50 million discrepancy in BFS's accounts on or before February 1, 1995. Although this discrepancy ultimately did prompt Barings' treasurer to investigate Leeson's accounts, the Board of Banking Supervision concluded that management was too slow in responding to this warning sign.
- *Communications from SIMEX.* The rapid buildup of Leeson's positions during January 1995 prompted SIMEX to seek assurances from Barings' management in London regarding the ability of BFS to fund its margin calls. In retrospect, it appears that Barings' management was too hasty in providing such assurances.
- *Market rumors and concerns made known to Barings' management in January and February.* By late January, rumors were circulating on the OSE regarding Barings' large positions in Nikkei futures. On January 27, the Bank for International Settlements in Basle, Switzerland, raised a high-level inquiry with Barings executives in London regarding a rumor that the bank had experienced losses and could not meet its margin calls on the OSE. On the same day, another

Barings executive received a call from the Bloomberg Information Service inquiring into the bank's large positions on the OSE.

Taken together, these warning signs suggest that Barings' management had ample cause to be concerned about Leeson's activities. But management was too slow to act on these warning signs. An on-site examination of Leeson's accounts came too late to save the bank.

The Board of Banking Supervision's report outlined a number of lessons to be learned from the failure of Barings. They emphasize five lessons for the management of financial institutions:

- Management teams have a duty to understand fully the businesses they manage;
- Responsibility for each business activity has to be clearly established and communicated;
- Clear segregation of duties is fundamental to any effective control system;
- Relevant internal controls, including independent risk management, have to be established for all business activities;
- Top management and the Audit Committee have to ensure that significant weaknesses, identified to them by internal audit or otherwise, are resolved quickly.[31]

The report also had some criticisms for the Bank of England's supervision of Barings. U.K. banking regulations require all banks to notify the Bank of England before entering into a transaction that would expose more than 25 percent of the organization's capital to the risk of loss. A Bank of England manager granted Barings an informal concession permitting it to exceed this limit in its exposure to SIMEX and the OSE without first referring the matter to the Bank's senior management. But while the report is somewhat critical of the Bank of England on this matter, it concludes,

The events leading up to the collapse of Barings do not, in our view, of themselves point to the need for any fundamental change in the framework of regulation in the UK. There is, however, a need for improvements in the existing arrangements.[32]

The report goes on to suggest a number of ways to improve the Bank of England's supervision of banks. According to the report,

- the Bank should "explore ways of increasing its understanding of the nonbanking businesses . . . undertaken by those banks for which it is responsible";[33]
- it should prepare explicit internal guidelines to assist its supervisory staff in identifying activities that could pose material risks to banks and ensure that adequate safeguards are in place;
- it should work more closely with the Securities and Futures Authority, the agency responsible for regulating the domestic operations of British-based securities firms, as well as with regulators from other nations; and
- it should address deficiencies in the implementation of rules dealing with large exposures.

The report also recommended an independent quality assurance review of the Bank of England's supervisory function.

The Board of Banking Supervision's report did not blame the collapse of Barings on its use of derivatives. Instead, it placed responsibility for the debacle on poor operational controls at Barings.

> *The failings at Barings were not a consequence of the complexity of the business, but were primarily a failure on the part of a number of individuals to do their jobs properly. . . . While the use of futures and options contracts did enable Leeson to take much greater levels of risk (through their leverage) than might have been the case in some other markets, it was his ability to act without authority and without detection that brought Barings down.*[34]

This point has been reinforced recently by news of a similar debacle at the New York office of Daiwa Bank, where a trader concealed large trading losses for over ten years before finally confessing to his activities.[35] Parallels between the Daiwa and Barings debacles are striking, as both incidents resulted from the unauthorized activities of a single trader. Daiwa's losses were in no way related to derivatives, however. The bank incurred over $1 billion in losses as a result of unauthorized trading in U.S. government bonds, widely regarded as the safest of financial instruments.

Some Final Observations on the Barings Debacle

The events surrounding the collapse of Barings have highlighted certain weaknesses in international financial markets that represent legitimate concerns for policymakers. Two of these weaknesses deserve special notice: (1) the lack of communication between securities and futures exchanges and regulators in different countries; and (2) conflicting laws on the legal status of customer accounts at futures brokers and clearing agents in the event of insolvency. These weaknesses can be addressed only by increased international cooperation among futures exchanges, regulators, and lawmakers.

At the same time, it does not appear that more stringent government regulation of futures markets could have prevented the Barings debacle. Leeson acted outside existing regulatory guidelines and outside the law in concealing the true nature of his trading activities and the losses resulting therefrom. Existing laws and regulations should have been able to prevent, or at least to detect, Leeson's activities before he could incur such astronomical losses. But Barings, SIMEX, and the Bank of England were all lax in enforcing those rules. Barings was lax in enforcing basic operational controls. In doing so, it violated not only official regulations but also commonly accepted market standards for managing risk. Similarly, it appears that SIMEX may have been too liberal in granting increases in position limits to BFS. Finally, the Bank of England granted Barings an exemption that helped make it possible for Leeson to continue his illicit activities undetected.

CONCLUDING COMMENTS

The cases of Metallgesellschaft and Barings provide an interesting study in contrasts. Both cases involve exchange-traded derivatives contracts. In both cases, senior management has been criticized for making an insufficient effort to understand fully the activities of their firms' subsidiaries and for failing to monitor and supervise the activities of those subsidiaries adequately. But while critics have faulted MG's management for overreacting to the large margin calls faced by one of its subsidiaries, Barings' management has been faulted for being overly complacent in the face of a large number of warning signs.

If these two disparate incidents offer any single lesson, it is the need for senior management to understand the nature of the firm's activities and the risks that those activities involve. In the case of Metallgesellschaft, the sheer scale of its U.S. oil subsidiary's marketing program exposed the firm to large risks. Although there is a great deal of disagreement over the efficacy of the hedging strategy employed by MGRM, it would seem difficult to argue that members of MG's board of supervisors fully appreciated the nature or magnitude of the risks assumed by the firm's U.S. oil subsidiary. If they had, they would not have been so shocked to find the firm facing large margin calls. In the case of Barings, senior management seemed content to accept that a single trader could earn huge profits without exposing the firm to large risks. With the benefit of hindsight, it seems clear that senior executives of both firms should have taken more effort to understand the activities of subordinates.

News of derivatives-related losses often prompts calls for more comprehensive regulation of derivatives markets. But the cases of Metallgesellschaft and Barings—which rank among the largest derivatives-related losses to date—involve instruments traded in markets already subject to comprehensive regulation. In the case of Barings, the debacle involved a regulated merchant bank trading in regulated futures markets. If anything, the Barings debacle illustrates the limits of regulation. Established rules and regulations should have been able to prevent a single trader from accumulating catastrophic losses. But both SIMEX and the Bank of England granted exemptions that helped make it possible for Leeson to continue his activities for years without being detected. It appears that regulatory organizations can also be subject to operational weaknesses.

Moreover, the instruments traded by these two firms—oil futures, stock index futures, and stock index options—are not the kinds of complex and exotic instruments responsible for concerns often expressed in connection with the growth of derivatives markets. In the case of Barings, the Bank of England's Board of Banking Supervision concluded that it was not the complexity of the business but the failure of a large number of individuals to do their jobs properly that made the bank susceptible to catastrophic losses by a single trader. As the recent misfortune of Daiwa Bank shows, weaknesses in operational controls can lead to losses in many areas of a firm's operations, not just those involved with derivatives. The losses suffered by Daiwa resulted from trading in U.S. Treasury bonds, widely regarded as the safest of all securities.

Unfortunately, no amount of regulation can remove all risk from financial markets. Risk is inherent in all economic activity, and financial markets exist to help market participants diversify such risks. At the same time, regulation can impose costs on market participants. The Metallgesellschaft case shows that attempts at stringent regulation can sometimes have undesirable side effects. According to critics, the CFTC's action against MG's U.S. subsidiaries has introduced uncertainty about the legal status of commercial forward contracts. As a general rule, government policy should attempt to minimize legal risk rather than create it.

To be sure, the Barings debacle did highlight the need for certain legal and regulatory reforms and for more international cooperation among exchanges and their regulators. But market discipline is also a powerful form of regulation. Highly publicized accounts of derivatives-related losses have led many firms to scrutinize their risk management practices—not only in the area of derivatives, but in other areas of their operations as well. Thus, while it is true that derivatives debacles often reveal the existence of disturbing operational weaknesses among the firms involved, such incidents can also teach lessons that help to make financial markets safer in the long run. As the foregoing accounts show, regulation cannot substitute for sound management practices. At the same time, government policymakers can act to minimize the potential for disruption to financial markets by promoting laws and policies that minimize legal risk.

REFERENCES

BNA's Banking Report. "CFTC Chairman Schapiro Tells Congress Barings-Type Disaster Unlikely in U.S.," *64* (March 6, 1995a), pp. 468–69.

_____ . "CFTC Undertaking Regulatory Review: Schapiro Address[es] Failure of Barings PLC," *64* (March 6, 1995b), pp. 469–70.

_____ . "World Futures Regulators Adopt Plan of Action in View of Barings," *64* (May 22, 1995c), pp. 1017–18.

_____ . "Schapiro Says CFTC, Industry to Craft Customer Protection Proposals," *65* (July 3, 1995d), pp. 15–16.

_____ . "IOSCO Endorses Value-at-Risk Models for Capital Adequacy Calculations," *65* (July 17, 1995e), pp. 120–21.

_____ . "Schapiro Defends CFTC Action Against Two MG Subsidiaries," *65* (September 25, 1995f), p. 503.

Board of Banking Supervision. *Report of the Board of Banking Supervision Inquiry into the Circumstances of the Collapse of Barings.* London: HMSO, 1995.

Culp, Christopher, and Steve H. Hanke. "Derivative Dingbats," *The International Economy* (July/August 1994).

Culp, Christopher L., and Merton H. Miller. "Hedging a Flow of Commodity Deliveries with Futures: Lessons From Metallgesellschaft," *Derivatives Quarterly, 1* (Fall 1994a), pp. 7–15.

_____ . "Letter to the Editor," *Risk, 11* (November 1994b), p. 18.

_____ . "Metallgesellschaft and the Economics of Synthetic Storage," *Journal of Applied Corporate Finance, 7* (Winter 1995a), pp. 62–76.

_____ . "Auditing the Auditors," *Risk, 8* (April 1995b), pp. 36–9.

_____ . "Hedging in the Theory of Corporate Finance: A Reply to our Critics." *Journal of Applied Corporate Finance, 8* (Spring 1995c), pp. 121–27.

_____ . "Basis Risk and Hedging Strategies: Reply to Mello and Parsons," *Derivatives Quarterly, 1* (Summer 1995d), pp. 20–26.

The Economist. "Revolution at Metallgesellschaft," December 25, 1993, p. 90.

_____ . "The Barings Collapse: Spot the Smoking Receivable," October 21, 1995, p. 79.

Edwards, Franklin R. "Derivatives Can Be Hazardous to Your Health: The Case of Metallgesellschaft," *Derivatives Quarterly, 1* (Spring 1995), pp. 8–17.

Edward, Franklin R., and Michael S. Canter. "The Collapse of Metallgesellschaft: Unhedgeable Risks, Poor Hedging Strategy, or Just Bad Luck?" *The Journal of Futures Markets, 15* (May 1995a), pp. 211–64.

Edward, Franklin R., and Michael S. Canter. "The Collapse of Metallgesellschaft: Unhedgeable Risks, Poor Hedging Strategy, or Just Bad Luck? *Journal of Applied Corporate Finance, 8* (Spring 1995b), pp. 86–105.

Falloon, William. "Who's Missing from the Picture?" *Risk, 8* (April 1995), pp. 19–22.

Fox, Justin. "2 in House Fault Futures Trading Panel on Over-the-Counter Derivatives Ruling," *American Banker,* December 26, 1995.

Futures Industry Association Global Task Force on Financial Integrity. *Financial Integrity Recommendations.* Washington: Futures Industry Association, 1995.

Global Derivatives Study Group. *Derivatives: Practices and Principles.* Washington: Group of Thirty, 1993.

Irving, Richard. "Beyond Barings," *Risk, 8* (April 1995), p. 6.

Kawaller, Ira. "Hedging with Futures Contracts: Going the Extra Mile," *Journal of Cash Management, 6* (July/ August 1986), pp. 34–36.

Mark, Jeremy. "With Leeson in Singapore Prison, Focus Shifts to Barings Executives," *Wall Street Journal,* December 4, 1995.

McGee, Suzanne. "Reform Sought to Prevent Future Barings," *Wall Street Journal,* March 17, 1995a.

————. "New U.S. Futures Chief Is Crafting a Global Role," *Wall Street Journal,* May 17, 1995b.

————. "Nineteen U.S. Exchanges To Share Data on Dealings," *Wall Street Journal,* September 6, 1995c.

Mello, Antonio S., and John E. Parsons. "Maturity Structure of a Hedge Matters: Lessons from the Metallgesellschaft Debacle," *Journal of Applied Corporate Finance, 8* (Spring 1995a), pp. 106–20.

————. "Hedging a Flow of Commodity Deliveries with Futures: Problems with a Rolling Stack," *Derivatives Quarterly, 1* (Summer 1995b), pp. 16–19.

Miller, Merton H., and Christopher L. Culp. "Rein in the CFTC," *Wall Street Journal,* August 17, 1995.

Rance, Brian D. "The Commodity Futures Trading Commission Order of Settlement with MG Refining and Marketing, Inc. and MF Futures, Inc.," *Derivatives Quarterly, 2* (Winter 1995), pp. 13–17.

Roth, Terrence. "Metallgesellschaft Sets Shareholder Vote Despite Worries Over Financial Package," *Wall Street Journal,* January 14, 1994a.

————. "German Firm's Bailout Package Gets Approved," *Wall Street Journal,* January 17, 1994b.

Sapsford, Jathon, Michael R. Sesit, and Timothy L. O'Brien. "How Daiwa Bond Man in New York Cost Bank $1.1 Billion in Losses," *Wall Street Journal,* September 27, 1995.

Springett, Pauline. "The Barings Rescue: 'Apologies, but the pressures have become too much to bear,'" *The Guardian* (London), March 7, 1995.

Stoll, Hans R. "Lost Barings: A Tale in Three Parts Concluding with a Lesson," *The Journal of Derivatives, 3* (Fall 1995), pp. 109–115.

Szala, Ginger, David Nusbaum, and Jack Reerink. "Barings Abyss," *Futures, 24* (May 1995), pp. 68–74.

Taylor, Jeffrey. "MG Corp. Aims to Stay Active in Oil Business," *Wall Street Journal,* March 14, 1994.

————. "Securities Firms Agree to Set Controls on Derivatives," *Wall Street Journal,* March 9, 1995a.

_____ . "Documents at MG Appear to Contradict Fired Chairman's Stance on Derivatives," *Wall Street Journal,* January 27, 1995b.

U.S. Commodity Futures Trading Commission. "Order Instituting Proceedings Pursuant to Sections 6(c) and 8(a) of the Commodity Exchange Act and Findings and Order Imposing Remedial Sanctions," CFTC Docket No. 95-14 (1995a).

_____ . "CFTC Order Imposes $2.25 Million Civil Penalty against MG Refining and Marketing, Inc. and MG Futures, Inc.; Other Remedial Sanctions Include Review of Internal Control Systems for Risk Management," Release No. 3859-95 (July 27, 1995b).

U.S. General Accounting Office. *Financial Derivatives: Actions Needed to Protect the Financial System.* GAO/GCD-94-133, May, 1994.

Wall Street Journal. "Metallgesellschaft A.G. Dismisses Chairman and Finance Chief," December 20, 1993.

_____ . "Former CFTC Chief Scores Agency's Move in Derivatives Case," December 1, 1995.

ENDNOTES

1. *See* Global Derivatives Study Group (1993).

2. *See* U.S. General Accounting Office (1994).

3. Recent losses by firms such as Gibson Greetings and Procter & Gamble have also raised concerns about sales practices and the disclosure of risks associated with complex financial derivatives. Neither of the cases examined in this study involves such concerns, however.

4. Many securities companies book their OTC derivatives through unregulated subsidiaries. Although these subsidiaries are not subject to formal SEC regulation, the largest brokerage firms have agreed to abide by certain regulatory guidelines and to make regular disclosures to both the SEC and CFTC about their management of derivatives-related risks. *See* Taylor (1995a).

5. As cited in Edwards and Canter (1995b), page 86.

6. Mello and Parsons (1995a) provide a detailed description of these contracts.

7. More recently, Edwards (1995) has become more critical of the decision to liquidate MGRM's forward delivery contracts.

8. *See* the *Wall Street Journal* (1993) and *The Economist* (1993).

9. A Futures Commission Merchant is a broker that accepts and executes orders for transactions on futures exchanges for customers. Futures Commission Merchants are regulated by the CFTC.

10. *See* U.S. Commodity Futures Trading Commission (1995a, b).

11. *See* BNA's *Banking Report* (1995f).

12. For a summary of Gramm's comments see the *Wall Street Journal* (1995).

13. *See* Fox (1995).

14. *See* Rance (1995) for a legal analysis of these issues.

15. This account is based on the findings of a report by the Board of Banking Supervision of the Bank of England (1995) and on a number of press accounts dealing with the episode. Except where otherwise noted, all information on this episode was taken from the Board of Banking Supervision's published inquiry.

16. Most of BFS' business was concentrated in executing trades for a limited number of financial futures and options contracts. These were the Nikkei-225 contract, the 10-year Japanese Government Bond (JGB) contract, the three-month Euroyen contract, and options on those contracts (known as futures options). The Nikkei-225 contract is a futures contract whose value is based on the Nikkei-225 stock index, an index of the aggregate value of the stocks of 225 of the largest corporations in Japan. The JGB contract is for the future delivery of ten-year Japanese government bonds. The Euroyen contract is a futures contract whose value is determined by changes in the three-month Euroyen deposit

rate. A futures option is a contract that gives the buyer the right, but not the obligation, to buy or sell a futures contract at a stipulated price on or before some specified expiration date.

17. The full text of Leeson's letter of resignation can be found in Springett (1995).

18. Board of Banking Supervision (1995), para. 1.77.

19. As cited in McGee (1995b).

20. *See BNA's Banking Report* (1995a), and Falloon (1995).

21. *See The Economist* (1995).

22. *See* the summary of Chairman Schapiro's testimony before Congress in *BNA's Banking Report* (1995a, b).

23. As cited in *BNA's Banking Report* (1995c).

24. *See BNA's Banking Report* (1995e).

25. *See BNA's Banking Report* (1995d).

26. *See The Economist* (1995).

27. Board of Banking Supervision (1995), para. 14.1.

28. Board of Banking Supervision (1995), para. 6.21.

29. Board of Banking Supervision (1995), para. 3.57.

30. Board of Banking Supervision (1995), para. 7.12.

31. Board of Banking Supervision (1995), para. 14.2.

32. Board of Banking Supervision (1995), para. 14.5.

33. Board of Banking Supervision (1995), para. 14.35.

34. Board of Banking Supervision (1995), para. 14.35.

35. *See* Sapsford, Sesit, and O'Brien (1995) for early details of the Daiwa debacle.

Glossary

TANYA STYBLO BEDER
ROBERT J. SCHWARTZ
CLIFFORD SMITH, JR.

All-or-Nothing Option: An option that provides for the payment of a fixed amount for a fixed period of time, only if the purchase or sale of an asset or index is beyond a stated level over the life of the option.

American Option: A contract that gives the holder the right to either (1) purchase from or (2) to sell to the writer of the option a specified amount of commodities or securities at a stated price. The contract is good for a specific period of time and may be exercised *at any time* up to its maturity date.

American Stock Exchange: AMEX or ASE is the second largest securities exchange in the United States. Listed stocks, bonds and options are traded on the AMEX.

American Window: An exercise period at the end of an option's life that allows the owner to exercise anytime within that window. Cheaper than an American-style option that allows exercise anytime over the life of the option.

Arbitrage: Strictly speaking, the simultaneous purchase of a commodity or security in one market and its immediate sale in another. Often used for the purchase of an underpriced security and the simultaneous sale of a security with similar characteristics with the expectation of a resumption of a more normal price relationship. Stock arbitrageurs are those who purchase a security with the expectation that it can be sold to a prospective corporate acquirer.

Asian Option: An option on an average of rates. Alternately, an option with windows of one or more American Options.

Asset Swap: Refers to (1) the application of an interest-rate swap to transform the rate of return on a given asset from fixed to floating, or vice versa; and, (2) the application of a currency swap to transform the rate of return on a given asset from one currency to a different currency.

Balloon: A payment to principal in a loan that is larger than the normal periodic payment. Typically occurs at maturity.

631

Bank Basis: See Money Market Basis.

Basis Point: One one-hundredth of a percent. [1/100 of 1%]. Used to measure the yield or cost of debt instruments.

Bear Spread: An options strategy utilizing puts and calls that provides the greatest return when the price of the underlying stock, bond, commodity or currency drops and experiences the greatest risk when the price rises. Contrast with bull spread.

Bermuda Option: An option that may be exercised on specific, non-contiguous dates. Contrast with European and American Options.

Bid: An offer to buy a security at a specified price.

Bond: A borrowing evidenced by an obligation to repay a determinable amount at a future date.

Bull Spread: An options strategy utilizing puts and calls that provides the greatest return when the price of the underlying security rises and the maximum risk when the price drops. Contrast with bear spread.

Bullet: Repayment of principal on a loan that occurs only at maturity.

Butterfly Spread: An options strategy utilizing two calls and two puts on the same or different securities with several maturity dates.

Calendar Spread: An options strategy utilizing the purchase and sale of options on the same security with different maturities.

Call: Definition (1): A contract that gives the holder the right to purchase from the writer of the option a specified amount of commodities or securities at a stated price. This contract is good for a specific period of time. Definition (2): A contract that gives the issuer of securities (e.g., corporation, mortgagor, etc.) the right to prepay all or a portion of its borrowing obligation. This contract may be good on specific dates or during specific periods of time, for which specific redemption/refunding prices are provided.

Call Provision: An issuer's right to redeem a security at a predetermined price utilizing a set formula on or after a certain date.

Cancellable Foreign Exchange Contract: A forward foreign exchange contract where the purchaser has the unilateral right to cancel the contract after a specified date.

Cap: A contract giving the purchaser the right to receive from the seller a payment that equals the amount that a floating-rate index exceeds a stated level (the agreed-upon cap level) during a specific period of time. In addition, the contract specifies the principal amount upon which the (potential) payments are to be made.

Capital Adequacy: The concept that all on- and off-balance sheet items entail an inherent credit risk and that a minimum amount of capital must be available to offset potential losses.

Caption: A contract that gives the holder the right to purchase from the writer a cap on a specific floating rate index for a stated period of time at a set price.

Ceiling: See Cap.

CTFC: The Commodities Futures Trading Commission—an independent government agency whose board is appointed by the President of the United States which has responsibility for regulating the U.S. futures exchanges.

Chicago Board of Trade: The CBOT is the United States' largest exchange for the trading of futures contracts. The CBOT trades commodity, currency and fixed income futures. Parent organization of the Chicago Board Options Exchange.

Chicago Board Options Exchange: An exchange sponsored by the Chicago Board of Trade (CBOT) and registered with appropriate regulators to trade standardized options contracts through the Options Clearing Corporation.

Chicago Mercantile Exchange: The second largest commodities exchange in the United States. Parent of the International Monetary Market.

Clean Risk: The risk in a settlement of a foreign exchange transaction that one party will fail to deliver its currency after it has received the counterparty's payment. The full amount is therefore at risk. Can be mitigated by escrow arrangements or by net payments through conversion to a common currency. Same as overnight risk.

Collateral: An obligation, security, cash or asset provided in conjunction with another obligation to secure its performance.

Collateralized Mortgage Obligation: A borrowing obligation backed by a group (or pool) of mortgages. Typically a "CMO" consists of a series of bonds (or tranches) that receive the cash flow of the mortgage pool sequentially. The payments made to investors may be in the form of fixed or floating interest rates (floating-rate tranches typically include a series of caps), plus principal repayments.

Commercial Paper: An unsecured and short-term note issued by a credit-worthy corporation or financial institution for up to a maximum of 270 days (if it is to be unregistered). Maturity and structure are negotiable.

Commodity Option: A contract to buy or sell a put or a call on a specific commodity at a predetermined price and date.

Commodity (Price) Swap: An agreement between two parties specifying the exchange of future payments based on a commodity index. Typically parties exchange a fixed for a floating rate (e.g., West Texas Intermediate spot vs. a fixed price per barrel). The calculation is based on a notional amount of the commodity and the commodity is not typically delivered.

Compound Interest: Reinvestment of each interest payment at the current rate.

Compound Option: An option on an option. Example: Caption.

Contingent Premium Option: The premium is paid only under specified circumstances. For example, the option expires in the money.

Contract Month: The month in which futures contracts may be satisfied by accepting or making delivery.

Conversion: As related to options, the process where a put can be changed to a call and a call to a put. In the context of the capital markets, a conversion is typically the exercise of the right to change a convertible bond to equity.

Covered: When a position with options is offset to a one-to-one basis with the underlying instrument.

Covered Writer: A call writer who owns the underlying stock or a put writer who is short the stock.

Convexity: Convexity is a measure of non-linearity.

Credit Derivative: The off-balance transfer of credit risk on an asset, such as a loan, from one party to another. This arrangement transfers all or part of the credit risk from the beneficiary to the guarantor.

Credit Risk: A risk existing in financial transactions where there is an exposure to receiving cash flow(s) from another party. Examples: an issuer may default on its borrowing obligation, or a counterparty/option writer may not meet the payment/delivery requirements of its swap agreement, cap contract, and so on.

Currency Exchange Agreement: See Currency Swap.

Currency Swap: An agreement between two parties that specifies the exchange of future payments in one currency for future payments in another currency. The exchange of interest payments and principal payments (typically at maturity) are included in the agreement.

Cycle: The expiration date of the three groups of options: Jan/Apr/Jul/Oct, Feb/May/Aug/Nov and Mar/Jun/Sep/Dec.

Debenture: Unsecured debt, typically long term.

Debt-Equity Warrant: A contract that gives the holder the right to purchase from the issuer of the warrant a specified amount of debt or equity securities at a given price. Debt-equity warrants may be issued for stated periods of time, or on a perpetual basis.

Delivery Risk: A risk that exists in financial transactions where there is an exposure to receiving cash flows/securities in different time zones. An example is the risk that a currency swap payment may be required to be made prior to the close of business in one time zone, while the related currency swap inflow payment may not be able to be made until the opening of business in a different time zone.

Delta: The expected change in the option value given a small change in the price of the underlying asset, with all other things constant.

Derivative Product: Typically an instrument that is created (derived) through a combination of cash market instruments. Derivative Products is used to refer to swaps, options, FRAs, futures and securities with the preceding instruments imbedded within. They may be interest, currency, commodity or equity based.

Difference Option: An option that provides for the purchase or sale of the difference between two assets relative to a fixed price spread for a fixed period of time.

Discount: An instrument trading at less than its face value.

Down and Out Call: A call option that expires if the market price of the underlying instrument falls below a predetermined level.

Downside Protection: Utilizing options or other hedges, the protection against a decrease in prices in the underlying instrument.

Dual Currency Bond: A security that typically pays interest in one currency and principal in a second currency.

Dual Index Floaters: A floating rate security that pays interest based on a spread calculation on more than one floating rate index. An example would be a certificate of deposit which pays the higher of (1) 3 month LIBOR, or (2) 3 month T-Bill rate plus 100 basis points.

Equity Swap: An agreement between two parties specifying the exchange of future payments based on an equity index and second index. The second index can be an interest rate (e.g., LIBOR), another equity index (e.g., S&P vs. Nikkei), a single stock or series of stocks, a commodity price index, etc. The calculation is based on a notional amount of the equities and the equities are not typically exchanged.

Eurodollar: A U.S. dollar obligation that is originated and held in a European country. Eurodollars may be created through U.S. dollar denominated bank deposits in foreign countries, or through other foreign U.S. dollar denominated transactions (e.g., loans, bankers' acceptances, bond underwritings, etc.).

European Option: A contract giving the holder the right to either (1) purchase from or (2) sell to the writer of the option a specified amount of commodities or securities at a stated price. The contract is good for a specific period of time and may be exercised *only* on its maturity date.

Exercise Price: As related to options, the price at which an option is exercisable.

Expiration Date: The date after which an option or futures contract is void.

Fair Option Value: The theoretical value of an option utilizing a probability based option valuation model.

Federal (Fed) Funds: Deposits by financial institutions at Federal Reserve Banks. Banks often lend these deposits to each other at overnight or longer Fed Funds rates.

Federal Home Loan Bank Board: Formerly the primary regulator for the savings and loan industry. Succeeded by the Office of Thrift Supervision.

Federal Home Loan Mortgage Corp: Freddie Mac, as the FHLMC is often known, provides liquidity in the secondary market for conventional mortgages.

Federal Reserve Bank: The central bank of the United States of America whose primary responsibility is to manage the money supply and financial markets and ensure the stability of the financial system.

Floor-Ceiling: For a given principal amount, a contract that gives the purchaser the right to receive from the seller a payment which equals the amount that a floating rate index exceeds a stated level (the agreed upon ceiling level) during a specific period of time. In addition, the floor-ceiling contract requires the purchaser to provide to the seller a payment which equals the amount that a floating rate index falls below a stated level (the floor level) during that same period of time.

FNMA: The Federal National Mortgage Association was established in 1938 to improve the liquidity of the mortgage market. In 1968, when the Government National Mortgage Association was formed (see "GNMA") FNMA became a government-sponsored, but privately owned corporation. Under regulation by the Secretary of Housing and Urban Development, FNMA buys and sells FHA-insured or VA-guaranteed residential mortgages. Funds for such purchases are raised via the sale of corporate obligations in the capital markets.

Forward Exchange Contract: An agreement between two or more parties to exchange payments in two or more currencies at a specified exchange rate (forward rate) on a given date (or series of dates).

Future: A contract traded on an exchange that gives the holder the right to buy or sell a specified amount of commodities or securities at a stated price and date in the future.

Gamma: The expected change in the Delta of an option or portfolio of options given a small change in the value of the underlying asset, other factors constant

(Gamma is the 2nd derivative of price with respect to underlying). Thus Gamma is the measure of convexity. Gamma demonstrates the Delta measurement's non-linearity, e.g. that the Delta is accurate only for small changes in the price of the underlying security. Note that Gamma is not necessarily symmetrical.

GNMA: The Government National Mortgage Association was established in 1968 as a corporation within the Department of Housing and Urban Development (it is 100% owned by the U.S. Government). The main businesses of GNMA are (1) to buy and sell certain Federal Housing Administration (FHA) and Veteran's Administration (VA) mortgages in order to support the housing market; (2) to provide a guarantee for mortgage-backed securities which are issued against pools of FHA and VA mortgages; and, (3) to manage the operations, assets and liabilities of the Federal National Mortgage Association's (FNMA) Special Assistance and Managing and Liquidating Functions which were transferred to GNMA in 1968.

Haircut: The difference between the amount received by the borrower in a repo transaction and the higher amount (typically the market value of the repoed securities) returned by the borrower to the lender at maturity. The term also refers to the amount of the security's value which may not be used to meet a collateral requirement.

Hedging: As related to futures, the sale or purchase of a contract as a substitute for the cash instrument. More generally, the substitution of one financial instrument with one or more cash instruments or synthetics so that the effect of subsequent movements in prices of the underlying instrument are largely offset by movements in the value of the hedge.

Hi-Low Floaters: A floating rate security that, at the time of issuance, pays a higher rate of return to investors (in the form of a greater spread to the floating rate index) but caps the possible ultimate return through the inclusion of a short put option.

Hi-Low Option: An option that provides for the purchase or sale of the difference between the high and low price of two assets relative to a fixed spread for a fixed period of time.

Immunization: The process of designing a portfolio of debt securities whose value is unaffected by changes in interest rates.

Indexed Amortizing Swap: A swap whose notional principal reduction accelerates or decelerates with changes in interest rates. It is intended to mimic a mortgage backed instrument, e.g. as interest rates drop, paydowns (notional reductions) increase.

Interest Rate Swap: An agreement between two parties specifying the exchange of future payments based on interest rates. Typically, parties exchange a fixed rate of interest for a floating rate of interest (or vice versa)—transactions are also done in which parties exchange *types* of floating rate interest (e.g., 3 month LIBOR for 6 month LIBOR; the Prime rate for the Commercial Paper rate, etc.). The exchange of interest payments is based on a notional principal amount; there is no exchange of principal.

Internal Rate of Return: Definition (1): The rate of return or cost of funds implied by the interest flows and principal flows of a given transaction. Definition (2): The discount rate required to make the price of a security equal the sum of the discounted interest flows and principal flows of the security.

International Swaps and Derivatives Association: ISDA is the leading global trade association representing participants in the privately negotiated derivatives industry, a business which includes interest rate, current, commodity and equity swaps, as well as related products such as caps, collars, floors and swaptions. ISDA was chartered in 1985 and in 1996 numbered over 270 member firms from around the world.

Intrinsic Option Value: The market value of the option less the strike price of the security.

Inverted Yield Curve: Occurs when short-term interest rates exceed longer-term rates. See yield curve.

Ito's Lemma: A rule by which functions of certain random variables can be differentiated. Specifically, random variables whose movement can be described as a continuous Markov process in continuous time. (Note that a Markov process depends at most on the most recent observation.) The sample path of such a process will be continuous (it can be drawn without lifting the pen from the paper).

Knock-in Options: An option that provides for the purchase of a specified asset at a fixed price but does not commence until the price moves beyond a stated level (the "knock-in" level) over the life of the option.

Knock-out Options: An option that provides for the purchase of a specified asset at a fixed price but expire if the price moves beyond a stated level (the "knock-out" level) over the life of the option.

LIBOR: (London Interbank Offered Rate); The rates specified for maturities ranging from overnight to five years, at which major banks offer to make deposits denominated in Eurodollars available to other major banks.

Line of Credit: The maximum amount a financial institution will lend to a borrower.

London International Financial Futures Exchange: The LIFFE is the London financial futures exchange which provides a market for futures on currencies and equity indices.

Lookback Option: An option that provides for the purchase or sale of a specified asset at the best price / strike achieved over the life of the option. For example, at the option's maturity the owner of a lookback call on IBM stock has the right to buy IBM at the lowest price that occurred over the life of the option.

Margin: The equity required to collateralize an investment position.

Marked-To-Market: The calculation and realization of the differential, if any, between (1) an asset's current value and most recently "booked" value; (2) a liability's current value and most recently "booked" value; or, (3) a risk management tool's current value and most recently "booked" value. The realization of the differential may be in the form of a positive or negative earnings charge, margin call, or collateral call.

Market Risk: The risk that exists in financial transactions in which there is an exposure to changing market prices of a security caused by changing interest rates and/or changing currency exchange rates.

Master Swap Agreement: A contract between two parties that specifies all definitions, non-trade detail elements and laws governing any swaps between the two parties. A master swap agreement enables the parties to execute one master agreement and transact multiple swaps through brief appendices to that master agreement, rather than executing multiple complete swap agreements.

Modified American Option: Also known as Semi-American Option, a contract that gives the holder the right to either (1) purchase from or (2) sell to the writer of the option a specified amount of commodities or securities at a stated price. The contract is good for a specified period and may be exercised at certain specific dates up to its maturity date.

Money Market Basis: The calculation method used to determine accrued interest owed on money market securities (T-bills, Federal Funds, Commercial Paper, Certificates of Deposit, Repurchase Agreements, and Bankers' Acceptances). The calculation requires that a security's rate of interest be multiplied by the actual number of days which have elapsed, and then be divided by the number of days in the accounting year for the particular market (typically 360 in Europe, and 365 in the United States).

Naked Option Writing: The act of writing an option without an underlying position in the security.

Net Present Value: The difference between the interest flows and principal flows of a given transaction discounted at a specified interest rate, less the initial investment/proceeds.

New York Futures Exchange: The NYFE is a wholly owned subsidiary of the New York Stock Exchange and provides a market for futures on Treasury bills, notes and bonds and on *GNMA* securities.

New York Mercantile Exchange: The NYMEX or MERC is a commodities exchange located in New York City that offers a market in futures on commodities and currencies.

New York Stock Exchange: The NYSE is the largest securities exchange in the United States.

Novation: In foreign exchange, when two or more currency payments are due on the same date novation provides for the cancellation of those trades and the substitution of one net payment.

Offset: Generally the right to net liabilities against assets of the same counterparty in a default.

Open Interest: The total number of a specific future contract not offset or satisfied.

Option: The right to buy or sell a security, asset, commodity or equity index at a given price (strike price) at or before a certain date.

Outperformance Option: An option that provides for the purchase or sale of the better performing of two assets over the life of the option.

Path Dependent Swap: A swap where a key component changes based on another variable. An example is an Indexed Amortizing Swap.

Perpetual Floaters: A floating rate security with no maturity date.

Plain Vanilla: The simplest version of the use of a derivative or the creation of a derivative product.

Premium: The price paid for an option.

Principal: The amount of debt that must be repaid.

Protected Strategy: A strategy to ensure that the value of a portfolio of instruments has minimal exposure to a change in prices. See Immunization.

Put: A contract that gives the holder the right to sell to the writer of the option a specified amount of commodities or securities at a stated price. This contract is good for a specific period of time.

Put-Call Parity Theorem: The relation between European put and call options of the same maturity written on the same asset.

Range Forward: A forward foreign exchange contract specifying a maximum and minimum rate at which a future currency exchange will be made. If the spot two days prior to close falls within that range it becomes the contract rate. Otherwise the maximum or minimum prevail.

Rate Bet: An open position taken with a view towards profiting from an absolute movement in rates. Contrast with a hedged position.

Reinvestment Risk: The risk that the reinvestment of interim cashflows (e.g., interest payments) is exposed to changing interest rates or currency exchange rates.

Return on (Credit) Risk: A calculation that measures the performance of a financial institution or corporation in determining the income received on the credit risk incurred. Financial institutions typically determine the credit risk associated with a derivative product as a function of the notional principal amount. Credit risk is existent throughout the life of the transaction. Therefore the Return on Risk measures the performance over time.

Return on Assets: A calculation that measures the performance of a financial institution or corporation in using its assets (net of financing charges) to create earnings.

Return on Equity: A calculation that measures the performance of a financial institution or corporation in using its equity to create earnings.

Rho: The expected change in the value of an option given a small change in market interest rates, other things constant.

Safe Harbor: Financial markets and/or transactions which avoid tax or legal consequences. Also refers to the transfer of assets to less volatile sectors of the financial markets.

SEC: Securities and Exchange Commission—an independent government agency whose board is appointed by the President of the United States and with responsibility for regulation of the securities markets.

Short Sale: The sale of a security that the investor does not own and that the investor expects will fall in value.

Spot Exchange: The foreign exchange rate for immediate delivery, two days for most currencies.

Spread: Options: the purchase of one option and the sale of another on the same security. Swaps: the differential over or under the government securities curve at which the swap is executed.

Spreadlock: A forward commitment to enter into an interest rate swap at a swap spread which is specified in the contract. Although the contract sets the swap spread, it does not set the interest rate level to which the swap spread is applied. (The interest rate level is determined when the swap is entered into.)

Strike Price: See Exercise price.

Strip: Technically, a combination of two puts and one call, often used to refer to a series of futures spread over various maturities.

Stripped Mortgage Backed Security: A mortgage backed security which has been divided into two separately traded parts, (1) coupon payments, and (2) its principal portion which is traded independently from its coupon payments.

Super Floater: A floating rate security that pays a rate of return equal to a multiple of a specified floating rate index, less a fixed interest rate spread (e.g., 2×3 month LIBOR $-$ 8%). These securities typically have caps (e.g., a maximum rate of 13%) and some have had floors (e.g., a minimum rate of 5%).

Swap Agreement: A contract between two parties specifying all definitions, trade detail elements and laws that will govern a particular swap between the two parties.

Swaption: A contract that gives the holder the right to either (1) purchase from or (2) sell to the writer of the swaption a specified amount and type of interest rate swaps or currency swaps at a stated price. The contract is good for a specific period of time and typically may be exercised only on its maturity date.

Synthetic Instruments: Two or more transactions that taken together have the effect of a financial instrument that may or may not exist by itself. For instance a floating rate note (FRN) with an interest rate swap synthetically creates a fixed rate bond.

Term Structure of Interest Rates: The relation between the yield to maturity of similar securities of differing maturities.

Theta: The expected change in the option value given a small change in the option's term-to-expiration, other things constant.

Treasury Bills: Full faith and credit obligations of the United States government with original maturities of three months to one year.

Treasury Bond: Direct obligations of the U.S. government with an original maturity of more than ten years.

Treasury Note: Direct obligations of the U.S. government with an original maturity of more than and one up to ten years.

Uncovered Option: An option written without ownership of the underlying instrument.

Unwind: To terminate a transaction before its original end date by an exchange of payments reflecting its mark to market value.

Up and Out Put: A put option that expires if the market price of the underlying security rises above a predetermined price.

Value at Risk: A statistical measure of financial risk over a specified time horizon. VaR can be viewed as an estimate of the expected deviation (or squared deviation).

Vega: The expected change in option value given a small change in volatility, other things constant.

Volatility: A measure of the likelihood that prices, yields, returns, etc., will change over a given period. Generally, volatility is represented in the form of standard deviation of possible ending prices, yields, returns, etc.

Warrant: The right (option) to purchase a security at a given date or set of dates in the future at a predetermined price.

Yield: The return on an investment. The discount rate at which the net present value of cash flows is zero. The internal rate of return of the cash flows.

Yield Curve: A graph representing the relation between maturity and yield for equivalent securities (e.g., a U.S. Treasury yield curve, a "AA" yield curve, an interest rate swap yield curve, etc.).

Yield Spread: Definition (1): The difference in yield between assets dissimilar in issuer or maturity. Alternatively the difference in yield between a financial institution's assets and liabilities. Definition (2): The graphical relation between yields on similar securities of different tenors. Most readily constructed utilizing United States Treasury instruments because of the depth and breadth of the market.

Zero Coupon Bond: A debt security issued at a discount and redeemed at a par (or another stated amount) at maturity. As no periodic interest payments are made, the investor receives the rate of return represented by the difference between the issue/purchase price and the maturity/sale price.

Zero Coupon Swap: An interest rate swap in which a floating rate of interest is exchanged for a single, fixed rate payment at the maturity of the swap, or vice versa.

Zero Curve: A graph that represents the relation between maturity and yield for equivalent zero-coupon securities (e.g., strips, zero coupon interest rate swaps, etc.).

Index